The Life and Times of
MEXICO

Also by Earl Shorris

FICTION

Ofay

The Boots of the Virgin

Under the Fifth Sun: A Novel of Pancho Villa

In the Yucatán

NONFICTION

The Death of the Great Spirit: An Elegy
for the American Indian

The Oppressed Middle: Scenes from Corporate Life

Power Sits at Another Table

Jews Without Mercy: A Lament

While Someone Else Is Eating (editor)

Latinos: A Biography of the People

A Nation of Salesmen: The Tyranny of the Market
and the Subversion of Culture

New American Blues: A Journey through Poverty
to Democracy

Riches for the Poor: The Clemente Course
in the Humanities

In the Language of Kings: An Anthology
of Mesoamerican Literature—Pre-Columbian to
the Present (with Miguel León-Portilla)

The Life and Times of
MEXICO

Earl Shorris

W. W. NORTON & COMPANY

New York · London

Parts of this book appeared in a different form in *Harper's* magazine,
the *New York Times*, and the *Nation.*

For information about permission to reproduce selections from this book, write to
Permissions, W. W. Norton & Company, Inc., 500 Fifth Avenue, New York, NY 10110

Manufacturing by The Maple-Vail Book Manufacturing Group
Book design by Charlotte Staub
Production manager: Amanda Morrison

Library of Congress Cataloging-in-Publication Data
Shorris, Earl, 1936–
The life and times of Mexico / Earl Shorris.— 1st ed.
p. cm.
Includes bibliographical references and index.
ISBN 0-393-05926-X (hardcover)
1. Mexico—Civilization. I. Title.
F1210.S543 2004
972—dc22   2004009873

W. W. Norton & Company, Inc.
500 Fifth Avenue, New York, N.Y. 10110
www.wwnorton.com

W. W. Norton & Company Ltd.
Castle House, 75/76 Wells Street, London W1T 3QT

1 2 3 4 5 6 7 8 9 0

FOR

Sylvia

SINCE 1956

AND

Samantha

SINCE 1996

CONTENTS

CONTENTS

CONTENTS

Saturday Stories

In 1943, when I was seven, my father drove to Agua Prieta every Saturday to fill the tank of our wobbly old Packard automobile with Mexican gasoline. While the car was parked beside the pump, I wandered up and down the block, my range limited only by the edge of the road. There were few cars on the streets of Agua Prieta in those days and not many more across the border in Douglas, Arizona; nonetheless, caution limited my excursions. As I whiled away the time, I noticed holes in some of the walls, like the holes the big red ants bored in the ground near the house where we lived. But these were bigger holes, deep into the thick adobe bricks. Here and there, beside a doorway or a window, there were rows of them, black spots in the brown.

An old man, who sat on a chair beside the door of his house, as constant as the dust of the high desert, asked what I was doing.

"Nothing."

The old man nodded and pulled his straw sheriff's hat down over his eyes. And that was all.

I had seen him several times before, but we had only watched each other across the distance of his dry dirt front yard, two desert creatures, the beginning and the end, squinting in the wind. One afternoon, when the car was raised up on a ramp while the attendant looked under it, I screwed up my courage enough to ask the old man why there were so many holes in his house.

"Pancho Villa," he said, and closed his eyes to the sun.

"And who is Pancho Villa?" asked the impertinent child.

"A great general," the old man said. "Do you know what that means, a general?"

It was the beginning of many conversations, a Saturday routine. The old man, or so he seemed to me, for his face was lined and his eyes had the weary, mechanical quality of the desert reptiles that lived in our brown garden, told in heavily accented English mixed with Spanish of the great battle that had been fought at Agua Prieta. While the war raged on the distant fields and beaches of Europe and the Pacific, the old man replayed the terrible night in November 1915, when Villa was defeated there. He described the searchlights, the machine guns, the dying men crying out, begging for water, praying, asking for their mothers to come and hold their hands and bind up their wounds.

How he knew this he never said. With all the questions I asked, I failed to ask that one. Had he been there? Had he fought? Had he called for his mother to help him? Although I like to think he had been a brave man on that November night, I do not know. Whatever he had done, he surely had seen the battle and remembered it. He was a historicist, a kind of magician, one who made dreams and gave birth to loyalties. He knew why things happened as they did. The war of my youth was not fought at Anzio or Iwo Jima, but on a dry, darkened Mexican plain, suddenly illuminated and made into a slaughterhouse.

The old man was obsessed by that night, the history, or was it mere memory? I do not know, I did not ask, and the next year we moved east along the border to El Paso, and the Saturday afternoon excursions came to an end. Only the story and the old man remained. He has been with me for almost sixty years, a guide to dreaming, and he now suggests how to look at an old country. We converse in memory, the old man of Agua Prieta and I, but he does not offer guidance in abstract ways; he tells stories and leaves them for his listener to apprehend, to learn why things happen as they do. He is an artist of memory: He shows, he never tells.

As the years went by, I learned more from the old man; time enriched my perceptions of his conversation. His advice now is clear: To look at Mexico, one must first know how Mexico looks at itself, for it is a country of historicists and fallen dreamers. Everything that happens in Mexico today has roots in the clash of civilizations that took place at the beginning of the sixteenth century, from the choice of a president to the killing of Indians in the jungles of Chiapas. The old man knew; his obsession with history was the Mexican obsession. He looked back, always back; he never spoke of the day he lived or the day to come; only the past interested him. Mexico's Nobelist Octavio Paz blamed the old man's way of thinking on the Counter-Reformation of the mid-sixteenth century, the failure of the

Spanish Catholics to develop a critical tradition, yet Paz also looked to the past. He was a great critic, but an infrequent dreamer.

The old man of Agua Prieta was another kind of critic: He could dream by means of the past. It seems a curious thing to say, mystical, but I do not mean it that way. The old man gathered his thoughts through memory, which is the value and the problem of being old. One must look very deeply to see patterns and predictions in old but unfinished things. Only the dead past is immediately clear, and even then . . .

Having been in the old man's thrall for so many decades, always writing this book, but not daring to begin it, to attempt the distillation, the inevitable whittling away of memories, readings, ideas, the Mexican obsession with time, I was surprised when the idea to write the book was suggested to me. I accepted it as if it were a dare. Only later, when I began to seek a structure for the work, did I realize that I knew too much.

Of course, a writer can never know too much about a scene, a person, an idea, love or war. It is possible to write a thousand pages about one filament of the down that lies along my beloved's cheek, but a country is another task. How can a country be said? The Maya use the ceiba tree as a metaphor to represent the world. A tree, as the old man of Agua Prieta could have told me, is nourished through its roots but identified by its leaves. And the leaves of the tree are multitudes. To identify an old country is to look at infinity; to write about an old country, not as a tourist but as an old lover, one who knows too much, is to attempt to find order in infinity.

Leaves, by which I mean people, the old man said.

Roots, by which I mean history, the old man said.

But what is the wood that binds? The structure? The metaphor of the tree would not do. After so many years, so many books, the old man of Agua Prieta had failed me. A tree is not a picture of a country.

I told him about my disappointment. He made no reply. For the first time, in memory, I saw the detail of his shirt, the torn corner of the pocket, the threads undone at the collar and the cuffs. Well, that is how life is over there, I had thought. Mexico is an old country; one of the world's few original civilizations grew up there. It is nothing like the United States, not even when it speaks English or sings rock and roll or drinks Coca-Cola at McDonald's. There is a difference in the vicinity of the heart between Mexico and the United States. If we ignore it and try to think of both countries in the same way, there are bound to be mistakes. Mexico is never far from its origins; the Mexican sun is very hot, and there is rarely a moment when Mexicans are not conscious of the sun and all its implications for the world. And Mexico is a difficult life for most people, as I saw on those Saturday afternoons; it lives in embrace with and opposition to the United States. Although I was a child, I remember wondering how the old man of Agua Prieta lived, how he put food on the table. I saw him once with a handful of dust, letting it drain slowly, taken by the wind. He told me to wear a hat.

When the memorious old man first spoke to me, his voice was hoarse and hopeful, as if he were still recovering from the effects of battle. But he and his country are older now, and the voice is more complex. There were nineteen million Mexicans then; there are one hundred million now. It was a rural country then; it is urban now. He said: Look at an old country long and short; neither history nor the moment alone will do; in an old country everyone is everything. He beckoned to me to come close and then to look beyond him, over his shoulder to the mountains.

He could not have been born in Agua Prieta. The town did not exist until 1905. The old man had come there from some other place, perhaps many places, Toledo and Tenochtitlán, Spain and Mexico. To look at an old country, one must see the origins of its parts and inspect the places where they fit or do not fit together, where it is complete and where it still struggles; in other words, politics, but not politics as in a new country, where the ideas are still strong and clear.

The old man of Agua Prieta is long dead, which suggests that to seek out an old country, one should listen to last words. What do they promise? Are they about goods or God? And if they are about God, what is his (or her) name?

Cantankerous and withholding old man, I thought. Or was he just worn out? Old man, old man, if Mexico is not properly a tree, what is the form of it? He said nothing. He sat. After a long time, he lifted up his hat and showed his face to me. It was he. He was Mexico. A person can be a country, as Plato knew. His Republic was "the man writ large." But the Mexican Republic was not a Greek; it had to be a Mexican written large. The old man's face was not a palimpsest, one world written over the other, nor did he wear the mask that is often said to hide the Mexican beneath. The face I grew to know in Agua Prieta was like light entering a prism, all the many components wanting to be revealed. If he had told me once, he had told me a thousand times, ten thousand times: Everyone is everything. Examine each almost invisible hair that lies along your beloved's cheek. Mexico is memories, resonances; you cannot know too much.

Begin with the wars, he said, as I began when I spoke to you, but even before that, look where you are standing. This is Mexico; begin with the land.

Then he looked to the mountains and took my hand, which was now the same age as his, and drew me into the conversation that follows.

First Homage to the Memorious
Old Man of Agua Prieta

As the old man well knew, for he had looked across the border for many years after he came north, Mexico differs from the United States in profound ways. It was his insistence to a child, advice to a writer. At the deepest level the United States was born in the making of its great eighteenth-century documents—the Declaration of Independence and the Constitution with its appended Bill of Rights—followed by the economic democratizing of the country in the early nineteenth century and a great Civil War. The United States sought the physical and cultural extinction of the native peoples as it conquered the land, justifying its actions with John Locke's ideas about property. Together, these acts and ideas, accompanied by enriching waves of immigration, have determined the course of its history and the character of its soul. The United States has enjoyed political democracy to a great degree since 1779.

Mexico has entirely different origins. It was, and to no small extent remains, a great indigenous American civilization. Its core ideas are still more religious than political, born in the clash and mix of native and Spanish Catholic culture. Independence did not produce stable democratic institutions in Mexico. The early presidents came and went with debilitating frequency. Then came Benito Juárez and Porfirio Díaz, who stayed too long, resulting in a ten-year period marked by conflicting ideas and civil strife. A social contract is written into the Mexican Constitution but has never been fully exercised.

Of no small importance is the fact that the United States invaded Mexico in the middle of the nineteenth century and took more than half of its most valuable territory, which became the American Southwest.

Octavio Paz, Mexico's Nobel Prize laureate, said his country looks to the past while the United States looks to the future. The interplay between his-

torical and contemporary Mexico remains definitive. A book about the
United States must turn on ideas; a book about Mexico must live among
echoes.

When a boy was born in ancient Mexico, the midwife said:

Here like a fragment struck from a stone, chipped from a stone, you are born.
Here you have only your cradle, your blanket, your pillow where you lay
   your head.
This is only the place of arrival.
Where you belong is elsewhere:
You are pledged, you are promised, you are sent to the field of battle.
War is your destiny, your calling.
You shall provide drink,
you shall provide food,
you shall provide nourishment for the Sun, for the Lord of the Earth.

If the child was a girl . . . the midwife . . . said to her:

My beloved daughter, my little girl . . .
You have come to a place of hardship, a place of affliction, a place of
   tribulation.
A place that is cold, a place that is windy.[1]

In a small examining room, in the city that had been the capital of the
Aztecs, five hundred years after the midwife spoke to the newborn children
in the ancient indigenous language, Dr. Andrea Navarrete took into her
hands the infant child of Fernando and Patricia Calvillo de Plancarte of the
suburb of Coacalco. She watched the infant for several moments, then laid
her gently on the examining table.

The elegantly trained pediatrician, a specialist in neonatal medicine,
caught the infant's hands in hers, feeling the grip, the flex, and the still soft
form of them. The baby's fingers were surprisingly long and thin, pale. The
doctor's hands had the slightly worn look of too many washings, too much
soap, disinfectant.

The doctor showed only ease with the child. In her hands the infant was

[1]This is from Thelma Sullivan's brilliant translation of the Florentine Codex, first published in *Estudios de la cultura Nahuatl*, UNAM, edited by Miguel León-Portilla, in Mexico, and later in *A Scattering of Jades* (New York: Simon & Schuster, 1994).

secure; she did not cry. There was not even a whimper; the child submitted to the tender intelligence. The doctor cooed and spoke, undressing the child rapidly, in a rhythm of snapping and opening, sure, studying the color of the child, the response of the skin to the slight pressure of a finger, feeling, comforting with the sureness of her probing touch. The doctor's hands moved quickly, passing over the child, touching the top of its head. She spoke a steady meter, reading aloud what her hands told her, informing the parents who sat before her, solemnly watching, certain of the health of the child, yet breathless.

"First, we shall examine the head. We are examining the fontanel inferior. When the babies are born, they have a head that is very malleable. The malleability can be checked by feeling the tension in the fontanel. This is normal. This baby has a normal fontanel."

Dr. Navarrete was younger than her skills; she showed a gentle face, a narrow, elegant nose, piercing eyes, physician's eyes in a mother's face. She touched the stethoscope to the baby's chest. "In the heart, we first listen to the amplitudes of the baby. Her cardiac rhythms are present. She has no murmurs." The pediatrician opened the child's diapers and palpated the liver, listened with a stethoscope to the chest, the wind sound. "The air enters her lungs. Good!"

The infant, a girl, is the second child of Fernando and Patricia Calvillo de Plancarte. They have named her Jacqueline, and they have already begun to dream for her. "She will surpass us," they said. This is their wish, no less. He is a soldier's child who found work in a bank and became a securities analyst. Neither Patricia nor Fernando has gone beyond secondary school (junior high school), but they can read and do sums, and they have dreams.

All the Plancartes are small and very neat. They speak not a word of the language of the Aztecs; they said that only their grandparents knew a few words of such a bygone language. The language that beckons to them is English. But it is never clear how much of the ancient world remains in anyone in Mexico, why the woman smiled at her husband's nod, how he sat so upright in his chair, why they dreamed of an orderly Mexico for their child, which god they thank. The middle class were merchants in the ancient market at Tlatelolco, the immense and orderly collection of shops that the invading Spaniards said was as large as the greatest markets of Europe or Asia Minor.

The child did not whimper. She wore pink. Her mother's clothes were starched, as was her father's shirt. They were the immaculate and newly risen class of the global economy, the keepers once again of markets as their ancestors had been at Tlatelolco. Fernando and Patricia thanked the doctor and took their leave. The child was well; she had been seen by a pediatrician who worked in the stream of new medicine, among magnetic resonance imaging (MRI) machines and electronically monitored incubators. The child was well; the ancient centers functioned. There were predictions, a modern version of the ancient book of auguries to offer wishes and warnings.

THE PLAN

Plato said the Republic was "the man writ large." It is a good way to think about a person or a republic. In this case, the Republic of Mexico. But the views are not quite the same. There is a Mexican way to look at a person, for the Mexicans were not Greeks or anything like Greeks; their civilization was of its own kind, one of the unique moments of the world. These are the three key parts of a person seen in the Mexican way. They provide a useful set of divisions for a book that attempts to touch on many, if not most, aspects of an old country. I have used the old names in the language spoken by the Aztecs, but one could almost as well say "the head, the heart, and the liver."

Book One: *Tonalli*, the center of vital power, is located in the head. Its attributes include physical growth, cognition, and here history and philosophy.

Book Two: *Teyolia*, the center containing what we would call the soul, is located in the heart. Its attributes include thinking, feeling, and here art and literature, family, character, and imagination.

Book Three: *Ihiyotl*, the center containing the spirit or breath, is located in the liver. It compares to the Greek *pneuma*, meaning "wind" or "spirit." Its attributes include vigor, passion, and here economics, education, politics, corruption, and race, but most of all ihiyotl is the center of survival.

Then come prognostications, here a look toward the future of Mexico. The Aztecs had a scheme of them, which they called the *Tonalamatl*.

The echoes, Mexico's history, will appear in chronological order in hope that when the writer and the reader come at the end of the book to look toward the future of Mexico, it will be in the same context of its life and times.

At the end, in an Appendix, there will be two brief oral histories: one from a small village in the Yucatán and the other from the center of the last fifty years of politics and government in Mexico. It is always useful to be able to compare what a writer has said to other, far less edited versions of the world.

Finally, the book will conclude where it could well have begun, in the house of my friend and colleague, Miguel León-Portilla, whom one of the country's major metropolitan dailies recently described as "the leading humanist in Mexico."

NOTE: To avoid awkwardness here and there, I have used the word "American" to contrast with "Mexican." Mexicans are Americans, since they live on the North American continent, but there is no English equivalent of *estadunidense*, which Mexicans use to refer to people from the United States. Aztecs prior to 1821 were Mexica; however, I have used "Aztec" interchangeably with "Mexica" in speaking of the period prior to 1821, the date of Independence and the choice of "Mexico" for the name of the new nation. In the use of diacritical marks, I have avoided them in very common words, like "Mexico," which is correctly written "México," and "Nahuatl," which is properly "Náhuatl." In spelling common words that are more correctly Mexican (not Spanish) than English, I have used the Mexican spelling, *chilli* rather than "chile."

Book One

THE HEAD

(Tonalli)

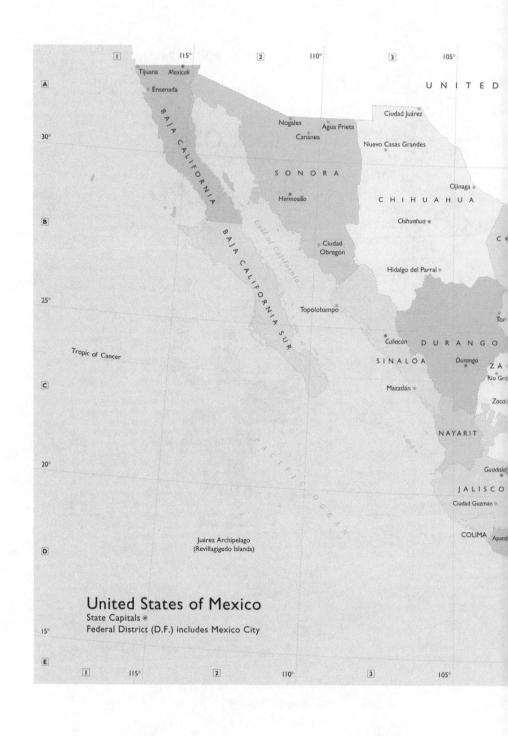

United States of Mexico
State Capitals ⊛
Federal District (D.F.) includes Mexico City

Tijuana   Mexicali
Ensenada

Nogales   Agua Prieta
Cananea

Ciudad Juárez
Nuevo Casas Grandes

UNITED

BAJA CALIFORNIA

SONORA

Hermosillo

Ciudad Obregón

Ojinaga
CHIHUAHUA

Chihuahua

Hidalgo del Parral

C

Topolobampo

Culiacán   DURANGO

SINALOA   Durango

Mazatlán

Tor

ZA
Rio Gra

Zaca

NAYARIT

Guadala

JALISCO

Ciudad Guzmán

COLIMA   Apatz

Juárez Archipelago
(Revillagigedo Islands)

Tropic of Cancer

Gulf of California

BAJA CALIFORNIA SUR

PACIFIC OCEAN

A
B
C
D
E

30°
25°
20°
15°

115°   110°   105°

A

TATES   OF   AMERICA

30°

B

Allende

HUILA

Sabinas   Nuevo
Laredo

Monclova

NUEVO
LEÓN

25°

Saltillo   Monterrey   Matamoros

*Gulf of
México*

Tropic of Cancer

TECAS

C

SAN
LUIS
POTOSÍ   Ciudad Victoria

TAMAULIPAS

AGUASCALIENTES
Aguascalientes   San Luis Potosí   Ciudad Madero
Tampico

Tizimín   Cancún

GUANAJUATO
León   Guanajuato   Mérida   YUCATÁN
Valladolid

QUERÉTARO   VERACRUZ

20°

Celaya   Querétaro   HIDALGO   Ticul   Peto

Pachuca
Tula

Morelia   MÉXICO   TLAXCALA   Jalapa   Felipe Carrillo Puerto

Toluca   D.F.   Tlaxcala   Veracruz   Champotón   QUINTANA ROO

MICHOACÁN   Cuernavaca   MORELOS   Puebla   Orizaba

Cuautla   PUEBLA

Tierra Blanca   CAMPECHE

TABASCO

D

Lázaro Cárdenas   Iguala   Coatzacoalcos   Villahermosa

Palenque   *Caribbean
Sea*

GUERRERO   OAXACA   Ocosingo

Chilpancingo   Matías Romero   San Cristóbal de las Casas

Acapulco   Oaxaca   Tuxtla Gutiérrez

Juchitán   CHIAPAS

BELIZE

Huatulco   *Gulf of
Tehuantepec*   GUATEMALA   15°

HONDURAS

Tapachula   E

1.

Definitions

Grown men do not discuss their business with children, but I think the old man of Agua Prieta must have been the proprietor of the dust that he so often gathered and let drain from his hand. He always held the dust when he spoke of war. He did not make the connection in his stories, only in the recurring gesture, but in retrospect it could not be more clear. The battle had been fought for the possession of land, not all the land, not a grand scheme, just land, more than the dust that drained from his hand, but not some abstraction, not everything. He always touched his piece of land in the same way. He took the dust into his hand, held it for a long time, and let it fall in a long caress. From the delicacy of his touch, it was clear that he loved his land as he would love a living thing. By his constant touching of the dust he signaled his embrace of land. Begin with the land, the old man said. He looked up, wistful, suddenly very old, older than I could ever be, and gazed north at what had once been Mexico. To begin with the land, one must first define Mexico, where it is, when it began, how it came by its name. And then engage his metaphor, the wind that took the dust, the tragedy of the land, the love and loss, as it happened in the old man's time and before his time, and now.

DATE OF BIRTH

Mexico was born in 1821 or 3000 B.C.[1] Either date will do, but 1821 suffers a lack of implications; it was merely the year in which New Spain won its

[1] The date may be earlier; recent methods using DNA suggest that corn bred from *teosintle,* the self-seeding grass from which it was developed, may have appeared in the state of Oaxaca as early as 5000 B.C. The dating of the domestication of corn continues to change with new methods and new discoveries. The 3000 B.C. date is conservative; however, the issue here is not the date, but the question of whether maize (corn) or political independence from Spain determines the founding of Mexico.

Independence from Old Spain. The earlier date has more meaning, because it represents the domestication of the wild grass that later became corn. The first plantings probably took place in Tehuacán in the current state of Puebla in central Mexico.

Three thousand B.C. also serves as a better date of birth because of the nature of corn, which is the only grain that cannot survive without the aid of a human being, because the husk does not open and the seed does not fall from the ear. According to the Popol Vuh, sometimes known as the Maya Bible, the first human beings were made of corn. The Maya metaphor had it right: With the planting of the grass, both the corn and the planter were domesticated. The hunter-gatherers had to stay in one place during the growing season, and the corn had to be cultivated by the formerly nomadic people. Corn transformed society, bringing about what was to become one of the world's original civilizations. Mexico was born.

GEOGRAPHY

The geography of Mexico presents a problem. Perhaps Mexico was or is Mesoamerica,[2] not defined so much by physical boundaries as by culture. Mesoamerica was made up of city-states that rose, flourished, and fell over thousands of years. It did not include any of the northern states of present-day Mexico or any of the land north of the Rio Grande (Texas, California, Arizona, New Mexico, etc.) that the Spaniards later claimed for New Spain. To the south Mesoamerica included city-states located in Guatemala and other Central American countries, far beyond the current boundary marked by the border with Guatemala.

LANGUAGE

The language spoken by most Mexicans is Spanish, but it is far from the only language spoken in Mexico. There are many Mexicans, about one million, who are at ease only in indigenous languages. Of these, the two largest

---

[2]Geographically, Mesoamerica extended from central Mexico down through much of Central America. More than a hundred distinct languages were spoken in the area when the Spaniards landed in 1519. There were many commonalities among the various language groups that existed in Mesoamerica, among them the adoption of a calendar and a deep interest in questions regarding time.

groups by far are Maya and Nahuas. Maya is a difficult language, tonal and accented, and there are many distinct languages within the Maya family. Nahuatl, the language of the Aztecs, which is spoken in a wide swath across the center of Mexico, is less difficult. It uses glottal stops, which are not easy sounds for English speakers, with the possible exception of people from certain parts of Brooklyn, who say "bot-l" for "bottle."

In the pre-Hispanic period, the people who spoke Nahuatl considered themselves superior, in part because of their language. Unlike most indigenous tribes and nations, the categorical name they had for themselves was not "the people," but "Nahua," which means "clear speaker." It could have meant simply that Nahuatl, their language, was unlike most indigenous languages in that it was not accented or tonal, but it may also have indicated that the Nahuas, like the Maya, had discerned something essential about human beings: the faculty of speech distinguished them from all other creatures.[3]

The number of languages within what are now the political boundaries of Mexico at the moment of the Spanish invasion probably exceeded 175. And by that time the languages of some of the most important civilizations had disappeared. Given its history, Mexico can be defined by its love of language, but it cannot be any one language.

HOW THE COUNTRY GOT ITS NAME

Choosing Mexico as a name necessitated changing the name of the people who lived in what is now Mexico City:[4] To avoid confusion the Mexica became the Aztecs. "Aztec" comes from Nahua origin stories, which say the

[3]There were many indigenous peoples besides the Mexica: to name but a few, Maya, Zapotecos, Purépechas, Raramurís, Yaquis, Mixtecos, Otomis, Popolocas, Mixes, Tzotziles, Mazatecos, Huicholes, and Tzeltales.

[4]According to Frances E. Karttunen's *An Analytical Dictionary of Nahuatl* (Norman: University of Oklahoma Press, 1992), "The etymology of [Mexihco] is opaque. Because of the difference in vowel length it cannot be derived from the word ME-TL 'maguey.' The sequence XIH also differs in vowel length from XIC-TLI, 'navel,' which has been proposed as a component element. The final element is locative -C(O)." Miguel León-Portilla said that the name is derived from Mexi or Mexitli, one of the names of Huitzilopochtli, the tutelary god of Tenochtitlán. We have used that derivation in our book *In the Language of Kings* (2001). For those who are not familiar with the word "maguey," I suggest the elixir derived from various versions of that heaven-sent plant: pulque, mezcal, and, from the blue maguey, tequila.

people came from a place called Aztlán, which probably means "Place of the White Heron" or something similar. The pre-Hispanic people who lived in what is now Mexico City had several names, in the way that "British" and "English" refer to the same people. Tenochtitlán was the name of the city-state, so Tenochas; Nahuatl was the name of the language group, so Nahuas; and Mexica referred to one of the names of their tutelary god. But they were not called Aztecs until 1821.

The choice of the name Mexico was not merely to recall pre-Hispanic power, although that certainly played a role. It was a curious choice in several respects. The government of the new Republic of Mexico was controlled by *criollos*, people of purely European ancestry. They despised the Indians of their own time (the very word *indio* had become an insult) but revered the ancient Indians, especially the newly named Aztecs. By 1821 Mexicans already preferred looking backward.

The idea resonates in the mid-twentieth-century work of Octavio Paz, who said that Mexico and the United States face in opposite directions: Mexico looks to the past, and the United States to the future. Paz made it clear that the issue was more complicated than one memorable assertion, but this connection to the past was, for him, the dominant factor in the makeup of the Mexican character. Another was the land; it was impossible to ignore the importance of the land in a country that had been born on the day of the domestication of corn.

THE LAND

In the recurring Mexican dream, the one that brings a smile to the dreamer's face, a gentle rain falls, the soil drinks, and all the land, whether torn from jungle or rescued from the high desert sun, is green. Mexicans dream the vision of green land in the crowded apartment complexes of one of the largest cities in the world, in mountain villages, and the squatters' camps that house the assembly plant workers along the northern border. Not so long ago the dream of land would have defined Mexico. That is what Emiliano Zapata would have said. And it would have been the definition given by President Lázaro Cárdenas when he turned over great expanses of land to the peasants in the 1930s. It is still the dream of every Mexican, rich or poor, in New York as well as Nuevo León, but the reality no longer defines the country. Perhaps it never did.

If one were to ask Encarnación Ruiz to define Mexico, she would speak of it in terms of land, of rivers and oceans, of ranches and tiny farms, and stolen squares of dust-covered rock. In Matamoros, in the state of Tamaulipas, in the heat, on land that once gave a few turnips in the best of seasons, Sra. Ruiz, born in Chiapas, in the far south, landless, a refugee from the primacy of men and the ravages of overpopulation, took for herself and her husband one Mexican dream.

This act, which in their minds was the reification of dreams, was entirely illegal. They stole a man's property. In the middle of a half-failed farm, not far from a stream that carried muddied brown water down to the Río Bravo, which is known in the United States as the Rio Grande, they erected three walls made of packing crates and cardboard. These were sufficient to defeat the north and west winds and support a roof to protect them from the sun and occasional rain. In a formal ceremony attended by them and their three children, they consecrated the land and blessed their home, attaching a crucifix to the packing crate wall. Sra. Ruiz, the dreamer in the family, declared then that they had founded a colony. Since it was constructed of dreams, she gave it the name of a dream, Valle Verde (Green Valley).

Sra. Ruiz recalled the origin of the colony, how she came to Valle Verde. Dreams begin in anger, she said, and after that comes longing. In Chiapas, where she was born, worldly property belonged to men. She was the child of a man who had five sons, one daughter, and a tiny farm. He was one of four sons of a man who had a larger farm that passed in equal parts to his four sons upon his death. And he, in turn, was the son of a man who had owned a rancho, which he divided among his six sons at his death. And he, in turn . . .

Each son, in his time, had been the inheritor of a fraction of the land of his father. The few acres belonging to Encarnación's father had not supported his family. Even so, the shards of the dream he left behind had been intended only for his sons. Encarnación was bereft. She married a man who was also landless, and they set out from Chiapas with a different dream, one in which rain was not required. "We wanted to explore our country and our future," she said. "We wanted to go across the border." They got as far as Matamoros, where they found work in a factory. The hours were long, and the pay was poor. Much of what they earned went to rent on a tiny house.

In time they met others like themselves and formed a community of the landless. Sra. Ruiz emerged as the leader, for she was the most eloquent. She was not fierce, not tall, not heavy, and she did not shout or use obscenities. It is difficult to understand how such a small woman, a woman with benign eyes, became the leader of so many people in a struggle to steal the land of a wealthy and well-connected man—until Sra. Ruiz speaks. Although her voice is neither loud nor deep, it commands. Her words march, measured, steady, and certain. She does not equivocate; she never uses the Mexican *o sea* (meaning "it could be something else, some other way"). She is a definite woman; she leads, she took the land first.

Others followed. More and more people moved out of the city, escaping what they called the trap of renting. Eventually the land was condemned by the government and given to the squatters. Then thousands came. They had no electricity, no running water, no sewage system, and no way to dig cesspools in the rocky ground. They had land.

As soon as Valle Verde was established, the same three-sided shelters built of packing crates and cardboard walls appeared in another colony adjacent to it. The people learned politics: In return for their votes they demanded electricity. And got it. When they were confident of their right to the land, they built tiny houses of adobe and furnished them with television. Then a new colony started. It too was filled with dreamers. They named the new colony Derechos Humanos (Human Rights), and after that came another colony, which they named Porfirio Muñoz Ledo, for the leftist who was the first member of the opposition to be the speaker of the Mexican House of Representatives. And then, with the battle apparently won, they began to name the new colonies in a Mexican way: March 5, May 17, and so on, for even now, among these internal migrants, there are remnants of the ancient importance of dates. Mexicans are the descendants of precise astronomers and powerful astrologers. The shamans who came up from the impoverished south to work among the squatters still use astrological tables, along with herbs and prayers, to say who will live and who will die and when there will be electricity and running water in the camps.

Conditions improve slowly for the squatters. Potable water is delivered by truck, and the summer sun cooks the water sour in the barrels outside the houses. The people still dump their waste and wash their clothing in the same filthy stream. Wooden carts, rolling on automobile tires, drawn by ancient horses, pass by the three-sided shacks. At night thieves filter through the darkness to rob and sometimes kill the residents. Yet people rarely leave their purloined land, packing up to cross the border to the other dream.

More come every day. Fewer and fewer can read; many do not speak Spanish; some have never seen a city before, even a city like Matamoros. They all lay claim to some small piece of land; no matter how little or how nearly useless, they claim it. And the land also claims them. In Mexico, land is the politics, land grants citizenship; land is the source of everything, it makes one real.

Or so it was.

By 1995 three-fourths of the population of Mexico was urban; five years later more than 10 percent of all Mexican citizens lived in the United States.[5] Separation from the land had redefined the country and its people. Most of Mexico now floated free, unconnected to the *patria chica* (personal homeland) of old. No international borders had changed, but the time-honored definition of the country in the language of land now belonged mainly to history and dreams. This loosening from its earthly origins would transform the country and its citizens more profoundly than Independence or the Revolution and civil wars of 1910–1920; nothing like it had occurred since the Spanish invasion.

A simple definition of Mexico remains elusive. Religion may serve to define Mexico, although not any one religion, but religiosity per se. The great distinction between the United States and Mexico at the beginning of the twenty-first century is that there is no country more concerned with religion than Mexico and no country more concerned with money than the United States; each is a paragon in its own way.

What has disappeared from the definition of Mexico during the fifty-two-year cycle that passed during my acquaintance is the sense of place. The

---

[5]An accurate estimate of the number of Mexican nationals living in the United States is virtually impossible. People living and working in a foreign country without proper documentation do not want to be found out by the authorities, including the Census Bureau. No one knows how many Mexican citizens cross the border each year in either direction. The Immigration and Naturalization Service (still known by that name, although changed officially) keeps count only of those whose crossing it interdicts. Since the crossing has become more difficult in recent years, fewer undocumented people engage in the long and difficult commute, preferring to remain in the United States for much longer periods, perhaps even to settle permanently there. The effects of this change in immigration patterns will be discussed later. See Book Three, Chapter 36.

art of Mexico makes this clear. Carlos Fuentes saw the beginnings of the lack of place in the urban loneliness of *Where the Air Is Clear*, then spent much of the rest of his career seeking through his fictions to find the cause of the loneliness. The work of the Mexican muralists, which was about the history of place and the struggle for land, long ago gave way to different schools of painting, abstract works and imitations of Europe, and now the erotic explorations of Francisco Toledo. Juan Rulfo's great Mexican novel *Pedro Páramo*, which begins, "I came to Comala . . . ," could not be written now, for the sense of place, the ground on which the mythical world of Mexican art stood, has been lost.

Of all the characteristics that once defined Mexico, only death, time, and religion remain. The sense of place, a God-given home, is gone. The people who came south to settle in the high plain and build the great Aztec nation were nomads, wanderers in the desert. At the beginning of the twenty-first century the Mexicans are wanderers again. Mexico is now, in the moment, but it is also in the past. Octavio Paz and the old man of Agua Prieta were correct: history and the moment. To think of Mexico only in one epoch or another is to lose sight of it entirely.

The story of this wandering can be written on a grain of rice.

RICE

The fair has no name. It moves, and wherever it goes it takes the name of the town or the celebration of the day. It is the Celaya Fair and the Cinco de Mayo[6] Fair, Carnival, Veracruz, Chihuahua, and Independence Day. It is the fair of Jesus, cold beer, auctions, bumper cars, history, hot food, and the carousel. No one knows exactly when or where it began, and everyone who travels with the fair prays that it will never end. The fair is work, and although the government says that only 3 percent of the work force is unemployed, there are no jobs to be found in Mexico. More than half of all Mexican workers belong to the informal sector, the nation of jugglers, street vendors, seamstresses, maids, day laborers, thieves, fire-eaters, bead

---

[6]On May 5, 1862, Mexican troops in Puebla under the command of General Ignacio Zaragoza defeated a French army of sixty-five hundred men, many of them veterans of the Crimea. The hero of the battle was Brigadier General Porfirio Díaz, who later became president of Mexico.

stringers, rubber tree tappers, clowns, charcoal makers, fortune-tellers, shoeshiners, and legions of aging men in makeshift uniforms who watch the cars that need no watching.[7]

A booth at the fair is steady work, like owning a stall in a market, or better. It can be done with no more investment than an arcane skill and the look of innocence in the barker's eyes. And a skill does not rot, like spurned vegetables, or turn brown and bloody, like cut meat in a case.

The fair spreads over many acres, and it is everywhere as clean as Franco's boulevards or Disney's streets. No empty cup, no scrap of paper mars the fairgrounds. The mix of cleanliness and cacophony begins in an open field approaching the fair. Local vendors spread their crucifixes and pots and wood carvings on blankets. They stay all day and into the night, showing weavings by lamplight, holding up religious paintings to the rainbow of lights beyond the main gate. The visitors pick their way through the vendors, whose blankets crowd together and leave less and less walking space as they near the entrance to the fair. The vendors call out in the darkness to the visitors as they come and go; they even appeal to those who emerge from the light burdened with toys, pictures, bolts of cloth, crucifixes, and crockery.

Inside the portable walls the beckoning noise dominates; even the flashing lights and neon signs cannot compete with the noise. The fair begins with long rows of booths, all bathed in the noise of the carousel and the auctioneer, the beer parlors, music halls, transvestite shows, video arcades. At the heart of the fair, the noise forces the visitors to shout; the pyramid of noise rises into a curious silence in which people speak with hand signs and facial expressions, a host of mutes, and everyone screaming.

[7]There is no generally accepted definition of the informal sector or informal economy. The International Labor Organization has one definition, economists have another, governments another, and so on. In general, the informal economy comprises persons who generate income through trade (exchange involving money) or barter to support themselves. Other definitions say the informal economy is outside government or corporate structures; yet others say the informal economy comprises activities that are only partly legal in that participants do not pay taxes, get proper licenses, and so on, although they are not criminals. In underdeveloped countries in Asia, Africa, and Latin America the informal economy supports a large part, often a majority, of the population. The degree of dependence upon informal economic activity is one measure of underdevelopment.

In countries trying to rationalize the informal economy, informal activities (a shoeshine box or a taco stand) become *microbusinesses*; a woman who sells goods she knits at home and a man who weaves straw hats at home become microindustries.

A man passes through the crowd, carrying two great white crucifixes over his shoulder, each with exactly the same representation of suffering Jesus, each with its own crown of thorns and sacred heart. The crosses are taller than the man and touch the ground behind him, leaving ruts in the swept earth. He bends beneath the weight of the crucifixes and walks slowly, accompanied by the sounds of hawkers and rock and roll. He stops to speak to the vendor of photographs of the Revolution of 1910, pauses to drink a cup of watermelon juice, nods to the leather belts seller, and stops again before the bracelet and earring booth. These are his stations.

The woman who sells religious articles wears a black lace mantilla supported by a comb stuck into her graying hair. She has no commerce with the people on either side of her booth. One sells illustrated novels, and the other displays silky red and black lace underwear. The woman under the mantilla carries herself as if on parade, looking neither left nor right. Beside her, the Virgin of Guadalupe, standing as tall as life, surrounded by flowers, appears the more gentle in the presence of the sanctimonious soldier.

Beyond the underwear stall and a meager display of carved wood from Asia, there is a booth with no counter. It stands open to the world, the only such booth among hundreds, vulnerable, a booth without guile. And in the center of the open space, standing at the imaginary line that marks the front of the booth, reaching ever so slightly into the flow of the passing crowd— a mild disturbance, like a stone in a stream, and no more aggressive—a young woman holds a tiny glass tube at eye level, thrusting it into the line of sight of the passersby.

Inside the tiny tube a cylindrical white object floats freely. She shakes the tube, showing the white object inside. "Look," she says, and points to the young man behind her, inside the booth. "This is what *he* can do. He will write your name on a grain of rice. Come, have him write your name on a grain of rice. A souvenir for her. A souvenir for him. A sign of love. Unforgettable." She holds up the tube. Indeed, the rice has a name. Illegible at almost any distance, it floats within the glass.

The young woman does not look into the eyes of the people who pass by her, walking around her. She sees them, she speaks to them, but she has no gaze. Although her face is the color of the face of the Virgin of Guadalupe in the next booth and the set of her features, the clean line of the nose, the unremarkable chin, black hair, and mothering eyes, speaks of the same benevolence, the young woman with the grain of rice does not claim innocence. She appears at the boundary of the booth, but she has no gaze: She hides something.

Perhaps that is what attracts people to the booth. It cannot be the grain of rice. No one could read the name written on the rice, not in the crowd, not in the admixture of colors that bestow the light. The young man inside the booth could not attract customers. His teeth are sharp; his hair is thick and straight, standing up like animal hair. He has the mien of a carnivore.

He is twenty-five; she is twenty-seven. She came with her parents from the state of Guerrero to the great Mexico City slum Nezahualcoyotl.[8] Her parents spoke Nahuatl; his did not. He was born in Neza, as the second generation of squatters, the rock and roll generation, refer to their section of the city. They found each other in Neza. But they could not find work in the slum or anywhere in the city, not even at the minimum wage. Miraculously, an old man, an artisan with trembling hands, came to settle near them. Because the uncertainty in his hands no longer permitted him to practice his craft, he took the young man as an apprentice. Within a few months, the apprentice could name the world on a grain of rice. But there was no money in Neza for the purchase of the artisan's efforts, and they could not pay the bribe for a place near the Zócalo in the historic center of Mexico City or even a stall in the thieves' market.

The apprentice, now the master, joined the itinerant fair. The young woman went with him. He could not attract customers, and she could not write on a grain of rice. They tried to learn from each other; but she did not have a steady hand, and he could not make a benign face of his sharp teeth and animal hair. When she brought customers to him, she stood beside the customers, chattering as they watched him write on the grain of rice, wetting the point of the fine pen on his tongue after each letter, his eyes as steady as his hand.

When he had inserted the grain of rice into the tube, sealed it, and attached it to the key ring, she took the money, fifteen pesos, from the customer. Almost always it was a couple, and she gave the key ring to the man to present to the woman. There was a little ceremony. She wished them God's blessing. The young man said little, nor did he show his sharp teeth in a smile.

At the end of every week they had a thousand pesos, from which they

---

[8]Named for the Nahua poet and *huey tlahtoani* (great speaker) of Tezcoco (1402–1472).

paid for the stall, transportation, and food. At the end of every night they gathered all the key chains and all the tiny glass tubes and all the pens and grains of rice and put them away under the counter in the back of the booth. Then they closed the front of the booth and counted the coins and bills. After the lights of the fair had dimmed and the noise had softened, the young woman lifted the heavy curtain that covered the space under the counter at the side of the booth. She and the young man stood together and smiled at the four-year-old boy who slept there curled up on a mattress of cardboard. The young man reached down and touched the dampness on the boy's forehead. The child lay deeply sleeping in its place and did not stir under the benign gesture of the father.

2.

In the Beginning . . .

There were many who for slight reasons of sadness, troubles, or sickness hanged themselves in order to escape and go and rest in their heaven where they said the goddess of the gallows, whom they called Ixtab ("female of the cord," related to the moon) came to take them.

—DIEGO DE LANDA[1]

Not long ago, in a tiny village in the Yucatán, a girl was born with the face of the sixth century, a face like those carved into the stone walls of ancient ruins and painted on vases and the interior walls of temples. A thousand years after the end of the classic period of Maya civilization, the face of the girl was irresistible. Whoever saw her was captured by time and beauty. She was more history than human, more beautiful than real. As she grew up through adolescence, she became aware of herself. She looked into mirrors; she stood close to people when she spoke to them, touching them with her breath.

To emphasize her history, she learned to show her profile, the curve of her nose and shape of her eyes, which were like horizontal teardrops. Whoever saw her could imagine the ancient world: a queen incised upon a wall, a string of spines pulled through her tongue; a king attended by his scribes; captives dragged by the hair.

The young woman who was out of her time did not look either happy or sad. Her face never changed; she was not uninteresting, but she was out of reach, like some ancient work of art, appreciated more for its form than content. Whoever saw her fell in love with the idea of her.

She lived across the road from Don Romulo the *h-meen* (shaman) of the village, and it may have been that when she was very young, no more than an infant, she had cried too often and Don Romulo had soothed her by letting out the black winds with the prick of a rattlesnake fang on the

---

[1] *Relación, The Maya,* translated by A. R. Pagden (Chicago: J. P. O'Hara, 1975).

17

bridge of her nose. Perhaps the ceremony of the fang had informed her face, made her into a work of art. I knew Don Romulo. He had sung to me. His voice was high and thin, but musical. He belonged to the time when Mayan traders traveled from the coast through the low jungle, bringing stingray spines as sharp as needles to the singers and healers of the interior. He had made such a trade in the weeks before he died, shortly after I saw him last.

They say that Don Romulo was a psychologist who could cure strange behaviors with songs and spicy honey made by bees that fed on the pollen of the habanero chilli plant. Perhaps he had sung for the girl with the sixth-century face. She was not like the other girls of her age. They giggled. She was a straightforward woman, although she was still a girl. She had the scent of perfume. She said, "The men come home to the village on Saturday nights with money in their pockets from construction jobs. They get drunk and fight in the streets of the village and beat their women. Don't ever come here on Saturday night." All the other girls in the village had a dreamy view, something like a lie. She was as honest as art. Men sought her, and she was as unresponsive as the stones of a Mayan temple. She was simply there.

One night, when the moon was full and the cycle of years was nearing its end, she and another young woman went out into the jungle in the darkness. They did not wear blue jeans or shorts or modern clothes; they wore embroidered *huipiles* (tunics) and carried jars and cans in sacks. By the light of the moon, they climbed the grassy side of a mound that covered an ancient *ku* (temple), one not yet molested by archaeologists or thieves, and then at the top of the ku, in the pale white light, they tasted each other as if their mouths were made of the stinging honey born of chilli and thought of the goddess Ixtab, who is herself a woman, death and the moon, and they opened the bottles and boxes and filled themselves with poison.

Neither long nor short, the old man of Agua Prieta said, history and the moment. Before the Spaniards arrived in the beginning of the sixteenth century, there had been many wars in the land we now identify as Mexico. These were not skirmishes among small tribes, but great wars involving thousands of troops, trained divisions, brilliant tactics, and great numbers of dead. In other words, Mexico was a civilized place, and it held civilized wars. More than thirteen hundred years before the so-called discovery of America, there were city-states and complex alliances among them. Some city-states had systems of inherited rule, kings and princes, and in others rulers were elected by an aristocracy of warriors, priests, and scholars. These city-states developed literatures, science, a religion with many branches, architecture, civil societies, sanitation systems, theater, music, dance. It was a world of its own, civilized and murderous. The concept of zero, the step beyond mere counting, was known to the Maya of Mesoamerica hundreds of years before it traveled from the Middle East to Europe.

Maya cities flourished between the third and tenth centuries and then were mostly abandoned, perhaps as a result of people fleeing devastating wars, more likely for some other reason that no one has yet identified. The end of the Maya classic period in the tenth century is still unexplained. But every few years for the past century someone has offered a new and incontrovertible theory of the widespread simultaneous collapse of the Maya city-states, many of them hundreds of miles apart. And a few years later another equally incontrovertible theory surfaces. Was it famine, disease, crop failure, overuse of land? Or war? Or could it have been something in their calendar, a prediction, one ominous date? No people in the history of the world has been more concerned with questions of time than the Maya. Their calendar was remarkably accurate, their astronomical calculations were impeccable; they could predict the movements of the planet Venus to the day. They had even set a date for the end of the world, our year 2012. But there is nothing in what we know of their work that dwells on the time of the collapse in the tenth century.

Can it have been written somewhere by the Maya themselves? They could write. They were in fact one of three civilizations, the others being the Mesopotamian and Chinese, to invent systems of writing. Recent readings of the carvings left in stone by the Maya speak of gods, dynasties, wars, and time. And although no details have yet been made out of the nature or the full scope of these wars, they were the work of civilized peoples, which means they were grand and terrible, highly organized, and their purpose was almost always conquest, tribute, power. And like all civilized nations of the world, they had a rationale behind their wars. The Maya based their wars on questions of time. Every major cycle of time was "seated"—that is, had its religious center—in one city-state. Power accompanied the seating of the cycle, and the standing armies of the Maya city-states, led by generals under the guidance of politically astute priests, went to war with one another over it.

In the city of Palenque, in what is now the state of Chiapas in southern Mexico, there was a king and conqueror named Pacal.[2] He ordered the building of pyramids and palaces, and according to the anthropologist Linda Schele, Pacal was a conqueror on the order of Alexander the Great or surely one of the Romans. The partially reconstructed ruins of his brilliant city rise out of the jungle now, a destination for tourists and an invitation to consider the mystery of the Maya. All we know of the history and thought of Pacal the architect and conqueror is what can be deciphered of the phonograms (phonetic writing) and logograms (signs used for complete words) carved in stone. And much of that is merely surmise.

After the tenth century the Maya civilization continued, but the brilliance was lost. Like a dancer after a terrible fall, all the turns, all the leaps, all the poses were perfect, but not brilliant, not breathtaking, not original anymore. People and ideas came down from the north. The names of new cities showed central Mexican influence. And then, as we know from oral histories that were written down in alphabetic language in the sixteenth century (and perhaps later), the Maya city-states of the postclassic period (tenth through fifteenth centuries) tore one another apart. There are records of intrigues, betrayals, leagues of city-states, and then entire cities destroyed. A visitor can still look at the unreconstructed ruins of Mayapán, in the center of the present-day state of Yucatán, and see the work of ancient war. After the battle and the defeat of Mayapán the victors lit huge fires inside the limestone structures of the city. The gases given off by the stone exploded and destroyed the pyramids and palaces as if they had been bombed or blown apart in a modern war.

When the Spaniards invaded, the Maya fought them and were defeated, and fought them again and were defeated, and fought them yet again, and again, all the way up into the first years of the twentieth century. But there was never again a great Lord Pacal. The classic Maya civilization had risen

---

[2]It is foolish and misleading to translate the names of individuals in any society; Mr. Schwarz is not black, and Mrs. Bird cannot fly. So it is with the ancient peoples of Mexico. For example, Nezahualcoyotl may mean "Hungry Coyote," but he was not a coyote, and he was probably not always famished.

and warred and bled and then mysteriously declined. The other aspect of civilization, the language and culture, never died.

The Maya, who were the great mathematicians and astronomers, inventors of writing, potters, painters, philosophers who dwelled on the very nature of time, were not the beginning of Mesoamerica, nor were they the conclusion of it. They were a starburst, a glorious moment, in a civilization that rose and fell in many places and many languages. The idea, the essence of what eventually spread across Mesoamerica appears to have begun on the east coast, in what is now the Mexican state of Tabasco. It influenced or evolved into all the cultures that followed, but no one knows quite how it happened. It was probably the Homer, the Abraham, and most certainly the Copernicus of Mesoamerica, but there are no individuals, real or imagined, to credit for beginnings. There are no books to consult, no oral history to be carefully written down by some Spanish friar. No one even knows what language was spoken there, in Tabasco, a thousand years before the birth of Christ, at the birth of Mesoamerica. The culture was given the name Olmec by the central Mexicans. It means "Rubber People," which hardly seems a name people would give themselves. The Olmecs worshiped a jaguar god and sculpted, among other things, the enormous basalt heads with thick lips and rather childlike features for which they are known. The headgear worn by whomever these immense heads represent is often described as reminiscent of an early leather football helmet. It is a foolish anachronism, but only through anachronistic comparisons can one begin to grasp the culture of Mesoamerica.

Why the Olmecs quarried the eight- or nine-foot-high pieces of basalt, somehow managed to bring them fifty miles overland, and then carved them into huge heads is another mystery. What is known about the Olmecs is that they developed a calendar, a sense of form in art that is absolutely peerless, and that they are the likely originators of Mesoamerican culture. How that culture moved south to become the Maya world, crossed Mexico from the east to the west coast to influence cultures in the present-day state of Oaxaca is not known, but at roughly the same time as the rise of the Olmecs, the Monte Albán civilization rose on the west coast. Two separate city-states and cultures, with different languages, were founded there: the Mixtec and Zapotec. Since they too were civilized peoples, they fought organized, long-lasting, and terrible wars. The ruins of both cultures remain, a delight for tourists and an occupation for archaeologists.

The Olmec world collapsed at about the time of the rise of the Maya to the south and another civilization in central Mexico, about fifty miles from present-day Mexico City. The central Mexican civilization was later named Teotihuacán, meaning the "Place of the Gods," but as with the Olmecs, no one knows what language was spoken there or what the people called themselves. The most curious thing about Teotihuacán, at least in terms of civilizations, is that it may have been a pluralistic society. There is evidence that people of different cultures, speaking different languages, lived in various parts of the city-state. What they did in Teotihuacán, why the Teotihuacán people were able to tolerate the presence of foreigners in their midst are another mystery, although it is clear that the guest peoples—and there were many, from many cultures—were neither slaves nor captives. But Teotihuacán, where the people were apparently pacific and the art was staid and gorgeous and monumental, also fell. Its grandeur lasted from the third to the sixth century, and then the pyramids of the sun and the moon and the enormous spaces devoted to the dead became dead themselves, silent and untouched, and much of what was there was not looked upon by humans for more than a thousand years. How it ended is another of the mysteries of ancient Mexico, for it was in the center of the high central plateau, where the great wars eventually took place, but there was no war in Teotihuacán, there are few signs of any kind of militarism. There are only the gods, the dead, the peace and beauty, and the end.

After Teotihuacán, the high plateau of Mexico, which was probably very green, very different from the land as it is now, did not know much peace again. There was what we now call a power vacuum. The great city-state of Tula, about sixty-five miles north of Mexico City, rose after the end of Teotihuacán, achieving its peak in the ninth century and falling in the twelfth century. The people who settled there were perhaps fleeing from Teotihuacán after its fall as well as fierce immigrants from the north who spoke Nahuatl, which became the language of central Mexico and the lingua franca of almost all of Mesoamerica, certainly the language of trade and probably of culture as well. Although they began as ferocious warriors, the people of Tula, the Toltecs (Craftsmen), soon came to merit their name. They were artisans and builders, and there was in Tula a great heightening of religious concepts.

The Toltecs, by means of trade, culture, and conquest, spread their ideas and talents across what is now Mexico, to the east coast and as far south as the Yucatán Peninsula. The linguistic evidence of their influence can be seen in place-names. Mayapán, which was destroyed in the fifteenth century, was a place-name out of two cultures. "Maya" is, of course, a Mayan word, but the suffix is Nahuatl, and the combined Mayan and Nahuatl name means "Place of the Maya." Chichén Itzá, which fielded the army that destroyed Mayapán, was a mixed Mayan and Toltec culture.

Although the Toltecs were warriors, practitioners of a form of economic and cultural imperialism backed by military might that bears more than a little resemblance to ancient European city-states (and, in the view of many people, to the current United States), there was something else going on in Tula during that period, perhaps the single most extraordinary conflict in the history of Mexico. There was a prince in Tula who had the name of a god, and everything that was to happen in Mexico after the birth of that prince, who was the prince of culture, perhaps even of peace, was influenced by the god, the prince, and the conflict.

The god was an old god, not so old as the jaguar god of the Olmecs or the rain god or the Old Old God, who is the god of fire, but ancient nonetheless. He is the shape of the steps of an ancient temple and the demiurge in the oldest extant Maya book of history and philosophy (The Council Book or Popol Vuh). His name exists in many Mesoamerican languages, and it has been famously translated by D. H. Lawrence as the Plumed Serpent. In Nahuatl, the language of the Toltecs, his name was Quetzalcoatl. If a visitor to Mexico and its history were to know only a single word in Nahuatl, the language of the Aztecs, it would be the name of the Plumed Serpent, Quetzalcoatl.[3] He is the only god of ancient Mexico who still shares the throne of culture and, in some places, of belief.

There are two versions of the life of Quetzalcoatl. One is divine, and the

---

[3] The quetzal is a beautiful bird with a long tail. The green feathers were very precious to people of Mesoamerica. The noun "quetzal" came to mean "precious." As an adjective it may also mean "beautiful." *Coatl* means "serpent" but may also mean "twin." Together the words mean Feathered Serpent or Precious Twin. To make the linguistics even more interesting, the mythical Quetzalcoatl became the Morning Star, Venus, which is the older of the twins of the morning, Venus and the Sun. There are representations of the Plumed Serpent in a series of temple steps arranged so that the sun at equinox climbs the steps. Intricacies such as these make the exegesis of Mesoamerican texts extremely difficult. It may be that somewhere in these arcana the reason may be found for the so far inexplicable fall of Mesoamerican city-states.

other a mixture of the divine and the secular. In the divine version, human life has ended on earth. Quetzalcoatl descends to the underworld, finds the bones of the dead, and resurrects human life on earth. He is also the discoverer of corn, which permits civilization. In the other version, he is a monk in Tula, where he is seduced into drunkenness and incest by three wizards and flees the city. One reading of this secular version has to do with human sacrifice. Quetzalcoatl opposed it, suggesting instead the sacrifice of butterflies. The wizards represent the other faction, which favored human sacrifice. It is also possible that the wizards represent other political forces in the city.

The true nature of the conflict may never be known. It may not be associated with political conflict at all. The monk may have been the one who adopted the cultural notions of Mesoamerica and the wizards the group that preferred the culture and gods the nomadic tribe or tribes had brought south with them. Or Quetzalcoatl and the wizards may represent different aspects of human nature: good and evil, peace and war. In the story that has been handed down, Quetzalcoatl, son of Mixcoatl, the founder of the city of Tula, shamed by his act of incest, flees the city, sets sail on the great ocean, immolates himself, and rises into the sky to become Venus, the Morning Star. The importance of several details of the secular/divine Quetzalcoatl comes clear after the landing of the Spaniards. He was known as the Plumed Serpent, but also by his birth date, Ce Acatl (One Reed). He is sometimes depicted with a beard. And it was prophesied that he would return on the date Ce Acatl in the Aztec calendar, which coincided with our year 1519.

Although its influence was vast, its soldiers fierce, its religion powerful, and its culture magnificent, by the end of the twelfth century Tula had also fallen. Unlike many of the other city-states, however, it left behind its language, Nahuatl, and a new version of the god Quetzalcoatl.

In 1325 the last group of nomadic people arrived in central Mexico. Several city-states had survived the end of Tula, but none of them was either large or strong. Once again there was a power vacuum, and a group came down from the north to fill it. The story of the arrival of the people who became the Aztecs is told in various manuscripts based on oral histories written down by Spanish priests. The invaders were said to be following a prophecy: When they arrived at the place where they were to settle and build their city, they would see an eagle standing on a prickly pear cactus holding a snake in its mouth. The scene they met upon their arrival is the illustration on the Mexican flag. And the name of the famous city they built is Tenochtitlán, which means "the Place of the Cactus."

Who these people were and exactly where they came from are very difficult to prove. There are both chthonian (from the Greek, meaning "originating in an underworld") and autochthonous (originating on the surface of the earth) myths. Either the Aztecs came up onto the surface of the earth through Chicomoztoc (Seven Caves), or they originated in Aztlán. Chthonian myths are generally older; autochthonous myths more likely to be based in some version of history. On those grounds Aztlán appears to be the more accurate, although less lyrical version.

For a large group of Mexicans, Mexican-Americans, and Chicanos living in the United States, the origin of these people in Aztlán, hence Aztecs, is of vital importance, for it enables them to lay claim to legitimate residence in the United States and for some people to ownership of the land of Aztlán, a not yet well-defined area in the Southwest.

These last invaders from the north were even more ferocious than the Toltecs. Persecuted wherever they went, they developed a stunningly harsh view of the world. When they arrived in the Valley of Mexico and found the promised eagle standing on a cactus, the place was already occupied. The people there had a king and a fairly settled life. When the new people arrived, the king did not know how brutalized they had become during their wanderings. After some skirmishing, he gave his daughter in marriage to a leader of the newcomers, an all but universal means to establish a long-lasting peaceful alliance. The newcomers accepted the offer. The princess was given, and the newcomers invited the king to a celebration, where they presented the presumably happily married princess to her father in the form of a priest dressed in the flayed skin of the girl.

Horrified, the king drove the newcomers from any habitable place. He left them to live on rattlesnakes and try to farm the middle of a lake. The Aztecs developed a taste for rattlesnake meat and a system of *chinampas*, artificial islands, to raise grains, legumes, and squash on a lake. They proved to be not only ferocious but imaginative, adaptable, and capable of building an organization far beyond the stage of the city-state. In less than a hundred years the Aztecs went from a nomadic people, wanderers, chased from place to place, to the founders of an empire. In the course of empire they could not rid themselves of several flaws that would eventually prove fatal. They did not make use of the wheel, perhaps because of the lack of beasts of burden in North America. They used what little metal they had, mainly gold, for ornamental purposes only. And while they were not a theocracy, they were utterly dominated by religion, driven by a millenarian certainty that life on earth for individuals, societies, and the species itself was doomed to extinction. They said the period in which they lived was the fifth and final sun, the last age, at the end of which the world would be destroyed.

The oldest of the stories of the origins of the Mexica, *The Legend of the Suns*, tells of the beginnings and endings of the world ". . . . two thousand five hundred and thirteen years before today, the 22nd of May, 1558."[4]

The first sun (4 jaguar, the Aztec calendrical designation for the year in which it began) lasted 676 years. Then the people were devoured by jaguars.

The people of the second sun (4 wind) were blown away by the wind and turned into monkeys.

The people of the third sun (4 rain) were destroyed by a rain of fire and turned into birds.

Those of the fourth sun (4 water) were drowned and turned into fish.

The fifth sun is the present sun (4 motion), and it will end in earthquake and fire.

As a result of these myths, the Aztecs, who had no sense of a certain life after death, were afflicted with a kind of melancholia and a deep concern with ontological questions. In this, they were not different from the other Mesoamerican cultures, like the Maya. All were bound together by a belief in multiple creations and multiple ends and in the certainty that a final end was coming, perhaps soon. One of the best expressions of this comes from a Mexica poet:

> I, Nezahualcoyotl, ask this:
> Do we truly live on earth?
> Not forever here,
> only a little while.
> Even jade breaks,
> golden things fall apart,

[4]Miguel León-Portilla and Earl Shorris, *In the Language of Kings* (New York: W. W. Norton, 2001).

precious feathers fade;
not forever on earth,
only a moment here.[5]

Given this sense of the order of the world, how one died became as important as, perhaps more important than, how one lived. Death was inevitable; endings were inevitable. They could only be staved off for a little while. In Aztec theology, the great god, the sun, depended on the offering of human blood to continue his rounds. Magic of all kinds was used to propitiate the gods. The sun maintained the world itself, but after the sun, there was the rain. The rain god (Tlaloc) could be induced to do his work by the tears of children. It led to sympathetic magic of the cruelest kind: causing children to suffer and weep.

Human sacrifice, which may have been at the center of the conflict in Tula, took a greater and greater role in the land of the Aztecs. They admired the Toltecs; to say that one was like a Toltec was the greatest compliment. To practice the sacrifice of humans, to surpass the Toltecs in this as in other things, including architecture, political organization, the scope of the hegemony, and the luxury of life at the top, was no doubt a kind of goal for the Aztecs. And they accomplished it.

Having leaped from a tribe of ferocious wanderers to the builders and managers of one of the world's largest and without question cleanest cities on earth in slightly less than two hundred years, the Aztecs were a still-unsettled society pursuing three distinct paths: one literary, artistic, philosophical; a second warlike and, when not warlike, a system of ferocious economic exploitation; and the third religious, but in an utterly bizarre fashion. The Aztecs had not invented Mesoamerican culture; they had won it, and they had not quite known what to do with it. Perhaps they were dazzled out of their sense of proportion by their success and terrified of losing it, through either war or the will of the gods. There was a neurotic streak in the culture. The sense of limits had been lost. They took too much, sacrificed too many, turned too harsh and too sybaritic at the same time. The sinewy invaders had become the nervous conquerors. They knew that at any moment their luck could change, and the prospect of such a change plagued their days and their dreams.

---

[5]"Cantares Mexicanos," León-Portilla and Shorris, *In the Language of Kings.*

At the beginning of the sixteenth century they had conquered most of Mesoamerica. For the first time in the history of the continent, a nation had grown far beyond the economic and political borders of a city-state. The Great Speaker of the Aztecs ruled an empire.

THE WOMEN OF CHALCO

Among the last great wars fought by the Aztecs was one in which they defeated the nearby city-state of Chalco. After the battle a woman of Chalco confronted the great speaker and military leader of the Aztecs, an immensely arrogant young man named Axayacatl.[6] The woman in the poem was brave, defiant, and bawdy. Perhaps she never existed, perhaps someone, an ancient feminist or an enemy of Axayacatl's, invented her speech. It does not matter. The important thing is what the poem tells of the woman of Chalco, for to taunt a conqueror, an Aztec fresh from battle, was a risk verging on suicide. And yet there is no record of the death of the woman of Chalco, no mention of punishment. Only the poem and the character of the woman remain.

The Chalco of that time is gone now. The ancient war between the Chalcans and the Mexicans is over. There is another kind of destruction now. It takes place in two stages. First, millions of people from all over Mexico come to Mexico City, where Axayacatl reigned, and when they do not succeed in the great city, when they cannot pay the rent on the most minimal living space, when they cannot find work, when they are robbed in the night and cheated in the daylight, they abandon their dream of living in the capital and find their way by the millions to places outside the center of the city, many to Chalco.[7] They are an irrepressible invading force. Axayacatl himself could not have mounted such a terrible attack upon Chalco.

[6]For those who are concerned with pronouncing the name of the conqueror, the *x* is pronounced as *sh*, and the penultimate syllable is stressed: ash-ah-YA-catl. Nahuatl, like German, is an agglutinative language, which makes for long and difficult words. Many names end with *tzin*, which is simply an honorific. Axayacatl thus becomes Axayacatzin.
[7]See Daniel Hiernaux Nicolas, *Nueva Periferia, Vieja Metrópoli: El Valle de Chalco, Ciudad de Mexico* (Xochimilco: Universidad Autónoma Metropolitana, 1995). I am grateful to Hiernaux for his guidance, his wonderful storytelling, and his deep understanding of Chalco and the phenomenon of the second migration (first to the center of the city and then outward to the periphery).

The once-beautiful place beside a clear lake, where the Chalcans lived within sight of the volcanoes and fished and raised corn and squash and beans and hunted in the mountains for deer and rabbit and armadillo and many kinds of birds, has become a slum for almost a million people. The lake was drained, and the squatters who could not survive the city built cardboard houses and then packing crate houses and outhouses. After the rains came and filled the dry lakebed again, the outhouses overflowed, and the waste of nearly a million people floated on the flood. When the waters subsided, the overflow of the outhouses dried, and as winter approached and the winds came across the dry lake bed, the fecal matter rose into the air in a poisonous cloud that sickened the people of the Valley of Chalco and caused eruptions on their skin.

In the century before the Spaniards arrived, Axayacatl had marched on Chalco with an army of tens of thousands. It is difficult to imagine him now, but every now and then one sees in a Nahua of the twenty-first century a face of dazzling intensity. Axayacatl must have been such a man, brilliant and arrogant, with dark, almost black eyes, and thick, very straight black hair that grew to a peak above his brow. His features would have been regular, but slightly thickened, as if he had been hewn of wood, and he would have been dressed in a cape of magnificent green feathers and ornaments of jadestone and gold. To have mocked him would have been a kind of madness, yet there was a woman of Chalco who stood before him, and taunted him, the victor in bloody war, questioning his manhood:

> How will you make love to me,
> my companion of pleasure?
> Let us do it this way, together,
> are you not a man?
> What is it that confuses you?
>
> . . . . .
>
> I am an old whore,
> I am your mother,
> a lusty old woman,
> old and without juice,
> this is my profession, me, the woman from Chalco.
> I have come to please my blooming vulva,
> my little mouth.
> I desire the lord,

the little man, Axayacatl.
Look on my flowering painting: my breasts.
Will your heart
fall in vain,
little man, Axayacatl?[8]

If the first woman of Chalco was a bawdy poem of defeat and daring, the second woman of Chalco, more than five hundred years later, was a hard and unsmiling novel. I asked if she spoke Nahuatl, which was the language of the first woman of Chalco, and she said, "Yes, but not in the classical form." Then I mentioned the first woman of Chalco, and she lowered her eyes. It was an awkward thing to have said, and I was immediately sorry. It is understood in Mexico, especially among indigenous people, that to study them is to conquer them. I did not want to be Axayacatl again.

The second woman of Chalco sat stiff, stately, and unsmiling at her small desk in the barren room of an office. Her body, the formality of her carriage, the rigidity of her arms as she typed on the electric machine told of some terrible tension inside her. She was like a match ready to burst into flame at the slightest friction. I tried to think of a safe subject. Silence.

Flor Morales[9] was not born in Chalco. She was a woman of the mountains, a Nahuatl speaker from a tiny group of houses, a village where the men and women still raised corn for their own food and kept chickens in the front yard and sheared sheep for wool, which the women combed and spun and loomed. They did not often eat meat; to kill a sheep was madness, to kill a chicken mere extravagance; they ate only the meat of the animals they hunted in the woods. The men drank pulque, the fermented juice of the maguey plant, and mezcal when they could afford it. No one of the older generation could read. Some of the children of the generation of

[8]León-Portilla and Shorris, *In the Language of Kings.* Axayacatl, who ruled the people of Tenochtitlán from the middle of the fifteenth century until 1480, defeated the Chalcans and others but met his comeuppance when he led twenty-four thousand Aztec troops into the present-day state of Michoacán to fight the Purépechas. His arrogance allowed him to fall into a trap. He was defeated by an army of forty thousand Purépechas fighting on their home ground. It was one of the few defeats of the Aztec armies prior to the Spanish invasion.
[9]Flor is not her real name. Daniel Hiernaux, the Belgian scholar who taught at the university at Xochimilco, told me much of what I know about her, for he knew her well and he was in awe of her life.

the second woman of Chalco attended a village school for three or four years, never more.

When Flor was still a child, her father got into a dispute over a patch of land. He was an evil-tempered man and not given to compromise. The dispute grew terrible, violent. There was an ugly scene, and the father was sent to prison. After ten years he was released, and he was unchanged but for one thing: He had learned to read. He returned to his village, a fierce man, a Nahua, and still the head of the family.

His daughter, Flor, was long gone. Her mother had taken her to the city and hired her out as a maid. The girl was slim and pretty, small, not delicately boned, but with the Asian elegance of some Nahua women when they are young. She was not timid, however, like many of the other young women of the village. She spoke easily, in both Nahuatl and Spanish, and she was quick. It was not difficult to find work for her in the city.

Flor was slim and strong, and she was not fair but the color of cocoa in sunlight. And her eyes were very dark. She used her eyes to belie her intelligence, to defend herself from being considered too smart, too quick, ambitious. It was not long before the woman of the household reported to her husband that someone extraordinary had come to work for them. He quickly agreed that she was too bright to remain a domestic servant; it seemed an injustice, the waste of a woman. Her employers sent her to school. She worked in the house and went to school.

Soon the family, which owned a thriving business with a busy warehousing operation, moved her from the kitchen to a job in the business. She had a knack for numbers. She was a disciplined young woman, and complicated: soft as a nursemaid with infants, hard as a Chichimeca warrior in business. She was the mix of mind and ferocity that had characterized the Toltecs. The family for whom she worked were Jews, merchants. As they had been hard pressed to overcome their prejudice against Indians, so she had found it difficult to overcome her prejudice against Jews. It worked somehow, an unlikely marriage, but successful.

Before long she was put in charge of the warehousing operation and all the accounting and inventory control connected to it. She worked, she supervised workers, and she met a man she could love. The young woman from a Nahua village in the mountains had, in the course of a decade, been changed into a businesswoman, an executive, in the largest city in the hemisphere. She had found everything in the world in the business and the family, even the man she loved. He worked there in the warehouse, a handsome man, older than Flor, not so successful, not so quick as she, but handsome and knowledgeable; he knew about love and loving, he knew the world.

She became pregnant with his child, but there could be no marriage, for he had a wife. She did not know what to do. She made demands. He beat her. She left the job. Beaten and sore and heavy with her child, she took what she had, and like tens of thousands before her, she went to the bus station at Tasqueña in the south of Mexico City, and there, among the pick-pockets and commuters, in the confusion of the hurrying thousands, car-rying what little she could drag along with her, Flor took the bus to Chalco. Now she prepared for the child. Everything was gone: love and work and the arms of the family that had taken her in.

Perhaps the beating was the cause or it was some error of nature, but when the baby came, it was dead. As soon as she was able to get up, Flor washed the dead baby and wrapped it in her *rebozo* and tied the great woolen shawl across her shoulders and set out for the village where she had been born. Her father was there. He was the head of the family. Together he and Flor would bury the child in the cemetery beside its ancestors, and every year on the Day of the Dead, they would bring food to all of them, all the ancestors and the baby. They would leave some and they would burn some so that the fumes would enter the graves and nourish the dead. Later, at the end of the day, they would return to the cemetery and make jokes with the dead and each other and consume the food that the dead had not eaten. It would be a great feast and happy. But that would be later. Now she carried the dead child in her rebozo.

The bus trip to the village took many hours. There was no first-class bus, and the buses that made the trip did not leave often. Meanwhile the dead baby lay stiffening in her rebozo. She was very careful with it; she kept it safe. When she arrived in the village, she climbed down from the bus and walked to the house where her father lived. The child was not heavy, and she was young, although the delivery had tired her and she was deeply wearied too by the death, but she anticipated the arms of her father, and it strengthened her.

She told him quickly. There was no other way, for she carried the dead baby in her rebozo, and it had begun to give off a slightly unpleasant odor although she had wrapped it very carefully. Before she finished telling him about the man and the way he had left her, he exploded in rage. He beat her. He beat her down from where she sat, and then he beat her to her knees, and then he drove her from the house with kicks and curses. She stayed in the village only long enough to bury her child.

When she returned to Valle de Chalco, she spoke very little. She lived alone in a dark place where no one else could enter. Instead of the stylish clothing of the businesswoman of the capital, Flor cut her hair short and wore denim so that from a distance she could have been a small man, compact, like a gymnast, and tense, like her father, like a match that could be fired by the slightest friction.

I have not seen Flor, the second woman of Chalco, for a long time, but Jaime Noyola, the director of the Casa de Cultura, where she worked, tells me that Flor has begun a career in politics. Eventually, he said, he will keep his job at her discretion.

TOLLAN

TIZAYOCAN

TZOMPANCO

XALTOCAN

TEOTIHUACAN

CUAUHTITLAN

ACOLMAN

CUAUHCHINANCO

EHECATEPEC

TEPECHPAN

TEZCOCO

AZCAPOTZALCO

TLACOPAN

TLATELOLCO

CHAPULTEPEC

TENOCHTITLAN

COYOHUACAN

CULHUACAN

CUITLAHUAC

TLAXCALLAN

XOCHIMILCO

CHALCO

CHIMALPAN

HUEXOTZINCO

CHOLOLLAN

TECAMACHALCO

3.

Realpolitik and Dreams

Aqiuque inin Tenime?[1] *(Who are these barbarians?)*
—ASKED BY AN AZTEC NOBLE DURING
THE SIEGE OF TENOCHTITLÁN

Mexican history could not possibly have happened as it did. The facts of the Spanish invasion make no sense. A few hundred Spaniards under the command of a lawyer, with no military experience, could not have brought down the great Aztec Empire. Yet it happened, and the events of that improbable clash between the two civilizations have determined the essential elements of the character of every Mexican since the fall of the empire. If an old man in Agua Prieta fortified himself with memories of war, this was the war that informed all wars, for it was the war within him, the war that gave birth to Mexico. He would never have spoken of it as conquest. Of that I am quite certain, for one afternoon I heard his wife call out to him in a strange tongue, neither Spanish nor the slow waltz with English he spoke to me, but something ancient and still not at ease, like the colors conflicted in his skin and the shape of his eyes when he looked into the wind.

In brief, here is the story: In 1517, a group of Spaniards lands on the beaches of the Yucatán Peninsula. They go inland to get fresh water and spend the night ashore. All night, as if in a bad dream, they hear drums and flutes. The drums are loud, an irritation, and the flutes play a strange harmony. They cannot imagine what the music means. At dawn they find themselves surrounded by black-painted Maya warriors carrying spears, arrows, stones, and war axes edged with stone or copper. The Spaniards make a brief stand, then flee to their boats. Twenty are killed by arrows, stones, and the sharp-edged axes. The rest barely escape with their lives.

[1] Florentine Codex, Book 12. James Lockhart, *Nahuas after the Conquest* (Stanford: Stanford University Press, 1992).

35

In 1519, a small party of Spaniards sails west from Cuba, fights several skirmishes with the Maya in the Yucatán, picks up a shipwrecked white man who has learned the Maya language and a woman from a Nahuatl-speaking[2] royal family who has been sold into slavery in the Yucatán. The company of Spaniards heads up the coast and lands in San Juan de Ulúa in the present state of Veracruz. They deal with the natives through the woman, whom history knows as La Malinche, and then begin a long trek through jungles and across mountains to a fabled inland kingdom.[3]

The head of this inland kingdom, Motecuhzoma II,[4] learns of the arrival of the Spaniards and sends emissaries out to meet them. By that time the native interpreter, who has been sleeping with Hernán Cortés the leader of the Spaniards, has learned Spanish. Speaking through her, the emissaries offer gifts to Cortés and invite him to leave. But Motecuhzoma has made a fatal mistake. Cortés, seeing that some of the gifts are made of gold, resolves to go on to the great city called Tenochtitlán. He has 530 men, sixteen horses, cannon, crossbows, arquebuses, and a pack of huge, vicious dogs.

The residents of the fabled city are known as the Mexica[5] (the word "Aztec" was not widely used until 1821, but for the sake of clarity I will use it throughout). They have an army of tens of thousands of skilled warriors armed with bows and arrows, spears, and obsidian-edged war clubs that can easily cut off a man's head or limb. Using this nearly invincible army, the Aztecs have

---

[2]Nahuatl was the language spoken in several city-states in pre-Columbian Mexico. The most widely known speakers were the Aztecs or Mexica; however, there were also Tlaxcalans, Cholulans, Texcocans, and so on. Nahuatl is still spoken by more than a million people in contemporary Mexico, although the classical form of the language is no longer common.

[3]Malintzin (her correct name) may have been the main interpreter, certainly the most fabled, but the shipwrecked sailor spoke Maya and Spanish, and many people along the coast were fluent in both Nahuatl and Maya, so the Spaniards must have had their choice of interpreters. However, these two-stage translations probably ended when the woman, whom Cortés called Doña Marina, learned Spanish.

[4]His complete name is Motecuhzoma Xocoyotzin. The second word means "revered (or honorable) younger one." The suffix -tzin means "honored" and is affixed to many Nahuatl names.

[5]The words "Mexica" and "Mexicans" are used interchangeably when referring to the people of Tenochtitlán and Tlatelolco, now in the center of Mexico City. The Spaniards were later to refer to the entire country as New Spain and to the capital itself as Mexico City. The entire country was not referred to as Mexico until Independence in 1821.

subjugated much of the surrounding area. People from coast to coast pay tribute to them. They have a highly developed civilization. Their capital city-state, Tenochtitlán, is the equal of the great urban centers of the world.

Before the little band of Spaniards has moved very far inland, Cortés demonstrates the thunder of his cannon to the Aztec emissaries, who report back to their ruler. But Motecuhzoma does not alert his vast divisions, he does not prepare his defenses. He waits, he is dreaming. It is the Second Coming of the man born on the date Ce Acatl: Quetzalcoatl, the good one, the monk who died for his own sins, who cast himself adrift in the sunrise sea and rose into the heavens to become the Morning Star.[6] He, Quetzalcoatl, has predicted his own return. It will happen in the year Ce Acatl (One Reed), and the year has come.

The Spaniards set out on the difficult and dangerous journey from the coast. They climb out of the jungle into the mountains, moving toward the cultural, economic, and military center, the place the Aztecs call "the navel of the universe," Tenochtitlán. But they cannot go directly from the sea to Tenochtitlán. They must first pass through Tlaxcala. The Tlaxcalans have paid tribute for many years to the Aztecs. But the Tlaxcalans are not docile. Unlike the Totonacs on the coast, the Tlaxcalans do not welcome the whites, whom they understand as invaders. They fight three separate battles with the foreigners. After the first, in which hundreds of Tlaxcalans and only a few Spaniards are killed, the Tlaxcalan military leader gathers an army of fifty thousand and attacks. When that attack fails, Xicotencatl sends ten thousand men on a night foray. But the Spaniards are not surprised. Although many are wounded and ill, they hold out against the onslaught in the dark.

The next day the Tlaxcalan leaders meet and conclude that their obsidian-edged swords and cotton armor are no match for the steel and gunpowder of the Spaniards. The question for the Tlaxcalans is whom they hate more: the invading Spaniards or their Aztec oppressors. Their decision to ally themselves with the Spaniards will determine the fate of Cortés, if not all of Mexico. What the Tlaxcalans do not expect is the Spanish response to an alliance: slaughter.

In his pitiless account of the massacre at Cholula, Bernal Díaz del

---

[6]Quetzalcoatl was said to have been celibate, devoted to the arts, committed to a life of utter simplicity, if not poverty, for himself; thus he is often said to have been a monk.

Castillo concentrates on the end result of killing one hundred unarmed nobles and after them three thousand common people: "This affair and punishment at Cholula became known throughout the provinces of New Spain, and if we had a reputation for valor before, from now on they took us for sorcerers. . . ."[7]

In the battles with the Tlaxcalans and later with the Aztecs, the strangeness, the luck, and the technology of the Spaniards overwhelm the natives. The obsidian-edged swords break when struck against Spanish steel, and the missiles fired from Spanish arquebuses and cannon easily pierce the cotton armor of the warriors. The natives, used to opponents at the same technological level, attack en masse, which only increases the effectiveness of the Spanish weapons, especially the cannon, firing ragged pieces of metal that tear through the cotton armor. With every thunderous shot, tens upon tens of warriors fall torn, bloodied, dying and dead. Nature too favors the Spaniards. Horses and huge dogs have never been seen in the Americas. Native commanders do not know how to deal with these strange beasts. The invaders, mounted on armored horses, trample the warriors in front of them and slash with their steel swords at those beside them. The dogs are as large as the jaguars of the Americas, and they are heavy beasts, with huge jaws and teeth that tear the flesh and crush the throats of the native warriors. In the open field, the hooves and steel, the fire-breathing cannon and blood-maddened dogs are terrifying enemies.

Cortés moves quickly toward his target. After landing on the coast on April 22, 1519, the Spaniards fight the Tlaxcalans, haul their men and equipment overland, and climb to the breathtaking altitude of Tenochtitlán in only six months, arriving on November 8 of the same year. Meanwhile, the leader of the tiny Spanish group that has dared to "invade" a country of perhaps twenty-five million people,[8] has to deal with desertions and the enmity

---

[7]His *Discovery and Conquest of Mexico* (New York: Noonday Press, 1956) and the letters of Cortés are the only firsthand accounts by the Spaniards. Important native accounts were recorded later in the Florentine Codex (informants of Fray Bernardino de Sahagún), the Aubin Codex, the Anonymous Manuscript of Tlatelolco, and in the works of Fernando de Alva Ixtlilxochitl and F. Alvarado Tezozomoc.

[8]The population of the territory now known as Mexico cannot be accurately estimated. Clavijero, the Jesuit who was exiled to Italy, estimated the population in 1518 at 30 million. Other estimates range as low as 8 million, with most now at about 25 million. The estimate by Woodrow Borah of 25 million in central Mexico alone seems too high on the face

of the governor of Cuba, whose orders he has disobeyed. His troubles are so great that to keep his small band from running away, he finally orders the Spanish ships anchored off the east coast to be burned.

But Motecuhzoma, the "Great Speaker"[9] who rules the Aztecs, still makes no move against the Spaniards. He has been hearing about them for more than a year, at least since a brief landing by Juan de Grijalva in 1518. Perhaps he has also heard news of the rout of the Spaniards at Champotón a year earlier. But he does not employ the power of the great Aztec army; instead he offers gifts to the Spaniards and allows them to form alliances with the Tlaxcalans and other subjugated peoples. Before long the Aztecs are defeated by a combination of Spanish steel, murderous dogs, armored horses, and vast numbers of native allies recruited from the vassal states around Tenochtitlán. Motecuhzoma invites the Spaniards into the city of gleaming white buildings and beautifully decorated pyramids and temples. Astonishingly, he allows himself to be made a prisoner in his own city, his own nation.

Unbeknown to the Aztecs or even to the Spaniards, the invaders bring with them a powerful weapon that is invisible to the naked eye and devastating to almost every indigenous person it touches. Like the horses and dogs and cannon and hardened metal, the invisible weapon is beyond the imagination of the Aztecs, worse than the nightmarish omens that preceded the arrival of Cortés. But even before that weapon is deployed, there will be

---

of it. Estimates of the population of the combined cities of Tenochtitlán and Tlatelolco range from 25,000 to as high as a million. Since there was no census before 1558, most population estimates claim to be based on the amount of food that can be raised in a given area, but most of the early estimates of pre-Hispanic agricultural production per acre appear now to have been far too low, leading scholars to put the population figures closer to the high estimates. One can only be certain that there were millions of people in the area between the Yucatán Peninsula and the current U. S.-Mexican border and that Tenochtitlán and Tlaltelolco were large cities, with a combined population of not much less than 100,000 and possibly more than 250,000.

The size of the Mexica army, including troops from allied city-states, was at least 32,000 and probably closer to twice that number. Troops were divided into legions of 8,000 following the vigesimal numbering system. The ratio of Mexica-controlled troops to the little band of Spaniards was probably close to 100 to 1.

[9]The Aztecs had no kings as we understand the word but elected a *huey tlahtoani*, which means "great speaker," to lead them. The title was not inherited but often was given to the son of the fallen great speaker. Motecuhzoma is often said to be the Aztec Emperor, but the word "Emperor" is no more accurate than "king."

the night of the Aztec Feast of Toxcatl. Troops under Pedro de Alvarado lock the Aztecs in their own temple. Fray Sahagún's informants tell what happened then.

> When things were already going on, when the festivity was being observed and there was dancing and singing, with voices raised in song, the singing was like the noise of waves breaking against the rocks. When it was time, when the moment had come for the Spaniards to do the killing, they came out equipped for battle. They came and closed off each of the places where people went in and out. . . .
>
> When this had been done, they went into the temple courtyard to kill people. Those whose assignment it was to do the killing just went on foot, each with his metal sword and his leather shield, some of them iron-studded. Then they surrounded those who were dancing, going among the cylindrical drums. They struck a drummer's arms; both of his hands were severed. They struck his neck; his head landed far away. Then they stabbed everyone with iron lances and stuck them with iron swords. They stuck some in the belly, and then their entrails came spilling out. They split open the heads of some, they really cut their skulls to pieces, their skulls were cut up into little bits. And some they hit on the shoulders, their bodies broke open and ripped. Some they hacked on the calves, some on the thighs, some on their bellies, and then all their entrails would spill out. And if someone still tried to run it was useless; he just dragged his intestines along. There was a stench as if of sulfur. Those who tried to escape could go nowhere. When anyone tried to go out, at the entryways they struck and stabbed him.
>
> But some climbed up the wall and were able to escape. Some went into the various calpulli temples and took refuge there. Some took refuge among, entered [the bodies of] those who had really died, feigning death, and they were able to escape. But if someone took a breath and they saw him, they stabbed him. The blood of the warriors ran like water, the ground was almost slippery with blood, and the stench of it rose, and the entrails were lying dragged out. . . .
>
> And when it became known . . . , everyone cried out, "Aztec warriors, come running, get outfitted with devices, shields, and arrows, hurry come running, the warriors are dying, they have died, perished, been annihilated, o Aztec warriors!"[10]

The barbarity of the Spaniards terrifies the Aztecs, but it also enrages them. Clearly, these foreigners have nothing to do with Quetzalcoatl, the

---

[10] Translation from Nahuatl by James Lockhart, in León-Portilla and Shorris, *In the Language of Kings*, pp. 296–97.

Prince of Tula, the one who opposed human sacrifice, proposing the sacrifice of butterflies instead of men. Motecuhzoma has misread the signs, made a dreadful error, but the Aztecs are still powerful, and they determine now to drive the invaders from the city.

A great battle ensues; the Spaniards are driven onto the causeways, forced out of the city onto the shore. The Aztecs remove the causeways. The Spaniards cannot retreat into the city. They must either fight their way around the lake to escape from the Aztecs or retreat and drown in the lake. According to Spanish accounts, Motecuhzoma is killed by a stone flung up at the rooftop where he stood to watch the battle below. The Aztecs claim he was simply murdered by the Spaniards. With no clear line of succession, the Aztec leaders do not make the critical decision to follow the routed Spaniards and destroy them. Cortés, once again in the open field, having escaped from the confusion of urban fighting and his untenable position between the Aztecs and the lake, knows he can now make full use of his horses and cannon. He and his remaining troops have survived.

By the time Cortés returns to complete his conquest of the Aztecs, the real killer has done its work. Within a year 40 percent of the population of central Mexico dies of smallpox. Motecuhzoma's brother, who succeeds him, lasts only eighty days on the throne, and for most of that time he is ill. The Aztecs are in chaos. And all the while, Cortés is cementing his alliances, making concessions when he must, defeating the smaller city-states where he cannot win them over with promises or guile. Since the Aztecs controlled the waters around Tenochtitlán with their canoes during the first battle and, though weakened, can still do so, Cortés devises a plan to overcome the Aztec advantage. He has saved sails and masts from the scuttled ships off the coast; he brings them inland and builds thirteen brigantines in Tlaxcala.

Meanwhile, he gathers the country he now calls New Spain to his side. More Spanish troops, animals, and supplies arrive. Against this growing army, the Aztecs, not merely decimated, now at little more than half the number that drove the Spaniards from the city, must stand alone. Cuauhtémoc, son of Ahuitzotl, is chosen as their leader, but the process takes two months, leaving him very little time before the main Spanish attack. He cannot consolidate his alliances, and fighting between the Tenochas (residents of Tenochtitlán) and the neighboring *altepemi* (city-states) continues even as the Spaniards carry out their plan.

Cortés completes construction of the ships, then employs thirty thousand Tlaxcalan laborers to dig a canal from the construction site to the shores of the lake surrounding the Aztec capital. He times his attack perfectly, launching the brigantines just as his commanders begin their attacks across the causeways leading into the city. It is the first day of June 1521, and the fighting will last until the thirteenth of August. It will be unlike anything the Spaniards have ever experienced. The Aztecs, fighting under the leadership of Cuauhtémoc and his council of nobles, will sacrifice everything to win, even their gleaming city itself.

Cortés has cut off the supply of fresh water to Tenochtitlán from a spring outside the city. No food can be brought in. His Spanish troops and their vast army of allies outnumber the Aztecs two hundred to one. Spanish technological superiority is great, but nothing matters more now than the sheer numbers of the attackers. The brigantines are faster than the Aztec canoes and protected by canoes manned by the Spaniards' allies. In the land battle, Cuauhtémoc's troops have learned that the Spanish cannon can shoot only straight ahead, so they go around them, dodging their thunder in the open places, but on the narrow causeways leading into the city, the cannon are devastating against massed troops.

During the days the Spaniards and their allies move forward, and at night the Aztecs raid their attackers, taking back territory, wounding their antagonists. But nothing can overcome such overwhelming odds. As the battle goes on, the numbers of the Aztecs diminish; there is no food in the city, little fresh water; their last native allies desert them, leaving the Tenochas and Tlatelolcas to stand against Spain and virtually all the rest of Mexico.

The Spaniards enter the city itself. To negate the terrible charges of the horses, Cuauhtémoc guides the fighting into narrow areas, jagged geography. He orders the construction of long spears to pierce the horses before they can trample the Aztec troops standing in front of them. He digs pits along the causeways so the heavily armored Spaniards who are forced into the lake will drown in the deep water. He installs sharp wooden spikes in the water of the canals to hold off the brigantines with their deep drafts.

Once the city is breached, there is little hope for the Tenochas, but they fight on. The city burns, the dead are everywhere, the stench of war fills the air, and yet the Tenochas and their allies in Tlatelolco will not give up the fight. Perhaps they are driven by their understanding of the temporary nature of life itself. Their poets have asked again and again whether it is true that humans "live on earth only a little while." Perhaps it is mere desperation. Seventy-three days after the first attack, Cuauhtémoc's canoe is found and overtaken, and he is forced to surrender. It is the end of the Aztec Empire.

A generation earlier a Nahua poet had written:

> Famously, the city of Tenochtitlán endures,
> Bringing glory on itself;
> Oh, you princes,
> As He the one God, commands you, His sons,
> Let no one fear the beautiful death.
> Whose efforts will truly gain
> The mat of the shield, the honored place of the arrows of God?
> Think of this, remember it, you, princes,
> Who can disturb the city of Tenochtitlán?
> Who can shake the foundations of heaven?
>
> Long live Tenochtitlán![11]

Yet the great *altepetl*, the place where the cactus (*tenochtli*) sprang from the heart of the killed wizard Copil, has fallen. Nothing is left of empire but memories and language. Now the Spaniards look for gold. Perhaps it is true that Cuauhtémoc has sunk the treasures of the city in a whirlpool. The Spaniards want to know. They torture him, to no avail. Several years later the most brutal of the Spanish captains, Pedro de Alvarado, whom the Aztecs called Tonatiuh (the Sun) because of his red hair, will take Cuauhtémoc south on an expedition in the Yucatán, where he will eventually kill him and leave him nailed to a ceiba, the cruciform tree the Maya know as the world tree. And that will be the end of the last Great Speaker of Tenochtitlán.

In the conquered city of Tenochtitlán the Spaniards murder the leaders of the Aztecs, but not before literally putting their feet to the fire in an effort to find more gold. No great golden treasure is ever found. In a quarter of a century one of the world's original civilizations disappears into the idea of New Spain. The Aztecs will attempt one more great uprising, at Mixtón. They will engage the Spaniards under the leadership of the killer Pedro de Alvarado, who will fall from his horse and die of his wounds.

---

[11] The quotation is from one of the poems in the "Cantares Mexicanos" as it appears in León-Portilla and Shorris, *In the Language of Kings*. The references to "the one God" are undoubtedly a result of Christian influences added during the sixteenth-century redaction of the poem.

The reasons given for the improbable history of the invasion revolve around political, cultural, and military errors, all of them by the Aztecs. The most prominent one is Motecuhzoma's belief that Cortés was the god Quetzalcoatl.[12]

According to the recorded accounts, Motecuhzoma dreamed of strange omens before the arrival of Cortés and was psychologically paralyzed by these dreams. It seems improbable. The Aztecs were a tough, aggressive people, who were known to have survived as recently as the early fourteenth century on a diet of rattlesnakes and forage food. They were steeped in religion but driven by practicality. Never before had dreams deterred them.[13]

It is more likely that the Aztecs made a good decision based on solid information about the Spaniards gained during their first gift-giving mission. Motecuhzoma even had drawings of the Spanish armor, horses, and cannon, accurate depictions done by Aztec artists while the emissaries engaged in the exchange of gifts and pleasantries. Whatever the Great Speaker's dreams, his decision at each stage of the Spanish advance on Tenochtitlán to give them gold and gifts and tell them to go home was not unreasonable. The invaders were strange creatures; they had demonstrated the power of their weapons. The idea of the flowery war, already in practice, was to avoid massive casualties. Motecuhzoma and his advisers may have considered making such an arrangement with the Spaniards.

After news arrived in Tenochtitlán of the defeat of the Tlaxcalans, certainly worthy enemies, and the slaughter at Cholula, all the Aztecs, not just Motecuhzoma, must have wanted to avoid open confrontation with the invaders. Moreover, the news that the Tlaxcalans and other peoples had allied themselves with Cortés may have been more than discomfiting, perhaps terrifying. Negotiation may have appeared to be a better course of action than war.

After the slaughter during the Feast of Toxcatl, however, the Aztecs knew

---

[12]Ce Acatl arrives every fifty-two years in the calendar cycle followed by the Mexica.

[13]The Aztecs had not won every military encounter, but one of their two major defeats had been at the hands of the Purépechas in the present-day Mexican state of Michoacán, and that was due to the arrogance of the Aztec military leader, who allowed himself to fall into a trap. The second defeat was by the city-state of Huexotzinco in 1506, and it was terrible. Thousands of Aztec warriors were captured, and a new series of alliances was made among the city-states of central Mexico. Huexotzinco was one of the city-states that joined the Spaniards in their defeat of the Mexicans.

they had no choice but to fight. Had it not been for the invisible weapon, the plague left by the first visit of the invaders, the outcome might have been different. Or at the very least, postponed. Fully prepared for war, and with the neurotic Motecuhzoma out of the way, the Triple Alliance of the three central Aztec states would have been formidable.[14] After the death of 40 percent of the population, however, their chances were greatly diminished. As it was, they fought valiantly against overwhelming odds in a cause that was fated to be lost. Cortés, trained in the negotiations of law, had a nose for politics as well as for war. He had learned the recent political history of the land he called New Spain.[15] He had seen the unhappiness of the other city-states under the Aztec yoke, and he exploited it brilliantly. Alone, the Spaniards could not possibly have defeated the Triple Alliance, not for all their guns or diseases or horses or dogs or armor and weapons of steel. The moment the Tlaxcalans decided to join Cortés rather than unite with their old oppressors the Aztecs, the war was decided. Mesoamerica became New Spain.

The Spaniards came to the Americas for economic reasons but fortified themselves with religious motives. They were experienced in dealing with the problems of other religions and cultures. They had a two-step conversion process: first the sword; then the embrace. In all Europe, only Spain was truly multicultural: Christian, Jewish, and Muslim; Germanic, Middle Eastern, African, European. Iberians, Celts, Visigoths, Jews, Romans, Moors all contributed to the *mestizaje*, the mixture of races and cultures, that was Spain, but never with comfort, never with ease. The Spanish mestizaje tore at its own flesh. The Christians killed the Jews; the Muslims killed the Christians; the Christians killed the Muslims. And all that was long after the Visigoths came down from the north and set about killing each other.

Many people have tried to sort out the strands of the Spanish mestizaje. Miguel de Unamuno thought the spirit of the Spaniard went back to his African origins. Octavio Paz wrote of the Muslim character of the Spanish will to convert by the sword. The Jewish aspect of the Spanish character

[14]Tenochtitlán, Texcoco, and Tlacopan.
[15]Fray Bartolomé de las Casas said that Cortés was a Bachelor of Law, but Hugh Thomas argues quite convincingly that Cortés had not completed his studies. Whichever view is correct, Cortés surely had spent enough time in study to know something about Roman law and to have gained some skills in argument, negotiation, and the art of a favorable settlement.

appeared in New Mexico in secret ceremonies in the sixteenth century, and the Roman ideas of relations between persons defined in law were at the core of much of the Spanish behavior in the Western Hemisphere during the fifteenth to nineteenth century and define much of Mexican law today.

Christianity had more or less triumphed in Spain by the end of the fifteenth century, but the Spanish mestizaje had not been completed. In 1478 the Inquisition was founded by the Spanish state, and although it was putatively religious, the Pope agreed that it would not be subject to the authority of Rome. The Inquisition was a state means for dealing with the lingering problems of multiculturalism. And it was a merciless melting pot: For the love of God any kind of torture or murder was not merely acceptable, it was a moral act. Philosophically, the Spaniards had reached the point at which anything was permitted. By the time the moral arguments of the friars Antonio de Montesinos and Pedro de Córdoba in the Caribbean and Bishop Bartolomé de las Casas on the mainland finally carried the day, the mission of the Spanish Church and state in the Americas had been completed: The Christian god of limitless power had proved superior.

In a colloquy held in 1524,[16] twelve Franciscans told the assembled Aztec nobles about the Christian God and His Son, Jesus. The priests explained that they were human, like the Aztecs, and that it was "neither jade, nor gold, nor quetzal plumes, nor any other valuable things, it is only your salvation that is his [King Charles's] desire."

The nobles responded by telling the great tragedy of conquest: "They are gone: The Lord, Our Lord, destroyed them, He disappeared them . . . the rulers who came to abide, to live on earth . . . for a brief day, a moment here. . . .

"If this had happened during their lifetimes, they would have . . . entreated you, based on your love for people, which we admire here. But what can we say now? Although we act like lords, we are the mothers and the fathers of the people; can it be that here, in your presence, we must destroy the ancient law, which our grandfathers, our grandmothers deeply believed, and which the lords, the rulers, studied diligently and beheld in wonder?"

---

[16]The Colloquy of 1524, undoubtedly reconstructed some years later by the informants of Fray Sahagún, rather than recorded in contemporary notes, is the only document in which the actual dialogue of conversion in Mesoamerica, or at least something representative of it, is recorded.

The Aztec priests asked the Franciscans why they must accept the gods of the Spaniards. "Is it not enough that we have been defeated?"

"And those who heard this were deeply disturbed, saddened, as if frightened, terrified by a fall," wrote the anonymous narrator of the colloquy.[17]

The attitude the Spaniards inculcated in the indigenous people, which has been reinforced again and again over the years by churches of all denominations, by the state through the educational system, and by the print and broadcast media, was first expressed by the Jesuit historian Clavijero at the end of his description of the conquest: "The Aztecs, with all of the other nations that assisted in their ruin, remain despite the Christians and the wise laws of the Catholic monarchs, abandoned to misery, oppression, and scorn, not only from the Spaniards, but also the most vile African slaves and their infamous descendants. God's vengeance leaves to a miserable posterity the cruelty, injustice, and superstition of the leaders of those nations. An unfortunate example of Divine Justice and of the precariousness of earthly reigns."[18]

According to Clavijero, it was not Spain, technology, germs, nature, luck, or even shrewd alliances that brought the indigenous peoples to their knees; he argued it was God. This had not been a war of equals or near equals in any respect but numbers (and there the indigenous people had been superior); this had been a war between the natives and their moral superiors. Clavijero went on and on about human sacrifice and cannibalism. His Aztecs had many fine qualities, but morality was not one of them.

The mestizo, born of European, less often African, but always native stock, in turn gave birth to yet more mestizos, and every one contained within his or her person the dark side of humanity, the side that suffered the vengeance of the Lord. This side of the mestizo could not be totally extirpated by conversion, not in the mind of the Spaniard. At best the mestizo could become like the New Christians (converted Jews) of Spain, always suspect, prey to the Inquisition. Over time the Spaniards had developed political, social, and religious methods for maintaining the power of the dominant group in a multicultural society. And nothing on earth or in

[17]León-Portilla and Shorris, *In the Language of Kings.*
[18]Clavijero uses the word *funesto,* which is most generously translated as "unfortunate." "Ill-fated" and "disgraced" would be other choices. *Historia Antigua de Mexico,* written in the 1760s; quotes are translated from the Porrua edition of the original Spanish translation (Mexico: 1945).

heaven matched the limitless power granted by the appropriation of the sincerity of one's love of God.

When Bartolomé de las Casas wrote his book in defense of the *naturales*, as they were called, he did at least convince the king of Spain that the Indians were human. The treatment of fieldworkers and miners improved somewhat. At the suggestion of las Casas slaves were brought from Africa to do the backbreaking work that had killed the indigenous peoples.[19] But the case for the moral equality of the native people at the time of the conquest was not considered until well into the twentieth century.

The indigenous people of Mexico accepted the Spanish church, language, and culture with astonishing alacrity. Only once before in the known history of the world had a people accepted a new religion and its corollary culture as rapidly. John Crow said in his history of Spain, "Christianity was taken up with an enthusiasm unparalleled in other countries."[20] He went on to explain the difference between Spain and northern Europe by the Spanish willingness simply to add Christianity to the pagan base. And again in Mexico, Christianity was taken up with amazing rapidity. The key to the Spanish conversion was offered by Seneca the Younger: "Spain was Christian perhaps before Christ."[21] The same can be said of New Spain. Mexico was Spanish perhaps before Cortés. The similarities allowed one religion and culture to be added atop another, like layers in an ecclesiastical pie, which included many aspects of life in pre-Hispanic Mexico.

Clavijero's condemnation of the world before the Spaniards had a corollary in the comparison of levels of technological and economic development.[22] No consideration at all was given to the religious or philosophical notions of the peoples outside of what is generally known as Mesoamerica—that is, mainly the north of what is now Mexico and the southwestern United States. As late as 1975 Carlos Alvear Acevedo, in writing about the Catholic Church in the history of Mexico, could describe these northern peoples as miserable, failing in all matters of "material progress."[23] In his

---

[19]Las Casas later regretted the notion, but it was too late; great numbers of African slaves had already arrived in New Spain.

[20]*Spain: The Root and the Flower* (Berkeley: University of California Press, 1985).

[21]Stoic writer born in 4 B.C. in Córdoba, Spain. Some sources say that he knew St. Paul, although it is unlikely.

[22]He also admired the pre-Hispanic peoples. He found them flawed but wonderful. Their contemporary descendants, however, earned only his scorn.

[23]*La Iglesia en la Historia de México* (Mexico City: Editorial Jus, 1975).

view, the Spaniards brought not only the "liberating presence of a kind God" but the knowledge that would produce a wealth of goods.

If the two societies were as their Spanish chroniclers described them—that is, if the naturales were the moral inferiors of the Spaniards—the mestizaje would be forever composed of people of unequal parts, and the more they appeared to be of pre-Hispanic origin, the more likely they were to behave like their ancestors. The completion of the miscegenation, the meaning of the word "mestizaje," could never take place. With every marriage, every birth, a new balance would be created, a different quality of person both genetically and morally. The degree of influence of the lesser part could be determined by the success or failure of the person in life: The greater the pre-Hispanic influence, the more likely the person was to fail morally, intellectually, and economically.

The prophecies of the Spaniards were, in large part, self-fulfilling; it is the function of colonization to make them so. New Spain was unlike many colonies because there was so much intermarriage, but that did not relieve the dualism; the two worlds existed side by side within the person. Mexico did not become a pluralistic society like its neighbor to the north, where many ethnicities lived in a single polity. Pluralism was to be the great strength of the United States, while the dualism of Mexico—religions, cultures, and races in deadly opposition—was to be its burden.[24] A pluralistic society diffuses oppositions and overcomes them. There cannot be a dozen different certainties. As certainty is transcended, science comes questioning; pluralism suggests seeking the new. Freedom, especially freedom of inquiry, is in the very nature of pluralism.

Dualism implies opposition; it creates a suffocating rigidity, positions become entrenched, and the society stagnates. The danger of pluralism is in the surrender of all sides to agreeable mediocrity. The danger of dualism is that it cannot accommodate to a changing world. In New Spain, dualism prevailed.

---

[24]This is not to deny the racist behavior of Americans (United States), only to say that they were able to accept the existence of various cultures in something more like a salad than a melting pot. Despite American racism, African, Latin American, and other cultures became integral parts of the salad of cultures.

4.

An Imperfect Likeness

The usual view of the invasion of Mexico holds that it was a clash between two entirely different and incompatible civilizations. The Spaniards raised their swords, cried "Santiago," for their patron, St. James of Compostela, and attacked, with no thought in mind but to kill or convert the savages. And it is true that the mestizaje, the seamless mix of races dreamed of by early-twentieth-century Mexican intellectuals, has not yet been completed. There is something unfinished about Mexico; however, the Spaniards and the natives, especially those of central Mexico, were not so incompatible as one might suspect. Although they were racists, inventors of forms of racism, the Spaniards did not attempt to exterminate the Indians. Something very different took place in Mexico, and without some idea of how this mestizaje, this mixing, began, it is all but impossible to grasp the tensions and possibilities of present-day Mexico.

All did not go smoothly after the capitulation of Tenochtitlán. It was not the end of wars. The Maya of southern Mexico and the Raramurí and Yaquis and Chichimecas of the north fought on for years after the invasion, but in central Mexico there was an astonishingly quick adaptation to Spanish ways. Perhaps the Aztecs and the Spaniards were not so different after all. A comparison of the way the two cultures thought and lived offers some perspective on the collision of civilizations.

DEATH

The Spaniards and Mesoamericans of the sixteenth century were both obsessed with the contemplation of death. A Spanish poet of the time, Luis de Góngora, wrote in his sonnet, "Carpe Diem": ". . . what in your shining years was gold, carnation, lily, luminous crystal will turn not to silver or limp violets, but . . . to earth, smoke, dust, gloom, nothingness."

His lines could have been written by the fifteenth-century Nahua poet-ruler Nezahualcoyotl, who said, ". . . not forever on earth / only a moment here."[1]

Góngora's views excited great controversy because there was no promise of heaven, but they were not so different from the Mesoamerican views that understood the existence of an underworld (Maya) and a milky paradise for people who drowned and mothers who died in childbirth (Nahua), with no clear picture of heaven and hell as reward and punishment for deeds done on earth. Both civilizations were desperate to solve the questions of death, terrified about questioning their own faith. They wrote about death, made prayers about it, feared it, and on both sides considered it a journey. In a corn-based society like Mesoamerica, the burying of the seed in the ground and the rising of the new corn indicated that something cyclical occurred. But there was no Virgil, no Dante to give it glorious moral detail.[2] Funerals were important on both side of the Atlantic. The Aztecs carried their dead from the battlefield to hold funeral services and cremation. The Spaniards gave last rites and said the mass for the dead. On neither side did warriors go uncelebrated, unmourned. Valor encountered nothing but valor on either side. As Cervantes said later, "My honor is dearer to me than my life." And the Nahua poet promised the young warriors, "Your name, your renown, will never be lost in the place of the rattles, the place of the flower of battle. . . ."

The difference lay in the clarity of the ideas of heaven and hell on the European side. The Nahua poets raised existential questions about the value of life, its brevity, the meaning of actions, especially in war, while their wise men devised a stern code for certain behaviors that included death by stoning for marital infidelity. On the Spanish side, honor was a reward in this life and heaven the reward of the next.

The Mesoamericans, like the ancient Greeks, had not learned the uses of promises about the afterlife. Their religion offered neither paradise nor pun-

[1]"Cantares Mexicanos," fol. 17r; León-Portilla and Shorris, *In the Language of Kings*.
[2]Even the magnificent Popol Vuh of the Ki'che Maya offers no ethical system, although such a system may have existed in what are now lost or as yet undiscovered works. The Nahuas had a system of conventions recorded in the Huehuehtlahtolli (Words of the Elders) that indicated rules for living existed among the Nahuas specifically and among other Mesoamerican groups by implication.

ishment in return for their actions. Those who died were dead, making death terrible, the end of time. In the Spanish world, death merely marked a station on the journey of the soul, a fork in the road, one that could be affected by one's religious beliefs and actions. The Catholic Church was the way to paradise; it offered eternal forgiveness for one's transgressions. Such forgiveness had little place in Mesoamerican literature or legend.[3] In practical terms, the theology was incomplete; there was no extreme unction except for a very few; a place had been left open for the Spanish death.

RELIGION

At the time of the collision the priesthood and the nobility held positions of nearly equal power on both sides of the Atlantic. Religious ritual had a role in every aspect of life. Some of the Aztec intellectuals had begun to raise questions that seemed to indicate something like a deist existentialism. A genre of Nahuatl poetry, *icnocuicatl,* "songs of orphanhood," spoke of personal abandonment, but also abandonment in a more profound sense, close to the ideas of the twentieth-century Catholic existentialists. But it is unlikely that those ideas had spread beyond a fairly narrow circle among the nobility.

The intimate connection of Church and State in Spain was evident in the name of the rulers, the Catholic kings. The Holy Office and its inquisitors were controlled by the state, not by Rome.

The Mexicans believed in Ometeotl, the god of duality, whom they also called Giver of Life and The Close and the Near, which may have meant omnipresent.[4] And then they had a great pantheon, made up partly of aspects of the dualistic supreme being. The Spaniards believed in a tripartite God, the Father, the Son, and the Holy Ghost. The saints of the Catholic Church were not directly comparable to the Mesoamerican pantheon, but there were many saints, and there were innumerable statues, paintings, and medals depicting saints. As every Mesoamerican and particularly every Mexican household and political jurisdiction had its particular god, so every

---

[3] Tlazolteotl (Eater of Filth) is the Mexican god to whom sins were confessed, but there is no evidence that the Nahuas thought Tlazolteotl could effect a change in life after death.
[4] Respectively, Ipalnemoani and Tloque Nahuaque.

Spanish household and political jurisdiction had its patron saint. As every Mesoamerican had a calendrical name, so every Spaniard had a saint's day.

HUMAN SACRIFICE

Quetzalcoatl opposed human sacrifice, perhaps the reason why he was driven out of his home in Tula. In his deified form, Quetzalcoatl continued to be associated with opposition to human sacrifice, but he and his adherents lost out to the followers of Huitzilopochtli, a god of war. In much of Mesoamerica humans were sacrificed to the gods, and in Tenochtitlán and the surrounding areas, thousands of human beings, including children, were killed in religious rites. Their hearts were torn out, they were often flayed, and the corpses partly eaten.

Anthropologists, most notably Inga Clendinnen,[5] have sought to understand the cultural and philosophical basis for human sacrifice and anthropophagy, but there is little to go on in the literature. Some basis may be found in sympathetic magic: Cause children to cry, and water will fall from the sky as the tears fall from their eyes. But the sacrifice of humans in large numbers was only described, not explained, in the oral literature redacted in the sixteenth century. The reasons, which have to do with imitating ancient sacrifices made by the gods and with feeding the "precious liquor," meaning blood, to the sun so that it might continue its daily journey, are arcane.

Mesoamerican culture had a powerful millenarian component. The Mexica thought this was the fifth sun, or fifth creation, and the final one. The Maya too described previous creations and set the date for the end of the world at 2012 in our calendar. If human sacrifice could put off the end of the world, the Mesoamericans were behaving in a perfectly rational way within their own philosophical system. But the flaw in the system that led from the sacrifice of butterflies to the sacrifice of children and warriors seems to us now incomprehensible, a kind of madness.

The Spaniards brought with them the Inquisition, which in service of the Spanish God burned living human beings at the stake. Unlike the Mesoamericans, the Spaniards also used torture in service of their God, utilizing such gruesome instruments as the boot, the thumbscrew, and the rack, as well as the application of red-hot steel instruments to naked flesh.

[5] *Aztecs: An Interpretation* (Cambridge: Cambridge University Press, 1991).

As the Mesoamericans learned about the Holy Bible—the Book, the Word that the priests spoke about in their earliest contacts with the indigenous people—they must have found some common ground. Abraham laid Isaac upon the sacrificial altar and raised the knife above him to slay his own son at the command of the Judeo-Christian god. It made no difference that God stayed the hand of Abraham after he had passed the test of obedience; clearly, human sacrifice was also part of the Judeo-Christian means of serving the gods.

Even more convincing, the omnipotent God of the Christians sent His only Son, Jesus, to die in agony on a Roman cross. It must have been difficult, indeed, for the surviving educated Mesoamericans to comprehend fully the opprobrium of the Spaniards toward the sacrifice of humans.[6] They may have thought torture, crucifixion, and the auto-da-fé utterly uncivilized. Or such cruelties may have seemed to some Mesoamericans brilliant extensions of the ritual of sacrifice. The point here is not to judge either society but to look at them side by side from a place outside our own ethical and metaphysical positions in the hope of understanding the nature of the mestizaje, which came of the forcing together of both religions.

CIVIL SOCIETY

Written reports by the Spaniards who saw pre-Hispanic Tenochtitlán describe the level of organization of the city. Díaz del Castillo wrote:[7] ". . . we

---

[6]Diego de Landa, bishop of Yucatán, left one of the most extraordinary cross-cultural notes about the Spanish invasion in his *Relación* but apparently missed the significance of it. He wrote: "Besides the killings done in the towns, they also had those two nefarious sanctuaries at Chichenza [*sic*] and Cuzmil [*sic*] where they sent an infinite number of wretched people to be sacrificed, in the one place by flinging them down the well and in the other by tearing out their hearts. May the merciful Lord, who chose to sacrifice Himself upon the cross to the Father of all . . . free these men from such miseries." Later he said that God stayed the hand of Abraham "because His Majesty was determined to send His own Son into the world there to let Him truly lose His life upon the Cross, so that men in their misery may see that for the Son of the Eternal God the command of His Father is a heavy one, though it is very sweet and of no account to Him." Although one sacrifice calls to mind the other, Landa never commented on the similarity. Like the other Spaniards in New Spain, he noted only the great difference between the father's willingness to sacrifice his son for one god and the indigenous sacrifice of strangers to another god. It is a stunning example of what Miguel de Unamuno meant when he spoke of "the tragic sense of life," the conflict between faith and reason.
[7] *The Discovery and Conquest of Mexico*, pp. 190–91.

saw so many cities and villages built in the water and other great towns on dry land and that straight and level Causeway going towards Mexico, we were amazed and said that it was like the enchantments they tell of in the legend of Amadis,[8] on account of the great towers and cues and buildings rising from the water, and all built of masonry. And some of our soldiers even asked whether the things that we saw were not a dream."

And here is some of his description of the market at Tlatelolco:

> . . . we were astounded at the number of people and the quantity of merchandise that it contained, and at the good order and control that was maintained, for we had never seen such a thing before. . . . Each kind of merchandise was kept by itself and had its fixed place marked out. Let us begin with the dealers in gold, silver, and precious stones, feathers, mantles, and embroidered goods. Then there were other wares consisting of Indian slaves both men and women; and I say that they bring as many of them to that great market for sale as the Portuguese bring negroes from Guinea; and they brought them along tied to long poles, with collars round their necks so that they could not escape, and others they left free. Next there were other traders who sold great pieces of cloth and cotton and articles of twisted thread, and there were *cacahuateros* who sold cacao. In this way one could see every sort of merchandise that is to be found in the whole of New Spain.

He went on to list foodstuffs, animal skins, tobacco, ointments, cooked foods, pottery, lumber, cradles, firewood, paper, salt, stone knives, axes, gourds. But it was the order of the marketplace that astonished: "There are also buildings where three magistrates sit in judgment, and there are executive officers like *Alguacils* who inspect the merchandise."[9]

The Spaniards were interested not only in the cleanliness of the city, the order of the markets in comparison to the medieval bazaars that still existed in Spain, but in the personal habits of the Mexica. Díaz del Castillo commented again and again about the Mexica washing themselves, changing their clothes, washing their hands before eating, laundering their clothes. It was the Mesoamerican habit and remains so even today among indigenous people. The Spaniards, on the other hand, were filthy. They rarely bathed or washed their clothing. The stench of the Europeans must have disgusted the

---

[8] *Amadis of Gaul,* with Portuguese and Spanish versions published in the fourteenth to sixteenth century. The work was derived in part from Arthurian legend.
[9] Ibid.

Aztecs, especially the nobles, who not only washed frequently but perfumed themselves. Some of the Aztec priests, on the other hand, must have given off a fearsome stench of dried blood, which clotted in their hair.

MORTIFICATION OF THE FLESH

Throughout Mesoamerica the mortification of the flesh belonged to the powerful rituals performed by priests and kings. In the bas-relief sculptures left by the Maya one can see a queen drawing a rope studded with spines through her tongue. The kings of Mayab (the land of the Maya) used stingray spines and thorns to draw blood from the penis, tongue, or earlobes in religious rituals. The bleeding noble then spun around, flinging blood onto pieces of amate (fig tree bark) paper, which were then ceremoniously burned.

Among the Aztecs, human life itself was thought to have begun with the mortification of the flesh of the god Quetzalcoatl. In *The Legend of the Suns*[10] the Mexica told the story. It was the end of the fourth sun. The last humans had been reduced to a pile of jade bones in the underworld.

And then Quetzalcoatl went off to Mictlan, the Region of the Dead, where he came before the Lord and the Lady of Mictlan. Then he said, indeed he did, "I come to take away the jade bones which you so honorably guard."

He sorted the bones into two piles, men on one side, women on the other, and brought them to a goddess, who *ground them in her jade bowl. And then Quetzalcoatl bled his penis over it. Then all the . . . gods performed penance. . . . And then they said, "The gods have given birth to men, the common people," for certainly they performed penance in our behalf.*

The Spaniards who arrived in Mexico as well as those who came to the Yucatán also practiced the mortification of the flesh as religious ritual. Octavio Paz quotes Juan de Oviedo, who wrote a biography of the seventeenth-century Jesuit Antonio Núñez de Miranda and his unceasing mortifications, especially the way he scourged himself "seventy-three times, in reverence for the seventy-three years of the Blessed Virgin's life . . . and the blows were so cruel and delivered so pitilessly that they could be heard outside the chamber, inspiring sorrow and compassion in all who listened.

[10]Translated from Nahuatl by Willard Gingerich, in Roberta Markman, *The Flayed God* (San Francisco: HarperCollins, 1992).

Those waiting outside the door feared they might find him dead." Núñez wore a hair shirt several times a week and when preaching, and according to Oviedo, he wore "a more painful hair shirt" in the form of "the vermin that bred on him and which the mortified father suffered with patience and joy."

In the town of Izamal, not far from Mérida, Yucatán, the Maya built two great pyramids. A road runs between them. No one yet knows well the history of the pyramids of Izamal, although the archaeologists and anthropologists have begun their work. The pyramid on the east side of the road has not been much studied. The steps leading up to the first platform have been uncovered, and the steps to the second, smaller platform have been partially opened. At the third level, the grass and earth still cover the platform and what may have been steps leading higher up, but nothing to enable the climb to continue has been uncovered there on the front of the platform. One must go to the side of the next rise to climb again, finally arriving at what may have been the base of the small area and even smaller structure where the business of worship or sacrifice or both may have been carried out.

At the corners of the pyramid, on various levels, the earth and stucco and layers of stone have fallen or been broken away. At these corners it is possible to see that the pyramid is not one, but three, each one covered carefully by another exhibiting a distinctly different kind of architecture. The pyramid on the east side of the road in Izamal began in the classic period. And then came the late classic and the postclassic, and each time there was an overlay. The pyramid became a palimpsest.

From the higher levels of the pyramid one can look across the road to the great green manicured platform before the main entrance to the Cathedral of Nuestra Señora de Izamal. The last builders here were not Maya but Christian. They tore down the stones of the top of the pyramid and used them to build a church in the very place where the Maya had worshiped. It was the same in Cholula and Tenochtitlán and a hundred other cities and towns. The church of Izamal, like the pyramid that faces it, is made of many architectural styles, as multicultural as Spain itself.

On Sunday at the noon mass, worshipers fill the cathedral. They overflow the pews and all the standing room and gather in the shade outside the entrance to listen to the mass broadcast over loudspeakers. Many people come to the Cathedral of Izamal, for it is a very holy place, made more so because Pope John Paul himself chose to preach there when he came to

Mexico. At the conclusion of the mass, the people leave the church, but a sweet sound comes from somewhere above. It is the choir of the young, playing guitars and softly singing, in sonorous Mexican melodies, praise of Jesus and the faithful.

Through the side door of the cathedral one enters a walled garden. It had been the garden of the convent of Izamal, but that was long ago. Now there are few nuns; the convent garden contains only silence, the cooling shadow of the porticoes, and in the center on a stone pedestal a realistic statue—more than three feet tall—of a flagellant. The skin color is as white as that of Jesus depicted on the cross inside the church. The hair of the statue is shown in gentle curls. It is clearly not a Mesoamerican who scourges himself there in the Mayan garden. In his right hand the statue holds a real whip and a real stick. The painted plaster torso is naked to the waist and red with marks that ooze sculpted blood.

In the place where the statue stands, in the convent garden, the kings and queens who worshiped Itzamná—demiurge, creature beyond time, god of Izamal—pierced their tongues and sexual organs in an ecstasy of adoration.

The Catholic Church and the Spanish language completed the work begun by the sword. There were rebellions by Nahuas, Maya, Yaquis, and others who wished to hold on to their old gods and their old ways, but these were few. Smallpox, typhus, and killing labor in the fields and mines weakened the indigenous people, making them more susceptible to the evangelical and political work of the Spaniards. Even so, the conversion of the people could not have happened so quickly unless they were somehow prepared.

In the seventeenth century the Spanish writer Carlos de Sigüenza y Góngora claimed St. Thomas the Apostle had journeyed to New Spain before his death and prepared the indigenous peoples, but the evidence shows a more probable course: In many respects, the two worlds had developed along parallel lines. The cultural mestizaje that accompanied the physical union was not so much the result of syncretism or even the layering of one culture atop another as the recognition, however unconscious, however unspoken, of deep similarities. To make unequals of equals was the triumph of conquest, for it was a marriage of unequals only in the eyes of the victorious civilization. Because of that victory, however, the product of the marriage, the mestizo, the one who contains both of the mirroring faces, lives as if one aspect were the greater and the other the weaker, as if good and evil, light and darkness were evident in the skin. The mestizo lives with pride in one and shame for the other, each person a cage containing the never-ending strug-gle, without peace, the product of a marriage often consummated, but never completed.

SATURNINO'S DREAM

If you meet a man at the invitation of a part-time taxi driver and he talks with you because you have known the bullfighters José Ramón Tirado and El Estudiante you do not necessarily become friends, but you may interest each other. What was interesting about Saturnino Mora was his dream.

If there had not been so much unemployment among factory workers and no work at all for farmers and if he had been married or even engaged, Saturnino Mora would not have dreamed of emigrating. And he certainly would not have chosen to come to Mexico if his mother's uncle Samuel had not written about his success in Aguascalientes. Samuel had died of old age in 1977, according to his grandson, who sent a notice of Samuel's death and asked if the family wanted to have a candle lit for him. The Mora family sent a few pesetas. The grandson did not write again after that; the family in Spain assumed it was due to the press of business.

Saturnino said that he did not write before he left Spain because he did not want to pester a busy man. Instead, he went directly to the return address on the envelope that had brought the one and only letter. He told the story only when he was drunk, and he always ended it with the same words: "The address was a sewer, a shit hole, nothing."

Someone always asked what had happened to Samuel and his descen-dants, just to hear Saturnino shout, "Killed by Mexicans, eaten by savages." Then everyone around him laughed and patted his shoulder, told him to go fuck his mother, and bought him a drink.

Among his pals were failed bullfighters, pimps, a roasted chicken vendor, a janitor, a thief, and a part-time taxi driver. Most had been to jail at one time or another, and all were tattooed. The thief liked to take off his shirt and pull up his pants legs to reveal a glorious portrait of the Virgin of Guadalupe on his back; snakes, hearts, and skulls on his arms and legs; and on his chest a line drawing of an unidentified woman in early middle age, with a smile more beatific than that of the Virgin.

Saturnino had met his pals while working as a busboy in a barnlike restaurant furnished around the perimeter with wooden booths painted black or brown and in the center of the ancient tile floor with a scattering of unsteady wooden tables and wire ice-cream chairs. He was glad to have the men for friends, although they made fun of his accent, whistling back at him when he whistled his sibilants and calling him Tetas Pesetas, *tetas* (teats) because he was barrel-chested and *pesetas* because the Spanish money rhymed with *tetas*.

He referred to Mexicans as *chinga-tu-madres*, because they were forever telling people to "fuck their mothers," but he was more careful with them than they were with him, because he was a stranger, a Spaniard among Mexicans, and lonely. He did not like or admire his friends, but he did not want to lose them.

One night, he claimed, he had a dream in which he was a famous bull-fighter and awakened the next morning knowing all the movements made by matadors in the bullring. "The dream must be true," he told his friends, who laughed. But every morning before he went to the restaurant, Saturnino went to the bullring at the edge of town and practiced his dream. He learned to use the big yellow and magenta cape, to make slow, graceful, sweeping movements and to snap the end of a movement with the cape so that the bull was stopped in its tracks, fixed there by the suddenness. Then he took up the *muleta*, the small red serge cloth on a stick, learning to extend it with the light wooden sword that would be replaced in the end of the last act of the bullfight with razor-sharp steel for the kill.

"I would like to fight in the Spanish style, to be like Manolete," Saturnino said.

But his friends reminded him that Manolete had been long and thin, dramatic, a man with a tragic face. They told him he would do better to think of himself like the first great bullfighter, the squat but inventive Juan Belmonte.

He accepted the correction, for Tetas Pesetas was not a fool; he knew his own girth, the depth of his chest, the square Basque shape of his face, the round innocence of his eyes. He was a gentle man, without the slightly aggressive thrust of a waiter in his manner, let alone tragedy in his face. He was a busboy; he rattled dishes and clanked glasses; spoons sang in his hands.

"They shall never tattoo me," he said.

"Fuck your mother," his friends replied.

"Savages. You ate my mother's uncle."

"*Rock and roll,* Tetas Pesetas."

On the afternoon of his first encounter with a bull, Saturnino prepared by playing hand-slapping games with his friends. They took turns putting their hands, palm up, under Saturnino's palms and smacking his hands before he could move them out of the way. He played the game with each of his friends until the slaps became too painful; then he put his hands in his pockets, turned away for a few moments until the stinging stopped, and took up the game with the next one.

A little before three o'clock the entire troop, armed with one cape, one muleta, and a wooden sword painted the silver gray of steel, gathered themselves and walked to the bus stop to catch the bus that passed closest to the slaughterhouse at the edge of town. Spider, the pickpocket, had heard from a friend who worked in the slaughterhouse that a half-breed bull, a *creyoyo,* had somehow found its way into the herd in the huge corrals. It was not as good a beginning as testing calves on a famous breeder's ranch, but it was a beginning.

On the bus Saturnino asked if Tirado had been afraid, and I told him the old line about fear: "The only one without fear is the bull." He smiled, but he looked terrified, like a man who had just dropped a tray full of dishes.

And then they began: "Don't shit yourself!"

"Better to fuck him then."

"Like his mother, the Spanish whore."

"What an asshole!"

"Which one?"

"The Spaniard's."

"Which Spaniard?"

"Both."

"Ay, those gachupines.[11] Smooth."

Saturnino did not respond to the insults, although they went on and on while the bus crossed through the city, from the Plaza de Armas to the end of the line, where the street turned into an open field and the stench of

[11] An unpleasant, mildly insulting word for "Spaniards." The derivation is widely debated. Francisco Javier Santamaría's *Diccionario de Mejicanismos* says it comes from the Nahuatl word *catzopin,* meaning "a man with spurs." Kartunnen's *Analytical Dictionary of Nahuatl* says it may have come from *cactli* (shoe) and *chopinia* (to pick at something), but the origin is questionable since there is no record of the word in the first two hundred years after the arrival of the Spaniards in Mexico.

stockyards and offal arrived on the wind. The yards were half a mile off, across the field. The buildings where the killing was done, geometrical shapes with two tall smokestacks, rose abruptly out of the plain. Beyond them, vague in the distance, almost at the horizon line, lay the mountains, dusty pale, almost pink, like an old woman's powdered cheeks.

"I am Spanish from Spain," Saturnino said.

"Like Manolete."

"No, man, like Belmonte."

As we neared the yards, they engulfed our senses. Head-high weathered wooden fences defined the perimeter, and within those fences, other fences, other perimeters, and inside the fences hundreds, perhaps thousands of steers standing quietly near the feeding and watering troughs, ruminating and dropping manure into the soft, stinking sea in which they stood; and from the dark, windowless buildings at one end, the unmistakable stench of old blood.

Spider gave directions to the pen where the creyoyo was held along with several hundred steers. He led the group around the side of the complex of pens to a gate that was padlocked, but easy enough to climb over. Spider was the dandy of the group. He wore a small earring with a stone made of cut glass and affected American gangster attire, although he could afford only *segundos*, used shoes and clothing trucked down from picked-over piles in Texas border towns. He wore his pants belted around his hips, but the cut was narrow and the fabric a middling brown with a synthetic sheen. His shirt was buttoned at the neck only, but instead of plaid cotton it was solid maroon rayon with French cuffs. Saturnino had dressed in his black bus-boy's trousers and white shirt and had somehow found a short gray vest that he wore open, tugging often at the corners near his waist, like a flamenco dancer.

It was easy enough to spot the creyoyo. Although its horns had been sawed off just after the place where they curved forward, giving them a grotesque, truncated look, and the bull had the curly coat and thick face of a Hereford, it had the great forequarters and tossing muscle of a fighting bull, and it was huge, as tall at the shoulder as a bull fought by a full-fledged matador, and heavier. The creyoyo stood quietly, along with eight smaller animals in a feed pen off to the side of the main corrals. Getting the other animals to move was easy enough. A few shouts, waves of the big cape and the muleta, and a couple of whacks with the wooden sword, and the steers in the big corral as well as the feed pen, already nervous around the odor of blood, started to run. As soon as the animals in the feed pen were moving, Spider and Chino opened the gate and drove them into the main corral. As the creyoyo came around close to the gate, Saturnino and Poison, the failed bullfighter, pulled the gate closed. With no place to go, no more noises or capes to frighten them, and the ground beneath their hooves a muck of manure and sand, the animals in the big corral soon drifted back into their bovine acceptance of death. The dust settled quickly in the light air of the late afternoon.

Saturnino and his companions climbed to the top rail of the fence surrounding the feed pen and perched there, crows in colorful costume, awaiting the debut of the new matador, Saturnino Mora, who announced, "I will call myself the Spaniard."

"Better the Gachupin," said the chorus.

Chali, who had taken the name of a murdered singer, Chalino, cupped his hands around his mouth to make a megaphone and sang, in an Iberian whine, "Da-da, da-da . . ." to the tune of the "La Virgen de la Macarena," the music that accompanies the parade of the bullfighters and their retinues across the ring. Saturnino jumped down from the fence, the big cape in his hands, and walked with great dignity, even grandeur—back arched, shoulders thrown back, head high—through fresh manure, rotting manure, sand, and straw. His feet sank into the muck; the cuffs of his black trousers grew heavy with the moist greenish brown filth.

Halfway across the pen stood the creyoyo, head up, still on the alert after the cutting by men on foot. Saturnino advanced slowly until he was no more than thirty feet from the bull. Carefully, keeping his eye on the animal, he opened the cape wide, held it out in front of his body, and, with a quick nod of his head, shook the cape once and shouted, "*Toro!*"

The bull remained in its place.

Saturnino moved closer, taking small steps. Ten feet closer he repeated the movements and the shout. He stomped his foot in time with the shout as he had seen the great matadors do on Sunday afternoon television, but there was no sound, no tremor in the sand, as his foot sank and splashed the soft manure. He moved forward again, very close now. In a few more steps he would be able to reach out with his hand and touch the bull.

"Toro!"

The bull took notice. It pawed the ground once, then returned to its patient watching.

"Toro!" He pushed the cape forward so that a rush of air touched the bull. And it charged. Saturnino stepped to the side, dodging the sawed-off horns and enormous shoulders. As it passed him, the bull stopped. The hindquarters stood next to Saturnino, chest high. He took several steps backward and waited for the bull to turn and repeat the charge, but it did not move. It stood utterly still; not even its tail moved.

Saturnino moved cautiously around the bull until he stood in front of it. He incited it to charge, waving the cape, shouting, stomping his foot in the muck, but the bull would not move. "Coward!" he shouted. "Cow!" But the bull took no notice.

Saturnino looked over his shoulder to his companions. "The muleta, please," he said. "And of course, the sword."

Again, Saturnino did as he had seen the matadors do on Sunday afternoons on television. He turned his back on the bull and walked away slowly, glorious and arrogant, like a fine horse prancing.

From the fence sitters came a sound he may have heard in his dream: They shouted, "Ole!" and banged their manure-laden tennis shoes on a fence rail.

Chali exchanged equipment with Saturnino, who took the stick of the muleta and the handle of the wooden sword in his right hand and with his left folded the red serge over the length of the sword. Saturnino approached the bull again, turning his body so that only his side was exposed to the animal, edging forward with the muleta held out in front of him. The creyoyo, which was as thick and heavy as a small automobile, moved its head from side to side, as if to loosen the great tossing muscle.

A few feet from the bull Saturnino stopped. A momentary breeze rippled the muleta and shook the ends of Saturnino's vest. The half-breed lowered its head. Saturnino shook the muleta once, twice. "Eh, heh, toro!" The animal charged, stopped, slammed the flat of its horn into Saturnino's belly, lifted him up off his feet, and threw him into the muck.

He lay facedown. The bull jabbed at his back and ribs with its blunted horns. Saturnino covered the back of his head with his hands. The bull jabbed at him again, three, four, five times, pushed him, slid him across the muck. Then, as suddenly as it had charged, the bull withdrew. Saturnino lay in the muck of the feed pen, the muleta and sword beside him.

The jeering started: "Gachupin, asshole, son of a whore, idiot, queer. Look! You eat shit!" Ruiz started the chant: "Te-tas, te-tas, tetas pesetas."

Saturnino rose slowly. He raised his filthy hands and studied them. He had no way to wipe his face. The jeering went on: "Te-tas, te-tas, tetas pesetas; ga-chu-pin!" Saturnino bent over and picked up the sword and muleta. With the clean side of the cloth, he wiped his face and then his hands.

When he was finished with the muleta, he threw it to the ground, raised the sword high above his head, and charged the fence, cutting the air with the gray-painted wood. "Santiago!" he cried. "Santiago!"

He was not Quixote; he was Cortés, history, the world as it ought to be, pure. "Santiago," he cried, and the natives fled.

I saw Saturnino's tormentors only once after that. Ruiz and I had some unpleasantness, and it seemed best to me to move on before it got any worse. I never saw Saturnino again, although I asked after him at the restaurant. Apparently, he had never gone back. Perhaps he went to Mexico City or Madrid or simply stayed there in the cattle country and blended into the crowd.

5.

The Shaman's Apprentice

The Indians took ill to the yoke of servitude, but the Spaniards had the villages which covered the land well divided up into repartimientos. There [was], however, no lack of agitators among the Indians, and because of this they were cruelly punished; and this was the cause of a decrease in the number of people. The Spaniards burned alive some of the chieftains of the province of Cupul and hanged others. A charge was brought against the people of Yobain, a town of the Chels. They took the chieftains and placed them in irons inside a house and set fire to the house so that they were all burned in the most inhuman way possible. And this Diego de Landa says that he saw a tree near the town from whose branches a captain hanged many Indian women, and from their feet he also hanged the infant children. In this same town, and in another two leagues away called Verey, they hanged two Indian women, one of whom was a virgin and the other recently married, for no other crime than that they were very beautiful and might cause disturbances within the Spanish camp and also so that the Indians should think that the Spaniards were uninterested in women. These two are well-remembered among the Indians and the Spaniards because of their great beauty and because of the cruelty with which they were killed.

—FRAY DIEGO DE LANDA, 1566[1]

Mexico is an Indian country. More than 12 percent of the population is purely indigenous, and the majority of the rest is mestizo, culturally and genetically indigenous and European or African. Whoever does not understand this Indian aspect and its effect on the hearts and minds of Mexicans cannot grasp the idea of Mexico, even now, in the twenty-first century. Apparently inexplicable things happen in Mexico, as in any other country, but in Mexico they are seldom attributed to chance. In the pre-Hispanic mind, which lingers all through Mexico, everything has an explanation.

Let me give an example.

[1]Translation of Landa's account of the affairs of Yucatán (the correct Spanish title is unknown, since the original manuscript has been lost) by A. R. Pagden.

A HURRICANE'S TAIL

We left Mérida early, heading south and east to a meeting with Maya artists and intellectuals in Quintana Roo. Although we were due to stop at a demonstration farm in the low jungle on the Quintana Roo border and later to have lunch in Dzulna, we hoped to be in Felipe Carrillo Puerto by nightfall, before the tail end of a hurricane crossed into the area. Our plan was to start a tiny university in the town of Felipe Carrillo Puerto, a place to train people in traditional Maya culture, as it was understood by the Maya. We did not know how strong the hurricane would be or if the Maya who had planned to come to the meeting would brave the weather. The others in the van were the historian Alejandra García Quintanilla; Raúl Murguía Rosete, who oversaw the United Nations Development Program on the Yucatán Peninsula; and Rosalba Robles Vessi, executive director of Women Fighting for Democracy. There was a certain symmetry in the visit of the leader of a Mexican women's movement to the town that had been renamed for Felipe Carrillo Puerto. During his term in office (1918–1923) Carrillo Puerto had been the first feminist to govern a Mexican state, as well as the country's first socialist governor.

More than three-quarters of a century had passed since Carrillo Puerto stood before a firing squad in the cemetery of Mérida on January 4, 1924. He had made the unforgivable political mistake: in a time of civil war he chose the losing side. It was the cruelest kind of execution because his brothers were killed alongside him, an end to the line, the mourners among the dead. Photographed in death, in the Mexican style of the time, eyes closed, bullet wounds still visible, dressed in simple prison garb, he no longer showed the face that spoke his politics. In life he had been quite formal, almost stern, a man in a high starched collar and firmly buttoned suit. But it was a public facade denied by dark and loving eyes, downturned at the corners in a promise of compassion or perhaps a prefiguring of martyrdom. Poor Carrillo Puerto! Born in Motul, east of Mérida, a Maya who spoke Maya, the last in a long tradition of Yucatecan rebels.

The town named for the martyred socialist governor should probably bear the name of a ventriloquist, for the ventriloquist, as we shall see, had a longer reign. It is that kind of town. The name changed again and again. There are gas stations and video stores and all-night *taquerias* on the main streets now, but the state of Quintana Roo beyond the beaches still belongs to the old mysteries. Five centuries after the landing of Spanish troops there were stories about the Maya who lived in jungle villages, organizing themselves in military fashion. It seemed impossible in the twenty-first century: shamans who called themselves captains, sorcerers who used time as their chief weapon in a never-ending conflict with the white Western world. It was a form of dreaming, this idea of an ancient Mexico still living only a few miles from the drunken spring break beach parties in the resorts of Cancún. But the history of the town indicated that it might be more than a dream, that ancient Mexico was not yet gone, that it existed pure and whole in some places, that the mestizaje was not yet complete. Whoever does not understand that about Mexico cannot understand the country.

"Maya" means "People of the Cycle." And Felipe Carrillo Puerto has gone through many cycles. At one time it was known as Chan Santa Cruz (Little Holy Cross). But not the Christian Cross. Chan Santa Cruz referred to the unusual small cross found on the trunk of a tree near a cenote.[2] Then there was another cross, and this cross was even more unusual. It talked! And it did not talk just once or twice. The Talking Cross gave military and political orders during much of the Caste War, the Yucatecan race war between the traditional Maya and the mestizos and whites. The talk of the Talking Cross was a trick performed by a ventriloquist, who hid near a cruciform figure, throwing his voice so that the cross itself appeared to speak.

The Caste War was the longest war in Mexican history, lasting from 1847 into the first decade of the twentieth century, and it was a war rooted in Maya folklore and classical culture. But Chan Santa Cruz was not the first name of the town. In 1677 the town was known as Chable. Even then it was one of the centers of resistance to whites and mestizos and their Christian religion. The traditional Maya organized into military companies patterned after the ancient Maya system. They came out of the jungle to attack and then stepped back into the green darkness and disappeared. They had names that make no sense to the Western mind: Many Skunks, Hanging Rabbits, Earth Lions, Flags. They fought, returned to their fields and homes, and then organized to fight again. They refused to pay tribute to anyone. Their rebellion was economic and political, but also calendrical. The rebel priests took

---

[2]Often called a well, a cenote is actually a hole in the thin layer of stone under the surface of the Yucatán. When the stone collapses, it leaves an opening into the water table below. The most famous cenote is at Chichén Itzá.

on military titles. The keepers of the all-important calendar became captains, soldier shamans.

Time and rebellion are the two hallmarks of the Maya on the Yucatán Peninsula and on the west coast, across the Lacandón jungle, in Chiapas. And both were to attend the meeting of artists and scholars that evening. The storm arrived just as we entered the building that served as community center and cultural home to Felipe Carrillo Puerto and the surrounding villages. Rain came light and cool, without wind.

The building was cavernous, twenty-five-foot-high ceilings and long, empty halls painted in drab bureaucratic colors. The ceiling of the room where we met was as high as the room was wide, the architecture of a mausoleum. Voices rose, held for an instant in the heights of the room, then floated down, faintly echoing. A square of tables had been set up in the center of the room. The four who had come from Mérida took chairs on the four sides of the square, and around the rest of the table sat the Maya: a painter, poets, teachers, even an accountant who was also a dreamer and author of stories. One of the Maya, the brother of the accountant, would not reveal himself until much later that evening. He was the youngest of the people in the room, but the most self-assured. Although his features were regular, he was not an exceptionally handsome fellow in any conventional way, nor did he have the classic Maya nose or eyes drawn on the walls of pyramids or carved in stone. Nevertheless, he demanded attention; he had the inexplicable magnetism of an accomplished actor. But he was different, young, in his twenties, Maya; he described himself as a student. Whatever the quality he possessed, it did not have the crutch of fame that makes stars of ordinary men and women; it was he alone. Or something he knew. "In the cask, in the coffer" is a Mesoamerican metaphor meaning "secret." He was a cask, a coffer; he held a secret. Although the boy said nothing, he controlled the room; the discussion leaned toward him, as if seeking his advice.

At the end of the meeting, Murguía and I invited everyone to join us for dinner. By then the hour and the hurricane had closed the town. The only restaurant still open was on the roof of a building a few blocks away. We hurried along under the portico of the building to the street, slipping on the wet tile, holding on to one another until we got to the sidewalk. Then we ran through the flooded streets.

The restaurant was no more than a series of small square tables under a thatched roof. But the wind had begun to subside; the hurricane had moved on, heading out to sea, leaving only the rain. The roof leaked here and there, but we had pulled several tables together on the leeward side, where it was fairly dry. The magnetic young man, the cask and the coffer, took his place at the head of the table, as if it had been planned.

At the other end of the table sat the painter, who passed around copies of a catalog of his work. He said he sold well, at good prices in Miami and Cancún; it looked like airport shop art. But he did not say much about his work; there were other things on his mind. Under the skin of commercialism, the painter carried the old rages of Quintana Roo:

"The hotels are lined up along the beach at Cancún, one next to the other, with no space between them. We Maya own nothing in the hotels. They belong to international corporations. All the good jobs go to people from other countries, Germans, French, Americans. To have a job as a clerk, even a waiter, a person must speak at least two languages, not counting Maya and Spanish. This rule applies to everyone who has contact with the guests, who are all foreigners. So, you see, the hotels are owned by foreigners, who employ foreigners, who cater to foreign guests.

"The only Mayas who work in these hotels are laundresses, dishwashers, gardeners, people who never have contact with the guests. Even the maids are mestizas. We are in the land of the Maya [Mayab], but we Maya cannot use our own beaches, because there is no space between the hotels to pass onto the beach. And if a Maya should enter the lobby of a hotel just to pass through it to go to the beach, someone will ask him what he is doing there and send him back out onto the street.

"The foreigners take everything. They use our name, our culture, the ruins of our cities, everything Maya, to lure tourists to their hotels, and they give us nothing. Maya Tours, Mayaland hotels, Maya Curios, Maya ruins, Maya food, Xtabentun, the liquor of the Maya gods. We have to take back our name. If they want to use the word 'Maya,' they should pay." He turned sullen, counting his losses, dark in the near darkness.

At the head of the table the cask and the coffer suddenly opened. It was not the young man, but his sister who let out the secret. "He does not attend a university," she said, "not a university as we know it. He studies to be a h-meen; he is apprenticed to a shaman in the village where our family lived."[3] We

---

[3]Literally, a "doer," a healer or shaman, a person who knows the arcana of Maya culture and can put it to use for good or evil. A h-meen cannot die of natural causes; he can only

asked if he would help to bring h-meenoob, the captains, to teach in the proposed school, and he said he would.

By then he had taken control of the conversation. He owned the attention of the four outsiders, although Murguía is a powerful figure, as are the feminist leader and the historian, García Quintanilla. Each, in his or her own style, could dominate a meeting, but once the cask and the coffer had been opened, it belonged to the apprentice. He made no response to a question about the military rank of the h-meen with whom he studied, nor did he say anything about h-meenoob and hurricanes. But he had something to say about the millennium. "The h-meenoob met to talk about this," he said, "and they agreed that the year 2000 would pass in a single day. And on the first of January, in the year 2000, the area of Quintana Roo was steeped in darkness. The cloud cover was so heavy that it never grew light. The year passed in a single day, and it was a dark day, as they had predicted."

Everyone nodded, but no one at the table understood the implications of what the h-meenoob had said. Interesting, strange, but of what relevance? Why had the h-meenoob chosen the year 2000? It seemed almost pathetic, the Maya trying to horn in on the West's great calendrical moment, to discount the worldwide celebration of the Gregorian calendar. The cask and the coffer closed; Murguía was again in control of the table. He announced that it was time to leave. The rain had slowed; the painter gave everyone a copy of his damp catalog; the young man stood up, his magnetism gone, his revelation fallen flat. Murguía put his arm on the young man's shoulder and called him *camarada* (comrade). They were man and boy again.

That evening, in my hotel room, lying on the stony mattress, listening to the roar of the ancient air-conditioning machine, I considered the day. What

---

be killed by another h-meen. Some of the rites practiced by the h-meenoob had come down from the pre-Hispanic period; others appear to have been influenced by Christianity; they are difficult to separate by such categories.

H-meenoob (the plural in Maya is indicated by the suffix *oob*) belong to a hierarchy, according to the depth of their knowledge. Every h-meen appears to have certain areas of competence. One might be best at curing psychological problems such as depression. Another might have a cure for colic in infants. All are herbalists; many are beekeepers.

Conferences among the h-meenoob take place now and then, although I do not know of an outsider who has attended one of these meetings. The works of several h-meenoob of the Yucatán and other areas have been redacted and translated into English (see León-Portilla and Shorris, *In the Language of Kings*, for the "Rituals of the Bacabs").

remained was the cask and the coffer, the passing of the year 2000 in one dark day. It had to be a key to Quintana Roo, perhaps to the Maya world, to Mexico itself; what other reason could the apprentice have had for telling us about it? With so many options—ancient history, herbal cures, prayers, the creatures of the forest—he had chosen to tell an illogical tale of a year passing in a single dark day.

For more than a year, although I thought about it with some regularity, the meaning eluded me. Then, while checking a quotation in Munro Edmonson's translation of the *Chilam Balam of Chumayel*,[4] I came across these sentences: "At Xcacal the *Books of Chilam Balam* are still read publicly each year. . . . It is ominous that both the year 2000 and the *baktun* and calendar round endings fall in the coming *katun* 8 Ahau."[5] It was a day of enormous importance to the Maya. A katun is a twenty-year cycle, and a baktun a cycle of twenty katuns, or four hundred years. What the apprentice had told was that the h-meenoob of Quintana Roo, the captains and commanders in their isolated cultural redoubts, had devised a battle for the possession of time itself. They had put the glorious accomplishment of Mesoamerica up against time as it was known in the European world and defeated the Gregorian calendar in the space of a single day.

The shaman's apprentice had passed on the word, arcana to us, but common knowledge in the jungle villages of Quintana Roo, that the war for time and power was not over. Who owned time owned the world. It had been that way in the Yucatán for more than two thousand years.

AUTO-DA-FÉ

No one comparable to the brilliant ethnographer Fray Bernardino de Sahagún lived and worked in the Yucatán during the sixteenth century. Diego de Landa was a very different representative of the Franciscan order. Although he left behind dictated notes that contained a clue to Maya writ-

---

[4] Austin: University of Texas Press, 1986.
[5] The calendar round is the completion of the cycle of days and months, which can be visualized as two interlocked wheels, like gears, turning at given speeds so that the cycle of days (twenty) and months (eighteen) plus five days with no name completes every fifty-two years.

ing, his work was hardly a Rosetta stone; no one could decipher the phonograms or logograms based on Landa's work. The Franciscan who later became a bishop is remembered chiefly for his cruelty to the Indians and the destruction of cultural objects, including the grand auto-da-fé of 1562, in which he burned the Maya codices.

The Spanish authorities found his behavior so reprehensible that they recalled him to Spain to stand trial before the Royal Council of the Indies. Otherwise, we might not have even the sketchy notes of his *Relación*, which Landa dictated in 1566 during his sojourn in Spain. And it was no more than a sojourn. The case was decided by the provincial of Castile, who allowed a group of theologians to think it over for several years before Landa was found not guilty. He returned to New Spain, where he succeeded Francisco de Toral, his original accuser, as bishop of Yucatán.

The peninsula he ravaged had been in a long decline. The great city-states had collapsed in the tenth century. By the time the Spaniards arrived, the Maya were in a weakened state. As in central Mexico, major sectors of the population were at war with each other, and the Spaniards knew how to take advantage of those divisions. The wars between the Maya forces were based on issues related to time.[6] Entire city-states engaged in war and destroyed

[6]Here one may attempt to understand as much as is possible for a person in the twenty-first century how power was exercised and celebrated in that period, for it demonstrates the Maya obsession with time and its hegemony over all things. There were two Maya versions of time, one belonging to the Itzá and the other to the Xiu. That is, there were two different calendars. The importance of the calendars and the datings cannot be overestimated. The Maya notion of existence itself relates to the calendars. In the Maya view, time began around 20,000 B.C. Their count then leads to a great ending in 13.0.0.0.0, which conforms to a date of August 15, 3115 B.C., according to Munro Edmonson.

This moment, this ending and beginning, connects to the great achievement of Maya mathematics and astronomy. The Maya had the concept of zero long before it occurred to Europeans. The date 13.0.0.0.0 in their calendar is zero. Prior to that date nothing existed but time. Nothing. And from there came the idea of a symbol to denote nothing: zero. The concept has an air of pre-Socratic thinking.

Of course, any comparison of Mesoamerica and ancient Greece is twice exciting: once in the contemplation and then in the risk of seeming the fool. Nonetheless, the Pythagorean notion of the existence of numbers prior to anyone or anything, man, god, or element, is in kind too similar to put aside without some consideration. Both were feats of staggering imagination, levels of abstraction previously unknown on earth.

Pythagoras is better known today for the goofy ideas of Orphism and an eponymous theorem than for his cosmological speculations. As the Pythagoreans allowed Orphism

one another over questions of time all through the history of pre-Hispanic Mexico. And battles over time have not ended but continue in other forms in Mexico, reminders of the long shadows of history, the genes of culture. In 2001 a skirmish over time occurred in the Federal District of Mexico. The mayor of Mexico City, Andrés Manuel López Obrador, and President Vicente Fox Quesada differed over the use of daylight saving time. As a result, all Mexico except Mexico City operated on daylight saving time. The argument over the control of time in Mexico City led to neighbors, businesses, and government bureaus choosing different versions of the correct hour. Leftists and rightists set their watches to different times. It was both ridiculous and chaotic, a contemporary form of the battles fought over the seating of the cycle of the years by the postclassic Maya.

Eventually the Mexican Supreme Court brought the left-of-center party (PRD) into conformance with the rest of the country. Perhaps the Maya would also have arrived at some agreement had not a much greater problem in the form of Francisco de Montejo arrived in 1526. By then most of the Maya had retreated to small villages carved out of the jungles of dense scrub growth and the other, deeper jungles of a darkening canopy of great trees. But the noble families and their subjects still lived in the remaining urban areas (Chichén Itzá and Mérida among them) and preyed on the people of the outlying villages, demanding tribute and labor.

Having learned to defend themselves against the demands of their own nobles, who retained their historic priestly and military organizations, the villagers were prepared to resist the invaders. The first excursion led by Montejo in 1526 ended in disaster for the Spaniards. The small force was defeated at Chichén Itzá, and Montejo had to flee the country. His second expedition fared no better. Montejo was forced to turn over the offices of *adelantado*

---

to blunt the thrust of their science, the Maya allowed their brilliant notion of zero and the preeminence of time to take an unreasonable amount of control over much of the rest of their thinking, at least in the postclassic period. The long measure of time, the *may*, or cycle, was 255 years, 205 days. The city in which the cycle was seated was holy, "heaven-born," and in control of the country surrounding the city. Its priests were the most powerful; its politics was the most important. The contention over the seating of the cycle was both political and what for the lack of a better choice must be called scientific. The Xiu said the cycle began on the date 6 Ahau and ended on 8 Ahau. The Itzá of Chichén said it began on 11 Ahau and ended on 13 Ahau. The Xiu priests or captains of Quintana Roo, as the apprentice shaman revealed in Felipe Carrillo Puerto, still keep the Xiu calendar.

(military commander) and governor and give the task of subduing the Maya to his son, known as el Mozo. According to some accounts, Francisco de Montejo, el Mozo, "conquered" the Yucatán, preparing the way for his father to become adelantado and governor again. The father did not last long in his restored position. He was accused of mismanagement, recalled to Spain, and stripped of his offices. After surviving shipwreck on the shores of an unknown world and soldiering in the invasion led by Cortés, he failed twice in the Yucatán and died in Spain, a poor, lonely, and miserable man.

Montejo el Mozo fared better. In 1542 he founded the city of Mérida on the site of the old Maya city of T'Ho. The Spaniards founded another town not far from Xocen, which the Maya called the Center of the World, and named it Valladolid. Four years later the invaders thought of themselves as conquerors, strong, secure, destined for wealth and the favor of God and king. They busied themselves with Christianizing and enslaving the natives, changing the landscape and culture to their own Spanish version of God, man, and nature. The climate was harsh, especially inland, where it was either hot and damp or hot and dry. Terrible storms came in autumn, and if it did not rain in the month of May, the wind blew away the ashes of last year's cornstalks and beanstalks, and the thin, unreplenished topsoil would not yield to the methods of Spanish farmers.

Mosquitoes abounded; poisonous snakes, blind when they shed their skin, biting at anything that passed nearby, crawled in the underbrush. There were no rivers; water had to be drawn from deep holes in the earth left by the collapse of the limestone crust that had formed over the water table in some unknown time when the planet first cooled and the waters receded. Even so, the Spaniards were conquerors, and they lived the lives of conquerors, dandies, and woodsmen, owners of the gift of the labor of the natives in the system the Spanish crown called *encomienda*. All seemed well on the night of the first full moon of November 1546.

Many of the *encomenderos* had gone out into the countryside, each with his retinue of servants. It was an ordinary night for the Spaniards, but not for the Maya. They had made a decision about the Spaniards. The priests said these were mere men, strangers who did not venerate corn or understand the gods, inventors of the meaningless mark of time they called the week, clothiers who insisted that the Maya wear white trousers, eaters of pork and beef, violators of Maya women, self-appointed slave masters. The Maya determined to rid the peninsula of the invaders, to obliterate them and every sign of them.

On the night of the full moon the killing began. The Maya, mainly from the Cupul district in the northwest inland area of Yucatán, spared no one, neither Spaniards nor those who served them. And after they had killed the people, they killed their domestic animals and destroyed their crops and even the trees they had brought from Spain. The rebellion might have succeeded had the Spaniards not been able to use their Maya allies to defeat the rebels. It was a repetition of the defeat of the Aztecs, a small contingent of Spaniards leading a large force of natives against other natives. As in central Mexico, the invincible weapon employed by the Spaniards was not superior technology or even disease, but the ability to take advantage of dissension among their enemies. They were the manipulators, the ultimate victors in what was really internecine war.

After the defeat of the Cupul rebellion came the shaming by Diego de Landa, the torture of women, the burning of the painted books, the long years of the painful conversion to Christianity. Three centuries after the Cupul rebellion failed, the Caste War began. The priests had not been obliterated; the old religion had not been destroyed. While the Spaniards called the Indians to worship in churches made of stones torn from the walls of ancient pyramids, the priests in the outlying villages, in the secrecy of summer houses made of sticks and thatch, in the squares of stone in which the urban Maya lived, in cornfields and caves, carried on ancient traditions; they kept the calendar, they counted.

In the twenty-first century, the Maya still know how to cure colic with the tooth of a rattlesnake and schizophrenia with the spine of a stingray's tail. They have not forgotten the curative powers of herbs or fragrant leaves or the hemostatic qualities of the red fuzz of the flower of wild pineapple. In everything, in the children and the tourist hotels, in the hammocks and huipiles, something Maya had remained, but it was no longer clear. The calendar existed in opposition to the foreign count. The vigesimal system, based on the twenty digits of a human being, which gave the name twenty (*winik*) to man and month and multiples, underlay the decimal system of the modern world, appearing now and then, like the unique crescent of a Maya nose in an otherwise European face. Nothing was clear, nothing was yet complete; the marriage of the Western ten and the Maya twenty had produced an unworkable fifteen.

6.

The God of Bread and
the God of Corn

No corn, but two stalks of wheat.
—MOTTO ON THE SHIELD OF THE MEXICAN
NATIONAL SCHOOL OF AGRICULTURE[1]

*Between January and November 2002, Mexico imported $688 million
worth of corn, mainly from the United States.*
—Reforma, JANUARY 15, 2003

Spanish Is Also Ours
—TITLE OF AN ESSAY BY NATALIO HERNÁNDEZ XOCOYOTZIN,
A CONTEMPORARY NAHUA POET

Twenty years ago the finest worms in Mexico City were prepared in the
form of a paste and served to the wealthy clientele of the San Ángel Inn
in the southern part of Mexico City, not far from the house where Frida
Kahlo lived with Diego Rivera. It is a grand restaurant of courtyards rich in
trees and dining rooms set under high ceilings. Such excellent worms as they
served in the San Ángel Inn could move an engineer, the president of a small
corporation, to tell of the winged ants his mother captured on the day of the
first rain of the season, when the insects, weighted down by drops of rain,
fell to the ground and lay squirming and vulnerable to gathering by the
women of the village. Every year after the first rain he went home to the
mountain town where he was born to enjoy the paste his mother made of
ground ants and chillis.

Delectable worms are also served in one of the best restaurants in the

---

[1]The Escuela Nacional de Agricultura was founded by the decree of Antonio López de
Santa Anna in 1853. The name was changed to the Autonomous University of Chapingo
in 1923. On the shield of the Autonomous Metropolitan University, founded in 1974, the
motto is written in Nahuatl.

industrial city of Monterrey, but not partially disguised in the form of a paste. The worms of Monterrey, fat and black, are fried and served on a little bed of guacamole. Elegant Mexican restaurants offer grasshoppers fried until they are as crunchy as peanuts and ants cooked and coated in chocolate. Mexicans also serve tamales filled with fruit at Christmas, but the five-fingered tamales described in the sixteenth-century Florentine Codex seem to have disappeared from all the menus of Mexico; perhaps the skill required to manipulate the corn husks into that shape has been lost.

The Florentine Codex contains a long list of the foods eaten by the people of central Mexico, only a few of which belong to the ill-defined category known around the world now as Mexican food. The small dogs (*xoloitzcuintli* in Nahuatl) cooked into tender stews seasoned with chillis and herbs have also disappeared from the diet, although they remain as a kind of overtone in the language. *Itzquintli*[2] in modern Mexican slang means "a little squirt."

Armadillo and agouti, which abounded in pre-Columbian Mexico, have all but vanished from the Mexican table. Villagers still forage for food in forested rural areas, but dishes like *brazo de reina*, made of wild chayote and egg and served with a sauce of tomatoes and chillis, do not appear on restaurant menus or urban dinner tables. There is a *mole* festival in Milpa Alta, high above Mexico City, and Oaxaca is famous for its moles, as is Puebla, but the meat under the brown sauce of chocolate, chillis, peanuts, cornmeal, and a dozen other ingredients is chicken more often than turkey, the *guajolote* of pre-Columbian Mexico.

Dog, alas, may not have disappeared entirely from the Mexican menu. As a young man I had a friend known as Veneno (Poison) whose mother sold tacos on the street. When it was discovered that the tasty filling of the tacos was made of dead dogs she found lying beside the highway, she was put in jail and her story told on the front pages of the afternoon papers. Presumably, Sra. Blanco served as an example, and no one stews or fries little dogs or dead German shepherds anymore and serves them with tortillas made of corn. Presumably . . .

The god of corn still lives in Mexico, but in the struggle between the great gods of sustenance, in the maw of culture, the god of bread took the cherished place. It could have been a titanic struggle, earthshaking, like the pre-

---

[2]Dog, the tenth day in the Mexica solar calendar; the prefix *xolo* means "small."

dicted end of the fifth and final sun, but the god of corn would not have it that way.

Nothing so distinguishes the European from the American worlds in Mexico as corn and bread. They are the primary symbols, native and imported, Mesoamerican and Christian, poor and rich, dark and light, ancient and modern, ignorant and intelligent. The conflict between corn and bread affects Mexican religion, regionalism, corruption, language, diet, personality, and politics. It is at the heart of Mexico. And it is learned early, even now. When I was a boy, the mothers of my schoolmates told their children to eat only tortillas made of wheat or bread baked in an oven; corn was for Indians, they said. As I remember their faces now, my classmates were all mestizo. Their mothers, especially the mothers of the girls, wanted them to be white, to live and think and look like people of pure Spanish ancestry, like criollos. It was a matter of class as well as culture. Wheat and white were the signs.

The god of bread arrived in Mexico on a horse, and he was unlike all other gods, for he had no twin and no female aspect; he was a trinity when gods had always been a duality. Before him, there had been only corn, a god tended by humans, created by humans, unable to survive without the creatures of his own making, a reciprocal god. Moreover, the god of bread was a jealous god; he had said so himself. His followers initiated a struggle with the god of corn, which they thought would be a struggle to the death, because they did not understand the history of the god of corn. But the god of corn was an inclusive god. Since the birth of the god of corn, humans had been including the new. Not just the change from hunting and gathering to agriculture, from a nomadic to a sedentary life; inclusivity meant the acceptance of new gods. Quetzalcoatl, the culture bearer, had been included all across Mesoamerica, sometimes by his Nahuatl name and at other times, in other languages, as Gucumatz or Kukulkan.

When the Spaniards were completing the invasion, they made clear the essential difference between the methods of the two gods in a colloquy in 1524. The priests of the god of bread told of Jesus, the Pope, the king of Spain, and the Holy Book, and the surviving Aztec priests and nobles were left to reply: ". . . can it be that here, in your presence, we must destroy the ancient law. . . ." Recognizing that they had been defeated, the native priests embraced the new god and His powers, asking only that they be permitted to include the new god rather than destroy the old one. Accepting a new member of the family of gods required the Aztecs to make a place for Him, no more than that. It was a process of inclusion; there was no conversion.

In the north and south the god of corn was also inclusive, but more reluctantly. It took long wars and many diseases as well as instruction in the south to force the god of corn to accept the god of bread, resulting in a half-hearted embrace. Many of the people of the north fought to the death the idea of inclusivity; they were hunter-gatherers for whom the god of corn did not hold sway; only the corn planters of the north believed in the inclusivity of their god.

From the first moments of the invasion of the god of bread the center differed from the south and the north. And the difference would remain and be noted, often in a cruel and uncomprehending way, by those most devoted to the god of bread. The division of Mexico into three distinct regions is based entirely on the reaction of those regions to the arrival of the god of bread. The three regions differ economically, culturally, and politically because of the way in which the native people accepted the new god. The distinction is as important today as it was in the sixteenth century. In his election campaign in 2000, Vicente Fox Quesada used what he viewed as the essential characteristics of the three regions to describe Mexico. He assigned intellect to the central region, industry to the north, and poverty and backwardness to the south. He was accused of racism in the way he phrased the distinctions, and there certainly was that aspect about his words, but Fox is not a man who knows or understands well the history of his own country. He is a salesman by profession; he thinks in terms of symptoms; causation eludes him, effects surprise him. Nothing of what he said indicated that he knew the worshipers of the god of bread, the Europeans, had an immediate effect upon every aspect of life in Mexico.

In the center, they changed everything so rapidly that the character of the land before they arrived can only be imagined. The animals they brought with them thrived on the rich forage land around the cities and towns. Cows, pigs, sheep, goats, and donkeys ate the vegetation and trampled the grassland until the grass dried up and died. The beasts made paths to the rivers and streams so that the water once held by the grassland ran off, carrying the topsoil with it. Only twenty years after the arrival of the Spaniards the indigenous farmers complained to the Spanish authorities that the animals were destroying their cropland.

Populations of people and animals, which had increased slowly over the centuries, suddenly rose and then collapsed. The people died of plagues of smallpox and other diseases that arrived in the bodies of the Spaniards.[3] The beasts thrived, then died after they had trampled and overgrazed the grasslands. On the traditional farms two or three varieties of seed corn had been planted in each hole made by a digging stick. One variety of corn or the other had grown best according to the temperatures and the moisture during the growing season, but almost always one. A season without rain or a plague of locusts might frustrate the will of the god of corn, but not forever. And beans and squash grew alongside the corn, in the same field, the same row. The *milpa* (small farm) was a complex and enduring place.

A wheatfield bore no resemblance to the milpa. The wheatfield was a simple place, vulnerable to error. At first the Spaniards planted their wheat in the wrong season, sowing in spring. Unlike corn, which welcomed the rains of summer, the wheat died. Then the Spaniards took to planting in the fall, expecting to harvest their wheat in spring, but there was no rain in winter; they irrigated the fields when they could.

What the beasts did not trample, the plow that had replaced the digging stick turned to dust. The Spaniards planted more wheat to satisfy their growing population. The wealth of the fields gave out; then the Spaniards set fire to the fields, hoping to rejuvenate them. The sky of central Mexico filled with smoke and dust, as if it were a pre-Columbian battlefield; it reeked of war.

No one knows for certain what grew in Mexico before the Spaniards

---

[3]Estimates of the decline of the population of central Mexico during the colonial period range from a high of twenty-four million to a low figure of three million. On the face of it, a loss of twenty-four million people seems high; however, the plagues of smallpox and measles, as well as other diseases imported from Europe, were terrible. People also died in great numbers from abuse and overwork, and with the decline in the food supply malnutrition had to have contributed.

Another factor, not so frequently mentioned, may have been a decline in the birthrate following the conquest. Several sources claim a loss of sexual energy resulted from the depressive force of defeat, enslavement, and the near enslavement of the encomienda system. How many anthropologists and demographers the average sixteenth-century Nahua couple permitted in their bedroom is not known.

The Olinalá (see León-Portilla and Shorris, *In the Language of Kings*), a complaint of sexual abuse by a Catholic priest, and the large number of children of mixed ancestry, although not of mixed marriages, indicate that the invaders, at least, suffered no diminution of sexual activity.

came. Some accounts say the grass was tall and there were great trees to break the wind and hold the soil in place. Toward the end of the sixteenth century the rains ceased, and a dry period began that was to last for two hundred years. In the places where trees had flourished mesquite and heavily thorned cactus grew. The desert came to central Mexico. Where corn had grown in abundance, supplying the cities and towns and the great market at Tlatelolco, wheat could not survive.

Native technologies apparently made no sense to the Spaniards. Instead of using the wetlands surrounding Tenochtitlán, continuing the practice of making chinampas of mud and straw and growing what they needed on these artificial fields constructed in the middle of lakes, they drained the lakes. Water became more and more scarce all over Mexico, yet wheat and sugar, the cash crops the Spaniards planted, required much more water than corn. Soon water as well as land became a cause of contention. The society of central Mexico took on some of the character of a standard American cowboy movie, in which the farmers and ranchers contend for water rights. The indigenous people, like the good farmers in the movies, could not count on the fairness of the authorities, who were appointed by the Spanish crown.

By the beginning of the twenty-first century the combination of modern U.S. farming techniques and vast population growth had turned Mexico into one of the driest lands per capita on earth. Egypt, according to Mexican President Vicente Fox Quesada,[4] had more water per person than Mexico. U.S. agreements with Mexico over water had fallen apart. The United States claimed that Mexico owed hundreds of billions of gallons of water under treaty agreements. Mexico said it did not have water to return. Fox, always the salesman, said the only way for the United States to recoup its water was to loan Mexico more than four hundred million dollars to improve its irrigation system. Mexico had suffered water problems since the arrival of the god of wheat, but solving the problem for two or three million people was different from dealing with the thirst of a hundred million. Farmers on the U.S. side claimed the theft of water was the most corrupt act in Mexican history. That was something of an overstatement of the issue, but water and corruption had a long history together in Mexico.

Local disputes over water rights were settled in the sixteenth century by the *corregidores*, provincial representatives of the crown, who were poorly

[4]Quoted in the *New York Times*, May 24, 2002.

paid and little respected. The corregidores lived by cheating natives and collecting bribes. They were the grass roots beginning of the system of corruption that only grew over the ensuing years. The famous *mordida*, the bite or little bribe, was not indigenous. It came with the god of bread and grew from the bottom up. The worst moral corruption of the time, the encomienda, the granting of labor, came from the top, the crown itself. In some cases the grants covered the entire population of an area, known as an altepetl,[5] like the encomienda granted Cortés, which gave him control of the labor and lives of twenty thousand people. In this way, the god of bread also became the god of servitude and corruption.[6]

As news of the exploitation of the natives by the encomenderos reached Spain, the king attempted to end the system by prohibiting grants of new encomiendas and terminating those already granted upon the death of the encomendero. But the New Laws of 1542 had no effect; the encomenderos would have none of it, and only three years later, new encomiendas were granted. In 1555, Charles I enabled the grant of the encomienda to be passed on to the children and grandchildren of the encomendero.

A few years later, when Philip II of Spain tried to abolish the encomienda system, some of the criollos were so incensed they plotted to overthrow the government and declare New Spain independent. The idea cost the plotters their heads, which were put on display, no surprise to the Aztecs, who had displayed the skulls of sacrificial victims on a great rack until the Spaniards, claiming to be appalled by the barbarity of the custom, put a stop to it.

The encomienda was finally abolished in 1720 in most of New Spain, although it continued until 1786 in the Yucatán and what is now the state of Tabasco. Special license was granted for the use of indigenous labor in the silver mines even after that. The encomienda system never bore the name "slavery," but it differed very little from that institution. Indigenous people were not paid for their labor, the encomenderos used the women and mis-

---

[5] A politically and geographically defined area, an "ethnic state," according to James Lockhart, in *The Nahuas after the Conquest*. Altepemi later became known as towns.

[6] The Spanish crown preferred granting labor rather than land, since land would have been given in perpetuity and could have caused the same tension between king and nobles that the crown had suffered in Spain. However, the crown's attempt to keep the *conquistadores* from accumulating great amounts of land failed, because the system allowed the grantees to use the money earned through the encomienda to buy land, quickly assembling great holdings.

used the men, and the bondage lasted as long as the people lived and on to the next generations. The extent of the cruelty of the encomenderos will never be fully known, since most of the native people could not write and the encomenderos were not likely to offer their behavior to the judgment of posterity. Nonetheless, as news of some situations reached Spain, the crown acted. The explorer Juan Ponce de León, for one, was imprisoned for the mistreatment of people given to him in bondage.

The Catholic Church, responsible for the souls of the colonists, did not shrink from enjoying encomienda privileges. Fray Bartolomé de las Casas, who held an encomienda in the Caribbean, was apparently made so unhappy by the notion of it, and especially by what he saw of the treatment of other people held in bondage, that he gave up his encomienda rights in 1514 and devoted himself to helping the natives. Fray Bartolomé's renunciation of the gift of human labor was the first extraordinary act in the life of a most extraordinary man. He never went so far as to choose the god of corn, but his defense of the humanity of the natives and his famous exposure of the cruelty of the invading Spaniards, known by its detractors as the Black Legend, had the effect of extending the life of the god of corn, who might otherwise have become an artifact rather than an enduring deity.

As Fray Bartolomé and others noted, slavery in its true form also flourished in New Spain. The number of slaves ranged from three million in all of the Americas to two hundred thousand in New Spain alone. The crown allowed captured enemies to be enslaved and permitted the sale of those who had already been enslaved. Cortés held slaves. Nuño de Guzmán, one of the great villains of the invasion, traded in slaves by the thousands.

At the beginning of the sixteenth century the god of bread was thrust into Mexico by slaughter and fire. With the meeting of the Nahua nobles and the Franciscans in 1524 the effort at the deeper insinuation of the god of bread began. For centuries historians believed the god of bread had quickly conquered Mexico, because most records came from the great cities, especially the capital, where the god of bread was strongest. Besides, the historians, most of them priests, liked telling it that way. But outside the largest cities, the god of corn remained vital. In central Mexico, Nahua social and political structures remained: The altepetl became the definition of the scope of the encomienda and of the parish. The Spanish form of local government, the *cabildo*, was accepted into the altepetl.

Nahuas quickly learned to deal in Spanish money, but here again the

European system was simply embraced by the Nahuas, who had used gold, cacao, and cochineal, as well as large squares of cotton cloth, as media of exchange. After the introduction of Spanish coins, cacao continued to represent smaller amounts of money—i.e., to make change of Spanish money, one might require a given amount of cacao. Spanish judges and other officials replaced some aspects of the Nahua governmental structure, but the head of the altepetl continued in office in most instances, and through most of the first century after the invasion, the leader of the altepetl was a descendant of previous rulers.

Language changed very slowly as the natives took Spanish words into their daily usage, and to this day Mexico remains a country of mixed languages. Seventy-five indigenous languages are still spoken in Mexico, almost all with borrowings from Spanish, but then Spanish cannot be spoken anywhere in Mexico without borrowings from indigenous languages. To begin, unlike Bolivia, Colombia, or the United States of America, the name of Mexico is an indigenous word. If immortality is defined as living memory, the indigenous gods of Mexico are not dead yet; they appear in the daily speech of all Mexicans, including those who would describe themselves as monolingual Spanish speakers. Every Mexican can easily pronounce the indigenous words that tie the tongues of foreigners.[7] Otherwise, it would be impossible to navigate through daily life. Mexico is not only an old country, it is an Indian country. Indigenous languages have named the world of Mexico.

No area of inclusivity had greater importance than religion. Fray Sahagún, the father of ethnography, who undoubtedly understood the native world better than any other European, knew the danger (from his point of view) of native religion's simply including the Holy Trinity as another set of gods. He tried to replace the native religion, even encouraging the Aztecs to translate the Psalms into their own language, but his efforts were not entirely successful. The Nahuatl version of the Fifth Psalm began, "The precious jades that I also shape with my lips, that I also have scattered, that I have uttered, are a fitting song." It went on to speak about looking into the face of God in heaven and of spirituality as the heavenly experience, but what it said was of relatively little importance. Poetry, even religious poetry, does not celebrate piety first. Poetry belongs to the realm of language, and

---

[7]Indian names are not so common in the United States, but Americans have no trouble saying Dakota, Iowa, Seattle, Menominee, Choctaw, Mohican, and so on.

the Nahuas had produced a poem about the scattering of precious jades, a metaphor belonging entirely to the god of corn.

Had the Spanish conquistadores understood the inclusive character of the god of corn, they would have behaved like the conquerors of what is now the United States, destroying language, religion, and culture as they went westward. Instead, they enjoyed the similarities between the two worlds. Mexico is now the most Catholic country in the world, but Mexican Catholicism is a syncretic religion. After five hundred years it is still not entirely clear whether the god of bread defeated the god of corn or was merely swallowed by him.

The Spaniards, for all that Fray Bartolemé de las Casas railed against his countrymen and the treatment of the people they called indios, did not pursue either physical or cultural genocide in Mexico. The crown sought profit and political sovereignty with which to manage its new source of wealth, and the criollos desired wealth, ease, and status. Nothing else really mattered. In every instance, they took the easy route, the quick one, in geography, administration, language, even religion. Only in the fields did the god of bread refuse the embrace of the god of corn, and there he made a desert.

7.

The Mesoamerican Origins of Generosity

The term "criollo," which originated among the Portuguese, was first applied only to Africans born outside Africa. Gradually it was extended to other people, including Indians, who were born outside their traditional homeland. Most of those whom it described were on the humble end of the scale. Before the end of the 16th century Spanish-born Spaniards began to call native-born Spaniards criollos, usually by way of insult. Bit by bit those insulted began to turn the term around and use it as a slogan.

—LISA SOUSA, STAFFORD POOLE, C.M., AND JAMES LOCKHART, *The Story of Guadalupe*

Mexicans have had a relentlessly negative view of Mexicans for centuries. Since the beginning of the twentieth century Mexican novelists, social scientists, philosophers, and filmmakers have developed great expertise in self-loathing. Octavio Paz, in his famous essay *The Labyrinth of Solitude*, describes the Mexican as lonely, living behind a mask. The Mexican is castigated by his own intellectuals for machismo, by his songwriters for betrayal, and by the scholar Samuel Ramos for his "inferiority complex." Justo Sierra, one of Mexico's great historians of the early twentieth century, wrote that Mexicans tended to run away on the battlefield. At the end of the century Guillermo Bonfil Batalla complained of Mexican racism, and everyone complains about corruption. The slogan of Mexican intellectuals could well have been spoken by Sor Juana Inés de la Cruz, one of the world's great writers, who spoke of herself as "the worst of all."

Can the Mexican possibly be so loathsome as he has been made out by generations of Mexicans? Is the Mexican of reality so vile or vulgar as the people portrayed by Mexican writers and directors in two movies that were widely released in the United States in recent years: *Amores Perros (Life's a Bitch)* and *Y tu Mamá También (And Your Mother, Too)*? Does the Mexican have even a single saving grace, something Mexican artists and intellectuals could have missed?

Of all the defined groups of people on earth it may be fairly said that the Mexicans are if not the most generous, surely among them. This applies not only to gifts and parties and the sharing of food and lodging but to what is commonly called generosity of spirit. And this characteristic seems neither to be left behind when Mexicans emigrate to the United States nor to disappear in the second or third generation in Los Angeles or Chicago or Fairbanks or a farm town in Iowa. Of course, this is a generalization about generosity, which means that the next Mexican one meets may be the epitome of meanness in spirit as well as worldly things. And then it will seem that Ramos and Paz and Justo Sierra had put their fingers on the essence of the Mexican.

The generosity of Mexicans does not extend to distant relations, as in the state and its citizens or subjects, or even to employers and employees, and certainly it does not exist between economic or social classes. It is the generosity of familiarity, and because of that, it is always vulnerable to betrayal. Among family members, Mexican generosity is limitless. If seven members of a family from Zacatecas want to move to Mexico City, they will be invited to stay with their relatives in Mexico City, even if those relatives have four children and a one-bedroom apartment. If they later appear without notice at the airport in Kansas City, intent upon visiting with a cousin who is married to an Anglo, they will again be invited to stay. And if it is their first visit, the Anglo will be surprised at how welcome they are.

Among family members and close friends, generosity may also include the requirement for vengeance, which is a curious form of generosity, but not uncommon. In practice, the generosity of vengeance works this way: A man, whose name I will not use, because he is an old friend and a public man, one who moves between the political and intellectual life of Mexico, told me what was once demanded of him. While in the United States to complete work on his doctorate at a major university, he received distressing news in a telephone call from Mexico. His niece had been raped. It happened in the small town, little more than a village, where my friend was born and lived until he left for the seminary in Mexico City.[1]

---

[1]Many Mexicans of modest means attend Catholic seminaries for several years before going on to private or public universities for advanced degrees. Tuition is not an issue, the classical aspect of the education provides a good foundation, and there is no penalty for leaving the order.

The young woman's father had died the preceding year, and she had only female siblings. My friend was both the closest and eldest of her male relatives. He was asked to come home immediately. Of course, he did as asked. When he arrived in the small town, where most people were of Purépecha descent, he was greeted by his own uncle, a very old gentleman who explained that the scholar had to kill the rapist. After he had finished laying out the rules of behavior, the old man put a pistol in the former scholar's hand.

Perhaps the young scholar had been away from the village too long or perhaps the study of philosophy and later sociology had worked too great a change in his understanding of his role in the family. He did not ponder the cause of his response. He could not murder a man, even the man who raped his niece. With the pistol in his hand, the gentle scholar, a former student of the Mexican historians Daniel Cosío Villegas and Miguel León-Portilla, was faced with the question of how to be generous without killing a man.

He leaves the end of the story with a kind of literary ambiguity. "It was taken care of," he said. And to the pointed question of whether he killed the rapist, he answered only, "It was taken care of." And yet again the same question, and he finally said, "No, I did not. It was taken care of in another way."

We are left to infer what we will, but the point he makes with his own life cannot be doubted: In the Mexican world, murder may be the greatest act of generosity, for the murderer in this instance must sacrifice himself as a moral person and perhaps incur his own death by starting a cycle of vengeance. His story confirms the theory and implies one of the basic questions about the development of the Mexican character: If it is true that between familiars Mexicans are one of the most generous of peoples, why should it be so?

Spaniards, who gave Mexico its most widely spoken language and much of its culture, are known for many things: courage, passion, jealousy, physical grace, a belligerent manner of speech, artistic talent, but not generosity. It is not that the Spaniards suffer the slurs that the French, the Jews, or the Scots must endure; the Spanish attitude toward time and money is simply not a distinguishing aspect of character. Only in Mexico do Spaniards become as generous as Mexicans. On the other hand, indigenous peoples in Mexico, who live in their own communities or nations, manifest their generosity in a variety of patterns. The Nahuas of Milpa Alta in the Federal District, which includes Mexico City, have the formal manners one finds in the old Aztec documents.[2] The Nahuas of Veracruz are unceremonious, but equally generous. Nahuas from the state of Guerrero are more aggressive.

Perhaps the sweetest people in Mexico are the Mixtecos from the state of Oaxaca, the least friendly the Jñatio (the unpronounceable correct name for the people known as Mazahuas) of the state of Mexico or the Huicholes, the great artists and ritual peyote eaters who live at the northern edge of Mesoamerica at the beginning of the dry lands of the mountainous north. The Yaquis of Sonora have a reputation for toughness. The Maya of southern Mexico may best exemplify the complexity of indigenous generosity. For centuries there was a curious myth among those who had only glancing knowledge of the Maya: These beautiful people, with their exotic eyes and scimitar noses, were perfectly peaceful, paragons of the Apollonian way of life. It was a myth much like the misunderstanding of the Hopi of Arizona.

In reality, the Maya have a history of ferocity, which they demonstrated briefly to Mexico and the rest of the world when they attacked San Cristóbal, Chiapas, in the Zapatista uprising of 1994. The early-twentieth-century Mexican educator and historian Justo Sierra would not have been surprised. In *The Political Evolution of the Mexican People*, published at the beginning of the twentieth century, he described the Maya as "savage tribes" and "implacable assassins."[3] "Rebels against white rule, a people insistent upon autonomy," would have been more accurate. And "savage" is not applicable to any of the Maya I know. Among friends and family the Maya display great generosity, worldly, when they have anything to give, and always of the spirit.

The generosity of very poor people, however, can be difficult to recognize. Some years ago, on the day after the celebration of the Day of the Dead, I spent a long day among Maya friends in a small village near the ruins of Kalkini without anyone's offering me so much as a tortilla to eat. I knew the people well, and with the exception of what I perceived as a curious lack of hospitality on that day, they were as open and friendly as ever. Later I found out that during the celebration of the Day of the Dead, when corn and

[2]See León-Portilla and Shorris, *In the Language of Kings*. The Huehuehtlahtolli (Wisdom Discourses or Words of the Elders) and the Bancroft Dialogues, so named because they were found in the Bancroft Library at the University of California, show the ancient courtesies of the Mexica.

[3]Justo Sierra and his father, a novelist, were Yucatecans and well known for their racist views.

chickens were roasted in the underground pit called a *pib* and the patriarchs of large families provided feasts for all their relatives and friends, the Maya had eaten everything in the village. The next day, when I arrived, there was nothing left, not for them or their guest; we were hungry together.

On another afternoon, in Morelos, Professor Herlinda Suárez of the National Autonomous University of Mexico (UNAM), her son, Javier, and I sat on the small piece of leveled rock outside a one-room house perched on a stone outcropping near the bottom of a cliff and talked with the family who lived there. Although Dr. Suárez knew everyone in the family, they did not invite us to come in out of the July sun because their babies slept in the darkness, in hammocks attached to the walls, and the sound of voices would have awakened them. The family stood in front of the house, while the sun cooked them and their visitors. Swarms of flies went in and out of the single room of the small house where the babies slept or gathered on the sweated skin of those who sat or stood in the sun. Although the flies crawled over our skin, they did not bite, sparing us, as if in gratitude for the offering of our salty liquor.

The people who lived in the one room of the house had nothing, no money, no food, only a few beads, which a group of Nahuas had paid them to string in simple patterns. They earned thirty centavos for each necklace, which the Nahuas sold to tourists for three American dollars apiece. As we talked, some of the people who lived in the house went inside and searched silently in the dark for something to give us, some gift of welcome, some act of generosity. They could not give us necklaces because the string, the beads, and the clasps belonged to the Nahuas who employed them. We could see into the house, where they searched for something, anything, but there were only the hammocks in which they slept and, hung from pegs on the walls, one change of clothes for each of them, if that. There was no running water, no light. They bought drinking water, washed in the polluted river at the foot of the cliff, and cooked outdoors. When it rained, stones and garbage from the house of the *curandera* (shaman) who lived high above them, near the road, rolled down the cliffside and crashed onto the cardboard roof of their house.

We had come to ask after the youngest daughter, who had not been seen for the last week. Was she ill? Troubled? Why did she stay inside the house, in shadow? She heard us asking after her, but she did not step out of the darkness, not for a long time. Finally, she came close to the opening, and we saw her in the reflected glare. Shadow cut across her face, complicating the bruises, the blackened eye. It was the work of her father, who came home drunk every night. One night he had beaten them all, mostly the young woman. She spoke rapidly and retired again to the darkness inside the room. We spoke then with her grandmother, who came out of the darkness to say that they had lost their land, their little rancho in Michoacán, and migrated to the city. They were exploited by the Nahuas, the old woman said; they worked too hard and were paid too little for stringing the beads.

She complained for a long time, about her husband, the heat, the Nahuas, but mostly about the cruel curandera, the witch who lived above them, and how the stones, sometimes great boulders, came rolling down the cliffside, gathering speed, and crashed through the laminated cardboard roof. She said they could hear them coming, rolling through the rain, rumbling, like thunder. The old woman, her daughters and granddaughters all complained of ailments and aches, of longings and the lack of everything, even water. And they looked out on the tiny flat place where their guests sat beside the slops barrel, among the flies, suffering in the sun. After a while a young woman came out of the darkness. She carried some pieces of cloth, gray squares that once were towels, and hung them over strands of wire she used for clotheslines. As she spread the pieces of cloth across the wires, she made a roof over the heads of her visitors. Having no worldly goods to offer, she gave them the gift of shade.

This generosity of the Mexican people has deep roots in the pre-Columbian world. The idea of sharing food appears often in the preserved literature of the time, as in Sahagún's Florentine Codex, in which one of the Aztec proverbs reads: "With someone's help I became a vulture," and according to Sahagún, "This is said when I have nothing to eat and through the offices of a friend I eat a little of his food. Should someone ask me if I have eaten, I reply: *With someone's help I was vulturing.*"[4] In addition to sharing whatever they had with family and neighbors, pre-Hispanic peoples built social relations around giving gifts, a trait that went all through Mesoamerica and north into what is now the United States.

The style of the Aztec nobles at the time of the invasion was vastly different from that of the tough, sinewy Chichimecas who had arrived in the

---

[4]Thelma D. Sullivan and T. J. Knab, *A Scattering of Jades* (New York: Simon & Schuster, 1994).

Valley of Mexico in 1325. The nobles wore cloaks of gorgeous featherwork, ate sumptuous food, lived in huge palaces, demanded entertainments, and in the case of Motecuhzoma collected strange species of birds and animals in an extensive zoo. He and other nobles decorated themselves with jewels, commissioned works of art and architecture, and often passed their days in the reading and composing of works we might now term poetry and philosophy. Generosity of mind and spirit was the sign of gentility among the nobles; it was the privilege of a people that had conquered much of the world around them.

For the Aztec upper classes life before the Spanish invasion was glorious, extravagant, and generous. Like Rome at the beginning of the modern era or Manhattan two thousand years later, there were poor and homeless people in the streets of Tenochtitlán; the operative phrase in the proverb recorded by Sahagún is "with someone's help." Generosity flourished among the rich and between rich and poor. The exchange of gifts, the giving of gifts, distinguished between civilized and uncivilized people. Mexico, like Rome in its glory and the United States now, was a generous and rapacious nation. Its character has changed since then. The gap between rich and poor is the largest in Latin America. The social security system leaves out most of the people who require help. Private charity, except through the Catholic Church, is all but unknown. More than half the population must "go vulturing," but "someone's help" is lacking.

8.

The Envious Origins
of Generosity

A literacy campaign conducted by Sandinista (leftist rebels in Nicaragua) youths taught nearly half a million people to read and write, reducing the illiteracy rate from 50.2 per cent—among the highest in Latin America—to 12 percent, second only to Cuba.

—PENNY LERNOUX, *Cry of the People*[1]

Transportation between San Andrés Larrainzar and the autonomous Zapatista village of Oventic is either a 1960s vintage Volkswagen bus or standing room in the back of a pickup truck. Of the two, the pickup truck is preferable because it is always less crowded. The standees in the bed of the pickup truck ride like straphangers on a New York subway car, holding on to a steel frame welded onto the truck bed. The passengers in the bus sleep, resting on each other, snoring and oblivious. Their desperate sleep comes of the changing character of the mountains of Chiapas. Until recently the people had a perfectly diurnal life. When the sun rose, they awakened. When the sun set, they went to sleep. They slept longer in winter than in summer, and they hardly slept at all when it was time to plant or harvest, but they slept. The sun regulated their lives.

When television came to the mountains, it usurped the ancient rhythm. The programs that interested the people, the adult programs, were broadcast in the late evening, and the people watched. In the morning, when the sun rose, the people rose with it. They slept only six hours, and on some nights only five or four hours, then spent the day in the fields. Whenever

---

[1]From the preface to the 1981 edition subtitled *The Struggle for Human Rights in Latin America—The Catholic Church in Conflict with U.S. Policy*. Lernoux devoted most of her work to issues connected with the Catholic Church. She was highly critical of its right wing and devoted to the ideas of Pope John XXIII. Literacy rates since then have climbed in Latin America, especially in Mexico, where the national average for people fifteen years or older in 2000 was 91 percent, according to UNICEF.

they stopped working, day or night, unless they watched television, they slept. They rode to Larrainzar or as far as San Cristóbal de las Casas like a wagonload of snoring corpses.

Life in the mountain villages is hard, physically more demanding since the advent of sleep deprivation, and more difficult to suffer because television promises that life can be easier, sweet, but only for the fair-skinned, fair-haired people who dominate the screens. Surely it was not television that brought about the Zapatista rebellion in 1994, but television proved that poverty was only relative. It exacerbated the itch of oppression.

In response to that itch, a group of rebels organized in the jungles and mountains of Chiapas. Their spokesman and, for all practical purposes, their leader was a man who identified himself as Subcomandante Marcos.[2] He wore a mask, smoked a pipe, and was literate to a fault. The rebels, who called themselves Zapatistas after the leader of the forces in Morelos during the Revolution of 1910, attacked San Cristóbal de las Casas, the main mountain city in Chiapas, in 1994. The attack was timed to coincide with the start of the North American Free Trade Agreement. The rebels held the town briefly, then retreated into the jungles and mountains of Mexico's poorest

---

[2]The Ejército Zapatista de Liberación Nacional (EZLN) was formed in the jungles of Chiapas in the 1980s (real dates and names among revolutionary movements are generally kept secret), perhaps earlier. Subcomandante Marcos (his real name may be Rafael Sebastián Guillén Vicente) appears at first to have been concerned only with the "liberation" of indigenous people throughout Mexico, beginning with Chiapas. Using the Internet, as well as other media, Marcos captured the attention of much of the world. His politics were leftist at a time when the left had few other heroes, and he was witty, charming, very non-Indian in his references and worldview, and he was out to change the world via the Internet. He did not advocate armed revolution so much as cultural revolution. The written word, albeit only in the positives and negatives of the electronic world, had not been so affecting or effective among the young (who had access to computers) for many years.

Marcos became a world figure. His life was in jeopardy: The Mexican Army and probably paid assassins hunted him in the jungle, he lived with the danger of malaria, snakebite, and the miserable jungle fly (*moscachiclero*) that deposited a viral infection with its bite, usually on noses or ears (it is not unusual to see a chicle gatherer with part of his nose or an ear mostly eaten away), and yet he wrote brilliantly. To be another Che Guevara (the hero of the Cuban Revolution, who was killed in the jungles of Bolivia while trying to start a revolution there), he needed only one thing: martyrdom. Presidents Salinas and Zedillo would have been only too glad to grant him that. Vicente Fox, as we shall see, had a better idea.

state measured by average wage and richest measured by natural resources. Shortly after the raid the rebels set up their own autonomous villages. One of them, high in the mountains, Sakam Ch'en (White Cave), was no more than a communal farm, but nearby another autonomous village, Oventic (Mountain Ridge), has grown into a community of fifteen hundred people.

Like many of the roads that climb to the top of the high central plain of Chiapas, the road to Oventic offers views of breathtaking beauty: Sudden, deep valleys turn dreamlike with mist as darkness comes; tall blue-green trees rise out of the mist; an icy cold follows the setting of the sun. Corn is planted along the steep sides of the road. In the woods there are flowers, butterflies, silence. And across the valleys, across other mountains, lost in the night mist, in daylight forests impossible to read in the blinding sun and shadow of afternoon, there are caves and other secret places washed in cool waters. It is a kind of paradise, beauty at the altitude of breathlessness, an ideal place for guerrilla war.

The Zapatistas built Oventic on the widest part of the ridge near the crest of the high mesa. It is not a good place for a town. There is no water nearby. The ridge falls off sharply into a deep valley. It is an aerie more than a town. One of the leaders of the town explained, "If the army comes here with tanks, we will see them coming, and by the time they arrive, we will have disappeared into the valley and up the other side into the mountains. They would never find us."

And if they came in airplanes, helicopters?

"How would they find us among the trees, in the canyons, in the caves?"

They were guerrilla fighters in Oventic, they carried light automatic weapons, and they feared only betrayal, the killing of them one by one. A family dead here, a tiny village of twenty, forty people wiped out there. The killings went on steadily in the towns and villages around Larrainzar. No one claimed responsibility for the killings. But sometimes it was not necessary, for everyone knew. The killers were often paramilitary units allied with the Partido Revolucionario Institucional (PRI), which had controlled Chiapas and the rest of Mexico for seven decades and was not about to turn over power to a few rebels in the jungle. Or the Mexican Army. Or feuding religious groups. Most often it was the paramilitary organization known as Peace and Justice, the group said to be connected to the PRI, but not always. The only constant was the killings. A journalist, Herman Bellinghausen, reported the worst of them, but a death here, a death there, in the mountains or the jungle, were not always news. In Oventic, the people were careful. There was a wooden gate and then a few yards of wooden fence and, at the end of the wooden fence, a wire fence. An autonomous community required a fence to separate it from the other Mexico and its government. An autonomous community also required money, and some of the little money that came to Oventic arrived through sales of handicrafts. The loving, the romantic, and the radical came to the two little shops to leave their money with the followers of Subcomandante Marcos, in whom they saw justice in their own time, a daring and witty postmodern guerrilla leader.

To enter the autonomous Zapatista community of Oventic, a visitor had to pass the checkpoint at the border marked by the wooden gate. For those who were not known in the community, nothing less than a valid passport would do. Horacio Gómez, a scholar just completing his dissertation on education in Chiapas, had agreed to accompany me to Oventic. He and I climbed down from the pickup truck, paid our two pesos each, and walked across the road to Oventic. The gate was unguarded. Twenty-five yards inside the village, several people worked in the noonday sun, painting an old truck. A woman dressed in blue jeans and an ironed shirt put aside her paintbrush, climbed down from the bed of the truck, and walked slowly up the dirt road to the gate.

She was armed with nothing more than a scowl. When she arrived at the gate, she said, "Your passport."

I did as she asked, and she opened the gate. Once we were inside, she told us to wait there, not to go any farther, not to enter the building closest to the gate or the one across the road. I asked to see the person in charge. She said she was in charge, the keeper of the gate, and then she went off with my passport, down the dirt road, past the truck, and into a shaded area, a series of stalls, where she sat down to study the passport.

There was no shade, no breeze, and it was hot. After a long time the young woman came back up the road. Still scowling, she put the passport in my hand. We glared at each other. The idea of the glorious innocence of the Zapatistas had started to fade among some of those who knew them well. They still approved of the idea of Zapatismo, but less and less of the manner in which it was carried out. The Zapatistas had begun to ostracize people who disagreed with them, including a young member of the family of one of Mexico's grand intellectual unions—the marriage of Emma, the daughter of the revered liberal historian Daniel Cosío Villegas, and the anthropologist Jan de Vos. The young woman had spent two years in the jungle with the guerrillas before they sent her away. De Vos had responded by calling Subcomandante Marcos "the white god of the jungle." The allusion to Conrad was unmistakable.

Until 2001 Marcos had been viewed by many people around the world as a figure incapable of error, a holy man of the left-liberal world, which was contrary to the kind of fierce critical appraisals that had distinguished that world. Marcos had been the darling of many of the clear-minded of the world, including Carlos Monsiváis, the stylish Mexican essayist, who had approved of both the politics and style of Subcomandante Marcos. Near the end of 2002, however, Monsiváis took Marcos to task for his style and for exhibiting the most dangerous characteristic of those who live a long time in the role of *leader*. According to Monsiváis, Marcos had used his position to utter crude personal epithets about a judge in a Basque separatist case, calling the judge "a clown" and worse.[3] Where were the wit and sense of place and dignity in this new Marcos? If De Vos and Monsiváis had detected a worm in the EZLN (Zapatista National Liberation Army), a dangerous tendency they did not want to take control of the rebellion, perhaps there was also a sign in Oventic.

"There is no one here today," the border guard said. "Everyone is in the fields."

"Everyone?"

"This is my job," she said, nodding toward the gate.

We stood for a very long time in the sun, speaking of health and education, but not of war. There was no war. The Mexican Army had large encampments in Chiapas, but public pressure in Mexico and the rest of the world limited the scope of their operations to taverns and whorehouses.

Why had the young woman joined the Zapatistas?

She fumbled for a reason. She had heard about it, she said.

What was their purpose?

The scowl faded. A blankness came across her face. As if to beg for time, she chose to smile. Her teeth were backed with gold. It made her middle-aged, beginning the long slide of deterioration. The conversation turned to war. "We know the mountains," she said. "The army does not."

"And Peace and Justice?"

[3] *La Jornada*, November 27, 2002.

She changed the subject. There was a doctor in the village, she said, a foreigner, a volunteer. But they needed medical supplies, they needed money. We talked about politics, about schools. She looked blank again, not dreamy, not dead, but masked. We went inside the little building next to the gate to get out of the sun. It was a shop and a meeting place, selling sandwiches, soft drinks, and curios. There were long tables and benches, like picnic tables. Clearly tours, batches of Zapatistas and supporters from Mexico and many other countries, came to Oventic. The Revolution was a tourist attraction.

Inside, in the shade, with a soft drink taken from the refrigerated case in the little shop, the woman took off her mask. We sat at one of the picnic tables. A reference book of perhaps two thousand pages rested on the table in front of her. The border guard said her name was Alicia and that she was twenty-seven years old. She was married but had no children; her husband worked in the fields. They had not been married long, she said, and they did not intend to have children soon.

"Is there a school for children here?"

She nodded.

"And do all of them attend?"

"No."

"Why not?"

"Some go and some do not. The leaders choose who can go."

"Have you been to school here?"

She shook her head. Neither she nor her husband had been to the school.

"Is it that you were not chosen?"

"No," she said.

I told her about a school for the Maya in the state of Yucatán that taught Maya literature and philosophy. Her face changed, softened, as if childhood had come over her, bringing its excitement of expectations. I said, "All that is required to attend such a school is the ability to read."

The expectation faded and was replaced by a childlike sadness, lost dog, saint's day neglected. I looked to Horacio and saw what he knew about the Zapatistas and had left for me to find out. The border guard of Oventic could not read. She had studied my passport as part of a charade. It had been all form, a dance without music, rote. "Don't all Zapatistas know how to read?" I asked.

"No," she said.

"But there must be a program to teach everyone to read. To have democracy without literacy is almost impossible. Is there a program down in the jungle?"

"No."

"To learn to read is easy," I said. "Here, look at this word on the cover of the book." With a finger, I pointed to the letters and made the sounds. She followed. She made the sounds. Then we put groups of sounds together. "D-ee-k, deek. See, oh . . ." When we had finished the word, all the sounds, it was she who triumphed over the mystery of the letters, who said, *"Diccionario."*

"Will you learn to read? Is there someone here who can teach you to read?"

"Yes, yes," she said. "Yes."

"And will you write a letter to me when you learn how? Here is a card with my address. And here are ten pesos to buy a stamp to put on the letter."

Horacio did not wait for the puzzlement to settle over her face. He told her how letters must be sent in something called an envelope, which he described, and then he explained as briefly as he could why one had to put a stamp on the envelope. She nodded to his explanations, a rhythm of understanding. And she promised to learn to read. She said I should expect the letter. Later, when we left Oventic, we parted with smiles and promises and hugs. There had been a time when foreign sympathizers had tried to build schools and teach in Oventic. Alejandro Carrillo Castro, then head of the National Immigration Institute, had said they required an FM3 visa to visit Oventic, to be human rights activists or to build schools. It was a matter not of morals but of sovereignty. The activists had placed the Mexican government in a difficult position. Like most Americans, they assumed they could do whatever they liked in Mexico. The Mexican government, jealous of its sovereignty, disagreed. A gringo could not do as he or she pleased in Mexico; there were limits.

One evening, years earlier, on the roof of a hotel overlooking the Zócalo in Mexico City, I had spoken with a woman from Boston who had been in Chiapas "to defend human rights" and was being deported for failing to get an FM3 visa.[4] The American Embassy had provided her with what she called

---

[4]The visa is required of foreigners who do various kinds of social and political work and investigation in Mexico. The visa is not automatic, like a tourist visa, and generally takes some time to complete, as it would in the United States or any sovereign nation. Mexico has not, so far as I know, had a policy of denying access to legitimate human rights organizations.

a safe house where she could wait for her plane home to Boston. For an entire day she had talked with "a very kind officer" of the embassy who wanted to know everything about Chiapas and her group and the Zapatistas. When I suggested that she had been with the CIA, she seemed surprised. The man had been so nice! And the Mexicans had been "so fascist" about an American citizen doing "human rights work" on a tourist visa.

On the way back to San Cristóbal I asked Horacio if he thought the gentle border guard would send a letter. The Volkswagen bus was crowded. We spoke over the roar of the motor and the sounds of the other passengers, victims of sleeplessness who lay on each other and on us, snoring and mumbling. "I am filled with hope," he said.

It has been a long time now, years. Perhaps the letter will arrive soon.[5]

As in all things in Mexico, the autonomous village at Oventic is neither indigenous nor Spanish, neither ancient nor modern, but a result of protests, revolts, victories, and defeats that occurred hundreds of years earlier in places the gatekeeper of Oventic had never visited and could not imagine. Her life and that of Mexico, down to the very state in which she was born and still lived, had been determined by events of the sixteenth to nineteenth century in Spain, during its struggles against Protestantism and the Enlightenment. Democracy, religion, oppression, internecine wars, the character of the Mexican could be traced back to a revolt of townspeople in ancient Spain or the envy one group of whites felt for the other in colonial New Spain.

In large part because of the wealth it extracted from its colonies Spain rose to military and economic glory and collapsed. The nation that was to impose its name and language on Latin America spent itself in wars, waste, and a formidable battle against all things modern but maintained the style and even increased the extravagances of the court during the entire period. During the seventeenth-century nadir of the Spanish Empire, while many people went without food, and the *picaros* roamed the streets, stealing, living by their wits, or starving, the women of the court wore hoop skirts and

---

[5]A few months later a conversation between members of an indigenous educational and cultural project, the Pan-American Indian Humanities Center (PAIHC), at the University of Science and Arts of Oklahoma, and the Zapatistas was opened. A member of the Centro de Investigaciones y Estudios Superiores en Antropologia Social (CIESAS) acted as go-between. CIESAS, like the PAIHC, is an educational organization unconnected to any political group. The Zapatista leaders considered the offer to teach reading, writing, and Maya culture to their members and rejected it.

jewels, the men vied to see who could display the finest long capes, and no *hidalgo* (from *hijo de algo*, a gentleman, inheritor of substance) would consider participating in an activity that might be called work.

The distaste for work led the hidalgos to look down on literacy, because of its use by scribes, accountants, lawyers, and the like. In Cervantes's *Don Quixote*, the fact that the hero was a reader of books implied harsh criticism by the nobility, who preferred to live like the gentle gatekeeper of Oventic.

Despite these failings, the sixteenth-century army and navy of Spain seemed invincible, even laying siege to Rome. Until 1588. In that year the Spanish king sent his armada to teach the English a lesson about power. Instead, Drake destroyed the armada, and as luck would have it, storms at sea and disease aboard ship completed Drake's work on the voyage home. Only half the ships and a third of the sailors and soldiers survived.

Carlos Fuentes wrote that 1588 was the third important date in the history of Spain's absolutist monarchy. It marked the beginning of a national collapse, the end of the sixteenth-century glory of Spain. Two earlier dates Fuentes pointed out marked the arrogance and error of empire. In 1492, Spain made the fateful errors that would determine its future over many centuries. Fuentes wrote, "Expelling the Sephardic Jews was the worst wound that the Spanish monarchy inflicted upon itself. It compounded the wound by passing intolerant laws in favor of religious dogmatism and against so-called impurity of blood."

In the same year the Catholic kings defeated the Moors at Granada, which was but prelude to their expulsion in 1502. Within the space of a few months Spain had stripped itself of most of its intellectual capability in matters of state, finance, commerce, philosophy, literature and got rid of the best of its artists and craftsmen. When Christopher Columbus made landfall in the Indies on October 12, 1492, the government that had sent him to gain its fortune through the spice trade was already doomed.

War, discovery, and expulsion in 1492 affected the administration of New Spain for more than three hundred years, but a single book by Antonio de Nebrija, a grammar of the Castilian language, was also to have enormous influence. When Queen Isabella asked what use there was in having such a grammar, Nebrija is said to have replied that the Castilian language was the ideal weapon of empire.[6]

---

[6]See John Crow, Hugh Thomas, etc.

The events of 1521, the third date, were to establish New Spain and set the pattern for its government. In that year the urban center of the Mexican world, Tenochtitlán, fell to the Spaniards and their Tlaxcalan allies, but of almost equal importance, the *comuneros* (townspeople) of Castile rose up in revolt. Fifteen Castilian towns gathered to petition the king for democratic reforms, perhaps a constitutional monarchy. But there was to be no Spanish Magna Carta. The nobles joined their king in putting down the rebellion. The comunero leaders were executed, and as they died, the idea of democracy in Spain and its colonies died with them. There were no more democratic uprisings during the three centuries of Spanish Empire. The effective democratic movements of 1776 in the American colonies and 1789 in France did not spread to New Spain. The separate political paths of Mexico and its neighbor were set 250 years before Jefferson's Declaration. The deaths of the comuneros had ended the democratic rebellion, and the tightening of the connection between the king and his nobles had begun an absolutist and centralist tradition in Spain, old and new.

There is a fourth set of dates that should be added to Fuentes's list. Spanish absolutism and orthodoxy were ratified in three meetings in Trent held between 1545 and 1563. The difference between the character and development of the United States and that of Mexico was determined by those three meetings. The Pope's most influential men at the meetings of the Council of Trent were Spaniards, proponents of the most severe forms of dogmatic control over religious thought, forms that furthered the control of the State and the State Church over the individual. Not for the Spaniards was Luther's idea of the "liberty of the Christian man." The Bible, tradition, and the world were to be as interpreted by the Pope.

The Spain of the Middle Ages had been preserved. A wall had been built against humanism and rebellion, the God of Thomas Aquinas had defeated the man of the coming Enlightenment, and democracy, the Athenian contribution to the politics of the modern world, had been shut out of the Spanish Empire. Religion and state had been interconnected, one dependent upon the other, in Spain as it had been in the pre-Columbian world of Mexico. In the world of the Protestant Reformation, life evolved in directions utterly opposite those of the world petrified at Trent and Madrid:

The Bible could, if only theoretically, be interpreted by individuals, suggesting a new organization of families and institutions.

Although individual rebellion was frowned upon, the legislature of the state could rebel against the king.

Earning money was good, but so too was thrift. The enjoyment of wealth was an offense to God; thus the accumulation of wealth and, according to Max Weber, the birth of the capitalist spirit.

Time was money, and time belonged to God, so to waste time was to waste God's own possession, a sin.

And some people were rich while others were poor, the rich being the elect of God.

To all these ideas, the Catholic Counter-Reformation issued opposing rules. Protestants and Catholics were almost equally authoritarian, but the Protestant Reformation, with its roots in religious rebellion, permitted political rebellion, the development of a capitalist middle class, and eventually, out of the mix of rebellion, bourgeois individualism, and Enlightenment rationality, the desire for democratic institutions. None of these notions came to Spain, old or new, but neither did Puritanism and its dour view of life have any purchase in the Spanish Empire. The Spanish nobility on both sides of the Atlantic were devoted to extravagance in all things. The Protestants made a duty of charity, which was more likely to be distributed to strangers than to familiars, while the Counter-Reformation continued the mendicant orders among friars and nuns and suggested generosity among familiars for the men and women of the court.

The first wave of Spaniards to arrive in New Spain were adventurers. Then came the religious, Franciscans and Dominicans and Augustinians, and later Jesuits, representing two different approaches to saving the natives. The powerful Franciscans wanted to Hispanicize the Mexican religion, and the Jesuits wanted to Mexicanize Christianity. Both views led to syncretism; they merely started from different places. The most syncretic of miracles took place in 1531 at Tepeyacac, outside the capital, where a Christianized Aztec, Juan Diego, said the Virgin of Guadalupe appeared to him. It was a small event at the time, virtually unremarked, but it was to become one of the most important events in Mexican history.[7]

[7]There has been great debate over the miracle, with some scholars arguing that Juan Diego did not exist and with Rome making a saint of Juan Diego. When asked if the mir-

During the first ten years of occupation the whites were almost all born in Spain (*peninsulares*), but at the end of the first half century there were as many criollos (born in New Spain). And by the beginning of the nineteenth century, New Spain had a white population of more than a million, about 95 percent of whom were criollos.

The growth of the white population took place along with the great decline in the number of indigenous people in central Mexico. Between the arrival of the Spaniards and the end of the eighteenth century, there were no fewer than seven outbreaks of plague: smallpox, measles, typhus, and influenza.[8] The peninsulares were immune to most of the plagues, almost all of them surviving, often pockmarked, toothless and frail, but alive. The criollos, however, had little more immunity to the plagues than the original people of New Spain. Many of them died, but the decline of the indigenous population of central Mexico caused by war, plague, overwork, and famine, along with what appears to have been a low birthrate, bordered on extinction. According to the estimates of Woodrow Borah, a professor at the University of California at Berkeley, the indigenous population of the area fell from twenty-five million at the time of the invasion to only one million in the middle of the seventeenth century.

Borah's estimates are probably too high at one end and too low at the other, but even if there were only ten million people in central Mexico at the time of the invasion and as many as two million in 1650, it would have been an average loss of more than sixty thousand people a year plus a number equal to all those born during that year. With Borah's extreme figures, the average number lost each year was over two hundred thousand.

While the birthrate of the original inhabitants declined, the birthrate of the peninsulares soared. In a momentary burst of Latin American romanticism or perhaps a tip of the hat to the Department of Tourism, Octavio Paz

---

acle had actually occurred, Miguel León-Portilla, who is the leading authority on the period, answered with a philosophical shrug, "What difference does it make?" and went on to speak of the powerful role of the Virgin of Guadalupe in Mexico.

[8]African slaves brought the concept of inoculation against smallpox to the British colonies in the Western Hemisphere. By the early years of the eighteenth century, inoculation was relatively common in the colonies, especially in the North. As in Africa, material taken from a pustule of an infected person was inserted into a small cut made in the skin of the person to be inoculated. The reaction to inoculation was often quite terrible, but seldom fatal. Why this method was not brought to New Spain from Africa is not clear.

attributed the rise in the Spanish birthrate to the climate and hot colors of Mexico and then was moved to devote a paragraph or so to the wonders of sexual congress, licit or, better yet, illicit.[9]

In the viceroy's court, the noble peninsulares had an enviably wonderful time, the operative word here being "envy." Court life included flirtations, parties, lavish clothing for both men and women, gambling, jousting, the excitement of the hunt, duels, grand processions, and innumerable excuses for celebration; the most taxing work for the courtiers was the requirement to invent new extravagances. Mexico City gained a reputation as the Athens of the New World, for it was rich in theater, dance, music, and art, but the viceroy's court was not the agora and there was no Socrates and surely no Pericles among the courtiers.

Even so, the court was the central feature of every aspect of the state in both Spain and Mexico City, the capital of its great colony. Nothing in the empire equaled the opulence and power of the court, either in the Old World or the New. The early-seventeenth-century playwright Juan Ruiz de Alarcón demolished the moral character of Spanish court life in *The Suspect Truth*, in part by describing the envious behavior of the courtiers and their extravagances, as in these details of a picnic:

> . . . a table was ensconced,
> square and clean and neat,
> Italian in device,
> Spanish in opulence.
>   . . . .
> My lady came in her coach,
> making envious the stars. . . .
>   . . . .
> The meantime have been served
> full thirty banquet dishes,
> first course and desserts,
> all but as many, beside.
> Fruits and wines in bowls
> and goblets fashioned from
> the crystal winter gives
> and artifice preserves. . . ."[10]

[9] *Sor Juana, or, The Traps of Faith* (Cambridge, Mass.: Harvard University Press, 1988), p. 71.
[10] English translation by Samuel Beckett in a joint project of UNESCO and the Mexican government, *Mexican Poetry* (Bloomington: Indiana University Press, 1958).

Envy had its place in the Spanish court, but the envy of the court of the viceroy in New Spain was far greater and more complex. Status, power, and money belonged to the peninsulares. A criollo who had amassed a fortune, even one who owned ten million acres of land in what is now northern Mexico, was merely new rich, and if he or his family tried to mix in the society of peninsulares, it was considered social climbing. Nonetheless, good criollo parents tried to marry their children off to peninsulares. As marriage material, a poor peninsular was worth more than the wealthiest criollo.

The crown maintained these social differences by appointing only peninsulares to positions of power. To assure the loyalty of the viceroys, the crown did not permit them to bring their families to New Spain. The army too was Spanish, and troops were not permanently assigned to the provinces; they were to be soldiers, not settlers. The Spanish kings were well aware of the prospects for trouble if they allowed the criollos to take control. The good life, the best positions, the route to wealth, the pleasures of the court belonged to the peninsulares.

The criollos were left somewhere in between the peninsulares and the people they called indios, and they desperately wanted to find a way to be more like their Spanish brethren. The criollos had land and money, but neither political power, nor influence, nor social status. Although they would soon outnumber the peninsulares, the criollos were outsiders in the land of their birth. The generosity of extravagance was their only means of competition. They built houses in the Spanish style, threw great parties, paid for public celebrations, sent their children abroad to study, and pursued an openhanded, friendly style that contrasted more and more with the narrow pleasures of the court. If the members of the viceroy's court practiced sexual intrigue and hid their actions by means ranging from coitus interruptus to abortion, the criollos sent their young swains and fair virgins to walk in the formal *paseo* of the late afternoon, when the sun had cooled and lamplight beautified the daughters of the criollo planters, ranchers, miners, and merchants.

Courtly generosity and criollo generosity had different structures: The court handed down its generosity, except in the form of extravagance, which is a display, not an exchange for service. The criollos practiced generosity among equals while learning the talent for what was to become the baroque style. They had come into the world too late to learn the extravagance of the Aztecs, but not too late to learn the indigenous custom of the gift as greeting, offering, or human connection. Everywhere the criollos went in the indigenous world they were greeted with gifts and all too often repaid the generosity of the givers with murder, torture, rape, or enslavement.

No matter how the whites tried to separate themselves from the people they administered—and over the years the effort at separation became greater, not less, as the use of native overseers and the *cacique* system of installing indigenous nobles as administrators became common—the languages and cultures entered each other, overlapped, meshed, married, shared, replaced, strengthened, weakened, each time different, every bargain unique, every form reformed in a Hegelian dance that has continued for centuries, reified at every stage in the enduring stone of cathedrals and palaces and the more enduring genetic heritage of mestizaje.

The generosity of indigenous people came more deeply into the Mexican character as the populations mixed: Spanish, African, and indigenous. The Calvinist character, which swept modern Europe and the United States, never entered Mexico. The nation did not simply fail in its quest for modernity, as many writers have said, but changed in another direction. Instead of a profound social rebellion, New Spain moved toward something even more modern, a culture built upon the accommodation of cultures, each one enriched by the best of the other. But the accommodation has yet to be completed. Mexico remains in process, suffering still from the paralyzing character of dualism, neither modern nor married, neither democratic nor autocratic, still lacking the glorious imperfection of an overwhelming middle class, still far from the seamless genetic melding implied by the word "mestizaje."

Ricardo García Sainz, a brilliant business leader and government administrator, who left the government of the PRI to join the left-of-center PRD and serve as a federal deputy,[11] could still say in the twenty-first century that he was a criollo but added that he would be pleased to have had Indian ancestors. After five hundred years the word "criollo" had taken on a discomforting aspect of another kind for García Sainz. It represented the great flaw in the generosity of Mexicans, the inability to extend the open hand beyond the boundaries of family, friend, race, and class. Between its first and most recent implicatory lives, the word had undergone many iterations. At one time during the colonial period the criollos tried to establish some pride in the word, but José María Morelos, who led the second phase of the war

[11]Akin to a member of the House of Representatives in the United States.

(1810–1821) for Independence from Spain, decided to get rid of all the various designations for race and national origin, to create a seamless nation out of an encompassing generosity. He ordered the revolutionaries to use a new word, *americano*. Morelos had a powerful sense of equality, but if democracy or the questioning character of people and nations produced by the Reformation entered his mind, he did not, or perhaps could not, say so, for he was a Catholic priest.

9.

The Chosen People

... just as the Spanish people had inherited from the Jews the belief that they were God's new chosen people, the Mexicans also believed they were a chosen people, having received the seal of divine predilection in the mineral wealth of their soil. —JUSTO SIERRA

The Padilla family is well known for its pessimism, so it was all but ordained that one of them would become an economist. It fell to Jorge, the son of a Padilla and an Olvera, to enter the profession as an undergraduate at the Instituto Tecnológico y de Estudios Superiores de Monterrey and then go on to Tulane University in New Orleans to earn a master's degree in the discipline best suited to the family disposition. In keeping with the pessimistic tradition of the family, he went from working as an economist for the giant Grupo Industrial Alfa to politics.

It is not necessarily pessimistic to enter politics in Mexico. Over the years many people have found it a sure and steady path to wealth; they refer to it among themselves as the system. Being a pessimist, however, Jorge Padilla Olvera chose to join the opposition in a country that had, in 1979, when he entered politics, enjoyed the rule of the same party for forty-nine years.

Shortly after becoming a member of the Partido Acción Nacional (PAN), Padilla left Grupo Industrial Alfa, the second-largest company in Monterrey, and became an entrepreneur, setting up a business to produce metal studs for Sheetrock. He was a sturdy young man, thirty-three years old, fair of skin, strong like a Basque, with brown, straight hair combed so that it fell across the right side of his forehead, accentuating the empathetic sweetness in the shape of his eyes. Young Padilla Olvera smiled easily, spoke frankly, and made many friends.

He also made enemies, because he belonged to the PAN, which is a party of conservatives with roots in the middle class, the radical right, the Cristero rebels of the 1930s, and Opus Dei, the extreme right wing of the Catholic

Church. Young Padilla understood the PAN as the opposition party, and as it turned out, that was what he found most appealing. "I like to be in the opposition," he said many years later, "because it is easier to destroy than to build."

In 1988 he ran for public office and was elected to the City Council of Monterrey, which is the Mexican city of industry and ambition. There are several explanations for the character of Monterrey, perhaps for Padilla himself. He subscribes to the Jewish theory, which leads inevitably to the basic tenets of his party, the PAN, and indirectly but still certainly to the course of Padilla's career. "Monterrey has been successful," he believes, "because of the Jewish influence. It was founded by Jews, Sefarditas, converted to Catholicism. The roots of the state of Nuevo León, the old families, have a lot of Jewish customs: hard work, savings, responsibility, that sort of thing.

"They say that makes us egotistical, that we treat the rest of the people, the ones who come from out of state, from farther south, as nothing but labor. But the leaders of the city, the original people, are hardworking. I understand that. They think, If you don't work, you don't eat. They think it's a virtue if one has ambition. That's what makes Monterrey different from all the rest of Mexico, the Sephardic people. I think the genes are still in us. That's why the people are different, a bit insensitive, not connected to social problems. Everyone goes his own way, every man for himself.

"But Monterrey and these people are known for their charity and social programs. Before there was social security, they founded a social safety net. Before INFONAVIT [public housing] in Monterrey, there was worker housing. It's a contradiction. The idea is that they were hard workers, so they deserved medical services, hospitalization, better housing. It's not socialism; it's the proper reward for hard work. That's why the only industrial groups that belong to Mexicans are here. The rest belong to the transnationals and the government."

Padilla's theory is based in part on the careers of the Carvajal family, Luis de Carvajal y de la Cueva, the founder of the town that became Monterrey, and his nephew Luis de Carvajal (the younger). They were New Christians, Jews who had converted to Catholicism rather than go into exile in 1492, and as such were always theologically suspect, easy targets for calumny and the Inquisition. For his troubles, the elder Carvajal was sent to prison after a disagreement with the viceroy; the prisoner was declared a crypto-Jew and exiled. The younger Carvajal did not fare so well. The Inquisition accused him of "obeying the Law of Moses," tried him, and found him innocent. A second trial in 1596 sent him to the auto-da-fé, along with more than sixty of his family and friends. On the way to be burned at the stake, the younger Carvajal convinced the inquisitors that he had indeed now truly converted to Catholicism. The Inquisition, ever forgiving, spared him from the fire and garroted him instead.

The testing of New Christians throughout the Spanish Empire was as much a political as a religious work. Had the Inquisition turned to priests in the capital shortly after the conquest, it would have had great effect, for the historian Diego Durán; the father of modern ethnography, Bernardino de Sahagún; and the great humanist of the time, Bartolomé de las Casas, all were said to be New Christians, men with histories that surely affected what they wrote and did. Had they lived in Monterrey, they might have suffered the fate of the Carvajals.

Given the history of its founding family, Monterrey became—and remains—the most sanctimonious as well as the most productive of cities in Mexico and by far the most conservative in matters of religion, politics, and society, closely followed by Guadalajara. Perhaps Padilla's pessimism grows out of his understanding of the fate of pioneers in Monterrey. He was, after all, a member of the PAN when it was less than fashionable, even dangerous, but not so dangerous as a whiff of heresy, a lesson he should have learned from the city's founders.

His first lesson in the politics of opposition came soon after he became active in the PAN. One evening in 1985, while putting up posters in the northern fringes of Monterrey, in what he called "real tough neighborhoods," he and a group of young volunteers noticed three buses coming their way. Padilla and one other adult stayed behind while the volunteers, all teenagers, fled. The busloads discharged a group of thugs, some of them drunk, some high on drugs, according to Padilla. "This is PRI territory," the thugs told him. "You can't put up your shit, your garbage here." They began tearing down the posters. There was an argument, and then, said Padilla, "They started beating us. They left us flat on the ground. Those were the good old days. They were rough times. These thugs were sent by the CTM [Mexican Workers' Confederation] union."

Padilla had suffered the PRI version of the auto-da-fé and survived. He continued to work for the opposition. Years later he had a telephone call from Governor Alfonso Ramírez Domínguez, "the one who ordered my beating. He invited me to have dinner with him in his house here in Monterrey, but I did not accept. I invited him to a meal in my house. As if nothing had happened, he arrived on time, alone. The first thing I did was to complain about that beating, and he told me, 'Oh, Jorge, those were other times.' He didn't say it was a lie, just another time and things have changed. He told me, 'Jorge, what drives the PRI is power. There are some who have fallen from power who are willing to give all of their money to recover a fraction of the power they once had. It's not always the money; it's the power.' And he told me the power of the PRI is from drugs. I don't know if it's true, but it is what he told me.'"

Padilla has many theories about the PRI and the very rich of Mexico. He retails the same stories told in Mexican political and journalistic circles about some of the richest men in the country belonging to a cabal of "homosexuals, dangerous men with twisted minds." Vicente Fox Quesada, when he was a candidate for the presidency, called his PRI opponent, Francisco Labastida Ochoa, a homosexual, then retracted the accusation. Labastida was one of the names on Padilla's list.

Meanwhile, Padilla was getting some practical lessons in economics. In 1988 the year he was elected to the City Council, his business began to sour: "It went down slowly, inexorably." He blames the failure on neoliberalism, the economic policy instituted by President Miguel de la Madrid during the 1980s. It is a curious attack, because the bête noire of the left is also neoliberalism. For Padilla it was not a question of social justice but a matter of pushing Mexico too soon onto the playing field with the international giants. "Mexico did not have the infrastructure. Our production costs were too high. We could not play with the big boys. It was like me getting into the ring with Michael Spinks."[1]

Three years later Jorge Padilla Olvera became a state representative in Nuevo León. He was charming, a man in his mid-forties, an economist, businessman, Catholic, husband, father, and he had shown himself more than once to be all but fearless, a quality admired everywhere in the world, but nowhere more than in Mexico. His political future looked excellent. And since there is a law against reelection in Mexico, he had to keep moving: The day after his election he had to begin thinking about his next post. For members of the PRI, the party made such appointments, after which

[1] The boxer, Spinks, had been briefly heavyweight champion.

election was all but assured. But the PAN was not in power, which meant the candidate had to be willing to risk the next step—up, down, sideways, or out. At the end of his term in the statehouse, Padilla had visions of a role in the national scene. Acción Nacional (the familiar term for the PAN) nominated him to run for federal deputy, and he won easily.

His political problems began when he was appointed to the Finance Committee. He took his job seriously, so seriously that he opposed accepting the U.S. multibillion-dollar loan to bail out Mexico in 1994, despite orders from the head of the PAN to vote for the idea. Padilla said the United States wanted too much control over Mexico in return for the money. It was, in his view, a further erosion of Mexican autonomy. He published an article in the magazine *Proceso* attacking the bailout, argued bitterly with then President Ernesto Zedillo in a private session at Los Pinos, the Mexican president's residence, and finally paid his own expenses to go to Washington, D.C., to lobby the U.S. Congress.

He endured insults, complaints, threats on his life, but he would not abandon his opposition to the bailout. Padilla became a public figure in a time of hilarity and rage in the Cámara de Diputados.[2] The PRD (Partido de la Revolución Democrática) and virtually everyone else in Mexico thought Cuauhtémoc Cárdenas had won the presidency in 1988 and had the office stolen from him by the PRI. The standing joke was, "The rich vote for the PAN, the poor vote for the PRD, and the computers vote for the PRI." Before the next election the PRI presidential candidate, Luis Donaldo Colosio, who made the mistake of criticizing the sitting president, was assassinated.

There were arguments on the floor of the legislature, Marcos Rascón of the PRD wore a pig mask during the president's state of the nation speech. The peso had been devalued, the country was in crisis, the middle class was being destroyed, interest rates had made mortgages impossible to pay, people were losing their homes and businesses, the standard of living had suddenly declined by at least 33 percent, and Padilla Olvera fought against accepting a loan from the United States.

His career seemed to be over, but it was not so. At the end of his term he returned to Monterrey and was elected a state senator. In 1997, the PAN held the majority in the state, an important part of the party's power base in the north. In the coming presidential election of 2000 they actually had a chance

---

[2]Chamber of Deputies, the lower house of the Mexican bicameral national legislature.

to win. And Padilla was unhappy. Perhaps bored is a better description of his feelings. He was a man of the opposition, as he said, a destroyer, not a builder.

Three young priests and an aging cardinal gave him a chance to join the opposition again. The young priests, led by the Jesuit Francisco Gómez Hinojosa, known as Padre Paco, produced a paper, *First Diocesan Synod: The Unity of the Church and the World,* and the liberal Cardinal Adolfo Suárez Rivera signed it. How the paper, a gentle and mildly liberal hypothesis about the role of the Catholic Church in the third millennium, became a scandal is not entirely clear. The right wing of the Church had long wanted to be rid of the cardinal, but that was not the entire motivation: Suárez was old, already waiting for his replacement to be named by the Vatican. Others could be got rid of by using the same paper. The governor of the state said, "Because of priests like these many people have left the Church." And the head of the Congress, who was also a member of Opus Dei, said the young priests and the cardinal were trying to turn the northern industrial state of Nuevo León into another Chiapas, where Bishop Samuel Ruiz had pronounced his solidarity with the Indians.

Padilla saw the move by the governor and the leaders of the PAN as a way to wound the reputation of the cardinal, who had been open about his distance from the conservative wing of the Church and from the PAN. And Padilla said so in private and in public. He defended Padre Paco and the cardinal, and the PAN and the right wing of the Church fought back.

"PAN is basically middle-class," he said by way of explanation. "Close to the Church. But what Church? The Monterrey church has always been very conservative, very traditional, and this cardinal [Suárez] has been in trouble since he arrived because he was interested in social problems."

Padilla's first auto-da-fé was administered by the PRI in the slums of Monterrey. Like Luis de Carvajal, the younger, he was to have a second test of his faith. Members of his own party, the PAN, circulated a petition demanding Padilla's expulsion. Felipe Calderón Hinojosa, then national leader of the PAN, accepted it, apparently with pleasure. Instead of asking for reinstatement, Padilla said that he had been told many times to follow the rules of the party but that he valued his liberty far too much to simply obey and remain silent. He said he believed in the constitution and fought corruption, and it made no difference to him whether the corruption was found among PRIistas or PANistas. It may have been the use of the word "liberty" that finally sealed the order of expulsion. The word has never pleased those in power in New Spain or Mexico. At the end of the eighteenth century a representative of the Spanish crown associated the use of the word by criollos with independence, rebellion against authority. Given the cyclical sense of history in Mexico, Padilla had chosen the wrong word.

In the Monterrey daily *El Norte,* of August 26, 1998, the expulsion of Jorge Padilla Olvera, who had been one of the most loyal of PANistas during its most difficult years, was compared with the "atrocious history of the Inquisition." Padilla completed his term in office as an independent, and then he was finished.

His career had been perfectly Mexican: It grew out of the sixteenth century and predicted the twenty-first. Religion and rebellion vied for power, as they always have in Mexico. Although Padilla lived in the criollo world of successful businessmen in Monterrey, he found Monterrey, in many respects, still very much like New Spain. As he said, the people from the south, by which he meant Indians, were there to be employed as labor, not to be owners, managers, the husbands of women who meet at five in the afternoon in the better restaurants or elegant houses to enjoy their *merienda* of sweet cakes and coffee.

As these fair-skinned matrons of Monterrey go about their lives, served at home and in shops and restaurants by dark-skinned people, they must frequently pass the statue of Fray Servando Teresa de Mier, who was largely responsible first for the intellectual and then the political independence of New Spain. Fray Servando, an imaginative fellow, claimed descent on his mother's side from Motecuhzoma II (Xocoyotzin). In his father's family there had been a member of the Inquisition and the former governor of Nuevo León. Servando was of noble birth on one side, if not both.

In Justo Sierra's political history of Mexico, written in the early twentieth century, Servando's sermon delivered in 1794 merits little mention. For Sierra, as for many historians, Independence grew out of a combination of the weakness of the Spanish government and the increasing tension between criollos and peninsulares.[3] The full importance of Fray Servando and his

---

[3]By then the criollos had adopted the term "gachupines" for the Spanish-born or the (Iberian) peninsulares. Since there is no Spanish dictionary equivalent to the *Oxford English Dictionary,* which operates on historical principles, a definitive source for the origin and history of the word does not exist.

role in defining the Mexican consciousness did not appear until 1974, in Jacques Lafaye's brilliant essay *Quetzalcóatl and Guadalupe*. Lafaye concentrated on the sermon delivered by Servando in which the Dominican gave his interpretation of the Apparition of the Virgin of Guadalupe and the true identity of Quetzalcoatl.

It should not be inferred from Fray Servando's role in fomenting Independence that he was a radical democrat, influenced by the revolutions of 1776 and 1789. On the contrary, Servando was frightened and appalled by the French Revolution. Perhaps that was why he did not trust the rule of the people. He never made his reasons clear, but he preferred a more authoritarian form of government. With little interest in a broad democracy, even by troublemakers like Servando, and no driving social impetus, the Independence of New Spain could only have come about in unique fashion.

It was not a popular uprising—that is, it did not include the urban poor, and there was no significant working class in New Spain. A few of the urban poor did eventually follow the leaders of the Independence, but their impetus was not social or economic and should not be compared with the feelings of participants in the U.S. and French revolutions, although the nonwhites, who made up the bulk of the poor, suffered every human indignity, from malnutrition to rape, and did eventually exhibit a terrible rage. It was a theological rebellion: The criollo church, eventually joined by the mestizo church, separated itself and its parishioners from Spain. Or perhaps the Spanish kings inadvertently decreed the separation, for during the entire colonial period, three hundred years of rule and the extraction of enormous wealth by the Spanish crown, no king of Spain had ever crossed the Atlantic Ocean to visit his provinces in the New World. Nonetheless, the crown made all the important decisions about life and death, God and money, in New Spain.

Had the crown been closer to its most profitable colony, the king might have noticed the signs of religious and intellectual unrest that appeared long before Fray Servando's sermon; the Jesuits had attempted to Mexicanize Christianity. Even more dangerous was Fray Juan de Torquemada's notion of the Indians' having undertaken a journey like that of the Israelites, making them the "chosen people." Torquemada's idea posed several problems for his fellow Spaniards, who considered themselves the "chosen people," evidenced by their *discovery* and conquest of the New World as part of their God-given mission to universalize Christianity. But then the criollos decided they were the "chosen people" on the basis of the finding of a seemingly inexhaustible supply of precious metals in the sixteenth century. If God had not chosen them, they argued, why would He have provided them with such wealth?

Only one people could be "chosen." But which one? Could the arguments be combined, as in the idea that the indigenous were chosen to receive Christianity? And if so, by whom? And did that make them the "chosen people"? It seems a foolish argument now, but not then. In the Thomist atmosphere of New Spain, such debates could go on indefinitely. Charles III, the Bourbon king, had embraced the Enlightenment, but thinking in the rest of Spain and its provinces was hardly "enlightened" at the time of Fray Servando's sermon. Aristotle's cosmogony, for example, was still considered all but holy.

During the colonial period, New Spain was the most unscientific part of the Western world. When the brilliant poet Sor Juana, who lived in the balm of worldly comforts and the excitement of ideas inside the convent of the order of San Jerónimo, took up the views of the Renaissance and the scientific revolution, the leaders of the Catholic Church turned on her. Humanism, which inspired much of the poetry of Sor Juana, and science, which provided content for some of her work, were dangerous in an absolutist world. Her faith was challenged by Church authorities; she struggled, wrote a historic defense of the role of women in the world, and then capitulated, signing her letter of surrender with her own blood.

The Jesuits, who had come to New Spain late but made their presence felt immediately, becoming the major educational force as well the owners of vast amounts of property, also threatened the crown and therefore the Spanish Church. The Jesuit threat came in the Mexicanization of Christianity, but even more in their direct connection to Rome, bypassing the Spanish Church. On June 25, 1767, the Society of Jesus was expelled from New Spain and the other provinces by order of the king. It took three years for the Jesuits to gather themselves and their belongings, to sell all but the little they could carry, make their way to the coast, and set sail in their unseaworthy ships.

Meanwhile, thousands of Indians and mestizos who had studied in Jesuit schools and worked on Jesuit-owned farms took up arms to stop the expulsion. The crown crushed the rebellion quickly and brutally. They hanged the leaders, beheaded the corpses, and put the severed heads on public view. The ferocity of the Spaniards and their utter lack of mercy revived old memories. It was the first time Spanish troops had been used in New Spain in more than two hundred years.

Had it been some overzealous military officer who sent the troops into action, the act might have had less effect, but it was the representative of the king who gave the order. José de Gálvez had been sent to New Spain by Charles III to reform a corrupt Church and even more corrupt secular administration. For the most part he succeeded. His work, known as the Bourbon reforms, ended much of the licentiousness of the clergy, stopped some of the corrupt practices that bled the poor and the Indians, and Gálvez convinced the king to end restrictions on trade and agriculture that had given rise to monopolistic practices in the province. But Gálvez, who had a brutal hand in defense of God's morality and the king's territory, could deal with only a few of the philosophical and economic problems of New Spain. And the Bourbon reforms could not bring rain.

In the *bajío*, the great breadbasket on the plateau between Celaya and León, crops failed. The year from the middle of 1785 to the middle of 1786 was a nightmare of hunger. There had been famine in the preceding century, riots in the streets of Mexico City, but during the last half of the eighteenth century Mexico suffered almost constant drought. Food prices rose; the value of the currency declined; the standard of living fell. With food in short supply, life for nonwhites in New Spain turned from grim to desperate. What had been a painful gap between rich and poor, whites and nonwhites, became intolerable.

Even so, the political, economic, and social problems of the province did not create an Independence movement. The spark came from Fray Servando and the theologians. There had been earlier thoughts of the conversion of the Indians by the Apostle St. Thomas, claiming he was really Quetzalcoatl, but they had come to nothing. The seventeenth-century writer Carlos de Sigüenza y Góngora, who revered the pre-Columbian Indians and had nothing but contempt for their descendants, had argued the unlikely tale almost a hundred years before Servando's sermon. At the end of the eighteenth century the St. Thomas as Quetzalcoatl theory had gone out of fashion. It made no historical sense. Then Fray Servando came up with an equally bizarre notion. Sigüenza y Góngora was in the right church but the wrong pew. It was not St. Thomas the Apostle but St. Thomas of Mylapore who had converted the Mexicans in the sixth century. The cloak on which the miraculous image of the Virgin appeared had been brought to Mexico by the sixth-century saint; it had not appeared miraculously.

For the people of New Spain the argument could not have been better.

The tall, white, bearded man known to the Indians as Quetzalcoatl had converted the people of New Spain long before the arrival of the Spaniards. As unreasonable as the argument sounds to the twenty-first-century mind, it had a powerful effect on the people of New Spain. It fulfilled their dreams of religious, social and—did they dare say it?—national equality. So they thought it was logical: Proofs of the evangelization of Spain by St. James the Apostle were very weak, but there was no doubt of the existence of the cloak of the Virgin of Guadalupe, the very cloak that had been brought with him by St. Thomas in the sixth century. A person could see it with his own eyes. What evidence was there that the headless skeleton found at Compostela in Spain really belonged to St. James?

If Servando's theory was correct, the Mexicans had not been evangelized by the Spaniards; they owed nothing of their understanding of God to the invaders. The Spaniards had come a thousand years too late to lay claim to the discovery and evangelization of the Mexicans. The argument made by Spain since the end of the fifteenth century that it had been chosen to carry out the will of God by evangelizing the natives of the New World no longer held true. St. Thomas, the real Quetzalcoatl, had done his work before the invasion. Truly, God had loved the people and the people had loved God long before the Spanish invasion. The justification for Spanish control had never existed. There was no longer any reason for the people of the place known as New Spain to be loyal to the Spanish Church or the crown.

Servando had conveyed the right to govern themselves to those born in New Spain, the criollos (he did not suggest that the land be returned to the indigenous people whom St. Thomas had evangelized). It made no difference that the historic Quetzalcoatl (of Tula) was born hundreds of years after the supposed visit of St. Thomas. New Spain in the nineteenth century did not concern itself with such matters. Servando had solved the questions around the evangelization and the Virgin of Guadalupe's cloak; he had pulled everything together with one marvelous explanation just as the Virgin herself was to pull together all the divergent parts of Mexico. The Inquisition recognized the power of his idea almost immediately and saw to it that he was sent into exile. For the next fifteen years Fray Servando wandered through southern Europe and Spain, now in prison, now fleeing for his life, hounded by Church and government. He finally made his way to England in 1811, the year after the *grito*, the "cry of Independence," was uttered in a church on September 16 in the town of Dolores. To support the Independence movement, he took to writing journalism or propaganda, the distinction then, as now, being somewhat unclear. When he returned to Mexico, after it had finally achieved Independence in 1821, Servando participated in the drafting of a constitution for the independent country, but had relatively little influence, since he could not make up his mind between centralism and federalism, although he thought the country would need a strong central government when it first became independent.

In the years between his sermon on St. Thomas/Quetzalcoatl and the grito at Dolores, Spain had endured one crisis after another. Not a little of the trouble grew out of the court affairs of Maria Luisa of Parma and her lover Manuel de Godoy. Maria Luisa had the thin mouth, tiny eyes, and cook's arms of a French washerwoman, if Goya's portrait of her is not too flattering. Justo Sierra said she "combined a remarkable intelligence with a surprising aptitude for sensuality (for it is always fierce in ugly women)." At fourteen she had married her cousin, who was to become Charles IV, a man whose lack of ability rivaled that of Charles II, the prognathous, depressed, idiotic end of the Hapsburg line.

Godoy, a handsome young military officer, was a favorite in both the council chamber and the bedroom. With his advice and help, Spain entered into a series of desperate alliances. Eventually the crown had to choose between England and France: war with one, alliance with the other. Spain chose France. The combined Spanish and French fleets, yet another seemingly unconquerable armada, engaged Nelson in the great sea battle at Trafalgar and were utterly destroyed. Spain was never again to be a power at sea; its ships and ports were prey to pirates, privateers, and the British Navy.

Charles IV abdicated in favor of Ferdinand VII, who reigned for six weeks before Napoleon took Spain. At the end of a long series of conspiracies and failures, Bonaparte put the country into the hands of Godoy, the queen's lover. But the Spaniards hated Godoy. Napoleon responded by restoring Charles IV, who then abdicated again, this time to Napoleon's brother Joseph. It was another mistake. Rule by a Frenchman was more than the Spaniards would tolerate. An uprising began in Madrid and turned almost immediately into a bloody national revolution. Spain had no king, no court, no government; it was run by committees.

The criollos, still loyal to the crown, saw no reason for loyalty to committees. Groups of criollos met in secret, disguising the meetings as literary salons. News of the movement against the Spanish committees was carried by the young military officer Ignacio Allende to the priest of the town of Dolores, Miguel Hidalgo y Castillo. The priest served under Manuel Abad y Queipo, bishop of Michoacán, a Spaniard loyal to the crown but filled with ideas about social justice. The conflicting ideas held by the bishop exemplified the problem of the whites in New Spain: king or country, St. James or St. Thomas, the Virgin of Remedios or the Virgin of Guadalupe, the Church of Spain or the Church of New Spain?

The king had resolved some questions for the clergy and many criollos in 1804, when he took control of the Catholic Church's funds in New Spain. Since the Church had been a major source of money used in the purchase of land, many of the people who depended on it could no longer make their mortgage payments. The ensuing financial crisis cost hundreds of landowners their property, among them Miguel Hidalgo and his brother. And then the crown ordered an end to the *fueros,* special privileges for priests and military officers. From the point of view of the court in Madrid, the power of the Church of New Spain had been vitiated. The troublesome theorist Servando was in exile, as were all the Jesuits; Bartolomé de las Casas was long dead, and the priests remaining in New Spain had been disciplined and disciplined again. Even as the crown of Spain was toppling, its richest province was safe. Or so it must have seemed in Madrid at the end of the first decade of the nineteenth century.

10.

The Fate of Independents

Smoke and mist: fame and glory.
—FLORENTINE CODEX, BOOK 6

It is difficult to imagine the sinister forces that lie in the past of the grandmother who must sit at the edge of her seat in order to reach the pedals of her small Japanese car. In the afternoon she drives to the private school attended by her grandson and goes inside to fetch him. He is newly adolescent and not much interested in the history of his grandmother, although he knows something about her career, for his mother does similar work, and she is far from home, among the refugees who still wander from country to country in Latin America. The boy is innocent, smooth-faced, lithe. His grandmother is a pretty woman in her late sixties. Her lower lip is thrust out, a promise of pugnacity when the occasion demands. Her nose is small and round, a memory of Catalonia. There are grandmotherly crinkles around her eyes, marks of compassion, but the eyes themselves are ever so slightly dulled, like the eyes of a boxer after many fights, as if to tell the pain of a committed life. To argue with her is a form of madness, for her mind is made of many razors, and they are honed to the finest edge.

Mercedes Olivera Bustamante is an anthropologist, and to be an anthropologist in Mexico is to study history in the mirror, for that is what "mestizaje" means, not only the mixing of races but of epochs too. It makes the Mexican a puzzle that functions like multidimensional chess, played on several planes at once. That is why so many of the best minds of Mexico are drawn to the study of themselves, to look in the mirror, because the questions are both within reach and difficult to solve. The trouble with becoming an anthropologist in Mexico is that like entering politics, it leads inevitably to a loss of innocence, as in the world of Mercedes Olivera.

As a young woman of twenty, she aspired to be a primary school teacher. Eight years later, in 1961, the mother of three children, she received a master's degree in ethnology from the School of Anthropology and History at the UNAM. By 1980 she was the director of the National School of Anthropology and History. Few academic careers had ascended more smoothly, especially for a woman who was by then divorced and raising three children. Her doctoral dissertation had been original, but not outside the scholarly realm. It dealt with the function of class in the means of production in central Mexico from the twelfth to the eighteenth century. Clearly the world she saw reflected in the mirror of Mexican anthropology had begun to affect her thinking.

A year later, in 1976, she published her first article dealing with feminist questions. Her life had become her subject; anthropology had moved from theory to reality, which is the end of innocence. She had emulated the journey from the theorist Marx to the revolutionary Lenin, from the philosopher of the greatest happiness Hutcheson to the revolutionary Jefferson. Mercedes Olivera was in the world. She saw not only the oppression of women but the long history of class in Mexico and then the upheavals of Nicaragua, El Salvador, and Guatemala. There was a revolution in Nicaragua; poets were taking up arms by teaching the poor. Right-wing death squads, using U.S. helicopters, were killing peasants in El Salvador, and in Guatemala, government troops were throwing Indians into volcanoes. Olivera, who was born in the moment of Mexico's embrace of the left during the administration of President Lázaro Cárdenas, was thirty-four years old when Mexican troops of the Olympia Brigade massacred students in Mexico City shortly before the opening of the 1968 Olympic Games. She knew something firsthand about repressive governments. In the following years the Sandinista movement grew stronger in Nicaragua, and both democratic nationalists and leftist idealists became more engaged and more hopeful in Latin America.

The possibility of the overthrow of dictatorships and oligarchies appeared to be realistic for the first time in many decades. The Sandinistas, named for a man who had resisted U.S. forces in Nicaragua, irritated and frightened the United States, inspiring the Reagan administration to interfere in the affairs of Nicaragua. But the United States was far away. Mexico was close. The government thought it had reason to be fearful. There were guerrillas operating in the mountains and the jungles, and the Communist League of September 23 and another radical left organization, the National Liberation Front (FLN), headquartered in the state of Nuevo León, had been wounded by imprisonment of some of their members but were still strong. It was the beginning of what has come to be known in Mexico as the dirty war. Only in 2002 did the Fox administration agree to open the government archives that held the details of the dirty war, which began in earnest after the massacre at Tlatelolco in 1968: arrests, disappearances, torture, exile, and murder. Anyone who expressed solidarity with armed rebels in Central America was suspect.

In 1970 the government captured two young Central American men allied with radical movements and, in the style inherited from the Spanish inquisitors, tortured them until they revealed a name, a highly placed person, influential in the academy, a Marxist and feminist, Professor Mercedes Olivera, director of the National School of Anthropology. Olivera was charged with betraying Mexico. She fled the country.

For the next ten years she lived in Cuba, Spain, Guatemala, Nicaragua, El Salvador, and Italy. "The groups in solidarity with the left in Central America helped me to survive," she said. But it was not an easy decade. The wounds come into her face as she speaks of it. And then she smiles, rueful and triumphant. This is her house, and for the moment it is safe. She sits in the small kitchen, remembering and drinking tea. It is a professor's house, and the professor is a feminist, and her feminism is in her conversation and her face, and she has declared it on the walls of her house, if one can judge by the paintings. It is an ethnologist's house, according to the artifacts. The living room is on fire with color, paintings and weavings, indigenous and feminist.

"It is still a repressive government," she said, referring to the Mexican government's use of Article 33 of the constitution to expel foreigners immediately, without a trial. She spoke of a group of Spaniards who had been accused of killing a Zapatista family when the truth was that the Spaniards had come to aid the Zapatistas. "The right is still very powerful in Mexico, the PAN in alliance with the right wing of the PRI."

She survived for two years in Cuba; then she went to Europe and back to Central America, mainly to Nicaragua, where she taught sex education to indigenous women. In 1988 she was hired by the Office of the United Nations High Commissioner for Refugees to work in Central America. When the UN moved her to Mexico to work in its southernmost states, "the government dropped the charges against me. I was protected by the UN high commissioner for refugees; what could they do?"

A leftist in Chiapas, she naturally became involved with the Zapatistas, but she did not always agree with the way they carried out their ideas. And their treatment of women angered her. She had supported the Sandinistas wholeheartedly, working with the revolutionaries when she left Mexico. Armed revolution had seemed correct to her in Central America. But times had changed. "Armed conflict is no longer the only path," she said. "There must be a better way." When the great wave of refugees went home from Mexico or moved north to the United States, and the size of the problem declined from two hundred thousand to thirty thousand, she went back to teaching. She worked with women's groups, founding the Center for Research and Action for Women (CIAM). And she worked with the Zapatistas. "I admire Marcos," she said, but nothing more. She remains of the left, a staunch feminist, a demanding and encouraging professor, a Zapatista heart and soul. But not a fool, not one to compromise her principles, never to compromise. She is pugnaciously independent, an adviser, a director, but not a member. She is not to be herded, not to be told what she must do. She has her own ideas; she is never anyone's woman but her own. In argument, the pretty grandmother changes, becomes sharp-toothed, ferocious.

In repose, she speaks of the "disequilibrium" between the independence of the mother and the father in Mexico. Despite her feminism or perhaps because of it, she locates the overweeningness of Mexican men in the actions of women: "The mothers teach the sons; honor comes from the woman. This has its Spanish as well as Arabic origin." There is no time to speak of the Aztec code, the Maya world, the Mesoamerican mother. Perhaps tomorrow. There is a restaurant that serves Chiapanecan food. And the Zapatistas? The equality of women in the eyes of the Zapatistas? Can there be democracy without it? The tea is growing cold. And the Zapatistas? Her eyes speak of all the sadness of all the failures of the left, of paradise lost and lost again, and still within the reach of dreams. And the Zapatistas, how they must adore this woman, this lover of equilibrium and independence!

"I cannot go to a Zapatista camp," she said. "They no longer permit me to enter."

The afternoon is dying; she has a class to teach, work to do; there will be no explanations. She smiles; the independence of a woman has its price.

A woman's intellectual independence in Mexico was tested in the seventeenth century by Sor Juana Inés de la Cruz, who recanted. The independence of the country itself was first put to the test in the late summer of 1810. After fifteen years of intellectual, theological, political, and military reverses, the Spanish Empire, which had been rescued from bankruptcy and near collapse by the brilliance of Charles III, was again in disarray. To make matters worse, an Independence movement in New Spain had begun. The young people who led the so-called literary club of Querétaro had established December 8, 1810, as the date to proclaim Independence. The plotters gathered weapons and ammunition and sought out allies across much of the central part of the country outside Mexico City. Two of them were military officers, Ignacio Allende and Juan de Aldama. Among the others were a grocer, a postal clerk, and the local magistrate, the corregidor Miguel Domínguez and his wife, Josefa. Only three months remained until the date set for the uprising when the news leaked.

After the plot was discovered, the corregidor had to launch an investigation. His wife, Doña Josefa, and other members of the local group were arrested, but she managed to get word to the plotters, for which Doña Josefa, known to every Mexican as La Corregidora, heroine of Independence, spent years as a prisoner, sequestered in convents in Mexico City.

The plotters reacted to Doña Josefa's warning by advancing the date. Three days later they pronounced Mexico independent. On September 16, 1810, the priest of the town of Dolores, Miguel Hidalgo y Castillo, raised aloft the image of the Virgin of Guadalupe and gave the grito (cry) of Independence. There is of course no contemporary record of what he said. But history or legend has it that he gave cry to either five or six sentences. And they are so important to every Mexican that it seems only right to reproduce them in Spanish here: "*Viva la religión! Viva Nuestra Santíssima Madre de Guadalupe! Viva Fernando VII! Viva la América! Y muera el mal gobierno!*" "Long live the religion! Long live Our Holy Mother of Guadalupe! Long live Ferdinand VII! Long live America! And death to bad government!"

The sixth sentence often attributed to Hidalgo was "Death to the gachupines!" Together the six parts of the grito suggest the entire history of Mexico up through the election of Vicente Fox Quesada. The priest himself may be the best place to begin the story. He was a criollo, fifty-seven years old, who appeared to be worn out by life. Bald, with only a fringe of white hair grown slightly longer at the collar, he looked out from eyes that seemed to be more in contact with death than life. Perhaps that is how great radicals must be in Mexico; perhaps they must accept sacrifice before they can offer it. So said Hidalgo's eyes, which were too dark, too open, too prominent, not at all in keeping with the sensuous and ironic shape of his mouth. To be a hero in Mexico, one must not merely die; he must expect death, and his lips must belie the expectation in his eyes.

Hidalgo was such a man. He was not an ideologue, and if he followed the rules of the Church of Rome and Spain at all, it was with a sense of irony. He made jokes about the self-mutilation of saints, occasionally raised questions about the notion of a virgin birth, and preferred preaching to saying mass. He was born into the middle class, inherited land, and among other things, he raised silkworms. How his politics evolved and how much they evolved have no more consistency than the features of his face. When the Spanish crown changed the financial structure of New Spain in 1804, Hidalgo nearly went bankrupt. The sudden call for the payment of mortgages did break Hidalgo's brother, who went mad. If the priest still loved Spain after that, it must have been difficult.

As a child and even as a young man he behaved in the most serious manner, scholarly, quiet, a young man training for the priesthood, but at some point he must have reconsidered not only his own life but life itself, for he became a professional gambler, a womanizer, a man often chastised by his superiors and seemingly without caring about their opprobrium or anything else. Complaints about the priest of Dolores came regularly to religious and civic authorities, and the priest went on dancing. He was a talented gambler, but a disorganized farmer. Long before he gave the grito, he seemed to have given himself over to fate or God. In his history of *caudillismo* (bossism), which owes more to Carlyle's worship of heroes than to reality after 1940, Enrique Krauze cites a telling comment about Hidalgo. His bishop and mentor, Manuel Abad y Queipo, recalled Hidalgo's disorderly method of feeding silkworms. He had no plan at all. Instead of picking the mulberry leaves at the point where they were best to feed the worms, he picked them up off the ground as they fell.

Hidalgo read, discussed ideas, but most of his thinking was confined to literature. The seventeenth century interested him more than his own. Abad y Queipo could not entice him into the world of Rousseau, although Hidalgo had often displayed an interest in serving the poor. The historian Justo Sierra was correct in his estimation of Spain's lack of philosophers at home or in its colonies. The intellectual production of the empire had been literary and theological, and in New Spain ethnographical and historical, but there was no Spanish philosopher to lead the minds of the people out of the domination of the fusion of Church and Crown.

The words of the Mexican cry of Independence began with religion. This was not a war against the Catholic Church, but within the Church. This was not a new Protestant Reformation or even a demand for reform within the

Church. Hidalgo sought only the change implied in the next sentence of the grito. The Virgin of Guadalupe, whose cloak Servando had placed in Mexico a thousand years before the Spanish invasion, proved the place of New Spain in God's own history of the world, and it came before Spain and was independent of Spain.

In the face of the Virgin and the time of the evangelization, the world could read the Indian history of the country. Her dark sweetness showed that God loved the indigenous people; Spain merely used them, killed them, debased them, so wounded them that within the space of three centuries they had fallen from glorious Mesoamericans to poor Indians. Neither Sigüenza's *Primavera Indiana* (Indian Spring) nor Francisco Xavier Clavijero's *Historia*, for all that they loved the ancients, were intended to rescue the indigenous people of the moment. That task fell to the Virgin and her followers in the fight for independence. St. Thomas/Quetzalcoatl was a conversion of the mind; the Apparition of the Virgin of Guadalupe was the union of brown body and God's own provenance. Only the Virgin of Guadalupe, the Holy Mother with a Brown Face, could have united Mexico; she was the bond among criollos, mestizos, and natives, body and soul. Jesus had died for the sins of the original people too; they would also be welcomed into heaven.

The wish for a long life and the implied return to power of Ferdinand VII bears out the conflicting ideas in the minds of the people of New Spain. America was the home of the Virgin and her dark-skinned people, and Ferdinand VII represented the usurpers, those who had tried to steal the chosenness of New Spain. Were they simply making a Spanish choice, which Miguel de Unamuno said meant not philosophizing about the tensions of life but accepting them as life itself? The tension between two peoples who saw themselves as the chosen of God could never be resolved, unless one capitulated or the two were independent of each other.

The last part of the grito, "death to bad government," at first appears to be earthbound, but who really governed New Spain? The Church or the Crown? In the era of the Inquisition, there were many who feared government by the Church. Then, as now, the question could be asked, "But which church?" Did priests like Hidalgo, who loved their parishioners and cared equally for the rich and poor, belong to the same church as the Inquisition?

In his own life, Hidalgo symbolized one of the key aspects of his Spanish origin, according to Unamuno's theory: the ability to heed simultaneously conflicting desires, to love God and Mammon, heaven and earth, abstinence and pleasure, Europe and America. What Unamuno saw as the tension of life in the Spaniard, Octavio Paz said was the mask worn by the Mexican. Is the tension between disparate wishes the life force of the Mexican or a mask to hide the inability of the country and its citizens to integrate the parts of their character? The career of Hidalgo offers further clues.

Aldama and Allende, having been warned by La Corregidora's message, headed immediately for Dolores. At 2:00 A.M. on Sunday, the sixteenth, they met in the parlor of Hidalgo's house. They discussed the situation for a few moments before they went into Hidalgo's bedroom to awaken him. While the priest dressed, he listened to their views, and he concluded: "We have no choice but to surprise the Spaniards." From there they went to see the local mayor, demanding that he release the prisoners from the town jail. The Army of Independence had grown to nearly a hundred when Hidalgo called the people to mass. Although they were unaccustomed to attending mass at that early hour, the parishioners came. Hidalgo was a blasphemous priest, a licentious man, but they admired the erudition in his sermons, and they enjoyed the warmth of his love for the poor. On that morning he had a different kind of sermon, a cry for Independence.

Armed with swords and a few pistols, the rebels wanted to move immediately on Guanajuato, but Hidalgo persuaded them to go more cautiously, to gather their forces before attempting to take the city. As the band of criollos made its way along the miserable roads and trails, mestizos and Indians joined them. The character of Hidalgo's army changed. The new recruits carried spears and machetes and hoes and arrows rather than swords and pistols. Some were barefoot. The local priests came too. And it was no longer an army of men, but also of women and even children. The horses they rode were bone thin, nags. No supply train followed them. The army had no name, no uniforms; it lacked even a flag. At Atotonilco, Hidalgo saw a portrait on canvas of the Virgin of Guadalupe, and he wrote the words of the grito across it, attached it to a long pole, and hoisted the banner of Independence. As the Spanish invaders had cried out the name of St. James (Santiago!) at the beginning of the sixteenth century, the rebels now cried out the name of their holy figure, their claim to be the chosen of God. They did not use the words "freedom," "liberty," "equality"; this was neither a political nor a social revolution. It was a war for the love of God; the Holy Mother had entered into battle with James, the saint of the gray horse.

The Army of Independence moved on from victory to victory. In Celaya it gained a semblance of legality when the city fathers pronounced Hidalgo the general in command of the troops and Allende his lieutenant. The army grew to fifty thousand and marched on Guanajuato. The *intendente,* the government official in charge of the area, considered his options. To defend the city was impossible. He had three hundred troops to withstand an onslaught of fifty thousand, but he had something like a fortress that he might be able to defend. He rejected Hidalgo's offer of a safe surrender, determined to make a stand at the Alhóndiga de Granaditas (public granary and exchange). By September 28 more than five hundred people had sought safety inside the Alhóndiga, a great stone building, with heavy wooden doors. Inside, the Spaniards and criollos, with their fortunes of silver, gold, and cash, whatever they could carry, even the archives of the city, awaited the attack of Hidalgo's army.

Promptly at noon the assault began. The intendente had deployed a line of riflemen in front of the granary. As the rebels came forward, the troops fired. One line of rebels fell, but there were thousands behind them. The intendente was killed, shot through the head at the very beginning of the battle. Then the rebel army attacked in force. It came like something from another time, medieval, dark even at noon, hordes of people, the poor of the city now part of the Army of Independence, screaming, hurling stones at the building, now the Spanish fortress of Guanajuato. With them, behind them, at their side, the armed troops of the Independence fired into the portals of the granary. The stones poured into the granary; the level of the floor inside rose, as if buoyed by the flood of stones, the endless number of stones carried up from the river. From above the Spanish soldiers fired on the attackers and hurled down canisters of gunpowder that burst like grenades in the crowd below.

The dead and wounded lay untended amid the chaos and the din, the shouting and raining cascades of stones and explosions of gunpowder and all the thousands of voices screaming. From the highest windows of the granary the Spaniards and criollos threw money and jewels to the crowd, thinking to satisfy the lust of the stone throwers and screamers below, hoping against all reality that the indigenous people were as they had imagined them, feckless and greedy, ready to abandon anything for the price of a few cups of pulque or a bottle of aguardiente. But the battle continued.

Through all the battering the stone walls of the granary held. The siege went on until the army outside slowly stacked wood against the gates to the granary, while those inside killed and wounded them from above. When there was a good enough stack of pine, they set fire to it. That was the beginning of the horror of the granary of Guanajuato. At five o'clock the crowd burst through the burned door and into the courtyard. The soldiers inside tried to make a stand on the stairs leading to the upper floors, but the attackers killed all the men they found there, beating them, chopping them apart with machetes. Once inside, the mob of attackers searched every room, every corner of the granary, looting and killing as they went. At five in the afternoon it was over. Only the women and children were spared; among them the boy Lucas Alamán, who was to become a well-known historian and conservative politician. It is his account of the massacre that has become the accepted history.

According to Alamán, the looting and killing went on all night. Hidalgo had put him and his mother under his protection, but he could not protect Alamán from the screaming and the battering down of the door of one house after the next, nor could he have spared him the horror of the first victory of the Army of Independence. The dark-eyed Virgin, surrounded by flowers, had looked down from her place at the head of the mob and witnessed a massacre as violent and as thorough as anything the Spaniards had committed. The Virgin of Guadalupe was no longer an innocent.

Every day the size of the army grew. Allende favored strict military organization, but the priest could not or perhaps did not want to make war that way. His followers loved him, worshiped him, thought of their general as a saint. And Hidalgo, the bookish one, the libertine priest, came under the influence of their rage. As they took city after city, his priestly demeanor failed him; he chose assassins from among his followers and put them to slashing the throats of prisoners in the night.

After he held most of the bajío, Hidalgo had only to march from the rich, high plains south on to Mexico City to complete the Independence. It had by then become a grand city again, not so grand as Tenochtitlán, but big, a city of universities, great buildings, elegance and poverty, where the rich lived sumptuously and perhaps thirty thousand unemployed people roamed the streets. Alexander von Humboldt, who had recently traveled through New Spain, envisioned a great future.

Perhaps some thought of the grandeur of the city went through Hidalgo's mind as his troops prepared to march on Mexico City. They far outnumbered the defenders of the city. The encampments of his army stretched for miles. They picked the earth clean as they moved, men and beasts eating everything, grain and grass, looting every city, every town. Hidalgo no longer controlled an army; he led a mob. If they entered Mexico City, they would destroy it. Hidalgo hesitated. He and his lieutenants had already suffered the opprobrium of the Catholic Church. Hidalgo's own bishop, his mentor in the study of social justice, Abad y Quiepo, had excommunicated him. In response Hidalgo had published a manifesto in which he defended his actions and proclaimed an end to slavery in New Spain as part of his social program.

Hidalgo had promoted himself to generalissimo and had a grandiose uniform made for himself, black and gold and scarlet, with an image of the Virgin of Guadalupe on the breast. At the end of October 1810 he waited on the doorstep of Mexico City. Royal troops under the command of the generals Félix Calleja and Manuel Flon had taken up defensive positions there. They had heavy artillery and well-armed troops. The Army of Independence was low on ammunition.

Hidalgo remained for days on the outskirts of the city, deciding. On the first day of November he gave the order: Retreat to Querétaro. The next morning the army decamped. Disappointed, without the loot they had come for, without the victory that would have changed New Spain forever, no longer awed by the priest in the gorgeous uniform, Hidalgo's followers began to desert. Within a few days half of his army was gone. The banners of the Virgin of Guadalupe and all the tiny representations of her that had adorned and made holy the hats and shirts of the great citizen army of Hidalgo disappeared.

No longer a saint in the eyes of his soldiers, Hidalgo proclaimed the end of taxation, promised a new government, held on, marched on, still welcomed new regiments, while the forces of the crown, terrified and energized by the possibility of a race war, the nightmare of more than five million Indians and mestizos killing the million whites, turned aggressive. The Army of Spain and the Army of Independence met at Calderón Bridge on the Río Lerma outside Guadalajara.

When they took the field, Hidalgo's army had grown again to as many as one hundred thousand, still poorly armed, still undisciplined despite the efforts of Allende and Aldama to shape them into a European-style army. Allende had cannon cast, filled wagons with ammunition, put rifles or ancient muskets in the hands of as many of his troops as possible. For the rest, it was still the machete and the hoe and the protection of the Virgin of Guadalupe. And the bow and arrow. Comanche warriors from the north, fierce, laconic, dressed in buffalo skins, had joined Hidalgo's army. The Comanches fascinated Hidalgo, and Hidalgo fascinated his great mass of troops, still fighting under the banner of the Virgin of Guadalupe, still hearing in the speeches of their fancy-dress green-eyed generalissimo all the words that moved them, the social undercurrents of the War of the Virgin.

On the other side, Calleja also had an army of almost entirely indigenous troops, but his troops were well supplied, disciplined, and they brought artillery. It was January 15, 1811, the dry season, and cool, when the two armies closed, tramping across the long, dry grass of the bajío. Calleja knew he would face an enormous army. Hidalgo had twenty thousand mounted men and eighty thousand foot soldiers. The forces of Independence stretched for miles, but they were not an army. They spoke many languages; they could not speak to one another. They wore knee-length loose clothing made of skins or carried serapes over their shoulders. All wore straw hats; some played drums, flutes, one-stringed instruments. Their horses were tiny; some rode burros. The riders carried poles, like lances. The foot soldiers carried spears or bows and arrows.

In a council of senior officers before the battle, Allende had argued for meeting Calleja's six thousand men, half of them cavalry, with their own disciplined troops, thirty-four hundred men. To the military men, the great mob would be less than useless in the field. And if there was a need to retreat, the mob behind the real army would block the way. Hidalgo had other plans: He wanted everyone in the field, and the priest won out over the soldiers.

At daybreak on the seventeenth the battle began. Calleja's troops fought through a hail of spears and arrows. The rebels sent grenades into the royal infantry and tried to disrupt its cavalry with explosions of shrapnel-filled bombs. From both sides the artillery bombarded the troops across the plain. With shouts and screams and the roar of cannon in their ears, the rebels could still hear the constant drumming and the whistle of flutes, and it drove them forward through the smoke of battle. They stopped and started and were turned from attack to retreat by the explosions of grenades and the brute power of the charging horses. The battle lasted through much of the day, each side fleeing one moment, attacking the next. At midday the grass began to burn. Spent gunpowder and burnt grass lay like a low cloud on the field. Corpses of the War of the Old World, blown apart by the cannon, smashed by pieces of lead, lay alongside the killed of the War of the New World, speared, lanced, or shot with arrows, chopped to death by machete or hoe.

Then a grenade exploded next to a rebel ammunition wagon, and the secondary explosions sent fiery projectiles through the rebel ranks. The men nearby fled the sudden, senseless hell coming from the wagon. And when the other troops saw them, they too ran. Calleja turned his artillery on the center of the rebel troops and attacked both the left and right wings of the rebel formation with infantry and cavalry. The rebels fled.

Calleja lost forty-one killed, while Hidalgo lost hundreds, perhaps thousands. Ten days later the military men among his officers removed Hidalgo from command in all but appearances. Calleja, sensing that the rebellion was coming to an end, rested his troops, then started driving the rebels north. The rebels took one city and moved on; they took the next and moved on; and then they just moved on, heading north. Their last hope for Independence was in Coahuila and Tejas (Texas), where they believed they could recruit more men to their cause. The northerners were tough, Indian fighters and cowboys. They held vast properties, hundreds of thousands of acres, and Spain had never done anything for them.

All night and even in daylight the rebel troops deserted, barefoot men and their families going home, defeated, unable to conceive of victory now that their Virgin seemed to have deserted the cause. As the rebels moved north through the dry country, the royalists tracked them, forcing them here and there, determining their course, like shepherds. At Saltillo, the rebel leaders decided to separate from the remaining irregulars, taking the money and an escort of the best troops as they headed toward the Río Bravo. In what was to become a classic maneuver, a royalist officer pretended to join the rebels, drew them into a trap, and on March 21 the rebellion was over.

The officers and the priest, no longer the generalissimo, only an old and weary man, were captured and taken to Chihuahua City. The end came slowly for Hidalgo, degradation by the ecclesiastical authorities, jail, perhaps torture, then the sentence of death. There would be no bullet to the back of the head. The royalists had other plans. He would face a firing squad, and they would aim for his chest.

In the end the "Father of Independence" recanted. He apologized for what had befallen New Spain because of him, because he could not control his troops, because it had been a kind of madness that had possessed the mob that followed him. He begged the forgiveness of God, for he had not respected the sanctity of religion or property. As he had once defended the poor, he now lamented their actions, the sacking of the towns, the slaughters at Guanajuato and the other towns they had taken. He had himself been the killer of Spaniards, ordering them murdered in the night, but it was the creation of a murderous mob for which he apologized.

When he stood before the firing squad, he refused the blindfold, then put his hand over his heart to give the executioners a target. The first volley wounded him in the arms and legs and in his body too. A bullet passed through the hand he held over his heart, but it did not kill him. He lay on the ground, bleeding and in pain. After a while they put the muzzle of a gun against his chest so they could not miss his heart, and killed him. When he no longer twitched or breathed, they hacked off his head and put it in a metal cage, as they did the heads of the military officers, and sent the heads to the Alhóndiga de Granaditas in Guanajuato, where they hung them on the four corners of the walls. And the heads remained there in the metal cages for ten years, which is how many years passed before an ultraconservative criollo with delusions of grandeur led the worshipers of the Virgin of Guadalupe out of the strangling embrace of the Spanish crown.

11.

The Conception of the Aztec

*The Mexicans or Aztecs, who were the ultimate settlers of the land of
Anáhuac and are the objects of our history, lived until the middle of the
XII century in Aztlán, located a great distance north of New Mexico. . . .*
—CLAVIJERO, ANCIENT HISTORY OF MEXICO, BOOK 2, 17

When the head of the defrocked priest Miguel Hidalgo hung in a cage
on the walls of the granary of Guanajuato, no country was known as
Mexico, and no people had ever called themselves Aztecs. The eschatological Catholics and the millenarian Mesoamericans had found common
ground mainly in the concept of virginity, the life that gave no life, the one
Unamuno viewed as dedicated to death. Nothing and no one had granted
the people of Mesoamerica surcease from this tragic obsession with death
and the death of everything for at least two thousand years. Only at the end
of the twentieth century did a worldly shudder begin to ripple through the
population. Perhaps it was the beginning of democracy, the human revolt
against eschatological thinking and the endurance of suffering in this life,
perhaps it was simply a wish to serve a gentler master while awaiting heaven;
it was not known then, on July 7, 1997, and it is not known now. But something happened on that day. If death did not suffer a defeat, it did lose one
battle, the first of many. Unlike the battle on the Internet waged by Subcomandante Marcos from his headquarters in the jungles of Chiapas, this was
an attempt to wrestle with death on a grand scale.

I spent the day and the long evening among the enemies of resignation
in Mexico City, where the signs of democracy—optimism, fratricide, and a
longing for justice—were already apparent.

On the morning of the day of his election to the Cámara de Diputados,
Gilberto López y Rivas was the busiest candidate in all of Mexico, or so it
seemed, because his campaign began the day crowded into two floors of a
very narrow house. Many stood on the spiral staircase that led from the first
floor, where the rooms were light but narrow, to the one small room on the

second floor, which was dark except for one dim desk lamp above a copying machine. Campaign workers, including many relatives of the candidate and a large number of idealistic young women, filled all the rooms, so that movement was restricted, as in the subway or the vast and dangerous housing project in the election district, the Delegación Iztacalco.

López y Rivas, the tallest man in the room, olive-skinned and balding, his appearance recalling that of a slim Miguel Hidalgo y Castillo, moved easily through the nonexistent spaces between people. He held a cell phone in his left hand and used the right for handshaking, backpatting, and now and then a calming or promising caress. Like Hidalgo, López y Rivas was an intellectual and a supporter of the rights of indigenous people. Later, as we drove through the district, he spoke about the way people lived, how there was sometimes nothing inside an apartment, neither food nor furniture. "Do not go here, do not go there," he said, admonishing me again and again about the danger in the district. Although he did not confide in me about the operation of his campaign, he did say, with pride, that he was an adviser to Subcomandante Marcos and the Zapatistas, who still hoped to make a revolution from their jungle headquarters. Of course, there were many advisers to the Zapatistas. Even I could have been an adviser to the Zapatistas, because Subcomandante Marcos had told several people he studied the military tactics in a novel I had written about Pancho Villa, *Under the Fifth Sun*. López y Rivas, however, was truly an adviser to the Zapatistas, although no one could say for certain how much of his advice the subcomandante followed. Certainly, their literary styles were not similar. The books written by the candidate were in the sedative style of the academic left, while Marcos harangued or made jokes on the Internet, more in the style of the priest José María Morelos, who had led the second effort for Mexican independence.

For many Mexicans who opposed the PRI, which had then been in power for sixty-seven years, this election promised a change. Some of the voters in López y Rivas's district said it would bring about democracy, but when they were asked what was meant by the word, they could only recount the dreadful things that had been done to them by thieves and thugs in the PRI. None had ever experienced democracy, leaving them unsure of how it would be different from the way they lived at the moment. They did favor it, however, and they were glad to say so, although in lowered voices, accompanied by inappropriate smiles.

Very few of them mentioned the name of the PRD candidate for governor of the Federal District (including Mexico City), Cuauhtémoc Cárdenas, even if they had voted for him. Cárdenas, the son of the revolutionary general who had brought many reforms to Mexico during his presidency in the late 1930s, had almost certainly won the presidency in 1988. Unfortunately, voting made little difference at the time. The PRI counted the votes, and it preferred not to lose.

This election was going to be different, said López y Rivas, the candidate from Iztacalco.[1] There were poll watchers, foreign observers; it was the first time the "mayor" of Mexico City would be elected rather than appointed. The president of the United States had met with Cárdenas, which greatly increased his stature, if not his *Mexicanidad*.[2] But Mexicanidad was not his problem, for his name was Cuauhtémoc, and he was the son of the general, which was as Mexican as one could be. Moreover, there were stories about his opponent, Alfredo del Mazo, who had been the governor of the state of Mexico. According to a high official in the PRI-controlled government, del Mazo, who lived a short distance from his office, had been picked up by helicopter at his home and delivered to his office every morning. During his term in office del Mazo had formed a special military unit of elite guards made up of men chosen from the army, the Federal Judicial Police, and so on. The elite group was charged with protecting him from all dangers to his person, "especially unkind words."

Cárdenas, like López y Rivas, was tall and slim, but he was not so far left of center as López y Rivas, and he had a full head of hair. Many people who knew him spoke of López y Rivas as intelligent, a professor, which is an honorable position in Mexico, but when they spoke of Cárdenas, they spoke of either his father or his honesty. In the heights, in Milpa Alta, where the people still spoke classical Nahuatl and harvested fields of nopales (prickly pear cactus), they remembered how the father of the candidate had once delivered a brief speech in Nahuatl and had even returned some of the land to the Indians, as Hidalgo and then Morelos had tried to do. In Iztacalco there were not so many people who spoke indigenous languages, and not

[1] A lower-middle-class and poor district housing many minimum or close to minimum wage workers, making bread, grinding corn and making tortillas, producing plastics, fabrics, structural steel, dairy products, printing, and so on. Housing projects had been constructed in many of parts of the *delegación*.
[2] "Mexicanness," from the Nahuatl *mexicayotl*.

many of them were Nahuas, but there were many poor people and many people who could recount the wounds that had been inflicted on them or their relatives because of the corruption of the PRI. The candidate from Iztacalco calculated that Cárdenas would win his district as well as Milpa Alta and many others, unless the PRI counted the votes as it imagined them.

López y Rivas not only had many poll watchers, but two crews of people who went from one polling place to the next to bring food and drink to the poll watchers and to check for any irregularities. Among these was his cousin Leticia Enríquez Guerrero and her beau, a physician named Broglio. "My mother's family was Italian," said Broglio. He had a square Italian face, like a movie star from the 1950s, and he drove his new sedan with the loving recklessness of an Italian, which is very different from the brilliant aggression of a Mexican. In the neighborhood streets every *tope* (speed bump) pained him as it humbled his car, but on the wider streets he drove like a man at Le Mans or Daytona.

Broglio practiced medicine only part-time; he lived mainly on his farm in Michoacán, where he raised mangos, but not the small yellow mangos de Manila, which he said were no longer favored by anyone, even the Mexicans. He said his neighbors were drug dealers, people of enormous wealth who kept armed guards around the mansion they had built nearby and came and went by helicopter. At the polling places he did not speak to the watchers from the PRD or ask them what they would like for lunch but left the work to Leticia.

Neither Leticia nor Dr. Broglio was a leftist, like López y Rivas or even a center leftist, like Cárdenas. Broglio was pleased by Leticia, and Leticia was enraged by the PRI, which she blamed for her present state of misery. They had met at the hospital where Broglio practiced medicine and Leticia, a biochemist, conducted laboratory tests. She worked very long hours, as much overtime as she could get, and he spent a good part of every week on his farm, meaning they did not see each other very often.

Leticia had a square face like Broglio, but delicate and dark, the color of long-steeped tea, and every morning she transformed herself with makeup. She painted highlights on her face, reds and blacks and paling pinks in the proper places, and she did it with genuine delicacy, but coldly, with the precision of a scientist. After delivering food to several PRD poll watchers, she and Broglio went to a large market to buy lunch for themselves. They sat at a long table, like a picnic table, where they ate whatever was left in the kitchen of the old woman who operated the restaurant there. She served a tepid soup. Fat floated on the water, translucent and magnifying, yellow islands in a red *chile de arbol* sea. The woman wiped the used disposable plastic dishes with a dirty rag before she ladled soup into them, and she laid warm tortillas gently on the enameled wooden table.

The biochemist and the doctor ate with gusto. She drank Pepsi-Cola; he drank beer. The old woman said she also had some sausage left; she held up a piece to show them the color and the shape of what remained, but neither Broglio nor Leticia wanted it. The old woman shrugged. With so little left, she could close her kitchen. When the doctor asked the old woman if he could drive her to the polling place where she voted, the old woman squeezed another hundred wrinkles into her face. Perhaps she smiled. She said she was eighty-four, too old to vote.

The doctor and the biochemist wiped their hands on pieces of brown paper he found at another counter in the market and went on. Since it was against the law to discuss the election at a polling place, Leticia could only ask how many had voted and inquire of her poll watcher about irregularities. The turnout had been good, the poll watchers said, but it had been a long day, and they were hungry; they asked for hamburgers and Pepsi-Cola. Between polling places Leticia and Broglio listened to the radio, hoping to hear news of the election. Underlying the excitement of a possible victory for Cárdenas and the PRD, a common and ugly theory ran through the campaign: The PRI wanted him to win. Mexico City was ungovernable; a victory for Cárdenas would mean failure, shame, and the end of his career.

Leticia hoped the theory was wrong. She hated the PRI. The devaluation in 1994 and the terrible fiscal crisis that followed had ruined her life. Her husband lost his business because he could no longer afford the bank interest on the goods he purchased to sell in his store. With no money coming in, they could not make the mortgage payments on their condominium apartment; the bank took the apartment from them and sold it for practically nothing. He had grown bitter over the fall, although she told him it was not his failure, the government had failed. They quarreled; he beat her; she took her son and went to live in her mother's house.

From there she had begun again, but the long hours at the hospital, the loneliness after years of marriage, the lack of help from her husband or from Broglio wearied her. She hated the PRI; it had done this to her life. When her cousin Gilberto threw a victory party that night, she would not be able to attend; her shift in the laboratory began in early evening. Broglio would drive her to the hospital, then go on to his farm. At the end of her shift, in the morning, she would return to the apartment she had rented near the great swimming pool and auditorium that had been built for the Olympics in 1968. Perhaps she would clean the kitchen, pick up the clothes piled on the couch and the bed, the shoes in the hall; perhaps not. The poor had always been poor, she said, but the PRI had murdered the middle class.

Toward evening the crowds began to gather at the party headquarters. The mood of false optimism at the PRI headquarters came of the information the party had learned through its network of operatives in the city. The Instituto Federal Electoral (IFE) had done its job all too well from the point of view of the PRI. Or had it? If the aim of the PRI had been to demonstrate the incompetence of Cárdenas and the left splinter group that had formed the PRD, the election had gone well. Such thinking had taken place at Los Pinos, the Mexican White House, if it had taken place at all. In the PRI head-quarters there was only the thought of jobs lost, the end of control over the quotidian life of the capital. And then there was the symbolism. The PRI had lost the center in a country that had spent years in confusion and conflict over the question of centralism versus federalism. The PRIistas waited. In 1988 the computers had worked a miracle for Carlos Salinas de Gotari, elect-ing him president, despite the fact that the opposition candidate had clearly carried the day; it was not likely that del Mazo would merit anything so nearly divine, but it was possible. The thick-set men, the men of the fright-ening glances, the men of the double-breasted suits, all the men who had come in from the farthest reaches of the vast drainage system of the sexage-narian party, waited.

In another part of the city Federal Deputy Ifigenia Martínez, known as La Maestra, because she had been the first woman to head the economics department of the UNAM, stood outside the PRD headquarters, where we had agreed to meet.[3] Her former student, now a professor at the university, Teresa Gutiérrez Haces, joined us there. They were the first and second pages of the history of women in economics and politics in Mexico. Like her teacher, Gutiérrez had moved in and out of the academic world. She had been one of the Mexican advisers who negotiated a better position for Mex-

[3]La Maestra tells her own history beginning on p. 717.

ico in the side agreements to the North American Free Trade Agreement (NAFTA). She had done her best in Canada and with the U.S. Congress, but she was not pleased by the agreement, for she saw her country wounded by it, and she did not think the wounds would heal for a long time, if ever.

Like other members of the PRD, among them Ricardo Pascoe, who had learned his economics at New York University and in the Allende government in Chile, Gutiérrez saw Mexico trapped into the position of servant to the United States. NAFTA, the ending of import duties on goods sold in Mexico, the agreed end to tariffs on agricultural products from the United States in 2003, the failure of Mexico to develop its own national industries had weakened her country. Both Gutiérrez and Pascoe agreed with La Maestra's view of the policies of the neoliberals, from privatization to the continuing failure to alleviate the problems of poverty, which meant to the *Perredistas* (PRDs) a bitter and perhaps dangerous future. They were not revolutionaries, they were nationalists, they favored an active government; in this they were like socialists, but they were not of the kind who wore uniforms or uniform clothing, nor were they of the other kind, the romantics. They were democrats and dreamers, and if there was anything they hated more than the PRI they had abandoned, it was the foreign debt their country could not abandon.

These gentle leftists, whose words could cut like razor wire, lived in the comfort of the wedding of academe and politics. La Maestra was the grandest of them, a woman whose beauty had changed in form and style over a long career but had not deserted her as it evolved. She and I had met at a dinner given by a mutual friend in Chimalistac (part of the San Ángel area in the southern part of the Federal District), and again at a meeting of delegates to a PRD convention. La Maestra, as everyone knew, differed from other politicians in that she wore her political heart on her sleeve. Her two flaws as a politician had been apparent almost since the beginning of her career: loyalty and a lack of talent for dissembling.[4]

Gutiérrez, who is married to the Belgian sociologist Daniel Hiernaux, lives far from the center of the city in a modern house with a lovingly tended private garden in the suburb of Padierna. Their son, Sebastián, was one of twenty Mexicans studying computer theory at the National Autonomous University in 1997. He and his parents were very aware of the difference

[4]She had also held appointive positions in the federal government.

between Mexico and China, which graduates thousands of students of computer theory, and of how the two countries would be affected by this and similar disparities in the next generation.

While the two women stood outside the PRD headquarters, it occurred to them that the government had provided no police protection for the PRD or its candidates in a country where guards carrying automatic weapons stand outside the banks. "If someone drove by . . . ," the women said to each other, and quickly moved inside the building. Gutiérrez and I waited while La Maestra went upstairs to a meeting of party leaders, after which everyone was to go to the Hotel Camino Real for a party to celebrate the expected victory. While we waited, Gutiérrez told her theory about the involvement of the United States in the election: The U.S. bankers had wanted Cárdenas because his election would stabilize or appear to stabilize Mexico in the eyes of the world, protecting U.S. investments.

Everyone had a theory about Cárdenas, and no one thought he would win on his own merits or because the citizens of the Federal District wanted him, except La Maestra. He is "a good man, an honest man," she said. I did not know then how much she had affected his career or that she had been a friend of the candidate and his family for many years. The moment was too exciting for such details. The governorship of the Federal District had often been a stepping-stone to the presidency. Cárdenas appeared to be winning the election; in the 2000 presidential election the country would belong to the PRD . . . theoretically.

Cárdenas had only one rival within the party then, the brilliant, mercurial Porfirio Muñoz Ledo. At that moment, Muñoz Ledo, La Maestra, Andrés Manuel López Obrador, Rosario Robles, and other party leaders discussed the most important question of the moment: Would the PRI steal this election from Cárdenas as they had stolen the 1988 presidential election? If that happened, what would the party do? What would Muñoz Ledo do?

The elevator door opened, and the party leaders emerged. A mass meeting had been planned for later that evening in the Zócalo, the main plaza in Mexico City. Cárdenas, Muñoz Ledo, others would speak. What they said would still depend on the announced outcome of the election.

We walked a few blocks to the arranged place where the cars and drivers waited for the party leaders. Night had come suddenly, as always in the Valley of Mexico. In the area where the drivers were to pick up the members of Congress and the party officials, people fell into groups around the conjunctions of headlights. Muñoz Ledo stopped to chat. He is a full-faced man, handsome, and intense. We were to spend more time together that evening, but at the moment La Maestra introduced us, she began to castigate him for the way he was dressed. "Porfirio, where is your tie? How can you go about with no tie? Did you lose it?"

The famed debater, known for his raging intelligence, answered meekly that he had not lost his tie; he had forgotten to put it on when he dressed that evening. A mock fury between the generations erupted from La Maestra: "How can you appear in public without a tie?"

Muñoz Ledo, the leader of the PRD who had dared challenge President de la Madrid during his 1988 annual report to the people, was speechless. "Here, take my tie," I said. "I will not be making any speeches tonight."

He looked to La Maestra, his friend of many years and his deputy when he was Mexican ambassador to the United Nations. "Yes, it goes well with your coat," she said. He put on the tie, and only after she had approved of the knot did we go to our separate cars.

The Federal District has few hotels more Mexican or imposing than the Camino Real, with its vast wall of red tile at the garagelike entrance, wide staircases, courtyards, and restaurants. Newer and more luxurious hotels have been built, but they have the elegance of New York or Tokyo, while the grand spaces and slightly worn appearance of the Camino Real belong to Mexico. The party opposed to neoliberalism, the party unsettled by the whiteness of the presidency since the election of Miguel de la Madrid in 1982, had selected a fine and Mexican place where the mariachis would not be a curiosity.

Carlos Monsiváis, the essayist, stood quietly with us in the elevator up from the main floor. Grayed and professorial, he smiled to people who greeted him but said little. At the long entrance to the main room a huge crowd had already gathered, pawing over a table laden with tidbits. The music of mariachis mixed into the din of voices; only the trumpets cut through; all the stringed instruments, even the violins, were lost. A huge screen covering the entire wall had been set up at one end of the main room, with rows of chairs arranged in front of it. The face and voice of the candidate would eventually appear on the screen.

Although the PRD was the party of the people, surely the closest to that place of the three major parties, the reception belonged to the upper middle class, mainly those people the Marxists contended belonged to no class, the artists and academics and politicians who had survived the crisis. No street workers, no poll watchers appeared in the Camino Real. The party of the people had an elite, but it did not show itself in ostentatious ways as the rich of Mexico do. It was a political gathering; ostentation had to do with contacts, not with clothes.

The most renowned Mexican actress of the day, María Rojo, star of the film *Danzón*, and her husband, the travel agency head, Esteban Schmelz, moved quietly in the crowd. René Columb, the architect and city planner, provider of a well-thought-out but never seriously considered solution to some of the city's problems, talked about ideas for the Federal District, the future. The daughter of the muralist Diego Rivera, as large as her father and dressed in the tan jumpsuit associated with the painter, held a place, like a monument, around which people flowed.

This was not the avant-garde, neither the political nor cultural edge of the country. No rock stars, no radicals celebrated here. These had been warriors; they had seen their comrades shot down in the streets of Tlatelolco in 1968, and they had retired momentarily, regrouped in the classroom and the studio, but they could not let go their dreams. This was the gentle revolution; it came at the end of the warrior's life, when weapons had been changed into words by the magic of time and democracy was expected to have a soft voice.

In the neighborhoods, in the streets, at the less elegant parties, like the fiesta for Gilberto López y Rivas, the tone was more exuberant, the past more distant, abstract, although never absent, because the people wanted López y Rivas to remain on the side of the Zapatistas, to carry on the struggle in the Federal Congress. In Iztacalco, the vote had not been about democracy. It had been for Cárdenas, but not with enthusiasm; it had been against the PRI, and the ballots had been marked with trembling hands and fearful glances at the men who sat in the shade on the July afternoon, remarking on everyone who marked and folded a ballot and put it into the clear plastic box. The defeat of the PRI in the city came with sighs and squeals. If victory had had a banner, it would have shown laughter and chewing, and it would have been held aloft by mestizos and Indians.

Among the elite of the party victory was more complex. Many of them had come from the PRI, "the system," and they had made the move out of anger and disappointment and heartfelt disagreement with the policies of neoliberalism. Cárdenas, whose entrance the crowd awaited, had not been the leader of the break with the PRI. One of the originators of the PRD sat in the first row of the small block of chairs in front of the screen: Porfirio Muñoz Ledo. I sat beside him. We passed a few remarks, made a lame joke about the tie, how it would become part of Mexican history, and then he fell silent. In the middle of the heart of the party he had all but created, he sat alone, accompanied by a stranger. No one came to greet him, he greeted no one; he sat. He had been the leader of the PRI, senator and representative at the federal level, ambassador to the United Nations, and he was looking at the end of the long career.

No one doubted his ability, the quality of his mind, the richness of his vocabulary; only the volatility frightened them: an incident with a gun while serving as UN ambassador in New York, the sudden rages, the distaste for authority. Both Muñoz Ledo and Cárdenas suffered the profound war within that defines the still-incomplete Mexican character, but the war was apparent in Muñoz Ledo and not in Cárdenas. The candidate, elongated and dour, had a quixotic air; Muñoz Ledo, the true knight, presented a soldier's face. They were of the same generation, they had both been members of the court of the PRI; only one could win.

Later another of the originators of the breakout from the PRI, Ifigenia Martínez, La Maestra, came to sit with us, but Muñoz Ledo had very little to say even to her, his ally and adviser for most of his political career. We sat quietly in the middle of the great party, while all around us the babble went. Then the face of Cuauhtémoc Cárdenas Solorzano appeared on the screen, projected in immense proportions, a floor to ceiling head, like an Olmec sculpture or a movie star, the god of the moment, not yet democracy, but an attendant god.

At this moment the PRD, the Democratic Party of the Revolution, cracked. The sign appeared on the face of Muñoz Ledo; the features contorted, became an ideogram for envy. The war of the elements within, the Mexican war, broke out with the appearance of the next governor of the Federal District. Muñoz Ledo was on fire, but no outward sign would show for years. The alliances and misalliances were yet to come. It would be at least two years before his ambitions and his lack of hope for himself, if not for Mexico, would drive him into the embrace of the inimical beast of ambition that had defined Mexican politics since the people first fought to free the country from Spain at the beginning of the nineteenth century.

In that struggle, José María Morelos y Pavón, a forty-five-year-old priest who had been a student of Miguel Hidalgo's, took up the leadership of the war the moment his mentor was imprisoned in the spring of 1811. Morelos had been engaged in the fighting from the beginning, having been sent by Hidalgo to win the south. Although like Hidalgo, he was to die before a firing squad and, like his mentor, recanting his rebellious acts and ideas, the similarity ends there. Hidalgo was a criollo, and Morelos, though he was listed as Spanish at birth, was probably a caste—that is, a person with some African ancestors. Hidalgo thought of himself as the leader of the people; Morelos said he was their servant.

Morelos made a little money in business, enjoyed women, and fathered at least three illegitimate children, one of whom, Juan Nepomuceno Almonte, would become a conservative general and an ally of the emperor Maximilian's. While Hidalgo came from a landowning family, Morelos started out his career as a mule skinner. He was a small, hard man, who always wore a handkerchief on his head, like a pirate or a Gypsy. As a military leader Morelos admired Frederick the Great and attempted to emulate his tactics and especially his discipline. He told the mobs of people who wanted to follow him and Hidalgo that they should stay home, work, and provide food for Hidalgo's well-disciplined, uniformed army.

A bitter humor, the sudden laughter and wildness of the *macho*, perhaps best characterized the priest Morelos. A womanizer, he took confession before battle; a follower of Prussian military techniques, he encouraged his troops to celebrate death and victory with bugles, parades, drunkenness, and oaths of fealty to honor, equality, and the Virgin of Guadalupe. He despised Indians. Morelos said they were lazy. And Indians hated him, complaining that he mistreated them, and forced them to work beyond their capacity. Even so, it was Morelos who declared that people of all colors, ranging from criollos to castes to Indians, should get rid of this "mouthful of names" and refer to themselves as Americans. The only distinction to be made among people should be based on their "morality or immorality." It was the first political attempt to create a nation of the disparate elements. Morelos apparently thought he could do by linguistic fiat what neither guns nor prayers nor even the beatific smile of the Virgin of Guadalupe had accomplished.

Had he succeeded in separating New Spain from the crown, he might have made the nation he dreamed. And he came close: At one point during his military campaign, he occupied most of the territory around Mexico

City. He was all but invincible; he endured a sixty-three-day siege at Cuautla, then led his troops out in a brilliant and dangerous maneuver. With his horse shot out from under him and his ribs broken, he was still able to rally his troops. In the most ironic turn of the war, Morelos was defeated at the Battle of Valladolid in 1813 by a man born in the same town, Agustín de Iturbide. Eight years later, Iturbide made good the claim of Independence for New Spain.

The later defeats and final capture of Morelos grew, also with some irony, out of his inability to separate his military talent from his dreams for New Spain. All through his brief career at the head of the insurgent army, Morelos tried to establish legitimacy for the new, separate country. He first addressed himself to his theories about egalitarianism and government according to the will of the people in a paper delivered to the opening session of the Congress at Chilpancingo. In his paper and in the documents to follow, including the constitution written at Apatzingán in 1814, Morelos combined ideas learned from the French and American revolutions with his utter devotion to religion and the Virgin of Guadalupe and the egalitarian notions symbolized in her.

He could not sort out the roles of Church and State as the late-eighteenth-century constitutions had done. Enlightenment notions of rationalism had come to Spain, where a new constitution was written at Cádiz, but New Spain had chosen a different road to government and glory. Its philosophers were priests and friars; there was as yet no secular intellectual or political leader. Fray Servando was the chief propagandist for the insurgents, writing from exile in London, arguing that the crown had decreed separation from the mother country early in the sixteenth century. If not, he asked, why would there have been a Council of the Indies? To his mind the two Spains had been separate and equal since the evangelization of the Americans in the sixth century. The implications of Independence in the decrees of the Spanish had merely recognized the true relation. New Spain had been independent for either three hundred or thirteen hundred years. Fray Servando was willing to take it either way.

Morelos added to the nativism of Fray Servando his more political arguments, but no argument preceded religion in importance. The first item in the constitution proclaimed the newly independent country Catholic. Those of other religions were not welcome in the independent country, an idea that came of the Counter-Reformation and of the Church and Crown's late-fifteenth-century change of heart about Jews and Moors. Hatred of heretics held a place at least as important as love of God in the atmosphere of eschatological fear; the end of this life, Judgment Day, and the fires of hell were as real as the earth on which a person stood.

Another fear that informed the constitution of Apatzingán grew out of long experience with the capricious and often cruel actions of kings. The document produced by the Congress while Morelos held off the royalist troops gave greater power to the legislature than to the elected administrator. After establishing the rule of a single religion, the 1814 Constitution proclaimed the guarantee of the "natural rights" of citizens. It spoke of the "expression of the general will to produce the common happiness" and went on to define happiness as the enjoyment of equality, security in one's person and property, and liberty. The echoes of the American and French revolutions were clear, as was the influence of the change in government in Spain, where a legislature had finally come to hold power.

Morelos had already proclaimed an end to slavery, the caste system, and onerous taxation of indigenous people. Finally, the Jesuits were welcomed back from exile. To protect the authors of the document, Morelos shifted battle plans, expended troops and ammunition, and in the end exposed himself to defeat and capture. The Congress he had so loved and defended vied with him for power and influence over the new government. It stripped him of his rank and command, and the Congress continued in session after he had paid his final homage to the Virgin of Guadalupe on his way to the firing squad.

With the death of Morelos, the War of Independence turned into a series of guerrilla actions. His second-in-command, Mariano Matamoros, had been executed despite the offer by Morelos to trade two hundred Spanish prisoners for the young priest. Among those left to fight were Vicente Guerrero and Nicolás Bravo. When the viceroy sent Iturbide to destroy Guerrero's army in 1820, Spain was already weakened by European wars and intrigues, in turmoil. Iturbide, who had been brilliant in the field against Morelos, was by then a Mexico City dandy, dissolute, and without money, and in his new assignment he was to find the opportunity to do something for himself. Unable to defeat Guerrero, he chose another path. Instead of engaging Guerrero in a major battle, he made a pact with him to declare Independence. They published their Plan of Iguala, with its three guarantees (religion, union, and Independence), and New Spain at last became a separate country. The planners did not consider democracy; Iturbide and Guerrero called for a constitutional monarchy and asked for the return of the Spanish king Ferdinand VII or another European monarch. But Iturbide really had something else in mind. The dandy of the viceroy's court, criollo and ultraconservative, had succeeded where the two radical priests Hidalgo and Morelos had failed.

Iturbide maneuvered quickly to get what he really wanted out of Independence. On July 21, 1822, he was crowned emperor, a title he held only briefly. A popular war hero came inland from Veracruz, where he had defeated an invading force of Spaniards, and forced Iturbide into exile. General Antonio López de Santa Anna gave the country over to its first president, a former general in the insurgent army, Félix Fernández, who had changed his name to Guadalupe Victoria (Guadalupe Victorious), the Mexican Virgen de Guadalupe had defeated the Spanish Virgen de Remedios. The independent country finally had a legitimate president, one whose name told the outcome of the War for Independence that had begun with the telling of Fray Servando's chauvinist dream and the arguments of history he constructed to honor it.

A newly independent state, however, must have a new name to move its suffering out of the moment and into memory. The *new* New Spain is the language of comedy. Then what would it be? Some argued for Anáhuac, which means "near the waters" in Nahuatl and denoted the Valley of Mexico before it came to stand for all of New Spain. Others, perhaps following the lead of Sigüenza y Góngora, wanted the name of the people who had built the great city of Tenochtitlán, Mexica. There was a debate over the origin of the word. Was *Mexitli* really another name for Huitzilopochtli, the tutelary god of the people who founded the city?

If they did not know the meaning of the word, they surely knew the application of it. Mexico, the name of a warrior god, one of the names of perhaps the most beautiful and orderly city in the world at the moment of its destruction—there could be no other name. But what of the Mexica? If everyone in the country was a Mexican, who were the Mexica? Francisco Clavijero had provided an answer. He used a new word for the Mexica. He called them Aztecs because one of the stories of their origin, the most plausible, said they came from a place called Aztlán. The categories were defined; it was not the Mexica who lived in the Valley of Mexico; it was the people from Aztlán. In an irony that would have pleased Cervantes, the victory of the Virgin of Guadalupe gave birth to the Aztecs.

12.

His Royal Highness

. . . only European blood can keep the level of civilization that has pro-
duced our nationality from sinking. —JUSTO SIERRA

The last time I saw Prince Lassalle he ended the evening, as expected, with a surprise and a flourish. He unscrewed the top of his narrow black cane, poured himself a small amount of French brandy out of the lower part, and drank it off as if it were medicine. With his perpetual ironic smile, he accepted the awe of his small audience and took his leave. A brief exchange of letters followed. He wrote from Venice, then London; then there was nothing. Silence. His obituary appeared in the *New York Times* a few months later. It did not mention the tiny rosette he wore in his lapel, indicating that the prince, former husband of the late Marie Agathe, princess von Ratibor and Corvey, of the Hohenlohe-Schillingsfürst line, had no Jewish or Moorish blood and had never engaged in commerce. Nor did it mention the color of his skin, which was darker than cinnamon, more chocolate; almost glazed in his youth, grayed and dulled by the waverings of his heart in later years.

Although I did not meet him until late in his career of charmings and marriages, my wife, Sylvia, and several Mexican friends had known the prince, whom we referred to by his given name, Edmundo, through several wives and careers. Sylvia was fond of the wives and other women with whom he was involved, save one, and that one does not appear until the end of his story.

The origins of Prince Edmundo Lassalle, Ph.D., were never quite clear. He was born in the state of Chiapas, perhaps in 1918 or 1920, the child of . . . And that was where the tales began. His friends in Mexico said he came from a family of wealthy landowners, who had sent him to boarding school either in the United States or France, probably the former, then on to Oxford and Columbia University, where he was awarded a Ph.D. in art history, which he took home to Mexico, where he married and divorced the princess and went off to Acapulco to enjoy the sea, the sand, and the adoration of ladies who came for the sun.

Acapulco was Mexico's most beautiful and fashionable resort when Edmundo and a very good-looking blond woman perhaps ten or fifteen years his senior set up housekeeping on the sand. Dressed entirely in white, sleeping on the moonlit beach, the tall, slim Mexican and the suntanned gringa were the stuff of which tourist advertisements are made. He surprised everyone by marrying again, but not with the blond woman of the beach. He married her stepdaughter.

A prince, even a Hohenlohe prince, if he is without funds, must work, which drove Edmundo from the beach to an office in Mexico City and from parties aboard yachts to parties in embassies and the new high-rise apartment buildings marking the boom of the Miguel Alemán presidency. At any party or perhaps at *every* party, Edmundo could be found at the center of a group of delighted and admiring women. He had a witticism for every moment of every occasion, and when necessary, he did not mind at all appropriating other men's wit for his own. To amuse foreigners, he explained the Mexican verb *chingar*, which means "to violate or rape" at its simplest level, but, like the Anglo-Saxon word "fuck," has at least a dozen other uses. The explanation astonished the innocents: How could a fellow so debonair as Edmundo know so much about this revelation of the soul of the country and spontaneously deliver such a brilliant essay on the subject? The answer is that it was a brilliant essay on Mexico, so brilliant, in fact, that it established the reputation of Octavio Paz, who wrote it.[1]

The women who gathered around Edmundo to enjoy his wit and gossip did not concern themselves with the origins of his entertainments. These moments were his works. As other Mexicans painted or wrote or built the grand resorts of *la epoca de oro* (the golden age), Edmundo entertained his

---

[1] The verb is used only in Mexico, and as Paz noted, it has roots in the affair between Cortés and La Malinche, his native concubine and translator. She is the one who is raped in the Spanish (white)/indigenous (brown) relationship. But *chingar* can be used in a dozen other forms, all of them related to the invasion or conquest of Mexico. A *chingón* is a tough guy. *No me eches chingas* means "Don't insult me." A *chingazo* is a "terrible blow." Recently the verb *joder*, which translates as "fuck," has become as common as *chingar*, perhaps because of the U.S. influence or the increasing distance from the time of La Malinche. And *chingar* has some curious connections. A *malinchista* is a betrayer of the culture. And so on.

listeners, all but the brigade of jealous men who stood among the less desirable women drinking scotch while patience failed them. Another version of
his early life emerged from the jealous brigade. A journalist of the kind who
wrote a column in a state-supported newspaper claimed to know the truth
about the prince. He had been born on a great *finca* in Chiapas, but his
father had been the chauffeur rather than the *patrón*.

As a young man, the journalist's version continued, Edmundo had developed a certain talent for charming women. The patrón, anxious to keep
peace among his servants while at the same time protecting his adolescent
daughter, had decided to kill two birds with one education: He sent the boy
off to a boarding school. There the chauffeur's son began to invent himself.
He took La Salle, the name of the car in which his father chauffeured the
patrón, added an *s* and *voilà!* Lassalle. "A piece of good luck," the journalist
said. "What if the car had been a Cadillac?"

In truth, the difference would not have been great. "Cadillac" is also a
French name, and Mexico had a passion for all things French. Even more
than they loved and imitated Spain, the Mexicans of the time adored France.
After the Revolution of 1910, as before, the children of the best families were
educated in France. The best clothes, the most brilliant books, the grandest
designs came from France. The city of Mexico had designed and built the
Reforma, its great boulevard, in imitation of France. The perfume of high
culture could have no other origin. A man named Lassalle could marry a
princess and drink brandy from his cane in scathing homage to the foppish
world of princes without funds.

Perhaps under the circumstances of the marriage, the princess would also
have married a Gómez, which was said, again by his antagonists, to have been
Edmundo's original name. If so, it was a detail he did not deign to discuss.
The princess interested him more. In 1947, according to Edmundo, she had
wanted to become a Mexican citizen, and the quickest way to accomplish her
goal was to marry a Mexican. The bargain could not have been more to his
liking; in return for the marriage, she gave him a title. He could not pass it
on to his children, unless she was the mother, but the title was his to keep.
The man from Chiapas had become a member of the nobility, more or less,
but not the nobility of Mexico; he had joined one of the great families of
Europe. As in the brief surge of the wish for kings before Iturbide declared
himself emperor or the tragic career of Maximilian, whom Napoleon
declared emperor of all Mexico in 1863, any European connection would do.

If the stories told by his antagonists were true or nearly true or even partly true, Edmundo of Chiapas had achieved the essence of Mexico, had become, in his own persona, the uncompleted nation; he was a man of parts, knitted together with irony. He had the grace and culture of Europe; he was a dandy who looked like a Mexican; he embodied the generosity of the Mexican; he lacked only the *machismo* of Mexicans. Had Edmundo been an Aztec prince or the son of a Mayan ruler, he would have been a model of courage and daring. Instead, he laughed, he gossiped, he surrounded himself with women and, according to the more desperate of his detractors, men.

His life turned on irony. He was perhaps the only prince ever to bring his friends to La Barba Azul, a dance hall frequented by Mexico's poor working people and more than a few petty thieves. If he went to a hotel in London and registered as Prince Edmundo Lassalle, the clerks confused him with sheikhs and rajas rather than the Hohenlohes. On a visit to Nantucket, a crowd gathered to inspect him, because they had never before seen a Mexican. As a student at Columbia University he lived in housing for international students, where he was asked to come to a party in "native dress." He wore a pinstripe suit. When there was an occasion to send a gift to his son with his third wife, he said he had sent him a wallet. "After all, the boy is Jewish."

All was wit, irony, fantasy. He called his close friends accomplices, as if life were one great caper in a world without solid ground. His worldview was not existential but millennial. The world might last awhile, but not forever. He could have been a prince of the Mexica, writing a philosophy calibrated to the coming end of the fifth sun. It made for the sacrifice of princes, but not the end of elegance, the abandonment of culture. His children were schooled at Le Rosey, a very expensive boarding school in Switzerland, but he did not choose to say so. He preferred the story about the wallet. In New York he and his third wife lived in two apartments on Fifth Avenue, one of them for the children and the nursemaid.

Sylvia ran into Edmundo now and then on the street or in a restaurant. Often years passed between sightings, brief visits with him and his wife, a movie, dinner. He divorced, married again, this time into an American publishing family. There was always money, always style. He loved funny stories, the Mexican stories most, the absurdities of machismo that had been so revealing to Octavio Paz. "A dwarf walked into a bar in Mexico City. 'Hola, Chaparrito [Shorty],' the bartender said, and the dwarf took out a pistol and shot him."

On his other side, the one on which his French was even more proper than his English, he had a joke about King Farouk of Egypt. The king was playing poker with some friends. At the end of the betting, only he and one other player were left. The other player showed his hand, a full house. Farouk laid down three kings and two unmatched cards. "I win," said the king. "You see, four of a kind. One, two, three"—and pointing to himself—"four kings."

Whether he had heard the story or witnessed it made little difference. He laughed. Thoughts of Farouk made him laugh. He told of the death of the king, who was so drunk he fell facedown into his food and drowned in a plate of pasta. The gluttony of the deposed king disgusted and amused the prince of the one-generation title. And the gossip, well, the gossip was the best part of any evening for him.

One night, not so many years ago, he came to dinner in New York, bringing with him his friend who ran the Hotel Eden in Rome. Edmundo was doing something—exactly what was not quite clear—to preserve Venice from filthy water and air pollution. His friend Peggy Guggenheim, he said, had put him up to this. He and his friend, whose name I do not quite remember—perhaps it was Ceccere—filled the dinner table with laughter. Among the other guests was a very plain—to tell the truth, "plain" is a compliment—woman whom we had seated between Edmundo and the Italian, possibly with a bit of irony of our own. Near the end of the evening, Edmundo and his friend began to flirt mercilessly with the woman. They praised her iron gray hair, lavished their eyes on her long nose, drank in the beauty of her sallow complexion, feasted on the small discolored depressions left by the pimples of her long-forgotten youth, licked their lips at the promise of her scrawny body covered with the unmanageable hair of the land of Aphrodite.

The evening came to the end Edmundo had been planning when we opened a bottle of champagne to atone for a paltry dessert. He took the neck of the bottle in one hand, pushed his chair back and to the side, and leaned down to slip off the scrawny woman's shoe. She giggled with pleasure as he brought the shoe and the bottle together, and prepared to pour. He told her he was about to drink champagne from her shoe, and the Italian leapt into the conversation to say that he would drink from her other shoe. She thanked them graciously, as if she often enjoyed such offers, and took back her shoe.

It was not up to his standard, but what else is a prince to do with an ugly woman? Irony was a requirement for life, like oxygen or champagne. He and the hotelier leaned away from her, performing a ballet on the word "alas!" And then they laughed, for now the prince had another brief tale, which he would tell with only a mild fiction to heighten the joke: "And that evening, my dears, I drank champagne from an ugly woman's shoe." And for all his wit and worldliness, he would not understand its lack of originality or what the tale revealed.

We were to see the prince only once more before he died. He was in New York permanently then, living at the Lowell Hotel. His heart had lost its rhythms, and the doctors had inserted a pacemaker to set it right. "Look! A pacemaker!" he said, pounding his chest with a fist, so that women had to look away, fearing his chest would rupture from the pounding and his heart would stop. He confessed to diabetes, as well as to this loss of music in his heart. But he had other stories. There was the chambermaid at the Lowell. He spoke of how much he liked sleeping with black women and how she had begun to oblige him on the very day he returned from the hospital with his electrically modified heart.

We talked about the book I had been working on, a long historical novel about Pancho Villa. I said how much I admired the Guzmán book about Villa, the great scene in which Martín Luis Guzmán meets Villa, and the general picks up the author by the lapels of his coat and raises him off the ground until their eyes meet. Edmundo said, "Of course he did. Guzmán was a dwarf, only so big." And he laughed until I thought his heart would stop.

It did stop soon thereafter, in London. And we thought that was the last of him. But some years later Aline Griffith from upstate New York, who married a Count Romanones, a Spaniard, published a book about her adventures during World War II, *The Spy Wore Red*. As Sylvia was reading through it, she came upon the name Edmundo Lassalle. He had been in Spain during the war, working for the OSS, the forerunner of the CIA. His code name, according to the countess, had been Top Hat. The only secret he had ever kept was the one about his own machismo. Perhaps it was like the pinstripe suit; he did not want to appear in "native" dress.

A second book by the countess told a different story about Edmundo. She put him in London, dead broke, reduced to shoplifting food from Harrod's during the last days of his life. The story angered us, but not so much as her telling of it. Was it true? We dismissed it as the act of a woman scorned. But his life could have ended so, perhaps proving again the mid-nineteenth-century idea of the Mexican Liberals, which was that Mexicans do not belong in Europe, as Europe does not belong in Mexicans.

It was an old question in independent Mexico: Should an independent country have a hereditary ruler? A king? An emperor? If so, Indian Mexico could no longer provide such a person; it would have to be a European, a Spaniard. Edmundo chose a Hohenlohe. Iturbide, having declared Mexico independent, offered the throne to Ferdinand VII of Spain but demanded a constitutional monarchy. The Spanish king had already made such a bargain with rebels in his own country, and he sent Juan O'Donojú to Mexico to set-tle the business of Independence the same way. He was to offer reforms but deny full Independence. O'Donojú arrived at the port of Veracruz feeling sick, and the climate, the yellow fever, and unfamiliar food made him sicker. He signed a document prepared by Iturbide, essentially giving Mexico its Independence while maintaining royal Spanish power over the country. Fer-dinand VII was back, but the document was essentially the Plan of Iguala that Mexico used as its declaration of Independence.

The Mexican royalists had turned against Ferdinand for making a deal with the Spanish rebels. O'Donojú's offer thus had no takers, not among the Liberals or the Conservatives. Instead, he signed a pact with Iturbide that provided for a Mexican emperor, but only if no European king wore the crown. That was how Iturbide named himself Agustín I, emperor of Mex-ico. Santa Anna, who had defeated the last of the Spanish troops in Mexico, managed to earn Iturbide's distrust. The emperor ordered him to Mexico City. Santa Anna refused. Iturbide sent troops to force Santa Anna to bend to his will. Instead, the troops joined Santa Anna, published a joint plan with him for the takeover of Mexico, and succeeded. Iturbide, the man of the right, who had won Independence when the left had failed, abdicated on March 19, 1823, and was sent into exile with the proviso that he would be exe-cuted if he returned to Mexico. A little more than a year later he returned and, as promised, was executed.

Agustín I, emperor of Mexico, generalissimo of the Land and Sea, emperor in perpetuity, monarchist, fool, unscrupulous incompetent, left behind a deeply divided country, independent, but not a nation, not even a coherent state. The racial and religious dualisms of newly Independent Mex-ico still resembled apartheid more than civil society. In addition to the tension between whites and nonwhites, no accommodation could be found between centralists and federalists, the bourgeoisie and the masses, adherents of the Enlightenment and the last holdouts of the Scholastics, the Scottish Rite Masons and the York Rite Masons; furthermore, Mexico, like ancient Gaul, was divided into three distinct and incompatible parts—the north, the center, and the south.

To make matters worse, the United States, increasingly powerful both economically and militarily, seemed intent upon unlimited expansion, and Mexico's northern territory lay in its path. U.S. citizens were moving into Texas and California at a rate that alarmed the Mexicans. Although much of it was high desert and mountains, there were also great expanses of grassy plains perfect for grazing or plowing, and the Americans wanted it. From the vantage point of Mexico City, nothing but troubles came from the sparsely populated north. With only a few troops spread across thousands of miles, the Mexicans could not protect their settlers from raids by "hostiles," indigenous tribes who had taken to the horse like no other people in history. All through the nineteenth century and into the twentieth, they continued their attacks, and the *norteños* fought back, becoming the hardiest, most independent people in Mexico, a character trait that would have great effect in 1910.

With constant war on the northern frontier and uprisings and invasions in the south and the center, the Mexican people needed military heroes, and there were many who were willing, if not able, to answer the call. Generals made their *pronunciamentos* (pronouncements of rebellion), took power, and then went into exile with all but comic regularity during the period following the end of Iturbide. Both of Morelos's remaining major generals fell. His son, Juan Almonte, emerged as a general, diplomat, secretary of war, Liberal, monarchist, and finally one of the men who led Maximilian to the firing squad. Almonte's political instability and shifting loyalties, if not outright betrayals, epitomized the problem of Mexico after Independence.

The blame lay with Spain, which had failed to provide a stable society in the Americas, according to historian Justo Sierra. But the Spanish government did not fail alone. It had the assistance of the Catholic Church, which had accumulated vast amounts of property and cash, so that it became the wealthiest entity in the country and the chief moneylender. The rich Conservatives and the official Church supported each other; the middle class turned on the Church, demanding the return of money and property, and the poor, whose devotion to the Virgin of Guadalupe had replaced the ancient religions, loved *la religión* more than ever. The military, for the most part, allied itself with the Conservatives and the Church, if for no other reason than to keep the Liberals from taking away the fueros (exemptions from prosecution by civil authorities) that protected its officers as well as the clergy.

Mexico turned into a comic opera, but with tragic results. The score was written by the United States, the lyrics by the two conflicting parties, and the conductor—resplendent in military garb befitting a clown figure in such an opera—was none other than General His Royal Highness Antonio López de Santa Anna.

Between Guadalupe Victoria (1824) and Benito Juárez (1858), the presidency of Mexico changed hands more than fifty times. Several men, most notably Santa Anna, served many brief terms, and more than a few were appointed president to hold down the office while the real president led troops in battle. There were uprisings of federalists every few years, attempts at secession—Yucatán did actually secede—but no disaster so great as the one that began with a grant of permission for "300 Catholic families" to settle in the northern territory of Texas.

Spain and then Mexico officially limited immigration to the green lands of Texas, but the Americans simply ignored the limitations. Settlers moved in by the hundreds until the American population far outnumbered the Mexicans, including the small, isolated garrisons of Mexican troops. The situation in Texas grew tense when the rumor spread that the Mexican government would use its army to put an end to slavery in its Tejas territory. The Texans found the prospect untenable. But it was not entirely the Tejanos' objection to manumission that led to secession. For more than two decades after its own Independence Mexico had lived under the threat of U.S. expansionism. Despite the bravado of Mexico's generals, primarily Santa Anna, everyone knew what would happen in a war between the two countries. If the United States chose to annex the northern territories, there was very little Mexico could do to stop it. Mexico lacked heavy, accurate artillery, had few first-rate officers, and its lines of supply had to cross hundreds of miles of desert south of the Rio Grande.

When Texas formed a provisional government in 1835 and refused to obey Mexican law, only one man could be counted on to put down the secession, the best Mexican general, the national leader, the heroic, powerful, meritorious criollo, Santa Anna. Up until that moment he had been the dream soldier, the one beyond logic, the hope of Mexico. Santa Anna marched north across the desert, with his army of conscripts from the southern coast of Mexico following behind, foot-weary, short of food, shivering in the northern winter. From Santa Anna's point of view, the war must have appeared to be going well. Wherever he marched, the Texans fell back. At a simple mission building, El Alamo, outside San Antonio, the Texans' leader, Sam Houston, left a small contingent of volunteers, Americans and Mexican secessionists, to engage Santa Anna and do what damage they could before surrendering or escaping to rejoin the main force of Texans.

What actually happened at the Alamo remains unclear. Santa Anna offered the usual terms of surrender, and when they were turned down, he had the bugler play the *degüello*, meaning "no prisoners, no quarter." The literal meaning of the word, from *degollar*, is "to cut the throat or behead." The result was not what Santa Anna expected, for as (imminent) death is said to concentrate the mind, it also increases the will to resist, apparently what happened at the Alamo. With cannon and a good stock of ammunition, fighting from behind the thick walls of the mission, the Texans did not go quickly or easily. Santa Anna's troops took heavy casualties before they breached the walls and killed the men inside. The heroics and the villainy, according to the mythology, happened during the final hours of the defense. There are many stories about Travis, Bowie, Crockett, and the other defenders of the Alamo, but almost nothing is known about the Mexican officers under Santa Anna who led their troops forward through heavy cannon and rifle fire. There is no Mexican John Wayne, and perhaps there should not be, for Santa Anna's triumph was short-lived. While he fought at the Alamo, the Texans signed their Declaration of Independence on March 2, 1836. Santa Anna had no need to hear the news. He set out from the Alamo to meet Sam Houston and his Texans in the last great battle for the Independence of Texas.

The Mexicans moved on quickly, intent upon putting down the rest of the uprising. The Texans, led by Sam Houston, met Santa Anna at San Jacinto and shattered all illusions about him and the Mexican Army. The Mexicans suffered terrible losses. Their foolish general was captured and returned to Mexico, but the legacy of his foray into Texas followed him for the rest of his life. In Mexico he lost his magical powers. In the United States they remembered the Alamo and wrote into their Constitution that slaves could be imported into Texas.

No doubt the United States would have annexed independent Texas sooner, if not for northern opposition to the entry of another proslavery state into the Union. When the annexation finally took place, in 1845, the Mexican representative in Washington, Juan Almonte, withdrew. The United States then recalled its man from Mexico. Washington lacked only an excuse to begin the war. The Mexicans, knowing the United States had designs on much, if not all, of their country, faced a difficult decision. To secure their territory, they would have to enlist the help of a European power, and that probably meant accepting a European monarch. They chose Independence and the risk of war.

The Americans meanwhile wanted to continue to expand westward and south. Many in Congress and the Polk administration wanted all of Mexico; it was simply a part of America's "manifest destiny." The situation on the border with Mexico was made to order for the imperialist forces in Washington. The Mexicans and the United States had agreed on the Nueces River as the southern boundary of Texas. The United States then declared the true border was the Rio Grande, well south of the Nueces. To establish the claim, General Zachary Taylor moved his troops into the disputed area. President James K. Polk had put the Mexicans in the classic double bind. What was it to be: war or the negotiated loss of more territory? The decision was quick in coming. Almost on cue the Mexicans gave the Americans what they had been waiting for. In the disputed territory between the rivers, Mexican troops engaged the Americans in a brief skirmish. In his report to Washington, General Taylor confirmed sixteen American casualties. Polk had his excuse; hostilities had broken out. When the declaration of war came before Congress, the young representative from Illinois Abraham Lincoln rose to complain against the situation, even to doubt the validity of the American claim to the disputed territory. It was too late. The Americans launched a powerful three-pronged attack into Mexico.

The war turned ugly at the start. Moving south out of Texas, U.S. troops under Taylor, many of them untrained and undisciplined recruits, slaughtered Mexicans wherever they found them—soldiers and civilians, women and children. A group of Irish immigrants in the U.S. Army were so disgusted by what they saw that they deserted, formed the Brigada San Patricio (St. Patrick Brigade), and fought on the side of the Mexicans. In the course of the war, all but seventy-three were killed in battle, and they were captured and hanged by the U.S. Army. The leader of the San Patricios, John O'Reilly, was made to watch them die, then whipped, branded on the face with a *D* for "deserter," and turned out into the world.

The Americans conducted a shrewd, savage, and ultimately shameful campaign against a weak and poorly armed foe. On the east, the American Army surrounded the Mexican port of Veracruz and then began a ruthless bombardment from the sea. General Winfield Scott, the American commander, kept the civilian population, as well as the military, penned inside the city while the U.S. Navy bombarded it. Foreign consuls tried to intercede on humanitarian grounds, imploring the Americans to allow the civilians— at the very least, the women and children—to leave, but Scott refused. The bombardment went on for two days and two nights. More than six thousand shells landed in the city. The count of the dead passed a thousand, and still the shells fell. Corpses lay in the streets. Scott would accept nothing but unconditional surrender. Of the fifteen hundred dead in the city of Veracruz, only five hundred were soldiers.

As the battles raged, American military officers moving down through north central Mexico under the command of Zachary Taylor wrote home about their shame at the needless violence and killing. One of them, Ulysses S. Grant, thought Taylor's troops were cowards. George Gordon Meade had no better opinion. Like Grant, he found them uncivilized, men who murdered "for their own amusement."

After the surrender of Veracruz on the coast, Scott marched inland, following the route taken by Cortés to Mexico City, destroying the Mexican Army as he defeated it. The short, ugly war had but one glorious moment, and it did not come until the very end. At Chapultepec Castle on what was then the edge of Mexico City, the cadets from the military academy, along with a thousand Mexican troops, awaited the attack of Scott's army. No more dramatic place could have been chosen. The castle, at the top of a long hill, had all the makings of a fortress, with a clear view of the surrounding area from inside the stone walls. The Mexicans placed land mines on the sloping ground leading up to the castle. If the Americans chose to take Chapultepec, they would have to pay.

On September 13, 1847, in the early morning, the Americans roared up the hill into the mined area surrounding the castle. The Mexicans had no luck that day. The mines did not explode, and the firing from inside the castle walls did not deter the Americans. Before long, Scott's troops were at the walls, tearing them apart with crowbars and pickaxes. Once the walls were breached, the Mexicans lost heart, all but the cadets, who fought until the last. In fact or fable, and it does not much matter now what really happened, for the meaningful truth is what is imprinted on the minds of Mexicans, these Niños Héroes, these Heroic Boys, climbed onto the ramparts, wrapped themselves in the Mexican flag, and leapt to their deaths rather than surrender.

In the following year, the Mexicans signed a peace agreement dictated by the Americans. The Treaty of Guadalupe Hidalgo ceded half of Mexico to the United States, including Texas, California, Arizona, New Mexico, and part of Colorado. For the Mexicans, who thought they had to choose between war with the United States and the acceptance of a European monarch, it had become a Hobson's choice.

The war left the Mexicans, including those who wanted to emulate the constitution and the federalism of the United States, with a deep hatred of the people they now called gringos. Mexico had been defeated on the bat-tlefield and shamed at the negotiating table. Everyone looked for villains. Who had done this to them?

As the sting of shame receded and the chronic pain of diminished aspi-rations settled into the bones of the society, the historians and politicians went to work. A list of causes emerged. First came Yankee imperialism. The Mexicans knew perfectly well what the Americans meant by "manifest des-tiny"; they had been the victims of it. The monarchists blamed the Spanish crown for leaving its colony ill prepared to govern itself; they still longed for an emperor. And the Conservatives, those who favored a centralist govern-ment, had a similar longing. The Liberals, soon to produce a radical branch known as puros, blamed the Catholic Church and the tax system. Fifty years later Justo Sierra wrote that Mexicans were incapable of saving because of the confiscatory taxes paid to one governing force or the other since 1521. He also spoke with mixed feelings about the Mexican soldier, whom he found brave in battle, but vulnerable to losing heart, after which he no longer had the Mexican disregard of death but chose instead to desert.

None of this affected the indigenous people, who suffered through war or the brief calm between wars and pronunciamentos. The whites and mes-tizos despised the indios, as they called them, even though they were still the majority in Mexico. No one defended them. Fanny Calderón de la Barca, a

Scottish-American woman married to the first Spanish minister to Mexico, arrived in Mexico City in 1839. Although she and her husband did not stay long in Mexico, she adapted quickly to Mexican racism. In her collected letters she described the indigenous servants in her household as "dirty and lazy." They worked for a while, she claimed, then quit to rest (*descansar*). The word both angered and scandalized Fanny. To get what she considered a good servant, she determined to train a twelve-year-old girl, but even these efforts came to nothing. The girl, corrupted by her own family, according to Fanny, soon wanted to *descansar*.

In light of this view of indios in the Mexico of his time, the rise to power and the presidency of Benito Juárez is all the more astonishing. A Zapotec, born in Oaxaca, Juárez learned Spanish, studied law, entered politics as a Liberal, became a prosecutor and a judge. His politics wavered early in his career. He supported Santa Anna in at least one of his presidencies, but then Juárez became a pure reformer and Liberal. Benito Juárez rose to prominence just as the old war-horses of Mexico's philosophical and political conflicts were dying off. Mexico by then had become an intellectual and cultural colony of France, a characteristic that became more pronounced as the century progressed. Both Liberals and Conservatives looked to Europe for their future. Even some Liberals wanted more European immigration to change the racial balance of Mexico from an indigenous to a white and mestizo majority.

The waltz of the presidents continued. In the final days of his final presidency, Santa Anna, once a hero, a fool in memory, attended the opera, where he heard the work of two young Mexican criollos, the composer Jaime Nuño y Roca and the lyricist Francisco González Bocanegra. Operatic, somewhat divorced from the realities of Mexican history, their work became the national anthem: "Mexicans, at the cry of war/prepare your mounts and steel/and let the center of the earth tremble/at the sonorous roar of the cannon!"

In the town of Ayutla, south of Guadalajara, Santa Anna's cacophonous career finally came to an end, for a group of rational men, mostly generals, published a plan. This one succeeded. Santa Anna put up a fight, but as more and more of the country declared for the Plan of Ayutla, he realized the impossibility of his position and accepted exile. Benito Juárez, former governor of the state of Oaxaca, and Melchor Ocampo, the purest of the puros, the most liberal of the Liberals, then returned from their own exile in New

Orleans. For both men the future of Mexico and the world lay in the economic liberties of capitalism, free trade, and the rights of man. Rousseau, Locke, Adam Smith, the thinkers of the new democratic, middle-class world, had been their texts in New Orleans, and they came back to Mexico prepared to implement these ideas. Melchor Ocampo had been working on a document to reform Mexico.

13.

Centripetal Forces

... la perfidia de tu amor.
—ALBERTO DOMÍNGUEZ BONNAS

The word "perfidy" has not appeared often in English since the late nine-teenth century, but in Mexico it is as common as "corn," a frequent description of personal and political relations. "Perfidia" is a famous song, and the exploding of the figure of Judas, the epitome of perfidy, to destroy evil in the world is the comic relief between Good Friday and Easter Sunday in Mexico. In a society based in two competing but curiously similar cultures, like those of Spain and Mesoamerica, cultural perfidy is a necessary act; choices between cultural values must be made constantly. In Mexico one is always choosing between corn and wheat, mole and McDonald's, but every choice is the betrayal of its alternative, and syncretism can be seen as the betrayal of both sides.

In relations between the sexes, perfidy suffers from a complexity largely unknown in the United States. The patron saint of Mexico is a virgin of two cultures, which is the beginning of conflict, but the idea of a virgin birth in Mexico preceded the appearance of the Virgin of Guadalupe by hundreds, perhaps thousands of years. Coatlicue, the mother of Aztec gods, was impregnated by a ball of feathers. She is thus a miraculous mother, a virgin who bears many children. Given the history of virgin births on both sides of the dualistic culture of Mexico, the man who has sex with the mother of his children symbolically violates the virgin; better to have sex with another woman, because it is possible then to enjoy the act without shame. A decent man goes to his mistress or to a whore, but he does not ravish the mother of his children.

All sexual relations are therefore perfidious. To visit one's mistress is to betray one's wife, and to enjoy the mother of one's children is to betray the Holiest Virgin, not *la santa* (the holy) but *la santísima* (the most holy). The importance of virginity produces interesting solutions to the problem of sexual desire. In the indigenous culture of parts of Oaxaca, the berdache is used to satisfy young men sexually so that they do not violate the young women. The role of the berdache, the male who takes the place of a woman, is common enough that the *Show de Frances* has become one of the more popular entertainments in Mexico. Frances, who is really Francis, stars in a transvestite show that plays in the popular Teatro Blanquita in Mexico City and in every state capital and large city throughout the country.[1] Franci(e)s is very funny and very political. She describes a meeting between Fidel Castro and former Mexican President Salinas de Gotari after the revelations of Salinas's vast thefts. Castro asks Salinas what he would like to drink. Salinas answers with the name of a popular Cuban drink, "Cuba Libre" (Free Cuba). He then asks what Castro is drinking. Castro replies with the name of a popular Mexican brandy, "*Un Presidente derecho* [A straight president]."

"What is that smoke coming out of the volcano Popocatepetl?" (s)he asks. The audience waits for the punch line. "It is Salinas burning his papers." The jokes are old, Salinas has not been the president of Mexico for several years, but the audience does not mind. They have come to laugh.

Between appearances by Franci(e)s, who is a lively entertainer in the costume of a grotesque, transvestites appear solo, in pairs, or as a chorus in cheap costumes and heavy makeup. They dance, without so much as an accident of grace, and lip-synch popular songs, mainly *rancheras* and old standards. The audience for the show at the Teatro Blanquita is the surprise. At eight o'clock in the evening, families fill the huge theater, children eating popcorn or ice-cream bars, sitting between their parents, laughing at the jokes they can understand, appearing to enjoy the singing of the stars. In a society devoted on both its cultural sides to virginity, homosexual behavior cannot be kept out of daily life. Homosexuals in Mexico suffer public opprobrium, but not all homosexuals in all situations. Some homosexual acts are considered male and others homosexual; bisexuality is acceptable as normal male behavior if the man is the aggressor. There is nothing wrong with being amused by France(i)s, as long as one does not permit the entertainer to become the aggressor.

The effect of the Virgin on women is much more closely related to self-

---

[1]Prior to World War II, there were tent (*carpa*) shows in Mexico, where sexuality was treated irreverently, like everything else. The Teatro Blanquita is a remnant of the carpa shows.

sacrifice. What could be a greater sacrifice than to give up one's sexual being and the life of one's own son for the glory of God and to save mankind from sin?[2] The Marian sacrifice translates into hard work, self-abnegation, the end of pleasures except for the giving of oneself to family. Such women take pleasure in scrubbing floors for the good of their children, preferably their sons. And again, it is not as if the Marian idea of sacrifice came only from the European/Christian side; the word in Nahuatl for the common people is *macehuales*, those who deserve the sacrifice of the gods. In sexual relations, the European and the indigenous are not reversed as in mirror images; they are structurally similar, yet they are in conflict; one must continually deny the existence of the other. Given the history of the invasion, it is tempting to assume the victory of the European over the indigenous, but in the world of culture there is a struggle for power. Every choice is perfidious in love, dinner, and politics.

When Vicente Fox Quesada first considered running for president of Mexico, he counted on perfidy as the basis for his campaign. In the years before his election, the PRI had always won by splitting the opposition, and in 2000 that was also its plan. But the PRI leadership made the wrong guess about the most dangerous opponent, thinking it was the left-of-center PRD and its candidate, Cuauhtémoc Cárdenas, and relegating the PAN with Vicente Fox, its cowboy from Coca-Cola candidate, to third. Fox and his advisers knew more about perfidy than politics. Their strategy was clear even before he announced his candidacy. The PAN would ask people to choose not between parties but between their own deeply held political and moral views and their love for their country. He would set up the contest in the election so that no matter how a voter behaved, it was a perfidious act. Vote for him, and betray your party loyalties and some of your political beliefs; vote against him, and betray your country and yourself. Since most voters were not registered members of the PAN, it came down to a question of the lesser sin.

Fox introduced the question of perfidy early on. A high-ranking member of the PRI at the national level, a man being groomed for a cabinet post,

---

[2]The version of the last days of Jesus, as written by the Nahuas and translated by Louise M. Burkhart in *Holy Wednesday* (Philadelphia: University of Pennsylvania Press, 1996), reprinted in *In the Language of Kings*, gives a picture of the origins of Marianism in Mexico in the sweet pleadings of Mary to her son.

was invited to attend a weekend party given by Fox in Guanajuato.[3] A large number of people had been invited to meet the possible candidate. The PRIista decided to go. After all, he said, "One never knows." He came back after the weekend having enjoyed himself. There was nothing secret about the weekend, members of all three major parties attended, but to mention his name might not be helpful to a bureaucratic career that has been battered by every form of perfidy, including his own. "He's a cowboy," the PRIista said of Fox after the weekend, "but I like him."

When Fox ran for office, he was supported by Porfirio Muñoz Ledo, who had been a cabinet officer, UN ambassador, and party chairman while a member of the PRI and the Mexican version of the U.S. Speaker of the House as a member of the PRD. Jorge Castañeda, son of a Mexican foreign minister and a Russian mother, had been to the left of the PRI, a Communist in his youth and an activist in his opposition to the North American Free Trade Agreement while teaching at New York University, when he joined the Fox campaign. In 2002, when the Fox administration ruptured the long love affair between the Mexican government and Fidel Castro, his ambassador to Cuba was Ricardo Pascoe. Before accepting the post in Cuba, Pascoe had been one of the members of the inner circle in the Cárdenas campaign for mayor of Mexico City in 1997. Pascoe's ideas about U.S.-Mexican relations were, at that time, antithetical to those of Fox. The task of getting rid of Pascoe fell to Castañeda, the former leftist.[4]

Perfidy takes place in bed and war in Mexico, but it is not the simple perfidy of the song, one lover betraying another. The perfidy of Mexico is of the universal kind, and it is not necessarily evil; Mexican perfidy is a matter of the constant choice between irreconcilable goods, Unamuno's choice between God and reason and the desperate choice between love and happi-

---

[3]He asked that I not use his name.

[4]Problems occurred early on between Pascoe and the Fox administration. Pascoe said that as Mexico grew closer to the United States, it grew farther from its long-standing relationship with Cuba. Mauricio Toussaint, who was Castañeda's undersecretary for North American affairs, which included Cuba, made accusations of financial mismanagement by Pascoe. Pascoe responded angrily. In no time at all, the one real leftist in the Fox administration (Castañeda had by then embraced neoliberal ideas) was on his way out. One September 6, 2002, Pascoe denounced the accusations as calumny. By the end of the month he had been removed from his post and the foreign service.

ness.[5] Perfidy in Mexico is not necessarily linked to either calumny or corruption, but to the ineluctable complexity of following two similar but divergent paths at the same time.

MEXICO'S JFK

The murder of Luis Donaldo Colosio, the PRI candidate for president in 1994, is thought by many to have been a punishment for his act of perfidy. Colosio, designated for the candidacy and presumably the office by Carlos Salinas de Gotari, committed the unforgivable perfidious act: He spoke out against the sitting president, a man of his own party, the very one who had chosen him for the office. It was simply not done. After his election a president could change policies, but during the campaign he had to maintain the tight-knit relationship of the party and the government in all his public utterances. Yet Colosio chose to break the rules. He was an interesting man, one who loved classical music and thought a great deal about the question of democracy in Mexico, but that was not so unusual among the younger members of the PRI.

Colosio represented the new PRI, the younger men and women who intended to take over the apparatus slowly and carefully, getting rid of the old stalwarts, the enormously wealthy "dinosaurs," but in evolutionary fashion; they were not radicals. Salinas, whose penchant for corruption is legendary, somehow had chosen Colosio. He was young, and when he was happy, not always, he had the broad, invincible smile one associates with victorious athletes. He was, in many ways, the ideal candidate, a reformer, but not a troublemaker.

In a speech delivered on March 6, 1994, Colosio suddenly broke with the party line. He wanted a democratic society, greater social and economic equality, but most perfidious of all, he wanted to separate the party from the government. On March 23, Colosio was dead, killed after making a speech while standing only a few yards from the California border. His wife, who had been ill when Colosio agreed to run for president, died eight months later. According to the government prosecutor's office, Mario Aburto, a twenty-three-year-old man who had lived in Tijuana for eight years, was solely responsible for the assassination of the candidate.

[5]See Miguel de Unamuno, *Tragic Sense of Life* (1913).

Following the assassination, Colosio came to be seen as the Mexican version of John F. Kennedy: sophisticated, compassionate, brave, and, according to some conspiracy theorists, dangerous to those who truly held power. Some said it was Salinas who had ordered the killing. After all, the argument went, Colosio's campaign manager, Ernesto Zedillo, had failed to accompany him on only one campaign trip, the one to Tijuana. In Tamaulipas, the northeasternmost state, there were more stories. The PAN had become strong early on in Tamaulipas, as it had in many northern states; it held the mayoralty of Matamoros, and the young mayor had political aspirations beyond his hometown. If the PAN had a patriarch, it was the old man Cárdenas, no relation to the former president, who owned a huge hacienda near Ciudad Victoria. The Cárdenas family had two political sons, Gustavo and Jorge. Gustavo was the public man, Jorge the manager. In the early 1990s, when Colosio was the national head of the PRI, the state of Tamaulipas was a political nightmare. The PRI controlled the state and the country, keeping its candidates in office against the surge of the PAN. Drug cartels not only bribed public officials at almost every level, but were involved in Satanic ceremonies. People were tortured, bodies found in bizarre circumstances. The president of the largest bank in Matamoros, Graciela (Chela) Gutiérrez, who had inherited the business from her father, said, "I saw too many cars with blacked-out windows on the street in front of my house, so I moved across the border to Brownsville."

Tamaulipas was near anarchy, or worse, in the hands of the PRI and the drug cartels. Opposition candidates stole ballot boxes and carried them across the border to the United States to be counted, fearing that the PRI would falsify the count. The Cárdenas family, anxious to move into a position of power, ran afoul of the PRI. Jorge, the brother who managed campaigns, was forced to flee across the border to the United States. After more than a year in exile the family entered into a negotiation with the president of the PRI, Luis Donaldo Colosio, who personally gave Jorge Cárdenas permission to return to Mexico.

Several days before Colosio was assassinated, he stopped in Tamaulipas on his northern campaign swing. Jorge, although a staunch member of the PAN, went to the airport to thank Colosio for his help. "He was a dead man," Jorge said. "His face was gray; he knew he was going to die."

"How did you know? Did he tell you so?"

Jorge did not answer. In Mexico everyone knew.

PAN VS. PAN

A few days later Jorge and I went to a meeting of the PAN leadership at midnight near the center of Matamoros in a neighborhood of solid middle-class houses. Jorge parked his SUV with the blacked-out windows, and we went inside. The house belonged to a man who owned a money-changing operation in the center of town, near the border. Half a dozen middle-aged men had gathered in his living room, a small but comfortable place stuffed with furniture, coffee tables, end tables, ornate lamps, stuffed. Candles for the dead had been placed on the mantle. There was a table laden with food in the next room. The women stayed in that other room. All the men who sat around the coffee table were beefy, big men, norteños, and all were fair-skinned. The man who owned the house looked Irish or German; in middle age, he had the full red face of northern Spain.

The men talked about the villain, Ramón Sampayo, the *presidente municipal* (mayor) of the city. He was slick, they said. He took money from the PRI; he was a PANista whom the PRI wanted in office. Of all the men in the room, only Jorge Cárdenas had apparent reason to be angry with Sampayo. He had run against Jorge's brother for the PAN nomination for presidente municipal. And Sampayo had won, forty-seven to forty-two. As with every such defeat in Mexico, treachery was suspected.

There was more talk about Sampayo, whom Jorge had once supported. They had been friends, even after Sampayo defeated his brother for the party nomination, but Jorge said that Sampayo had used city money to give business to his asphalt and cement plants, and that had ended their friendship. The question was how to keep Sampayo from allowing the PRI to win the next election, for he had refused to endorse the PAN candidate, a dumpy little man who suspected all poor people of dishonesty. The candidate appeared briefly at the meeting, embraced everyone, mumbled his hatred of the poor, embraced everyone again, and went home. His pants were too short; his white socks puddled around his ankles.

He would be a sure winner, his supporters said, if not for Sampayo. "This Sampayo looks diabolical, with a little beard, like the devil himself. He thinks he is so handsome, a movie star."

In the morning I went to see the devil himself, Ramón Sampayo. We had agreed to meet for breakfast in his house, an American-style single-story house with a small, enclosed front yard patrolled by two large German shepherd dogs and several armed men. The guards were polite, and the dogs were obedient. The mayor was a slim, elegant man with a tiny beard and thick black hair stiffened and shined with mousse in the Hollywood style. His wife was a tiny woman, well educated, fashionable, and, as she said, "in love with politics." We immediately sat down for breakfast in the dining room of the house. Sra. Sampayo paused for a moment to repeat her statement about politics; then their three-year-old daughter, a remarkably pretty child, gave each of us a kiss on the cheek before she headed off for school.

Sampayo had been educated at ITESM (Monterrey Institute of Technology and Graduate Studies) on its central campus in Monterrey, worked in the accounting department of one of the large Monterrey multinational corporations, then had come home to Matamoros to make his fortune. It did not take long. He had learned in Monterrey that the production of basic materials is a business that cannot be ruined by competition from the United States. He chose cement and asphalt, a sound idea in a city undergoing vast increases in population and industry. Like many cities along the border and in other parts of Mexico, the assembly plants (*maquiladoras*) that sprang up largely as a result of the North American Free Trade Agreement had brought work, population, and infrastructure problems to Matamoros. The plants, many of them foreign-owned, -financed, and often -managed, imported parts or materials from the United States, then manufactured or assembled them and shipped them back across the border. The entire operation was duty-free. The maquiladora assembly plants in and around Matamoros drew people from Tamaulipas and Veracruz and points south; there was a market for materials in both the infrastructure and the construction of factories. Sampayo was, like many PANistas, the owner of a small business. And that, he said, was the answer to Mexico's economic problem.

"It is not the maquiladora," he said. "Maquiladoras can provide only twenty to thirty percent of our requirement for new jobs." Sampayo went through the other possibilities: "We cannot meet the prices in the international market. If we create a Mexican auto industry, we will never be able to compete with the United States. Textiles? The Mexicans go to the U.S., where they can buy them more cheaply. We have no heavy industry. The answer is microindustry. With one hundred twenty-five dollars a woman can open a shop to cut hair. With one hundred dollars, a man can mow lawns. To satisfy our employment needs, people will have to employ themselves, but we don't have the resources now to fund that.

"We can't borrow the money to start big businesses, and if the state starts a large business, the bureaucracy will devour it. We pump oil, but we cannot refine it, so the oil goes to the United States and comes back as gasoline. It costs more to buy gasoline here than in the United States.

"I meet young men who are hopeless, because they don't know what to do. They say such things as, 'I'm an industrial engineer, Señor Presidente, what can I do? I'm thinking of a job in a factory, but I don't want to work in a factory.' They would like to start a business, but they have no resources. The capacity to start a big company, a macro, is very small compared to a national strategy to build micros."

The city was hard pressed. It had improved somewhat during his term, but not substantially. The first of the maquiladoras to abandon Mexico for cheaper labor in another country was already in the process of leaving. The maquiladora situation was not thought to be the fault of the mayor. It would not hurt Sampayo's future, and that was important, because he had aspirations for higher office. He said he had followed what he believed to be the golden rule of politics, which was to leave office with no more money, perhaps even less, than he had on the day of his inauguration. For at least a while after his term, he said, he would have to tend to his business. And there were other problems. He had a sick child who concerned him very much. Politics might have to wait.

Sampayo's term was nearly over. His hand had been light. He worried about jobs, infrastructure, and cleanliness. He did not meddle in the great business of the city, which was the traffic in narcotics. After three years in office no one really believed he was a thief, but he had not been able to solve the problems of the city. There were too few jobs, too many narcotics traffickers, and a great many of his constituents lived in three-sided cardboard shacks and washed in filthy water.

Ramón Sampayo did not run again for public office; instead he turned his efforts toward medical and charitable institutions. The illness of his son, which he chose not to discuss, had drawn him to the work. Despite the change of emphasis in his work, he maintained his interest in politics. He believed in the evolution of the system in Mexico. "Mexico is changing," he said. "The people are maturing faster than the political parties. We will have to get used to political pluralism. A PRIista is not necessarily corrupt, a Perredista [member of the PRD] is not necessarily a guerrilla, and a PANista is not necessarily a saint." Perhaps he foresaw that Mexican political pluralism would lead to legislative deadlock. For very soon, after more than seventy years of the rule of the PRI, no one was in power.

CHURCH POLITICS

To be the president in Mexico without a solid majority enabling one to rule had been a problem from the first day of Independence. The emperor Iturbide did not last long, and then came what seems in retrospect to have been the worst of times, the Mexican-American War and Santa Anna again. When the Liberals finally got rid of Santa Anna, they put Juan Álvarez in the office of president, and he appointed a cabinet of puros, the purest of the Liberals, including Melchor Ocampo, the attorney Benito Juárez, and the economist Miguel Lerdo de Tejada, who was, in 1855, to write the most anticlerical, anticorporate law in Mexican history.

The Ley Lerdo decreed an end to corporate ownership in Mexico, including the ownership of Church property other than that actually used by the Catholic Church for religious purposes. It also forced many indigenous groups to break up their lands held in common (*ejidos*). The disentailment of Church property was intended to weaken the stranglehold of the Church and its wealthy allies, the hacendados, but it did not work that way. Lerdo, the economist, had misread the economic consequences of his law. The hacendados bought the properties the Church was forced to sell, increasing the size of their estates. The Church suffered far less than Lerdo had intended because so much of its capital had been converted into liquid assets. Since the Church functioned as Mexico's main moneylender, it could profit from financing mortgages on the property it sold.

The next Mexican president, General Ignacio Comonfort, gathered a mixed cabinet, hoping his notion of political pluralism would enable him to stabilize the country. And then Comonfort vacillated. He was either the most moderate of Mexican presidents or the Mexican Hamlet, depending on whose view of history one reads.[6] But it was during his presidency that Mexico accepted the document that moved it closer to a true democracy than it had ever been before, and perhaps since.

[6]Enrique Krauze sees him as a great moderate; Eduardo Ruiz and Justo Sierra thought him more like Hamlet. Comonfort was in a difficult situation. It was while he was provisional president that the constitution was written. He was then elected according to that same constitution. The Conservatives did not accept him or it, and he was soon out of office.

The constitution that passed into law in 1857 grew out of the ideas of Melchor Ocampo. It was he who had proposed the law barring priests from voting. But the Liberals had more on their minds than attacking the Church. The 1857 Constitution put a legal end to the caste system, declaring all persons equal before the law. It granted freedom of assembly, freedom of expression, abolished debtors' prison and the privileges of the military and the Church (fueros). Under the new constitution all persons were granted a fair trial and free representation if they so chose. Given the history of Mexico since Independence and the national disgust with Santa Anna, it is not surprising that the authors gave the legislative branch far more power than the executive. But the check on executive power would not last.

The Conservatives, backed by the Church, took power yet again, sending the elected president fleeing into exile in the United States. Juárez, the head of the Supreme Court, then declared himself president, according to the 1857 Constitution. The war between the Liberals and Conservatives, known as the War of the Reform, began. From January 1858 to January 1861 the two sides killed each other in a series of outrageous massacres. The Liberals shot captured Conservative officers; then the Conservatives under the command of General Leonardo Márquez captured Tacubaya (now a neighborhood of Mexico City), where they slaughtered Liberal officers, soldiers, even the doctors and medical students who cared for the wounded.

This time the Mexicans went to war for ideas as much as for money and power. They fought to decide two of the great issues of the time, the Ley Lerdo and the Constitution of 1857. Only twenty-five thousand people, a tiny percentage of the population, engaged in the conflict, yet the War of the Reform gave birth to the Republic. Until then Mexico had been little more than a colony adrift, with no agreement on how it would govern itself, existing somewhere between anarchy and autonomy.

The Conservatives, with the military behind them, soon took control of Mexico City. Juárez fled to Veracruz. There, in the port city, where the Liberals could still collect the customs fees to keep them more or less solvent enough to fight on, Lerdo argued that the Liberals had little to lose by proclaiming the ultimate anti-Church laws, the Veracruz decrees. It must have been difficult for Benito Juárez, who remained a Catholic, inspired by *la religión* to legalism and prayer. But Liberal anger against the Church, which had been financing the Conservatives, won out, and the government proclaimed the final separation of Church and State in Mexico: All assets of the Church, not just land, were nationalized; marriages and births had to be registered with civil authorities; religious holidays were limited; and religious processions were banned.

A DECLARATION OF DEMOCRACY

A modern Mexican state, democratic in both intent and law, had been declared, but this turn toward the contemporary world struggled to take hold in Mexico almost from the moment of its declaration. Juárez had made the declaration reluctantly, and much of the country had not accepted it. At every turn the Liberals found themselves in trouble. Neither the Church nor the rich obeyed the law; almost all capital was still held by the hacendados in the form of land or by the Church in liquid assets, mortgages, gold, and jewels. The government borrowed money and imposed taxes but could not pay its foreign debts.

As the War of the Reform progressed, the Conservative general Miguel Miramón devised a strategy to finish off the Liberals at their stronghold in the port of Veracruz. He brought ships in to blockade the port, cutting off the Liberals from outside aid. What he did not count on was U.S. involvement in Mexican affairs. Juárez had a brilliant representative in Washington, Matías Romero, who served as a go-between, linking the two governments, providing information, ideas, writing pamphlets to spur foreign investment. Whether it was Romero's work or the thought that the Liberals were less likely to ally with a European nation, or some of both, the United States intervened. To counter Miramón's move at Veracruz, Washington sent three armed ships. After that, the Conservatives fought on, but with little success. The government would soon belong to the Liberals.

On the battlefield the younger members of the Liberal Party, among them General Porfirio Díaz, took charge. And in the field of geopolitics Washington took charge. After the intervention at Veracruz, the United States would never again hesitate to involve itself in Mexico's internal affairs. It was a new aspect of an ancient pattern of force exerted on the center of Mexico from outside.

CENTRIPETAL REFORMERS

Unlike the centrifugal patterns of great European cities—Paris, London, Rome—the Mexican pattern has been centripetal. Of all the plans declared to accompany the pronunciamentos of rebels and revolutionaries during the entire history of New Spain and Mexico, not one was labeled the "Plan of Mexico City." Everything came from outside.

The pattern had been set in the fourteenth century when the Aztecs came down from the north. The Spaniards came from across the eastern sea, Independence from the sermon by Fray Servando in Nuevo León and the grito in the small town of Dolores in the bajío, Benito Juárez and Porfirio Díaz from Oaxaca, Maximilian from Europe, Emiliano Zapata from Morelos, Pancho Villa from Chihuahua, Madero from Coahuila, the Constitutionalists from the northwest, all the way up to the Zapatista movement in Chiapas, the PAN from the northern states, and Vicente Fox Quesada from Guanajuato. The major current exception, and there were many along the way, is the PRD, formed in Mexico City although led by people who came from outside, and the most prominent figure in the PRD after the final defeat of Cuauhtémoc Cárdenas in the 2000 presidential election is the mayor of Mexico City, Andrés Manuel López Obrador, who was born and raised in the state of Tabasco.

Power comes to the center in Mexico; it is not born in the center. The centralist Conservatives could hold the capital, but it did not mean they held Mexico. Juárez fled, taking the government with him, largely in his own person. Resolute, dour, legalistic, a deeply religious Catholic, he lived a federalist scenario during the war. The Conservatives were soon enough defeated, but Mexico had other problems. Some men, even those close to him, did not approve of the way Juárez governed; reelection especially did not seem democratic to them. In the presidential campaign of 1861, Lerdo de Tejada ran against Juárez, but the campaign came to an abrupt close when Lerdo died on the eve of the election. The two great intellectual voices of the Reform were silenced; Melchor Ocampo had been murdered by a defeated Conservative general and then Lerdo was suddenly dead. Juárez, elected president for the second time, would have to rely on his own determination and thinking; no one left in his coterie could influence him as Ocampo and Lerdo had, not even Lerdo's brother, Sebastián. And Juárez had a new problem, one that would plague Mexico and all of Latin America throughout the rest of that century and into the present . . . the external debt.

Mexico was not only in debt but broke. Juárez suspended payment on the debt to England, Spain, France, and the Swiss bankers. The European creditors, however, were determined to force Mexico to resume payments. In autumn of 1861, with the United States engaged in a civil war, no longer able to enforce the Monroe Doctrine, the Europeans took advantage of the situation to land a joint army on the eastern coast of Mexico.

The English had no stomach for a long war, and the Spaniards did not want to fight against the poorly armed, even poorly clothed Mexican troops; only the French wanted to go on from Veracruz. The other countries withdrew, and Napoleon III ordered his troops to move on Mexico City. The idea of a French Empire in the Americas intrigued him. Mexican Conservatives in exile in France urged him to occupy the country and set up the European monarch of their dreams. With the United States otherwise occupied, and Mexico without European allies, Napoleon poured troops and supplies into the country.

Could all Mexicans, not just the Conservatives, accept a foreign monarch? Justo Sierra described the attitude of Mexicans, even Liberals, toward France in the 1860s: ". . . they had been educated, as lawyers, engineers, or statesmen, in France or by French authors, and so were intellectually good Frenchmen. They believed in the infallibility of French thought and the immortality of French military power."[7] France was a possibility, even to some Liberals, but not to Juárez.

CINCO DE MAYO

The first great battle took place on May 5 (*cinco de mayo*), 1862, at Puebla. The French sent seven thousand well-equipped, highly trained infantrymen and artillery against a ragtag Mexican army under the command of a thirty-three-year-old veteran of the War of the Reform, Ignacio Zaragoza. The French infantry attacked with abandon, rushing the Mexicans, who had taken positions on the hills. But the Mexicans repulsed the French infantry, withstood the French artillery, and saw the "immortal" French retreat from the field. After that one great moment, however, the war went badly for the Mexicans. Zaragoza pursued the French to Orizaba, engaged them, and suffered heavy losses. He became ill and died soon afterward. Napoleon, stung by the defeat at Puebla, sent another twenty-

[7] *Political Evolution of the Mexican People*, translation by Charles Ramsdell (Austin: University of Texas Press, 1969).

five thousand troops to Mexico, and General Leonardo Márquez, the Tiger of Tacubaya, returned from exile to lead Conservative troops into battle alongside the French.

Once again, Juárez fled from city to city, carrying the government on his back and in his head. As the war went on, only the north was safe for him, and he stayed for a while on the border at Paso del Norte (now Ciudad Juárez). To the French and their Conservative allies it meant the end for the Reform Party, as the Liberals now called themselves. Juárez appeared ready to cross the border into exile. But the Mexicans had not forgotten the fifth of May at Puebla; something had happened to the spirit of the Mexican Army there; they did not surrender easily, even though they were pressed into tiny corners of the country. And contrary to the opinion of Justo Sierra, the Mexican soldier, sometimes dispirited after many defeats, did not desert. The victory at Puebla, although followed quickly by defeat, had created a sense of autonomy far greater than the Independence of 1821 or even the Constitution of 1857; the idea of independent Mexico became reality at Puebla; they had held against the "immortal" French Army. A powerful aspect of the Mexican character would manifest itself after Puebla: The Mexicans would suffer, they would die, but somehow or other, they would hold their ground (*aguantar*). It was not yet over.

"ADIÓS, MAMÁ CARLOTA," BELLS FOR THE EMPEROR

Because of the victory at Puebla, it mattered far less that a group of Conservatives, who described themselves as the most illustrious men in the country, went to Miramar Castle near Trieste to meet the young archduke von Hapsburg and give him the news: They had voted him emperor of Mexico. The Conservatives and the Church had achieved their dream. And the archduke had achieved his. From that moment until his death, he thought of *his* Mexico, *his* beloved empire. It was the beginning of a long series of illusions in the life of the archduke. In reality, the crown had not been bestowed upon him by the Mexicans at all. Napoleon III had made the decision, and he and the archduke had negotiated the terms under which it was offered. Nonetheless, in his heart and mind Maximilian von Hapsburg believed he had been chosen by the Mexican people.

He and his wife, Charlotte (Carlota), arrived in Veracruz at the end of May 1864 with two sets of dreams in their vast luggage. Carlota, the daughter of King Leopold of Belgium, coveted power, and Maximilian coveted love. The second emperor of Mexico (Iturbide had been the first), who loved *his* people from the moment they were given to him, was never to have the love of more than a few of his subjects. His reign would have little effect on the course of Mexican history, for it was brief and tragic, more in dreams than reality. He imagined himself a Mexican, he took a Mexican woman, *la india bonita*, for his mistress, and he loved the Indians. Of all the men who ruled Mexico, from the fall of Cuauhtémoc to the presidency of Lázaro Cárdenas more than four hundred years later, not one truly loved its indigenous people, except Maximilian. He made laws protecting their communal lands, and he gave land to those Indians who had none. He said the military officers, judges, and Catholic Church hierarchy were the worst of Mexico and the Indians its best.

Everything indigenous appealed to him and Carlota, who went to the Yucatán to visit the ruins there, and everything about the Church and the Conservatives disgusted him. He argued with the Pope and the papal nuncio; he sent Conservative generals into exile; he tried desperately to form some alliance with Juárez. Maximilian had long been a liberal himself, he believed in liberal ideas; it confounded him when most of the Mexican liberals found the idea of a foreign emperor or any emperor, for that matter, odious. He found no meeting ground for the two lives that were joined in him, the emperor and the man; he did not know who he was, except in illusion, the only place in which he could not hear the cacophony of his conflicted life.

Like many dreamers, he did not understand the meaning of events around him. His wife, Carlota, descended into madness. She sailed for home, and the Mexicans made up a song about her and the end of empire, "Adiós, Mamá Carlota." The song described a stupid and reactionary Maximilian expecting his defeat. In fact, it was coming. The surrender of Lee at Appomattox signaled the end of Napoleon's ambitions in the Americas and with them the demise of the emperor of Mexico. It all happened so quickly for Maximilian: The world shattered; the rules of power and lineage could not hold. He needed the troops; he needed Napoleon. The Republicans failed to understand how dearly the emperor loved them, loved *his* Mexico. Did he not oppose the Church, exile Conservatives, despise Bishop Labastida? What more did they want of him?

He was in many respects a gentle man, but not without vindictiveness, not without the ability to terrorize his beloved Mexicans. He passed a law enabling the military to kill people who belonged to armed bands—in other words, civilians. He went about his business. And Napoleon took his time. The French did not expect the Americans to begin acting on the principles of the Monroe Doctrine immediately after a long and debilitating war, but they knew it would not be long before the United States made good on its promise to oppose foreign powers in the hemisphere. Napoleon had made the decision to sacrifice Maximilian, if necessary, and withdraw his troops from Mexico rather than risk war with the Americans.

Without the French, the Conservatives fought on, but the trajectory of the war had turned. The Republican army laid siege to Maximilian's army at Querétaro. Maximilian, by then ill and alone, longing for the iron-willed advice of the mad Carlota, considered abdication but decided to hold on, to take the field and break the siege; his plans failed, and the emperor was captured. At the end, in 1867, the emperor, who so loved *his* Mexico and the descendants of the people who had been there before the invasion, faced a military tribunal. With Juárez in control, there would be no summary executions, no appearance of revenge; the process went according to law. Maximilian had a team of attorneys to defend him. The efficacy and sincerity of their defense showed in the split decision of the members of the tribunal. By a single vote a sentence of death was imposed just before midnight on June 14. The defense appealed to Juárez for clemency, but the president, who had once pardoned the Tiger of Tacubaya, would not be moved: It was not his decision; the law required the death of Maximilian.

On June 19 a Republican firing squad executed Maximilian and two Conservative generals on the Hill of the Bells. Márquez, the slaughterer at Tacubaya whom Maximillian, perhaps in a moment of ironic amusement, had once sent to Jerusalem to build a Franciscan monastery, survived and went into exile in Cuba, where he lived a long and presumably uninteresting life as a men's tailor. Carlota lived on, lost in madness. Porfirio Díaz, the brilliant young Republican general, retired for the moment to Oaxaca. Juárez, whose term as president had expired during the war against the French, remained in office, putting off elections during the emergency. He had been at war almost continually since claiming the presidency in 1858.

With Maximilian and Juárez, Mexican history lurches into the age of heroes. Until then forces beyond the control of any human being had determined the course of Mexico: the domestication of corn; the expansion of civilizations across the temperate zone; colonialism's inevitable failure. The most prominent men and women affecting Mexico in the centuries prior to the War of the Reform had been carried on the flow of the wind and water and then the history of development of the arts and sciences. The names of the rulers of Teotihuacán were not known. Lord Pacal of Palenque had come and gone, and his great city lay in ruins. The great Aztec ruler Nezahualcoyotl had left behind nothing more than a few poems, if indeed he was their author. No one signed the beauty of the ancient Maya city of Uxmal or the gleaming buildings of Tenochtitlán. No Ozymandias spoke for the Mexican past; it flowed on the cycle of time. Until Juárez.

CARLYLE'S MAN IN MEXICO

He, the Mexicans believed, had affected his time; he had changed history; the times had not changed him. Over the years he became invested with powers and virtues beyond those of any ordinary man. His stern, scarred visage looked out at the world with the certainty of a god. Tragedy and power belonged to him. Juárez lived above the world, a traveler dressed in black, riding in black carriages, with his lovely Italian wife beside him, and all Mexico following in his wake. As Maximilian thought Mexico was *his* country, so Juárez thought Mexico belonged to him. He was the father, the instrument of the law. The other fathers, the priests, could no longer appear in public in their fatherly garb; that was the law. There was but one father, Juárez.

Was Benito Juárez a true hero of the earthshaking stature described by Thomas Carlyle or, like most leaders, a man cast and carried by history? If Juárez was a hero, then the history of Mexico belongs to the *caudillos*, the strongmen, and there is little likelihood of Mexico's becoming a democratic society soon, or ever, for there is something lacking in the people, an inability to catch the currents of history, a need to be driven, to suffer the rages of lambs.

An examination of the Juárez years after the execution on the Hill of the Bells may put the question in clearer light, for it was during those years that he was free of the constraints of war and survival. The American Civil War and the response of Napoleon III no longer determined what happened in Mexico. The Reform had been accepted. Juárez had choices, and he had to make them without the powerful, all but overwhelming drive and intellect of Miguel Lerdo de Tejada or Melchor Ocampo. Romero continued to advise from Washington on foreign and financial matters, and Sebastián Lerdo de Tejada played a role in all his decisions up until the end, but the postwar years raised the great issues of race, education, finance, and democracy.

Juárez had no greater success than the improvement of education for the middle class. Under the direction of Gabino Barreda the number of students in school in Mexico quadrupled during the Juárez years, but the Zapotecan president had no interest in educating the people he referred to as "our brothers." The egalitarian notions that had fueled the early struggle for independence had no place in the Juárez regime. He was a free marketer, listening to Barreda and the other *cientificos*, sliding rapidly toward their worldview, one in which hope could not be extended to Mexico's poor and indigenous. Juárez, in reality or by the self-invention so common to the famous, was a descendant of Zapotecan royalty, different from other indios. He saw himself as a separate class, both Indian and not Indian, a man with the features of an Indian, but without the characteristics that barred them from participation in the progress of the modern world. Juárez did not suffer from the self-loathing of oppressed peoples; he abandoned egalitarianism and took up self-aggrandizement.

With the help and advice of Matías Romero, who had come home to serve as treasury secretary, the Juárez government devised a plan for the Mexican economy that may have seemed perfectly reasonable in the near term but set a pattern for economic development from which the country has yet to emerge. With Mexico in the shadow of what Romero had seen during his years in Washington as a growing behemoth in the manufacturing field, he advised Mexico to develop its mining and agricultural resources rather than attempt to meet U.S. and European manufacturers in open competition. Since the Juaristas were free marketers, the idea of shutting their doors to imports while growing their own manufacturing sector was apparently not considered an option.

On the political side of his life, Juárez may have spoken of democratic ideas, and he may even have wished to imitate the democracies of the United States and France, but he suffered the tragic flaw of men who accept their own greatness: He could not conceive of anyone other than himself who was capable of governing. He established an upper chamber of the legislature with no real purpose but to weaken the power of the lower chamber. He governed by fiat. He and his fellow Liberals had written the laws. Juárez not only administered the law, but as coauthor and executive responsible for administration he *was* the law. His own closest friends and advisers, among them Sebastián Lerdo de Tejada, opposed his apparently endless term of office and ran against him.

The newspapers, which he allowed—and the word "allowed" reflects the power he held as president—to operate freely, began to criticize him. People compared him with Julius Caesar and then praised the daring of Brutus. He became the emperor Juárez. Porfirio Díaz, the brilliant young general from Oaxaca, also ran against Juárez. Using a strategy that the PRI adopted in its last years in power, Juárez let the two opposition candidates share the vote that went against him, assuring him of a plurality. According to the Constitution of 1857, the choice then went to Congress, where a Juarista majority returned its president to another term, his fourth.

Voting, however, represented something other than modern democracy in late-nineteenth-century Mexico. The percentage of voters among the population was small. Whoever controlled the bureaucracy had a huge campaign organization at the grass roots. Government employees campaigned hard; implied threats and promises could not be ignored. Without women's suffrage, with few indigenous people voting, most of rural Mexico unconcerned, democracy was for the few, which is no democracy at all.

At least 5 percent of the entire population had been killed since the Liberals began their fight. Juárez thought he was the only one who could stabilize the country and end the nightmare. His contribution to that stability should not be underestimated, but he did not achieve a just or a democratic or an economically sound government. He reduced the external debt through extremely careful budgeting and cut the military from eighty thousand to about fourteen thousand, a vast saving. When Juárez died in office, Sebastián Lerdo assumed the presidency, but not for long. He was soon to be replaced by Porfirio Díaz, the choice of Mexico's youthful generation.

The cientificos, as the followers of Auguste Comte and his ideas of order and progress were known, had the new president's ear; during his regime they would come to dominate Mexican thinking. There would be a "scientific" view of society; "order" and "progress," the watchwords of Comte's philosophy, would become the rationale behind the next phase in the history of Mexico.[8] In style and philosophy, Mexico belonged to France more than ever. But the full impact of this new philosophy was yet to come; meanwhile, the country was still moving only slowly into the modern world. Economically, Mexico had chosen to survive through the exploitation of its seemingly limitless natural resources. The most modernizing actions at the end of the century belonged to the builders of Mexico's railroads, all of them foreigners, all of them seeking to exploit Mexico as a supplier of raw materials and a market for manufactured goods. Foreign investment was the dream of the restored Republic, an idea that proved to be both right and wrong, right about the moment, wrong about the future. Yet Juárez had gathered the country together; he had for the moment found some equilibrium of stresses. With war and will and the blind belief in himself of a man on the verge of dictatorship, he had avoided the final dissolution of the state.

---

[8] Auguste Comte (1798–1857) coined the word "sociology" and the idea he labeled "positivism." His philosophy, along with that of Herbert Spencer (1820–1903), who was a student of Comte's work, formed the basis for Latin American social and political philosophy of the late nineteenth century, most prominently in Brazil and Mexico.

Comte, an engineering student as a young man, wrote a vast six-volume study of the history of human thought, which he published in 1830. His work grew out of his study of the Enlightenment and the writings of Henri de Saint-Simon. His pessimism has been compared with that of Joseph de Maistre, whom Isaiah Berlin saw as the foundational writer of fascism. Comte's work did not have great vogue in Europe, although the English philosopher Richard Congreve subscribed to it. Comte's scientific view of language was later to become important in the philosophical school known as logical positivism.

During the last third of the nineteenth century and the first decade of the twentieth, Comte became so influential in Latin America that churches were dedicated to his philosophy, which he called the Church of Humanity. His Mexican followers were known as the cientificos for the scientific basis of positivism. Gabino Barreda, a Mexican physician, met Comte in France and returned to Mexico convinced that Comte's ideas favored education. The Mexican dictator Porfirio Díaz surrounded himself with cientificos, who provided a basis for his policies with the philosophy of Comte and Spencer.

Spencer, a believer in the evolutionary aspects of society, coined the phrase *survival of the fittest*, which provided Charles Darwin with a handy explanation of his theory of evolution. Spencer was a racist as well as a believer in the natural aspect of class. In *Progress: Its Law and Cause*, published in 1857, he compared "the evolution of child into man" with the "evolution of savage into philosopher."

Spencer said Comte's work was about "the progress of human conceptions" while his was about the "progress of things." Working back from Spencer, whose ideas were easier

His weapon in defense of the state had been law, not justice. The peasants and workers of Mexico had no unions, no effective rights, and no hope except for a rare moment of generosity by the president of the country or the patrón of the hacienda, the mine, or the factory. The Ley Lerdo had been used to break up the Indian ejidos (communal landholdings) and sell off what little they owned to wealthy hacendados. The federalist president had turned to centralism to maintain order. As he saw it, Mexico was ungovernable except by force. The country was for sale to the rest of the world on a piecemal basis, but it existed, and it was capable of continuing. Juárez, the Zapotecan Indian who did not love his own, had left it so.

----

to follow, the cientificos took up the two major ideas in Comte's philosophy that were useful to them in the making of Mexico into a modern nation, although at terrible cost to indigenous people and the urban and rural poor of Mexico.

Comte saw the human mind progressing through his famous three stages: theological, by which he meant primitive believing in many gods, when militarism predominated; metaphysical, which meant abstract thinking, a legalistic society; and finally, positive, the stage based on science, with its emphasis on manufacturing, the division of labor, the most highly technological aspect of his time.

The age of science, according to Comte, had an ascending order, according to its complexity or degree of interdependence with other sciences. He put mathematics at the base upon which the sciences were built (he was trained as a mathematician), followed by astronomy, physics, chemistry, biology, and, at the very top, sociology, the most complex of sciences, the one he invented. Like Maistre, Comte thought it quite all right to impose order on society. For Comte it was a matter of order and progress, always moving toward a more scientific understanding of humanity and from humanity outward to society and the world.

He based the need for his own philosophical system on the lack of a system that followed the French Revolution and the fall of the ancient regime. He wrote that nothing could be destroyed unless it was replaced, and he was about to replace what had gone before with his own system, his own religion of science. The fit of Comte and Spencer's ideas with Mexican history was all but perfect. It required very little effort to see the three stages in Mexico, with the positive stage only in its infancy.

Unfortunately, neither Comte nor positivism nor Spencer is defined even in the slightest way in histories of Mexico. The men and their philosophies appear as shadows, words only, making it difficult to recognize the force of them during the height of their influence and minimizing the quality of the intellectuals in Mexico during the nineteenth century.

14.

The Defeat of Auguste Comte

. . . de cuali-oquichtin ihuan de cuali netechhuiloanime.[1]
—EMILIANO ZAPATA, FIRST MANIFESTO

In the town of Anenecuilco, Morelos, where Emiliano Zapata was born, the *campesinos* still use the word "boca" (mouth) to denote a person. They do not use the word in the English way, as in "mouths to feed." In Anenecuilco "mouth" serves as a synonym for the whole person, as when the word "sails" is used to mean a ship. Unlike other metaphors, synecdoche refers to the whole, the whole ship or in this case the whole person. In Anenecuilco a boca, a mouth, is not merely what eats or speaks, appetite or words; a boca is all of a man, bone to soul.

The use of "mouth" as a synonym for "person" might have grown out of the Nahuatl language spoken in the area until fairly recently, but that would have been in the sense of "speaker," for the Nahuas were concerned, one might even say obsessed, with language. James Lockhart offers many examples of loan words crossing from one language to the other, but "boca" is not among them.

Why, then, would a man become a mouth? What has been inferred by the one who speaks of a person so? A wolf has a mouth, and a river too. The children at the dinner table are mouths to feed. "Mouth" may be a verb as well as a noun, and there are constructions, although clumsy, in which "mouth" becomes an adjective. Wolves and children and even rivers are not merely mouths. A mouth is an entrance for food and an exit for words and the water of a river. It is not possible to think of a mouth thinking; there are no original mouths; mouths do not kiss, except in France, everywhere else kissing is the business of lips; mouths are the servants of words and appetites; an autonomous mouth would lack a place of origin for its words and a repository for its swigs and chews. What every mouth needs, longs for by its very

[1] ". . . of good men and good revolutionaries."

nature, is to be put to use. In Anenecuilco a campesino speaks of a mouth as a man.

Thirty thousand people are registered in Anenecuilco now, although many of those whose names appear on the register of citizens have gone to the cities or to the United States of America. A man who has gone off to another place is not said to be a boca. Perhaps a mouth cannot go into exile; it would seem so. In the logic of language as practiced by the campesinos, those men who still cut sugarcane in Morelos, a boca is inseparable from his family and home. No boca is an orphan or an exile. Every boca has a family. In Anenecuilco the idea of a boca as an individual, separate from family and community, is laughable.

A man, a boca, may be weak, tired, hungry, cut, swollen, or otherwise wounded, but never lonely. Revolution is appropriate, but not whining, because a boca is a part of the whole and whining is a particular sound; whining suffers the loneliness of the distinctive, for no two sour notes sound the same.

A democracy of such men, who speak of themselves as mouths, has never existed. The metaphor used in Anenecuilco holds true: A body made entirely of mouths, of nothing but hungers, could not long survive. In time, as the old Greeks knew, any mass of such persons will eventually seek order, a ruler, a system, something to which they can surrender. A mouth is not a man, as the campesinos always come too late to know, which accounts, in the manner of art, for the beauty in the faces of the old men and the overwhelming thickness of their mustaches.

In the town of Anenecuilco, where the campesinos still speak of one another as mouths, on a July afternoon in the year 2000, when much of Mexico participated in an election that finally had more to do with disgust than democracy, the mouths of the village did not give much energy to thinking about the outcome of the vote. The sugar mill accepted loads of cane in the afternoon, and the sun was very hot. A great load of cane came wobbling down the street—on a cart perhaps?—led or pulled by a mouth. The mouth wore a straw hat, not so broad as a classic sombrero, but sufficient to shade his face and neck. He wore thin and ragged trousers, a tattered shirt, and carried a machete in his belt. Of his face, nothing could be noted other than the great white mustache. His feet, brown in sandals, not *huaraches* made of straw or leather, but simple things, thongs tied to pieces cut from rubber tires, showed the power and the beauty of the great toe, which propelled him, with long and measured strides, down the road. As he passed by, the load of cane, which reached to the ground on all four sides, shuddered, shifted slightly, and for a moment revealed the darker brown legs and pale hooves of an animal, a burro or an inconsequential horse.

Mouths, as might be expected, speak similarly of the world, in natural unison, which may be the reason why they fall easily into patterns of organization: family, village, clan, indigenous nation. One mouth thus speaks for the many. After the cart had passed, another campesino, a man who referred to himself as a boca, spoke of the business of the day. He had reached the age of fifty-nine, a grandfather. Zapata had been assassinated long before the mouth was born. Nonetheless, the mouth belonged to the time of Zapata, to the harsh history of revolution as José Clemente Orozco had painted it, not to the urbane sensuality and wit of Diego Rivera. His face repeated the shape of the machete or the sudden peaks of the angular mountains near the Río Yautepec. His eyes had yellowed too soon; his mouth moved but could not be seen beneath the great mustache. Time and use had torn the straw of his small sombrero and much-used huaraches. The earth of Morelos, black and clean, rimmed his fingernails.

He spoke in bursts, in the style of runners and men who pass briefly in the fields. He said: "Democracy is impossible in the villages, perhaps in all Mexico. It will never come. This is what we campesinos find instead: One thing is that they [the government] don't deliver what they promise; another thing is that we are not part of the politics, we are left on the sidelines. We have no business; we have nothing; we are just country people.

"The government sends benefits to our village, but they do not get to everyone. I think it is about discrimination, because everyone doesn't get them. Why? Because some are timid, others . . .

"Well, how good it would be if some person would come and say there was help for everyone, those who tend their animals, those who tend their fields!

"Even if they put a factory here, it would not help me, but I have children, grandchildren who would benefit. But these benefits will never reach here. Cuautla, Ciudad Ayala, Mexico, Cuernavaca, there they have good jobs, but here we do not enjoy them; we are campesinos, my friend.

"The big industries grow—and God willing, those workers earn more— but for us it is always the same: Our animals have no value; our crops are worthless.

"When I was twelve years old, my father took me out to work. How can I speak about democracy? We have no experience of it; we are ignorant, although for us it would be something very nice. We are not political. We are not literate. If we speak bluntly, perhaps they will kill us.

"If the PRI wins, if the PRD wins, even if the PAN wins, no matter who wins, it will be all right with us, because they will treat us the same, always the same. If they want to have members [in their party], they will have to look good.

"Those of us born here work for the minimum wage, forty pesos, and we travel farther and farther to the fields. But we are not going to move away, my friend, because that is the measure of a mouth." Aguantar (to stand fast, to endure) has been the campesino's way of judging himself for centuries, since the time when the land was held communally, since before the time of towns and states, when civil society and its geography were called the altepetl.

He had many children and no land, and there had been no land in his family since it was taken from them before his great-grandfather was born. He did not know when it happened. The history of the family was kept in names, not in years, and there are only a few words for ancestors in Nahuatl, *tocoltzin* for revered grandfather and *achtontli* for the one before that, the first one, the oldest one. He did not speak of recovering the land. Such thoughts belonged in the town museum beside the remains of the house of Emiliano Zapata. Mexico had been different then. The mouths were not timid; there was blood on the land.

What is called a revolution had been born in Anenecuilco or in the miners' strike at Cananea or in the work of radicals from their place of exile in St. Louis, Missouri; the world had begun to turn in many places at once in the way of most revolutions. The Mexican Revolution of 1910, the one with the date separating it from the greater or lesser turnings characterized as Independence or Reform or conquest or restoration, began in the last quarter of the nineteenth century. In Mexico, as in the rest of the world, history moves along in fits and starts, a series of dreams and dissatisfactions. If there is an end to history, it is less likely to come in some series of oppositions and syntheses than in the Aztec vision of earthquake and fire. Or perhaps the world will end with our destruction by the things we have made, our technology, as in the rips and tears of faces, the rising up of the things in the Popol Vuh of the Maya. Should the end come in Mexico, it will be known not as the end of history but in the Mesoamerican way as the end of the cycle, the last turn of history.

THE EDUCATION OF PORFIRIO DÍAZ

The Mexican Revolution, like most upheavals, perhaps all, had a lever to begin the turning. It takes a lever of Archimedean proportions to start a revolution and a civil war. They are not set in motion by chance or the movement of a butterfly or an infant's squall in some distant place. There must be a lever, a symbol, most likely a man, or an idea, or the combination of thought and man, hatred and hope; nothing less will do: not Carlyle or Tolstoy, Carlyle *and* Tolstoy, history and the man, or so the Mexican Revolution would say. And who would the hero be? Why, the villain, of course; there must be someone or some system to overturn; otherwise revolutions would have to begin out of thin air.

There were, in fact, two kinds of villain in Mexico: the dictator Porfirio Díaz, as virtually all historians agree, and in the realm of ideas, turn-of-the-century Mexico had several. One set came from Auguste Comte, who provided a rationale for the oppression of workers and peasants in the name of progress. The other came from Herbert Spencer, who invented the phrase *survival of the fittest*. And in the way of suffering, pure desperation, Porfirio Díaz and his intellectual mentors did not create the conditions, as the Marxists are wont to say, but they exacerbated them. In the last quarter of the nineteenth century and on through the first decade of the twentieth, Mexico was filled with people in debt peonage or situations even more closely linked to slavery in the *henequén* (sisal) fields of the Yucatán, the cane fields of Morelos, the ranches of Chihuahua, and the farms of the bajío. Legal slavery had been replaced by the bookkeeper and the whip. At the turn of the century the Tolstoyan view of a great wave of human feeling producing the person or people to lead them seemed unlikely. The idea of a war fought by men on their knees was enough to make a dictator laugh, let alone someone who applied the rule of the survival of the fittest to the underpaid and overworked industrial workers and half-starved campesinos. In the eyes of the world Mexico was a comic country, a burlesque of human organization.

The lever of the period known as the Mexican Revolution of 1910, Porfirio Díaz, came to power through a coup d'état. He had no plan, although he published one. He had no idea of government, although he controlled one. The Liberal general from Oaxaca had been born poor. And then, to make matters worse, his father died when Porfirio was only a boy. The widow Díaz had nothing; she left the boy at home while she went out to work at an inn. He grew up all but motherless, half wild; tamed momentarily by the Catholic Church, Porfirio considered law but could not bear the rigor. He chose war, and Benito Juárez chose him. Golden epaulets and a sword soon adorned the widow's child. He was the most mercurial follower, the most ill-mannered leader. Historian Luis González described him as a man who spit on rugs and once tried to leave a party through a mirror.

During his first four-year term he made twenty-two changes in a six-man cabinet. Seven times he changed the secretary of the treasury, and still he could not solve the financial problems of a country battered by civil wars and invasions. Mexico generated too little revenue and accumulated almost no capital. Nonetheless, Matías Romero, financial wizard as well as first Mexican ambassador to Washington, made payments on the debt to the United States and calmed Rutherford B. Hayes, the American president, who had doubts about Mexico and Díaz. When Hayes decided to recognize the Díaz government, the Mexicans were greatly relieved, and with good reason. Until then the Americans had harbored serious thoughts about annexing the remainder of Mexico.

The small successes of his first term taught the general some lessons in the form of the government he wanted to impose on Mexico. He learned to manipulate both the cacique (political boss) system and the more sophisticated men who served him. As a general he had learned that men are expendable. To change cabinet ministers and to order the execution of a disloyal cacique were not, in a soldier's mind, exceptional acts. He brought the murderous efficacy of the battlefield to civilian government with his order *Mátalos en caliente* (Kill them in the heat of the moment!). It was not the first of the many slogans to come from the general's lips. Earlier, when ambition first possessed him, he had said, in regard to the career of his former mentor Juárez that the country needed "effective suffrage and no reelection," for Juárez had been reelected so often that voting no longer had any effect in the world.

At the end of his first term, when Díaz could not legally stand for reelection, he turned the government over to Manuel González, and busied himself with more personal business. During his presidency Díaz had lost his first wife. Having mourned one wife, he did not want to suffer such a loss again. He took another path, this time marrying a younger and stronger woman, an eighteen-year-old girl from a wealthy family. She was his "Carmelita, treasure of grace and virtue." People who saw them together often asked if she was his daughter. They missed the essence of the relation-ship; Carmela was his tutor.

There was no doubt about their public roles, but in the secret places of the marriage, she remade him: She dressed him in the manners of a presi-dent and a gentleman; she honed him, as one might hone a razor or an ax. He cut his hair, trained his mustache, took to wearing fine suits, and refined his language. They traveled through the United States, but the trip did not convince him to apply its policies to Mexico.

At home, in Mexico City, with Carmelita, he moved in circles entirely new to him, among the wealthy and educated of the city, the Mexican elite that had survived the wars and changes of government almost entirely intact. The resilience of the Mexican rich, their immutable hold on power, must have impressed him. Wealth had proved more enduring than God, for the Church had suffered the Ley Lerdo, and the rich had simply added the lost wealth of the Church to their holdings. He began devising plans for the future of Mexico. If wealth endured in men and nations, the question was how to achieve such stability for Mexico. He turned to France for ideas. No other culture appealed to his new allies and friends among the rich; certainly not the original cultures of Mexico or the still-muddy boots of the democ-racy next door.

When he and the other Mexicans looked to France, they no longer saw the revolutionary ideas of Rousseau; they were not much interested in his social contract notions, nor did the Mexican elite, who lived in a country still largely populated by indigenous people, like Rousseau's idea about "the youth of the world" and "its decrepitude." They preferred a general's will to the "general will" of Rousseau. Like Juárez before him, Díaz found efficiency in centralism; centralized management was control, safety, like accumulated wealth. Even so, there had to be a method, and that was where Díaz found his way through Auguste Comte and his followers, the cientificos. Comte had never been to Mexico, but Gabino Barreda had been to France, and Díaz liked the idea he had brought back: "Liberty, order, and progress."

PORFIRIO THE POSITIVIST

In his second term Díaz looked to the younger generation of positivists for ideas, but not in awe of their erudition or family background; his Carmelita had brought him up out of awe. One of the unspoken plans for his second term was to put others in awe of him. He saw that he could use positivism to back his own ideas for governing.

Comte's philosophy determined much of the social thought of the country between 1880 and 1910. Comte has largely been set aside now, an artifact in the history of philosophy, but not in Mexico, where his sociology and the eventual reaction to it determined the course of the country. At the heart of Comte's thinking was his idea of the three stages of human development: the theological stage, dominated by militarism; the metaphysical stage, in which laws predominate; and then the positive stage, in which industry reigns.

These stages correlate, in positivist terms, with the history of Mexico: The pre-Hispanic period coincides with the theological stage. During the conquest and colonial period metaphysical thought prevailed. From the end of the Reform forward Mexico sought the positivist dream.

The cientificos read Comte "in the raw." Díaz had a less abstract way: He attacked the workers and peons and indigenous people of Mexico as incompetent. Enrique Creel, one of the cientificos, said, "100,000 Europeans were worth more than half a million Indians." Attacks like this were used to justify mistreatment of workers, virtual enslavement in some cases, as in the deportation of the Yaquis to the Yucatán, where they died in the hot, humid fields. Díaz came back to office with a two-part plan: First, improve the standing of Mexico in the eyes of the world. Only after the world understood Mexico as a country of capable governors, managers, and workers—orderly, financially stable, a place in which one's person was safe from harm by bandits—could the vital second part of the plan succeed. Díaz believed Mexico could not move into Comte's third stage unless it attracted foreign investment; for him and the cientificos, Mexico needed vast investment from outside the country to industrialize.

The Díaz plan was exactly the same as the policies announced by Mexican Foreign Minister Jorge Castañeda and President Vicente Fox in 2000, the first year of the Fox presidency. Castañeda spoke of a "politics that presents a good image abroad of Mexico." And went on to explain that Mexico, having neither economic or military power, had to use *poder suave,* (smooth, delicate, or suave power). Fox looked for foreign investment.[2] He and Cas-

---

[2]Reported in *La Jornada* and other papers, October 11, 2002. Castañeda went on to say that the image Mexico had established in the world because of the 2000 election and its commitment to solving the conflict with the Zapatistas in Chiapas over indigenous rights was very good. Then he added, as if it were a confession, that the government's image in the world was better than its image at home.

tañeda were in perfect agreement on that subject, especially when it came to the United States. But in 1995 Castañeda had seen only one investor worth courting; he described Mexico as "a country divided between those with access to the United States and those who were deprived of it."[3]

The Fox administration was not quite so successful as the Porfiriato had been in attracting foreign capital, which flowed into Mexico at an ever-increasing rate under the Díaz dictatorship. And the foreigners who invested maintained control of their investments. It was part of the bargain. The Mexicans wanted the foreign capital, both money and intellectual capital in the form of technology and management skills, and in return they gave up ownership and the driving spirit of turn-of-the-century industrialism. Encouraging foreign investment and constantly lessening the limitations on what foreigners could own and manage in Mexico had two deleterious effects—the failure of Mexico to develop an entrepreneurial mentality and the consolidation of wealth in fewer and fewer hands—as well as one very good effect, the modernization of the country.

Under Díaz Mexico vastly increased its gross national product, averaging 8 percent a year for more than thirty years, but the tripling of production had little effect on the millions of very poor, poor, and lower-middle-class Mexicans.[4] In the main, Mexico improved its gross national product through exploitation of its natural resources: silver, gold, and copper mining; forestry; cement; and farming and overfarming the arable land, which decreased steadily from harvest to harvest, each one leading to more erosion and debilitation of the nutrients in the soil. Northern Mexico exported great amounts of beef. The Creel and Terrazas families of Chihuahua exported beef to the United States in astonishing amounts. When American buyers

---

[3] *The Mexican Shock* (New York: New Press, 1995), p. 265. Castañeda described the situation as part of his plea for democracy in Mexico. He envisioned a new political party as the most likely path to democracy but thought there was also a chance that people of various parties outside the PRI might join together to defeat the single-party system.

[4] Mexicans speak of *pobreza* (poverty) and *pobreza extrema* (extreme poverty) and divide the middle class into upper, merely middle, and lower. The distinction not made in industrial countries comes between poverty and extreme poverty, the latter currently pegged at two dollars a day or less. Many Mexicans, especially indigenous people living outside urban areas, make do on less than one U.S. dollar a day. During the Porfiriato and for hundreds of years prior to the "modernization" of Mexico, many people lived in what can only be described as a noncash economy, for they survived by foraging or subsistence farming or, when they had no land, by debt peonage.

negotiated with the great ranches, which were many times the size of the King Ranch in Texas, they famously made arrogant jokes: "A hundred thousand head of cattle? What color?" Today the balance is reversed; Mexico imports beef and pork from the United States in large amounts.

Maximilian had begun to modernize Mexico City by building a road from Chapultepec Castle to the center of the city. Under Díaz, the road became the Paseo de la Reforma, lined with trees and shops, dotted with the kinds of traffic circles Napoleon had invented as points of defense, a Champs-Élysées for Mexico. During the Porfiriato, the telephone, electricity, trolleys, railroads all arrived in Mexico. The French owned most of the Bank of Mexico; the British and the Americans owned the railroads; the Guggenheim family's American Smelting and Refining and its subsidiaries owned many of the mines. Rockefeller and Hearst had vast land and oil holdings. Industry had something close to a center in the city of Monterrey. It was not far from the U.S. border; the percentage of indigenous people in its population was lower than that of almost any other Mexican city of any size, and it had a work ethic more European than Mexican. There were so many Germans in Monterrey that the Hohner Company started an accordion factory there. German brewmasters participated in the founding of Mexico's finest and still-foremost, although now largely foreign-owned, breweries. The foreigners left the corn, the cows, and the cane for the Mexican elite.

The middle class, which Justo Sierra thought would mean progress for Mexico, grew very slowly. José Yves Limantour, the son of a Frenchman who had emigrated to Mexico, took over the role of secretary of finance. With the debt to the United States paid off, he could concentrate on moving the country's treasury from debt to surplus. The Porfiriato had indeed begun to stabilize the country, but at the turn of the century it had become obvious that Díaz had made a curious trade. In return for modernization and the increasing wealth of the upper classes, he had de facto returned Mexico to colonial status. Independence existed in name only; Mexico belonged to its foreign investors, and Díaz was their majordomo.

In one of his many slogans Díaz recognized the situation: "Poor Mexico, so far from God and so close to the United States." Which is not to say that it stirred nationalist feelings in him. He governed Mexico as a ferocious viceroy might have done in earlier times. He favored educating the populace—that is, the whites and mestizos in urban areas. In the rest of Mexico he preferred an iron fist. For bandits, he offered another of his mottoes: "Caught in the act, shot on the spot." The lack of due process spread from bandits to other enemies of the state, and Porfirio Díaz was the state. Neither house of the Mexican Congress, which was made up of the weak, the retired, and the timid, had any function other than to toady to the dictator.

His cientificos were no better. They celebrated him and his every action. When he amended the constitution in 1890 to permit reelection, there was no outcry from the wise young men of Mexico. A satire on the presidency appeared in Mexican newspapers, describing a new constitution and speaking of the "Indispensable Leader." Article 1 of the satirical constitution called him the "Necessary President," and Article 2 said his term of office was to last "until God wanted him." It was a daring piece to publish, but it was simply politics, and Díaz shrugged it off.

Another of his mottoes explained his method of governing: "Little politics and much administration." By "administration" he meant dictatorship, which he played almost perfectly over many years in office, constantly balancing and rebalancing power in the central government, the provinces, and the military. He appointed Bernardo Reyes general in charge of the entire army, with the mission to modernize it, and Reyes did as he was asked, creating a powerful force in defense of the Porfiriato. And when Reyes had to use the army, he did it ruthlessly, especially against Indians and rural uprisings.

Life in Mexico under Díaz was good for the few and nightmarish for the many. Whippings were common in the Yucatán, where henequén production grew year after year as Mexico supplied most of the world with twine for its reapers and other machines. On the ranches and haciendas punishments were equally harsh. A system known as the *tienda de raya* (company store) kept the poor mired in debt. Those who worked on the haciendas were forced to buy from the store on the ranch or farm. Prices were much higher than in the villages or towns nearby, and failure to purchase sufficient goods could result in punishment, including loss of pay and sometimes the whip. The system worked perfectly: The peons never got out of debt. No matter how hard they worked or how little they ate, the system took it all back, and more.

To make life even worse for the majority of Mexicans under the Porfiriato, there were several drought years and a series of plagues of smallpox and typhoid that killed over one hundred thousand people. Yet production increased in the mines and the fields. Exports grew. Mexico was the second-largest producer of copper in the world. It exported lead, antimony, gold, and silver, as well as coffee, chicle, and dyes. Most of its export-import business then, as now, was with the United States, although it still did considerable business with England, France, and Spain.

The grand economic errors of the Porfiriato, errors that have not yet been corrected, may have caused the downfall of the Indispensable Leader. Or he may have lost his grip on the country because of an interview he gave to a reporter. There are at least nine probable causes of the Mexican Revolution of 1910. Every one is valid; none could have succeeded without most or even all of the others. No proper order of causes can be made since they affected all or some of the revolutionaries at the same time. Destiny had some role, and as death is destiny, the list should begin there.

THE INDISPENSABLE LEADER AND THE REASONS FOR HIS FALL

Age

Porfirio Díaz was born in 1830. At the time of the Revolution he had lived far beyond the life expectancy of people born in Mexico early in the nineteenth century. He had problems with his neck. Abscessed teeth took all of his attention and much of his strength in his last days in office. He was deteriorating physically, although not mentally. The whispered complaints about his age started when he turned seventy, and ten years later, at the beginning of yet another term in office, Díaz was on the verge of the ineluctable fall.

The age of the Indispensable Leader and his cabinet, which averaged nearly sixty-eight, was all the more pronounced in a very young population. In 1910, a third of all Mexicans were less than ten years old, more than half were under twenty, and less than 10 percent were over fifty.

Economics

In the last two years of the Porfiriato the Mexican economy had suddenly contracted. Silver prices had collapsed. Exports were down. The surplus in the treasury had continued to grow under Limantour's guidance, but much of it had come at the expense of government employees. Limantour had streamlined the government but also limited the flow of money into the economy. For the poor and the middle class, the effects of the contraction made life more difficult than ever. The Mexican economy rebounded in 1910, but the forces of change were already in place.

Appearances

Although Díaz had violated most of the principles he had brought with him into office, making a new alliance with the Catholic Church and seeking to centralize the government, he had not been able to exercise complete control over the provinces. A dictatorship must be centrifugal in form, and Mexico remained a centripetal country. Díaz was vulnerable at the outskirts, and he knew it. He reached here and there, sending troops, moving entire populations, punching at the problems, but he could not gather the entire country into a complete authoritarian system. He limited freedom, but he did not understand how to abolish it.

The Porfiriato, for all its social and economic flaws, had no relation to a modern totalitarian state. Díaz exerted only limited control over the press, although some of his minions would have preferred more. The great Mexican caricaturists worked all through his administration, lampooning the Porfiriato. He paid more than lip service to the liberal Constitution of 1857, holding himself and his government in check, always mindful of the appearance of Mexico in the world, always concerned about the withdrawal of foreign investment that might follow an end to constitutional guarantees, always worried about the will of the United States.

He was a strong man who came to power in a weakened country. Díaz followed the example of Benito Juárez, who refused to give up the office of president, and set an example for the oligarchic rule of the PRI. It was during his regime, however, that the middle classes of Mexico came to believe in their rights and to have a sense of their power. Díaz owned the majority of the intellectuals, he had crushed the poor and embraced the rich; the unavoidable error of his plan for Mexico was the creation of an insolent middle.

Haciendas

Much of Mexico outside the major cities remained a feudal system, grim and stable, using ancient farming methods and the harshest organizational principles. In 1893 and 1894, Díaz legislated the settling of unused lands (*terrenos baldíos*). For the six thousand hacendados who owned most of the country in estates of up to four million acres, the laws vastly increased their holdings. The amount of unused land they could take was now without limit. They were in fact required to take the adjoining empty land and put it to use. A second aspect of the laws was more insidious: It enabled the hacendados to take land from peasants who either had not staked official claim to it or had made some administrative error in the title. Thousands of people lost their land; among them were many of the holders of small parcels near the town of Anenecuilco. When combined with the rules of the Ley Lerdo against corporate ownership, which included the ejido system of communal lands as a corporate owner, the number of people whose land had been "stolen" was enormous. And to Mexicans nothing is more precious than the land, even now, when the 75:25 rural to urban ratio at the end of the Porfiriato has been reversed.

Philosophers

In France, near the end of the Porfiriato, a new philosophical view emerged that would change the way Mexican intellectuals viewed the world. It had a major influence on French thinking when it was finally published as a book in 1907 and may have led to the formation in Mexico of the Ateneo de la Juventud (Atheneum of Youth). Four of the leading thinkers of the post-Díaz era belonged to the group: José Vasconcelos, Antonio Caso, Alfonso Reyes, and Martín Luis Guzmán. When Henri Bergson published *The Creative Mind*, it was the end of positivism as far as these young men were concerned.

There were links in Bergson to the deepest Mexican beliefs; time and astronomy played important roles in his work, as they had in the development of Mesoamerican philosophies, but most important for the Mexicans, his ideas were of the spirit rather than of the material world. He was, in short, closer to religion than science, and the brief waltz with science and sociology brought about by the love affair with Comte had to end, for it was contrary to the Mexican character and tradition. Bergson's *The Two Sources of Morality and Religion* was not published until 1932, but the basis of his idea of open and closed societies was established early on in his writing. He opposed an open (creative) society to the closed society supported by Comte. Closed societies were based on intelligence, repetitive, not creative, while open societies were creative expressions of the élan vital. The young activist scholars of the Ateneo understood Mexico, both ancient and contemporary, as a highly creative society. Comte bored and irritated them. Antonio Caso argued against positivism by insisting that modern man was capable of love and altruism, emotions that Comte wanted to replace with scientific thinking. For Caso it was clear that intuition was the basis of philosophy.

The turn away from positivism affected an entire generation of future writers and educators. Bergson so influenced García Naranjo, later to become secretary of education, that he set out to educate the Indians of Mexico, a practical application of Bergsonian notions that upset the other members of the Ateneo, who thought him too political.

The connection between Bergson's writing and Mesoamerican thinking produced a new understanding of the Mesoamerican worldview. Bergson said in *The Creative Mind* that his entire philosophy was based on his understanding of time. A key sentence—". . . this duration which science eliminates, and which is so difficult to conceive and express, is what one feels and lives . . ."—comes on the third page of his review of his philosophical journey, a journey that culminates in the idea of the élan vital, the force in us and in all things, which finally means God. It is not really stretching the point to speak of the élan vital as a European version of the pantheism or earlier animism of Mesoamerican thinking.

The idea of open and closed societies, the frontal attack on positivism, the deistic notion of the élan vital are a matter of record rather than speculation; the effects on Mexican thinking at the highest level are undeniable. Moreover, Bergson promised a "creative, progressive" society in comparison to the "stable society" proposed (and instituted) by the positivists. The Bergsonian spirit had a grandeur utterly lacking in Comte. Had a philosophy been invented solely to appeal to the minds of young Mexicans, to rid the country of the intellectually and morally stifling rigidity of positivism, it would have been Bergson's. Here, at last, the Mexicans had a modern French link to their roots. Henri Bergson had given art and religion back to Mexico; it was to be beautiful again, but first it would be bloody.

Public Relations

In the March 1907 issue of *Pearson's Magazine*, James Creelman, who wrote admiringly, almost in awe of the old man who still resided in Chapultepec Castle, published the following quote as part of an interview with the Indispensable Leader:

> No matter what my friends and supporters say, I will retire when my presidential term of office ends, and I shall not serve again. I shall be eighty years old then. I have waited for the day when the people of the Republic

of Mexico should be prepared to choose and change their government at every election without danger of armed revolution and without injury to the national credit or interference with national progress. I believe that day has come. I welcome an opposition party in the Mexican Republic. If it appears, I will regard it as a blessing, not an evil. And if it can develop power, not to exploit, but to govern, I will stand by it, support it, advise it, and forget myself in the successful inauguration of complete democratic government in the country.[5]

The statement was quoted in almost every Mexican newspaper. At the time of the interview, Díaz may have meant what he said, but when the opposition formed, he did not react as if it were a blessing. Instead of supporting a move toward democracy, he tried to kill it. The Necessary President had not changed his mind; he continued to think of himself as necessary. Democracy did not interest him except as a catchphrase.

He could not, however, undo the effect of the interview, which was read by Francisco I. Madero of Coahuila, Emiliano Zapata of Morelos, Abraham González of Chihuahua, and the Flores Magón brothers of Oaxaca, among tens of thousands of others. The man who had caught the fancy of the entire world, the sloganeer, dictator, modernizer, had given hope to his enemies, a fatal error of dictators.

Liberals

Shortly after the turn of the century the Liberals, who had not disappeared from Mexico during the last years of Juárez or the first part of the Porfiriato, expressed their anger at the new relations between the government and the Catholic Church. The rumblings came from San Luis Potosí and Guadalajara and Mexico City, from engineers and jurists and three brothers from Oaxaca, who published a weekly they titled *Regeneración*. In one place the complaint was against the social character of the Porfiriato, in another they opposed positivism and the cientificos, and the three brothers, Jesús, Ricardo, and Enrique Flores Magón complained about every aspect of the regime. They complained in their newspaper and in another, *El Hijo del Ahuizote*, which had begun to publish satirical pieces about the Indispensable Leader, including the constitution that said he would remain in office "until God took him."

---

[5]The full text appears in Ralph Roeder's biography of Porfirio Díaz and in vol. 19, no. 3 (March 1908) of *Pearson's Magazine*.

The brothers allied themselves with Camilo Arriaga, who had started Liberal clubs in several cities, and the Díaz regime began arresting and imprisoning them all, although not all at once, in 1901. Three years later, having been in jail three times, the brothers left Mexico and set up shop in San Antonio, Texas, where the Mexican-American community was large and stable, still composed in part of descendants of people who had been granted U.S. citizenship under the Treaty of Guadalupe Hidalgo.

Permitting the Flores Magón brothers to leave Mexico rather than keep them in prison was one of those curious errors dictators seem destined to make. Thinking themselves safe in San Antonio, the Flores Magón brothers changed the tone of their newspaper from critical to seditious. The influence of Kropotkin and Bakunin became stronger, more apparent. They used the most inflammatory language they could muster, speaking of "slavery" in Mexico, describing Díaz as "bestial," puncturing the myths of democracy and federalism in Mexico by calling the state governors "cronies" of the president.

Like many radical documents of the time, *Regeneración* had a slightly messianic tone: "the day of liberation was coming." And the tone appealed to many Mexicans, both rich and poor. Contributions came from all over Mexico, sometimes a few pesos, sometimes substantial amounts. Among their wealthiest readers were the Madero brothers, sons of a hacendado from Coahuila, and one of the five richest men in Mexico. One of the brothers, Francisco I., who was educated in Paris and the United States, had developed an interest in the welfare of the people who worked on the family properties.

The editorial policies of *Regeneración* coincided almost exactly with the ideas that came to Madero through observation of the conditions of the poor. Like many of the wealthy hacendados in the north, he opposed the Porfiriato, the dictatorial policies, the reconnection to the Church, the centralist ideas, and the Díaz method of maintaining control through a system of loyal local political bosses. But to the Flores Magón brothers, who had connections to the International Workers of the World (IWW), Madero was still a rich man, a capitalist. He may have read their newspaper, but it did not make him trustworthy. Ricardo Flores Magón later denounced him.

Díaz, who kept track of the activities of the Liberal clubs and the Magonistas, realized his mistake in allowing them to live and sent an assassin to San Antonio to rectify his error. In the eyes of the Porfiristas, it was the proper action politically, if not morally. Fifteen years later Emilio Rabasa, an apologist for Díaz, blamed the success of the revolution on the freedom the Indispensable Leader had permitted the press. Such freedom, he wrote, "was taken for weakness and incited audacity."

The Flores Magón brothers survived the attempt but thought better of staying so close to Mexico and moved north to St. Louis. The tone of their work heated up, and before long they were in jail again, this time for being in violation of U.S. neutrality laws, but the charge did not stick. In 1906 they published a Liberal Plan for Mexico. There was to be an end to child labor and economic injustices. The plan opposed the death penalty, demanded the return of ejido lands, but perhaps most astonishingly proposed an eight-hour day and a six-day week, with wages paid in money instead of company scrip. In his plan, Ricardo Flores Magón emphasized education, asking that more public schools be opened, religious schools be closed, and children be required to attend school until they were fourteen years old. There was to be no religious instruction in public or private schools.

Many of the ideas in the Liberal Plan found their way into the Mexican Constitution of 1917, often said to be the first socialist constitution, but of itself the plan did not bring about either the industrial workers' movement or the Revolution. In 1918, while living in the United States, Ricardo Flores Magón published a manifesto directed to anarchists the world over, and it cost him his freedom and perhaps his life. He was arrested and sent to prison in Washington (state). When his health failed, he was moved to the federal prison at Leavenworth, Kansas, where he died four years later, with sixteen years left to serve on his sentence. He was not yet fifty years old.

Tomochic

In 1892 a young lieutenant born in Querétaro and educated at the Colegio Militar, was sent to the state of Chihuahua to put down an uprising in a village of two hundred people. His battalion completed the assignment, but the experience so moved the young lieutenant that he wrote about it first in *El Demócrata*, a liberal newspaper, and then later expanded it into a novel, which he titled *Tomochic*. The publication of the book cost him his commission in the army. After the second edition was published in 1895, he was sent to prison.

The lieutenant, Heriberto Frías, survived his prison term and had a long and active life as a journalist, novelist, and diplomat in a postrevolutionary Mexican administration. The book for which he is known, *Tomochic*, was not a best seller, but it kept the story of the battles at Tomóchi (the Indian name of the town) alive. Practically everyone in the state of Chihuahua knew about the uprising and the courage of the townspeople in the face of the overwhelming military superiority of the Mexican Ninth Battalion. Along with the Frías novel, a *corrido* (an anonymous popular story song), a form of communication no political administration could impede, told the story of Tomóchi.

Most histories of the Porfiriato, including those written by Mexicans, do not pay much attention to the battles at Tomóchi. Only Friedrich Katz[6] finds a starting place in the struggles of the tiny town, for it was from there that the idea of revolution spread to San Andrés, Chihuahua, and at San Andrés a few men joined Pancho Villa and Pancho Villa fought alongside Pascual Orozco, who had been accused of reading the work of Ricardo Flores Magón. No revolution has one place, one moment when it is born, but there are birthplaces. One of these was in Tomóchi.

The impetus for the uprising was the sudden imposition of a new mayor by one of the Indispensable Leader's state-level bosses. The new mayor grazed his sheep on other people's land and threatened conscription into the regular army for anyone who left the town because of the untenable conditions he had brought about. When the people complained, he asked the government to reroute shipments of precious metal on their way to Chihuahua City to avoid Tomóchi, implying that the residents would hijack the silver. The Raramurí inhabitants of the town would not bear the insult to their character. They showed their displeasure, and the mayor called for federal troops.

The troops arrived, a few shots were fired, and the townsmen fled to the mountains. The mayor, the governor, and the head of the small detachment of soldiers all claimed victory. But the villagers went off to see Teresa Urrea, an eighteen-year-old curandera, who lived at Cabora. The fame of the girl had spread as far north as Las Cruces, New Mexico, where a story about her appeared in the local newspaper. People spoke of her as Santa Teresa de Cabora.

On the way to see her the villagers were pursued by federal troops, fought

[6]Renowned historian, head of the University of Chicago Mexican studies department. His huge biography of Pancho Villa, in which he tells the story of the battles at Tomóchi, is without peer, as is his book about German involvement in Mexico, *The Secret War in Mexico*. The Villa biography was published by the Stanford University Press in 1998 and immediately became the definitive work, much like John Womack's biography of Zapata.

and defeated one detachment, avoided another, and finally arrived at Cabora. But Santa Teresa was not there. On their way home, the men of Tomóchi agreed to put their faith in their own leader, who now raised the stakes, saying the townspeople were no longer beholden to anyone but God. They prepared for the inevitable assault of the *federales*.

After two defeats the governor did not want to take any chances. He asked that an entire battalion of federal troops be sent to put down the rebellion in Tomóchi. The townsmen destroyed the battalion, humiliating the army, the governor, and the president of Mexico. In the humiliation, Díaz saw something more, the possibility of a statewide, perhaps even a national movement. He sent a personal friend, General Felipe Cruz, to solve the problem. On the way to Tomóchi, Cruz started drinking. As his cavalry troop climbed up through the fields and along the mountain trails, Cruz continued drinking. When he finally saw the townsmen assembled before him, he led his troop in a powerful cavalry charge. Cruz slashed left and right with his sword, but it was not heads that fell. In his drunken stupor, he had mistaken a cornfield for the Indians of Tomóchi.

Next, the government sent General José María Rangel, who was rumored to have over a thousand troops with him. Another contingent, all of them veterans of the wars against the Yaquis, was sent from Sonora. The federales advanced on the town, and the skittish army full of stories about the powers of the villagers' protectress, the Saint of Cabora, met the most astonishing sight: thirty women, all dressed in black, marching forward, closing on the federal lines. When they came within the range of their hidden Winchesters, the townsmen threw off their women's clothes, aimed the rifles, and poured .30-30 bullets into the federal troops.

After the bizarre beginning of the battle, the federal officers had great difficulty maintaining order among their troops. The men of Tomóchi almost routed them again. But it was not to be. For ten days the federal army assaulted the town.[7] They had lost over two hundred killed and wounded, when on October 29, 1892, General Rangel offered to spare the lives of the women and children and the few men remaining in the village. The villagers rejected the offer. Rangel, appalled by the destruction, knowing the number of his own casualties and able to imagine what had gone on inside the town,

[7]Historian Jean Meyer puts the number of federal troops at fifteen hundred in *La Revolución Mexicana* (España: Colmex, 1973).

offered again to spare his enemies; this time he said the men would be allowed to escape to the mountains if they would lay down their arms.

The few remaining men had very little ammunition; there was no food, the women and children were suffering; still they refused. When the last of the rebels' ammunition was spent, Rangel and his troops moved in. Seven men were left alive in the village. Rangel saw to it that each man had a cigarette before he was executed.

In his book, Farías wrote an often quoted description of the battles: "... every rebel was worth ten federal soldiers." It was the last thing the Indispensable Leader wanted to hear about Tomóchi. The idea spread throughout the Mexican north: The government was not invincible. The other summation of the fight, however, came from the man who commanded all federal forces in the state, General Rosendo Márquez: "Tomóchi is horrible beyond belief." It could as well be said about the civil war that was to come.

Modernization

During the Porfiriato, Mexico ventured into the industrial world, following the positivist model. The period is generally characterized as the "modernization" of Mexico, although the gap between rich and poor bore more resemblance to a feudal society. Nonetheless, change took place. Mexico may not have been truly modernized; it had been colonized in the modern style, through its economy. Even so, for many Mexicans dreams became expectations. And the expectations became realities: Railroad routes increased from six hundred kilometers to twenty-five thousand. The textile industry grew from 8,000 to 80,000 workers. At the time of the last election of the Indispensable Leader, in 1910, the census counted 15,160,369 people, of whom perhaps 800,000 were industrial workers. Ramón Eduardo Ruiz, a leftist labor historian, suggests that 16 percent of these were children, and his numbers are generally reliable.

Wages were poor, and buying power was falling. Average daily wages[8] ranged from fifteen to eighteen cents for agricultural and most industrial workers, with the industrial workers at the high end. The exception came in the mining industry, which paid thirty-five cents a day. Pay for public employment had fallen precipitously in the preceding years as Limantour

[8]University of California at Los Angeles Chicano studies department statistical data bank.

tried to maintain the budget surplus. There had been an international economic contraction, and Mexico felt it deeply everywhere, especially in the mining industry. And there had been a drought, which severely limited the amount of cotton produced in Mexico, forcing Mexican mills to buy raw cotton on the open market, raising their costs, which were passed on to the average Mexican, whose wages did not rise at the rate of inflation.

Strikes

Almost a third of the land in Mexico was owned by foreigners. Investors outside the country owned 90 percent of the value of its industries. The French owned the textile industry; the Americans owned the mining industry; the railroads were owned and managed by foreign companies. The small but growing oil industry was owned by the British and the Americans. In all these enterprises, the foreign owners had put their own people in management and technical positions.

In return for his openness to their investment, foreign governments heaped medals upon Díaz. In addition to Mexican awards and those from the Catholic Church and Spain, he had received awards from Switzerland, Norway, Portugal, Venezuela, France, Japan, Italy, Belgium, Prussia, Hungary, Austria, Persia, Great Britain, Netherlands, China, and Russia. He was procapital, antisocialist, antiCommunist, and he both feared and despised organized labor, which he said would make it impossible to operate industries in Mexico.

While he held office, there were at least 250 strikes or demonstrations by workers. Most were attempts at improving working conditions and pay for industrial workers, but some were nationalistic: Mexican workers did not want the best jobs, the least dangerous jobs, to be held by foreigners. Limantour, the secretary of the treasury, had tried to solve part of the problem by buying back the railroads from foreign investors, but even the Mexican-owned railroads were run by foreign managers and technicians.

The middle class, which had ambitions, saw the wealth of its country taken by foreign investors, and the little that was left shifted, without great subtlety, to the owners of the large haciendas. Mexican Independence had produced instead a state owned and run by foreign capitalists. Díaz had only his vast network of caciques (political bosses) and the professionalized army to maintain his position. The peasants were unorganized; the middle class was angry but tentative; only the industrial workers were a problem.

Cananea

On the first day of June 1906, at the American-owned Cananea copper mine near the U.S. border, fourteen men elected by the miners to represent their demands went to the commissary expecting to negotiate with the local mayor and mine officials. The miners demanded a higher starting wage, shorter hours, better working conditions, all standard union demands, but they also insisted that 75 percent of the work force in the company must be Mexican and that Mexicans and foreigners receive the same pay for the same work. They were the highest-paid industrial workers in Mexico at the time, but they were quick to say, "Mexico is a mother to foreigners and a step-mother to Mexicans."

The union representatives went optimistically to the meeting. They had two thousand workers in their camp and good connections to the towns-people of Cananea. A company lawyer heard their demands, which were made solemnly in the language of workingmen. The men were well acquainted with the Partido Liberal Mexicano (PLM), which Ricardo Flo-res Magón had founded, but it was not a PLM strike. It was nationalist, patriotic, Mexican, local. No political theorists confronted the lawyer and the mayor and the manager of the mine; fourteen miners made their case. At the end of the presentation of the miners' demands, the attorney for the mineowners laughed. The mayor and the company men threatened reprisals. The Indispensable Leader had branded union members Communists, a danger to the country; there was no question of support from Mexico City for antiunion activities. The owners and the authorities could fire the workers, imprison them, have them conscripted into the army, or worse. And they told them so.

The miners knew these were not idle threats. The history of the Porfiriato in Sonora was known to everyone in the room: The Yaqui revolt had ended in death, deportation, and emigration to the north. But the threats and derision did not cow the miners; they planned a demonstration in the town.

On the other side, William C. Greene, an American who managed the mine, made his case to the mayor of Cananea, who telegraphed the governor of Sonora, asking for help. The town, which lay only a short distance south of the U.S. border at Agua Prieta/Douglas, was isolated by the Cananea mountains. Thousands of people lived in an overgrown miners' camp, outfitted with banks and seed stores, dry goods companies, grocers, a lumberyard, and, looming over all, the towers of the smelter, fouling the air of the high desert. Cananea had grown suddenly to become one of the largest towns in the state, and it depended on the mine and the mine alone.

Early in the afternoon, having paraded through the streets of the town, two thousand strikers headed toward the mine, where they hoped the remaining five thousand workers would come out and join them. They arrived first at the lumberyard, where two Americans, the Metcalf brothers, stood on the balcony and poured a powerful stream of water down on them from a pump hose. The strikers responded with stones. As the strikers broke through the gates of the lumberyard, the Metcalf brothers put down the hose and began shooting hollow-nosed bullets into the crowd below. The battle of stone throwers and shooters lasted only briefly, because the hot shell casings ignited some dry sawdust, and the fire spread quickly to the wood in the lumberyard. The Metcalf brothers killed ten strikers before they died in the fire.

With the Mexican Army far away and local police unable to contain the eruption, the governor of Sonora made one of the great mistakes of the Porfiriato. He appealed to the American consul in Cananea to ask the U.S. military to cross the border into Mexico to quell the riot. The next day 275 U.S. Rangers arrived. There were more demonstrations; strikers were thrown into jail. The mining company sent its own "sheriffs," a huge contingent of armed men, to join the U.S. troops. When the Mexican Army arrived, the officer in charge demanded that the U.S. troops retire.[9]

On the next day the Americans left, and the Mexican Army finished the work. The strike was over. A few buildings, most notably the lumberyard, had been destroyed; nineteen Mexicans and four Americans were dead, and twenty-two were injured. The leaders of the strike were sentenced to fifteen years in prison.

Although the Cananea strike failed and the next great strike, a few months later, against the French owners of the Río Blanco textile mills near Orizaba,

---

[9]Michael C. Meyer and William L. Sherman, in their history of Mexico, say that Lieutenant Colonel Kosterlitzky, in charge of the Mexican Army contingent, hanged large numbers of strikers from trees outside the town. They offer as a source Cornelius C. Smith, *Emilio Kosterlitzky: Eagle of Sonora and the Southwest Border* (Glendale, Calif.: Arthur H. Clark, 1970). Mr. Smith's information is unique.

Veracruz, had even worse results, the memory of the strikes survived. The labor issues and even the killings at Cananea fell into the background. American troops had crossed the border into Mexico. They had done it almost surreptitiously, arriving in small groups, and leaving in the same manner, but the style made no difference in the minds of Mexicans. The Indispensable Leader's man, the governor of a Mexican state, had not only permitted American troops into the country, he had invited them in to protect U.S. interests from Mexican workers who wanted nothing more than a living wage and the economic and social dignity of equality with foreigners.

Five years passed, and there was no revolution, no general strike, and no improvement in the lives of the vast numbers of the rural and industrial poor. It had been a hundred years since Hidalgo uttered his grito in 1810, almost four hundred years since the destruction of Tenochtitlán. Mexico had lost half the territory once claimed by Spain; it had become a victim, an exploited nation led by an old, old man wreathed with garlands, draped with medals. The country much of the world saw as a comedy had evolved into a secret tragedy.

The city that had been Tenochtitlán gleamed with fine buildings, coddled poets, admired novelists, adored historians, and venerated liars in service of an Indispensable Leader. In the opera house the great voices of Europe sang, and in the parlors and salons and ballrooms the rich danced and chatted lightly in French and English as well as Spanish, but never, never in the languages to which the country had been born. The secret of perpetual motion had been discovered in Mexico: the admixture of elegant laughter and unseen labor. As all the rich men and beautiful women knew, the distance between laughter and labor was a gift of God, and it would last as long as there was white skin and green eyes to tame the savage population.

No one looked north to Chihuahua and Coahuila; they were too far away, the provinces. No one even looked nearby, south and west, not far beyond the gentle town of Cuernavaca, just over the sharp and green peaks of the mountains of Tepoztlán, among the cane fields, in the town of Anenecuilco, to a young man who "wore good clothes—a fine broad hat and spats" and agreed to negotiate the land claims of his neighbors. Emiliano Zapata, not yet thirty years old, had been elected by them, sugarcane farmers, laborers now, although they had once owned a little land, some for corn, some for squash, some for beans (the Three Saints), as well as cane. These men, according to one witness, Doña Luz Jiménez, who saw them later in her own village, were "dressed in white—white shirts, white pants, and they all wore sandals [huaraches]. All these men spoke Nahuatl."[10]

They did not know politics; few of them could read. They labored. There were among them hawk-nosed men with great hands and small dark men, with black and burning eyes. One such man owned a house, trained horses, fought bulls, wore charro suits on festive days, cultivated his mustache, and could read. Emiliano Zapata was like them and not like them: He was not poor; he inspired memories of esteem; he did not understand the concept of futility.

[10]See León-Portilla and Shorris, *In the Language of Kings*, for Fernando Horcasitas's translation.

15.

Revolutionary Dreams

*"You say the government will help us, teacher? Do you know the gov-
ernment?"*

I told them I did.

*"We know it too. It just happens. But we don't know anything about
the government's mother."*

*I told them it was their country. They shook their heads saying no.
And they laughed. It was the only time I saw the people of Luvina
laugh. They grinned with their toothless mouths and told me no, that
the government didn't have a mother.*

—JUAN RULFO

. . . only for a little while here on earth . . .

—"CANTARES MEXICANOS"

There was no Mexican Revolution in 1910. It was a dream, and the dreamers are many; I am among them. One of the first was Martín Luis
Guzmán, and then there was Juan Rulfo and after him Carlos Fuentes, and
between them and after them, hundreds. It has been the dream of millions,
always with pretensions to reality, even connections to reality, but nonetheless
a dream. It was a Revolution written, painted, sculpted, filmed, but not real,
not yet. Hundreds of thousands, perhaps a million, or even more died for art.

Of the many artists who created the Revolution, there was one who lived
in the mountains between Canutillo and Hidalgo del Parral. I saw him there,
many years ago, when I was learning the life of Pancho Villa, preparing to
write a novel, before I had begun to dream him. A more detailed account of
Villa's life appears later, but this is how I first found him and came to understand something about the role of the Revolution of 1910 in the mind of
Mexico. I had been traveling the course of Villa's life, from the tiny town
close to where he was born to the jail at San Juan del Río, where he had been
imprisoned as a young man, to the battlefields of Torreón, Celaya, Zacatecas, and the cities and small towns of Chihuahua and Sonora.

These were familiar towns; I had known them since I was a child, when the old man of Agua Prieta introduced me to history written with the scars of Villista bullets. At the end Villa had come north over the Sierra Madre, bringing his troops through ice and desert, promising them an easy victory, a new beginning for the Division of the North. The division had been at its most powerful only a few months earlier. He had taken it to the city of Celaya to meet Álvaro Obregón in the field, and it had been a slaughter, for Obregón had learned the methods of modern war. He had German officers, machine guns. His troops dug trenches and strung barbed wire, and when the Villistas came running forward, with the cavalry at full gallop, they met the lines of the trenches, the barbed wire, and the bayonets were thrust into the bellies of the horses, disemboweling them in a vast ocean of gore, leaving them to die among the men, and the men to die among the horses. This was war as the Villistas had never seen it, never heard it, with the heavy machine-gun fire tearing through everything, worse than the cannon. Villa lost much of his army in the first battle there, and then he attacked again, exactly as he had the first time, intent upon delivering his *golpe terrifico*, his terrible blow, his overwhelming blow, and instead, after the terrible defeats at Celaya he never recovered.

Everything had happened at Agua Prieta as the old man described it. At the end of Villa's war he made one more attempt, and he did not know, could not have known, that the American president Woodrow Wilson had changed his mind about Villa or that Agua Prieta no longer had a garrison of twelve hundred. There were almost ten times that many, and they had heavy artillery and machine guns, and electricity from the generators in Douglas, Arizona. On Wilson's orders the U.S. government had allowed troops from the faction opposed to Villa to move by train out of Coahuila across Texas, New Mexico, and Arizona to reinforce the small garrison at Agua Prieta.

It was as the old man of Agua Prieta had said: When Villa launched a night attack on Agua Prieta, charging from the south, across the high desert plain, he expected no more than token opposition. Suddenly searchlights illuminated the Villistas, blinded them, pinned them in the glare. Then the machine-gun fire came out of the light. They died; they bled; the bullets broke their bones and tore their flesh. They did not know where to turn, where to fire. Villa, still believing in his strong ties to the United States, had ordered his troops not to shoot in the direction of the United States. He did not want to antagonize Wilson. But Wilson had betrayed him. He had seen to it that Villa would never again fight a major battle. After Agua Prieta, after the searchlights went dark, only a nightmare remained, the vague shapes and terrible cries of the dying Villistas begging for water.

As is the case in dreams, Villa's Revolution ended in the night. He made the brief convulsions of guerrilla war after Agua Prieta, but never again anything grand, with trains rumbling and cannon roaring. There was the bitterness of guerrilla war, and then he laid down his arms and accepted a reward for the end of dreaming, a great hacienda at Canutillo on the plain between the states of Durango and Chihuahua. He was soon dead, and the hacienda died with him. Only the walls of the great house and parts of the stables remained, some dried wood mostly eaten by desert insects, crumbling adobe, and everywhere the dust of the dry season, as it had been in Agua Prieta during the failed rains and the winds of winter. A small church, something like a shrine, still stood. I went to the hacienda alone; there were no other visitors. It was far from any town, and the last part of the road was not good. Scavengers had picked the grounds clean of iron, glass, leather, anything of value. They had taken everything but the dust and the wooden shells the insects left.

Villa had not died at the hacienda, among his books and maps and rows of farm machinery. He had gone to the mining town of Hidalgo del Parral—he kept a woman there—where the assassins waited for him. Half a century later old men and old women sat on small chairs on Gabino Barreda Street beside the great tree and discussed the details of Villa's death. "The car went this way," an old man said. And an old woman answered, "No, it went here. It crashed into the tree." And another old man said, "He was shot with a thirty-thirty. Would you like to buy a thirty-thirty?"

"Is it the rifle that shot Villa?"

"Of course."

In Chihuahua, the capital city of the state, where there is a tomb dedicated to Villa, one of his former wives, Luz Corral, lived comfortably in her old age in the Villa house on Tenth Street. She had turned the house into a museum, complete with the Dodge touring car in which Villa had been riding when he was assassinated. In display cases around the car, she kept knives and pistols and belt buckles and boots and hats that had belonged to Villa, earning her living by the relentless sale of her treasures. Everything was for sale, even the car and all its bullet holes, said to be the third such wounded touring car she had exhibited as the death car, the first two having been sold to collectors. The supply of knives had no end. New pistols, although old, replaced the pistols taken home by tourists. *Bilimbiques*, as the bills issued by Villa were called, had no value, had only briefly been valued equal to the great numbers printed on them, until Luz Corral put them in the display case beside the dagger Villa carried when he was murdered, next to the knife he used at Celaya, beside the knife he kept under his pillow before the Battle of Zacatecas, near the knife he used in his meat market in Chihuahua. There were so many knives, so many bills, and she swore they all had belonged to Pancho Villa as she swore he had had no legal wife but Luz Corral; all the others were fakes and frauds. Only she was not a dream. So she said, all the width and the weight of her, all the harsh white hair no longer perfectly in place, as it had been in the photographs, when it seemed to have been sculpted, parted ferociously down the middle; now it was like unruly threads of steel.

I sought him out, the man and the Revolution as they had really been. Eventually I came to the tiny village of Los Charcos (The Puddles). It lay north of the hacienda and east of the road between Canutillo and Hidalgo del Parral: fifteen houses, perhaps twenty, scattered across the puddled plain. Pigs walked in the mud. A chicken appeared here and there, in the dry places. There were no fields beyond the houses. The mountains rose suddenly on every side. The Curandero de Pancho Villa lived in Los Charcos, and he was said to know everything about Villa, all the secrets of the man and the Revolution. I went to see him.

He lived in a house behind a low wall that enclosed what appeared from a distance to be a small patio. When I arrived at the gate, I saw that it was not a patio but a pen built to hold the small black and white pigs common to that part of Mexico. The curandero (healer, shaman) came to the door of his house to inspect his visitor. He was sixty years old, perhaps more. We looked at each other for a moment, one man imagining the intentions of the other. He wore a sleeveless undershirt, his cheeks bristled with the white stubble of days, perhaps a week, and his left eye was partially covered by a thick cataract, a strange and somehow magnetic thing, the color of a chicken's beak.

We spoke about Pancho Villa, the Revolution. He said he could arrange for me to converse with the spirit of Pancho Villa. And then he begged my pardon, stroking his cheek with the flattened fingers of one hand and with the other pointing to a razor that lay on the narrow bed in the front room of his house. He had been ill, he said. "Physician, heal thyself," I thought to say, but kept silent.

A woman entered, slim and pretty, a third his age, even less. He introduced her as his wife. Perhaps she was as old as he, perhaps I was in a magical place; were it not for the scurrying and grunting pigs just outside the door, it might have been so. The curandero put on a shirt and invited me into a small room at the back of the main room of the house. The room was windowless, and the ceiling was very low, not five feet from the ground. We walked bent over at the waist and neck.

He turned on the electric light and directed me to one of the two chairs in the room. Both chairs were straight-backed, made of wood, mine next to the door, his against the far wall, facing me. My chair was unadorned; his had a gray cloth skirt that reached to the floor on all four sides. On the plastered green-painted wall beside him, in a niche, he had placed a photograph of Pancho Villa on a rearing horse. Siete Leguas, I thought, Villa's favorite, the horse the mariachis sang about. The tune came to mind.

> *Siete Leguas, el caballo*
> *que Villa más estimó*

Behind me, on a shelf near the ceiling, Villa looked down on us from another photograph. The Virgin of Guadalupe was also there, beneficence and roses among the photographs of the general of the División del Norte.

The curandero fixed me with his yellowed eye, the thickness of the cataract, the bright color, attractive, like plumage or the cobra's eye. I watched his eye; I studied the image of Villa. He spoke of the Revolution of General Francisco Villa. As I thought I knew the facts, if there had been facts, his history was faultless. He spoke of details, the first fight at San Andrés, the Yaquis in their striped overalls bayoneting Villa's horses at Celaya, the character and courage of Felipe Ángeles, the brutality of Rodolfo Fierro.

He said, "The spirit of Francisco Villa appears in the form of a black bird. You can ask questions of his spirit."

In the grasp of the curandero, caught by the cataract, astonished by the accuracy of his history, concentrating on every word, not wanting to misunderstand, although he spoke clearly and in simple sentences, I did not see the spirit of Francisco Villa appear. But there it was, in the corner of the room, a black rooster with a brilliant red comb. How could it have appeared?

There were no windows. I sat beside the only door. The room was empty but for the curandero and me.

"The spirit of General Villa would like a gift of six hundred pesos," the curandero said.

"That's a great deal of money."

We negotiated for a moment. I was again fixed by the cataract, caught by the yellow thickness of it. And when I looked around again, the black bird was gone. Fool, I thought, for a few hundred pesos you lost the spirit of Pancho Villa. You have no imagination; you do not understand dreaming. All is lost. In sadness, I sat across from the curandero, no longer fixed on the cataract. At that moment something even more extraordinary happened. The gray cloth skirt around his chair began to move. This was no mirage, I thought. There was movement. Then the chicken stuck its head out from under the cloth. The curandero pulled on a string and the chicken was yanked back under the chair. But it was too late. The spirit of Pancho Villa had proved to be a chicken on a string, thrust into the room while I stared at the cataract, pulled back under the chair when I failed to put up the money.

The curandero and I laughed, and I gave him some money and went on to Parral to look at the place where someone had opened a grave and stolen the head of the general of the Division of the North. There was a rumor in Parral that up in the mountains, through a narrow canyon, in a cave on the side of a cliff, lived a curandero who spoke daily with Villa, a true curandero, not a roadside magician. Could I speak Purépecha? Then a translator was required. For only a few hundred pesos a day . . .

I did not then know that it was a dream, that it had always been a dream: Villa, Zapata, the Revolution. If not a dream, a song; if it had not been a dream, why were they singing? In what other country did people still sing the details of their revolution three-quarters of a century after the last shot was fired? As a child, a quarter of a century after the signing of the Constitution of 1917, I had heard the music and the singing: "Adelita," "Siete Leguas," "La Rielera," "Carabina .30-30," "Marcha de Zacatecas," songs to Villa, Zapata, to horses and camp followers, bloody songs, love songs, songs of victory and vengeance, but mainly songs of longing. Please let the Revolution be real, the songs said, for if it was real, there will be food on the table. Instead, it was a song, a painted revolution, books of dreaming. The reinvention of the past is an old business in Mexico. Tlacaelel, the gray eminence behind the Aztec throne, had ordered the history of the Mexica rewritten. In the *Chilam Balam of Tizimin,* which Munro Edmonson titled *The Ancient Future of the Itzá,* the Maya rewrote history as they saw fit. In Mexico the telling makes it so. It is not a matter of propaganda, as it might be in a European country; in Mexico the rewriting of history is a matter of faith. The logic of this faith has yet to be refuted: If there is no Rain God (Chaak, Tlaloc), why does it rain? Does the rain not come from the sky? If there was no revolution, why is it remembered? Nothing that is can come from nothing. If there was no revolution, who died?

Of course, there was a revolution—for a moment in the 1930s, during the Cárdenas presidency—but it was only a moment; by 1940 the dream had vanished again, nothing had changed, there was no revolution.

The dream of revolution, like the basic building block of Mesoamerica—time—is a road in multiple directions.[1] There was the dream of political democracy and the dream of social reform, of anarchism, land reform, labor reform, and none of the dreams survived the daylight, for each of the many figures who passed through the dreams brought a different expectation of what was to be found upon awakening. Many figures moved among dreams as well as within them. They rearranged their faces to match the direction of the road, the sequence of time and, even so, found themselves dead at some early place along the road. But almost every one of those who died in dreams remained as the ghost of what might have been. And over time all the ghosts became beautiful.

It is difficult to see the dream figures clearly now. In thinking about them,

---

[1]The Maya wrote: "Time is a road in five directions." The translation is by Munro Edmonson with the assistance of Eleuterio Po'ot Yah. The directions are the four cardinal points and the center. The notion of time and space as one is peculiar to the Maya, although people interested in Einstein's approach to relativity will have their own views on the subject.

The Maya understood time in two forms, which might be stated as Time and time, the latter occurring within the former. An analogy could be made to Heidegger's idea of being within Being.

In the Maya conception of the universe, time existed, and all else appeared within time. In the concrete form of Maya expression, the notion was laid out in a metaphor: When time began, there were already footsteps in the sand. Nothing so occupied the Mesoamericans as questions of time. Everything in Mesoamerican philosophy can be related to the question of time, from millenarianism to human sacrifice to politics and war.

one cannot help but be struck by the idea that gods originate in dreams. They take on dream names: Villa became the Centaur of the North, Zapata the Attila of the South, Madero the Apostle of Democracy. Who can sort dreams from reality? Who can discern the motives of ghosts? The historian's problem is doubly complicated in Mexico, because the dreams are so powerful. The revisions began with the first utterances, the first deaths, the first betrayal. Letters signed by one hand have two voices. And then there were the survivors, the eyewitnesses who saw different dreams of the same moment and later revised their dreams.

In all the stories, biographies, and histories of the Mexican Revolution, there is but little mention of ideas, although the time was rich in theories, to set beside the dreams. It is as if the revolt came out of the air or, worse, was an animal reaction: starved farmworkers; brutalized factory workers rising up in rage, snarling as they killed their torturers. American movies took away Zapata's ability to read, made the teetotaler Pancho Villa into a carousing drunkard. It is another kind of dream, the history of the ignoble savage.

The fall of Porfirio Díaz had many causes, human destiny undoubtedly first among them. No one in Mexico thought Díaz would live forever. The end was approaching; the interview he gave to James Creelman made it clear. But the end was certain only for the Indispensable Leader himself, not for the vast machinery he had put in place to support his administration. He controlled the Congress, the courts, the statehouses, the local governments, and all foreign businesses in Mexico were obligated to him and his system, save one. The representative of the most powerful foreign interest, U.S. Ambassador Henry Lane Wilson, had no interest in Mexico other than to pursue what he thought were the interests of American business, and he would pursue that policy even if it meant the dissolution of a Mexican government. When the Indispensable Leader became interested in European investors and trading partners, the Americans stopped supporting him; they were willing to let him fall. And should it have been thought necessary by the U.S. government, there would have been a great invasion, like the Mexican-American War, like the landing of the Spaniards under Cortés. Plans were made in Washington.

In the final years of the Porfiriato, Mexican insurgents had no external support and no internal organization capable of overthrowing an entrenched government. Positivism, as adapted by the Porfiriato, had served a powerful segment of the population, and the world outside the country credited Díaz with what historians still refer to as the modernization.

To make a revolution, one must have something in mind, an alternative structure, even if the alternative is anarchy, in which there is no state at all. In Mexico, the philosophers, those peculiar dreamers, lost faith in positivism. Another wave of thought had been set loose in the world, in a strangely non-Western way in the United States and in several forms in France: spiritualism. It had begun in the United States with "mediums" who spoke with the dead, made tables rise, observed a curious cloud they called ectoplasm, and generally worked slightly beyond the edge of reason. In France, the idea had come from Maine de Biran in the early nineteenth century and was then elaborated by Félix Ravaisson-Mollien, who began to separate the material world from the vital world or spirit, which we discover in ourselves. Although the idea common in much of Mexico was not so sophisticated as Henri Bergson's élan vital, it bore more than a little relation to it.

For the adventurous but not necessarily scholarly mind at the end of the nineteenth century spiritualism was the new, the future. Spiritualism could be taken up in several forms, ranging from the séances of the American Allan Kardec's more than slightly irrational views to Bergson's more seriously formulated vision, with its debt to Kant. Moreover, those who were interested in either or both kinds of spiritualism found more to think about in Hindu philosophy. Many people who considered themselves avant-garde thinkers were able to connect all three versions of spiritualism into a worldview contrary to the harsh intellectualism of Comte. And nowhere did it take greater hold of the minds of the young thinkers than in Mexico.

While Flores Magón and his followers were forming Liberal clubs based partly on the ideas of Kropotkin and Bakunin, a middle-class opposition to positivism grew from an even more fundamental change in their worldview. At one end of the Mexican enchantment with spiritualism the young men of the Ateneo de la Juventud thought about Bergson, and at the other Francisco Madero,[2] and the future generals from the northwest, Álvaro Obregón and Plutarco Elías Calles and the Benavides brothers, thought about Kardec. There was yet another group in Mexico interested in spiritualism: Robert

[2]In *Mexico: Biography of Power* (New York: HarperCollins, 1997), Enrique Krauze wrote at length about Madero's spiritualism, but his attention is rare among historians; for most, Madero's philosophical interests were simply a curiosity, an explanation for weakness.

Owen's socialist colony in Topolobampo on the Sea of Cortez. Owen himself was a spiritualist, indicating the possibility of some philosophical connection between anarcho-syndicalism (Flores Magón) and Madero's less radical followers. It was 1910, a hundred years after the grito in Dolores, the Indispensable Leader had organized a great celebration in Mexico City, unions had gained strength, political clubs had sprouted wherever the middle class gathered: Mexico had put aside the hard face of positivism to examine its soul. The forces were all in place, the bloody wars that would over the decades become the dreamed Revolution of 1910 were about to begin.

If there had been a true revolution in Mexico, the events would appear in chronological order, with most pointing toward the overthrow of the sitting government and the institution of a new government, according to the tenets of the revolution. Since Mexico had not a true revolution, but a series of civil wars, in which the forces divided again and again and turned against each other, it will be of use to the reader to have a clear, if simplified, view of the order of events. There were many defections, betrayals, and political events other than those below, but these should be sufficient to overcome the disorienting aspect of the maelstrom.

A BRIEF CHRONOLOGY OF THE YEARS 1900–1920

1900 – Flores Magón brothers found *Regeneración*, Liberal Party
1906 – Strike at Cananea mines
       Francisco I. Madero attends 1st National Congress of Spiritists
1907 – Río Blanco textile workers' strike
1908 – Madero publishes *The Presidential Succession of 1910*
1910 – Díaz elected to eighth term
       Madero publishes Plan de San Luis Potosí
       Aquiles Serdán, antireelectionist, killed in Puebla
       Madero enters Mexico from United States on November 20 to overthrow
          Díaz
1911 – Troops under Villa and Orozco take Ciudad Juárez on May 10
       Díaz resigns May 25, appoints Francisco León de la Barra interim president
       General Victoriano Huerta sent to Morelos to "control" Zapata
       Madero wins election, takes office November 6
       Zapata publishes Plan de Ayala, including intention to overthrow Madero
1912 – Orozco rebels, publishes radical plan, allies with Liberal Party and former
          cientificos

Huerta leads federal troops against Orozco

Villa accused, convicted by Huerta military court

Villa escapes from prison December 25, flees to United States

1913 – Casa de Obrero initiates strikes in Mexico City

Generals Félix Díaz, Bernardo Reyes, Manuel Mondragón attack national palace, but are repulsed, Reyes killed

Ten Tragic Days of street fighting in capital

Madero gives command of Mexican Army to Huerta

U.S. Ambassador Henry Lane Wilson and Huerta conspire to overthrow Madero

Huerta puts Madero under house arrest, assumes presidency on February 19

Madero and Vice President José María Pino Suárez executed secretly by Huerta forces on the night of February 22

Abraham González, governor of Chihuahua, Madero supporter, murdered

Pascual Orozco joins Huerta

Venustiano Carranza of Coahuila leads revolt against Huerta

Plutarco Elías Calles, Álvaro Obregón join Carranza

Villa returns to join in revolt against Huerta

Carranza names himself First Chief, leads forces under Constitutionalist banner

Villa defeats Huerta forces in state of Chihuahua, becomes provisional governor December 8

1914 – Villa forms División del Norte

Felipe Ángeles, Madero loyalist, joins Villa, bringing his formal military training to División del Norte

U.S. Navy attacks, occupies port city of Veracruz, April 21, strangling Mexican government supply lines, revenues

Carranza condemns occupation, Villa is silent

Villa defeats federal troops in major battle at Torreón

United States turns against Villa, blocks supply lines from north

Villa and Zapata break with Carranza

Huerta resigns, July 15

Carranza installs his government in Mexico City August 20, but moves to Veracruz in November after U.S. troops leave

Convention of all major factions (Villista, Carrancista, Zapatista) in Aguascalientes begins October 10

Convention names General Eulalio Gutiérrez provisional president, but Carranza has not resigned

Conventionists (Villistas and Zapatistas) enter Mexico City December 6

Workers from Casa del Obrero Mundial join Constitutionalists (Obregón and Carranza)

1915 – Obregón defeats Villa twice in major Celaya battles
    Membership in Casa del Obrero Mundial passes 150,000
    U.S. President Wilson backs Carranza, Constitutionalists
    Villista attack fails at Agua Prieta, signaling end of Villa as important
       military force
1916 – Guerrilla actions by Villa and Zapata
    Constitutional Convention begins November 21
1917 – Constitution signed January 31
    Carranza smashes Casa del Obrero Mundial (anarcho-syndicalist union)
    Carranza becomes president under Constitution of 1917 April 26
1919 – Zapata murdered April 10
    Obregón publishes manifesto attacking Carranza, announces presidential
       campaign June 1
    Felipe Ángeles executed despite worldwide protest, November 26
1920 – Plan de Agua Prieta, Calles leads rebellion April 23
    Carranza flees capital, killed by forces loyal to Obregón and Calles, May 21
    Obregón assumes presidency, December 1

Villa retires to hacienda at Canutillo and is assassinated on July 20, 1923.

16.

The Spirit of Madero

Mucho trabajo,
poco dinero,
no hay frijoles;
Viva Madero!
—POPULAR RHYME

Francisco I. Madero's political thinking was minimal, at best; the excitement in his mental world, the subject of his contemplative moments, was spiritualism. The reigning characteristic of Mexican thinking did not vary during the Mexican Revolution of 1910; religion in one form or another, including the negation of religion, dominated the mind of the country. Díaz had brought the country closer to the Catholic Church, but anticlerical feeling was still very strong, especially in the northwest. And Madero had no quarrel with the religion. He had been educated by Jesuits and the University of California and was steeped in spiritualism and East Indian philosophy. He is known as the Apostle of Democracy, but his view of the world was religious, and his democratic notions were not as strong as those of the 1857 Constitution. He had few ideas about what we would now call social justice. It was for him more akin to charity, which was in his case a religious rather than political concept.

The Mexicans who were concerned with social change, from Ricardo Flores Magón to Emiliano Zapata to the trade unionists, eventually split with Madero over his unwillingness to pursue land and labor reform and to replace the political infrastructure of the Porfiriato with his own people. On the other side, the old Porfiristas wanted him out of the way so they could pursue their own policies as before. His allies were in dreams; they came to him in the night to tell him what to do. He wrote under pseudonyms drawn from the Bhagavad Gita, Arjuna and later Bhima, and it is unlikely that he knew exactly who they were, other than warriors. Or perhaps he knew them far better than it now appears, and he moved from the name of Arjuna, the

227

questioning warrior, to Bhima, the cruel, relentless brother, when the wars began in 1910. No explanation for the change was found in his papers.

Perhaps the idea for the change was sent to him by his dead brother, with whom he said he communed, or the new pseudonym came to him while reading. In the material world the Apostle of Democracy was much more single-minded; he seemed to know only that reelection was not a democratic idea, and not much about democracy beyond that. Madero adopted the slogan Díaz had used in his campaign against Juárez: "Effective suffrage and no reelection." Although he published an extremely popular book on that point in 1908, he did not call for revolution; his goal was a free election without the possibility of reelection, an end to the dictatorship of Díaz, who had come to power through an electoral process. After publishing the book, Madero toured the country, gathering huge crowds in some of the larger cities, always sponsored by the antireelectionist clubs, which had by then split from the more radical Liberal clubs. Madero was a strange mix of empathies: He cared for the poor when he was close to them. He took in orphans, saw to it that working conditions were acceptable on the vast agricultural, mining, and manufacturing holdings of the Madero family. But he could not or would not extend his concerns beyond the immediate world of the family enterprises. He was an Apostle of Democracy but not of social justice; he was not in any way a revolutionary; there was nothing about revolution in spiritualist thinking, which was much more concerned with the inner person, the spirit.

Díaz finally lost patience with Madero's popularity as an antireelectionist and had him arrested in Monterrey, Nuevo León. When Madero was transferred to San Luis Potosí, his family's wealth and influence enabled him to go free on bail. He rode around town for a while, then escaped across the border to the United States, where he wrote his Plan of San Luis, calling for the overthrow of Díaz. The plan contained a reference in Article 3 to righting the wrongs of the Law of Vacant Lands, under which many Indians had been deprived of their property. But it also said, "In every case the agreements contracted for by the Porfirista Administration with foreign governments and corporations will be respected." It set the date of the Revolution as November 20, 1910, at six in the evening and named the author, then thirty-seven years old, provisional president of the United States of Mexico.

When Madero made his triumphal revolutionary reentry into Mexico on November 20, there was no one on the Mexican side to meet him. He retired to New Orleans, where he read, wrote letters, and rarely failed to take his daily exercise. He was interested in health, practiced homeopathic medicine, and kept his small body (he was not quite five feet tall) in excellent physical condition. Meanwhile, the Indispensable Leader had been elected to the presidency for yet another term.

Madero was certain that Díaz was incapable of governing. He had interviewed him early in the year and found the president a doddering old man; if the antireelectionists could get a revolution started, the Porfiriato would not be able to withstand their assault. Three months after the abortive uprising, he entered Mexico again, this time with more than a hundred men. To begin the Revolution, perhaps simply to demonstrate his own commitment, he planned and led an attack on Casas Grandes, where he suffered an arm wound and the loss of several men. Although the Casas Grandes fiasco demonstrated his lack of ability as a military commander, he was the last man to retreat, and he quickly gained a reputation for courage, something unexpected in a political leader who regularly communed with the dead.

Antireelectionist forces had already risen in more than half of the states, and even had their first martyred hero, Aquiles Serdán. When federal forces attacked the Serdán family house in Santa Clara, Puebla, the antireelectionist family, fully armed, had fought back, firing down on their attackers from positions on the roof. Under a thunderous fusillade from police and federal troops, all but one of the few remaining members of the family surrendered. As the attackers entered the house, Aquiles hid behind a false door in a first-floor bedroom, where he stayed for fifteen hours until he thought the soldiers and police had gone. But when he came out, pistol in hand, he was met by a policeman. "I am Aquiles Serdán!" he shouted. As he raised his pistol to fire, the policeman killed him and gave the antireelectionists an example of courage and devotion to their cause.

The next major step toward the end of the Porfiriato came early in May 1911. The Díaz regime had been crumbling under the pressure of rebel uprisings all over Mexico, and Díaz wanted to negotiate an end to the troubles. He even proposed returning lands to indigenous peoples. It was a sign that he had come to the end. He was old and weary, and his teeth hurt. The revolutionaries made demands. Díaz gave in to them here and there, but he did not offer to resign, at least not immediately. Perhaps later, perhaps at some time in the future when he could be sure of the kind of government that would replace him. . . . He wanted an end to rebellion, a return to order; then he would consider resigning.

The first of Madero's mistakes in the role of commander in chief came at Ciudad Juárez. His two revolutionary leaders had assembled their troops for an attack on the city across the river from El Paso, Texas. On May 8, General Pascual Orozco and his second-in-command, Colonel Francisco (Pancho) Villa, attacked the city. The federal garrison commander was General Juan J. Navarro, who had established a reputation for cruelty when he ordered the execution of rebel prisoners in the state of Guerrero. But it was his action at Cerro Prieto, Chihuahua, that the rebels carried into battle with them. After defeating Orozco there, Navarro ordered his troops to use bayonets to execute all captured revolutionaries. It was as much to avenge their murdered comrades as to support Madero that the fifteen hundred revolutionary troops came to the border town. Although Madero wanted to give more time to Díaz to surrender the city and make a gracious exit from the presidency, Orozco and Villa knew what their troops wanted: The rebels taunted the federal soldiers into breaking a cease-fire. Shots were exchanged; men were killed and wounded. Finally, Madero had to give the order to attack the city.

As the rebels moved into the streets of Ciudad Juárez, they found that federal gun positions controlled virtually every street. If they moved up the street, the federal troops killed them almost at will. What Navarro had not counted on was the ability of guerrilla fighters to improvise. Instead of moving through the streets, they went from house to house, literally passing through the walls. They used dynamite or crowbars to tear holes in the adobe wall of one house, then moved on into the next house and the next, without exposing themselves to federal fire.

The revolutionaries fought an utterly unorthodox war. After a firefight they rested and ate and drank before returning to battle, while the thousand Mexican Army troops stayed at their posts, cut off from all sources of water. The May sun brought the daytime temperature in the high desert to a hundred degrees. After two days of heavy fighting, the federal soldiers collapsed. Navarro surrendered his troops and arms to Madero. Orozco and Villa, recalling Navarro's shooting of prisoners, asked Madero to execute the general. When Madero refused, they demanded it. Again Madero refused. In the next moment they considered taking Madero prisoner, perhaps killing him. Orozco put a gun to Madero's chest, but another man in the office pointed a gun at Orozco.

With the two guns producing a standoff, Madero walked past his victorious officers, a tiny man in impeccable riding attire, passing between two men each more than a foot taller than their leader, and out onto the street, where he climbed up on a railroad car and delivered an impassioned speech. The assembled soldiers cheered him and the Revolution. Villa is said to have been so moved by the "tiny man with a great soul" that he wept and begged his forgiveness. In the early summer heat, speaking in his thin voice, shouting to be heard, Madero had won the day from two revolutionaries still fresh from battle, Orozco, the tall, thin, almost gaunt Protestant cowboy and Villa, a ruddy, curly-haired man who had a reputation for banditry and womanizing.

It could have been the end of Madero, perhaps the saving moment for the Porfiriato. Nothing Madero had done since the taking of the city pleased his revolutionary generals. Yet after he had saved the day with a speech, he irritated them again. He took Navarro in his own car, drove him to the Río Bravo, and allowed him to cross the river to freedom on the other side. A few days later the incident did not seem to matter, for the Indispensable Leader, his will to fight sapped by age and abscess, signed the Treaty of Juárez, naming Foreign Secretary Francisco León de la Barra, a fat-faced dandy with ties to the National Catholic Party, interim president. The Porfiriato came to its end before the last day of May 1911.

The Mexican Revolution, if it was a revolution, went on until the signing of the Constitution of 1917, and it smoldered for years after that. The course of it can be seen in the events of its first major battle: The Apostle of Democracy had no politics beyond his understanding of electoral politics. The cientificos had been undermined philsophically by the spiritualists, both philosophical and popular. But a government could be constructed using policies drawn from positivism, while spiritualism served only as a negation of positivist ideas, not an alternative.

Liberal clubs, inspired by the radical Flores Magón, did not merge with the Antireelectionist clubs and the unions to form a single, coherent movement. All sides favored democracy, but after democracy, what? And what was democracy anyway? Mexico had many philosophers in 1911; the sophistication of its small middle and upper middle classes was astonishing. Its wealthy had the most luxuriant beards, the grandest medals decorating the most beautiful uniforms. There was hardly anyone among these classes who did not speak fine French and useful English, as well as Spanish, and everyone knew Latin and perhaps a little Greek. But there was no one powerful, unifying idea to carry the Revolution beyond the end of the Porfiriato. The middle class had one idea, the unionists another, the anarcho-syndicalists another, the land reformers another, and the vague democrats yet another. The old dictator, who did perhaps love Mexico in his perverse way, had raised the question in the last days of his rule: What would follow him? He asked for some proof that there would continue to be order. Democracy, Madero said, and there was a democratic moment, an election freer than Mexico had ever enjoyed or would enjoy until the next century, but that was all.

Before the end of May, Madero dismissed his revolutionary troops, preferring the federal army to the army that had put him in power. He paid off the soldiers and rewarded Orozco and Villa as if they had been mercenaries. Orozco went back to his family ranch, and Villa used his money to open a meat-packing business in Chihuahua City. Venustiano Carranza, a hacendado and former Díaz senator, was appointed secretary of war. Trouble was brewing with Zapata in Morelos. General Bernardo Reyes, who had been exiled to Europe by the Porfiriato for his anticientifico tendencies, had returned and was not happy with the new government; neither was Porfirio's nephew Félix. Tensions had been increasing between the United States and the Díaz administration, but they were minor compared to the anti-American positions the Madero interests had taken as they pursued their various businesses.

In Mexico City, U.S. Ambassador Henry Lane Wilson was extremely unhappy about the events in Ciudad Juárez. He wrote in his memoirs of his distaste for Madero and the "elements" that had forced Madero to attack the city. Madero was not fond of Ambassador Wilson either. By 1913 he had dispatched his man in Washington to ask for the replacement of the ambassador. At first, according to some accounts, the Taft administration, anxious to be rid of Díaz, had favored Madero, aiding him in subtle ways, even allowing munitions for Madero's forces to pass across the border. But Taft did not recall Ambassador Wilson, nor did he rein him in as Wilson worked to undermine Madero's presidency. Madero's troubles began before he took office. The interim president of Mexico (May 25–November 6, 1911) between the resignation of Díaz and the election of Madero, Francisco León de la Barra, who liked to call himself the "White President," set out to undermine Madero, managing to open a rift between the government and Zapata by sending General Victoriano Huerta to Morelos, where he brutalized the peasants. De la Barra hated Zapata, who was soon to be described by the presidential-military power bloc as the Attila of the South. After Madero was elected and took office in November 1911, there were uprisings by General Bernardo Reyes and later by Porfirio's nephew Félix Díaz. The army put down the rebellions, and Madero sent both men to prison. He could have executed them but chose instead to let them live. Their ingratitude would cost him dearly. The problems with Zapata grew worse. Huerta was finally removed from command of the federal troops in Morelos and replaced by Felipe Ángeles, a French-educated artillery officer, who had been in command of the cadets at the Chapultepec Military School. Beginning then, and continuing over the decade, Ángeles proved to be one of the most decent and competent men in Mexico. He betrayed no one, never dodged his duty, moved slowly across the political spectrum to socialism. Like many Mexicans on all sides during the chaotic years, Pancho Villa, whom he served as chief artillery officer, revered him.

Madero had been greeted as a savior and a conqueror of the dictatorship, a philosopher-revolutionary who would institute agrarian reforms, push the remaining cientificos out of office, and bring democracy and social justice to Mexico. Even before he took office, he began to lose control. He appointed cientificos to the cabinet he would install and left Huerta in charge of the army. There was no land reform. Worse, Madero's plans to sell government-owned land put it in the hands of rich hacendados and American speculators. His failure to carry out that part of his platform led to an open break with Zapata. In often quoted statements, Zapata characterized Madero as having lost most of the people who supported him in the beginning, and then he explained why: "He is the most fickle, vacillating man I have ever known." Zapata promised to attack Mexico City, pull Madero out of Chapultepec Castle (the Mexican White House), and hang him from one of the tallest trees in the park.

With Otilio Montaño, a schoolteacher, Zapata produced the Plan of Ayala, which was published on December 15, 1911. The beginning of the plan accused Madero of traitorous behavior, the murder of peasants, ineptness in office, reproducing the dictatorship of the Porfiriato, and so on. The first part of the document concluded with the announcement that he would be overthrown. As with all such documents, it was intemperate and often wrong about its enemy. Madero was described as failing to obey the law when one of his worst flaws was to follow the law out the window. The idea that Madero was a traitor is absurd. On the other hand, he did maintain Porfiristas in office, there were some ugly manipulations of capital that may have benefited the Madero family, and there was no movement toward resolving the land problems of the campesinos in a country where few things mattered more to the largely rural population.

The Plan of Ayala dealt with the land issues very forthrightly in its items six, seven, and eight, giving back the "fields, timberlands, and water" to their rightful owners in item six. In the next item it blamed the poverty of the "great majority" on the powerful few and ruled that a third of all of the great landholdings of the rich would be expropriated and given back to the people. Item eight called for the nationalization of the goods of the "landlords, cientificos, or bosses" and the distribution of the goods to pay for pensions for widows and orphans of revolutionaries. Zapata's plan called for Pascual Orozco to assume the presidency and, that failing, for the task to fall to Zapata himself.

The political alliance between Orozco and Zapata contained the seeds of a powerful radical coalition because Orozco had been a member of the Liberal Party before Madero appointed him general of the revolutionary forces. Ciudad Juárez had been a point of contention between Madero and Orozco, and Madero's disbanding of the revolutionary forces, maintenance of the Porfirista official structure, and failure to carry out land reform had further alienated him. While all of these radical ideas played in Orozco's mind, he appears to have carried on secret negotiations with the Terrazas/Creel family, the largest landholders in Mexico and the very heart of the cientifico world.

What had begun as an alliance against the dictatorial government of Porfirio Díaz began to take a peculiar form. The revolutionaries of all classes and origins (indigenous to criollo) were people of two cultures, able to hold separate and conflicting ideas within them, as they held conflicting cultures inside a single mind. They wavered, staggering from one pole to the other, souls and shadow souls, conquerors and conquered, an admixture but not a blend. Madero loved the poor but could not bring himself to give back their land; Zapata allied himself with peasants and dressed as a hacendado; Villa proposed to be a capitalist and a revolutionary, an entrepreneur and a radical. The deceptions, betrayals, and calumnies came with power and the lack of power; only two major figures, other than his own brothers, remained loyal to Madero: Pancho Villa and Felipe Ángeles. Pascual Orozco's father had gone so far as to offer Villa a huge sum of money to join the uprising against Madero only to have Villa reject the offer, declare his loyalty to the president, and promise to fight on the side of the government. Madero, utterly unable to read the signs of the political world or to judge the motives of the men around him, put his faith in his brother and Victoriano Huerta, his general, the one he believed could hold the army together, put down every rebellion, and give Madero the time he needed to change Mexico, if indeed he truly wanted change.

He sent Huerta to fight Zapata in the south. And when Orozco pronounced against Madero in Chihuahua, the president sent Huerta to bring down the tall, stringy cowboy. Orozco's plan was perhaps the most radical document of the period, following Flores Magón's Liberal Party platform, and even going beyond it. He sought minimum wages, unions, shorter working days, distribution of the land, a free press. How he convinced the great Chihuahua landholding families Terrazas and Creel to finance an uprising based on that document will remain one of the most extraordinary secrets of the decade. Could he have promised to convey the country to the cientificos after he had conquered it? Or did Terrazas and his son-in-law Creel hate Madero so passionately that they were willing to risk an Orozco victory?

From his chair in Chapultepec Palace Madero saw the military-political problem with Orozco in Chihuahua. He knew the history of the federal General Felix Díaz's rebellion in the north, and for once he acted with great shrewdness. Díaz had failed because he had not allied his federal troops with local forces. The federals appeared as interlopers, invaders rather than representatives of the government. Madero did not make the same mistake. When Pancho Villa offered to put himself and his troops under the command of federal officers in the fight against Orozco, Madero quickly and gratefully accepted. Villa had already been a major factor in a federal victory over the Orozquistas at Parral. With him and his cowboys and miners at the side of the federal troops, the countryside would open up to them.

Unfortunately for Villa, he was to told to report to General Victoriano Huerta, a man he despised. Villa knew how Huerta had treated the peasants in Morelos. The brutality angered him, but he was more concerned with Huerta's past. The general had been one of Porfirio Díaz's favorites. It made no sense to Villa for Madero to have such a man at the head of a federal army. He neither trusted nor liked nor respected his new commander. For his part, Huerta did not care for informal armies or local heroes, especially those who were very effective in combat. Although his war against Orozco went better with Villa at his side, he hated both the man and the idea of him. Huerta first treated Villa with flattery, raising him to the rank of honorary general and providing him with a general's uniform. To Huerta it was a joke, a perfectly Mexican irony. Soon the joke was not enough to satisfy Huerta. He began harassing Villa and his troops.

He arrested one of Villa's lieutenants and threatened to execute him. Villa interceded, and Huerta let the man go. Then there was an incident with a horse, which Huerta claimed Villa had stolen. And then there was another incident and another, until Villa finally said that he had volunteered his men and now he was leaving with them. Although it had been understood that volunteers were not the same as conscripts and could leave whenever they chose, Huerta took Villa's resignation as an act of treason during time of war. There was no trial, no opportunity to explain, to appeal to the courts; Huerta had no use for such formalities. He condemned Villa to death by firing squad. Villa appealed to Madero to reverse the order and got no response. As the moment of the execution neared, Villa lost his composure. Weeping, he fell to his knees, held on to an officer's boot, and begged for his life. Within moments, he had regained his dignity, and when he was taken to the wall, he stood quietly, waiting. At that moment a reprieve arrived from Madero. But it did not set him free. The death sentence had only been commuted to a prison term.

In prison, Villa met radical thinkers and learned about socialism and anarchy. According to some sources, he learned to read during his months in prison. Time and again, he appealed to Madero to free him. There was no evidence of insubordination, no reason for him to have been executed or even imprisoned, and his loyalty was unquestionable. The moral and legal arguments from Villa and his attorney had no effect. Madero acquiesced to other views about Villa: Huerta thought him dangerous, and the hacendados and officials in Chihuahua considered him a bandit, but it was mainly U.S. Ambassador Wilson who once again thrust himself into Mexican affairs. Many years later, in his autobiography, Wilson told his version of the story.

According to Wilson, who appears not to have had much interest in reporting events as they actually happened, "I then quietly but formally requested him [Madero] to 'arrest Villa and have him tried by court-martial.' When he demurred to my request, I said to him that he was forcing me to the unpleasant course of asking my own government to send troops across the border to furnish the protection to American citizens which he declined to give." He went on to tell Madero that Villa's alleged actions against American citizens constituted an "act of war." At that point, wrote Wilson, "a perceptible change took place in his manner and he said: 'Very well, Mr. Ambassador, I will have the man arrested and tried.'"

On Christmas Day 1912, Pancho Villa, dressed in a severe black suit of the kind worn by lawyers, finished sawing through the bars of the window of his prison cell, climbed out into the yard, where he was met by a young attorney, and, partially covering his face with a handkerchief, walked out of the prison, all the while chatting animatedly with his companion. With the Mexican Army and police hunting him, Villa, who would have been expected to go north to the mountains of Chihuahua, went west to the coast, caught a steamer north, and finally crossed the border at Nogales into Arizona. A month after Villa arrived in the United States, General Manuel Mondragón attacked the prison at Tacubaya with a force of three hundred men, freeing two important prisoners, General Felix Díaz and General Bernardo Reyes. Then the three generals led an attack on the Madero government in Mexico City, beginning the series of street battles that became known as the Ten Tragic Days.

While the Díaz and Reyes forces attacked the government strongholds in the city, turning the capital into a bloody battlefield in which no one—soldier or citizen, Mexican or German or French or American—was safe, Henry Lane Wilson led a plot to finish off the Madero government. Although he claimed in his autobiography to have merely agreed with the ambassadors from other countries stationed in the city to ask Madero to resign for the good of Mexico, it has been long established that Wilson was at the heart of the plot to overthrow the government. He had opposed Madero, claiming in various letters and telegrams that the Mexican president was corrupt, inept, anti-American, and utterly incapable of governing the country. And his communications were exactly what President Taft wanted to hear; Taft was determined to get rid of Madero before his own term ended and Woodrow Wilson took office.

As the battles went on in the streets of the city, the American ambassador involved himself more and more deeply in the attempt at a coup. He appears to have understood General Huerta's intentions in the coup from the outset, although he never warned Madero. It was the president's brother, Gustavo, who discovered that Huerta, the leader of the government forces, had made a pact with General Felix Díaz, the leader of the rebellion. Gustavo confronted Huerta with the accusation and brought him at gunpoint to the president's office. Madero listened to Gustavo's charges against Huerta, whom he still held at gunpoint. Everything Gustavo said comported with what the president knew about Huerta. He had insulted Madero. He had been part of the Porfiriato. Apparently, everyone in Mexico suspected Huerta's motives, including Madero's mother, who warned him about the general's disloyalty. Instead of ordering Huerta's arrest, Madero offered him the chance to defend himself against the accusation. Huerta swore that he was loyal to Madero, embraced the smaller man, and promised to finish off the counterrevolutionary forces within twenty-four hours.

Given Huerta's actions during the preceding two and a half years, there was no earthly reason for Madero to believe him rather than his own mother and brother. No historian has been able to explain Francisco I. Madero's behavior in that moment even though it changed the course of Mexican history. Could Madero have thought he had no alternatives? Villa was in the United States, and Orozco and Zapata were at war with his government. But there was a clear alternative. Felipe Ángeles was still a federal officer, a general; Madero had turned to Ángeles to replace Huerta in Morelos. Why not in the capital?

Perhaps no one could have saved him. Madero was betrayed on every side, and always with subtlety, always with sad eyes and tears of sincerity. Perhaps he lacked the ability to sense the ironic moment, for betrayal is always difficult to apprehend, the betrayer being both himself and another, an unrevealed comedy of identity. Apparently, it was clear to almost everyone but the president himself that he had been betrayed. When he spoke to an assembly of federal senators who had come to ask him to resign, he promised them that General Huerta would end the counterrevolution, unaware that the legislators, many of them old cientificos, were already allied with Huerta. When he spoke to Henry Lane Wilson, he knew that Wilson opposed him, but he apparently could not imagine that the U.S. ambassador was involved in a plot to overthrow him. And as if to help Madero with his self-delusion, U.S. President William H. Taft sent Madero a telegram of support for his government.

There was no place, no person to turn to for help. The brief attempt at democracy was dying, and the president could not spare it or himself. While he remained at his desk, brave, believing and dreaming, Henry Lane

Wilson, in a private meeting with Huerta, made the deal for the end of Madero. According to his own memoir, Wilson "determined that I must take a decisive step on my own responsibility to bring about a restoration of order." He went on: "I decided to ask Generals Huerta and Díaz to come to the embassy. . . ."

The next day the coup took effect. The president, the vice president, and General Felipe Ángeles were arrested. In return for their resignations Huerta offered the president and vice president exile rather than execution or imprisonment. After the resignations had been accepted, he kept them under house arrest in the National Palace. Perhaps he considered sending Madero into exile as he had promised, but the lesson of Reyes, who had been killed on the first of the Ten Tragic Days, and Felix Díaz, who had led the assault against Madero, was clear. Madero had had the chance to execute them, and he had not taken it. They had survived to bring him down. Neither exile nor prison was a guarantee of the end of opposition.

Madero's wife wrote to Ambassador Wilson, asking him to protect her husband. Wilson said later that he had complete faith in Huerta to do the right thing. On the night of February 22, probably on orders from Huerta, Madero and his vice president were taken from the National Palace. The men who came for them said they were to be transferred to a federal penitentiary. Madero must have expected the worst, for he knew by then that Huerta had arrested his brother and had him killed. Before he was led away, Madero embraced Ángeles, perhaps the last man he could trust to be faithful to him, and went along quietly, weeping as he went. He and Vice President Pino Suárez were driven outside the city and murdered.

Madero's career has been summed up by many writers. The first was Antonio Caso, a member of the Ateneo de la Juventud. Caso, who was one of the pallbearers at Madero's funeral, began that day to speak of the martyred president as a saint. Ramón Eduardo Ruiz, a labor historian, said Madero followed Porfirista policies with regard to unions and workers' rights; Ruiz found Huerta more progressive on that issue. Jesús Silva Herzog vilified the Apostle of Democracy in his brief history of the Revolution. John Womack is understanding of Madero's plight, but he sees no lasting importance from either Madero's presidency or the wars and ideas of the decade 1910–1920; like many contemporary writers, he does not think there was a Revolution. Friedrich Katz concentrates on the nature of the decade rather than the man, concerning himself with the motives of those who went to war, separating the southern rebels and their search for the return of their land from the northern cowboys and landholders and workers whose motives were so mixed they took different sides in the civil wars that followed the death of Madero. As is often the case with Mexican history, the clearest statement came from Daniel Cosío Villegas, who said at the very outset of his famous short essay *La Crisis de Mexico*, "The Mexican Revolution never had a clear program. . . ." He went on to explain that at some future date such a program would be worked out by "conservative writers." Of Madero himself, Cosío Villegas said in the essay only that there was no person who was equal to the demands of a Revolution in Mexico. Perhaps the demands were too great for any man, but it is more likely that the time was not right for a modern social revolution, that the classes were not defined, the issues not yet clear.

In the years that followed the murder of Madero, no program emerged that could capture the imagination of all sides. Tens of thousands, a million died, most of them without really knowing why or for what. Shortly after the coup, in Chihuahua City, Abraham González, who had been one of the most revered of the antireelectionists, was murdered. Ángeles went into exile in France. Huerta, the interim president, consolidated his position with the army, appointed cientifico and National Catholic Party members to administer the country, and set out to seek recognition from the United States for his new government. There was no attempt in Mexico City to overthrow Huerta and save the democracy. The movement would come from outside the capital; as always in Mexico, the force was centripetal. Huerta had to contend with Zapata in Morelos, and soon Villa in Chihuahua, and then a new, and powerful political force in the taciturn, bearded former cientifico from Coahuila, Venustiano Carranza. The coup had established nothing; it had begun the shattering of Mexican society. The experiment was over. Madero had been incapable of creating democratic institutions. There had been no democratic revolution just as there had been no social revolution; there had been a dream embraced by a desperate people, a reaction to the long dictatorship, middle-class except for the Zapatistas in Morelos and middling in intellect and leadership.

In the failure of a freely elected president to manage the country, future Mexican political leaders found a lesson in domestic governance they followed until the end of the century: The people cannot be trusted with power; only a strong man or an oligarchy can manage Mexico, and a constitution may be written, accepted, and revered without anyone adhering to its rules. A lesson in foreign policy also emerged from the decade of civil war: The most powerful force in the Mexican government was and always would be the United States. It would control the economy, the politics, the physical environment, a large part of the culture, even the ecological factors that determined the life and health of the butterflies and birds that wintered in Mexico. During the Depression of the 1930s, one Mexican president would attempt to remove the United States from some part of Mexican life by nationalizing the oil industry. But his nationalism and social reform would not survive his presidency. The first Mexican president of the twenty-first century would have the surname Fox, which had been in use in the English language since the ninth century, and he would have spent almost his entire career as part of one of the names symbolic in the world for U.S. cultural imperialism, Coca-Cola.

Jorge Castañeda, his first secretary of state, who had been a leftist professor in New York City before joining the conservative candidate in the 2000 election, exemplified yet another lesson learned from the collapse of Mexico's moment of democracy: Political allegiances are fluid, and as Mexico's great comic social commentator Cantinflas said with his confoundingly hilarious double-talk, words spoken in public by powerful men in Mexico have little or no meaning. In war or politics, dissembling and betrayal are important tools, for history shows that Mexico, like Rome, can fall only when both internal and external pressures are applied at the same time. At least since the sixteenth century, conquest in Mexico had always taken place in that form. It was not the Spaniards but the Tlaxcalans who brought down the Mexica, as it was not the generals who had declared themselves against him but his own man, Huerta, who brought down Madero with the help of the American ambassador.

Only one aspect of Mexico proved capable of including all factions as the attempt to establish a democracy deteriorated into civil war. At the moment of Madero's downfall, the Catholic Church had among its devoted members the Madero family, Huerta and his entire cabinet, and Zapata and his peasant-soldiers in Morelos, who went into battle wearing pictures of the Virgin of Guadalupe pinned to their great straw sombreros. No institution had proved so resilient, no other idea so powerful. Neither capitalism nor socialism nor consumerism, oligarchy, democracy, autocracy, or chaos had shaken the Mexican love of its religion. Although priests had not been able to appear in public in clerical garb since the middle of the nineteenth century and many men died on the battlefields without benefit of last rites, they were still religious. Even the northern troops who held liberal anticlerical beliefs and raged against the Church were guided by religious ideas. Obregón, the powerful general from Sonora and future president of Mexico, was a spiritualist, as were many others, no longer members of the Church of Rome, yet still concerned with ideas beyond this world. But the civil war was ultimately a war of desires in the material world; it did not have a religious explanation for being. This time neither the Virgin of Guadalupe nor Quetzalcoatl was required to validate the Mexican existence.

Unlike the wars of Independence, which were led by priests, this war belonged to the soldiers. Five generals and one political figure dominated the fighting: Generals Victoriano Huerta, Pascual Orozco, Pancho Villa, Emiliano Zapata, and Álvaro Obregón and First Chief Venustiano Carranza. In the beginning, the others were aligned against Huerta and the federal army. By the end they had destroyed each other, and Plutarco Elías Calles, a spiritualist schoolteacher with leftist ideas, a northerner, had emerged as the victor, the beginning of an all but invincible oligarchy that eventually became known to those close to it as "the system."

Between the death of the infant democracy and the beginning of the oligarchy, the Mexican civil war and business as usual went on side by side. Only a few states were deeply involved in the war. The battles were bloody, but the Division of the North, commanded by Pancho Villa, developed the first hospital train for military use, which helped to reduce the number of dead, especially at the two battles of Torreón in central Mexico. On the side of death, however, the machine gun came into use during the Mexican civil wars, as did the military use of aircraft. Economically, Mexico suffered terrible inflation as its own reserves fell and Carranza and then Villa issued their own paper currency. The value of the peso (in U.S. dollars) fell from forty-nine and one-half cents in 1913 to less than half a cent in 1916. On the other hand, the production of oil increased from 3 million to 157 million barrels over the decade. There was a decline in production of almost everything else during the three years of the height of the war, 1913–1916, but by 1920 production of most goods and commodities was far greater than it had been at the beginning of the decade. The bloody, terrible civil war was far from pervasive, and it made no fundamental change in the society, yet it defined Mexico for the rest of the century.

The continuing tragedy of the war, as Carlos Fuentes made so real in his novels *The Death of Artemio Cruz* and *Where the Air Is Clear*, lay in the corruption that grew out of it. By the middle of the century Fuentes and others saw that a civil war with no clear program had been a moral mistake, and little good could come of it. The Mexican society that emerged from the war turned on intrigue and betrayal. Carranza declared against Huerta. He called Huerta a traitor and named himself First Chief of the Constitutionalist forces. He had many generals, many divisions, among them Pancho Villa's Northern Division and a western army composed at first of Yaqui Indians and led by a farmer, who had been a primary school teacher and later the mayor of Huatabampo, Sonora, Álvaro Obregón.

Huerta raised an army of enormous size for a country of only fifteen million people. At one time he had a quarter of a million regular army troops plus militias and irregulars. A third of the entire national budget went to the army. He promoted hundreds of men to the rank of general and accepted almost any kind of behavior in the field. In Morelos he set up concentration camps to hold the Zapatistas. At the same time, he made bargains with the unions, which supplied him with a brigade of irregular troops to be used against Villa in the northern states. He dealt with the British over oil, bought munitions from Europe, and completely alienated American President Woodrow Wilson, who permitted Huerta's enemies to buy arms from U.S. merchants. Even that was not enough for Wilson, who threatened Huerta again and again in the summer and fall of 1913, demanding that he resign and turn the government over to Carranza. On April 21, 1914, Wilson sent U.S. marines ashore at Veracruz and Tampico as part of a plan to move troops by train to take Mexico City, following the route of Cortés and Scott.

The landing of the marines in "the halls of Montezuma" was too aggressive even for Carranza, who had until then been firmly allied with the United States. The day after the marines went ashore Carranza called it a violation of Mexican sovereignty. Only Pancho Villa remained a staunch friend to the United States and its president. The Mexican public was enraged: The United States had plotted against Madero, preferring Huerta; now they had Huerta, and they demanded his resignation in favor of Carranza, and to get what they wanted, they had invaded Mexican territory, closing off its main port, shutting down international trade, and depriving the government of tax revenues.

The lines of betrayal had been drawn. A dour and formal military man, killer of Maya and Yaqui rebels, a heavy drinker, if not an alcoholic, down-

ing glass after glass of brandy every night, square-faced, staring out of rimless eyeglasses, dark and frightening, descended partly from the mystical
and terrifying Huicholes of the western mountains, Huerta sat in the
National Palace. As president he preferred to be photographed in top hat
and tails, a stern leader, comfortable in the formalities of government. He
had no clear politics; nothing appeared to interest him but power.

17.

The Land of Zapata

Be realistic: Demand the impossible.
—CARLOS MONSIVÁIS

To die in a revolution is to die pure in Latin America; the moral danger is to survive. The idea has been borne out so often that it has become a truism, necessary to know, but no longer surprising. It is also true that revolutions in Latin America begin in argument, progress to secrecy, and end in victory or betrayal. Long after the death of Madero, in northern Mexico, in the city of Juárez, a group of young men, inspired by the victory of Fidel Castro and the daring of Che Guevara, planned to overthrow the government of Mexico.

One afternoon they invited me to visit with them. They thought I might be able to help them buy guns in Arizona. We met in the cellar of a tavern, in the dark. The man who extended the invitation said the room would be dark to protect the people at the meeting. After the glaring sun of the high desert, I could not even make out shapes in the room; I had to feel my way, stumbling on the stairs.

They were students, all but one or two, who were primary school teachers. We talked about the United States. "You rob us here and you rob us there," one student said, his voice coming out of the dark. "You buy our raw materials at any price that pleases you and sell the manufactured goods back to us, also at any price that pleases you."

And another spoke of corruption and poverty and the theft of land from the peasants in Mexico. In the middle of the series of brief speeches or harangues, a waiter carrying a bottle of beer opened the door to the room. There was a sudden shaft of light, a flash of the rebels: mustaches, some beards, checked short-sleeved shirts. Much of the clothing appeared to be brown, perhaps a trick of the brief light.

The group had formed in Monterrey. Their aim was to buy rifles from a

245

Czechoslovakian arms merchant, but the high price had surprised them; they complained that the Czechs were not true comrades. Could I arrange for weapons from Arizona?

The complaints and promises of revolution went on and on. To change the subject, I said, "There was news this morning from Chihuahua. A woman says that her husband, a PANista, was killed by the army. He was campaigning, running for some local office. The soldiers came in a truck, and they had an officer, a major, with them. They had a machine gun mounted on a tripod inside the truck. They lifted up the canvas flap at the back of the truck and opened fire."

The overhead light went on.

"Why did you turn the light on now?" I asked.

"Because we are Mexicans," someone said, perhaps to tell me they were patriots, revolutionaries, and unafraid, no matter how brutal the killing of the PANista had been. It was, I thought, a nice bit of theater, pure bravura, but I did not think they would ever do more than talk.

Seven years later, on September 23, 1965, some of the young men who were not afraid of the light took part in an armed attack on the Mexican Army barracks in the town of Madera, Chihuahua, in the foothills of the Sierra Madre. They gathered before dawn, in the darkness, armed with .22-caliber rifles, Molotov cocktails, and a few grenades, hoping to take the garrison, capture arms and ammunition, make a quick broadcast over the local radio station, and escape into the mountains. The attack followed the model of Fidel Castro; it expected the glory of Che.

But something had gone wrong. There were more than a hundred soldiers assigned to the tiny garrison. They lay in wait for the still-young revolutionaries. There was a brief battle, but the radicals were outnumbered and outgunned, soon surrounded, caught, exposed to a killing crossfire. I heard later that several of those who were killed, perhaps only two, may have been among the young men who were not afraid of the light.

The Liga Comunista 23 de septiembre took its name from the date of the attack. On December 6, 2001, a government commission investigating human rights abuses released information about people who had "disappeared" in Mexico. The list included Alberto López Herrera, member of the Liga Comunista 23 de Septiembre (L-23), detained in May 1978 in Monterrey; José Fernando López Rodríguez, L-23, detained April 5, 1978, in Monterrey, seen for the last time in Military Camp Number One; Jesús Piedra

Ibarra, L-23, detained April 18, 1975, in Monterrey, last seen in a secret prison in the Federal District in 1984; Ramiro Salas Ramos, L-23, detained April 5, 1978, in Monterrey, last seen in Military Camp Number One.

It was not clear what the young men who attacked the barracks at Madera had planned for the future of Mexico; their argument was with the present. It is equally difficult to know what went through the minds of the men who led the bitter civil wars from 1910 to 1920. Except for Álvaro Obregón they did not live to write their memoirs, and even he was assassinated. Huerta survived briefly, fleeing the country in 1914 only to die of cirrhosis of the liver two years later, and he had nothing to say. Huerta's position in 1914 was precarious. He had Villa, Obregón, and the Benavides brothers commanding large armies on the north. Pablo González on the east. And on his southwest flank, in Morelos, Emiliano Zapata and his coterie of anarcho-syndicalist intellectuals, displaced farmers, and sugarcane cutters were almost constantly engaged in battles with the government. It may have been the anarchist influence, as some writers have said, that set the Zapatistas against each successive government, from Porfirio Díaz until the death of Zapata, but it is more likely the Zapatista connection to land and the failure of one government after another to promote land reform. When they accepted the slogan of the Magonistas, "Land and Liberty!," it may have been the melding of an anarchist idea with dreams of a return to their own origins: the calpulli as part of the altepetl.[1]

At one time during the civil wars, the Zapatistas had driven their enemies from Morelos and established a kind of government that was no formal government (as we know it) at all but ran on something closer to a village elder system. Emiliano Zapata was the elder, functioning as a judge in mediating land disputes and even family quarrels. In his private life, Zapata behaved like many men in power—emperors, sultans, Pancho Villa, John Kennedy, Bill Clinton—taking as many women as he wanted, when he wanted them, and as he wanted them. He passed his days dark-eyed and serious and his nights drinking, telling stories of his days as a bullfighter, enjoying his women.

There was in him a streak of distrust that verged on paranoia. It was this

---

[1]Since these may be unfamiliar words, they are defined again here for the reader's convenience. The calpulli was the Nahua neighborhood, a part of the altepetl, which was a complete political and economic unit, much like the city-states of ancient Europe.

flaw or perhaps this lesson learned through centuries of oppression that complicated him; it was the source of his goodness, his rebellion, and his power over people and animals; it drove him into the role of revolutionary, allied him with anarchists, connected him to the only entirely trustworthy thing in the world, the land, and finally, twisted by men who both understood and hated him, led to his death.

In the way of civil wars, the rebels split into factions and tore at one another. They defeated Huerta and the federal troops; then Venustiano Carranza, who had declared himself First Chief, turned on Villa. A new war began, Carranza and the northwestern generals and their armies against Zapata and Villa, with Zapata clearly leftist and Villa leaning more and more in that direction. Carranza ruled briefly from Mexico City, then was driven out by Villa and Zapata.

Zapata met with Pancho Villa at Xochimilco south of Mexico City before their triumphant entry into the capital. The meeting had been carefully staged by the Villa and Zapata forces and became one of the most famous moments of the civil war. Otilio Montaño made a speech to welcome Villa to the Zapata camp; then there were apparently some awkward moments while the cowboy and the bullfighter waited politely for someone to speak. Villa wore plain soldier's attire. He had no embroidery, no jewelry. Zapata, who sat with his sister and his four-year-old son, was the most elegant man in the entire encampment. His shirt was lavender; his scarf was blue; his short black *traje corto* jacket was embroidered. Although it was December, it was warm, and Zapata wiped his face with a flowered handkerchief at one time and with a white and green handkerchief at another.

Zapata offered a glass of brandy to Villa, who was a teetotaler. Out of politeness Villa drank it off and choked and coughed and laughed at himself for his reaction. They made some comments, perhaps for the stenographer who sat with them, waiting to take down their words, or for the American observer or for their staffs, who would spread the word to the rest of their forces. Villa said that the little bits of land should be given back to their rightful owners, and Zapata agreed. The leader of the farmers of Morelos spoke only of "the land," while the cowboy, used to the vast stretches of northern ranchland, spoke of them as little bits. Much has been made of the different phrasing, but it is based on a misunderstanding of Villa's frame of reference by Mexican writers, who do not realize that the four hectares (ten acres) the farmers wanted was barely sufficient to support one steer in the high desert surrounding the Sierra Madre.

For the benefit of the crowd of listeners around them and the stenographers who captured their words, Zapata said Venustiano Carranza was a son of a bitch, and Villa agreed. Despite the function of the meeting as a show, there was an important political moment: Villa accepted the Plan of Ayala, in which Zapata had set forth his position on land reform. When the show was over, the two men went inside a nearby house to discuss their plans to defeat Carranza. They had pushed him out of the capital and were about to make a triumphant entry into the city. These were to be the most glorious days of their war, and perhaps they knew it. As they entered the city, the armies became a great parade, long lines of cavalry led by Villa, Zapata, and their generals. Gustavo Cassasola, who documented the revolution in photographs, shows Villa and Zapata riding side by side, Villa in military dress, with garrison cap, riding on the highest horse, the tallest man in the parade, and beside him Zapata, in an embroidered charro suit, wearing a great sombrero. Villa is looking to his right and slightly downward, in the direction of Zapata, and he is smiling. Zapata's face is hidden in the shade of the sombrero.

Later, in the National Palace, they are photographed again. This time Villa is sitting in the Eagle Chair, the thronelike presidential seat, and Zapata is on his left. In the photograph they look out at the camera, but they lean toward each other, their arms touching. Villa smiles broadly, obviously at ease with the irony of himself in the chair. It is his great joke. Zapata's head is tilted slightly downward, his black eyebrows pulled down by the beginning or the remains of a frown and his eyes turned upward, showing a long sliver of white moon below, all of which makes his appearance both dangerous and fearful. One man expects good news; the other expects trouble. Tomás Urbina sits next to Villa, and Otilio Montaño sits next to Zapata; these are the close ones, the trusted men. Their leaders will agree to the execution of both men before the civil war is over. With the help of Woodrow Wilson, they had defeated Huerta, but Carranza and his military leader, Obregón, ousted for the moment, would outlast them. As the war went badly in the north for Villa, the Zapatistas fought harder, harder perhaps than they had earlier when Villa needed them, when the general of the Northern Division had expected them to attack the Carrancistas. And in Morelos, Carranza's generals were brutal, worse than Huerta, killing hundreds of civilian prisoners, burning houses and fields, destroying the economy of the region. They took Cuernavaca, the state capital, then moved on to force Zapata to abandon his headquarters at Tlaltizapán. Zapata's men operated in small bands, never more than a few hundred. They attacked trains, operated ambushes, but they could not mount a sustained attack on large concentrations of troops. With the war going badly for him, Zapata's forces came apart from the inside. There are no records of internecine war among the common soldiers, but among the leadership it has been well documented.

There were betrayals, executions, defections, and murders; it was as if Zapata's sense of imminent betrayal had become ineluctable. Genovevo de la O, a dead ringer for Cantinflas, with his curiously innocent eyes and failure of a mustache, was one of the most ferocious of the Zapatista generals. He dragged one man behind his horse to kill him in that most terrible way, because that general had killed two other Zapatista generals. Francisco Pacheco, a general who had been close to Zapata, exchanged accusations with de la O, then failed to carry out his own duties and was executed. Lorenzo Vázquez, who had been a member of Zapata's inner council, took in two of Pacheco's officers after the execution, blamed the radical intellectuals for the Zapatista defeats, then failed in battle; he was hanged for treason. Otilio Montaño, the author with Zapata of the Plan of Ayala, was accused of treason. Zapata agreed to a court-martial for his old friend, then left his headquarters, apparently unable to bear being involved in the probable verdict. Montaño was found guilty and sentenced to death. He was not permitted a priest, and he died in a rage, protesting his innocence until he heard the order to fire.

Officers dismantled sugar mills and sold off the scrap metal for profit. Emiliano Zapata's brother, Eufemio, a big, bony, square-shouldered man with a typical Zapata family mustache, caught and punished the looters. But by then he had lost control of himself; he made accusations, beat old men, drank too much, insulted his own brother, and was shot by a man whose father he had beaten. Then by some accounts General Eufemio Zapata was dragged out of town to an anthill and left there, mortally wounded, to be eaten by the ants as he died.

In the end Zapata's fear of betrayal was not great enough. His error began when he heard news of a split between Carranza's man in Morelos, General Pablo González, and one of his cavalry officers, Colonel Jesús Guajardo. Sensing the opportunity to bring an officer, perhaps the entire Fiftieth Regiment over to his cause, Zapata wrote to Guajardo, asking for a face-to-face meeting. The letter was intercepted and turned over to General González, who set in motion a brilliant plot. He knew how much Carranza wanted to put an end to Zapata and how killing or capturing Zapata could affect a Carrancista general's career. After receiving the approval of his president, González moved ahead with his plot. The spat between the general and his colonel had been true. Guajardo had been found drunk instead of leading his troops in an attack as ordered by his general.

Now González found Guajardo, whom he had returned to duty, in the officers' mess at Cuautla (Morelos). He ordered the other officers out of the room and then showed Zapata's letter to Guajardo. His proposition to the cavalry officer was simple: Either Guajardo was a traitor, in league with Zapata, or he was willing to participate in the capture of Zapata by going along with the request for a meeting. Guajardo agreed to the plot. He sent word back to Zapata that he would meet him. A series of delays, feints, demands of proof, ensued, and finally Zapata agreed to a meeting, if Guajardo would turn over a group of former Zapatistas, traitors whom Zapata despised. Guajardo delayed, not wanting to arouse suspicion by appearing to be too willing, but finally gave the order to execute the men.

After killing his own troops as a display of fidelity, Guajardo met with Zapata, negotiated, begged off an immediate surrender of his men and ammunition, and set a date to accomplish the defection the next morning at his main camp at Chinameca. On a Thursday morning in April 1919 Zapata and 150 mounted men descended from the hills toward Chinameca. The winter had passed; the harshly shaped hills were greening again. It was still morning when Zapata and Guajardo met in a little shop outside the main wall of the hacienda. Guajardo said there were rumors of federal troops in the area. Zapata agreed to send out patrols. By early afternoon they had found no one. Now Zapata was invited inside to complete his business with the colonel. Zapata complied; he and an escort of ten horsemen entered the hacienda. The remaining Zapatistas waited under the trees outside the gates. The horses grazed; the men took their ease in the shade.

Zapata and his small escort entered the hacienda. An honor guard and buglers waited for them there. Three times the bugles played for him, and at the end of the third call the men of the honor guard raised their rifles and killed Emiliano Zapata. There is a story of a thousand men firing at him there in the courtyard of the hacienda, and it is a good story, but a thousand is a great number and not needed for the killing of one man, even Emiliano Zapata.

After the killing was done, Guajardo had Zapata's body loaded onto a horse, perhaps the very horse he had given him for a gift, and brought the body to Cuautla, where he dumped it in the middle of the street. It was almost dark by then, and General González had to use a flashlight to look at the face of the corpse to be sure it was Zapata. Later the body was taken to the police station at Cuautla, where a photograph was made. The face in the photograph is swollen, and Zapata is not dressed in one of the short embroidered charro jackets that he wore in almost every photograph. He appears sullen, stupefied, as if from drink rather than death. It is the most informal photograph of him in all his thirty-nine years.

18.

Villa's Angels

With my .30-30 I shall swell
the ranks of the rebellion;
if they ask for my blood,
my blood I shall give
for the exploited of our country.
—"CARABINA .30-30," A POPULAR VILLISTA SONG

After Zapata, there was only Pancho Villa. The Centaur of the North had lost his division by 1919. The crack troops he called *dorados* (golden ones) were long gone, yet all the news was not bad. Ángeles had come back from the United States, and Carranza had problems. General Álvaro Obregón was not happy with his president. Obregón and Villa had a long and unhappy history together, but that had come late in Villa's career. General Villa had begun as a bandit, mule skinner, salesman, stagecoach driver, and only after all those attempts at a life found his calling in war.

Like Zapata, whose chief biographer was John Womack, Villa is the subject of a biography by Friedrich Katz. All biographers of course are burdened with the need to revise what has been written before, but in these instances the work is solidly researched and destined to stand as the canon for a very long time. The problem even with such careful work is that it cannot escape the moment in which it is written, while readers continue to revise their views of the subjects. Villa will be a socialist when socialism wants him and a brute when no one feels need of him; his troops will be workers to the unionists and cowboys and peasants to all varieties of romantics. And everyone will be correct. The dream of Zapata wanders from Attila to something close to sainthood. The very house in which he lived, reconstructed in part in the Zapata Museum in Anenecuilco, grows larger or smaller, according to the politics of the person describing it.

Zapata had the luck to become young Marlon Brando, although in a historically inaccurate film, while Villa suffered the guise of the fat, loud, and astonishingly crude-looking Wallace Beery in a film that bore almost no relation to history.[1] Only long after their deaths did Villa and Zapata become heroes in Mexico, and even now there are families whose histories were bloodied by the depredations of the armies of heroes. Villa suffers most, for his army covered more territory and made more headlines. No painters have seen fit to make heroes of the Villistas; the great Mexican muralists Siqueiros, Rivera, and Orozco did not paint cowboys. The muralists preferred men in white, with great hats and machetes. The Villistas preferred big horses and repeating rifles. They liked to move by train, support their troops with artillery, and, when they could, send up biplanes to spot enemy troop concentrations.[2]

Pancho Villa's operations and politics bounced up and back between the styles of the nineteenth and twentieth centuries, sometimes capitalist, sometimes socialist, democratic in theory, autocratic on the battlefield, always romantic. He was astonishingly agreeable to other men's political notions, although he generally edited them to fit his own thoughts. He liked laughter and love, was probably sincere in all of his marriages and affairs, and preferred that other men do his killing, although he was quite capable of doing the work himself. For a time his greatest champion was Woodrow Wilson.

During the starburst of Villa's life, the five years from 1911 into 1916, Pascual Orozco betrayed Madero and thus Villa; Zapata failed to support the Villista plans in the south; Carranza turned against the Division of the North; Obregón defeated Villa in the field again and again; Woodrow Wilson abandoned Villa after those defeats; and Villa's longtime friend, and perhaps his closest ally, Tomás Urbina, became so utterly corrupt that Villa finally ordered his death. Even Felipe Ángeles left Mexico for a time to live in exile in the United States during Villa's desperate years. It can be fairly said that in love and war, the coruscation known as Pancho Villa was a Mexican life.

He was born in Durango and grew up a widow's son. He knew farms, ranches, animals, oppression, dust, summer sun, floods, gambling, and suddenness. To survive, not merely to endure in such circumstances, required cunning and quickness, and something more: A man had to be unpre-

---

[1]He was also the "hero" of a movie made in 1914. The story of the movie ended with Pancho Villa as president of Mexico. Villa, who enjoyed publicity, appeared in the film as himself.

[2]The horses rode in the railroad boxcars, and the Villistas rode on the roofs.

dictable, capable of laughter and murder within the moment; otherwise he was not a man, not dangerous, he lacked the mercurial soul of the macho.

Villa was nothing like Zapata; they were the duality of *mexicayotl* (Mexicanness): solemn and uproarious, dark and bright, thin and thick, bullfighter and mule skinner, elegant and gruff, green and brown, and, in the postconquest world, south and north, corn and wheat. Villa's intellectual development came first through meetings with Abraham González, then in conversation with Madero himself, later, in prison, with the Zapatista Gildardo Magaña. His ethics, which were those of the macho, were eventually transformed by the decency of Felipe Ángeles.

During his brief ascension to national and international importance, he moved politically to the left, eventually embracing socialist ideals, but then in retirement backed away from them. Although he was a general, he was not a militarist. When he was in control of the city and state of Chihuahua, he put his army to building the infrastructure of the city and helping to set up schools for the children. The money he issued was valued at fifty cents on the U.S. dollar when Villa was in his ascendant period. It was backed by little more than his word and his military exploits, and when his luck ran out, the value of the money fell to pennies and then to nothing. Everyone, or so it seemed, was printing money in Mexico; in addition to Villa, Carranza and the Constitutionalists printed vast sums. Money was everywhere; millions were printed; the inflation was wild.

A brief résumé of Villa's career leads to some insight about the failure of revolutions. He began as an instrument for Madero. Along with Pascual Orozco, he captured Ciudad Juárez, leading to the fall of the Porfiriato.

In the Orozco rebellion, which published leftist manifestos and had the support of the hacendados, Villa fought alongside Huerta in support of Madero, whom he considered saintly.

After Huerta sent Villa to prison and Madero was murdered, Villa returned to Mexico to fight alongside Venustiano Carranza, who had declared himself First Chief of the Constitutionalist army.

Carranza's Constitutionalists could not take Torreón, but when it was time, Villa took the city and control of the railroads centered there. It was the beginning of a long series of victories and the establishment of the Division of the North.

As victor and administrator Governor Villa began implementing his land reform policies in the state of Chihuahua. According to some sources, he divided up the great Terrazas hacienda into twenty-five-hectare (about sixty-acres) farms or ranches, giving them to loyal members of the Division of the North or to their widows and orphans. For the most part, however, the confiscated haciendas were administered by a complex collection of government agencies. The peasants, who formed the Villista army along with the cowboys and miners, did not receive land grants. They continued to work, producing grains, vegetables, and meat, but they did not become the owners of the land. Although Villismo and Zapatismo claimed similar agrarian policies, the implementation in the south was real. Zapatismo produced a semblance of equalitarian life by fiat; the Villistas had a different view, believing that education would eventually lead to equality. Zapata gave the land back to the farmers; Villa sent their children to school.

In war the Villista forces were brutal. His method was the golpe terrifico (terrific blow), sending overwhelming numbers of cavalry and foot soldiers in attacks that his enemies could not resist. And after the battles were over, when the burning and burying of the dead had just begun, he permitted mass executions, as if for him the spoils of war were the enemy dead.

The influence of Felipe Ángeles later moderated the Villista forces in victory, reducing the number of executions. But no one could control or even influence such men as General Rodolfo Fierro of Villa's División del Norte. Martín Luis Guzmán described the cruelty of Fierro in several instances, but none so terrible as his tale of the prison yard. On the night after a major battle, Fierro told hundreds of prisoners that he would give them a chance to escape. The prisoners had only to run the length of the small yard and climb a shoulder-high wall to freedom. The unarmed men, said Fierro, would be let out into the yard in groups of ten. No one but the general would attempt to stop them. Fierro, tall and narrow-eyed, a former low-level railroad worker in Sonora, stood at one end of the yard with his pistols holstered.

When the first group of men ran out, Fierro killed them. Then the next and the next. He killed them all afternoon and into the early evening. He killed them until his trigger finger cramped and he had to rest while the muscles relaxed; then he killed again. He killed two hundred, and then he killed more. He kept on killing, calmly, efficiently, often with a cigar in his teeth and the smoke rising into his eyes, pooling in the dark space under his felt cowboy hat, but never interfering with the accuracy of his shooting. Of all the men who ran across the prison yard that day, galloping, dodging, hoping, their hands poised, ready to grasp the top of the wall and pull themselves to freedom, only one escaped Fierro's killing ground.

If Villa's was a Mexican life, Fierro's was the macho life unalloyed, and for that Villa admired him and took him into his inner circle. Fierro was no more than a common cavalryman when he caught Villa's eye during the planned ambush of a train. As the engineer aboard the train realized he had entered an ambush, he opened the throttle, hoping to roar through, but Fierro rode alongside the train, spurring his horse, faster and faster, until he caught up with the engine. Then he leapt from his horse to the steps of the locomotive, killed the engineer and crew, and stopped the train. It was enough to endear him to Villa forever. Fierro murdered, stole, lost battles, gave rotten advice, but never lost the loyalty of his general. In the end, crossing an artificial lake on the way to the fiasco at Agua Prieta, Fierro's horse stepped into quicksand. Fierro dismounted and tried to make his way to solid ground, but he could not swim, for he was weighted down by a belt and vest filled with stolen gold. He sank through the water into the sand and disappeared.

After the defeat of Huerta, Carranza agreed to a convention in Aguascalientes to determine who should be the interim president of Mexico, the First Chief's assumption being that he would soon be elected to sit in the Eagle Chair at the National Palace. Villa and Zapata had by then become allied, with Carranza and his General Alvaro Obregón leading the other faction. The Convention, held in the autumn of 1914, produced the split between the two main factions and led to the last and most murderous phase of the civil war in Mexico.

They chose Aguascalientes because it was neutral ground, neither Villista nor Zapatista nor Carrancista. It was, they agreed, the place from which a new government, a new Mexico would emerge. At the beginning of the Convention the Villistas were compliant, agreeing to the distribution of delegates and virtually everything else proposed by the Carrancistas and the peace faction. The Zapatistas, who were convinced by Felipe Ángeles to join the Convention as well as to ally themselves with the Villistas, came late. By the time they arrived, the members had sworn their allegiance to Mexico, even signing a Mexican flag as a symbol. Villa came to the Convention, wrote his name, and left, putting the negotiations in the hands of his intellectuals.

Zapata followed the same policy, although he did not attend the Convention at all. During the debates it became more and more clear that there were

two great and incompatible factions: the Villa-Zapata group and the Carrancista group, which was headed by Carranza himself and his chief military
leader, Álvaro Obregón. The factions were divided over land reform and distrust, but there was something deeper perhaps. The problem that had dogged
Mexico since its Independence had never been completely resolved: Was it to
be centralized or federalized? What was the basic structure of the state?

Villa had said he had no national ambitions for himself. When he had the
chance to become president of Mexico, he made a joke of the possibility
and saw to it that the office was held by a man he thought more qualified.
Zapata had no national ambitions for himself either; he was concerned with
power only as it affected policy. Carranza, on the other hand, saw himself at
the head of a powerful central government. Obregón agreed with Carranza
about centralization but saw himself rather than Carranza at the center.

As the debate went on, Villa proposed that both he and Carranza resign
from the Convention. He went even further, suggesting that they both be
shot, solving the problem forever. There were many at the Convention who
approved of Villa's offer; in their eyes, he was a wild animal, and Carranza a
potential dictator; nothing would have pleased the large peace faction more
than the deaths of the two opposing figures. Carranza did not accept the
idea of twin executions, although he did agree that he and Villa should
resign. No resignations were forthcoming, however, because neither man
trusted the other. And through it all, the Zapatistas were able to put their
sociopolitical policies forward, convincing the entire Convention to adopt
Zapata's Plan of Ayala with its radical land reforms. The Convention
produced agreements that no one expected would be put into effect. The
middle-class views of the Carrancistas (Constitutionalists) could not be rec-
onciled with the peasant and cowboy views of the Zapata-Villa alliance. The
political and personal hatreds of the two main factions were deeper than
ever. The stage was set for the most brutal and bloody phase of the long
civil war.

Conventionist forces took Mexico City. Wilson pulled the U.S. marines
out of Veracruz after hundreds of Mexicans had been killed, and the Constitutionalists took control and set up their capital in the port city.

Villa made a fool of himself over a woman in Mexico City, causing an
international scandal.

The Constitutionalists took on a two-front war, Zapata in the south and
Villa in the center and the north. Woodrow Wilson remained a supporter of

the Convention and of Villa, although there were plans for an invasion in the event the Mexican civil war could not be settled to America's satisfaction.

Two great battles across the same ground determined the future of Mexico. Obregón brought his Army of the Northwest down to Celaya in central Mexico and waited there for Villa and his Division of the North to come to him. He had learned from German officers attached to his army that machine guns, barbed wire, and the use of trenches had changed the nature of warfare in the twentieth century. Villa, although advised against it by Felipe Ángeles, chose to remain with the golpe terrifico strategy that had brought him such success on the battlefield. He had men, horses, artillery, and he had his dorados, the devastating cavalrymen who had destroyed enemy forces all across the north and center of Mexico.

Obregón later produced a cool military account of the battles in his memoir, "The Eight Thousand Kilometer Campaign."[3] He counted artillery pieces captured, numbered the hours of bombardment, but he did not say much about the nature of the battle. Obregón referred to the Villistas as "traitors" or "reactionaries," although they were actually representatives of a more radical political view at the time. He noted that his vanguard troops engaged in a skirmish with three columns moving south toward the city, and he had to relieve them. He began to place his troops, with the German Colonel Maximiliano Kloss commanding the artillery and providing the lessons in the use of the machine gun.

Meanwhile, Villa moves south, planning a three-pronged attack to begin with artillery fire, followed by cavalry, and then a massive charge of infantry. Ángeles, keeping the terrain in mind, warns Villa against an attack across the soft fields and through the irrigation canals outside the city. There will be mud, sand, ditches to cross. Villa will not hear of it. He will destroy Obregón. He knows him, he has met with him, looked in his eyes, threatened him when Obregón came to Chihuahua, then spared his life, and now he will destroy him.

Obregón orders his troops to retreat from the skirmishes, to draw Villa's forces into battle. He places his Sonoran Yaqui troops in the front trenches behind the strings of barbed wire. They are dressed in pin-striped railroad worker's coveralls cut off at the knee, and they are perhaps the most fero-

---

[3] *Ocho Mil Kilometros en Campaña* (Mexico City: Fondo de Cultura Económica, 1959). First publication in 1917 in folio.

cious fighters in Mexico. The Yaquis wait in the trenches, bayonets fixed. Villa's cavalry will come across the fields when the artillery barrage is over. The horses will be slow in the soft ground, and there will be no purchase for their hooves. They will not be able to leap over the trenches.

The Division of the North waits for the bombardment to finish. The artillery fire is heavy, but there is more noise and terror than actual damage. When the Villista cavalry charges, the Yaquis are still there in the trenches. The machine guns cut down the horses, and those that survive the bullets are torn open by the bayonets. It is a slaughter. The ground turns muddy with blood, the corpses pile up, and then Obregón sends his cavalry from the left and right. The Villistas die by the thousands; hundreds surrender. Obregón's cavalry turns up toward the Villista artillery. Villa has pulled the cannon back to save what he can. After fifteen kilometers, the Constitution- alists end their pursuit. A battered Division of the North pulls back. It is April 7, 1915.

Villa had made the error of attacking instead of following Ángeles's advice and drawing Obregón north, extending his supply lines. He lacked sufficient ammunition, and Zapata, who had agreed to cut Obregón's com- munications with Carranza's capital in Veracruz, had let him down. Perhaps a greater problem was the lack of Ángeles beside him in the field. Ángeles had been thrown from a horse and could not make the trek to Celaya for the first battle. A week later he was still not there.

Instead of bringing in reinforcements from other areas on the east coast and in the cities to the north and west, Villa executed the same battle plan a week later, on April 13. This time it was worse. Villa lost fifteen thousand men killed, wounded, or captured. He could not save his artillery at the end of the second battle, and the number of horses and rifles left behind for the Con- stitutionalists was enough to equip an army.

Why Villa followed the same plan that had cost him so dearly the first time is not clear. No trained military officer would have done so. The First Battle of Celaya proved that the nineteenth century, with its great cavalry charges, was over. The tactic could not succeed against machine guns and trenches and barbed wire, and Celaya, with its irrigation system and soft ground, was a terrible place in which to learn the lesson. Yet Villa appears to have learned nothing from the first battle. He did not even bother to study the disposition of Obregón's troops, to find out that his cavalry waited, hidden in a forest at the edge of the battle scene, until the Villista troops were all out in the field, battle weary, vulnerable, an exercise in slaughter for the cavalry.

After Celaya, Villa fought on but never recovered. There were other battles; Obregón lost an arm; Villa enjoyed some victories, lost Chihuahua City, retook it, and lost it again. Torreón fell to the Constitutionalists; even Ciudad Juárez fell. Villa was cut off from ammunition and supplies. Then Woodrow Wilson recognized the Carranza government, and it was all over.

Obregón and Carranza proved more calculating, more brutal than Villa and Zapata imagined. They executed prisoners and civilians. After the Second Battle of Celaya, Obregón lined up 120 captured Villista officers and promised to spare their lives if they identified themselves. The officers complied, and when they were done, when Obregón had what he wanted, he sent them to the wall. Unlike Fierro, he did not do the killing himself, it was not an amusement, the executions were orderly and efficient: No one survived.

There was a small victory for Villa over Obregón after that. The Sonoran general lost an arm in battle against Villista forces. Or it may not have been a victory at all because the severed arm was preserved in a jar and put on display as a sign of Obregón's indomitable spirit. Villa lost battle after battle. His generals defected; his men stole; he no longer knew what to say. The Apostle Madero was dead; Villa's secretary, Aguirre Benavides, had deserted him; Ángeles went to the United States to negotiate for Villa and found no one would hear his pleas.

In those last years Villa permitted a massacre of Americans at Santa Isabel, and then, perhaps spurred on by the Germans who wanted to involve the United States in a war with Mexico or by American businessmen who wanted the spoils of another U.S.-Mexican war, Villa led or sent two hundred men across the border at Columbus, New Mexico, in the predawn hours of March 9, 1916.[4] Since the slaughter at Agua Prieta, he and his remaining men had been in a rage against the United States. He may not have needed the spurs of German spies or American businessmen. It is also possible that he chose Columbus because he had long done business with an arms merchant there, and the man had recently cheated him.

Columbus, a small town about ninety miles west of El Paso, never recov-

---

[4]There is no conclusive evidence that Villa himself crossed the border from Palomas, Mexico, to Columbus, New Mexico, but there can be no doubt about the actions of his troops.

ered from the attack. It began as a stop on the railroad going west, and the tracks have long since been torn up for scrap. Dust, rattlesnakes, and coyotes dominated the town then and now. In the area around Columbus the desert offers little besides snakes, rabbits and Gila monsters. Even the cactus is sparse. Ten acres of land are required to support one steer. And in the spring months, especially in March, the wind comes unceasingly across the long desert, and the signs outside the few stores rise and fall on the iron rings that hold them and make a mournful iron lament that dies in the wind.

The town had no military value, no wealth, nothing worth taking but the sense of invulnerability of the country that had turned its back on Villa. Seventeen people were killed in the raid. The Villistas took what little of value they could find and fled back into Mexico. For his pleasure in tweaking the country he now saw as the great betrayer, Villa incited a punitive expedition into Mexico. John J. Pershing, who was to become a hero of the war in Europe, brought a powerful force to Columbus. With cavalry and even airplanes, the six thousand men of the punitive expedition left Columbus, crossed through Palomas, Mexico, and searched for Pancho Villa. It was a modest force compared with the suggestions made in the U.S. Congress to send half a million men to occupy the country.

As the American troops moved south, Carranza's mild protests turned to outrage. He too was searching for Villa, and when Mexican federal troops encountered the American expedition, there were nasty skirmishes, but no great battles and no successes in tracking Pancho Villa. No Mexican would betray him to the gringos or the Carrancistas. They said he had turned into a small dog that followed along behind Pershing's cavalry.

In fact, Villa had suffered a leg wound in a battle with Carrancista troops in late March and had been unable to walk or ride. His men loaded him on a burro and brought him up to a cave in the mountains, where two cousins tended him. For two months he lay in the cave, sometimes delirious, weeping, and at other times lying at the entrance, peering through the brush at the U.S. troops passing below. Once or twice Pershing's soldiers climbed the mountain, looking for tracks, and passed so close to the mouth of the cave that Villa could have touched them.[5]

The Americans suffered heat, thirst, snakebite, and hunger. They cooked leather for food and found no one who had raided Columbus. The Villistas

[5]Perhaps not quite so close, but it is a good detail in the storied life of Villa.

stayed far to the south and were quiet. Between the Villista and Carrancista troops there was a kind of détente, a sense of mexicayotl that came of having a common enemy on their soil. It would not last, they knew, but for the moment it mattered only that they were Mexicans.

Pershing went to war in Europe, and Villa survived to fight again, but only briefly, and when he did fight, he no longer shot Carrancista prisoners, perhaps because of the response to Pershing, but more likely because Felipe Ángeles had returned from the United States. He had lived in New York City uptown on 114th Street and at other times on the Lower East Side, where he learned practical socialism from the garment workers and delivered speeches on the theory of socialism to groups of Mexican liberals in the city.

They were together again after a long time, and Villa listened to Ángeles as never before. The wild man the world had complained about seemed calmer, more sophisticated. Angers remained, however, against the United States and, curiously, against Madero. Over the years he had turned over the Madero collapse in his mind, considering and reconsidering what had happened in Mexico, from the taking of Ciudad Juárez at the beginning of the battle to the inclusion in Madero's inner circle of so many officers and officials who had been Porfiristas. He had come to the conclusion that Madero was a fool.

In the middle of June 1919 Villa attacked Ciudad Juárez again. This time U.S. troops came across the border, ostensibly to defend U.S. citizens, and drove the Villistas out of the city. It was, Ángeles realized, the end. He had become convinced that the United States would never permit the Villistas to come to power, and he said good-bye to Villa and the Revolution. They parted friends, but in sadness, and with Villa concerned for the safety of Ángeles. There was some talk about Ángeles going to the United States, but he had concluded that he was a Mexican and would stay in Mexico. Accordingly, Villa helped him to find a secure hiding place in the mountains of Chihuahua.

The betrayal and capture of Felipe Ángeles came quickly. Perhaps more than anyone, even more than Villa or Zapata, Ángeles was the man Carranza wanted dead. There was little doubt that Ángeles was capable of serving as president of Mexico and that he enjoyed the admiration, if not the loyalty, of large numbers of people in both Mexico and the United States. While both Zapata and Villa were regional figures, with no more than regional ambitions, Ángeles had a more encompassing view, and he had

been thinking about the presidency: He opposed part of the Mexican Constitution of 1917 because it invested too much power in the executive branch
of government.

Like so many figures in the history of attempted revolutions, he was
betrayed and captured by the group in power, in this case Carranza/Obregón/
Calles and the northwestern junta. Although President Carranza would have
preferred to avoid a trial, he could not simply send Ángeles before a firing
squad. Ángeles and the men captured with him were taken in a boxcar to
Chihuahua. As they passed through Hidalgo del Parral, people gave him food,
and some even offered to help him escape. He declined. In his view, he had
committed no serious crime; he had only to fear the vindictiveness of the
president.

In one of very few trials held during the period known as the Revolution
of 1910, Felipe Ángeles appeared before a military court in a theater in the
city of Chihuahua. News of the trial spread rapidly. Letters and telegrams
asking Carranza to spare the life of one of the most honorable men of the
decade came from Mexico, the United States, and Europe, but Carranza
paid them no mind; he wanted Ángeles dead, and soon, before the international pressure became any greater.

While he awaited the trial, Ángeles spent his days and long into the nights
in a tiny cell, reading Renan's *Life of Jesus*. He had been permitted a type-
writer and access to both the mails and the telegraph. Clean military clothing had been given him. He no longer had the ragged look of a man who had
spent months as a guerrilla, moving from one mountain hideout to the
next. During these last days spent in his cell, he wrote a great deal, and it is
said that he did not sleep much, if at all.

The government did not hold the trial in a courtroom, for it was a show
trial, the certain end of a danger to the men in power, so it was set in the
Teatro de los Héroes, and five thousand tickets were printed and distributed.
Before the trial began, General Manuel Diéguez, military commander of
Chihuahua, wired Carranza, explaining to him that Ángeles was no longer
a soldier but a civilian and had to be tried by a civil rather than a military
court. In response, Carranza ordered the immediate formation of a court-
martial and insisted that the trial go forward with all possible speed. As if
they had been prompted by Diéguez, the first thing the defense lawyers did
was to argue that the trial was improper under Article 13 of the very constitution Carranza had helped to bring about in 1917. But in November 1919,

Carranza and his handpicked Supreme Court paid no attention to the constitution; the excuse was that the telegraph lines were not functioning, they hadn't heard the appeal in Mexico City. The trial went forward.

Speed was on Carranza's mind. He pushed Diéguez to hurry the trial along, to avoid long recesses. There were still pockets of resistance, guerrilla bands in the north and south, and all the intellectuals had not yet been killed. To make matters more difficult for Carranza, the people were not pleased with him. Inflation had made their money all but worthless, and the brutality of the Carrancista generals in dealing with civilians as well as soldiers had made military opposition to the government appealing once again.

On the first day of the trial Ángeles answered questions by giving full and clear expositions of his history and his ideas about everything from politics to ontology. It was clear that he knew this was his end, and he seems to have written a kind of intellectual memoir in the protracted answers. Although the photograph of him in the Casasola Graphic History of the Revolution shows a man slumped in a chair in what appears to be a military uniform denuded of all insignia, a tiny figure among two other defendants on the great stage, with the painted backdrop of the Teatro behind them; he was not defeated morally so much as physically. He spoke of democracy in its classical form of direct representation and as it existed when the people had no direct voice, only representatives. In a society still based largely on communal notions, he spoke of the individual will. He said that men must learn not to be servile.

A great part of his intellectual memoir was given over to socialism, which he had found strong at the Aguascalientes Convention and even stronger among the people of the United States. He said, "The truth is that some work while others eat well." And when the applause from those in the farthest seats died down, he went on to speak of the mediocrity of bourgeois society in Mexico. He complained of the lack of education in Mexico, the poor quality of mind of the men who made the Revolution, the paucity of true intellectuals in the fight.

He spoke of his split with Villa, largely over their views of the Americans. Ángeles said Mexicans and Americans did not know each other. He defended the character of Americans far from the border; he said they were different, better, yet he said the Americans thought of Mexicans as "an inferior race." He spoke of the error of hate and of the teachings of Jesus. "I cherish hatred for no one," he said. "I had no hate, not even when Madero sent me to fight the Zapatistas. The concern I showed there led the people to call me a Zapatista, because I spoke with the poor and humble people. . . . In Monterrey, I spoke of the enemy as our mistaken brothers. . . . I love all humanity. . . . I love all the things of the earth. . . . I love the planetary system, the nebulae, the stars, the worlds that turn in the immensity of space. I love it all."

During his last hours Ángeles wrote to his wife, slept for a while, then put on the old clothes he had worn in the mountains. A priest came to his cell to hear his last confession, but Ángeles refused, explaining that he opposed the idea of confession. He told the priest he would have preferred a visit from a psychologist, who for the good of humanity could have studied "a man who loves life and is not afraid to lose it."

At 6:00 A.M. on November 26, 1919, Felipe Ángeles was executed. Although Villa lived on for a few more years, it was the end of the great duality of the Division of the North. The general who loved and the general who raged no longer fought together. The age of heroes was over. Zapata was dead, betrayed and murdered. Madero and Abraham González were dead, and Flores Magón would soon die in an American prison. Only the aging young men of the Ateneo de la Juventud lived on. The cientificos had finally been brought down; the world of Auguste Comte had come to an end in Mexico. Even the military leaders of the northwestern oligarchy, Obregón and Calles, were spiritualists. In little more than a year Carranza, who was one of the last connections to the Porfiriato, would be dead, and Villa, the last of Madero's warriors, would have surrendered. Much of what was left in Mexico seemed the same, although many had died, including thousands who fell to influenza, and thousands had fled to the North or Europe. There is no accurate count of the number of civilians or combatants who died in war during the decade that ended in 1920. There is only the census, which showed a decline from 15,160,000 in 1910 to 14,335,000 in 1921.[6]

As many contemporary scholars have pointed out, the businesses that dominated the Mexican economy in 1910 still controlled it at the end of 1919. The vast differences between rich and poor had not been erased or even

---

[6]*Diccionario Porrúa.* John Womack, *Cambridge History of Latin America* (1991) puts the decline in absolute numbers at 300,000 (15,000,000 to 14,700,000) between 1910 and 1920. Given the high birthrate during that period, the loss of population because of war, disease, hunger, and emigration was in the millions, with at least 1,000,000 killed.

mitigated. Government had shifted from a dictatorship to an oligarchy. There had been some changes, however, and they were important. A major union of workers had been formed, and it was, at least in its early years, helpful to working people. As the historian Friedrich Katz said to me in a private conversation, the great landholdings had been broken up, the army had been weakened, and there had been a change in the people's view of themselves, leading perhaps to the true, although brief, real Mexican Revolution of the 1930s. The problem with the breaking up of the estates is that they were given as gifts to the myriad of generals and colonels who fought on the ultimately triumphant side in the wars. One form of corruption replaced another; it was the failure of New Spain again, as if the country had been colonized from within. Of all the lasting accomplishments of the wars begun by the angry middle class and some poor farmers and workers and won by the angry middle class and the old and new rich, two stand out: the survival of the country itself, which provided a modern mythology of the kind necessary to the continuation of a state, and the Constitution of 1917.

19.

Carranza, Obregón, Calles, and the Constitution

Carrancear: *Avanzar, hurtar, apoderarse de lo ajeno. La revolución constitutionalista, cuyo primer jefe fue don Venustiano Carranza, creó este verbo festivo y ofensivo para el caudillo, pero se hizo muy popular.*
—DICCIONARIO DE MEJICANISMOS[1]

C arranza was already an old man with a long white beard when he decided that the First Chief of the Constitutionalist army should wear a uniform similar to that of a Confederate officer during the American Civil War, but a uniform without the insignia of a general. He was a civilian chief, and he did not believe that a military man should ever be the real chief, the president of Mexico. In the house devoted to him now on Río Lerma, not far from the British and American embassies in Mexico City, the sense of the man has been kept well: It is the formal house of a formal man, a tall man, bespectacled, pale and bearded, the father of daughters who had to borrow money to bury him more than three-quarters of a century ago, before he became a hero, long before it would have occurred to anyone to gaze across the distance of history at the chair in which he sat or the bowl from which he lifted up dripping handfuls of water to wash his face and cleanse his beard and mustache of the remains of meals taken formally with silver forks and spoons from their place on fine flowered china set out on embroidered white linen.

Venustiano Carranza was among the whitest of men in an era of white-skinned presidents and their cabinets. Indigenous men lived in distant places, where they proposed to remain; white men came from distant places

---

[1]Carranza permitted such rampant theft and corruption during his presidency that his very name became the verb meaning "to steal, to take from another what belonged to him." The dictionary says it was both amusing and offensive to the leader (caudillo) but was very popular.

to take control of the center. Carranza was a middle-class man from Coahuila, a norteño, although not a Sonoran, like the men who supported him and later followed him into power. Like all norteños, he could not forget the Mexican-American War, the loss of territory, the blow to dignity; it affected him all through his life, in his dealings with the Wilson administration and his dalliance with the Germans.

The First Chief, known as the Bearded One and the Old Man, came from a generation born before most of the warriors and theorists of his time. They were in their thirties or even younger, and he was in his fifties, although he looked older. His politics, like those of many men of his time, were not clear. They were made of bitterness over an earlier war, admiration for Benito Juárez, a desire to govern or even to rule, distrust of the military, and, in his great political and historical moment at the Constitutional Convention of 1917 in Querétaro, accommodation. He accepted Villa briefly, but he wanted him only as a weapon against Huerta, and it is clear that he wished him gone as soon as possible.

Villa and Zapata were of a different world, two socialists, even if one believed in an indigenous version of socialism and the other, as has been often said, was a socialist without knowing it. Carranza belonged to the time of Juárez and to his ideas. He and the Sonorans were violently anticlerical. They tore churches apart, made jokes of Roman Catholicism by parading through the streets in priestly vestments. They saw the Catholic Church as Mexico's second greatest problem after the proximity of the United States, and they were determined to vitiate its powers forever, even though the majority of Mexicans, including the Zapatistas and most Villistas, remained loyal to the Church.

Carranza wished not only to separate Church and State forever but to make the State dominant and the Church all but nonexistent. His view of economics and politics was not laissez-faire. He proposed a strong state, one that could influence, if not determine, the course of events large and small in the country. And he saw the role of the chief executive as powerful, much stronger than under the 1857 Constitution, which had given so much power to the legislature—although the Porfiriato gave the lie to the principle in practice. Carranza succeeded in doing away with the office of the vice president, but he was not a man who cared at all about social revolution, and when it came time to write a new constitution, he made that clear with the draft he presented to the convention.

What finally emerged from those meetings was an extraordinary document, the first "socialist" constitution in history, even before that of the Soviets. The arguments during the convention were laid out brilliantly by Charles C. Cumberland in *Mexican Revolution: The Constitutionalist Years.*[2] With an escort of fifty horsemen, Carranza made a symbolic journey from Mexico City to Querétaro, following the path of Maximilian, to attend the convention. The First Chief rode beside his general, el Manco, the one-armed man, hero of Celaya, Alvaro Obregón. Around them, a swarm of people walked and ran: barefoot boys, members of the press in suits and ties, men in wide sombreros, fedoras, workman's caps, campaign hats, a pith helmet, and western cowboy hats of every size and shape. It was a long journey, days on horse, intended to gain the attention of Mexico and the world. According to press reports, Carranza and his entourage were greeted by ten thousand people upon their arrival in Querétaro. His daughters, one in heavy taffeta and the other in a wrap of fur, were there to embrace him. And when he did at last enter the Teatro Iturbide, where the convention was held, he passed through a presidential honor guard all resplendent in boots, white jodhpurs, and embroidered tunics and holding swords in salute. Nothing could have been further from the tenor of the document that was about to emerge.

There were fights over credentials and other minor disagreements, but the convention, under the guiding and curiously light hand of the First Chief, quickly got down to doing its work. They were to produce the completed document and sign it in only sixty days, an extraordinary accomplishment given the innovations in the articles relating to labor and land. Some of the document came as a reaction to what were viewed as the flaws in the 1857 Constitution while other aspects of it were undoubtedly produced by the involvement of peasants and workers in what was largely a battle between elements of the middle class and those in power. In response to the power invested in the legislature, which had hampered the president's ability to govern, the convention abolished the vice presidency and gave great power to the executive, power that every president through the end of the century used to his advantage.

The document prohibited reelection, but past presidents had already learned to put handpicked successors in office, return to power, then find

[2]Austin: University of Texas Press, 1972.

ways to circumvent the prohibition. The new constitution would force a change in the form, creating single-party rule in oligarchic fashion perhaps suggested by the oligarchy from the northwest that ruled the country until the Cárdenas administration in the thirties.

As the convention opened, each state delegation posed for a photograph with the First Chief, who sometimes wore his curious civilian version of a military uniform and at other times sat, silver-handled cane in hand, derby hat on his knee, dressed in a three-button dark suit. His collar is generally obscured by his long white beard. He is a huge figure, tall and heavy, and he sits in the center of the front row of all the photographs like an enlargement of a man. The character of the convention itself is revealed in the attire of the delegates. There are wealthy men and unionists who carried on the strikes that preceded the beginning of the revolution, but those in attendance are distinguished not so much by the quality of their clothing as by the style. It is a convention across the line of the centuries. There are plainly nineteenth-century men in winged collars and turn-of-the-century men in celluloid collars and more than a few who have entered the second decade of the century, with their chins held up by nothing more than starch. A few have adopted the great bows of the French style associated with paintings by Manet, and here and there a man wears a pince-nez. Only a few wear eyeglasses, the First Chief most conspicuous among them. The Constitutional Convention has the atmosphere of a changing of the guard, the moment when the old contingent, the century past, and the new stand in the same place. Carranza himself is that moment; he is the man out of his time and not into the next, an in-between man, "the ancient future of Mexico," and sixty days after the photograph is made, the completed Constitution of 1917 will speed up time and presage the political aspirations of the century. But it will not be a revolution; it will be but a blueprint for the revolution that could have been.

Some of the articles of such a constitution were expected: The anticlerical aspects of Article 3 had a long history in Mexico, but only after some argument did the Convention vote, 99–58, to approve a version of the article providing that all public instruction would be secular and free and that primary and secondary education were obligatory. Some of the writing in the article is well worth considering. For example, speaking of the nation to be founded, section II a) reads: "It will be democratic, in consideration of democracy as not simply a juridical structure and a political regimen, but a way of life founded on the constant improvement of the economic, social and cultural life of the people."

Article 5 created a debate over labor law that eventually ended up in Article 123, which covers a dozen pages in one of the popular paperback versions of the constitution and begins, "All persons have the right to dignified and socially useful work . . ." and goes on to set standards never before codified in a national constitution: an eight-hour day (seven at night); the prohibition of dangerous and unhealthful labor; rules against certain forms of child labor; a minimum wage set at what is required to satisfy the needs of the head of a family;[3] equal pay for equal work without regard for sex or nationality; cash for work, the end of the company store and scrip; overtime pay; responsibility for workers injured in accidents on the job; the right to collective bargaining; the right to strike; social security, including workers' compensation, old age pensions, unemployment insurance.

Of all the ideas in the constitution, however, the most controversial came in Article 27, which made fundamental changes in the laws controlling property rights. It began by subordinating property rights to the public interest, "with the objective of equitable distribution of the national wealth" and conservation of natural resources. The article gave control of all subsoil rights, including oil and gas, to the government; limited foreign ownership of property, especially that along the coastlines and northern and southern borders; then prohibited ownership of land by churches (with an eye to Rome). As Cumberland wrote, it "declared Mexico for Mexicans." It was an article that protected the "integrity of lands of indigenous groups" and guaranteed the rights of ownership of land held and worked in common by ejidos. But it went even further, providing for the distribution of the land in what has to be considered one of the primary influences of the Zapatistas and the Aguascalientes Convention.

The Constitution of 1917 provided for a strong government, one that would be involved in every aspect of the social and economic life of the country. The influence of the early social revolutionaries, especially Flores

---

[3]The minimum wage does not meet that provision in the constitution. It had risen from 37 to 43 pesos a day between April 15, 2000, and April 15, 2003. Meanwhile, the daily cost of the thirty-five goods and services in the food basket required by a family of five had risen from 173 to 228 pesos, according to the Center for Multidisciplinary Analysis of the UNAM. *La Jornada,* June 22, 2003.

Magón, could be seen in some few aspects of the 1917 Constitution, but it was a far cry from an anarchist document and equidistant from the nineteenth-century liberalism of the 1857 Constitution. A new state had been defined. From that moment forward Mexico would be a democracy with a socialist constitution, and it would pass nearly a hundred years without enjoying democracy, as defined in the 1917 Constitution. As the signers emerged from the theater at the end of January 1917, a new duality had been born in Mexico: the law as codified and the law as practiced.

Under the new constitution the First Chief soon became the president of Mexico in the middle of an ongoing civil war. Although it may have tempted him, he did not make an agreement with the German government that might have prolonged the war in Europe; his hatred of the United States did not overcome his fears for Mexico if a pact with Germany became public. He dealt as best he was able, given the conditions of civil war and all the attendant problems, from inflation to influenza, and in some small measure he succeeded. Mexico changed because of him: The 1917 Constitution created an activist government; under the leadership of Luis Morones a union, the Confederation of Regional Workers of Mexico (CROM), came into being and slowly gained prominence and power; and the seeds of yet another form of corruption were sowed with the giving of various kinds of rewards—mainly land—in return for the service of military officers.

Carranza had become president because of his generals and the northwest junta, and when he came at the end of his term to selecting a new president, his objection to military men in the highest office led him to choose a civilian who was outside the circle of Sonoran generals. And the generals, led by Obregón, would not permit it. They published their Plan of Agua Prieta and drove Carranza from office. He wrote his manifesto to the nation, and then he had much of the wealth of the nation loaded onto a convoy of trains and headed again for Veracruz, the port that had sheltered beleaguered presidents since Juárez. He was not alone. General Francisco Murguía and others remained loyal. But not Jesús Guajardo. The man who had betrayed Zapata on behalf of Carranza now destroyed half of the convoy, killing hundreds, and tearing up the tracks, making it impossible for Carranza to continue by rail.

With a small military escort, Carranza made his way to a ranch at Tlaxcalantongo in the state of Puebla. On the night of May 21, 1920, he settled down to sleep in a small wood hut with a high thatched roof. It offered less space than the bedroom he had slept in only a few days earlier in the capital. He had difficulty sleeping, but finally the exhaustion of the flight to Veracruz caught up with him, and he closed his eyes and listened to the sound of the rain and sank into rest.[4] Shortly after three the next morning, a small group of men crawled through the low brush, past the tree stumps at the perimeter of the house, silent in the slippery earth, and when they were close to the thin wooden side of the house, they opened fire, screaming imprecations at the old man inside. When they entered, Carranza was wounded in the leg, the gut, and the liver. They did not finish their work. He lay dying, unable to speak, until finally he used his own revolver to quicken the end.

Carranza's body was brought back to Mexico City, where his daughters gave him a fine funeral, although they had to borrow the money to pay for it. The civil war was over, the decade finished, and Mexico had survived. The representatives of the states had written and sworn loyalty to a great change and the word "Revolution" had been enshrined as the most delicious and mercurial in the language.

---

[4]The Mexican novelist and critic Fernando Benítez described in moving detail the suffering of the last days of Carranza in his historical novel *El Rey Viejo* (The Old King) (Mexico: Fondo de Cultura Económica, 1959).

20.

The Dream of a Word

Friends, listen to the dream of a word.
— "CANTARES MEXICANOS"

In the summer of the year of the millennium, the word "revolution" suffered a great fall in Mexico. It happened suddenly across most of the country, and it was not a quaking or a rearrangement but a fall, for it was
precipitous and resounding, and after the fall the word settled in another
place. I saw it happen in cities and towns, but especially on election day,
along the paved road that rises from the center of Cuernavaca up along the
cliff above the river, then turns and climbs into the elegant part of the city.
In the early evening of that July day, the word lost its grip on Mexican politics. At a distance, walking up the steep slope, I heard the saying of names, a
slow and laborious counting, sometimes interrupted by a scattering of
applause. The polls had closed, and they were counting the votes. Until that
day, for seventy years, all but a handful of the votes of the people who lived
on the steepness above the now-fouled river had been for a party that contained the word "revolution" in its name.

Section 0364, known as La Lagunilla, where the poor of Cuernavaca lived,
had been the scene of many irregularities during the 1988 election, when the
loser came from the Democratic Party of the *Revolution* and the winner
from the Institutional Party of the *Revolution*. In the next election, in 1994,
"revolution" was overshadowed by the word "assassination," because of the
killing of Luis Donaldo Colosio, leaving 1988 as the last great moment of the
word "revolution."

How "revolution" came to mean all things good and desirable in Mexico
is a history of the country after 1910 or 1917 or 1929 or 1934, depending upon
one's politics. For the PRI it is 1929, when the party was born; for the PRD
it is 1934, when Lázaro Cárdenas came to power; and for the PAN it is a question that must be decided by the market, which is a synonym for "democ-

racy" in the PANista lexicon. Only lawyers and dreamers connect the word with the year of the constitution. Nineteen ten is the romantic year, and November 20 of that year, the day Madero set for his uprising, the celebrated date. Villa, Zapata, Flores Magón, Carranza are without years, timeless, as if a revolution had an immortal soul.

In the first decade after the end of the fighting and before the Cristero Rebellion of the 1920s, the dominant political party, formed by Obregón and his group in 1916, was the Liberal Constitutionalist Party. Before that, there was a Liberal Party, a Democratic Party, a Labor Party, a National Catholic Party, an Anti-Reelection Party, but no political party that used the word "revolution." Madero used the word in his Plan of San Luis Potosí, but he defined it to mean "throwing the rascals out of office."

The common use of the word came later, history or justification, a ceremony for the dead. By the time a national political convention was held at Querétaro in March 1929, all the danger had seeped out of the word. According to Daniel Cosío Villegas, "revolutionary" was a word that could include all the other political words.[1] It could be invested with whatever one wanted, and the new party was designed along just those lines; it had no specific program. Former President Calles, who was by then no longer quite so radical a leftist but still the gray eminence lurking behind the presidency, presided over the 1929 convention. In addition to the all-encompassing character of the word, he found a new rhetorical use for it. The word had the sound of victory, for the Revolution or some part of the Revolution—political or economic—something other than the Porfiriato, had won the wars. But it was not victory alone that General Calles endorsed. He was not the father of parades; he was a political man, one who adored power, and such men quickly learn to salute the past and promise the future. And what word held more promise for the landless and the poor, the great mass of Mexicans, than "revolution"? The party became the party of hope. He named it the Partido Revolucionario Nacional. It was the precursor of the PRI, and the name went through several versions before it became the Partido Revolucionario Institucional, but every version contained the word "revolution."

Calles had discovered something about language as well as politics: The Mexicans could invest the word with whatever enabled them to continue to expect a better life for their children, if not for themselves. If revolution was

---

[1] *El Sistema Político Mexicano* (Mexico: Cuadernos de Joaquín Mortiz, 1973).

not the accomplishment of paradise on earth, it was at least the promise of paradise. It did not mean "now"; it meant "someday." And whether Calles was conscious of it or not, the idea of paradise on earth appealed to memories of pre-Hispanic religion. While Christianity spoke of heaven and hell, of God, Jesus, and the Holy Ghost on one side and the devil on the other, the ancient religions held no promise of an afterlife except in rare instances: death in childbirth or by drowning for the Aztecs, for example. For the rest of the Aztecs, "it was only a little while here," and then human life, like jade, feathers, and even gold, would be destroyed, over.

"Revolution" edged into the place formerly occupied by heaven and hell in the fractured consciousness of the Mexican. It sustained the party of Calles for seven decades, yet no one ever quite defined the word in Mexico. And that was the source of its power and its usefulness. "Revolution" was the enormous basket of heaven on earth; it could hold every dream and almost every imaginable route to the dreamed life. Even after the word had lost its hold over the people, it was possible for the Mexican left to say that the campesinos still believed in the Revolution. But the word had become an instrument of oppression; if they believed, it was a terrible irony, as if they hoped to be freed by the very chains that bound them. And even if the campesinos believed, it was of less and less importance, for there were fewer campesinos every year. Mexico had long been an urban country; the campesino was the hero of the sweet Old Left and a few bands of guerrillas; urban Mexico was a more difficult proposition: There was little romance in fast food, traffic, television, and street gangs. The Thieves' Market had charmed generations; Oscar Lewis, the slightly racist, eminently leftist sociologist, had been enchanted by Tepito, a slum in the center of Mexico City; but now the Thieves' Market was mottled with AIDS patients, and in Tepito criminals and the police fought pitched battles in the streets.

The last great revolutionary hero in Mexico was not an apparent revolutionary at all, but Cantinflas, who more than any other writer or thinker in recent Mexican history embodied in his work the incomprehensible meaning of the word "revolution." He spoke a torrent of slang, broken sentences, and neologisms that often made no sense at all. He was the poor campesino come to the city only a generation ago, a slum dweller with his pants falling down and his tiny two-gallon hat perched miraculously on the back of his head. Cantinflas was the revolutionary who made comedy of the language of the Revolution, an ironist who defined the word "revolution" by making language, especially official language, incomprehensible: The Revolution went round and round and round, and nothing ever changed; a sentence never ended, it only gave birth to another and another, an infinite and unintelligible sequence of puns and ironies.

No single phrase could have been more influential in Cantinflas's understanding of the deceptions of language than the name of the political party that ruled Mexico, the Partido Revolucionario Institucional. If a revolution is to overturn and an institution is to remain, how could one possibly have a remaining overturning? A steadfast change? An immovable motion? The name of the political party for which almost every Mexican voted, the very heart of Mexican government, was an oxymoron, an incomprehensible statement, exactly like the comedy of Cantinflas. No one could defeat him in argument because no one could understand what he was saying. Only he knew. The secret of the Revolution was bound up in the Revolution, and only those who controlled it could understand it. If anything earthly was as mysterious as the ways of the Lord, it was the way of the Revolution, whatever it was and whatever it said. One could not question God or the Revolution; one could only believe in it. Was the message of Cantinflas one of unrest? Was he a Chaplinesque character, comedy on screen, socialist in the world? The Party of the Institutional Revolution did not see him that way. Cantinflas, the bumpkin in the big city, the victim of the great urbanization, pointed out the comedy of the system, but he was never, not in any of his films, destroyed by it. He could in fact be understood as the happy ending. The incomprehensible Revolution would work out in the end. There was a heaven. To be sure of that interpretation, a film was made to show Cantinflas in hell. It was a dream, but the double-talking scamp with the falling-down pants defeated the devil himself. The Revolution triumphed over evil. And what was evil? Whatever opposed the Revolution! It was a catechism. When Miguel Alemán in 1946, about to become president of Mexico, changed the name of the party to the PRI, he could have had no greater inspiration for the making of the phrase than the comedy of the most beloved man in Mexico. For the rest, he had learned as a child that Revolution could have the power of faith and the durability of dogma.

Octavio Paz found another and somewhat different meaning in the word. In *The Labyrinth of Solitude*,[2] he calls "revolution" the "magic word." Every-

---

[2] *El Laberinto de la Soledad* (Mexico: Cuadernos Americanos, 1950).

one is following the heroes of the Revolution, according to Paz, but where are they going? "No one knows," he concludes, but it somehow brings "an immense happiness and a quick death." The most interesting point he made about the Revolution had to do with its purpose. He said it was to integrate the two parts of the mestizo, the pre-Hispanic and the Spanish Catholic.

Everyone who has written about Mexico since 1910 has written about the Revolution. In 1947, Cosío Villegas began his famous lament *The Mexican Crisis* by speaking about the Revolution. He said that its aims had been exhausted, that the Revolution had many programs but never a clear program. And if there was no clear program, what was meant by "revolution" other than something good, beyond the horizon? And for whom was it good? More and more it became the idea that had been good for the rich and the poor alike. "Revolution" became the foundation of the new world, a reversal of the punishment for the error in Eden.

Unlike the Revolution to the north, which had been a War of Independence (July 4 is Independence Day, not Revolution Day in the United States), the Mexicans had a war for independence in 1810 and a revolution in . . . ? The answer depends on how one views the "magic word."

In 1992 the historian Lorenzo Meyer published *The Second Death of the Mexican Revolution*. At the end of the book, he addresses a chapter, a kind of coda, "To My General," by whom he means Lázaro Cárdenas. He denies that the deaths he has described are the finish of the idea of Revolution in Mexico. Meyer has a definition of "revolution": It is what the "general" wanted for Mexico in the 1930s, a mix of Marxism, nationalism, land reform, and the New Deal.

What is interesting about Meyer's notion is that he thinks the Revolution was not really born until the mid-1930s, more than seventeen years after the 1917 Constitution and only six years before its first death. However, the Cárdenas vision was for a rural Mexico, and Mexico has since become a highly urban country. And Meyer, who adores Cárdenas, also blames him for the centralization of enormous power in the person of the Mexican president, the one who is charged with carrying out "the Revolution."

Sixty years had passed since the end of the Cárdenas *sexenio*,[3] when the word truly described the society. There on the steepness of the road that ran

[3]The six-year Mexican presidential term.

up along the cliff the counting of the ballots went on into the evening. The light seemed to fade along with the word. The vote count was a surprise, for the Institutional Party of the Revolution had offered threats and bags of rice and cooking oil, and on the left the Party of the Democratic Revolution had the name Cárdenas embodied in the son of the general. But the election clerks announced the new name of power again and again. They called out, "Green.[4] PAN. PAN. PRI. PAN. PAN. PRD. PRI. PAN."

The polling place had been set up on the curve of the hill, where it was almost level for twenty yards before it climbed to the plateau above the city. The members of the election commission and the poll watchers sat behind long tables, pulling folded ballots out of clear plastic boxes, opening them, laying them out in piles. The counting of the ballots for state and local elections had been completed. Only the presidential ballots remained. The official counters looked uphill toward the heights, where armed guards stood at the iron gates of the weekend villas. They could not see what lay behind them. Nylon tenting made a white roof over the tables and a wall behind them; it shielded the election officials from the sun and from the sight of the cliff and the river. They could not see the descent to the staggered rows of narrow trails and cardboard roofs, the polluted river where the vermin swam. Nor could they see the far side of the river, where a jungle grew untouched, as green as Eden, and gave home to the creatures that survived the river.

Green and PAN and PRI and PAN.

The Green Party had used the polluted river at the bottom of the cliff, with its mix of chemicals and disease, to win votes. The river had caused terrible sickness among the people who lived in the voting district. A party devoted to ecology appealed to them, even though it was a tiny minority party, unlikely to win more than a few seats, if any, in the legislature. The PRD had offered only the Prince of the Revolution in Cuauhtémoc Cárdenas, the son of Lázaro. And of the PRI, the people said they had endured enough of "Revolution"; there is no Revolution, there was no Revolution. Carlos Salinas de Gotari had awakened them from the long years of dreaming. If that was the Revolution, if the only meaning of the Revolution was now "theft," then it was all right for the word to fall.

The word "revolution" fell as the peso had fallen in the first days of the

---

[4]A party originally devoted to matters of ecology. Its elected representatives have sometimes voted with the PRI and sometimes with the PAN. The full name is Partido Ecologia Verde.

Zedillo administration. The poverty level, according to the conservative figures of the World Bank, had risen from 50.97 percent in 1994 to 61.88 percent in 1996. A significant part of the Mexican middle class had been
destroyed. Millions of people had fallen into poverty, and the poor who
were struggling to reach the lower middle class had lost hope. The old politics was dead. The boys from Harvard and the American business schools
had killed it. The death was accidental, to be sure, but it was a killing nevertheless, and it had caused a fundamental change.

What had occurred there on the edge of the cliff was not politics, however; something had taken place at a deeper level. I saw it in the face of Fernando Macedo, the PRI poll watcher who stood at the end of the row of
tables at the place where the road began its long downward slope. He leaned
heavily on the table, as if he had trouble standing. Now and again he
straightened up, pulled a handkerchief from his pocket, and wiped the sweat
from his face. It was not the face he had worn for all the years he had worked
in the district, nor was it the face of the PRI that morning. The menace had
gone out of it; nothing was left of the icy stare, the heavy jaw, the face that
greeted like a fist. He said nothing, questioned nothing. He did not speak;
he did not sigh; he leaned on the table more heavily with every name the
election clerk tolled. There were no surprises; it was after his fall from power,
but all the votes had not yet been counted, the agonizing fall of Fernando
Macedo had not yet been completed.

Macedo had been the PRI's man in the district for thirty years. In that
time he had gained weight, raised a grand mustache, then trimmed it back,
made it neater, more corporate. "What did I do for thirty years?" he asked,
his eyes glancing up at the sky, as if he expected an answer from someone
who dwelled there. "I did social work, helping people. Where will the help
come from now?"

On the same road, farther down, going toward the level center of the city
where Hernán Cortés built a palace, there was a woman who lived in a cave
at the side of the road. She paid no rent. She had raised her children and now
her grandchildren there. In conversation, she did not use the word "revolution." Macedo had not performed his social work for her, but neither had he
done much for himself. His teeth were rotten, missing here and there; some
were corn-colored, one was black, another gold. When he closed his mouth,
he had to grimace to bring his teeth together. It could not be pleasant to
watch him eat.

He sweated and stood to mop his brow and leaned again on the table. He still had the sweet smell of cologne about him. He must have washed and shaved very recently, just before the closing of the polls. Perhaps he thought of the manly hugs, the congratulations he had enjoyed in other elections, other times, before the fall of the word. No one spoke to him, although he had ruled the district for thirty years. The look on his face was not as it seemed at first; it was not defeat but shame, as if he had been in love with a sin. "I must look for another post," he said. He offered no smile, no tears. He looked down; by the demeanor of his shoulders he said that at least he was not without shame.

The fall of the word would not be real for a long time after that July day, not until the new man took office on November 20. In the intervening months it became more and more clear that "revolution" was not understood as a political word, for such a word would have been defined more clearly; a program would have been connected to it. It was, if not in fact, at least in feeling a religious notion, as almost all things must be if they are to have profound effect in Mexico. "Revolution" was not the messiah, not the Second Coming, not heaven on earth, but it was the messianic feeling, and it was always used that way: The Revolution had been and the Revolution would come again, and when it came again—that is, when it was realized—there would be Peace on the Mexican Earth, Goodwill toward Men, and the table overflowing with the products of the fatherland. Paz was correct in that the Revolution was an attempt to integrate the past into the Mexican persona, but it was not a real past; not a known past, the nostalgia inspired by the Revolution was for a time and place and a sense of well-being that had never existed for any but the few. Only a religious notion could make such promises; "revolution" stood not for politics, but in contrast with politics; it did not compete with laissez-faire economics or liberalism or anarchy; its only competitor was the Catholic Church.

In the failure of historians to find a single theme, to paint an indubitable portrait of its drives and intellectual details, "revolution" was left to be portrayed as Quetzalcoatl or Jesus or Moses had been across the centuries—to fit the styles of the time. In Mexico the rivalry between divine and worldly things, between worship and politics, had gone on for centuries. "The religion," as Catholicism was called, had one advantage that could not be overcome, however: The Church had a central thesis laid out at Trent, the "clear program" Cosío Villegas had not found in the revolution. In the clash between the two religions, Church and Revolution, the outcome should never have been in doubt.

. . .

Every year, for generations, on the anniversary of the day Francisco Madero set for the beginning of the Revolution of 1910, the President of Mexico has celebrated the heroes of that bloody decade: Madero, Zapata, Villa, Carranza. In 2001, Vicente Fox, whose party did not carry the word "revolution" in its name and whose affiliation with the Catholic Church was stronger than that of any Mexican president during the preceding seventy years, made no mention of Zapata, Villa, or Carranza, and in his lexicon the anarcho-syndicalism of Flores Magón never existed. He spoke only of Madero. During his presidential campaign he had spoken only of Madero. When he took over Los Pinos, he removed a portrait of Benito Juárez from the presidential office and replaced it with that of Madero. "Democracy," he said, and there was no doubt that his election had been a triumph of the democracy of the ballot box, but it had also been the fall of "the dream of a word." Mexico had put itself in God's invisible hand. If the PRI or the PRD were to come to power in 2006 or 2012, it would be as a different religion, not merely neoliberalism, but something sterner yet, perhaps a new and dangerous nationalism.

21.

Totalitarian Threads

At this time we Tlatelolca set up skull racks; skull racks were in three places. One was in the temple courtyard at Tlillan, where the heads of our lords were strung; the second place was in Yacacolco, where the heads of our lords were strung, along with the heads of two horses. . . . It was the exclusive accomplishment of the Tlatelolca.

After this they drove us from there and reached the marketplace. That was when the great Tlatelolca warriors were entirely vanquished. With that the fighting stopped once and for all.

That was when the Tlatelolca women all let loose, fighting, striking people, taking captives. They put on warriors' devices, all raising their skirts so that they could give pursuit. . . .

And all this is what happened to us and what we saw and beheld. What we suffered is cause for tears and sorrow.

—Anales de Tlatelolco, 1528,
TRANSLATION BY JAMES LOCKHART

Although the national university was in danger after the strike had closed it down for ten months, it did not seem likely that it could ever die. Under various names it had survived since classes were first offered in Mexico in 1553. If it finally collapsed, if the year of emptiness and chaos brought some end—a bow to private education, a federation of campuses—it would take decades for Mexico to recoup. The Aztecs had their *calmecac* (school for nobles) to carry on their culture, and when the Spaniards came, they brought their own tradition. Founded by royal decree, the first university was a weapon of colonialism, used to spread European culture to New Spain, producing a class of educated criollos, mestizos, and natives who could carry on the business of the crown in an organized, God-fearing, and profitable manner. During its first 250 years the university served both functions.

The children of the rich were often educated in Europe, but the university was the center of culture in New Spain and the birthplace of the language of discontent. The original university, having produced a cadre of intellectuals who successfully opposed the rule of its founders, was secularized and divided into several institutions following Independence and then reorganized into its present form as part of the Ministry of Education under Justo Sierra in 1910. But it was not until 1929 that the university had been granted autonomy. President Manuel Ávila Camacho strengthened the autonomous character of the university by enabling the leaders of the UNAM to choose the rector. The many faculties were fully integrated in 1945, and in 1953 the entire university was moved to the present campus in the south of the Federal District, where it grew into a vast organization, employing more than fifty thousand people.

The Mexican government, which always has an eye on the past as well as the future, watches the university carefully. Most of its troubles over 350 years have come either from the United States, the Catholic Church, or the university. Even the Zapatista rebellion in 1994 was led by a university-trained middle-class man, Subcomandante Marcos.

The problem for the government has always been the character of the intellectuals and the university under their tutelage. Among the rectors who were appointed after the reorganization of the university by Justo Sierra in 1910 were two of the most prominent members of the Ateneo de la Juventud, José Vasconcelos and Antonio Caso. Since they were both scholars and in their time radical thinkers, having led the intellectual opposition to the positivist notions adopted by the Porfiriato, Vasconcelos and Caso gave the university a sense of independence and a certain moral authority that the institution held dear until it succumbed to creeping bureaucratization after the 1968 strike and then, at the end of the century, complete shutdown by student and faculty strikers.

VASCONCELOS, FROM LEFT TO RIGHT

The man behind the reestablishment of the university in 1910, Justo Sierra, remains best known as a historian, while the man remembered for his influence on public education and the arts is José Vasconcelos. He was one of the founders of the Ateneo de la Juventud, which, despite its short life, had lasting influence on Mexican thought.[1] But none of its illustrious members had more influence, more ambition, and a more curious political road than Vasconcelos.

Trained as a lawyer, he wrote the Ateneo's devastating essay on Gabino Barreda, who had been one of the chief architects of positivism. During the

---

[1] The Ateneo was founded under another name in 1907, took the name Ateneo de la Juventud in 1910, and disbanded in 1914.

Revolution he sided with Madero, became a Villista, joined Carranza, went into exile after a split with the Constitutionalists, and finally emerged from the civil wars as Obregón's secretary of education. In that post he oversaw the building of a thousand rural schools and the opening of two thousand libraries. He directed government presses to print vast numbers of books, many of which were packed into crates to be carried by mules into the remote villages of Mexico.

Since the literacy rate in Mexico after the civil wars was under 28 percent, Vasconcelos had undertaken an all but impossible task. In his wish to make Mexico into a nation, he not only convinced Obregón to double the education budget so that schools and libraries could be built and staffed but conceived a program to use the plastic arts as a form of pedagogy. If the people could not read, then he would teach them with pictures. He employed a group of young painters to decorate the walls of public buildings with large murals depicting the history of Mexico and the struggle of the people for Independence and freedom. Two of the painters were Communists, and President Obregón was a thoroughgoing capitalist, ordinarily an unhappy marriage, but the all-encompassing concept of Revolution was enough to avoid confrontations over politics and economics.

Vasconcelos may have had only didactic aims, but his project produced the school of Mexican muralists, including Diego Rivera, David Alfaro Siqueiros, and José Clemente Orozco. The indigenous world, from pictures of a pre-Hispanic paradise to the dark and resolute figures of the wars, appeared on the walls of Mexico. Vasconcelos had not yet published his vision of Mexico and the world, but the choice of painters, politics, and subject matter reflected what he had learned in the villages as well as his study of the classics. None of this gave even a hint of the strange political turn of his ideas toward the end of his life.

As a man Vasconcelos was a microcosm of the enduring problem of Mexico. He was born in Oaxaca in 1881 and raised in Coahuila, bringing both the north and south experiences with him to the capital. He opposed positivism, which was a European view, with the more artistic and spiritual ideas of Bergson. As an educator he insisted upon the classical texts of Europe as the only worthwhile texts. His devotion to this idea was so deep and unyielding that it sometimes led his critics to find him ludicrous. In one of the best-known (probably apocryphal) stories about him, Vasconcelos is said to have traveled to a very remote village, where he asked a native several questions, including the name of the village in which he lived. To all the questions the man replied that he did not know. At the end of the interrogation, Vasconcelos turned to an aide and directed him to implement a solution to the villager's problems: "Send two cases of books to this village. Immediately."

Upon taking his post as rector of the National University, Vasconcelos said, "I do not now come to work for the university, but to ask that the university work for the people." He then wrote the motto on the university's seal, *Por mi raza hablará el espiritu,* foreshadowing his idea of the cosmic race, for which the spirit will speak, and later inspiring the use of the word *raza* as the slogan of Chicanos in the United States. The motto concludes with the Bergsonian and indigenous idea of spirit.

So it is curious that now the complaint about him in some quarters is that his teaching was "too Eurocentric." But the very people who attack him for his Eurocentrism compare the genius and importance of their own views to his *Raza Cósmica,* a short book published in 1925, after his experience teaching the classics to the (mainly indigenous and mestizo) rural poor. His idea of the cosmic race was of a genetic genius in which there was added to the races of the world a fifth race made up of all the others. Nowhere was this cosmic race of races more prevalent and more likely to be the first to achieve its full potential than in the Americas, particularly Mexico. He wrote at the conclusion of his book of "a race composed of the treasure of all that preceded it, the ultimate race, the cosmic race." He was leery of whites, claiming that in qualities of the spirit the mestizo, the Indian, the black exceeded the white.

The problem for many of his current critics may lie more in their reading (or lack thereof) than in Vasconcelos himself, at least in the early and vital Vasconcelos, before a series of failed revolutions, lost elections, banishments, imprisonment, and self-imposed exile led him to bizarre political ideas. By 1940, when he returned to Mexico from one of his many exiles, the man who hired Rivera and Siqueiros had joined the extreme right. He worked to spread fascist propaganda, editing *Timón,* a magazine rumored to have been funded by the Nazi Party. Perhaps it was an inevitable philosophical end for a man who had been torn between two opposing worldviews and had resolved them in a grand wedding of all peoples, all origins. Perhaps he had simply exchanged one utopia, one *Übermensch* for another.

His idea of the genetic and spiritual power of the mestizaje, which he called the cosmic race, has risen and fallen over the years. It was probably never stronger than during the Cárdenas presidency (1934–1940) and never weaker than today, when whites dominate business and politics. The idea of a cosmic race remains alive, but Vasconcelos himself seems an anachronism, like Comte, in the shadow of the poverty of education in Mexico and the globalization of practically everything.

A STRIKE AT THE HEART OF THE UNAM

The strike had been going on for ten months (since March 1999), and the students inside the university now believed it would end badly for them. Hundreds were in jail after a riot at one of the Mexico City preparatory schools that fed the UNAM, and the federal government had formed a new unit, the PFP (Federal Preventive Police), to deal with such problems as the strike. Moreover, the students had no important allies beyond the barricades. The PRD had turned on them. "Naughty children need to be spanked," said a longtime leader of the party. And they had no allies in the press, not even in *La Jornada*, the left-of-center daily known as the voice of the UNAM.

One writer, Enrique Krauze, had called the strike "a bland revolution," but said it might turn tough. He connected it to the Zapatista rebellion in Chiapas. Mexico's leading journalist, Elena Poniatowska, said it was a "political thermometer" for the country. Early on the forty-one professors emeritus of the university had met to try to work out a solution to the strike. The rector who had called that meeting had been replaced, and the new rector had summoned a group of ten professors, whom the students described as *los grandes*. Miguel León-Portilla, the only professor who had been a member of both groups and who claimed his political party was the UNAM, said he was deeply disturbed by the injury to the university he had served for so many years, yet he found the student representatives sensible. During the private negotiations he told the students he agreed with much of what they demanded of the university. "If you were not on strike," he said, "I could be sitting on your side of the table."

The situation had occupied the headlines of the Mexican papers every day for months. The strikers had broken into two distinct groups: the reformers and the ultras. Critics of the strike on the center-left found a comfortable situation because of the emergence late in the strike of the ultras: The critics could maintain their left credentials by condemning the ultras rather than the strike itself. Thus, the center-leftists could have it both ways; they could both abandon *and* support the students. For the PRI, the PAN, and many of the small parties the strike was an affront to intellect as well as order. The strike belonged to the egalitarian left, the humanistic left, and mostly the furious left.

What concerned the students most was not the opinions of the moment, but the advice of history. Many of their parents and some of their professors had been part of the 1968 strike that ended in the modern massacre at Tlatelolco. In what seemed to be a repetition of ancient history, hundreds of students had been killed,[2] thousands had been put in jail. The Mexican Army had used tanks and turned machine guns on the crowd just as the Spaniards had turned their superior killing capacity on the Tlatelolcans in the sixteenth century. Now the strikers feared another massacre.

With no allies outside, the students chose to permit no enemies inside. When the strike leaders gave interviews, they did so in the city, away from the campus, in the privacy of the public world. Meanwhile, ten months had gone by and more than 225,000 students at the University City campus of the UNAM had not been to school. The newspapers spoke of a "lost generation." In fact, there had been a lost year.

Given the size of the university, there would be some lasting effect, for the UNAM was truly a *national* institution, but with one main campus. According to Luis Villoro, the philosopher and professor emeritus, each year the UNAM admitted 33,500 to its professional schools, 33,000 candidates for bachelor's degrees, 18,000 to science and humanities, and 15,000 to its preparatory schools. Half the doctorates granted in Mexico came from the UNAM, and one-fourth of all graduate degrees. What Villoro did not say in his 1999 summation of the importance of the university was that its reputation had been in decline for nearly a decade as other campuses, other universities had risen in esteem. For those who could afford it, the private universities now offered superior education in many fields.

The loss of a year was difficult for many students and, for most people involved in scientific research, a painful waste. For others it was only a loss of time because Mexico could no longer provide employment for its educated middle class. Since the collapse of the peso in 1994, engineers drove taxicabs, architects owned little shops; times were worse for historians and

[2]The number is still in dispute.

experts in the poetry of the Mexican romantics. Worse yet, the UNAM was known as the birthplace of radicals. Who wanted a revolutionary in the office, some kid with a balaclava in one pocket and a pistol in the other? Better to find someone trained by the Jesuits at Universidad Iberoamericana or better yet a graduate of the elite Instituto Tecnológico y de Estudios Superiores de Monterrey (ITESM or El Tec).

Since they had so little to look forward to after graduation, thousands of middle-class students—and the strikers were mainly from the middle and lower middle classes—felt no academic pressure to end the strike.[3] The poor were another matter. The strikers claimed the poor were shut out of the preparatory schools that fed students into the UNAM, but it was not one of their major issues. Unlike the 1968 strike, which spread beyond the UNAM to other institutions and had deep social and political as well as academic issues at its core, the strike that began in 1999 belonged to the postmodern revolution. *La Onda*, the Wave of the sixties, had no meaning for students at the end of the century. The leaders of the 1968 strike had included men named Cervantes Cabeza de Vaca and Sócrates; the spokesman for this strike was El Mosh.[4]

The music had changed, issues of race and personal economics had come to the fore; focus had turned inward, become more personal; the university itself was the issue; the outside world was exactly that, outside, peripheral. And in the postmodern world irony was permitted; the five-hour orations of Fidel Castro had been replaced by the wit of the Zapatista rebel Subcomandante Marcos. Instead of standing in a crowd of thousands, one could attend the Revolution alone, on the Internet. The organization of the strike had also changed. Argument rather than union was the rule, and by choosing consensus over democracy, the strikers had made the duration of every argument all but limitless. They claimed consensus as the indigenous method; therefore, they (all but one faculty, *Ciencias* [Science]) preferred it. This too was a postmodern notion, for

[3] At the end of 2001 the Mexico City daily *Reforma* reported that only one-third of graduating seniors expected to be employed in their chosen fields within the next ten years.

[4] According to some sources, Sócrates Campos either did not hold up well under torture after his arrest or may have been a provocateur.

El Mosh, a name taken from a recording star popular at the time in Mexico, was Alejandro Echavarría. He was jailed after the strike, tried, and finally released in 2003 after paying a fine of twenty-five hundred dollars.

modern Mexico had abandoned its indigenous people by 1940, leaving them to assimilation and history.

Yet there was something of the sweet anger of the young in the students. Many of them belonged emotionally to the old generations of dreamers and warriors who had tried again and again to invent their own idea of paradise in Mexico, to accept Trotsky when Stalin did not want him, to praise the Communists Diego Rivera and Frida Kahlo and not to keep David Alfaro Siqueiros in prison very long. That the students were brave, there was no doubt, for they knew history and now loneliness. The government had appointed a new rector to deal with them, a psychiatrist with PRI connections. No matter who sat in the rector's chair, Mexican law made a long strike dangerous. Social dissolution was not permitted in Mexico; the government was legally entitled to defend itself. If President Ernesto Zedillo chose to see the strike as social dissolution, he could send in the army.

The students shut down the university early in the strike, manning checkpoints, installing barricades at the gates. With the campus closed to the press, rumors of rampant destruction, orgies, stockpiles of weapons appeared in the media. Ten months into the strike, on February 5, 2000, Professor Camilo Pérez Bustillo and his wife, María de la Luz, arranged for me to visit University City with them. Two students from another university picked us up and drove us to the campus. At the one gate that had not been barricaded, we passed through with no questions asked. The students at the checkpoint looked into the car, smiled at María de la Luz, whom they recognized, although she was not part of the strike, and moved the barricade to allow us to pass.

It was late afternoon, and dusk does not last long in winter in the Valley of Mexico. We drove slowly, touring the emptiness. No other cars passed us on the roads, which were wide and smoothly paved, boulevards in the woods of University City. The ambience was very much like that of one of the Mesoamerican ruins at the end of the day, after all the tourists had gone, after all the interminable repetitions of guides and guidebooks had been put to rest. At another entrance a barricade of benches, logs, and stone stood ready to block the way of the cars and trucks that did not come. We all had read stories of mounds of garbage piled up in the streets and buildings, of terrible destruction. But we saw only the woods and the wide road.

The most radical faculty, according to the press, was Ciencias. Most of the ultras and many of the founders of the strike movement were said to come from Ciencias, perhaps because one of the major issues of the strike was the possibility that the university would "privatize" its scientific research, selling it off to Mexican and foreign corporations and using the profits to cover the increasing cost of operation.

The act that precipitated the strike was the announcement on March 15, 1999, of a plan to increase student fees, although the increase was not very much (680 pesos—$68—per semester) and applicable only to those who could afford to pay. But it was the last straw for the students. They demanded that Francisco Barnés, then rector of the university, rescind the fees. He had refused, and the students had declared a strike. Barnés soon capitulated, making payment voluntary, but by then fees were only part of the problem in the eyes of the strikers. They walked out on April 20. As the strike grew more sophisticated, it included questions of academic freedom and the organization of the university. Nothing so worried the student and faculty strikers as the bureaucratization of what had been an autonomous university. Neither students nor faculty had any influence over the policies that ruled the UNAM. The university had fallen into the hands of managers, and the managers were tied to the government, and the government was the PRI, and the PRI was the home of neoliberalism, and there were few things the students and most of the faculty despised so much as neoliberalism.

On the evening of my visit the Consejo Central de la Huelga (CGH), the central council of the strike, was to decide whether to negotiate or remain committed to their demands. The faculties, each having reached its own internal consensus, were to gather in the Che Guevara Auditorium in the Humanities Building to seek a general consensus.

Inside the main part of the Humanities Building, the graffiti artists had been hard at work. Slogans were written everywhere, but nothing obscene, nothing threatening. The themes ranged from academic freedom to social justice. There were no signs of the guerrilla groups the newspapers and the rector had said were behind the strike.

Two students stopped to talk with us. We followed them through the kitchen, where older people, mostly parents of strikers, cooked the food that was brought daily onto the campus and distributed free to whoever was hungry. The students kept their backpacks and blankets in a small office on the third floor of the building. The office was crowded, and it was not neat; after ten months the university maintenance crew was sorely missed, but there were no unpleasant odors, nothing had been destroyed. Telephones, copiers, chairs, everything was in working order. The students invited their guests to sit down, and after we were seated, they took the remaining chairs or sat on the floor.

One of the students, a young woman, was slightly plump and slightly pretty, and very bright behind her large eyeglasses. She was in her last year, majoring in education. Her voice was clear and penetrating, and she had the diction of a middle school teacher. As the hours wore on, she became the star of the conversation.

She said, "The fees implied a total reform of the university, its structure as much as its academics, but most important, the structure; basically what's implied is the privatization of the public university." The national university, she said, should be entirely free; that was the law, which the students believed should not be changed. It was a matter of social mobility.

The other student who had led us to the office, a history major in his senior year, sat on the floor. He said, "The university corresponds to a neoliberal society."

Then the one with the clear voice spoke, and everyone agreed: "What we have now is a university with a vertical structure, and we want to open it up to greater participation. Generation after generation the students are different, but the professors stay here and have less and less voice; the administration listens less and less to their demands. What has been lost is the critical capacity of the university, its students, and faculty. We want a true democracy, one that includes diverse voices."

When they spoke of the humanities, it was often with heavy irony, for Francisco Barnés, upon being appointed rector, had suggested doing away with the humanities entirely since there was no money to be made from studying them.[5] The young woman said, "In general, a society without philosophers, without teachers, without historians is an incomplete society, lacking specific thinking about social necessities.

"We are opposed to a change from education to training. We are seeking the kind of education that will help the society. For example, those that

[5]This is not an uncommon view in Mexico. Jorge Castañeda, when speaking as a potential candidate for president in 2006, takes a position only slightly different. He wants to use market techniques to determine what will be most productive for the country and then give scholarships or other inducements to move students into those fields.

study chemistry go to work for the big companies. This is not what we want. We are humanists.

"Oh, yes, they [the administration] want a humanities faculty, but what is the humanism they want, the humanism of Preparatory School Three, the humanism of beatings?"

Then the students began to speak of the spying that had gone on before the strike, of the surveillance cameras and the spies that watched every movement of the students. One of the students who had crowded into the door of the inner office to join in the conversation showed a dossier the strikers had found. We looked through page after page, all addressed to the government, some containing personal reports about students, others referring to flyers or other published materials considered subversive.

The students said they demanded an end to the spying, a return to the academic freedom provided by law. There was not much that pleased them now in Mexico. They had no more respect for the press than for the authorities. The people who appeared in the newspapers and on television, the one known as El Mosh and others, were self-appointed leaders, they said, media creations, not the real leaders at all.

Then I asked if they were afraid that the army would enter the campus, and the demeanor of all the brave young men and women changed. The smiles turned wan; the carefully spoken, academic phrasing changed, if only for a moment. "Tlatelolco," they said. They knew what had happened in 1968. "Yes, of course we are afraid," the one with eyeglasses said. She had spoken earlier of going home on weekends, of the support of her parents for the strike. The child appeared in all the faces of the students when they thought of the army.

The students listed the possible ends of the strike in the order of their probability, with the most likely first.

1. Victory for the strikers.
2. The entrance onto the campus of the army and the killing of the students.
3. Expulsion of the strikers and privatization of the university.
4. Some accommodation between the strikers and the authorities.

There was no irony in the list. They were sure that some of them would die, but they did not know when.

With the list complete, there was not much more to say. We went to the Che Guevara Auditorium, where the plenary session was to seek consensus from all the faculties on their next move. The question was what to do about the events of the past few days. The clash between students and police at a preparatory school had led to the arrest of 247 students. At least 30 had been hurt. The jails were now full of students accused of a variety of crimes, including terrorism, which carried a sentence of as much as forty years. Of the students held in the various city jails, 76 were under eighteen years of age. Some of the speakers referred to them as minors. Others, more dramatically, called them the innocents. The speakers proposed that yet another demand—for the release of all the imprisoned innocents—be added to their nonnegotiable list.

A communiqué was read from El Sub, as Subcomandante Marcos is affectionately known. It was brief, witty, ironic, dismissive of Mexican President Ernesto Zedillo's remarks about the Zapatistas during his stay at the annual conference of the world's wealthiest people in Davos, Switzerland.

But even Subcomandante Marcos, beloved of the students for his wit and willingness to put his radicalism to the test in the jungles of Chiapas, had no purchase on the strikers compared to the taped voice of a little girl. The tape had been made surreptitiously and smuggled out of the juvenile jail. The girl spoke of a hunger strike and delivered a long, ironic litany of the crimes of which she and the others were guilty. Then she promised never to abandon the strike, never. At the conclusion of the tape, the auditorium, filled with weary people who had been eating, chatting, sleeping, finally came to life. "Strike, strike, strike," they shouted, raising their hands above their heads and making the victory sign.

And then there was another speaker and another, into the early-morning hours. The speakers went on and on through the night. Shortly after six o'clock that morning, with support helicopters flying overhead, hundreds of heavily armed men in riot gear, the troops of the newly formed Federal Preventive Police, stormed the campus. More than seven hundred people were arrested. The news media finally entered the campus along with the armed police force. Two hours later the evidence of the depraved and dangerous character of the strike was displayed on television: three marijuana plants, a piece of pipe, one machete, and a couple of knives. Nothing else was reported about what had happened on campus, how the strike worked, why it always took so long for the strikers to respond to offers of negotiation, or how the professors and students had, for the most part, maintained the order and decorum of an academic institution during ten months of occupation and siege.

THE CAPITALIST

Other than the work of Vasconcelos, there was little dreaming during the Obregón presidency. He was a practical man, with a talent for war and little experience with peace. During the first three years of his four-year presidency the United States refused to recognize his administration. The American secretary of state referred to Mexicans as nonwhites and thoroughly distrusted them and the provision in Article 127 of their constitution that applied to foreign-owned property, especially oil. In the summer of 1923, U.S. and Mexican commissioners met on Bucareli Street in Mexico City to agree to an interpretation of Article 127 that would reassure U.S. interests in Mexico. In return, the United States granted full recognition to the Obregón government, which resulted in greater import-export business and a more favorable exchange rate. Despite its salutary economic effect, Mexican nationalists found the Bucareli agreements unfair to Mexico, another U.S. incursion. Obregón, ever the field general, moved quickly against the nationalists, several of whom were soon murdered, including Pancho Villa and Obregón's friend and general Benjamin Hill.

As his administration neared the end, Obregón followed the pattern set by Juárez and Díaz: He chose a successor who would in turn choose him as his successor, thus maintaining power without violating the antireelection clause in the constitution. He named Plutarco Elías Calles, a man from Sonora, like himself. For most of his career, Obregón had been able to count on the loyalty and shrewdness of the former primary school teacher.

The election of Calles to a four-year term in 1924 marked the beginning of stability, if not of democracy, in Mexico. There was peace, if not happiness, among the workers. Luis Morones, the head of the CROM (Regional Confederation of Mexican Workers), had supported Obregón, and Obregón repaid him generously. Morones grew fat and overconfident. His fingers were loaded down with diamonds, and his head was filled with dreams of glory. He looked like the madam of the richest whorehouse in Mexico.

The peace was limited largely to the presidential palace. Control of the workers by Morones was uncertain, and the Catholic Church and the hacendados who still controlled most of the wealth and the arable land of Mexico considered Calles a dangerous radical, likely to carry out the letter of the 1917 Constitution his predecessor had obeyed with winks and shrugs and half measures guaranteed not to cause trouble in a country beginning to enjoy the fruits of capitalism.

MOTHER CONCHITA'S CORSET

In 1928, at the end of the Calles presidency, there were many celebrations of the election of Álvaro Obregón as president. There were public demonstrations on July 16, and on the seventeenth a grand celebratory luncheon was planned for the president-elect at La Bombilla, a restaurant in the elegant neighborhood of San Ángel. A huge floral piece spelled out in daisies the purpose of the celebration: "Homage and honor from the people of Guanajuato for Álvaro Obregón." The newly elected president, his thick, blunt mustache now turned gray, sat at the center of the head table between the *A* and the *V* in his name on the floral decoration behind him.

It was not the best of times in Mexico. Relations with the United States had improved after the Bucareli agreements, but they were not good. A Mexican had pinned the general's stars on the Nicaraguan rebel Sandino. A new U.S. ambassador, Dwight Morrow, was to meet with Obregón the next day to try to settle some of Mexico's external problems and to act as a go-between in the country's internal disputes.

Obregón was a hard, unforgiving man, a soldier from Sonora. He had led an army against the Yaquis, engineering the brutal conquest of the people who had stood in the trenches of his first line of defense at Celaya. Calles, who came in as a radical and changed into a confirmed capitalist during his term in office, had been even tougher. People who opposed him were sent to prison, where most of them "committed suicide." Calles had distributed eight million acres to the peasants, but it had been largely vacant land. No one knew how Obregón would behave in his second term. The men from the rich farmlands of the bajío had reason to entertain the incoming president; they did not want him to distribute their haciendas to the peasants.

It was a good party on a sunny afternoon in the spacious and airy restaurant. An orchestra, led by Maestro Esparza Otero, played popular songs. A young caricaturist, José de León Toral, who had been making a drawing of Obregón in his sketchbook, stepped up to the head table to show his sketch to the president-elect. As he neared the table, the artist took a pistol out of his pocket and shot Obregón several times. Obregón fell to his right, then slid under the table, dead.

In the days that followed, there were many accusations. It was an ideal time for Calles to rid himself of those enemies who had survived his presidency. More than a few people resigned from the government to avoid suspicion. Among these was unionist Luis Morones of the CROM, who, having made the error of opposing the Obregón candidacy, lost his post as secretary of labor.

During his interrogation the battered assassin confessed and implicated a Roman Catholic nun, Concepción Aceveda de la Llata. Mother Conchita, as she was known, had a deep, almost hypnotic influence over León Toral. She was his adviser, confessor, symbol of the Virgin of Guadalupe. All this at a time when Mexico was in the middle of a deadly struggle between the Church and the Constitution. With the help of the nun, the young man had come to believe he had to sacrifice his own life to save "the religion": Obregón was responsible for the troubles that had befallen the Church; the president-elect had to die.

León Toral said he believed the religion was in danger. He had worried over it, but he had not thought it proper to kill, not then, not until February 1926, when everything changed for the young man and for Mexico. The archbishop of Mexico, responding to the implementation of anticlerical laws in the 1917 Constitution, declared that Roman Catholics could no longer accept the constitution. Calles responded immediately. There would be no more religious processions in Mexico, foreign priests and nuns were to be deported, Church schools were to be closed, monasteries and convents were to be closed, and all priests were to register with civil authorities.

On July 31 the archbishop declared a strike. For the next three years no last rites were given, no babies were baptized, and no masses were said. Calles was delighted. He said that the suspension of Catholic rites would cost the Church thousands upon thousands of members, a full 2 percent every week. The Church and its adherents outside the capital responded, *"Viva Cristo Rey!"* Calles told them they had two choices: They could go to the Congress (where Calles controlled a huge majority in both houses) and seek redress or they could go to war. They chose war, and more than fifty thousand people died in the Cristero wars. The conflict began spontaneously in villages and small towns, where the army met the rebels with machine guns and cavalry. Atrocities were committed on both sides. Neither the religious Mexicans nor the liberal Mexicans displayed any sense of limits.

All this while León Toral was on trial. He said, ". . . if things went on this way, I feared that Mexico would lose its religion," and his statement set the tone for the trial. The lawyers could not argue the guilt or innocence of the defendant; religion was the only issue. While León Toral's lawyer made his case, a plea rather than a defense, the onlookers in the courtroom shouted, demanding the death of the assassin, his lawyer, and Mother Conchita, whom they blamed for inciting the twenty-seven-year-old innocent. At one point the crowd broke through the police lines and attacked the nun, breaking her leg and smashing several vertebrae so that for the rest of her life she lived in an iron corset.

The prosecutor argued that the assassin and Mother Conchita were not true believers, that the Church would never permit murder: "These people are not Catholics, but heretics." He called Mother Conchita the "infernal machine."

León Toral was sentenced to death, and the corseted Mother Conchita was sent to prison for twenty years. In his last moments the young assassin maintained his religious fervor. When the firing squad was ordered to make ready, León Toral lifted his arms to make his body into the form of a cross. And in that position he died. The young man's version of the Virgin, Mother Conchita, fared better. She was able to leave prison early, married, and became a painter. Until the shadow of a newly erected building obscured her light, she worked in a studio in Mexico City on Avenida Álvaro Obregón.

EL MAXIMATO

A norteño who believed Mexico should become another version of the U.S. state of California, Calles thought the Protestant Reformation had been good and useful, if only a halfway measure toward the end of religion.[6] The Enlightenment and the Reformation embodied the modern world, both

---

[6]The innermost thoughts of Calles on questions of the existence of God, the divinity of Christ, or the afterlife at the time are not known. His actions, however, were in opposition to the Catholic Church, its powers and its rules. For example, at the first opportunity, when he was still a young state governor, he changed the laws to permit divorce. El Jefe Máximo, who was orphaned at the age of four, took the name of the man who adopted him, Calles, and added it to his original family name, Elías; thus Plutarco Elías Calles.

philosophically and economically, according to Calles. But his thinking, while leftist when he first took office, never quite comprehended the idea of either a social contract or democracy.

After the murder of Obregón, Calles arranged for Emilio Portes Gil to become interim president of Mexico, but he was chief executive in name only, as were his successors, until Lázaro Cárdenas took office in 1934. Calles ruled the country as if he owned it. When cabinet members met with Mexican presidents, they had already received instructions from Calles. The legislature voted according to his instructions. His whims were orders. He was a strongman in every way, big and burly, demanding, unforgiving, loud, yet his body betrayed him. He suffered one ailment after another. Liver trouble and back problems kept him in bed for days at time. He could control everything but his health and everyone but the Cristeros. The war drained the national budget, and no matter how many were killed the number of Cristeros grew. When the army took over a town, they killed all the Cristeros, and on the day the army moved out the town belonged to the Cristeros again. It was an impossible task: The army promised death, and the Church promised a better life after death. There was nothing Calles could do. When the government distributed land, the local priests often said that accepting land from the government was a sin. In some villages the Cristeros killed campesinos who accepted land grants and joined ejidos (communal farms).

To make matters worse, Vasconcelos, the educator and inventor of the idea of the cosmic race, had announced his candidacy in the coming presidential election and demonstrated enormous popular support. Calles was afraid that Vasconcelos would form an alliance with the Cristeros and force a close election or another civil war. Calles gave in to the Church in a deal negotiated by the American ambassador: He abandoned his interpretation of anticlerical provisions in the 1917 Constitution, and the Cristero soldiers and irregulars packed up their gear and went home.

Calles, whose ten-year reign was known as the *maximato* because he was the man with maximum power, had information from the U.S. Secret Service about the Vasconcelos campaign and perhaps a little advice from his U.S. friends on how to handle the problem of a popular opponent. The result of the election in which Vasconcelos had such great popular support that he threatened to defeat Calles's newly formed National Revolutionary Party and its candidate, Pascual Ortiz Rubio, presaged the future of Mexican electoral politics: The official count gave Vasconcelos 5 percent of the vote.

Meanwhile, a worldwide depression did not spare Mexico. Oil and gold prices began declining in the 1920s. The Calles regime saw the peso devalued. His method for distributing land gave more to the rich and less to the poor, with the northwest favored over the rest of the country. And the character of Mexican agriculture changed. Between 1910 and 1929 the production of corn fell by 40 percent while the population grew by 9 percent. Production of export crops—coffee, tomatoes—increased as corporate farms became more dominant. Mexicans left the country in great numbers for opportunities to the north. But then between 1930 and 1934 the United States deported more than four hundred thousand Mexicans. El Jefe Máximo had to contend with more unemployment and less money coming in. Mexico's treasury surplus disappeared, and it could not pay the interest on an accumulating foreign debt. The Revolution had resulted in an even greater gap between rich and poor, as the rich got richer in a pattern that was to dog Mexico for the rest of the century. In order to hold on to power after the civil wars had ended in 1920, vast amounts of wealth were distributed as gifts or bribes, and even more was simply stolen by the government and its cronies. Land distribution schemes were corrupted and used to turn the campesinos against each other.

Corruption went unchecked. In Cuernavaca, an elegant area was known as the Street of the Forty Thieves because everyone who lived there had gained his place through corruption. It became a standard metaphor in Mexico when speaking of high government officials. When the charming and outgoing Miguel Alemán was replaced by the dour, diminutive Adolfo Ruiz Cortines in 1952, one newspaper, saddened at the loss of the playboy president, wrote "Better Ali Baba and the Forty Thieves than Snow White and the Seven Dwarfs."

The foreign and domestic policies of the Máximato were not very different from those of the Porfiriato or the Fox administration: Balance the budget, stabilize the currency, and improve the image abroad to encourage foreign investment.[7] Calles had a general idea about the future of Mexico

---

[7]The Fox administration of course has the lessons of history to instruct it. In a global economy, countries like Mexico survive economically almost at the whim of the financial markets. A sudden run on the currency of the country brings it to its knees in a matter of days as the national banks are unable to meet the demands of foreign investors who want to cash out. Interest rates go higher and higher to continue attracting foreign investment until finally there is no place to go and the currency collapses. Mexico has been through several such crises, most recently in 1994.

The only way to insure against the danger of a run on the currency is to maintain the image of economic health, which has less to do with reality than perception. If on any

when he entered office. He envisioned a great agricultural nation, but he saw no future for heavy industry in Mexico. It would be a country of exports—agricultural products, oil, and precious metals—and the provider of low-cost labor to "finish" goods made elsewhere.

His vision would lead Mexico into economic disadvantages that would not be overcome for a century, if ever. Nonetheless, he was anxious to make a nation of the disparate parts of the country. He did not like the idea of a Mexico made up of distinct economic and social classes. He thought he could use government to overcome those antagonisms without changing the economic or social system. His sworn enemies in that respect were the class-conscious Communists, who were making inroads in the intellectual and artistic worlds and had begun to recruit members at the fringes of the labor movement. Calles turned against them early in his presidency, and his antipathy grew every year of his life.

By 1934, his last year in control of the government, Calles was praising fascism and imprisoning large numbers of Communists. He had read *Mein Kampf,* and he liked what Hitler had to say. It was one subject on which Calles and his rival, Vasconcelos, could agree. Neither of them complained when the Gold Shirts, the Mexican version of the German Brownshirts, roamed the countryside, threatening Communists and Jews. The fascists, most of them former Villistas, had only a few thousand public adherents, but they did not submit to ridicule or insult. They fought in the streets when they had to. Like Spain, which many Mexicans still called the mother country, Mexico was separating into the great factions of the time. Mexican trade with fascist countries (Japan and Germany) increased while the socialists and Communists within the unions and government grew more powerful. Mexico was on the verge of social revolution. The question was whether the country would turn to the left or the right.

---

given day the international currency and bond traders were to decide that Mexico was not stable, they would begin to sell Mexican currency and bond positions. The Mexicans would have to raise interest rates in an attempt to stop the downward spiral, but almost nothing the Mexicans could do would stop the currency hemorrhage. It would seek a loan from the International Monetary Fund and then agree to the usual devastating austerity measures. The ensuing social costs would be added to those suffered since the crises of the 1980s and 1990s.

When President Fox of Mexico embraces President Bush of the United States and calls him "my friend," there is more than friendship on the table. They are really talking about the stability of the Mexican currency.

THE REAL MEXICAN REVOLUTION

Had there been a central idea during the period known as the Revolution of 1910, the political transpositions that took place among many of the leading figures of the period would be inexplicable. Several minor general officers who fought under Pancho Villa became fascists, but Lázaro Cárdenas, a general who fought against both Villa and Zapata, rose through the ranks to become governor of Michoacán when he was thirty-two years old and the leftist president of Mexico at thirty-seven. His sexenio (the first six-year presidency after Calles forced a change in the constitution) was certainly the closest Mexico has come to a social revolution.

In the great reversals of the politics of the survivors of the wars of 1910–1920, Lázaro Cárdenas moved as often as any man. Had it all been different, a genuine revolution with a clear plan, Cárdenas might have fought with Zapata instead of against him. Or perhaps he would have remained a Villista, like General Nicolás Rodríguez, who became the leader of the Gold Shirts. Instead, Cárdenas joined the Constitutionalists, who had destroyed the last great charge of the Villistas at Agua Prieta, and became the most important figure on the left in Mexican history.

The tools of meaning came late to Cárdenas. The young officer rose through the ranks as a half-wild creation of war. He took orders, he reacted, he killed and was nearly killed himself; he made war, but he could not find an ideological home. For more than a quarter of a century after the signing of the Constitution of 1917, the Mexican presidency was occupied by former generals. Cárdenas, like many others, had risen quickly to the rank of general officer, without having the time or opportunity to develop a clear understanding of the reasons behind the civil wars. He fought out of loyalty rather than political conviction. A young man, largely uneducated, he looked for a father rather than an idea, attaching himself first to Calles and later, after the wars, to the radical socialist governor of Michoacán, Francisco Múgica.[8] Cárdenas read Marx in 1925 or 1926, studied the French Revolution, and later learned about the New Deal when Roosevelt came into office in 1932. These were the political and economic touchstones he brought with him when he

---

[8]Cárdenas was a protégé of Múgica, who had been one of the most influential and obstinate anticlerical voices in the 1917 Constitutional Convention and was then governor of Michoacán. Long before that Cárdenas was a protégé of Calles, who called him "the kid," but only in private conversation.

began the Mexican Revolution of 1934. This time the Revolution had a clear central idea. It rose gloriously in 1936 and began its fall before the end of the Cárdenas presidency in 1940.

Perhaps the kind of Revolution Cárdenas made could not survive in Mexico; perhaps it was bad economics to give so much of the richest land in the country, even land owned by former generals, to the poor. But it did not appear to be so when he began the distribution of the land. He gave back vast tracts in the cotton-growing Laguna region of Coahuila, and he was careful not to allow anyone to pervert his cause. The president of Mexico, Lázaro Cárdenas, went to Coahuila himself and stayed there until the distribution was done. It took months, but Cárdenas was determined. He made a revolution with the force of his will and the clarity of his purpose. He distributed more land in the brief Revolution of 1934 than all the presidents who had preceded him. And it seemed to work. Not only were the campesinos now landowners, but they were productive. The tragedy of the Cárdenas vision, which harkened back to Zapata and the 1917 Constitution, has become apparent only in recent years in Mexico, long after the bank failures and the corruption and the killings of the *ejiditarios* (communal farmers) by one another. The ejido had its roots in the Aztec system of land utilization. It was not designed for mechanized farming or to play a role in a largely capitalist system, certainly not in the era of globalized production and marketing.

Forty years after the 1934 Revolution, in a tiny town, more like a village, in Central Mexico, a man who had been one of the recipients of the land distributions said to me: "Tata[9] Lázaro [Cárdenas] was a great man. He could speak Indian. But he was no help to us. He gave us land, but we had no money. We could not buy seed or fertilizer. In the end, we had to sell the land back to the rich."

"Then he was not a great man."

"Yes, he was a great man. Before General Cárdenas, every president was a thief."

"Even Benito Juárez?" It was, I thought, a telling question, although the moment I asked it I felt bad. The man facing me, squinting in the sun, was more than seventy years old, perhaps eighty, a campesino. The sun had dried

[9]From the Nahuatl *tatli*. The *Simeón Diccionario* says that "tata" is used when a child calls for its father.

him out, made something interesting of his skin, the way the sea produces the aesthetics of driftwood.

He said, "I am an old man, but I did not know Benito Juárez. Did you know George Washington?"

"He was not a thief."

"Porfirio Díaz was a thief. And the Maderos were also thieves. And after them, every one but General Cárdenas. He was the only one who loved the campesinos."

"But he failed. You told me so."

"That is not what I told you, my friend."

Sixty years after the Revolution of 1934, in the little town of Santa Anna Tlacotenco, an enclave of Nahuas who still speak the language in its pre-Hispanic form, I asked the scholar and translator Francisco Morales Baranda what he thought about the coming election for mayor of Mexico City. Would the people of the town vote for Cuauhtémoc Cárdenas?

"Yes, of course," he said. Morales lives with his family in a house off the street at the end of a narrow lane. The house has been in his family for generations. On a plot of land outside the town he cultivates nopal (cactus) as his ancestors did before the first Spaniards arrived in the Americas.

"Because his name is Cuauhtémoc."

"No. The people here will vote for him because they think he will be a better mayor."

"And what about his father?"

"He cared about indigenous people; he made a speech in Nahuatl."

"But indigenous people still suffer in Mexico. What did he do for them?"

"He respected us."

There was no other Mexican president like Cárdenas, certainly not the nineteenth-century Zapotecan Juárez, who wished to be a *peninsular*, not merely a criollo. Cárdenas was mestizo, but he showed solidarity with the Nahuas, Maya, Otomis, Raramurí and others, as well as the Purépechas from Michoacán, where he was born. Even though he had been nominated by the National Revolutionary Party (PNR), which guaranteed his election, Cárdenas traveled eighteen thousand miles, campaigning across the country. For the first time a Mexican presidential candidate went up into the hills, to tiny mountain villages cut off from the rest of Mexico. He said he wanted to hear for himself what the people thought, to learn what he should do as president. There are photographs of him in the mountains, a man with a soft face, a sudden mustache, and a curiously elongated head. He was not an especially tall man, but in conversation he appeared to be bending over to be closer to people, to listen. The fat of his neck rolled over his shirt collar, and he often stood with his hands in his trouser pockets as if he did not know what else to do with them.

Of all the presidents of Mexico, there was never one so ethical as Tata Lázaro, who took for himself little more than a ranch in Michoacán. He was a Mexican general loyal to one woman,[10] modest in his wants, and incorruptible. But his ethics did not prevent him from shrewdly manipulating the government establishment to push out the old conservatives and replace them with men who agreed with his policies. He brought the army over to his side first. He had seen enough military uprisings, including several that he had personally put down, to know that he could not accomplish a major change in policy without the agreement of the army. After using pay raises and military education to win the army's loyalty, he went to work on labor.

Within the CROM, Vicente Lombardo Toledano had led a left-wing faction of the union. In 1933 the Communist professor and intellectual broke away from the CROM and founded a leftist national union, With the support of the new president, Lombardo's union soon had over a million members; that did not make Calles happy. In fact, very little that Cárdenas did pleased his mentor. As one man went to the right, the other turned to the left. Soon Calles was criticizing the president in public, telling the newspapers that he was taking the country toward communism. Cárdenas could not merely shrug off the complaints of an ill and aging former president. Calles had already thrown one president (Ortiz Rubio) out of office for disobeying his wishes; he would have had no qualms about doing it again. But Cárdenas moved too quickly. He took the army away from Calles; then he removed the Callistas from the cabinet, all the while courting the unions and the campesinos. One day in April 1936 he finished the task. He ordered the arrest of Calles and the corrupt boss of the CROM, Luis Morones, and had them put on an airplane bound for exile in the United States.

Everything went as planned for Tata Lázaro as he made the Revolution.

[10]There were rumors of affairs with other women, which may or may not have been true. However, a Mexican president who was not rumored to have such affairs might not have maintained the respect of many voters.

He was able to control the economy. The minimum wage rose, although it was still fifty centavos a day short of a living wage, which was then calculated at four pesos. Overall, the rise in income was greater than the increase in the cost of living. Industrialization continued, spurred now by the government. For the first time in its history Mexico had a nationalist development program. The economy expanded from within. Mexico was integrating its own productive system. Although still an exporter of raw materials rather than finished goods, it was moving toward a modern economy that would enable it to survive the urbanization of the twentieth century. The industrialists of Monterrey were annoyed by the activist role of government, but their profits rose faster than ever, soothing their purses, if not their politics or religion.

Cárdenas had been anticlerical since he was a boy, but he arrived at a sort of détente with the Catholic Church. There had been 642 strikes in 1935, but the next year the rising standard of living had calmed the workers. Internal development was a workable idea. Both the industrialists of Monterrey and the unions found it acceptable. The huge loans taken out to support the growth of the infrastructure and the ejido system were not pleasing to the men of Monterrey, but they did not complain loudly as long as the profits rolled in, the real Revolution did not seem so bad after all.

Education remained a basic flaw in the capability of the country to modernize. Neither Justo Sierra nor José Vasconcelos had succeeded in raising the literacy rate above 50 percent. But there were problems about what to teach—Socrates, sex education, or socialism—and who was willing to go into the rural areas to teach ideas that went against the beliefs of the local power structure and the inheritors of the Cristero orthodoxy? The teachers who told the village children about sex education were boycotted, beaten, or killed by religious Catholics, and those who taught socialism and tried to start cooperative ventures were boycotted, beaten, or killed on the orders of the local mercantile monopolist.

The long-term failure of the land distribution system can be blamed in part on corruption, inadequate funding, the collapse of the banks, the shrewdness and greed of the hacendados, and so on, but nothing, not even droughts and sudden devaluations of the peso, so devastated the system as the failure of sex education, which really meant birth control.[11] With each succeeding generation, the tiny plots of land were either divided among the

[11] See the story of Sra. Ruiz of Matamoros, formerly of Chiapas, in Book One, Chapter 1.

children of the owner or given entirely to the firstborn son. The Mexican population increased from 16.5 million in 1930 to 100 million in 2000. By comparison, the U.S. population merely doubled, from 123 million to 260 million over the same period. Land expected to support one person in Mexico would by 2000 have to support six. Subsistence farming, a little piece of land, *mi ranchito*, the Mexican dream, fueled by the promise of the 1917 Constitution and again by Tata Lázaro, died a little with every new birth.

Cárdenas distributed almost 50 million acres of land, about 5 acres for every man, woman, and child outside the cities. Before him, 25 million acres had been given out—a total of 7.5 acres for each person. For a family of five, that added up to a little less than 40 acres, which was barely enough, but for two generations: a family of thirty? Perhaps the Cardenistas had no idea about the arithmetic. A generation later the economist Ifigenia Martínez published a small book placing the blame for many of Mexico's problems on overpopulation. But the Revolution of 1934 had more immediate problems.

Everything had appeared to be going well for the Cardenistas in early 1937. Union relations were good; the Monterrey business community was grumpy but nothing more than that; the ejido system required a huge but not impossible amount of money. The Civil War in Spain had brought Mexico into world affairs, and the Cárdenas administration had made clear its opposition to the Fascists, sending arms and supplies to the Loyalists and defending them in League of Nations meetings. Mexico still did business with Germany, one of its major importers of oil and agricultural products, but Cárdenas would not go along with Hitler's invasions or his treatment of Jews. Mexico became a haven for exiles, accepting Trotsky, thirty thousand Spanish Loyalists, and large numbers of Jewish refugees. Cárdenas announced that all were welcome; they had only to comply with Mexican laws.

In every area—ethics, wages, international relations, distribution of land and wealth, even labor and industry—everything was going Mexico's way. It had survived the Great Depression better than the United States. Education was a problem, but the opposition of the Catholic Church was still localized. The most immediate problems began with the sun and the rain. The Bank of Mexico had made a huge bet on a good harvest, good enough to pay off unsecured loans, and Tlaloc, the Aztec god in charge of rain, and Xipe Totec, the god of the harvest, had not come through. It was the beginning of inflation.

And inflation played a role in the oil workers' decision to strike in May 1937. The oil industry, which could not then be properly called the Mexican oil industry, was owned almost entirely (over 98 percent) by foreign companies. Wages were better than average, but profits were phenomenal, and Mexican workers were treated as second-class persons. The situation was almost a perfect duplicate of the 1906 Cananea strike. This time it was not a copper mine south of Arizona but the entire Mexican economy that suffered. There was nothing symbolic about an oil strike. Oil was Mexico's leading source of income, and without the wages and the taxes on exports, the country could not get along. A federal commission advised both sides to give a little: a 33 percent increase in pay, far better than the companies offered, improved pension and welfare, but generally fewer social benefits than the workers demanded. The oil companies said no. Cárdenas sent the case to arbitration. The arbitration board agreed with the commission. The oil companies claimed it would cost them seven million U.S. dollars a year. Neither side would give in.

To raise the stakes in the strike, the oil companies began a massive public relations campaign in the United States and Mexico. Cárdenas responded by saying he would burn the oil fields before he would give in to the demands of the companies. It was, the general said, "a question of honor." The oil companies took the case to the Mexican Supreme Court, which upheld the findings of the arbitration board. Under Mexican law Cárdenas had what he needed. Either the oil companies could give in or he could expropriate them for refusing to comply with the law. At that point the lawyers for the oil companies knew that Cárdenas would not back down. They tried to negotiate a deal.[12]

On March 18, 1938, President Cárdenas, giving as grounds for his action the violation of the sovereignty of Mexico, signed a decree expropriating the property of seventeen oil companies. He had been warned by businessmen and by members of his own cabinet about the risk, but on that day at the end of winter there were few dissenters. It was a great moment for Tata Lázaro and for Mexico. The president of Mexico was a man! There were celebrations, congratulations; at last, a Latin American country, and one so close to the United States, had stood up to the gringos.

There were also qualms. U.S. Ambassador Josephus Daniels had made it known that he was not happy. The oil lobby was very powerful. What would the U.S. Congress do? How would Roosevelt react? There were a dozen ways

[12]Here the situation differed from Cananea. No Americans crossed the border ready to shoot Mexicans, and no strikers went to jail. No one was killed.

to punish Mexico economically—blockades, boycotts, border closings, tariff manipulations—and intervention was always a possibility. But Roosevelt held to his Good Neighbor policy. The oil companies would have to be compensated for the loss of their property, nothing more. Cárdenas did not disagree; the only question was the amount. The U.S. oil companies asked for two hundred million dollars. The Mexicans offered ten million, and settled for twenty-four million.

For a moment the Mexican Revolution of 1934 appeared to be a success. Then the moment passed, and with the taste of victory still lingering, all the dire predictions Cárdenas had refused to hear came true. Mexicans rushed to get their capital out of the country; inflation ate much of what was left; no one knew how to run the oil business; there were no Mexican tankers to carry oil to foreign customers; the United States stopped Mexican credit and slowed its purchases of silver. Cárdenas cut the budget for education, and then the budget for infrastructure, and the distribution of land slowed and slowed some more. If there was no oil money and no credit, then Mexico would make money from tourism. *Indigenismo*, the archaeological–anthropological–nation-building dream of Manuel Gamio, turned into a means for attracting tourists.

To deal with his economic troubles, Tata Lázaro looked to his politics. He reorganized the PNR into the Mexican Revolutionary Party (PRM) and brought every sector of society into it so that the party was corporate, commanding, irresistible, and yet, in the curious way of single-party systems, representative. As the end of his term neared, he had to choose between naming his successor or holding on to power until the "national emergency" was over, as Juárez and Díaz had done. If he named a successor, it was assumed that it would be his mentor, the leftist intellectual Francisco Múgica, or even the other radical thinker at the 1917 Constitutional Convention, Gildardo Magaña. Instead he pointed his finger at the secretary of war, a cautious, conservative, relatively unknown former general, Manuel Ávila Camacho. The Revolution of 1934 was over.

AFTER THE REVOLUTION

The end of Cárdenismo and the foundation of all that would determine Mexico in the first year of the twenty-first century came in the same breath, the sigh of failure again, the sense of falling, the desperate desire to stop, to hold on, to climb up again, to live. It is perhaps in the nature of states, the rise and fall of the kinds of power that were discerned long ago when Plato suffered a disappointment about democracy. In Mexico there had been this rising and falling and birthing and dying since Palenque, since the Olmecs, since the time before stonecutting and calendars. The up and down pace had been astonishing until the machismo of the expropriation in 1938, when it looked as if the cycles had come to an end and Mexico were on a great rise. Then the cycle began again with the collapse after the nationalization of the oil and perhaps even before that, with the founding in 1937 of a secret society in the twin shadows of the Catholic Church and the Falangists.

The National Union of Sinarquistas formed in opposition to the leftist government, which was for a moment a Revolution in Mexico, an idea so odious to the fanatical members of the Church that they imitated what they saw as the organization of the evil that had beset the world: They formed cells, like the Communists, no cell knowing more than one connection to the center, not knowing the center, connected only by orders, newspapers, and devotion. They were at one time a million, or so they said, or so it was assumed, believed, or feared. Once, for a moment in 1941, they captured Guadalajara and then Morelia, but only for a moment.

It is not certain who they were, except for the few who said they were its leaders. All the others were hidden, except for the moment when they took a city, and then were gone again, defeated, but not defeated, believers nonetheless. There were priests among them, although the Church officially disavowed the Sinarquistas. They stood for family, against communism, in favor of free enterprise and some strange adherence to justice, which was justice as they defined it, and that only. They wished for the elimination of the idea of classes within a society, saying they broke the society apart. They liked liberty but not libertines. And they admired nothing so much as the government of Francisco Franco. It was perhaps in their minds, although they did not say so, to integrate the Church and State again, as in the glorious days of Spain. They planned to take over sectors of the Church as their method of taking Mexico. If the Sinarquistas had not been so near to religious madness, they might have won the country.

Another, less radical force on the right arose as the Sinarquistas went underground. More than a few Mexican historians and intellectuals think the second force was encouraged by the United States as a way of guaranteeing stability in Mexico. The Americans had a two-party system; why not Mexico? In 1939, Manuel Gómez Morín, who had been the rector of the UNAM, formed a small political party in opposition not to the Communists or even to Tata Lázaro's Revolution but to his Partido Revolucionario Mexicano (PRM), the not quite official party, which was to be renamed the PRI a decade later. Gómez Morín called his party National Action, PAN, and it did not have many members or much of a chance to win even a single office at any level of government when he began. In the first elections, the first round of losses, the PAN did not offer a candidate for the presidency. If there were Sinarquistas in the PAN, they did not identify themselves; it was not their way.

The character of the PAN was Catholic, but more business than religion. It mingled with the Church, its members came from the Church; but while they were from the right wing of the Church, they were not openly fanatical, there was no madness in their meetings. They were capitalists, and the madness of capitalism is first about counting, not killing. They were middle class and upper middle class. Their money came from Monterrey, where the economic powers approved. If Guadalajara was home to the well spoken and fanatical, Monterrey was a place for the well heeled and acquisitive. The business barons of Monterrey could make peace with both the semiofficial PRM and its antagonist, the PAN. There was nothing duplicitous in their minds about supporting both sides in political conflicts; they were exactly like General Motors and General Electric in their view of politics: Government served business. And their neighbors to the north liked the idea of another party. Cárdenas had not pleased the oil industry; the United States smiled on the idea of the PAN.

Over the next sixty years the PAN grew slowly, first taking offices at local levels at the farthest ends of the country: It won an election in Mérida, Yucatán, and another in Baja California. Gómez himself was from Chihuahua. The money came from Nuevo León. As always, the forces in Mexico were centripetal; the capital was the end, not the beginning.

On the day of the election of Manuel Ávila Camacho in 1940, all the forces of present-day Mexico had been let loose, including one that came from the port of Veracruz, where Bernardo Pasquel and his brothers had established a highly profitable import business, soon to become the largest smuggling operation in the history of Mexico. Among their friends was a young senator and former judge who was interested in the governorship of Veracruz, as were the Pasquel brothers. Unfortunately, another man had been elected. But before he could take office, the governor-elect was assassinated in the Café Tacuba in Mexico City, and the young attorney and former magistrate, Miguel Alemán Valdés, became governor of the state of Veracruz. It was the beginning of the destruction of the last shred of ethics in Mexican government. All the seeds had been planted; there would be no more limits.

Upon taking office in 1940, Ávila Camacho announced his view of Church-State relations. "I am a believer," he said. It was not the end of tensions between the two major governing bodies in Mexico, but it was enough to calm the Sinarquistas and the religious businessmen of the PAN. Tensions between left and right in Mexico had grown fierce during the last years of the Cárdenas sexenio. The German government had made another effort to use Mexico against the United States. The right-wing candidate who opposed Ávila Camacho in the July 1940 election had been approached by the Germans with offers to supply arms and money for a fascist uprising. The Mexican government entered into a much closer relationship with the United States, which sent oil industry technicians to Mexico again, guaranteed purchase of raw materials at protected prices, and dispatched the FBI south to begin watching the beaches for Japanese and German landings.

The Hitler-Stalin pact stunned the left and the right in Mexico, as in the rest of the world. Mexicans had switched sides again and again during the 1910–1920 civil wars, but the joining of Fascists and Communists was beyond imagination. What were the Mexican radicals to do? A détente of stupefaction settled over them, and both sides looked to the United States as partner and protector. To demonstrate his friendship for Mexico, Roosevelt sent his vice president Henry Wallace to the inauguration of Ávila Camacho at the end of 1940. Cárdenas had expressed strong antifascist sentiments during his term, attacking Nazi persecution of Jews and the Japanese invasion of Nanjing, but he had also done business with Germany. The Cárdenas of the last years of his term was not the same man who had taken office; business made demands just as labor made demands, and Tata Lázaro could not dismiss the demands of business or the commercial power of Germany. Nonetheless, as the world became involved in the war, Ávila Camacho relied on Cárdenas to direct the defense of Mexico as secretary of war, cooperated fully with U.S. military forces, broke the Mexican rule of neutrality to join the war against Japan and Germany, and sent Mexican pilots to train in the United States.

With trade to Europe cut off by the war, the United States had to fill the gap. More than a third of all the war materials used by the United States were supplied by Mexico, and without help from foreign capital, management, and trade (except for defense business with the United States), Mexico became more self-reliant. The Mexicans took over and then expropriated German-owned industries, including Mexico's largest chemical company, and learned to manage them. Business profits increased during the war years, but there was no accompanying rise in the general wealth. U.S. demands for shifts in crops hurt farm income, while the percentage of national income from the manufacturing sector barely grew (18.6 in 1940 to 19.9 in 1946). The number of people employed in manufacturing grew by 2 percent over the same period, but the value of the goods manufactured did not.[13]

Mexico enjoyed a great increase in per capita income during the Ávila Camacho sexenio, but only a small decrease in the poverty index. The major change during his presidency lay in the attempt of Mexico again to produce most of the goods for internal consumption, with some excess for export. Tariffs and limits on foreign ownership of industry were Ávila Camacho's methods for accumulating capital and encouraging native industrial development. At the end of his term his brother expected to be the one at whom the finger of power pointed, but the brother, like the governor-elect of Veracruz, did not live to enjoy the office.[14] With his brother out of the way, Ávila Camacho gave the government to his longtime friend and secretary of the interior, Miguel Alemán Valdés, the son of a quixotic general from Veracruz, and the first civilian to hold the office since Carranza.

THE PUP OF THE REVOLUTION

If one were inclined to a psychoanalytical view of history, perhaps a slightly messy admixture of Carlyle and Freud, the relation of Miguel

[13]The value of the goods jumped by more than 50 percent in pesos, but there was almost 100 percent inflation during the same period. Productivity remained stable or even declined slightly.

[14]Máximino Ávila Camacho, secretary of public works during his brother's presidency, detested Miguel Alemán so much that he threatened to kill him. Instead, curiously, Máximino died; that must have pleased Alemán very much, according to some people, too much.

Alemán Valdés to his father, Miguel Alemán González, a general who fought on all sides, would explain much of the Golden Age of Mexico or the Mexican Miracle, as the twenty-two years between the inauguration of Alemán and the fateful day in Tlatelolco were known. The general had begun his adult life working on the railroad, then become a grocer, a member of the Liberal Party, and a man who dreamed of nothing more than taking part in the overthrow of the Porfiriato.

When the wars began, the grocer was among the first to take up arms. He fought and won and went home to tend to his business, but it was not one revolutionary war, it was a series of civil wars, and when the fortunes of war changed and a new faction gained the upper hand, he took up arms in a new cause and fought and won and went home to further his business, and when that side was forced out of power, he strapped on his pistol and took up his rifle and went to war again. And when that war was over, the general went home to his cans and bottles and fresh eggs and cheese. But Don Miguel was the Quixote of grocers. All his days he prepared for war, although he had other plans for his son, whom he sent to a fine preparatory school and then to the national university. The business did well enough, but it was nothing compared with war. If the general did not exactly dream of a return to chivalry, he clearly dreamed of a return to war. Like a Spanish nobleman of the sixteenth century, he could validate himself only in war. When the opportunity came to declare against Calles in 1929, he took it. But that uprising had been a mistake. Trapped in the mountains, with federal troops closing in, the general for all sides, gallant to the end, refused to surrender. He took his own life.

Stated in the simplest way, the psychoanalytic notion is that we take our parents inside ourselves and rebel against them. Perhaps. In his own way, the senior Alemán lived entirely according to principle: He died rather than abandon (or perhaps explain) his code. His son, who was twenty-six years old when the general shot himself, had no code at all. Had the son been immoral, a violator of his code, he would have been as dour as the men who followed him into office, Adolfo Ruiz Cortines and Gustavo Díaz Ordaz. But Alemán, *el cachorro de la Revolución* (the pup of the Revolution),[15] was famed for his charm and good looks. Compared with Cárdenas, who never owned formal clothes, Alemán was at least as handsome as a Mexican movie

[15]"Cachorro" (pup or cub) can also mean "small pistol."

star. His mustache was neatly trimmed, like that of the male lead in a light comedy of the late 1930s. He danced; he laughed; he had a famous affair with Linda Christian, the half-Mexican, half-Dutch "actress" who later married actor Tyrone Power. Alemán loved women, sunshine, law, business, and himself—above all, himself. Cárdenas, like many of the old generals, took the presidential pension (a large hacienda) for his services, the senior Alemán could not wait to die in war, but the young Miguel, forty-three years old when he became president of Mexico in December 1946 had no sense of limits. If ever it occurred to him that he was doing something immoral, he gave no outward sign; he stayed in his version of the grocery store and made a fortune.

Even before taking office, he reorganized the party that Cárdenas had first made corporate. The difference between the two views of Mexico was so deep and his determination to abandon the ideas of the old generals so great Alemán thought it necessitated a change of name. The Mexican Party of the Revolution (PRM) became the Institutional Party of the Revolution (PRI). He kept everyone—business, labor, campesinos—in the party, and everyone who belonged to the party did just a little bit better for it. The party became as ubiquitous as the Church, as corporate as the Ford Motor Company. In northern cities, where the PAN was making inroads, garbage collection was only for those who belonged to the PRI; nonmembers carried their own garbage to the dump. Polio vaccine in the 1950s was distributed at party headquarters. Rats and dead children, hellish punishments, awaited those who did not belong to the Institutional Revolution, whatever the phrase meant.

Cárdenas had looked to tourism for income when oil prices fell, and Mexico, which had once supplied a fourth of the world's oil, no longer had the money to continue its land distribution and educational programs. But Alemán had a different view of tourism. Instead of inviting tourists to look at Mexico's antiquities, he wanted them to lie on its beaches. He turned the hot, humid Mexican resort village of Acapulco into one of the world's most desired playgrounds. Lizards walked on hotel room ceilings, and the tap water was often green, but Teddy Stauffer, the dashing former ski instructor, ran a spectacular outdoor nightclub on the cliffs of La Perla. Foreign tourists gaped at movie stars, sipped their drinks, and watched the local boys take their daily concussions, diving into the water from great heights.

For glamour, Alemán saw to it that a tiny, tired man, who had slipped into

Mexico to avoid legal problems in the United States, moved his focus from hotels and restaurants in Mexico City to building the Hotel Casablanca atop a hill in Acapulco. A. C. Blumenthal looked like the cartoon figure Mister Magoo by the time he moved to Mexico, but he had not always been a squinty-eyed fellow who preferred lying in his bed surrounded by books to attending lavish parties on yachts anchored off Acapulo. Blumenthal had been part of a famous orgy that included the silent film star Louise Brooks, and he had been the lover of Commodore Vanderbilt's daughter (the first Gloria Vanderbilt). He was also rumored to have "taken the fall" for one of the Schenk brothers in a Hollywood financial scandal that sent one brother to prison. To avoid prosecution and lawsuits, Blumenthal had retired to Mexico. He was known on Wall Street and in the film business as a financial wizard, but in Mexico, Alemán took care of the money. The president gave the weary little man from Hollywood two tasks: Bring the glamour of the movies to Acapulco and provide women for businessmen and politicians whom the president wanted to please. In return, Blumenthal could remain dourly in Mexico, safe from his antagonists across the border. With confidence in his bargain, Alemán bought property in Acapulco, holding it until he and Blumenthal could turn Acapulco into a fortune for Mexico and Alemán. It was not long before tourism brought in almost as much money as oil.

Alemán had a genius for business. Land speculation, although "speculation" was hardly the proper word in this case, was his favorite endeavor. He bought land northwest of Mexico City, paid almost nothing for it, and then oversaw the construction of Satellite City, a gigantic suburb, where every house was built on land sold by the president to grateful citizens. As the father shunned business for war, so the son reduced the size of the Mexican Army until it took up only 2 percent of the budget; he made a business of both government and life.

The key to Alemán's fortune at Satellite City was the Mexican Miracle, the error from which the country may not recover until the middle of the twenty-first century, if ever. If nothing but growth of gross domestic product (GDP) is meaningful, there was indeed a miracle. The GDP tripled from 1940 to 1960 and tripled again between 1960 and 1980. Manufacturing grew to 25 percent of the total by 1980, stimulated first by the lack of goods from the United States during World War II and then by import substitution policies (quotas and tariffs). Even considered from a statistical point of view, the Mexican Miracle was a mistake. Mexico made consumer goods but not the machinery that made the goods. Heavy equipment, manufacturing machinery, and technology continued to be imported at very high cost, devouring most of Mexico's export earnings. Worse, the failure to produce the machinery that produced the goods meant that the Mexican economy could not become self-sustaining. It could only build with what it bought, entering the process at a late stage; it could not build from the beginning, nor could it develop its own products for export. The Mexican Miracle was not made by God or the Mexicans; it came in crates, most of them marked "Made in the USA."

Mexico's contribution to the "miracle" came mainly in the form of labor. Using imported machinery, Mexicans made consumer goods for a protected domestic market. The agrarian policies of the past faded as Miguel Alemán put the dream of 1917 into reverse. By 1960 almost 42 percent of the land was owned by one-tenth of 1 percent of the population. Under Alemán, the ejido system of communal lands crumbled, like ancient Rome, from both internal and external pressures; the small individual plots of land parceled out after the ejido system was broken up could not sustain the growing population. The old hacienda system was renewed, with some of the great fincas transformed into agribusiness. Small farmers could not compete with mechanized farming; they sold off the land, and the haciendas grew larger.

To speed industrialization Alemán moved away from the support of unions that had characterized previous administrations. The Communist intellectual Lombardo Toledano had been pushed out of his post as leader of the CTM by President Ávila Camacho in 1942 and replaced by a much more malleable (from industry's point of view) leader, Fidel Velásquez. Alemán opposed labor stoppages, declaring them illegal, sending the army in to break up demonstrations and arrest the strike leaders. And the CTM under Velásquez went along with the policy, refusing to support unaffiliated unions or its own members. By keeping labor costs down, he kept prices down, maintaining the internal market, but at a heavy cost to the lowest-paid workers and the rural population. All the per capita numbers went up, but the distribution of the increase was not across the board. Statistical progress does not necessarily imply social justice. Prosperity affected the rich and the middle classes.

Industrial workers became a ragged elite among the general population.

Alemán and Velásquez turned the unions into a means for holding down labor costs rather than improving the lot of workers. Mexican economists may have read the work of John Maynard Keynes, but the idea of the modern industrial state and the need to have constant internal markets for goods had not reached the government. Velásquez, who headed the CTM until he died in 1997, was simply a tool of the PRI and hence the government; workers were organized but not represented. If workers attempted to start independent unions, the organizers were beaten and sometimes killed.[16] Real wages, adjusted for inflation and devaluations, fell from 1940 through the Alemán sexenio and on through the Ruiz Cortines years into the next administration.

Mexican products were shoddy, poorly designed, and, given their quality, expensive, but import substitution worked. First-rate imported goods were available only to the upper middle class and the rich. The government devalued the currency twice, until the exchange rate rose to twelve and one-half pesos to the dollar. Wages rose after each devaluation, but slowly. With the peso worth eight cents, those who earned their wages in pesos were unlikely to want to buy foreign goods. Devaluation was another form of import substitution, another tool in creating the "miracle."

Thousands of factories stood at the heart of the "miracle." For reasons that made little economic sense and no social sense at all, a great many of them arose in Mexico City, where essayist Alfonso Reyes had once welcomed travelers to the "clear air." Before long the Reyes invitation became the ironic title of a novel by Carlos Fuentes, *Where the Air Is Clear.* The factories brought in the millions of people who drove the millions of cars, which led to the mix of industrial and automobile pollution that poisons everyone who breathes in Mexico City. Water had to be piped in, labor had to be imported from the countryside and from small towns, housing had to be built, and everything, from raw materials to machinery, had to be brought by truck or rail thousands of feet up the sides of the mountains and then down into the high valley. There was probably no worse place in the country for industry.

Millions and millions of people came to the capital for low-paying jobs.

---

[16]A detailed, but fictionalized, version of the effort to start an independent union is given in a novel I published in 2000, *In the Yucatán* (New York: W. W. Norton); *En Yucatán* (Plaza y Janés).

It stood to reason: Some money was better than no money at all. Agrarian policies had failed and continued to fail in the ensuing years until Mexico became a net importer of food and grains, even corn. There was little choice for the campesinos. Wages below the minimum were better than starvation. A factory job in the capital paid two or three pesos for an eight- or ten-hour day. A day spent braiding straw hats in a village in Guerrero brought in a few centavos, the price of a little corn and a few chillis, but less than the cost of an egg. The campesinos poured into the Federal District. The capital of Mexico was on its way to becoming one of the most populous cities on earth, for no good reason other than the greed and lack of foresight of the government and the centripetal movement that had characterized Mexico at least since the Aztecs came south at the beginning of the fourteenth century.

Instead of industrialization, which seemed for almost twenty years to be the Mexican Miracle, the postwar years were a period of rapid and continuing urbanization. The pattern was set early on. Campesinos came to the city, found a place to sleep, a room, a place on the floor of a relative's apartment, anywhere, and looked for work. Daniel Hiernaux, a sociologist who has followed the Mexican pattern of internal migration for many years, tells the story of one campesino who came to the city.

The man, a Nahuatl speaker from the state of Guerrero, somehow made his way to an affluent suburb on the southern outskirts of the capital. He was still a young man and strong, and if he did not have plans for greatness, he did expect to earn a living. He went into the suburb, found what seemed to him a likely door, and knocked. A woman answered. The campesino, who spoke only a few words of Spanish, removed his hat, smiled, and made gestures indicating that he was looking for work. The woman smiled in return but said she had no work, and told him, "Good day."

"Good day," the campesino said, and put on his hat and went on to the next door.

He knocked, and after a moment a woman opened the door. It was the same woman who had just bid him good day. This time she did not smile. She said something he did not understand and slammed the door.

The man was astonished. He had never before seen a house with two doors.

All day he went from house to house, knocking on doors, smiling, asking for work. His gestures were now practiced, his smile was still expectant, but he found no work. He had no money, no food, not even anything to drink, and he did not know exactly how to ask for water. It grew cold and dark, and he did not know what might befall him in the city. That night he slept in a tree.

As Hiernaux learned, the man was part of the pattern of migration. Those who found work and could earn enough to pay rent and buy food remained in the city; those who failed moved out to the edges of the capital to live in shelters made of cast-off cardboard or tin cans. Plumbing of any kind and electricity were out of the question. Between 1940 and 1970 the Mexican population doubled, and from 1970 to 2000 it doubled again. A few million people emigrated, almost all of them to the United States; the basic pattern was internal migration. At the end of the century almost a fourth of the entire population lived in and around one city.

During the postwar years Alemán operated Mexico as if the country were a huge business unconstrained by either market or government forces. History interested him, but history is not a limit, it is a judgment, unless the person in power is obsessed by history, like a Mayan ruler or a Chinese dictator. Then history yet unwritten reaches back to beset a man with imagination, building long trees of decisions in his mind, emboldening him with expectations or paralyzing him with anxiety. Unwritten history, the anticipation of consequences, no matter how deep in dreams a person lives, has a limiting function. It is the expectation of public knowledge, the enforcer of ethics in all but two instances: The limits of history do not apply to madmen or to business, which lives by markets; there is no unwritten history of markets, the future is now. Alemán was not mad, yet he did as he pleased, much like an old-fashioned Mexican caudillo (the term applied to Francisco Franco and the Mexican generals), but not like a king or even like a true caudillo, for his reign could not last beyond the sexenio.[17]

---

[17]There is a view of modern Mexico as a succession of caudillos. The journalist Enrique Krause embarked on a series of brief books about Mexican presidents. It was a wildly popular series, well written, cheap to buy, each one half an hour of reading. The design of the series, marketable as it was, forced Krauze into a view of Mexico based on the idea of the caudillo when in fact it was ruled by a corporatist state party, the PRI, under its various names. A caudillo would have remained in power over many years, like Francisco Franco or Porfirio Díaz. The antireelection laws written into the 1917 Constitution gave ultimate power to the party, no matter how much power it put in the hands of the executive. If the view of Mexican government as a series of caudillos were entirely correct, the election of a president who was not a member of the PRI in 2000 would not have been important, merely one caudillo replacing another.

Guided by the rules of business, convinced of the holiness of the delicious moment, Alemán set the ethical tone of Mexico more thoroughly than the Catholic Church had ever done. The Church offered extreme unction, but Alemán, the businessman, said there was no need to wait; his ethics promised paradise in the here and now for those who knew how to take it. And if there were sins involved, Christ had already died for them; a man could be forgiven.

He let the ejidos dwindle, putting his constructive energies into the national university, which had been the cradle of his success. The son of the general for all sides filled his cabinet with law school classmates, hoping to make certain there would never again be military rule or even great military influence in Mexican government. If his actions sometimes benefited the general society, there was always doubt about his motivation. He was interested in the glorification of Miguel Alemán Valdés. His presidential campaign had been the first in Mexico to depend on U.S.-style hoopla.

If Alemán had any sense of the judgment of posterity, he planned to take care of it by completing the construction of the new national university campus. He personally oversaw the design and building of University City in Pedregal in the far south of the Federal District. To be sure the project would be remembered as his, el Cachorro de la Revolución commissioned a statue of himself to stand at the center of the campus. Then, to be sure the statue was properly presented to the public, he unveiled it himself. In a speech praising the president, José Vasconcelos congratulated him on the design of the campus, saying that it would enable the various faculties to work together. It was a standard speech, a bit sententious as was expected, but there was one sentence that stood out. Vasconcelos said Alemán's "powerful personality will bring to the university discipline, order, and progress." It had been decades since the motto of the cientificos had been proclaimed in public. To Vasconcelos, Miguel Alemán had rejuvenated the grandeur of the Porfiriato.

The country was a property of the president and his minions in the PRI. Highways and dams bore the name of Alemán. He owned a hotel in Acapulco and an entire suburb of Mexico City, and he and his friends were together in many other private businesses. The Cadillac automobile exemplified the way business worked during the Alemán presidency. The import tariff doubled the price of the car, but the importer of Cadillacs in Mexico was an agency owned by the Pasquel brothers whose involvement with the president was more than casual.[18] The Pasquels not only had a national monopoly on Cadillac cars but also monopolized the distribution of petroleum products. Through their intimate connection to the president, el Cachorro, they had become both the General Motors and the Standard Oil of Mexico.

The amoral view from the top spread through the echelons of bureaucrats, it swept through the character of all the new rich of the twentieth century, generals and entrepreneurs, lawyers and engineers. Manuel Casas Alemán, a relative of the president's and the regent of Mexico City, had an affair of the heart, so to speak, with Irma Serrano, a thirteen-year-old girl from Chiapas. As luck would have it, Serrano grew up into a woman both vivacious and loquacious. She told in detail of that affair and others in an immensely popular memoir. True to his name, Casas (which means "houses") built gaudy mansions for himself and then, to amuse and entertain his cronies, held live sex shows after lunch in the garden of one of his suburban houses. All the guests were male, except for a few women who were expected to find the show so stimulating they would gladly bring the entertainment to a climax for the friends of Sr. Casas. Some of the women knew why they were invited. With others Casas took his chances. If they stayed for the show, they augmented the huge coterie of "party girls" in Mexico. If they felt duped by the invitation and left in a rage, it was no matter. There was nothing they could do. It was Mexico City, and he was in charge; his name was Casas *Alemán*.

His thirteen-year-old girlfriend, whose story is told by Jonathan Kandell in *La Capital*,[19] went on to become a well-known singer and actress. But her real success came privately, until the publication of her memoir. She was the mistress of the sour man of the rimless eyeglasses, Gustavo Díaz Ordaz, during most of his presidency. Nothing Serrano wrote in her memoir

[18]The American press, including *Time*, suggested that Alemán's rise to the presidency depended upon two killings: the governor-elect of Veracruz and Ávila Camacho's brother. Rumors in Mexico linked the Pasquel brothers to Alemán's business dealings, but no one spoke aloud of a connection to the murders. If anyone had engineered the two deaths that led to Alemán's presidency, it was probably the Pasquel family. The Pasquels occasionally visited New York City, where one of the brothers, apparently in a good mood, once took a pistol from his pocket and shot holes in the ceiling of his suite in the Sherry-Netherland Hotel.

[19]New York: Random House, 1988.

harmed her career. Mexico was 90 percent Catholic, the Catholic Church had a national campaign to raise the moral standards of the country, and Serrano, Casas, Díaz Ordaz, Blumenthal all flourished.

Under the Alemán regime—and the party, as he had captured it, controlled the country with sufficient thoroughness to be called a regime—everything seemed to flourish. Mexico City, which had become internationalized by the willingness since Cárdenas to accept refugees, gave a home to Spanish philosophers and American screenwriters fleeing subpoenas from the House Un-American Activities Committee. Alemán's worldview, a kind of ill-defined nihilism that would have interested Dostoyevsky, permitted not only license but an undercurrent of freedom to think, write, paint, film, and dance in the otherwise grimly conformist decade of the fifties.

Freedom in Mexico existed in layers of contradiction. Under the surface of the liberty and democracy that Alemán described on a visit to official Washington lay a sinister limitation of freedom.[20] Those who raised political objections to the policies of the president, from the Sinarquistas to the Communists, were outlawed. Newspapers that spoke ill of the president might find themselves unable to import newsprint. Or, like *Novedades*, bought by Alemán. Mexican theater suffered similar limitations. Political satire, once a staple of popular theater on stages in the center of the capital and in little neighborhood tent shows, like the one in which Cantinflas first performed, had to be done with care. Only things relating to the president were off-limits to the comics. Otherwise, libel was a popular sport; celebrities lived off their public sins in the amoral atmosphere created by el Cachorro. But a man who made jokes about the president was likely to find himself in a jail cell, battered by the police.

In the next layer, Mexico developed a comedy of signs and signals, an underground of bitter satire that the government goons could see and hear but could not understand. Cantinflas was a subversive in Mexico in the way that Pushkin was a subversive in Russia. He was beloved, a national hero, a treasure, but even after he had accumulated great wealth, he belonged to the people rather than the government. He made the rich and powerful appear

[20]He was the first Mexican president to visit the United States in more than a century. Both Roosevelt and Truman had been to Mexico, one to talk about the war effort with Ávila Camacho and the other to see a volcano and visit the pyramids at Teotihuacán. The last Mexican president to visit Washington before Alemán was Santa Anna, who was brought in defeat and disgrace before Andrew Jackson.

ludicrous, and in that respect he was Chaplinesque. Deeper inside the layer, beyond Cantinflas was the underground of jokes. Unlike the United States, where Bob Hope and Fred Allen were expected to skewer the famous, the pompous, and especially the politicians, the Mexicans had to depend on one another. Jokes were whispered across the country. The poorest campesino living in a cardboard hovel knew who slept in the president's *other* bed. Alemán launched vast public campaigns to promote ever greater love and respect from the Mexican people, and the people adored him and praised him and in fits of enlightenment and envy whispered about how he got rich and what the Pasquel brothers had done for him. They did not know which Alemán was real and which was painted on the papier-mâché of publicity.

The next layer belonged to the artists and intellectuals. On the surface, Alemán supported and encouraged them. He appointed them to government posts, although most often outside the country. Under a less complex regime, Octavio Paz, then an ardent leftist, might have been jailed or even killed; instead, Alemán sent him to Paris in a mid-level job in the Mexican Embassy. There was no need to send everyone abroad. Some writers, like Martín Luis Guzmán, caved in to the unwritten rule of the regime and became apologists for Alemán. Daniel Cosío Villegas, surely one of the most brilliant and fearless men of the period, went to the United States to think about Mexico. Much of the best thinking about the country has been done from north of border, from the work of Cosío Villegas to Paz's *Labyrinth of Solitude* to Frank Tannenbaum's devastating attack on the Mexican Miracle published in 1951 to the histories written by Friedrich Katz and John Womack to the journalism of Alan Riding. But there were other ways to cripple freedom besides outright repression or co-optation through career appointments or scholarships. Cosío Villegas's work went all but unread from 1940 to 1946, the years of el Cachorro's presidency; his criticism of the regime had no audience beyond a small cadre of intellectuals. For the rest, the rich didn't care and the poor couldn't read.

Unlike the United States, where the defeat of the intellectuals was accomplished by the joint forces of democracy and the market, which grinds everything down until it can be swallowed without chewing, Alemán's government had to work at anti-intellectualism. Yet there was another layer underneath the co-opted and the silenced, and it was like the one that underlay the Soviet dictatorship, except that it was filled with good times. This was not Akhmatova writing poetry despite Stalin, teaching Isaiah Berlin that totalitarianism did not prevent art from being made. The PRI regime—and it is perhaps most accurate to refer to the party rather than the person, even though one person controlled both government and party—allowed art to exist under the surface of the government, even stimulated both art and thought as opposition.

To be an artist under the PRI of postwar Mexico was to live in a mix of socialites, actors, exiles, and other artists. A painter could survive on what he ate and drank at parties; a poet could find, if only for a little while, a woman or man to provide foolscap and finery. It was, some Mexicans said, a Golden Age. There was always a party, one kind for those who could afford to give it and another for those who could be afforded. One could hear the lovely, sentimental music of Agustín Lara or look at the face of the actress María Félix, for whom he wrote the song "María Bonita," and give the hours over to wishing. If the actress made her peace with the government by giving her body to Jorge Pasquel, whose family connections to Alemán and the PRI gave him almost unlimited power, it was understood, for beneath the submission to power, lived a rebellious woman who slept with the Communist painter Diego Rivera and lay beside Frida Kahlo to comfort her in her last days.

If the repression was intended to discourage the undercurrent of freedom among painters, writers, and political thinkers, it failed. It produced a surface of political pimps and panderers, but in the deepest layer of the society, after all the contradictions, repression generated the reaction that made art. Repression encouraged the making of outlaws in Mexico, for thinking was an outlawed activity, and the outlaws told their thoughts in the only way they could, in bold colors and sad tunes, in the mask of metaphor. Mexico was an old country, although it was then a country for young men and a few young women. No Mexican lived without the conscious and unconscious whispers of history always in his ear, insisting upon cycles and ultimate nothingness. Artists had evidence that metaphor would outlast the meanness of the moment. They laughed and danced and drank whiskey or pulque, whichever they could afford, and in the secret place where outlaws live, in the deeps of society, they worked, in imagined light, to spite the surface world. It was a good time for poets.

TO THE LEFT (WITHIN THE CONSTITUTION)

For the next twelve years a veneer of calm and decency came over Mexico; the face of the country did not betray anger or suffering. Tourists came and went, happy for the devaluation of the peso to eight cents; voting rights were finally extended to women, who made no change in the system begun by Cárdenas and turned into the tripartite ruling elite of president, party, and bureaucracy by Alemán; wages continued to increase, but not as fast as inflation, which meant the standard of living fell slowly but inexorably during the Ruiz Cortines years; and the population grew and grew and grew, until even the good Catholic President Ruiz Cortines recognized it as Mexico's fundamental problem. When the bookkeeper and statistician from Veracruz took office, there were three million people in Mexico City, and at the end of his sexenio the population of the city had increased by half.

Richard Nixon visited Mexico to carry on his fight against communism, and Ruiz Cortines took him to a Mexico City slum to show him the real problem of Latin America. The government, to its credit, devoted more and more of the budget to education, and the percentage of illiterates decreased. But in the literacy problem, as in almost everything else, population growth made a mockery of every effort on behalf of the poor. Despite the new schools and the adult literacy courses, there were thirteen million illiterates in a country of thirty-five million people in 1960. With so many people and so little industry, Ruiz Cortines decided that the best way to keep them employed was to stop the use of machinery in building public projects; a return to the old methods of backbreaking hand labor would enable many of the poor to enjoy the benefits of inefficiency.

Although Ruiz Cortines followed most of the policies set by his predecessor, there was one great difference between the two men. The greatest thief (at that time) in the history of Mexico had been replaced by a man known for his honesty. One of his first acts as president was to put an end to the oil distribution monopoly Alemán had permitted the Pasquel brothers. He had some troubles from unions, but Adolfo López Mateos, whom he appointed as secretary of labor, had a great talent for soothing both sides in difficult issues.

Nothing in the Ruiz Cortines presidency mattered so much, in the end, as his free market views and his deep conservatism. He sent the PAN and the left into action in response. The left, led by Tata Lázaro, did as might be expected when a conservative took power; it became bolder. The PAN, instead of growing stronger under a conservative administration, lost its purchase with the business community, which could not see beyond the moment in all its markets. Labor costs remained low, the 1954 devaluation

made foreign products too expensive for all but the extremely rich, and government stayed out of the way of industry. Business was good. It was so good
that the moguls of Monterrey no longer saw any reason to support the PAN.
They got what they wanted from the PRI, and the cost of the *mordida* had
gone down since Ruiz Cortines took office. The PAN had to look elsewhere
for support.[21]

The party turned to the Church. With the Sinarquista movement outlawed, conservative Catholics had no political vehicle in Mexico, and they
turned to the PAN. The fanatical aspects of Sinarquismo did not infect the
party, but its membership was conservative about religion as well as economics. The Church had been on a moral crusade, and it all fit nicely with
National Action. Monterrey remained an important city for the PAN even
though the businessmen were, for the moment, content with Ruiz Cortines
and the PRI. It was one of the places where the Spanish Inquisition had been
strong in Mexico, and Opus Dei, the right wing of the Church and, some say,
the inheritor of the Holy Brotherhood, was strong in Monterrey, as in
Guadalajara. Opus Dei had dormitories for women students even in the
twenty-first century in Mexico City, where it insisted that they follow its
dress code and its very stringent rules of behavior. The writer Penny
Lernoux, a deeply religious Catholic who nevertheless was critical of the
Church, understood Opus Dei as powerful, conservative, but not sinister.[22]

---

[21]The PANistas were largely owners of small and medium-size businesses, supported by
a few who had larger holdings. They were bitter about the government, but fearless, at
least on the surface. Rumors abounded even then about the party growing out of the
Radical Catholic Sinarquista movement. It was the common language of their enemies
in the government and on the left: Fascistas! Sinarquistas! PANistas!

Proving the allegations was more difficult than making them. One evening, in the
mid-1950s, I was invited to meet the leading members of the state organization of the
PAN at a party in Ciudad Juárez. There were more than a hundred people at the party.
The entertainment was a well-known musical group of the time, Los Tres Aces, and the
food and drink were plentiful. I was introduced as a journalist. No one claimed to know
anything about the Cristeros or Sinarquistas, although several spoke proudly of belonging to Opus Dei. I asked their opinions of the groups rather than confront them about
membership. All were "good" Catholics, as they explained, but not so much interested in
God as in the new taxes aimed at shutting down businesses owned by members of the
PAN.

[22]See her *Cry of the People* (New York: Doubleday, 1980) and *People of God* (New York:
Viking, 1989).

Perhaps the reason for the joining together of the PAN and the Church had as much to do with the suffering both had endured under the Mexican government as with politics. In the latter half of the 1950s, the PAN and PRI confronted each other in Ciudad Juárez, where the PRI simply stole elections. The PRI put its owned man, René Mascareñas, into the mayor's office. Mascareñas was a charming fellow, with a little fringe of hair closely cropped around a large bald dome. He was the color of the south of Spain, and he had the small features and roundness more generally representative of Sancho Panza than the don from La Mancha.

I used to enjoy visiting with him. It was while he was mayor of Ciudad Juárez that the *paracaidistas* (parachutists, slang for squatters) first fell on a section of nearly useless grazing land west of the city. They occupied an abandoned ranch house and spread across the land in houses made first of cardboard, then of old packing crates, and finally of blocks of adobe. The paracaidistas of the north, like all Mexicans, dreamed of land of their own, even if it was no more than the space required to build a tiny house, but they had little or nothing in common with the campesinos of Morelos, who still cherished Zapata's dreams. These squatters belonged to the Church.

A priest had come to work with them. A stern man, he arrived in a sturdy automobile, dressed in street clothes, the only kind of clothing a priest could wear on the street in Mexico. He stepped out of the car, carrying only a small bag, went inside the house, and waited for dusk. Meanwhile, a table was carried out onto the long front porch of the old house and made into an altar. Young boys carried out tall, heavy, gold-colored candlesticks and thick white candles from inside the house, and after the sun had gone down behind the house, they lit the candles. There was no wind, and it was quiet except for a cow that called out somewhere in the middle distance, out of sight, its voice soft and therefore mournful.

At one moment there was still light on the eastern field in front of the porch, and the light grew red and colored the long, flat place, and in the next moment it was dark. No church bells rang; no call was given. In the darkness, the shapes were barely discernible. Here and there some white fabric— a shirt or blouse—glowed, as if it had somehow managed to capture the afternoon light. The priest, splendid, dour, and quick, came out of the house. He spoke softly; he did not immediately begin the mass. He waited, while the shapes came out of the night, all the women's heads covered with dark shawls, as if they had entered a church.

The mass began, and all the shapes, the men and the women, knelt on the stony ground. There was some fear in the air; lookouts had been posted on the road below. The police had been to the squatters' camps before, and they had not been tender with either the men or their women; only the children had escaped the boots and bludgeons. The little bell sounded, and the squatters rose, and prayed aloud, and knelt again. They did all this, as they had been instructed since childhood, in perfect unison, which may have been what frightened René Mascareñas and the PRI. When I told the story in the press of the squatters and their politics, the mayor sent word by a newspaper reporter that if ever I were found in his city again, I would spend a long time in jail, or worse.

In 1958 a new president, Adolfo López Mateos, was elected to replace the dour old capitalist Ruiz Cortines. There was a scandal having to do with money found missing from a milk fund for children, but there is always a scandal at the end of one presidency and the beginning of another in Mexico; it is part of the ritual. Ruiz Cortines was not much affected by it; history looks upon him as honest, although rightist, the second businessman to hold the office. He is remembered as the man who explained what was necessary to get along in politics in Mexico: "You have to learn to eat toads."[23] His successor took a different view of the country and the economy. López Mateos told Mexico and the world that he would take the country to the left but then carefully qualified his statement, adding "within the Constitution." It was the caveat he kept in his pocket, ready to use when needed, and beside it there was the law of social dissolution in the penal code, a law so vaguely phrased the president could use it to jail anyone, even a famous painter, like Siqueiros. After the left roared in anger, claiming the president had violated his promise, he had only to reach into his pocket again to show the letter of the caveat: Siqueiros was not acting "within the Constitution."

The strongest voice on the left during the López Mateos sexenio was Tata Lázaro. He had made certain that Fidel Castro, then a young relatively unknown Cuban radical taking refuge in Mexico, had not been extradited. And in 1959, when Castro proclaimed the triumph of the Cuban Revolution, the beloved former president of Mexico, Lázaro Cárdenas, stood next to him on the platform, looking out over a huge and adoring crowd. As the sexenio went on, Cárdenas condemned the United States for the Bay of Pigs

[23]Quoted by journalist Fernando Benítez and many others.

invasion, demanded the release of political prisoners, and carried out the duties of father to the young of the Mexican left. He was their Beatles and their Castro, the hippest old man in the world, and he was *Mexican*!

The Cuban missile crisis caused the world's heart to stop for a moment while Kennedy and Khrushchev played poker, and it hurt the left in Mexico, as in the rest of Latin America. Even Tata Lázaro was momentarily stunned to think that the Russians and the Cubans, both of whom he loved and admired, had brought the end so close. During the López Mateos sexenio, the country moved both left and right at the same time. Kennedy agreed to return the Chamizal Zone, a small piece of disputed territory north of the river between El Paso, Texas, and Ciudad Juárez, Chihuahua. It was a few hundred acres of cheap stores, taverns, and small adobe houses with inadequate plumbing. Nonetheless, it was a victory for Mexico, the first return of Mexican territory since 1848. Most important, however, the negotiation had taken place on more or less equal terms.

The Mexican Miracle changed during the López Mateos years. The role of government grew; that was in itself a move to the left. Business continued to do well, but often with support from government. Regulation increased. López Mateos did not expropriate foreign property, as Cárdenas had, but he bought out the privately owned electric utilities and nationalized them. Mexico celebrated: The country owned oil production and electricity; the government controlled basic industries, regulated prices for tortillas, and kept the cost of movie tickets low enough for every Mexican, no matter how poor, to go to the movies. And to keep the theaters from showing only foreign films, it nationalized film production. Arturo Ripstein and Luis Buñuel directed, and they had Gabriel Figueroa and others like him to film and edit the pictures. The industry enjoyed a huge stock company of actors to populate and popularize whatever they produced: Cantinflas, Jorge Negrete, María Félix, Tin Tan, Miroslava, Pedro Armendáriz. In 1962, Mexico produced 124 movies, 29 percent of all those shown in the country that year. The industry never again reached either that absolute number or percentage.

Social security, a system that included health care as well as small pensions for workers, vastly increased its reach. Hundreds of clinics and hospitals opened to care for people who had previously been treated by curanderos or not treated at all. Infant mortality rates and the overall death rate fell, contributing to the population boom. For every bit of good news, something wounding, something sinister happened. It was not entirely a lack of foresight; Mexican presidents worried publicly about the birthrate but were helpless to do anything about it. The Church officially opposed birth control, but the Church had less sway than the culture over the over-production of children. Mexico turned into an urban society without losing its rural attitudes toward children. On a farm or ranch every child was another human being to do manual labor; children were the only wealth a poor man could accumulate; the culture responded to the demands of sur-vival; men produced children with their wives but *fucked* other women, they did not make love to them. Octavio Paz had his theories about the verb *chin-gar* and the rape of La Malinche as well as the sexual stimulation of a hot cli-mate. But the cause of overpopulation was not merely a theory; it grew out of a need that no longer existed.

López Mateos spoke of birth control to no avail and maintained his popularity by reaching into crowds to pull out and kiss the prettiest women. He had affairs with many women, and he all but announced them to the public. After a president who was "older than the mountains," it was good to have a real man in office, comforting. The logic could not have been more apparent. López Mateos had *huevos* (balls), as indicated by the number of women he wanted and enjoyed; therefore, he was the kind of man who could dispute the Chamizal and take back the electric utilities from the foreigners.

He called in the army to break up strikes, and he did not hesitate to use the social dissolution law to imprison people he thought had gone too far to the left or were too deeply opposed to the one–party-government-president system. And at the same time he distributed more land than any president but Cárdenas. There was of course a complaint from the left and the organization of campesinos about the quality of the land distrib-uted, and there was more than a little truth in the complaint: The land often came closer to vertical than horizontal or could be properly described as desert, or both. But the problem lay in the geography of the country as much as the will of the president: Only 15 percent of the land in Mexico is considered arable. Pre-Hispanic agriculture had been suited to the deserts, mountains, and jungles, and the percentage of arable land was undoubtedly greater. Overpopulation may have been a problem in some parts of the Mesoamerican civilization, but the corn, beans, and squash combination used in the milpa (small farm) could apparently sustain a large population.[24] However, there had never been a population like the one that was growing in Mexico. In 1963 there were 1.5 million live births.

The López Mateos administration recognized the problem of the concentration of industry in Mexico City and tried valiantly to stop it, even to reverse the damage. But it was too late: From 1950 to 1960 over half a million people had moved into the Federal District. The pattern had been established. When combined with the high birthrate and falling death rate, no one could doubt that the city was on the way to desperate overcrowding. To deal with the question, López Mateos built government housing and charged low rents, attempting to get the people out of the squatters' shacks that ringed the city. Beggars worked the streets of the city, women with dark wood faces sitting on street corners wrapped in their rebozos, children selling individual boxes of Chiclets held out in tiny blackened hands, the blind and the legless holding out their cups, and here and there someone proudly selling old flowers. The failures of the society were everywhere on the streets of the capital: the picaros and *leperos* of New Spain in different dress after four hundred years.

Almost in desperation, López Mateos traveled the world to find capital for Mexico, to loosen the hold of the United States, and to promote his ideal government. In 1963 the largest single item in the budget was education. By then women were being educated in many urban areas of the country; it would change Mexico, freeing women, eventually moving them into positions in universities and government. But education did not extend beyond the middle class. There was more equality for women of the higher classes, less for poor women; change in Mexico continued to take place mainly among comfortable classes; there was no continuing social revolution.

Left, the president had said, but "within the Constitution," he had insisted. In the month of May 1962, after the May Day celebrations and parades, when the mountains had turned green again in central Mexico, especially in Morelos, the problem of Rubén Jaramillo had come to the fore yet again. Jaramillo had always been trouble; he had been born to trouble,

[24]Until recently overpopulation and poor agricultural methods were thought by some historians to have led to famine, which in turn brought about the fall of the Maya city-states. But recent studies show the average height of the Maya decreasing during the last five hundred years, indicating a lack of proper nutrition following the invasion. Whether that is due to the deprivations of colonization or the change of agricultural methods is difficult to ascertain. In all likelihood, both were contributing factors.

or so it seemed, for he was only seventeen years old when he was made a captain in Emiliano Zapata's cavalry. With the disintegration of the Zapata forces in 1918, many of his former troops turned to living off the land, but not Jaramillo. He is said to have gathered his own troops together and told them: "Few men have triumphed without ideas based on justice and social good, and so we cannot take the road of bad revolutionaries who cannot sustain themselves without harming the people and who sooner or later fall on their knees before the enemy. We are going to separate from each other, with the aim of maintaining ourselves for a better time. And from today on it will not be an armed revolution, but one of ideas of justice and great social liberation. . . . The people, future generations, will be unable to live as slaves, and then, our cause renewed, we will be on the march. And even though we will be apart, we will not lose sight of each other, and when the moment arrives, we will reunite. Take care of your ammunition; keep it where you can pick it up again. . . ."

Jaramillo never gave up the ideas learned in Zapata's army. He bought mules and became a trader of rice and beans, traveling long distances, helping the ejiditarios to sell their products direct to markets, avoiding middlemen. The wealthy businessmen around Jojutla, Morelos, where he lived, joined with the politicians against him. He brought his ideas to Lázaro Cárdenas, who put them to use. Jaramillo ran the cooperative for a group that took the name of Emiliano Zapata. It worked for a while; then the bankers and politicians crushed it and forced him out. Jaramillo went to work as a cane cutter, laboring in the fields, but continued to oppose the institutional powers in Morelos.

In the 1950s the police came to his house once, twice, looking for him, and after a third visit Rubén Jaramillo went into the mountains. It was the moment he had called for in the speech in 1918. He brought the old Zapatistas together again. There had been unrest among the campesinos since the Mexican military draft during World War II, and Jaramillo knew how to tap it. He put together a small cavalry unit, with plans to attack several towns at once. He led one unit into Tlaquiltenango, planning to rid the town of corrupt caciques, but no one attacked the other towns, and Jaramillo had to quickly retreat. He tried to raise an army, going from town to town, but he soon realized that there would be no general uprising, no great army, no repeat of the days when he had fought with Zapata.

Defeated in the field, Jaramillo took up politics. He was a sturdy man who wore his straw hat on the back of his head, showing his face full, as Pancho Villa had. He raised a family; lines came into his face, first from laughter, then deeper lines, permanent marks around his mouth, like brackets. His eyes narrowed, saddened at the corners; his mustache turned gray. He wore striped shirts, buttoned at the collar but never decorated by a tie, and he spoke and stared. He studied all the faces in crowds, knowing that the army was waiting for him. In 1945 he had founded the Agrarian Workers Party of Morelos. And from then on he fought political battles. Jaramillo organized groups of squatters to take over land in Morelos. Like Zapata, always like Zapata, he fought for land for the peasants.

In 1958 the president who said he would take the country to the left within the Constitution embraced Jaramillo, asking for his help in settling the agrarian question in Morelos. Jaramillo was by then growing tired. He had been a rebel for almost half a century. In the offer from López Mateos he saw the ideas of Zapata coming to fruition at last. His friends warned him against it. They had heard the qualifier, "within the Constitution," but Jaramillo had heard the word "left." He accepted the guarantees offered by the president.

Only after the president told him to calm the cane workers and then reneged on one promise of land distribution after another did Jaramillo realize that López Mateos had trapped the last of Zapata's officers in much the same way that Carranza had been involved in the trap laid for Zapata himself. Jaramillo fled to a safe house in Mexico City. The police found him there, but he escaped and went home to his house and his family in Tlaquiltenango. Again, the government found him. Federal troops and State Judicial Police took Jaramillo and his family to the ruins of Xochicalco, not far from Cuernavaca, on the road to Acapulco. What happened there would have been but another incident in the dark side of the López Mateos administration, a part of the system, but Carlos Fuentes went to Xochicalco a few days later and wrote an article about Jaramillo for the popular magazine *Siempre* (Always).

"They pushed him down. Jaramillo could not hold himself back, he was a lion of the field. . . . He threw himself at the party of murderers; he was defending his wife and his children, and especially the unborn child; they brought him down with their rifle butts, they knocked out an eye. Epifania flung herself on the murderers; they tore her rebozo, they tore her dress, they threw her on the stones. [Jaramillo's son] cursed at them; they opened fire and he doubled over and fell beside his pregnant mother, on the stones. While he was still alive, they opened his mouth, picked up fistfuls of earth, pulled open his mouth and laughing, filled it with earth."[25]

After the story ran, López Mateos punished the magazine financially but did not close it. As always with attempts to obliterate the life of a martyr, López Mateos's effort failed. Jaramillo became a national hero, schools and towns were named after him, the Fuentes article was reproduced again and again, and in the United States, Phil Ochs, a popular folk singer in the 1960s, wrote a song to Jaramillo.

López Mateos did not pause in pursuit of Communists. He jailed Demetrio Vallejo of the railroad workers' union, and he put away as many Communists as he could find. But Mexico had by then begun to slip out from under the immense monolith of the inseparable party-presidency-government. López Mateos would not tolerate open disagreement, but he had softened the position of men in power, he had new ideas for the state. The undercurrent of discontent was everywhere; the government could not help seeing it. Pope John XXIII had made the most fundamental change, putting the Church at the service of the poor. *Comunidades de base* (base Christian communities) existed all over Latin America; the Jesuits, traditionally the educators in the organization of the Roman Catholic Church, had turned their considerable power and influence to the task of alleviating the suffering of the poor. The sense of change was everywhere.

In 1965, a year after the end of López Mateos's term, while the still-young (fifty-two years) former president lay immobilized by a stroke, Pablo González Casanova published *La Democracia en Mexico*,[26] in which he redefined democracy for the new generation of Mexicans, taking it out of the realm of mere majority rule and adding to it dimensions of political and cultural participation. He found the idea of progress in Mexico a political sham, and he tore apart many of the statistics that had been used to support it.

At the very beginning of the cool, devastating book, he wrote that progress was judged by gross national product, yet there never was a case in which gross national product was distributed equally. Distribution, for him, was at the heart of democracy, and it included the distribution of everything. The vote—and the vote had to be genuinely free and fair—was only

[25]English translation from Krauze, *Mexico: Biography of Power.*
[26]Mexico City: Ediciones Era, 1965.

a means to assure distribution. The vote, however, was the place where democracy began; suffrage had to be universal, including the poor. He quoted Disraeli on suffrage for "the honest and brave people of England." As for the idea of revolution, González Casanova complained of the stereotypes of "the Revolution" that had permitted paternalism and authoritarianism in Mexico. And of course he argued that a democratic society had to be secular.

A social structure could not be democratic if it deprived the poor of books and information, he wrote. Among the "structural obstacles to democracy," he put first "a plural society that impedes a uniform political expression." By a "plural society" he meant one in which there was both indigenous culture and what he called national culture. He equated monolingual and bilingual speakers of indigenous languages with the marginalized poor. They were, he argued, the remnants of colonialism, part of the continuing internal colonialism of Mexico. He concluded that the "indigenous problem" more than anything else, even class structure, explained the problem of Mexico. In the end, he wrote, Mexico could progress only by becoming urban, literate, a nation of rising per capita income.

Change came, as he had urged, but in a Mexican way. It began as the milpa begins, as everything Mexican has always begun. Eat what has grown; then burn the field, stoke the future. And under the ashes of the field, on the first day following the rain, when the ground is rich with the nutrients of the ash, the seeds will germinate. It was the way from the beginning, always to have to civilize the forest, to grow in ashes, to plant the seed in the most selective way, in the hole made by the digging stick as it feels for the weakness between the stone plates under the ash. Then put five seeds in the hole so that out of the many, one will surely survive and grow to feed the future: Daniel Cosío Villegas, Fidel Castro, John XXIII, Rubén Jaramillo, and Pablo González Casanova.

In the decade of discontent that encircled the world, the long hair and genital freedom of the great middle-class child's rebellion also came to Mexico, but it was an import, like the movies and toothpaste and Coca-Cola. The Mexican rage had other origins; it did not grow in suburbs, but in ashes. The central myth of Mesoamerican civilization told of the blossoming and burying and rebirth of corn and humans. The underworld was filled with monsters to be overcome by hero twins, by the gorgeous twin of first light. The Mexican rebellion spread through the society, a rumbling in the ashes left by civil wars, the Cárdenas Revolution, drought, a burst of orchids, drought, and then the inexplicable ambiguities of López Mateos. The agricultural method was known as *tumbar y quemar* (slash and burn). There had never been democracy in Mexico, not even for a little while, and only Tata Lázaro had raised the question of whose tree would be cut down and made into ashes.

ONE WHITE GLOVE

In July 1968 the Second Mexican Revolution began. Although the first fruits of the Revolution would not appear for thirty-two years, there can be little doubt now that when the mayor of Mexico City sent the riot squad (*granaderos*) to stop a fight during a soccer game between a technical school and a preparatory school, the citizens of the Federal District began to take a more critical view of government. The granaderos broke up the fight, followed the students into the school building, and beat them. Then there was a student demonstration in the center of the city that turned into a fight between police and students that lasted for days. Students burned buses, police beat students, and students were arrested and jailed. The confrontations had all the earmarks of student-police battles in Paris and San Francisco and New York. It was 1968.

The battles in the center of the city had settled down when the police blasted their way with a bazooka into an UNAM feeder school and occupied the campus. The government blamed it all on the Communists, but no one outside the government accepted the argument. It was no longer a student riot. The rector of the National Autonomous University of Mexico appealed to students to join in the defense of freedom, and he led a march toward the city. Fifty thousand people marched with him. The government had made a problem for itself, and Gustavo Díaz Ordaz, the ugly president with the mistress who went public, used the problem to express his hard line about everything: the presidency, the Communists, the students, and the state. Mexico was a democracy, free and growing, in the view of the president, and no one had the right to challenge the state.

On August 28, the students from the UNAM and the National Polytechnical Institute brought together the faculties of their university and thousands of citizens they had been recruiting for their cause in a massive demonstration in the Zócalo. Perhaps half a million people gathered there.

The government sent tanks into the streets to break up the demonstration. A student was killed. On September 1, 1968, President Gustavo Díaz Ordaz delivered the annual State of the Union message (*informe*), and it was not calculated to win over the students and their supporters, now at least a million people or more. He appeared not to care about them. He had something else on his mind: The Olympics were coming to Mexico. The games were not a spectacle that Díaz Ordaz had promoted or desired, but he did not want the world to see Mexico as a lawless country, something out of a bad movie about Pancho Villa, with people killing each other in the streets.

The students and their supporters held open meetings, and the public found them sensible, orderly, exactly as they wanted university students to be. The government, which still controlled all the newspapers and every magazine but *Siempre* and *Política*, used the press to condemn the students and their followers, hinting always at Communist domination, control from distant and dangerous places. At one point the government argued that there had been no bazooka or mortar fire in the first confrontation. It had been a Molotov cocktail thrown by a student, the government said. But everyone seemed to know exactly what had happened. And there was evidence: The ancient wooden gates of the school had not burned; they had been blown off in an explosion. And the students seemed to know exactly what to do to keep the goodwill of the public. To show their wish to avoid confrontation, they held a silent march. The students and their supporters moved through the streets of the ancient capital, and there was no sound but the low rumble of the footsteps of a quarter of a million people.

Since the unrest surfaced, Díaz Ordaz had made one wrong move after another. In response to the silent march, he had a new idea of how to bring calm to the situation. He dispatched thousands of army troops to invade and secure the UNAM campus. The rector of the university resigned. The students had won; the criticism of the government had reached to the top of the intellectual world. Not only the rector but Professor Cosío Villegas, the revered historian himself, had come over to their side. Yet Díaz Ordaz and Luis Echeverría, his secretary of the interior, the post from which presidents came, were relentless. Troops occupied the Polytechnic Institute. The newspapers wrote day after day about foreign agitators, Communists, a student plan to wreck the Olympics, to embarrass Mexico before the world.

On October 2, in Tlatelolco, where the Spaniards had seen the most orderly and clean marketplace in the world of 1519, in the city-state where the conquest was completed, in a place known as the Plaza of Three Cultures (Aztec, Spanish, and Mexican), a student gathering began in the afternoon. The crowd was not very large, the speeches were not very stirring; it seemed the rebellion had grown weary. As the afternoon ebbed into evening, a helicopter appeared in the sky over Tlatelolco near the center of the city. Some of those who had been standing in the plaza looked up at the curiosity. Tanks waited outside the entrances to the plaza as did soldiers and the Olympia Brigade, a group of men each of whom wore a white glove on the left hand only. The tanks and the soldiers were ordinary business for the government, the one white glove was strange, as were the helicopter and the flares.

The machine guns opened fire first, and the soldiers and tanks came rushing in, closing off the exits, turning the crowd into a mob. Parents and their children screamed, gunfire came from every direction; then the men each with the one white glove invaded the crowd, and there was more gunfire. No one was permitted in or out of the plaza, no ambulances for the wounded, just the thousands who had been there and the tanks and soldiers and the men who wore one white glove.

> The people were trampled; one ran just on top of people. . . . Thus were defeated the Mexica Tlatelolca, who relinquished their altepetl [city-state]. . . . When it was done, when it was over [they] delivered Quauhtemoctzin to the place where the captain [Cortés], don Pedro de Alvarado, and Marina were.
>
> When they had been taken into custody, the people began to leave, heading for where there was a way out. Some still had some rags to wrap around their bottoms.   —*Anales de Tlatelolco*

The special presidential guards of the Olympia Brigade tore the clothes off the people they thought were student leaders. Journalists in the crowd photographed the nearly naked students, the shreds of the clothing hanging around their shoulders, their trousers gone. That was how the army identified them when they took the hundreds to the jails. They gathered them up in trucks and took them away. Five hours after the helicopters had dropped the flares, the first ambulances were allowed into the plaza.

For more than thirty years the government insisted that the crowd had fired first at the army. Snipers hidden among the crowd, the government said, student provocateurs; it even implied that it might have been the white-gloved Olympia Brigade that put the slaughter into motion, but not the Mexican army, not the police. All the records kept by all the police and the army and the staffs of the president and the secretary of the interior (*Gobernación*) remained secrets. In a diary published after his death, Echeverría, the secretary of the interior, blamed the massacre on the president. He could not have given such an order, he said; he did not have the power. Only the president could have done it.

Elena Poniatowska collected everything that was not secret, and a few secrets too, and edited it and made a book about the massacre.[27] The police said twenty-six were killed, or forty-five, a small number. The leaders of the strike were tortured, beaten, burned, shocked, humiliated. But they had no secrets, no money from foreign governments; they had read too many books, and the books had engendered too many dreams. That was all.

In time it came clear, although not certain, that the number who were killed was closer to three hundred, or five hundred. But the official number remained the same: a few. Only twenty-six autopsies had been performed. Journalists and politicians asked questions, and the government always had the same answer: Produce the bodies! Produce the bodies! What did not come clear was who started the shooting, who planned the massacre; was it Díaz Ordaz or Echeverría?[28] Were the uncounted bodies dumped into the sea? In

---

[27] *La Noche de Tlatelolco* (Mexico City: Ediciones Era, 1971); English translation, *Massacre in Mexico* (New York: Viking Press, 1975). In his introduction to the Poniatowska book, Octavio Paz compared the massacre in Tlatelolco with the 1692 strike described by Carlos Sigüenza y Góngora. There were similarities, certainly, but as Paz was quick to say, the 1692 riot was driven by a shortage of corn, and the rioters were the very poor. In 1968 the strike was mainly of the middle class (students and faculty), and it was driven by the will of the students and their professors to establish a democratic society in Mexico. Paz credits the 1692 riots with being a precursor of the Mexican Independence movement of 1810. The massacre at Tlatelolco was surely a precursor of the end of the reign of the PRI.

In a footnote to his introduction, Paz blamed the lack of a critical tradition in politics and philosophy for the failure of Mexico and other Latin American countries to become true democracies. It was a point he had made before, but never with such vehemence. He was angered by the massacre, resigning his ambassadorial post, and deeply moved by the conception and execution of Poniatowska's book.

[28] In *Parte de Guerra, Tlatelolco 1968*, a book published in 1999 by Aguilar, a large and prestigious house, the journalist Julio Scherer García and the Mexican essayist Carlos Monsiváis quoted the memoirs of General Marcelino García Barragán, who was

the end it did not matter. After Tlatelolco no decent man or woman in Mexico was ever again quite at peace with the system of the party-government-president all wrapped together in a country that was both free according to its laws and very close to totalitarian in the way it worked. Everything that took place at Tlatelolco was an official secret and public knowledge. The whispers were unending, inexorable; they did their business slowly, but no government could survive them unchanged.

The 1968 strike and the killings in Tlatelolco had given rise to an opposition movement on the left. The 1999–2000 strike would, at least in the first few years after the millennium, provide ammunition for the right. A man who had marched in the 1968 strike and who claimed to have seen people gunned down beside him in the street, cursed the millennium strikers. The strike had cost his daughter a year of school, and it had done nothing but lower the reputation of the UNAM, making it more difficult than ever for UNAM graduates to find work. He said he would send his daughter to a private college, but he did not know how he would pay the tuition. "In 1968 it was different," he said. "We had an agenda; we were organized; thousands joined us; we became the left opposition. Do you understand? They tried to destroy us, and instead, we became stronger. Yes, that's how it is. And don't use my name because they have lists. They read everything, you know. Listen to me: In Mexico, nothing turns out the way it was intended. The best die before their time."

---

secretary of defense under Díaz Ordaz. He said the order to fire on the students came from General Luis Gutiérrez Orpeza, the president's chief of staff. According to the book, it was ten men armed with machine guns who were assigned to start the killing and the subsequent riot. García Barragán said the men were specially trained members of the presidential staff, not members of the Mexican Army.

Book Two

THE HEART

(Teyolia)

22.

The Werejaguar

The beautiful flowers, the beautiful songs,
come from the heart of the sky.
Our yearning makes them ugly,
our inventiveness ruins them.
——"CANTARES MEXICANOS"[1]

Arturo Rivera, who was born in Mexico City and who lives and works in the Condesa section of the city in a two-story house dominated by the artist's studio, is not a Mexican painter. When he describes himself that way, it seems a foolish thing, a conundrum, meant to start a conversation, perhaps to end one. In his work, which some critics say is post avant-garde, the draftsmanship is superb. He produces figurative works, very accurate, realistic in a nineteenth-century way, but parts of the human figures have been excoriated, revealing their anatomically correct innards.

If the viewer of his work were to visit the museum at the site of the Templo Mayor in the center of the City of Mexico, in the last room of the entire exhibition, there are two awesome and terrifying statues that were found among the artifacts long buried there. The room is dark but for two lights shining down on the statues of Mictlantecuhtli and Mictlancihuatl, Lord and Lady of the Underworld. Aztec music—flutes, drums, rattles, and whistles—fills the room, obliterating conversation. The statues stand on a platform raised several feet above the floor.

Each one rises another six or seven feet above the platform. They are white, but not entirely so; they give the appearance of whiteness, of the colorless character of death. The figures are human, larger than life, but both have bills rather than mouths, and the bills contain teeth. The sight of the short bills and teeth terrifies. The effect is unaccountable. It should be comic, but it comes of nightmares, of hallucinogens and millenarian numbers, of nothing ever seen, death's forms.

[1] Fols. 9v–11v, León-Portilla and Shorris, *In the Language of Kings.*

And all the while that the impossible teeth and the strange height of the dead white rulers of the underworld capture the viewer, something else lurks, yet more frightening, but not at first obvious, death's undercurrent. In each figure one organ of the body is exposed. Not the expected heart but the liver, the part known to the ancient Mexica as ihiyotl, the place of the winds of life, the place devoted to the defense of life in all its manifestations, what Freud taught a later world to think of as the ego.

What was the exposed liver meant to tell? That some live and some die? That the Lord and Lady of the Underworld have appropriated the winds of the lives of all who descend there? Or is it merely the opening of the body cavity common in Mesoamerican sacrificial ritual? In life, the heart; in death, the liver? The excoriation of the one whose life culminates in public, gloriously, a gift to the world of the living, is the Mexican moment. That is what Arturo Rivera paints. Yet his claim is valid: He is not a Mexican painter. However, he is a painter, and he determinedly lives a painter's life, as if he had read the cartoon somewhere and now laid on the paint with a delicate brush.

The question of who is a *Mexican* painter or writer or composer has become very important, in many instances dominant in the thinking and the work of Mexican artists' work at various times in the twentieth century and continuing into this century. It has determined not only the subject matter but the form. In the life and work of Arturo Rivera the complex interrelationship of Mexicanness and art appears in stark relief.

Rivera connects his work to Germany, Italy, to his studies in Europe, nothing Mexican. He lived and worked in New York for several years, earning a living as a painter of fakes, a master of old masters. "I painted four Klimts in one day, but they were all very poor imitations. They were bought by businesses, hotels for decorations." It was a beneficial exercise, but he did not like New York. Once he stepped out of the studio there, he was no longer a painter; the color of his skin and the accent of his words made poverty and illiteracy of him. "The gringos . . . ," he said. Yet he enjoyed the energy and the prosperity of New York. He sees Mexico as a depressed nation, especially the indigenous people. "They have no place to turn. They can keep their culture and be destroyed or they can give up their culture and be destroyed." He saw no solution for them, or for democracy in Mexico or anywhere in the world. "Democracy is an illusion," he said, "because people have different mental capabilities."

We drove down darkened streets, quickly. He was fifty-two years old then, slim, slightly hunched, as if he were always leaning forward, brush in hand, intent upon the canvas. His hair was long, but thinning; his beard was full, but graying.

"I am a hypochondriac," he said. "I have always been a hypochondriac, but now I have a bad valve in my heart, and I must go to Monterrey to a hospital, where they will repair it." He laughed. "So I am no longer a hypochondriac." He was not drinking then or smoking his beloved *mota* (marijuana), for the weak valve frightened him. He thought of his brother who had been killed, speaking of him as he drove the new Volkswagen sedan up and back across lanes, the driver who passed all others, the car in the sure hands that wielded the brush. "I died once," he confessed. "I committed suicide, but they revived me."

At the Hotel Nikko, the attendant took the car, and we went to the upstairs lounge to wait for the person he was to meet. It was awhile before she arrived, and he had grown nervous expecting her. She was dressed all in black, in what was then the downtown New York style, and she was as thin as a New York woman, with the parenthetical lines around her mouth and the abnormally open eyes that come of dieting. She had left her blouse open to the third button. The effect was theatrical, not erotic. She began almost immediately to talk about drugs.

"When Arturo comes back after his operation, we'll go to the drug supermarket. You can buy herbs, mushrooms, whatever you want, drugs from the Indians. You must come with us."

The next time I saw him, he had recovered from his surgery. We walked around his studio, looking at his new work, which he described as "homage to the masters." Here was Vermeer, but on a canvas in Mexico, and with organs exposed, the Mexican moment again, as I said to Rivera, and he replied, "I am not a Mexican painter; I am a painter who happens to be a Mexican."

After we smoked together, we had a look at the treasures he had gathered in his studio: insects, stuffed birds, various skeletons, and an assortment of books of human anatomy, photographs, drawings, and medical illustrations, from Vesalius to the most recent renderings of human life under the skin. He had by then separated from his fifth wife, replacing her with a black Labrador puppy. He allowed the dog out of its cage to walk around the studio while we smoked and talked, but it was not a place to allow a young animal to run free. The painter was meticulous. There were no multicolored splatters, no piles of books or crumpled tubes of paint; even the palettes had been put away.

It was a lonely house. A young man who worked as a bartender a few blocks away, but still in Condesa, came to care for the rooms, to answer the telephone or open the door to guests, but the refrigerator had only a few cans of juice in all the space of it, and there were no odors of living, only of paint. After we looked at the work, a young painter, Guillermo Scully, just becoming known for his paintings of dance hall scenes, and a young woman from Univision News, Citlalli Peña, arrived, and we went off to an art show.

On the way to the show, Arturo said he had got the money together to do a monograph containing all of his work, everything, and with it his autobiography. "But not criticism, not a work of art criticism, just my life." He had been talking to an art dealer and critic about putting the monograph together, but he feared that it would turn out to be a critical appreciation, and that was not what he wanted. Abruptly he changed the subject.

He spoke about his childhood in Mexico City as he maneuvered through the traffic, peering out into the darkness and oncoming lights through slightly tinted eyeglasses. His uncle, an anatomist, had employed him to bring skeletons from the paupers' cemetery. When he was eight and nine years old, he had regularly walked miles across the city with a bag of skulls and bones slung over his shoulder. The work, he thought, had begun his fascination with death, his interest in suicide, the fixation on the death of his brother. He spoke at some length about the bones, the weight of them, the memory of them, the few pesos the uncle paid to the boy who delivered skeletons.

"A *tzompantli* [Aztec skull rack displaying bones of sacrificed persons]. It is very Mexican," I suggested.

"I do not want criticism in the monograph," implying that he did not want to hear it from me either.

He drove more aggressively, perhaps to emphasize his point. He established a rhythm in the traffic, in and out, zoom and swerve, like a stoned drummer, cursing in cadence with the moves: *Car-a-jo! Pen-de-jo!*[2] They were not words, but music, meaningless lyrics, rhythm, like the rhythm indicators in Aztec poems. And then we were lost. Neither the journalist nor

[2]"Prick, cunthair."

Scully, the dance hall painter, knew the neighborhood. When we finally found the place, we were among the last to arrive. It was the house of the painter, an amateur, the mother of a cellist and an actor, both of whom Rivera knew and admired, as he admired her.

He walked through the rooms of her house, where all her paintings were hung. He was generous to her, warm, but he said he was not a critic, he did not want to offer a critical comment. The work was amateurish, his kindness surprising, although he was careful not to flatter her. A young woman, a girl, joined him at the painter's house, as thin as the others, but younger, wearing a blue denim jacket and tight, low pants. He spoke of her as one of his *hijas,* and it was true, she could easily have been his child. Like the woman at the Hotel Nikko, she was speeded up, although her style was different, the next iteration of Mexico City youth; she would have found the Hotel Nikko insufferable, boring, a place for dead persons and parents.

After the exhibition she told Arturo she wanted to go to Milan, a popular hangout for young people. He complained about the music, the noise. He said he wanted to go back to his studio and smoke more mota. He took her home, politely, opened the car door for her, walked with her to the entrance to her house. When he returned, he drove to the Argentine, a restaurant in Condesa, near his house.

The evening slowly fell apart; the young television journalist with ringlets of bright yellow hair, the fairest skin, and blue eyes did not go home with the handsome young painter of dance hall scenes. The Mexican painter who said he was not a Mexican painter said he did not like to spend all of his time working. He had lived in Paris; he loved cafés, women, mota. "I am not an angel," he said. "I have done bad things, unethical things. I want to tell everything that relates to my work, even the attacks of critics, how I have managed to survive them." He smiled. He wore tinted eyeglasses for a mask. He opened the chest cavities of his subjects, exposing the heart, the vital organs. This was his work, his ritual. He had performed it countless times. The odor of it was part of him, in his fingernails, in his hair. He said he was not a Mexican painter.

Then what is a Mexican painter? Definitions abound, but the best of them is very old. It was shown in Mexican work more than thirty-five hundred years ago and confirmed by a great British art critic at the beginning of the twentieth century. To understand the definition in a Mexican way, it is best to go close to its point of origin. However, the Mexican approach to art is not Mexican alone. People identify the same approach in Cézanne and abstract painting, but it has had a unique and lasting influence in Mexico, both in the plastic arts and, in some respects, in literature.

A museum would be a good place to study the Mexican approach to art, but there is, I think, a far better way to begin. In the city of Villahermosa, which is not far from La Venta or from the Rió Grijalva, there is a black jaguar. It paces on heavy paws, a huge cat, sleek and dangerous even in its cage. The jaguar stops and stands motionless; it stares at someone on the other side of the cage. The stare of the black jaguar changes the relation between the animal and the person. In daylight it terrifies, and in the dark of night the light from within the animal, the gleaming in its eyes, comes from an unknown place. Whoever doubts the jaguar has only to see the black jaguar of Villahermosa in its jungle garden, where the beast has been caged, but not the form.

The jaguar teaches the art of Mexico, and it has done this work of instruction since the people whose name we do not know, but whom we call Olmecs, came under the tutelage of the jaguar in the fifteenth century B.C. or perhaps long before. The first people to learn the difference between the animal and its form lived near Villahermosa, perhaps not far from a river, in a place stolen from the jungle. They knew of the war between man and the jaguar, how either one might kill the other. It was as clear to them, as it was to Plato, however, that form is eternal. They saw jaguars dead, rotting. They saw monkeys throwing shit at the animal just as monkeys throw their shit at visitors to the park where the black jaguar lives in Villahermosa. Again and again the form proved superior to the beast, perfect. They saw god in the form.

Over time they came to worship the jaguar's form and then form itself. They were not reporters; reproduction of the world did not interest them, although they were ever more practiced technicians, capable of delicate work in greenstone, in basalt, perhaps in colors on stone, pottery, or skin. Only form captivated them; the artists among them, sculptors, potters, spoke through form. And they also thought of the ruin of form, perhaps in war or ritual, the killing of it with drills or chisels. Evidence remains of this killing of the work done by people who thought first of form.

In San Lorenzo and at La Venta, great monoliths were buried, heads the size of small automobiles, faces unlike the faces anyone knows, not human faces but forms that could suggest human faces, all of them looking somehow childlike, all of them wearing helmets, like the first football helmets, many of them conveying just the hint of a snarl. How these forms came to their resting places is unknown, for there is no stone like that stone for fifty miles around. But these colossal forms were not the only works the Olmecs made. There is also the form of a man, which we know as the wrestler, a bald creature wearing a breechcloth, seated on the ground, his torso half turned, modeled like life, but not lifelike. The artists produced a form other than real life, a metaphor.

As if to tell the viewer the provenance of form in the Olmec world, the sculptors produced werejaguars, forms made of the jaguar and the human combined, unlike either, pure inventions, the work of craftsmen, but not mere craft, art. Meaning interested the Olmecs, but not verisimilitude. The werejaguar illustrates almost perfectly the appreciation of form and the absence of modeling after anything known outside the mind of the artist. If these beautiful forms were gods, then it is an argument for the invention of gods as works of art, because the only gods they saw were in dreams. The god of rain did not look like rain. The form of the god of rain contained no rain; it was not wet. Gods are a priori, forms. To argue otherwise, to say that we infer the forms of gods from their earthly works, is to diminish the imagination of man, which may be the most godlike of acts.

Three thousand five hundred years later an English art critic, Clive Bell, was captivated by their work. In his famous essay *Art*, he called it "significant form," and he praised it for creating the "aesthetic experience" in the viewer. No works, no examples of significant form excited him more than pre-Columbian art. In a sense he discovered Mexico.

Bell distinguished the content of the work from its form. There are many kinds of valuable work, he conceded, naming portraits, illustrations, pictures that convey stories, and so on, any kind of descriptive work. The content of these works may convey information, according to Bell, but "They leave untouched our aesthetic emotions, because it is not their forms but the ideas or information suggested or conveyed by their forms that affect us."

He saw art in Cézanne's painting as well as Olmec sculpture, but he did not mention the portraiture of Rembrandt, and he did not think of political painting as art. Now the questions are raised: What were the Olmecs thinking when they did their work? How can we have an aesthetic experience from form when we cannot grasp the content or there is no content?

In the garden of Olmec work, not far from the caged black jaguar, the

viewer looks carefully at the sculptures, thinking of what is known or con-
jectured about the Olmecs. The viewer is at once analytical, an anthropologist, archaeologist, a critic, and then, after all these approaches pass and
there is just the viewer and the work, the forms succeed, each one set there
among the trees, in greenery, on solid ground, each one in its own cul-de-
sac off the main pathways. Nothing can elicit the aesthetic emotion but the
form, nothing else is known but time, earth, sky, and the form the jaguar
teaches. The Mexican essential of art was defined thirty-five hundred years
ago, the a priori, the work of the human mind set in stone, form.

From its beginning on the east coast the Olmec conception spread south
and west, always seeking to make forms that produced what Clive Bell
called the aesthetic experience. In Teotihuacán, artists made masks with no
breathing places, forms, neither practical nor descriptive, yet exciting to
behold. And the architects took up the building of the great form that does
not exist in nature, the pyramid. They invented the order of cities, always
mind-made, not following the existing course of a river or a rut. In Teotihuacán the architecture and urban design were as devoted to form as the
mathematical depiction of the pattern of the solar system.[3] Like the Olmec
sculptors, the architects did not work only with what was found in a place;
they brought what they needed to the place where the form would be produced: basalt, greenstone, seashells, gold. The world came to the imagination of the artist.

The literature is not different from the plastic art. In the Maya play *Rabinal Achí* (Warrior of Rabinal), everything that is said is beholden to the
form, which is less drama as we know it than pageant, formalized dances and
speeches, choruses and costumes. The play may contain what appears to the
modern reader to be history, but to the Maya audience the information was
already known. The history meant little, because it was not new; it was common knowledge. The aesthetic experience of the playgoer could not have
come from anything but the form.

The single greatest literary work known to us from the Maya is the Popol

---

[3]In many Mesoamerican city-states structures and sculptures were designed and placed
to capture the rise of the sun at solstice or equinox, to produce patterns at certain times
of the year. Form had a mathematical basis in calendrical calculations. At one temple the
light of the sun at equinox climbs the narrow steps, which are the serpentine body of
Quetzalcoatl.

Vuh or Council Book. The quality of imagination in the work leaves little doubt that form took precedence over information or description. The book, which was probably first written in the Maya mix of logograms and phonograms (a rebuslike form), begins at the beginning of the time of the world, which is within a greater universal time. It covers creations, generations, migrations, and the adventures of the hero twins in their battle with the underworld.

A reader can think of the Popol Vuh as inferred from the cycle of nature, for the hero twins descend to the underworld and emerge again, having outsmarted the vicious creatures there. Corn, the man-made grain, the one that cannot grow without the help of man, has the same cycle. The story of the hero twins is only a metaphor. The cycle is the form.

Man can provide everything for corn but rain. Everywhere in Mexico there are rain gods, rain rituals, corn gods, corn rituals, and every representation is a form invented to control the world of reality; every form is presumed to be superior to the world, to determine the world, from the shape of stone to the life of man. In Tenochtitlán, perhaps in the fifteenth century, three thousand years after the birth of the werejaguar, the Aztecs took form to one of its most glorious moments in the carving of Coatlicue. To stand in the presence of the image of Coatlicue is to be in the presence of form, more pure by far than a Henry Moore, terrifying as a crucifixion, a standing mountain of dark stone—serpents, hearts, skulls, claws dug into the earth—unreal, impossible, yet looming there, more Mexican than a pyramid, silent, an opera in form.

According to the literature, Coatlicue was the mother of Huitzilopochtli, the tutelary god of the Aztecs, the god of war. She became pregnant with him when she swallowed a ball of white feathers or the feathers fell between her bosoms. Her other child, Coyolxauhqui, jealous of the younger sibling, planned to kill him when he was born, but Huitzilopochtli was born with sword in hand. He cut off Coyolxauhqui's arms and legs and severed the body from the round head, which became the moon. All is form, story and stone, and Coatlicue is the mother of form, a summit in stone for the art of Mexico. That is the content of the Coatlicue, and it is powerful. Yet to stand before the Coatlicue in the Museum of History and Anthropology in Mexico City is to be in awe not of the content, which is no longer meaningful to most, but of the form, which is the Mexican aesthetic.

No one knows how much the Olmecs or Teotihuacanos thought about questions of form and content, whether their thinking was critical as well as artistic. The Popol Vuh contains a discussion of the suffering one must endure in the process of becoming an artist, but no discussion of the role of art and the artists beyond that. Only with the Aztecs, whose ideas have been better preserved, does it become clear that the pre-Hispanic peoples of Mexico had developed a critical awareness of their work. In the late-fifteenth-century "Dialogue of Flowers and Song," a group of Nahua princes discuss in poetic language the provenance of art. The opening lines of the discussion speak to a symbolic singer (poet), asking where he comes from. The princes then admit to hating everything that changes, everything that dies, and take comfort in the idea that art endures. Form.

23.

Diego Rivera's Dogs

—because the gods have been condemned to live among men—
—JAIME SABINES

Colonists do not adopt the forms of the colonized; by definition it is the other way around. But not always and not forever. Memory and the artist can change a world. It happened in Mexico in 1955. A writer from the state of Jalisco, Juan Rulfo, published a slight and unique novel, *Pedro Páramo*. "*Vine a Comala...,*" it begins (I came to Comala...), and goes on to marry the formal beauty of the indigenous world to the language brought to Spain and then to Mexico from its Latin origin. It would be an error to deny entirely the political, social, historical, descriptive content of the novel, but those aspects were not to be its destiny. *Pedro Páramo* is a dream; the form of it is an exact reproduction of the approach to form found in the art of the Olmecs. If it is not quite so grand as the statue of Coatlicue (and few works are—in any medium), it is at least as universal. Out of *Pedro Páramo* came an entire school of literature, magical realism, a literature in which it could rain butterflies. The Cuban novelist Alejo Carpentier also took up the idea and described such a rain. And then it famously rained butterflies in the work of Gabriel García Márquez.

Everyone came to Comala, the entire Latin American "Boom," as well as writers from the rest of the world. Magic came into the prose of Carlos Fuentes, especially the mystery of *Aura*, the most Mexican of his novels. Writers who did not employ magical realism but found analogues in myth were said to be disciples of Juan Rulfo. But Rulfo's name was not often mentioned. Unlike the Maya painters who signed their work with a proprietary air, Rulfo gave away the form of his invention. Outside Latin America Rulfo was almost anonymous, like an Olmec sculptor or the one who found a form for Coatlicue. But from the time he published the novel, in 1955, there was a uniquely Mexican form on the page. Rulfo took into his novelist's mind history, geography, psychology, dreams, and the terrible longing to come home that has driven fictions in the West since Homer and in Mesoamerica before that, and he did it in a completely modern and utterly ancient Mexican way.

Before there was writing, there was a form for fiction in Mexico. In a group of Olmec statues, carefully buried and just as carefully unearthed, one can see the beginnings of a novel. All the figures are of the same material, save one, and that one faces the others. What is being said? What is the relation of the granite figure to all the rest in greenstone? Is the variation in the carved faces, in the sizes, in the precise positioning, a forerunner of the layering of the novel? Nothing remains but the form. It is anonymous work; we know only the name we have imposed upon the culture and the thrill of the form. The situation is real or magical, the blending of the a priori and a posteriori that universalizes and immortalizes art. And it is a Mexican novel, like *Pedro Páramo.*

Octavio Paz said of him in *Inframundo*, a book of homages to Rulfo and a collection of his photographs, "Juan Rulfo is the only Mexican novelist that has given us an image—not a description—of our passage."[1] In the same series of homages, Gabriel García Márquez wrote that he committed paragraphs of the novel to memory, that he could recite them, recite the whole novel, "forward and backward." In his own inimitable style of dreaming overstatement he wrote that he could say on which page of which edition a certain scene appeared. Some years later, in an interview given to a newspaper in Argentina, the Colombian Nobelist said that magical realism was the invention of Rulfo. And of course he was correct.

More famous than Rulfo, perhaps more famous than any other Mexican artists, the muralists represent Mexican art to much of the world. But there is something less clear in the character of of the muralists: Were they Mexican artists or did they paint Mexican subjects? And who can judge? Some years ago I had the opportunity to visit the famous Diego Rivera murals in the National Palace in Mexico City in the company of a little Mazatec girl, an extraordinary "critic," one who was still possessed of the innocence that eluded the Clive Bells and Clement Greenbergs and Benedetto Croces of this world. This critic of the muralists and I met through her "aunt," a woman who lived in the same barrio near the Tepito market and the wrestling arena in the old part of Mexico City.

[1] Mexico: Instituto Nacional de Bellas Artes, 1980.

I invited the two of them to lunch, the girl and the aunt, who was not really an aunt, but a childless woman of fifty who had taken a shine to the girl. It was a bright and cool afternoon; it had rained recently, and the filth had been washed from the air. We walked slowly from beyond the park in Tepito toward the Zócalo, which was then still a gigantic bazaar, an open-air marketplace, like something pre-Hispanic, but not clean, not orderly, as the market had been at Tlatelolco. On the way we passed a storefront where instant lottery tickets were sold. "Let's try our luck," I said. I gave the little girl, whose name was Marta Irene, twenty pesos and told her she could do with it whatever she liked. She could put it in her pocket to buy ice cream later in the day or she could try her luck on the lottery.

Since twenty pesos is not much and the lottery can return a few hundred pesos, even several thousand pesos, hardly a fortune, but to a child a solution to all the problems of her future and that of her family, she chose to buy the tickets. "Then I will buy some tickets too and some for your aunt," I said. "We'll put them all together, and if we win . . ." I gave the shopkeeper a hundred pesos, and her aunt explained to Marta how to choose the tickets, which games to play and which to avoid. It took awhile, because there were many tickets, and the aunt confessed that she had never played the games before, although she had studied them.

Out on the street again, in the darkening afternoon, I gave Marta a coin, and we watched, the aunt and I, while the girl scraped away the waxy substance covering the numbers underneath. After many disappointments, she uncovered a winning combination, but the win was very small, and she decided to use the winnings to buy more tickets. We went into the store again, and this time Marta chose the tickets she wanted. Out on the street she rubbed off the waxy coverings. None of the tickets was a winner. She shrugged. She did not smile, for it was not in her character to smile, although she could laugh. The disappointment showed only in her slightly raised eyebrows, a gesture that increased the vulnerability of her eyes.

The aunt made a joke about such luck bringing rain, a country joke, a view of the world before the great migration to the cities. In the city, rain meant floods, scurrying, the closing of outdoor stalls (*puestos*) for the day. We hurried on. The sky grew darker. Then we came to what appeared to be a restaurant of some quality. It was large, with huge windows showing white tablecloths inside and some Mexican families having Sunday dinner. I thought it was a reasonable place, and to be sure they were comfortable, I reminded Marta and her aunt that I had invited them.

The headwaiter met us at the door, or rather he confronted us. Marta's mother had outfitted her in a salmon-colored organdy dress tied with a blue sash at the waist, but she had neither a jacket nor a sweater nor an umbrella, and her shoes were worn at the sides and toes. Her aunt wore a dress of many colors of red, some almost black and others as pale as pink. It fit loosely at the shoulders and too tightly across the belly. The aunt had no noticeable bosom, and the dress hung limply across her chest, before it began to fill out at the waist. She wore flat black shoes aged to gray, and she carried a brown sweater across her arm, but she did not have an umbrella either, and everyone knew it was going to rain. The two women were very dark, the aunt a Nahua and the girl Mazateca.

For myself, I do not cut a dashing figure, to say the least, and I am unable to appear prosperous even in a dinner jacket. The headwaiter put his face too close to mine in an act of deliberate rudeness and waited for me to speak. "Good afternoon," I said.

"We are full up. Reservations."

"*Joven* [young man], we would like to sit there, near the window." I pointed to the table, then turned to my companions. "Young ladies, is that all right?"

A foreign accent is always helpful in Mexico, unless it sounds like border Spanish. The waiter seated us as I had asked. But when Marta Irene surveyed the table, the folded cloth napkin, the full place setting, she appeared to be puzzled. Although she and her brother and sisters had come to Mexico City to join their parents almost two months earlier, her aunt explained that she had never before been in a restaurant.

The aunt, who had lived in Mexico City for several years, coming from a farm in the state of Mexico, was not much more comfortable. She and the girl stared at the place settings, concentrating on the utensils. Although the restaurant boasted its dishes were "typically Mexican," neither of my companions was impressed. They glanced at their menus, then laid them down very carefully beside their plates. "May I make suggestions?"

They nodded.

I went down the menu, which was fairly extensive, but either the food did not appeal to them or they were not conversant with these "typical Mexican" dishes. Finally, they recognized the name for grilled flank steak (*arrachera*) and greeted it with smiles. It was part of the *comida corrida* (the daily special), which I explained included soup and dessert.

Marta asked for a soft drink with her food. The aunt asked for coffee. The waiter, now a different fellow, this one with a squared mustache and a fat face, greeted the order with a sneer. "Coffee now?"

"Yes," I said. "And for me a cup of black tea."

He left, returning with the drinks and, moments later, with bowls of soup that Marta and her aunt found bland and thin. It was when he brought the salad that I understood the consternation of my guests. Neither of them had been able to read the menu, and now it came clear that Marta had never used a fork. Her aunt tried to explain the utensil, but she was not much more familiar with it than the girl.

I showed Marta how we "use the fork in the United States." "This is American style," I said, demonstrating clumsily.

After that, the meal went easily enough, although Marta Irene said that the tines of the fork stung her mouth. We talked about school and Marta's parents, who were part of the "informal economy." I asked if Marta Irene or her aunt had ever been across the Zócalo to see the Diego Rivera murals in the National Palace. They did not know of the painter, nor did they know what was meant by a mural, but they were eager to go.

We gossiped about Marta's father, who drank, and the neighbors who tried to put their noses into everyone's business in the *vecindad* (a small, generally two-story grouping of apartments) where the aunt lived. Neither of them had been in Mexico City during the last earthquake, but they had noted that it struck mainly in the neighborhood occupied by the poor. The aunt said she had heard it was God's will to destroy the small clothing factories owned by the Jews. I said I did not think that had been the case.

A very light rain had begun to fall as we crossed the Zócalo to the National Palace. We all huddled under my umbrella as we made our way through the street vendors packing up, fleeing the rain. A crowd had gathered in the doorway to the National Palace, and it took awhile for us to get through to look at the murals. At the landing we came upon the grand panels depicting the world of the Mexica. Although Marta was very bright and a good student, she did not know the functions of any of the figures in the painting, neither the huey tlahtoani (great speaker, ruler) nor the warriors, nor the symbols floating in the sky.

As we went on up the stairs, passing by the history of Mexico, as recorded by Rivera, I told her the names of the people on the walls. Finally, on the second floor, away from the crowd, we came to a long panel showing the life of brown-skinned people in a kind of paradise, almost like a Gauguin, bare-breasted women, a gorgeously fecund setting, the idealized indigenous life. Marta and her aunt looked for a long time at the murals but said nothing. There was an interruption when a troop of Mexican soldiers marched out through the center patio of the palace in the ritual lowering of the flag.

When we returned to looking at the murals, I asked Marta what she thought. She was Mazateca, raised in a tiny village, forced to leave when the river that had fed her family for hundreds of years no longer provided enough fish for them to survive. They still had their houses, and the family lived for the time when they could return home even for a few days, but they could no longer live in the ancestral way.

Marta's skin was darker than that of the people in Diego Rivera's paintings. Her face was wider, and she had a certain lightness in the way she walked; her steps were small and quick, a girl dancing. She looked at the murals, passing silently along the walls. She did not close in on them, putting her nose to the paint, as children often do, but kept a critical distance, taking in the whole. I asked what she thought of the work she had seen, especially the indigenous people, whom she referred to as indios. "They are not like us," she said.

"But they are Mexicans."

"Yes, they are Mexicans, but they do not look like me."

"They are indios."

"Yes, they are indios, but they do not look like me."

"But this work, these murals, are great Mexican paintings."

"Yes, sir, but they are not like me."

Since then I have visited many times with Marta Irene and her aunt. They often mention the lottery and the restaurant, especially the forks, which they found foolish and prickly, but they never talk about the paintings. After a while I began to wonder why. Little Marta became a very good student, a sweet child and diligent. The family business thrived; she ate well, gained weight, barely fit into her clothes. Her parents and her aunt indulged Marta Irene's passion for ice cream. She took on the shape of the figures in Diego Rivera paintings, yet she never mentioned them.

Marta Irene's criticism raises the question: Was Diego Rivera a Mexican painter or a painter of Mexicans? And if he was not a Mexican painter, who was?

Had the Maya not painted murals on the famous walls of Bonampak in the Lacandón jungle of Chiapas? What was the difference between the Olmecs, the Maya, and Diego Rivera's mural in the Detroit Institute of Arts celebrating the workings of the Ford factory? Both the Maya murals and Rivera's were descriptive, historical; both were rich in content; both had form. Yet no viewer could apprehend the murals in the same way. The content of Rivera's work overwhelms the form, but any viewer can appreciate the form of the Bonampak murals without understanding the content. There is a line between art and history, art and politics, a never-ending contest between form and content. Mexican art begins in dreams and culminates in form, but a Mexican may produce any kind of art. Diego Rivera came home from a long stay in Europe, where he learned portraiture and cubism, to paint on the walls of Mexico. At one point he tried to paint like a Nahua, mixing the juice of the nopal into his paints, but the paint quickly aged and left large areas discolored and flaking. He wanted desperately to be a Mexican painter, but he had to be content with painting ideas about Mexicans. Perhaps to assuage his wish to be a Mexican painter, he collected pre-Columbian work, much of which he left to his last mistress, Dolores Olmedo.

She installed the pre-Columbian objects, along with many works by Rivera and Frida Kahlo, in the rooms of a grand old building in the southern part of the Federal District of Mexico. The house, now known as the Dolores Olmedo Museum, sits in the center of a beautiful, manicured park, where peacocks engage in glorious mating rituals and ducks sing their tuneless song. Olmedo herself, La Lola, who was more than ninety years old when she died in 2002, has been named a part of the national patrimony of Mexico. She was not only Rivera's mistress but his patron. La Lola was rich, perhaps because she served as mistress to at least two Mexican presidents.

Behind a fence in the garden of La Lola's museum, there is a small black animal, about twenty inches high at the shoulder, like a dog, in the form of a dog, but with no fur other than a small crest on the top of its head. It is a xoloitzcuintli, and there are but few of them left in Mexico. The xoloitzcuintli in the house of La Lola bears the Nahuatl name Citlalli (Skirt of Stars). It is a common name now in Mexico, and in this case the name is proper, for few things could be more Mexican than these animals, which provided protein to the Mexica before the invasion and the introduction of Old World animals.

Although it was once common, the xoloitzcuintli has been crossbred almost out of existence. There are only a few left in all the world. The animal in the foreground of Rivera's famous *Dream of an Afternoon in the Alameda* presumes to be such a Mexican creature, but it looks more like a European dog, perhaps a dachshund; as the critic Marta Irene might have said, it may be a xoloitzcuintli, but it does not look like a xoloitzcuintli.

24.

The Nationality of the Rose

. . . the world illuminated and myself awake.
—SOR JUANA INÉS DE LA CRUZ

. . . soy yo, peor de todo [It is I, the worst of all].
—SOR JUANA

If the entire history of Mexico and its character were to be found in a single person, if everyone is indeed everything, as the old man of Agua Prieta advised, the exemplar would be Juana de Asbaje, whom the world knows as Sor Juana Inés de la Cruz. The path to Sor Juana's door begins in seventeenth-century Mexico City, winds through the mountains of present-day Chiapas, and ends on a letter signed in blood. Not since Quetzalcoatl, the monastic Prince of Tula,[1] had there been such a creature as Sor Juana in Mexico: self-aware, preternaturally intelligent, comfortable with life's accouterments, sensual, bisexual, rational, attacked by the arbiters of behavior in her time, then trapped into suffering and death. The greatest war in the history of Mexico raged inside her; she is the tragedy of the defeat of reason.

Juana de Asbaje died, a widow of Christ, in the time of the full glory of New Spain and before the ascendance of the Virgin of Guadalupe. Sor Juana's discovery was of the intellectual and poetic powers that came of the marriage of Quetzalcoatl and European rationalism. Not only did she envision the Mexicanization of Christianity, as the Jesuits had, but she also embraced the new humanism of the seventeenth century. She was perhaps the perfect example of Miguel de Unamuno's idea of the "tragic sense of life": the conflict between faith and reason.

To reach Sor Juana, Mexico's first great poet in the Spanish language, requires a circuitous journey through analagous conflicts. "Tell the truth/but tell it slant," a poet of a later time said. And it is good advice, for there are,

---

[1] He is also known as Topiltzin, which means "Our Honored Prince."

in Sor Juana's life and work, adumbrations of Dickinson as well as echoes of holy wars. Her life contains all the other profound conflicts in Mexico then and now; she is the goddess of the war within. She is the mestizaje, the uncompleted mix not merely of races, but of faith and reason, of man and woman, hedonist and virgin, sacrifice and survival, and the two roads to heaven.

In Mexico, everyone must choose first between faith and reason, and if the choice is faith, then he or she must choose between the two routes to syncretism: the primacy of Quetzalcoatl (the Mexicanization of Christianity) or the Virgin of Guadalupe (the Christianization of Mexican religion). Jacques Lafaye concluded his work on these two great religious icons, *Quetzalcoatl and Guadalupe,* by predicting: "Some day Guadalupe will become an extinct star, like the moon, with which she is associated . . ." while Quetzalcoatl "seems to have a better chance of a future sacred 'recharge' in a laicized society like that of present day Mexico. . . ."[2]

Evidence of the tension between the two is often hidden by the overwhelming presence of one or the other. The least religious of Mexicans may have a shrine to the Virgin, or a picture of her, and few Mexicans other than historians may recall that in their time Francisco Madero and Lázaro Cárdenas were compared to Quetzalcoatl or that President López Portillo believed he was the reincarnation of the Mesoamerican savior of human life and bringer of culture. In Chiapas the conflicted soul of Mexico is bared; it is the state richest by far in natural resources—oil, timber, cattle, wool, coffee—and the state where the people are poorest. There, in the steep mountains and impassable jungles, in the nakedness of conflict, no one can doubt the dual citizenship of the Guadalupan rose or Quetzalcoatl's ascent into the sky to become the Morning Star; it is only a matter of the struggle, which deity will subsume the other. The newspaper version of the contest in Chiapas centers on politics and economics, but the deeper contest, the oldest war, is between the two paths to syncretism: Quetzalcoatl and Guadalupe, Mesoamerica and Rome, autonomy and colonization, mask and miracle, death and the rebirth of nations. And over all, there is Unamuno's tragic

[2]*Quetzalcóatl et Guadalupe* (Paris: Gallimard, 1974). English translation by Benjamin Keen (Chicago: University of Chicago Press, 1976), p. 310. Lafaye should not be taken literally. The moon of course is not a star. Whether or not Mexico is laicized is a question, and his idea of the eventual triumph of Quetzalcoatl is speculation far into the future. The association of Quetzalcoatl with indigenous ideas and that of Guadalupe with European (Christian) ideas is at the heart of Lafaye's book.

sense, although in Chiapas, both faith and reason are under siege; no one knows what will happen next.

THE MEAT OF LARRAINZAR

San Andrés Larrainzar is one of the battlefields in the many-sided war in Chiapas. The center of the town perches on a small, dry plateau perhaps two hundred feet above the surrounding land but far below the mountain peaks to the south and west. The trees have been gone from the plateau for centuries, and there is no living vegetation on the few streets and squares. From the escarpment behind the old municipal palace one can look down on the modern gray building where meetings were held between government representatives and the Zapatista rebels to work out the San Andrés Accords, which promised autonomy, the right to maintain their culture, and decent living conditions to indigenous people in Mexico.

The plateau is the oldest part of the town, which began as ancient towns often did, at the most defensible position. The church stands there, and the schools and the market; the Mexican Army has set up its camp half a mile away, along a dirt road leading up to the center of town. As Saturday nears, the market grows busier. It is more businesslike than colorful, although a group of drummers and flautists can be heard playing music as old as Quetzalcoatl in a house no more than twenty-five yards away. The produce and grocery sellers, intermixed with soft-drink and toy vendors, occupy the square. Some stalls are empty; some women sit on the sidewalk on the north side of the market, their goods in baskets or displayed on pieces of cloth. Shoppers encounter them first and last; their opportunity is great, but their space is limited; more than the others, they depend on luck.

An apple costs three pesos, and the price of meat, which is sold from a series of stalls across the street from the market, is very high. The sides of beef and lamb hanging in the early morning sun are sold in chunks for thirty pesos a kilo (2.2 pounds), more or less depending on the amount of bone and the richness of the fat. The shoppers and the butchers study the meat, the yellow fat, the white fat, the dark organ meat piled on the makeshift tables, the lighter lines of ribs, the thick meat of the heavy muscles oozing blood, the uneven surfaces of brains, the segmented tails, ears. No meat is cut until it has been chosen; the whole side of the beast hangs here, hooked by the leg.

There are no modern scales in the meat market, only ancient balances on which brass weights are compared against the red meat. The weights, the meat, and the money all pass through the butchers' bloody hands. As the sun rises, the owners of the meat stalls erect cloth shields to keep the meat from cooking in the searing light. There are few flies in Larrainzar in winter, because it is high in the mountains of Chiapas and the nights are very cold. The weather does not deter the dogs, however, and they gather around the meat stalls in anticipation of errors; there are no scraps in Larrainzar. Like all dogs in rural Mexico, they are timid, even when they are large and ugly. At the approach of a person or the sight of a walking stick, they jump back, cowering, ready to dodge a kick or escape a blow. And when no blow or kick comes, they return to waiting. There is a blood smell in the air. The dogs drool, sniffing the blood, the unseen tendrils of the scent of gall, the odor of washed gut. They wait, poking in the dust, careful not to show their teeth.

On the west side of the square, between the market and the meat sellers' stalls, there is a street of two blocks that begins at the Zapatista Municipal Palace on the south and culminates in the PRI Municipal Palace on the north. Between the two municipal palaces, on the block closer to the PRI, the PAN has opened an office. In the first municipal election of the new century, the PAN got five hundred votes and the PRI thirty-two hundred, but the PRI refuses to allow any members of the PAN to sit in its council meetings, even though they deserve two places, according to law. That is how the PRI operates in Chiapas, as in much of rural Mexico. The governor of a state may be a member of the PAN or the PRD or an independent, but in the villages the power of the PRI has only lately begun to diminish. Everyone knows that the PRI can kill.

In Larrainzar[3] the PRI had won everything for as long as anyone can remember, but the Zapatistas took the Municipal Palace by force (without firing a shot) and declared it autonomous. The PRI and the government, which were difficult to separate at the time of the Zapatista move, com-

---

[3]In newspaper accounts and conversation in the capital the town is known as San Andrés, but in Chiapas it is known as Larrainzar, for Manuel Larrainzar, an attorney who served in government at the local, state, and national levels during the nineteenth century. At one time Larrainzar owned a gigantic finca comprising most of the land between San Cristóbal de las Casas and the town that bears his name.

plained, stamped their political foot, but eventually shrugged and decided to make the best of it. The PRIistas built another municipal palace at the north end of the street. Each city government now has its own tall radio antenna, and each is empowered to give out such forms as birth certificates. When the IFE (Federal Election Institute) brings its mobile registration unit to town, people line up at both municipal palaces to obtain the documents needed to register to vote. Since the secretary of state in Chiapas was an executive in the IFE before he joined the state government, the state is careful about voting fraud, but not so careful that the PANistas were able to obtain their two seats on the city council. Like many towns now in Chiapas and other parts of Mexico, political life in Larrainzar is extremely complex. There is no peace or parity in the villages, and the various factions are always maneuvering. The people of the villages employ several different methods to deal with the ongoing tensions: murder, religious conversion, and expulsion or ostracism. Murder gets the most headlines, but it is a difficult and sometimes counterproductive business. The most persistent murderers in Chiapas are said to be paramilitary groups under the control of the PRI. According to Emma Cosío Villegas, daughter of the Mexican historian, wife of the internationally known anthropologist Jan de Vos, and the director of a large group of social service organizations with headquarters in San Cristóbal, people are murdered with terrible regularity in Chiapas.

There are few prosecutions, little public outcry. One death in a remote village is not a news story. But the murders are not secret; that would not serve the purpose of the killers. They are not public either, not like urban killings. There are no photographs, no depositions. Often the families of the dead do not speak Spanish. Sra. Cosío de Vos is not given to hyperbole. She is as straightforward as her spare, scrubbed office, with its plain walls and two chairs, one for her and one for conversation. She is gracious and literate, and she counts the toll of the siege of faith and reason. She does not tell the news happily. Her eyes, which are large and dark and bespeak a gentle intelligence, become momentarily opaque when she talks about the murders, as if she does not want anyone to see her mourning strangers, to know that weakness in her, to look under the lamentations at the angers.

The infamous massacre of forty-one defenseless people on December 22, 1997, at the village of Acteal horrified her. There had been other groups of people killed, but the hardest reality was the regularity of the business of murder. Presidential candidates and human rights leaders and drug dealers had been murdered in Mexico, a group of doctors had been found murdered in Ciudad Juárez, and an insane bus driver had murdered many young women there, no one knows how many of the more than two hundred whose bodies had been discovered by the end of 2003. Nonetheless, the common, quotidian killing of innocents in the village politics of the provinces makes a deeper wound in decent people, and it is a moral wound; the pain comes of sadness and not of fear.

Only the pursuit of heaven can compete with political murder in the ruin of happiness, for it has a longer history and greater lastingness. But heaven has come only recently to Mexico, for there was no sense of an afterlife until the Spaniards arrived, exempting heaven from complicity in war and sacrifice; religion then had to take its toll without the help of heaven. For three thousand years before the arrival of the Christian God there were gods to spur the work of killers in Mesoamerica, but nowhere has it been more exquisite during the last seven hundred years than in Chiapas.[4]

Chiapas has been a place of factions, competing gods, the misery of colonialism, racism, self-proclaimed saints and saviors, and murder. Scholars have studied the killing, and they offer many explanations, but it is always difficult to know what crosses the boundary between Mesoamerican and European thinking, how the world varies, wobbles, and wounds understanding. To comprehend the modern city of Monterrey, Nuevo León, is relatively easy; to understand Chiapas requires a lifetime and a few years more.

THE RIBBONS OF AUTHORITY

One evening, over dinner in a restaurant in San Cristóbal, Gaspar Morquecho, the owner of the town's Zapatista bookstore, delivered his view of the recent history of the village of San Juan Chamula, Chiapas, which is in the mountains west and slightly north of San Cristóbal.[5] Morquecho is an Indianist, one of Quetzalcoatl's intellectuals, an unquestioning Zapatista, but more than that, a believer in the permanence of pre-Columbian religion despite Spanish, Catholic, Protestant, Marxist, and, most recently, Muslim

---

[4]The anthropologists Gary Gossen, Mercedes Olivera, Robert Laughlin, Jan de Vos, Jan Rus, and others have recorded much of the oral history of the area.
[5]The Chamulas belong to the large language group (at least six hundred thousand) of Tzotzil Maya.

assaults. He thinks criollos and mestizos should not involve themselves in directing indigenous affairs.

Morquecho stands solidly with Quetzalcoatl; he is skeptical about everything and everyone non-Indian. He gives as an example the photography project in the village of San Juan Chamula directed by Carlota Duarte of the Center for Research and Graduate Studies (CIESAS). Duarte, a Mexican-American nun (Society of the Sacred Heart) with an M.F.A. from the Rhode Island School of Design, gives cameras to the Chamulas and lets them photograph whatever they like, teaching them only the techniques of the camera. Morquecho said, "When she leaves, there will be no more cameras, no more film. And the Chamulas will go back to being exactly as they were before she came."

Perhaps. It takes a grumpy man to criticize Duarte's project. The results have been exceptional, both as photography and as recording of culture. Duarte is a quick, efficient woman, thin, with graying hair, and a healing face. She wants her Chamula photographers to become ever stronger, self-sufficient; she tries to step back from directing them, although goodness is difficult to resist.[6] But Morquecho may have a point. Larrainzar has been the setting for national negotiations, military oversight, if not occupation, rebel occupation, autonomy, political conflict, and it still belongs to the Maya.

At ten in the morning in Larrainzar, which is the middle of the Chiapanecan rural day, the *autoridades* (traditional religious authorities) come to pray. They are as gorgeous as the peacocks in Dolores Olmedo's garden, and they are traditional Maya. The autoridades arrive in sets: men and women, husband and wife, mother and child. The men are the most startling, dressed in thick black wool knee-length doublets and bright sashes, carrying embroidered shoulder bags and wearing flat straw hats adorned with brilliantly colored ribbons. The women wear ankle-length black skirts fastened at the waist with brilliantly colored embroidered sashes wrapped twice around and wrapped again with long cords made of the braided wool of the sashes. Their white cotton blouses have square necks and wide lines of embroidery around the neck; the embroidery identifies them; every village has its own pattern.

The women walk behind their men, and behind each woman, slung

[6]Duarte's work extends to ten different groups of Maya speakers. Although she is a nun, the project has no religious orientation and no connection to the Catholic Church.

across her back, is a baby lying quietly in a rebozo made of cloth of a single color, each length of cloth different from the others and each one as rich in hue as the next. They enter the church and stand behind a gauze screen, perhaps seven feet high and ten feet wide. The men stand closest to the screen, and behind each one his wife and child. They stand perfectly still and chant in Tzotzil. The sound is at first recognizable only as imperfect unison, and then harmonies emerge, beautiful instances in the otherwise unmusical chanting, not Gregorian, or reminiscent of other forms of the singing or intoning of prayers, but Tzotzil, theirs. They are the authorities, the traditional leaders, they have powers beyond the reach of the IFE or the PRI or the PAN; there is no acronym so gorgeous or so close to the saints as they.

Morquecho's argument rests on the ribbons that hang so decorously from the low crowns and straw brims of the hats of the autoridades. The test of it lies in the longevity of culture. How it has survived the last five hundred years may predict what will happen when television comes to the houses in which the autoridades and their families live. Morquecho, who was born in Mexico City, but has lived in Chiapas for the last thirty years, bows his head and runs his hands through his graying hair as he speaks. He is a man of arguments and lamentations. His car is an ancient, flat-sided Volkswagen; he eschews all modern conveniences in his store: cash register, credit cards, alarm systems. He concedes to the modern world only the telephone, herbal tea, eyeglasses, and purified water.

His view of San Juan Chamula covers the contentious last half century, and many people in Chiapas say he knows the conflict as well as anyone. Much of what he says is widely corroborated, but not all. And whether it is truth or the stuff of myth matters less than where it leads in understanding the art and literature of Mexico.

Tensions and terrors have existed in the Tzotzil villages since Bartolemé de las Casas was named bishop of Chiapas in the sixteenth century. When Jesus arrived in Chiapas, there was a revolt, war, and then the people accepted him, for many gods had come to the mountains and the jungles, and they had always found followers. The space in which the gods lived was vast and accommodating. Like the plumed serpent (Quetzalcoatl/ Kukulkan), who came south or west to Chiapas, or the rain god, whose name in Tzotzil sounds like Ángel, Jesus found a place, and was not lonely in Chiapas. There were problems with Jesus, because his followers among the Spaniards were very strong, and many of them were killers. But before long Jesus was the leader of many sects. He was first among many in the pantheon of Catholic saints, who were old gods under new names. Before too many years had passed, a man proclaimed himself Jesus-king, and there was a revolt of Tzotziles. In 1868 the rebellion was called the War of St. Rose, in 1910 the rebellion was called Pajarito's War, and in 1935 there was a rebellion against the government's closing of the churches.[7]

In fact, the conquest of the indigenous people of Chiapas has never gone well, although it has been the goal of many groups over the last five hundred years—the Spanish invaders, the Spanish Church, the Mexican government, the PRI, the Protestants, the Zapatistas, television, Coca-Cola—and now the Muslims want to send Chamula Indians to Mecca to complete their conversion. Who, if anyone in Chiapas, actually cared or cares about indigenous people as such, meaning in their own choice of how to live and think, is not at all clear. Manuel Gamio, the founder of modern Mexican anthropology, cared deeply for indigenous people and eventually came to be one of the first to hope to maintain their languages and what he thought of as the best of their cultures, but Gamio classified some indigenous peoples as savages and others as semicivilized.[8] When he spoke of the people he called indios, he said there did not exist among them a reasonable concept of art, "and when it did, it was folkloric." They had no notion that "pointed toward the universal, the entire world, foreign countries, the Republic, nor even the nation." He was anxious to educate their "choreographic manifestations of profane-religious dances . . . endeavoring to rid them of their ritual character, developing an exclusively artistic sensibility."

Gamio argued more than once that indigenous people were inherently the equal of whites or mestizos. But for all that he reveled in the beauty of what was long gone, he also grieved for it, and the distress led him at times to speak patronizingly of what had been left after the conquest. It was a curiously conflicted idea of indigenous people. He both admired them and wanted to change them into a different race, a different culture, an assimilated part of a third race, which included both Indians and whites, whom he

---

[7] A result of the anticlerical policies of Lázaro Cárdenas. The churches were closed in 1934 and reopened in 1936.

A part of the hostility to Protestants is carried over from this period, because the Tzotziles blamed the closing of the churches on the Protestants. This was in fact not true.

[8] *Forjando Patria* (Mexico: Porrua Hnos., 1916).

called the "bronze and the iron." He wanted desperately to find a way for them and some part of their world, as much as possible, to survive. In all this, he was a man ahead of his time, both lover and conqueror, admirer and proselytizer, another version of Unamuno's "tragic sense of life" as it appears in the dualism of the Mexican mestizaje.

CHAMULA CHOICES

The Tzotziles of Chiapas refused to die, either culturally or physically. They fought and proved they could be as ethnocentric as the people who claimed to have conquered them and reduced their worldview to folklore. In the Tzotzil version of the "Origin of the Ladino" (white or mestizo),[9] the Spanish-speaking mestizo came about when an indigenous woman's dog mounted her from behind and got her pregnant. The child of this union was a Ladino. Many of the original people of the area were afraid of the Ladinos, who were brave and strong, according to the legend, which ends by saying that the Tzotziles of Chamula were afraid of the Ladinos because the Chamulas did not speak Spanish. Nonetheless, say the Chamulas, the Ladinos are loud and shameless, people without manners, because they were fathered by a dog.

To counter the view of the Chamulas, the Ladinos invented their own story, which describes the Chamulas on their hands and knees being impregnated. Both tales probably came from the basic myth, which tells of a terrible flood that left only one person alive, a man. He had to do everything for himself—cook and clean and farm and wash clothes—and he was lonely. Then a dog appeared, and from out of its skin a woman emerged. She was very simple, able only to respond to commands from the man. Her speech was limited to a few monosyllabic utterances. The man taught her to cook and clean and sew. He was so pleased with her that he even taught her many more words. To make certain she did not change back into a dog, he took the skin high up into the mountains and buried it in a secret place. Eventually the man and woman had children and began to repopulate the world.

The legend not only establishes relations between men and women but

[9]See the translation by Gary Gossen in León-Portilla and Shorris, *In the Language of Kings*.

makes very clear that the world is divided into those who serve and those who are served. It is a more fundamental notion than the story of La Malinche. There is no sense of an interchange among equals. Someone is always on hands and knees about to be had. If not the woman of the household, then one's enemies; if not individuals, then an entire country.

All this is prelude to the history of the town of San Juan Chamula in the last half century, 450 years after the apparition of the Virgin of Guadalupe. Yet conflict between the followers of Quetzalcoatl and the Virgin still rages. In Chamula the two sides of the Mexican soul conduct open warfare. Gaspar Morquecho tells his version of the conflict. He shifts in his chair, studies his listener, at first uninterested in his own tale, then growing more agitated as the complications of the story emerge. As he comes to each major point, he lowers his head and runs his fingers through his hair. And all the while he sips herbal tea and eats deep-fried cheese.

"In the 1960s a group of young Chamulas started joining the Protestant churches, which were receiving money from the United States to use in building their temples and converting traditionalists to their religion. This alerted the Catholic Church.

"Until 1966 a priest came only now and then to San Juan Chamula. But in 1966 the Chamula Mission was established, and there was a priest for the town. The people were Catholics, but they were traditionalists, *santeros*. They believed in the Virgin of Guadalupe and in many saints, but these saints and the Virgin were only new names for old gods. The Chamulas were Catholics, but they were not Catholics as the Church wanted them to be.

"The town was controlled by the caciques [traditional bosses], who were PRIistas and traditionalists. They had come into power during the Cárdenas sexenio, when the PRI became very strong, and they remained in control. But in 1969, Bishop Samuel Ruiz sent priests from the Catholic Church to convert the traditionalists to [Roman] Catholicism. It was the beginning of a battle between the Chamula gods and Ruiz.

"In the beginning of the 1970s, Echeverriá [Mexican president] put in his own group of caciques; then he threw them out and put Bishop Ruiz's people in their place. For the next three years the Catholic caciques were in control of Chamula. There was an election in 1973, but the government controlled it. The election was fraudulent.

"In 1974 the state and federal governments realized they had lost control of the town by abandoning the traditional caciques and their religion, so they brought the traditionalists back into power.[10] Soon afterward the traditionalists held a meeting in the center of the municipality to discuss religion. They said they were going to destroy the church of San Juan.

"In that same year the traditionalists attacked the Catholics in the villages, putting hundreds of them in jail, destroying their houses. Bishop Ruiz called the governor, asking him to save the prisoners. Dr. Velasco-Suárez did as Ruiz asked; the governor managed to save the prisoners, but the traditionalists expelled the Catholics. They said they would kill them if they came back.

"The next year was calm. Then, in 1976, the traditionalists attacked the Protestants and expelled them. Now the expelled Protestants occupy all of the north side of San Cristóbal. Their colonies have reached higher and higher up the mountains, and you can see many Protestant churches on the north side of the city. All the sects erect churches with money from the United States.[11] Despite everything, there are still groups of Protestants and Catholics in San Juan, because the caciques do not have total control. Until 1994[12] all three groups were PRIistas, but after that other parties entered. In 2001 the PRI, PAN, PRD, and Green parties all campaigned. The PRI won." Morquecho smiles; ironies amuse him, and they are not so great a problem anymore, for there has been, in his view, a solution to the problems of indigenous people since 1994. However, the Zapatistas, his allies, his intimates, his faith, have as yet relatively few supporters in Chamula.

Religion remains the primary issue. Morquecho's view of Bishop Ruiz is uncommon. When Ruiz retired on his seventy-fifth birthday, he was considered a candidate for the Nobel Peace Prize for his efforts to stop the low-level war between the Zapatistas on one side and the Mexican Army and PRI paramilitary forces on the other. He was instrumental in bringing about the accords (never implemented) arrived at in San Andrés Larrainzar. In the villages he did astonishing things. Bishop Sam, as those who admired him spoke of Ruiz, loved the people more than he cared for the rules of Rome or the secular world.

[10]The governor of Chiapas at the time, Dr. Manuel Velasco-Suárez, a physician educated at the UNAM and Harvard and founder of the Autonomous University in Chiapas, was also one of Mexico's leading figures in both neurology and public health during his long career. Dra. Herlinda Suárez de Valencia, who appears elsewhere in this book, mainly in Cuernavaca, is his daughter.

[11]Not all expelled Protestants have fared well. They make up the bulk of the poorest people in San Cristóbal, begging, foraging for food, doing the worst, lowest-paid work.

[12]The date of the Zapatista uprising.

Since Bishop Ruiz was interested in peace and social and political improvements for the indigenous people (Tzotziles, Tzeltales, Tojolobales, Lacandones, and Choles, by Maya language group) while promulgating his religion, he appointed many "deacons" among indigenous people. His reasoning was clear: There were not enough priests to serve the Maya. He needed help to proselytize the traditionalists, so he took a leaf from the Protestant rulebook and appointed married men, with their wives as assistants, to serve in place of priests. His idea worked very well, continued under the new Bishop, Felipe Arizmendi, and did not run into trouble until Rome became interested in the winter of 2002. No new deacons can be appointed, said the Vatican, and the future of those currently in service to "the religion" is unclear.

There is no doubt where the Vatican stands; Juan Diego, to whom the Virgin appeared, has been made a saint of the Church. But what of the Zapatistas? Guadalupe or Quetzalcoatl? Must the road to paradise begin in Europe? In an interview given to a magazine mentored by Gabriel García Márquez, Subcomandante Marcos described his intellectual and artistic roots as completely European. He had nothing to say about indigenous art, literature, philosophy, or religion. Zapatista literature belongs to the Internet; from the jungle of Chiapas no one writes to the world but Marcos, "the white god of the jungle."

SOR JUANA, THE WORST OF ALL

Centuries before Vasconcelos hired Rivera and the other muralists, the Church understood the idea: When the majority of the people are illiterate, one proselytizes with pictures. In New Spain, the word of the Council of Trent (1545–1563) and the first Council of the Mexican Church (1555) made clear that "painting is an art in service of God and the religion and they [the artists] must do work that exalts the Virgin and Christ." The admonition applied as well to poets, for after the painters come the singers. Although the Mexican Church concerned itself with converting the natives, one of the effects of didactic art was to turn the artist's priority from form to content—that is, to convert it from Mexican to European.[13]

[13]The first poet generally described as Mexican, Bernardo de Balbuena, was born in Spain, brought to Mexico as a small child, raised in the Church, and eventually became bishop of Puerto Rico. Bernardo wrote of Mexico (then meaning Mexico City) as "par-

Matías Bocanegra, a Jesuit priest, gave New Spain a lesson in what could happen if an artist failed to heed the admonitions of the Church. He wrote his "Song on Beholding an Enlightening" in the early seventeenth century. The poem foreshadowed the tragedy of Sor Juana Inés de la Cruz, the feminist who became a nun, then wrote of science, feminism, and humanism, suffered the opprobrium of the Church, recanted her intellectual freedom, and was soon dead. Bocanegra described a goldfinch, once secure in its cage, that escaped, was attacked by a hawk, and killed. "He dies for living free," said Bocanegra of the bird, telling the reader how the protagonist of the poem was enlightened.

Nonetheless, poetry in Mexico escaped the cage for a time in the work of the famous and influential Carlos de Sigüenza y Góngora, born in 1645, and Juana de Asbaje, born three years later. Sor Juana is not so much studied or admired now as Frida Kahlo, the subject of a popular book and a prizewinning movie, although Octavio Paz's critical biography, *Sor Juana, or, The Traps of Faith*,[14] restored interest in her for a while. Placed beside the life and work of Sor Juana, the literary rather than painterly works of Kahlo pale, and her loves and glories, while both difficult and fascinating, are not of the order of classical tragedy that befell Sor Juana. Kahlo was not a Mexican painter. Her style, surrealism, belonged to Europe, and Kahlo's subject matter was Kahlo.

Frida Kahlo lived much of her life in the penumbras of Diego Rivera and Leon Trotsky and in the dark shadow of her battle with physical pain. Sor Juana lived in the penumbras of the Spanish Catholic Church and Plato and in the dark shadow of her adoration of physical pain. Both were artists. One invented the modern feminist consciousness, and the other enjoyed its next iteration. Both loved women (although no one knows the details of Sor Juana's love for María Luisa, countess of Paredes); they differed only in the balance between mind and emotion, soul and body. One was beautiful, if we can trust the extant portraits, and the other fought to convince the world of her beauty. One wore the nun's habit of her time; the other braided her hair and hid behind indigenous clothing, which she used

---

adise" and spoke of "immortal spring" in his *Grandeza Mexicana*. But there was really very little yet that could be considered Mexican. The style owed everything to Europe. Bernardo lived in Mexico for much of his life, but he was a poet of New Spain, not a Mexican poet, surely not in the way the Aztecs had been Mexican poets.

[14]Cambridge, Mass.: Harvard University Press, 1988.

to advertise herself. They were brave women, inventors of their time; one wore a surrealist mask, and the other eventually disappeared into the abyss of faith unmitigated by reason.

In the latter part of the seventeenth century, one could consider joining the new "cult" of the Virgin of Guadalupe and also believe in the possible connection of Quetzalcoatl to St. Thomas. Relying on papers collected by a Jesuit priest, Manuel Duarte, Sigüenza wrote a now-lost book-length essay, *Phoenix of the West, the Apostle St. Thomas, Found Under the Name of Quetzalcoatl.* Sor Juana, his friend, surely read the book and perhaps some of the documents it was based on. Both she and Sigüenza were confirmed Indianists until 1692, when the wild, drunken behavior of the native people during food riots in Mexico City led him to reverse his view of indigenous people and St. Thomas/Quetzalcoatl. Until then Sigüenza had been so impressed by ancient Mexico he celebrated the ancient gods and even advised the viceroy to adopt Aztec methods of governance.[15] His change of heart after the riots came only three years before the death of Sor Juana, too late to influence her written works. Until then he and Duarte provided Sor Juana with powerful arguments on behalf of Quetzalcoatl.

Sigüenza wrote the *Phoenix of the West,* but also *Triunfo Parténico* (Triumph of the Immaculate Conception), which became part of a collection of prize works that included a poem by Sor Juana. She, however, is known to have written only that one poem to the Virgin of Guadalupe, which is not surprising, since the "cult" was still new during her writing life. The apparition had occurred in the sixteenth century but remained relatively unknown, masked by differences in language between the religious, who controlled scholarly pursuits, and the Nahuas. Almost a hundred years later, at the time Sor Juana was born, Miguel Sánchez published *The Miraculous Apparition in Mexico of the Image of the Virgin María Mother of God.* The book gave new impetus to the importance of Juan Diego's story, which had languished since it was first written by Antonio Valeriano in the second quarter of the sixteenth century. Sigüenza became one of the best authorities on the text, its authorship, and the quality of the Nahuatl used in the manuscript, although he retained his interest in Quetzalcoatl.[16]

---

[15]Sigüenza was a Jesuit until 1667, when he left the order to enter the university. He became a priest upon completing his studies, but he was not admitted to the Company of Jesus again until he was near death in 1700.

[16]*Tecpilatolli,* meaning "language of the *pipiltin,* or nobles," as taught in the calmecac, the school devoted to teaching the Mexica nobility.

Sor Juana demonstrated in her poem how well she grasped the dual nature of the Virgin. Only the balance was in doubt. In her one poem to the Virgin, she spoke of her as the "divine American protectress." But Sor Juana knew the provenance of the Mexican Virgin of Guadalupe: ". . . a rose of Castile," she wrote, "is transformed into a Mexican rose." Guadalupe of Mexico is "a marvel made of flowers," but what is the marvel?[17] The apparition? The changing of the Castilian rose into the Mexican? Did she predict the uniting of Mexico under the symbol of the Guadalupan Rose? Sor Juana leaves it to the reader to discover the underlying meaning of the words. Paz pays scant attention to the poem in his biography. And perhaps he is correct in that, for the poem to the Virgin was written to celebrate an occasion; it did not hold the same place as Sor Juana's interest in the pre-Columbian world. Sor Juana not only wrote a poem in Nahuatl but was one of the writers who compared the eucharist to the Aztec festival of the god of war (Huitzilopochtli), in which an image of the god was made of corn and human blood, then shot to pieces with arrows and eaten as a form of communion.

The Aztec idea appears to have been very close to transubstantiation, the most mystical and controversial act of worship conducted by the Roman Catholic Church. The Catholics took into themselves the "body and blood of Christ" just as the Nahuas took into themselves the body and blood of Huitzilopochtli. There are two possible explanations for Sor Juana's interest in the similarity of the ceremonies: Her passion for "scientific" truth led her to investigate these acts, which seemed to her to go beyond mere coincidence, or she sought to discover the foundation of a universal faith. Since she was a criollo, there could not have been an ancestral connection; her fascination with Mexica ideas, gods, and ceremonies was intellectual, cool; it did not have the fire of faith or atavism.

Quetzalcoatl was the key figure in the connection the intelligentsia of New Spain (mainly the Jesuits) made with the Aztec religion. Quetzalcoatl was, in one legend, the savior of humankind. After the end of the fourth sun, when all humans were dead, he descended to the underworld, where he came upon their bones. To bring them back to life, he bled his penis and let

---

[17]She used the word *maravilla*, which is generally translated as "wonder" or "marvel." Some translations of the poem and commentaries on it use "miracle" as the translation. It would seem to be stretching a point. The Spanish word for "miracle" is *milagro*.

the blood fall on the bones. As Jesus bled on the cross, so Quetzalcoatl bled over the bones of the dead. Both merited the name savior.

In all of Mesoamerica there was no story equal to that of Quetzalcoatl. He overwhelms the figures of the saints, including Thomas, for Quetzalcoatl is fundamental, the source of human existence and culture. The Church is Mexicanized by Quetzalcoatl, no matter what political or theological import is given to the alleged visit of one St. Thomas or the other.

In the other great story, the one told by Juan Diego of the Virgin of Guadalupe, Tonantzin (Our Revered Mother) has been replaced and all but forgotten. Ask Mexicans about Tonantzin, and they will describe her, if they can associate anything at all with her, as an earth goddess or fertility goddess. Virtually no one but a few scholars will know that she is one of the aspects of the god of duality (Ometeotl), the supreme god.

With the "cult" of the Virgin of Guadalupe, the European mystery of trinity replaces the Mesoamerican mystery of duality. The newly arrived concept of heaven is given a brown face. Doubt remains about the authenticity of the story, even the existence of Juan Diego. In reality, as Sor Juana was eventually to think, it makes no difference, for faith is not subject to reason. She bowed to faith, and her decision to choose it over reason led to the destruction and death of Mexico's great poet and essayist.[18] The effect upon the country of closing the door to rationalism is immeasurable. Mexico has consistently accepted the role of the laborer in the fields of one lord or another—the Church or the United States—rather than that of thinker, originator. Its science has been first-rate only in the area of astronomy, and the connection of that accomplishment to its ancient history is obvious.

Juana de Asbaje was born in the state of Mexico, in a time of men, in a country of machismo and its Spanish brother, *hombría*. Both notions have to do with manliness, the former more concerned with reputation and the latter with honor. By the seventeenth century the Spanish nobility's distaste for literacy had subsided, and court life in Spain and New Spain was sophisticated, witty, corrupt, and very literate. Mexico (City), the capital of New

---

[18] Sor Juana died in 1695, just forty-five years old, yet she left behind a large body of work, including her long poem *First Dream*, plays (comedies), and essays, all in defense of humanism, enlightenment thinking, and the indigenous world. Her most widely read work now is the *Response to Sister Filotea*, her brilliant defense of freedom of thought and the equality of women.

Spain, had become one of the more exciting intellectual centers in the world, but men were the intellectuals. Few women were formally educated: They could read, do sums, and so on, but they did not enter the universities. Juana was different. Her genius showed early. At three she could read; at eight she had composed poems. To get around the prohibition of higher education for women, Juana de Asbaje dressed as a boy and enrolled in the university.

She joined the viceroy's court, but the life of the court was hardly suitable for a young intellectual. She wrote that the affairs, deceptions, gossip, and ostentation were more than she could bear. But something else may have affected her decision to leave the court. She was a "natural child," illegitimate, which was then an insurmountable social obstacle, a "stain." Declaring that she did not want to remain at court and that she did not want ever to marry, she entered the Carmelite Convent of San José, and two years later, in 1669, she moved on to the Convent of San Jerónimo, where she remained until she died.

The facts of her life are themselves the outline of a Greek tragedy. After leaving the court and the Carmelites, she thrived in the pleasantness of the Convent of San Jerónimo. She had servants, a private library, an affair of the heart with María Luisa, her poetry was published, she spent her life in reading, writing, and conversation with the best minds of New Spain. And then she descended into the question of faith put to her by the nightmarish leaders of the Church in seventeenth-century Mexico, flagellants in hair shirts, nuns who engraved crosses on stones with their tongues, licking the stones until their tongues bled. While Sor Juana lived free and celebrated, she looked into both astronomy and astrology, a true woman of Mesoamerica, finding in the heavens both the genius of a mathematician-creator and the arcane connection of the movements of the heavenly bodies and the daily lives of mortals. She lived and thought in that regard exactly as the people of Mesoamerica had lived and thought for two thousand years and more. Heaven and earth were joined through human observation and reason, but connected too by arcane forces. On the one hand, knowledge accumulated in the way of the modern world, and on the other, everything was explained, as in the Neolithic world. If astrology was also European, it was more Mesoamerican; only in Mesoamerica could one predict the past.

Juana de Asbaje must have seemed even then a paradigm of the emerging conflicts within the soul of New Spain. She had accepted the convent, and as the "bride of Christ" married the religion, yet she could not put aside the other world. In her *Respuesta a Sor Filotea de la Cruz*[19] she wrote: "I have been brought closer to the fire of persecution, to the crucible of torment, and to such lengths that they have asked that study be forbidden to me. . . . I obeyed . . . in that I did not take up a book; but that I study not at all is not within my power to achieve, and this I could not obey, for though I did not study in books, I studied all the things that God had wrought, reading in them, as in writing and in books, all the workings of the universe. I looked on nothing without reflection. . . ."

She could not, she said, watch a top spinning without considering the how and why or look at the confluence of lines at a distance without wondering why it happened. "This manner of reflection has always been my habit, and is quite beyond my will to control." At one point, commenting on the scientific approach to cooking, she wrote, ". . . had Aristotle prepared victuals, he would have written more."

She was brilliant, witty, suffering from the shame of her birth, and she broke the rules. This was no tabula rasa found inside the skin of a dog, as in the Tzotzil legend; she could not conceive of a difference between the minds of men and women. She was an artist with a mind for science, a love of reason. In that, she embodied the hope of Mexico in the modern world. She was a glorious critical intelligence, Quetzalcoatl in a nun's habit. In its failure to embrace her, New Spain made a choice between faith and reason that would plague the land and its people for centuries.

The Church, in the form of Archbishop Francisco Aguiar y Seijas and the bizarre Jesuit Antonio Núñez de Miranda of the Brotherhood of Mary, saw in her the risk of questioning, the danger of humanism. We cannot know what conversations went on between the beautiful humanist poet and the mad ascetic, the flagellant whose death revealed a corpse beset by vermin, their heads buried in his flesh, their bodies engorged with his blood. In the end the poet wrote a confession and famously signed it not with ink but with her own blood.

The artist had been charged with becoming a secular humanist, a woman of modern Europe, but she had been unable to emerge completely from a

---

[19]Sor Filotea de la Cruz was a pseudonym used by the bishop of Puebla in a letter to Sor Juana castigating her for her humanist and rationalist and feminist views. The translation is by Margaret Sayers Peden. The quote appears in the *Norton Anthology of World Literature* (New York: W. W. Norton, 1995), vol. 2, pp. 414–15.

religion that demanded the renunciation of worldly things and then the sacrifice of her life. The humanist abandoned reason for the demands of faith. She left the comforts of her book-lined rooms, the shield of fame, and died while caring for the sick. No doubt she wished to die, to become the bloody mortar of the cornmeal image of Huitzilopochtli, herself the Mexican eucharist. In the moment of her confession, when she turned to writing in blood, when she called herself "the worst of all," she became the impenetrable mystery of faith, art conceding not to life but to death. No other act brings about so perfect an end to content, so glorious an embrace of form. It is—she was—the gorgeous nightmare of Mexico.

25.

Once There Was a Circle

Was it dream or reality?
—IGNACIO RODRÍGUEZ GALVÁN,
The Prophecy of Cuauhtémoc

Feeling foolish and at the same time irritated by the confusion at the Mexico City airport, the man in the business suit and I complained to each other about the inefficiency. He looked prosperous, chic, if that word properly applies to a man in middle age with gray-streaked hair and the slight puffiness at the jawline indicating a life of sufficiency and a little, but not too much more. The fabric of his suit was fine, a light wool, gray with a very proper pinstripe, and his tie and shoes were obviously expensive. He must have made excuses to himself for the age and slightly improper fit of my tweed jacket.

We found our bags together in an inappropriate corner. We laughed, and I said, "Good-bye." Given his attire and his slight and graceful Spanish accent, I thought he would be hurrying off to a waiting car, but instead he asked where I was going. "Cuauhtémoc," I said. And he asked if I wanted to share a taxi since he was going to the same district.

In the taxi we spoke in Spanish. We were in Mexico, and he and I felt obliged to speak in the language of the country. "I have not been back for a long time," he said, "since I completed university. Would you mind if I asked the driver to pass by the house where I lived? I'll give him a few pesos for his time. It won't cost you anything."

I agreed to the detour. The driver crossed to the other side of Reforma, Mexico City's still-beautiful boulevard, and drove into the Condesa district. As darkness came quickly and the winter air turned cold, the taxi driver asked us to lock the doors. It was dangerous, he said. "Look at the delinquents. They go to these places, they don't eat anything, just a soda; then they gather on the street. They're delinquents; they rob and kill. You should never come here at night."

The man in the gray suit looked out the window. He did not have a thin face, but it seemed to grow thinner as he watched the little knots of young men gathered on the sidewalk, the neon colors, street vendors, open fronts of fast-food restaurants, young men alone perched on stools, backs to the counter, staring out at the street. They wore billed caps turned sideways, imitating their North American counterparts. The man in the gray suit did not understand how Mexico City had changed after the construction of the subway, when huge numbers of the poor, especially the young, dressed in poor imitations of currently stylish clothing, came pouring into Condesa and the Zona Rosa, changing the character of the center of the city, bringing with them fear and fast food. These were the *nacos*, the new name for the people despised by the Mexican middle and upper classes. The nacos had come to his neighborhood; they had stolen his history. He would eventually have to choose between fear and compassion, but not then, not at that moment; he was lost in time.

"There were houses on this street," he said. "I think it was this street."

He turned away from the window and leaned forward to speak to the driver. "Can you go in, away from this street? I lived inside Condesa, not in a place like this. I don't remember the street. It was not so far from here. There was a small grocery store on the corner, across the street a kindergarten. I went to the kindergarten."

The driver turned right, entering the heart of the neighborhood. The streets were darker, quiet. Parked cars lined the blocks. We passed a street of art galleries and another of restaurants.

"Is this it?" the driver asked.

"No."

Another street and another.

"I haven't been gone so long. I was a boy here, a young man, a student at the university. This was my neighborhood. My mother, my father . . . Across the street, in the gray stone house, my cousins lived."

"How long have you been gone?"

"Thirty-two years."

"It's a long time," I said, although it did not really seem so long to me, for I had first come to Mexico City then.

He turned to look at me. His face was lined, deep vertical marks around the mouth, cut into the cheeks, stern lines, business. He reached into the breast pocket of his suitcoat and took out a pair of eyeglasses: two hexagons, gold wires, and pink plastic pads where the eyeglasses rested on his nose. He put them on carefully, one side at a time, manipulating the second wire piece to fit over his ear. It made a dour figure of him, a schoolteacher or a clerk, disapproving. Long after my comment he answered, "Not in Mexico."

We went a few more blocks. "Turn left here," he instructed the driver. "No, no," he said. "Not there, you missed the turn. Go around the block."

The driver did as he was instructed, but when we came to the place where he thought the driver should have turned, the man in the fine gray suit said, "I told you it was not here."

"Where are we going?" I asked. "If it's going to be very long, why don't you drop me off at my destination?"

"We are here."

"Here?"

"Yes," he said, "but it's not here. Don't you understand? There is something very wrong. The street is not here. It has always been here. My grandfather lived here. He was a member of Carranza's cabinet. He was a Constitutionalist minister."

"Perhaps you mean on the other side of the Reforma, on Río Lerma; that's where Carranza lived. The house is a museum now."

"My great-grandfather lived in the same house, and his grandfather too. They were with Benito Juárez."

"From Oaxaca?"

"No, never from Oaxaca. We were not Zapotecos. We were always here."

"Your ancestors came with Cortés?"

"No, later, with the viceroy. The ones who came with Cortés were pigs, illiterates; the only ones who could read and write were the crypto-Jews and Cortés himself; he was a lawyer."

"Yes, yes, I know."

"But what you do not know is that you are in Mexico, and Mexico City is disappearing. My house is gone, everything has gone with my house. My great-great-grandfathers, everything has disappeared."

He removed one of the wire earpieces so that the eyeglasses hung from one side, took a handkerchief from his pocket, and wiped his eyes. The driver asked where he wanted to go next. "Around," he said. "Look for my house."

"But, sir, I do not know your house. Perhaps you remember the number? And if not the number, what is the street?"

"There was a kindergarten, a grocery store."

"Things change, sir."

"You cannot change the past," he said, lecturing the driver. "Don't you know about history? How can you change history? Do you see the light that comes from the stars? It has been traveling for thousands of years, perhaps millions. You cannot change the path traveled by the light. This is a famous statement about history my friend. It was meant to demean the practice of history but not history itself."

The driver pulled up at a corner. He sighed, a great sour breath that filled the front seat of the taxi and floated back over his passengers. "Sir," he said, and sighed again, "your house is gone."

The man in the fine suit leaned back. He rested his head on the top of the seat, exposing his throat as if he were about to be shaved or slaughtered. He said, changing to his softened English, "Then who am I?"

He did not speak another word. I thought of asking him a question, why he knew this tidbit about history. Was he a professor? An artist? He had paraphrased George Kubler on the history of art. Who knew more than Kubler about art and time in Mexico? I looked over at the man in the gray suit. His eyes were closed. I saw him swallow once, the anatomy exaggerated by his outstretched neck.

When the driver let me off, the man in the fine wool suit did not bother to look around, as if I had not been there at all. The taxi door opened, and a pale, yellowing light fell on the man. It changed the color of his skin and removed all the lines, all the marks of time from his face. He had begun to disappear, like his house. There was something wrong. Could it be that he had no relatives left in Mexico? No old friends, schoolmates, neighbors? Mexicans go home, I thought, but not all, and not forever.

"Well, good-bye," I said in English. "I am sorry you could not find your house."

He did not answer immediately. Perhaps he did not answer at all; perhaps I did not hear correctly because he muttered, he did not speak. It is also possible that I imagined what I heard: "*Huellas.*"

Footprints?

Mexico is an old country and memorious, unlike its neighbor to the north. For the last three hundred years or more the inhabitants of Mexico have been historicists,[1] like the man in the gray suit, by which I mean that even

---

[1]The term "historicist" is not used here as it would be used to describe the work of Martin Heidegger and his idea of the randomness of events.

when they do not know history, they are obsessed by it. There is a way to think about the historicism in Mexico that will be useful to keep in mind here: the eighteenth-century German philosopher Johann Gottfried Herder's idea of understanding through empathy, of respect for the uniqueness of every culture. Herder also thought that the nearer the historian got to the "primitive" or original aspects of a culture, the nearer he got to its "genius."

Mexican artists and writers since the Maya scribes have been historicists. When the Spaniards came to Mesoamerica, they began immediately to write down what they had seen, what they had done, and what went before the invasion. With the exception of a few novels and poems, the major literary work in Mexico has been historical, if not in the commonly held Western sense, certainly in the sense of describing mythical origins. The few outstanding Mexican musical compositions—Carlos Chávez's *Sinfonia India* and *Xochipilli* and Silvestre Revueltas's *Cuauhnáhuac* and *La Noche de los Maya*—have been historical, reproductions of ancient music rather than references to times and sounds past, examinations of the history of Mexican music.[2]

Recently, some young writers have questioned the historical aspect of Mexican literature, but until now it was mainly in the plastic arts that history as a driving force came into question in Mexico. There were transitions, inventions in pre-Hispanic work, but the role of history was minor in New Spain and during the first hundred years of Mexico as an independent country. The material portrayed in paintings and some sculptures was almost exclusively religious: saints and virgins, angels and the Christ, madonna and child, as the Church of Mexico advised. The exception was portraiture, which served for the history of the wealthy before photographs filled family albums. Painters in New Spain and independent Mexico had no interest in the formal considerations of the original inhabitants. They emulated Europe; in their minds pre-Hispanic Mexico had existed, but it and its significant forms were dead.

At the end of the nineteenth century Mexico went through the first of a series of conflicting views about art and history. The cientificos were theo-

---

[2]Other composers of roughly the same era, Béla Bartók and even more obviously Charles Ives, used old themes, but the use of folk tunes was not nearly so important to their work, and although Ives did once do something of a satire on Fourth of July band music, the joke was not central to his thinking.

rists, devoted to the ideas of positivism. History meant little to them. The past was what had to be overcome. In their eyes the indios were simply a problem: backward, largely illiterate, and seemingly forever recalcitrant. Art was of little interest; they were cientificos.

BERGSON'S INTUITION

In the closing days of the Porfiriato, there were several new philosophies in Mexico: democracy, socialism, anarchism, and syndicalism in the political arena and, as a powerful underlying notion, spiritualism. Influential members of the young Mexican art world, not just the members of the Ateneo, knew about Bergson and thought about the idea of the creative spirit, the élan vital. Art critic Juana Gutiérrez Haces describes a book by Francisco Díez Barroso, published in 1921, in which he chose Bergson, along with Croce, as a philosopher to follow.[3] And Gerardo Murillo (Dr. Atl), who was to have enormous influence on Mexican art, traveled from Rome, where he was a student at the university, to Paris for the sole purpose of listening to a lecture by Henri Bergson.

Positivism had failed, not in the attraction of foreign capital or industrial development but in the creation of a participatory democracy and a decent standard of living for the majority of the citizens. It was not, at its heart, Mexican. A democratic society, with full credence in the value and capability of the human spirit, was the goal of the intellectual revolution that swept the Mexican leadership. And the idea of the spirit was everywhere. Philosophers, painters, even generals were aware of it. Professor Gustavo Valencia of ITESM in Morelos said his ancestor Benavides, first a Villista general and later a Carrancista, had been interested in spiritism.[4]

Along with spiritualism came the beginnings of another idea, one that has grown stronger in recent years. The late Guillermo Bonfil Batalla, in *Mexico Profundo*, argued for a pluralist state, for empathy with the original people, respect for their genius. The historian Miguel León-Portilla has

---

[3]She quotes Díez Barroso describing three aspects of art, including "genius—that he will later define as the psychic process of the artist." Juana Gutiérrez Haces, *El Arte en Mexico: Autores, Temas, Problemas*, ed. Rita Eder (Mexico: Fondo de Cultura Económica et al., 2001), p. 146.
[4]On the other side of Valencía's family, Felipe Ángeles remained loyal to Villa.

argued for years on behalf of a pluralist society in Mexico, explaining the difference between autonomy and sovereignty to those who would or could understand. Historicism is very much alive in Mexico, but it contends now for supremacy with social ideas much closer to those of the cientificos.

VASCONCELOS'S DEMAND

The second change in the Mexican view of art and history came at the conclusion of the civil wars. President Obregón moved José Vasconcelos from his position as rector of the national university to a post with much broader responsibilities. Vasconcelos, who had helped bring an end to the worship of positivism, took up nationalism in its stead. And he wielded enough power to force his ideas into practice. He had control of the humanities: the theory as rector of the university, the practice as the director of the national educational system, and finally the activity, which took place on the walls of Mexico's public buildings.

He commissioned the Mexican muralists, but not to paint what pleased them. He wanted a very specific kind of mural, work he considered "Mexican." Vasconcelos criticized the first mural done by Diego Rivera because the subject matter was not Mexican enough. He wanted more history, more bronze, something befitting the *raza cósmica*. He planned to educate Mexico, to end illiteracy, to create a Mexican art. Rivera and the other muralists soon learned that by art he meant nationalism.

Three great painters were among those who took on the task of history and dominated this stage of art in Mexico. Diego Rivera became the most famous of the muralists; David Alfaro Siqueiros the most troublesome, a painter who spent a good part of his life in Mexican prisons as punishment for his radical politics; and José Clemente Orozco, a man who had lost his left hand in a childhood accident, a student of agriculture before he became a painter, a taciturn, although not unpleasant, man, became the most intellectually mercurial, the most unfathomable, and in his painting the most interesting.

No life in painting could be much more public than the frantic years of Diego Rivera after his return from Europe. His marriage to Frida Kahlo, his dabblings in the Communist Party, his love affairs, the grand confrontation after painting his mural on the wall of the RCA Building in Rockefeller Center. Abby Aldrich Rockefeller, who admired Rivera and his work, was behind the commissioning of Rivera to paint *Man at the Crossroads*. Rivera started the work, including a portrait of Lenin in a prominent position, in 1933. Nelson Rockefeller objected to the portrait, demanding that it be removed from the mural. Rivera refused. E. B. White wrote a poem about the confrontation, "I Paint What I See." In the poem Rivera defends the mural, saying it is his work, and Rockefeller responds, ". . . but it's my wall." Rockefeller ordered the destruction of the mural.

There have been many biographies of Rivera and much critical and political attention paid to his work, all of it well deserved and rarely tedious even when the information is not new. Rivera was a huge man, physically and metaphorically larger than life; there was room enough in him for a thousand critics and millions of romantics to stand side by side admiring the encompassing genius.

He learned politics early on from Siqueiros, visited Russia; hosted Trotsky's exile in Mexico; endured the attack on Trotsky's life by a group led by Siqueiros, Trotsky's affair with Frida, and the ax murder of the old revolutionary. Rivera was expelled from the Communist Party, allowed back in, painted perhaps his best work in Detroit, married his art dealer in his last years, and all the while maintained an affair with Dolores Olmedo. There can be little doubt that he was a major painter, but there can also be little doubt that he carried out the Vasconcelos viewpoint. He never became a rightist, like Vasconcelos, but he never became a Mexican painter either. He painted many Mexican subjects, but not only Mexican subjects.

The industrial world fascinated him. The mural of the Ford factory is an advertisement for the genius of the engineer, but also for the organization of the factory, the employment of the worker. If Rivera, off and on a Communist, a Marxist for most of his life, understood anything about the alienation of the worker from his labor, it surely was not evident in his portraits of factories and technological devices. He was a romantic Communist, an artistic leftist. Although he was said to have been a brilliant talker on any subject, including politics, the deadening aspect of the life of the factory worker appears not to have bothered him very much, if at all. Perhaps it had to do with the complex organization required to paint a mural: the assistants, the flow of cash, the scaffolds and ladders, and plaster and paint. He was an artist and also a construction manager, a boss, a genius of many sorts, but unable to understand the plight of the day to day. Alienation from one's labor was beyond his magnificent imagination.

Was Rivera a painter or a propagandist first? Did he care most about pictures or ideas? He had theories; he lived by theories; he loved dabbling in politics. He lived according to a mix of theory and desire. Rivera had true empathy for the original people of Mexico and for their works. He collected the work, he adored the people, but he was not of them. Rivera had a politics, and he illustrated it brilliantly, breathtakingly, but the politics never fell before the power of form; he lived art and painted nonfiction. He was surely the greatest nonfiction painter of his time. The question he leaves behind is whether a nonfiction painter can be a truly great artist. The answer for most people is yes, although not for everyone. He was witty, a caricaturist, a magnificent technician, and a devout artist, but after World War II a new generation of Mexican painters was to come along and say no to Rivera's immortal walls.

In the world of popular art or rather the art of the popular, Diego Rivera became the Mexican painter and a great celebrity. Siqueiros spent a good deal of his career in jail and became known as much for his politics as for his painting. Orozco, who is less well known than Rivera but more famous than Siqueiros, in purely painterly things, was the most adventurous of the three, but it is virtually impossible to know what went on in his mind. He had to leave the country after his anti-Catholic paintings inspired a riot in Mexico City, yet he never quite left the culture of the Church. In his depiction of a Franciscan friar, the small face, the size of a child's face, eyes downcast, eyebrows like arches, a beneficent smile on his lips, Orozco painted the figure he most admired, among the few in which he allowed the loving side of his own character to appear. The friar's body is huge, his clasped hands in the blunt, powerful style one associates with Orozco. If there is irony in the figure, it does not make its way through the paint; the Franciscan's smile *is* beneficent and the long, soft shape of his figure is more loving than any other Orozco painted. The Franciscan is dreamed, a form containing a figure, an idea for inclusion in the form, because the lines required direction.[5]

There is no irony in the face and figure of the friar as there is no irony in any of Orozco's work. He is a painter of a particular style born of a particular place. His close friend the historian Edmundo O'Gorman said he was "the voice of America" and then qualified it to speak of "our America." O'Gorman, the Mexican-born son of a transplanted British foreign service

[5]Hospicio de Cabañas, Guadalajara.

officer and brother of the architect and muralist Juan, had an existentialist view of Mexico and Mexican history, having been greatly influenced by Heidegger, whose work he translated into Spanish. O'Gorman saw the genius in the original culture of Mesoamerica, and he searched for it in the works of writers and painters.

In Orozco, he found almost everything he sought in an artist.[6] He found Orozoco's creatures and caricatures, which he thought of as dreamed monsters, the same kind of work he revered in pre-Hispanic art. O'Gorman's theories about the various states of being, European and native (he largely neglected the African), inhabiting Mexicans become less easily applicable to Orozco as the painter's career blossoms. The most monstrous of Orozco's figures is an ink on paper drawing, *The Devil*, which critics have compared to the great Aztec statue of the goddess Coatlicue, because it includes many legs, a pair of arms, and snakes either wrapped around it or emerging from its back. Orozco's devil, however, has a European feeling, as if Dante rather than an ancient Nahua sculptor had dreamed it. The drawing itself lacks the clean lines and inexorable conception of the pre-Hispanic goddess. Orozco's devil is tortured, but Coatlicue is an exact opposite. She is majestic, and we the observers are tortured. She is the goddess and the mother of gods, heaven and the underworld, and all that lies between, hearts for the blood that moves man and the universe, twin snakes for the duality of all things in all realms, and magnificence to separate the gravity of the gods from the ephemeral existence of mere humans.

If Orozco dreams monsters, they are not of such magnificence, although they are larger than life and the observer must often look up at a ceiling or to a place high on a wall to be affected by them. Nonetheless, there is very little precise description in Orozco's work. He is not a portrait painter. He was brought to painting by the caricaturist José Guadalupe Posada and spent more than a few years drawing caricatures for the anti-Porfirista newspaper *El Hijo del Ahuizote*. The monsters he painted on the staircase of the Governor's Palace in Guadalajara have as much of the sense of caricature as of monster about them. They are ugly, with gaping mouths, black holes, terrible caves of endless depth, maws, but they lack the unexpected form of

[6]See Renato González Mello for his book *Orozco: Pintor Revolucionario?* (Mexico City: UNAM, 1995), articles on the career of Orozco and his connection to O'Gorman's ideas, and other works on the muralists.

monsters; they are commentary, conflict, fear. And not everything he painted was caricature, the making of description into monstrous lines and colors; the enormous figure of Hidalgo that appears in two Orozco murals is a beneficent creature, among the very few historical figures he did not paint with hateful faces, the other being Emiliano Zapata.

Vasconcelos demanded nationalism, and Orozco gave it to him now and then, but it was rarely pure. Orozco subscribed to no theory but painting. Although much of his work appears to be based in historicist thinking, he did not always admire the genius of his indigenous ancestors. In the Dartmouth College murals he painted a history of Mexico in which the human sacrifices conducted by the Aztecs were brutal, with the faces of the killers obscured by angular masks in a foreshadowing of Paz's theory about Mexicans hiding behind masks. In the same series he painted Quetzalcoatl, but it is not a Mexican Quetzalcoatl one sees in the mural. The culture bearer looks more like Moses parting the Red Sea. His raft of snakes waits in the background, but the face and attire are Mesopotamian; the monk of Tula, often imagined as bearded, becomes something other than the great, good Toltec. When one looks at Orozco's Quetzalcoatl, it is almost impossible not to think of the reports of Motecuhzoma's series of nightmares before the arrival of Cortés, whom he identified with Quetzalcoatl. Orozco has made a ferocious foreign god of the soul of Mesoamerican culture.

In painting the murderous civil wars of 1910–1920, Orozco found little good to show. He painted bloodshed and destruction. There is no spirit of revolution in those murals, no glory, nothing but horror. What is it that Orozco thought? Why did his Christ take an ax to the cross? How is it that he is as disgusted by the Russian revolutionary leaders as by the Fascists?

He was born in Jalisco, and he did some of his best work there on the walls of the Governor's Palace and the Orphanage. Of all the muralists, and there were many others beside the famous three, Orozco was the most Mexican, in the sense of his time and his connection to the original genius of Mesoamerican art. No one could paint the true Mexican Revolution, the great intellectual changes that brought Mexican thinking into the twentieth century and married it more securely to the ancestral culture. In that venture Mexico made another attempt to heal the wounds of colonialism. There had been the Apparition of the Virgin, the journey of St. Thomas the Apostle and St. Thomas of Mylapore, and in 1910 there came the result of a new recognition of the creative power of the human spirit. It led to a revolt against the cientificos, with their hardened philosophy of the ultimate advance of man as the establishment of the world of manufacturing (what we would now call technology). And this twentieth-century recognition of the spirit in all humans of every epoch connected the contemporary with the pre-Hispanic world. There at last was Mexico! Or so they hoped.

Had it been the miracle dreamed by Vasconcelos and his painters, art would have erased the wounds of centuries of colonialism and served to create the cosmic race. But it was not to be, not then. Orozco represents both the hope and the impossibility of the goal. He was an artist, a success that can never be discounted, and he was a mestizo, a problem that still requires resolution. The conflict between Europe and America tore him into pieces and set the pieces at war with each other. No theory could pacify him; no promise could calm him. He was a man in opposition, finding fault with everything that had gone before, everything in his own time, and the future as far as he could imagine it. He raged at the world that had been given him, he staggered from wound to disappointment to despair, and all this quietly, a bespectacled man with a little square mustache who went unmasked, unclothed, excoriated, to his easel or to climb his muralist's platform to put his conflicted Mexican soul before the world.

THE RUPTURE WITH SUCCESS

Orozco painted the horrors of civil war but could not say how the ideas changed, except through form, through his own ambiguity and historicism. Rivera, the historian, became the world-famous painter, but together Rivera and Orozco were perhaps the most widely viewed showing ("export" would be the wrong sense here) of Mexican culture since the invasion. After them, only the novels of Carlos Fuentes would find a huge worldwide audience. Octavio Paz would win the Nobel Prize for Literature, but never find the great audience. Nor would Rufino Tamayo or the later painters Juan Soriano and Francisco Toledo find a large audience outside the narrow world of art.

As the muralists grew old and their work became ever more popular, the battle among artists of different generations took place in Mexico. If their thesis was nationalism, the antithesis was universalism. Octavio Paz named the next wave in painting la Ruptura (the Rupture), and the name stuck. Art critics, following Paz, sought to make ever more grand and complex the break with what had become traditional. They spoke of the break with the muralists as "the negation" of what went before, which is always a comfortable way to speak in historical terms, since it avoids the idea of a continuous process of thesis, antithesis, and synthesis that leads finally to the "end of art."[7] But then critics in every field are forever discovering the end of some grand category when the only real end is the end of us. Critics die; audiences die; art discovers. It may seem an overly simple way to put it, but the facts are difficult to dispute. The question of course is how art discovers, and why.

If la Ruptura is considered a negation of the muralists, all that is left is to think why, and the answer for most critics is World War II. A less frequently given reason is that Mexican nationalism peaked during the Cárdenas years (1934–1940) and then declined as Miguel Alemán sought foreign investment, strengthened the bureaucracy, and made tourism part of his economic miracle. Or it may have been Coca-Cola and all it represented that left Mexican artists feeling less Mexican, more universal. La Ruptura was, in that sense, a form of capitulation. Rather than seek to discover Mexican art, the painters abandoned Mexico for universal themes, and perhaps what they thought would be universal recognition. The particular had lost its universal meaning for them. Siqueiros had said, "Ours is the only way." The leaders of la Ruptura made the same statement about their own work, but they began it by saying, "Since then . . ." They were painters, and they had embarked upon their own voyage of discovery.

Although they were fine painters, the world did not recognize their discoveries as unique. And that may have been what they really desired. Nationalism and the chimerical Revolution of 1910 had brought the question of mestizaje to the fore. Were they European or indigenous? Was the person created by the sixteenth-century invasion syncretic, the two systems of belief fused into one, or simply two-sided, a war-torn victim of colonialism? If Rivera faced the question standing on European ground and Orozco some-

---

[7]The theory belongs to Hegel, who said that after the end of art there would be a relinking to the past. The critic Arthur Danto described a blank canvas presented as a work of art as Hegel's end. According to Danto, nothing new was left for painters. It had all been done, just as Hegel predicted. The relinking was about to begin. There was something inherently silly in their certainty that it would all work out according to plan. The wonder of art of course is that it does not come to an end in reality, only in theory—and never according to plan.

where in the center, battered by his internal war, the painters of la Ruptura finally solved it. They were not mestizos, not Mexicans, not Europeans; they were universal. They transcended the idea of the cosmic race, they were no race at all, simply universal men and women; the Ruptura was an extraordinary human act: The painters had deracinated themselves. They no longer had Mexican roots or Mexican concerns; they floated somewhere in the ether, without home or memory.

Had the painters of la Ruptura made a mistake about art? Was a change of form different from the change of nationality, memory, life they insisted they had accomplished? There are two important painters who were contemporary with la Ruptura, one at the beginning and the other at the end. They were the most successful of the painters claimed by la Ruptura, but they were unwilling members. The striking distinction between them and the painters who considered themselves part of la Ruptura was that both men had studied in Paris and returned to Mexico, happy to be home.

TAMAYO AND TOLEDO ON THEIR OWN

Rufino Tamayo was the first Mexican after the muralists whose work attracted international attention in the art world, perhaps because it was Mexican, although it was also beautiful by any standard. Tamayo was able to work in a philosophical vein, thoughtful, almost metaphysical in his questioning of origins both spiritually and temporally. He worked, as well, on brilliant, beautiful surfaces, painterly, never reportorial, giving the viewer ideas and experience through form. And he could be charming, romancing the colors of his watermelons, which were also the colors of the Mexican flag and the shapes of quarter moons and half-seen planets. He worked in form, but abstract only because of the dominance of form, never a guessing game, never so personal and so intimate that like some painters of his time, he was comprehensible only to himself, if at all.

Tamayo came to light before the time of la Ruptura, which brings into question Octavio Paz's dating and even his notion of a rupture, with its connotation of explosive suddenness. Tamayo, even more Mexican than Rivera had hoped to be, found the genius of the original artists: The forms he painted were both *significant*, able to produce aesthetic pleasure, and based in comprehensible dreams. They were simply beautiful, and they were his alone. The theories of art that have hounded Mexican painters for the last half century were transcended by Tamayo, and they have been transcended again by Francisco Toledo, who has ascended to the place left to him by Tamayo. He is Mexico's most important living painter, and he is his own school, a card-carrying member neither of the first Ruptura nor the second nor the third, as critics in Mexico have tried again and again to narrow painting into time periods.

It is a silly business in Mexico, where criticism too often attempts not to serve but to surpass art. In an interview given to Delmari Romero Keith, Francisco Toledo, generally considered the leading painter of the Ruptura, spoke about the concept. Since Toledo has given very few interviews during his long career, it is a rare opportunity to delve into Mexican art. Toledo is from the state of Oaxaca, where he lived in the small town of Juchitán as a child. In 1960, at the age of twenty, he went to Paris, where he studied for five years before returning to Mexico. While he was in Paris, Olga and Rufino Tamayo took him under their wing, and when Tamayo left Paris, he left all his painting gear to Toledo, one Oaxaqueño to another, and Toledo accepted it as a sign of the passing of the mantle. Toledo spent a short time in New York City in the 1980s, but his career has mainly been in the state of his birth.

He told Romero Keith, "I always lived isolated and away from the group today called la Ruptura. I lived in Europe and later in Oaxaca, I was never really close to the artists who 'broke away.' I never broke with anything, perhaps because of my traditional mentality, I see the history of painting as a kind of continuity. Miró said, 'Painting is the same from the era of the caves to our time.' I never felt the need to break away since I admired the muralists and I saw the same things in the paintings of [Juan] Soriano, Gunther Gerzso,[8] and Tamayo; although those three were far from muralism, I never thought they painted 'against' something. I felt that it was a grand family, although every one had different features. For me it is clear, painting may or may not have an ideology; what is finally important is the plastic quality.

"For me the term Ruptura means nothing in the history of art. If we look at Tamayo; in his painting there existed at the same time abstract images, semi-abstracts, and even images with metaphysical references, finally what interests me is his poetry, that is to say, the manner in which he plays with the line, the color, and the material."

[8]Gerzso also worked as an art director for some notable movies, including the movie version of Malcolm Lowry's *Under the Volcano*.

Mexico now boasts of only one world-renowned painter, and he is the most Mexican by any measure, the primacy of form, of the plastic quality, as he puts it. Or it may be the monstrous quality of dreams. Luis Cardoza y Aragón, one of Mexico's most prominent art critics, said of Toledo, in 1987: "He lives and loves his magical culture. . . . He has broken the monotony of art in Mexico. . . . He copies nothing, imitates nothing, always invents. You cannot capture Toledo with reason alone."

Like the first Mexican artists, Toledo is filled with surprises: A coyote with hooves steps on a fish. A man and woman undress together in preparation for going to bed. He has wings and the beak of a bird; we see her only from behind, him from the side; thus we see his bird beak and wings, the width of her buttocks, and in the upper left a window with a flower pot slightly to the left of center in the window, a painting Toledo has of course named *The Flower Pot in the Window*. The joke of the name is indigenous humor; whatever is off center, unlikely as the figures or events in dreams, is either comical or religious in the indigenous world. Form is the substance; wit is whatever breaks the rules. Octavio Paz described the macho as a man who shoots another man in the head at a bar and laughs. That may be Paz's sense of humor, but it is not the wit of Toledo or of most indigenous people, where comedy is whatever is out of turn, doesn't make sense, as in Cantinflas or Tin Tan or the pre-Hispanic "Story of the Tohuenyo," who "went about naked, dangling the thing."[9]

Toledo is sly, witty, a painter of many frogs and many women with voluptuous thighs. He learned engraving early; he is enamored of the expression of line. There are moments in his painting when the attention to form leads him toward abstraction, but he is never at a loss for something to say. He belongs to no school, although every school would have him. There is no Toledo but Toledo, as there is no Mexico but Mexico.

[9]See León-Portilla and Shorris, *In the Language of Kings*.

26.

Real Magic

It is all surreal.
—ANDRÉ BRETON UPON
ARRIVING IN MEXICO

Shortly after Don Paulino passed the age of eighty, the cooperative of the town of Tetiz hired him to tend to the fruit tree in the patio of the community center. Since it was a magnificent mango tree, perhaps the only fruit tree in the Yucatán that had grown to such great size and bore fruit of such unusual sweetness, Don Paulino took this job, as he did most things, with great seriousness. And that is what caused him to lose his ability to sing.

That year the rains began in the spring exactly on time, so there was little for Don Paulino to do but visit the tree now and then to admire the sprouting of buds, leaves, and blossoms. In early summer the tree bore fruit, as always, but birds came and ate the fruit. Don Paulino stood under the tree and shouted and clapped his hands, but the birds paid no attention. He climbed up into the tree and chased the birds away. As soon as he climbed down, the birds came back.

He climbed up again and chased the birds away again, and then he climbed down, but he had not yet reached the ground when he saw the birds eating the fruit. He went home and got his cat. Then he climbed up the tree and crawled out on a branch and left the cat there. The birds did not come while the cat was out on the branch, but the cat soon tired of sitting there and jumped down. No sooner had the cat reached the ground than the birds came back.

Don Paulino caught the cat in a noose, strangled it, skinned it, and stuffed it. But when he put the cat in the tree, the birds saw that its mouth was closed, and they were not frightened. Don Paulino climbed up the tree again and crawled out on the branch to put a stick in the cat's mouth to hold it open. That was when the branch broke and Don Paulino fell out of the tree and lost his ability to sing.

Although he cannot read or write, Don Paulino of Tetiz, who has but one tooth and many broken ribs and can no longer sing, is a literary man—that is, he is literature. It is not the best literature, nothing more than a simple tale, like a fable, but Don Paulino's loss of the ability to sing is like the fables told by many indigenous writers in Mexico. The difference between Don Paulino and literature is like the difference between life and literature. Except in Mexico.

For all the world Don Paulino must appear to be a made-up character, a cautionary tale about chasing birds and killing cats, but art is different in Mexico. The keeper of the fruit tree of Tetiz could be a painting by Francisco Toledo or a fable by the Mayan writer Miguel Ángel May May, but he is not. I have a photograph of Don Paulino standing in the center of the patio of the cooperative building in Tetiz. It shows a man of more than eighty years, a slightly skeletal man, hands at his side, smiling without showing a sign of tooth, tongue, gum, or gullet, posed next to the trunk of a great fruit tree. And it is true that before he fell out of the tree, he was a singer and composer. According to one of the members of the cooperative, "Don Paulino knew all the songs he heard on the radio as a boy, and when he could not remember the words, he composed them."

The story of Don Paulino, although it has aspects of low comedy, is also a story about death. The hero kills a cat, then tries to make it appear as if the dead cat could kill a bird. The eighty-year-old keeper of the tree has arrived at a time in life when death is near, if not today or tomorrow, then soon. He has outlived his expectations; without hesitation he risks his life to save a few pieces of fruit. Finally, he loses his ability to sing; he is already partly dead, sinking. And it all seems just a little bit mad, surrealistic, which André Breton said is the reality of Mexico. Mexican life and thought are centered on death and the gods; magical realism has only to be recognized and pointed out to the world by the artist.

Literature began in Mesoamerica with prayers and went on to think of the brevity of life on earth. In Europe, by comparison, Lucretius wrote these lines in *On the Nature of Things*: "Death/ is nothing to us, has no relevance/ to our condition, seeing that the mind/ is mortal."

The death of Socrates was not concerned with death, but with how to live. He made it quite clear that he was an old man and expected to die soon no matter what happened. He thought he might just go to sleep, at worst, or have a chance to meet Homer, at best. His famous argument about sleeping and waking, dying and living seems almost casual, a dismissal of an issue that did not concern him very much.

In Mesoamerica, however, the Popol Vuh deals largely with a journey to the underworld. The battles of the hero twins are with the creatures of that world, monsters of death and nightmare. The heroes return to earth; their story imitates the life cycle of corn. The Quetzalcoatl myth is about immolation, descent into the underworld, rebirth of humans.

When literature concentrates on death, it always has as its corollary the existence of God or the gods. Miguel León-Portilla's general introduction to an anthology of Mesoamerican literature speaks at length of the gods, while Bernard Knox's introduction to an anthology of classical (Greek and Roman) literature does not devote even a full paragraph to the gods. The literary and philosophical lines of Western classical and Mesoamerican thinking diverged almost from their respective inceptions. Both cultures were concerned with ethical questions; neither had solved the question that propelled Christianity and then Islam into dominating religions in much of the world: Socrates brought heaven down to earth; the Mesoamericans studied the never-ending rotations of the heavens from their place on earth. For the Greeks, the questions became ethical, scientific, artistic, political; for the Mesoamericans, ethical, ontological, artistic, millenarian. The Greeks investigated the nature of matter, the Mesoamericans devoted themselves to questions of time, and the Christians and Muslims worried about the next life.

When the European and Mesoamerican civilizations clashed, they entered into the process of killing and wedding. The mind of Spain was still in the Middle Ages, in the clutches of God and Aristotle; the Mesoamerican mind was locked in the cycle of flowerings and destructions, in the hands of the gods. The only possible intellectual meeting ground of the two worlds lay in religion; all the rest, from the bedroom to the battlefield, was war.

Mesoamerican literature suffers the problem of attribution. It is difficult to find the names of the poets among the Nahuatl speakers, although some poems have been assigned to various princes of the Aztec world. No author is even suggested for the Popol Vuh, which is known as the "Maya Bible," and may actually have served such a purpose during the pre-Hispanic period. The single largest collection of "oral literature" was made by Fray Bernardino de Sahagún, and it was nearly lost to the world, because the

Catholic Church determined to get rid of it despite the fact that Fray Bernardino had in mind to get rid of the indigenous religion by first understanding it.

Luckily, the Church was not successful. There was no horror like Diego de Landa's burning of the Maya codices. What Sahagún left behind was not entirely uncorrupted. There are countless references to "Diós" in the manuscripts by him and the people who worked for him, transliterating, translating, and writing down in Latin script both the original spoken literature and the Spanish translation of it.

Approached as ethnography, the work of Sahagún and other priests is detailed, presumably accurate, well illustrated, and often difficult to fully comprehend. As with all literature out of our own time, what seems perfectly clear to us may not have been what was meant by the original speakers or (in the case of the Maya) writers. But we know something, and the something we know is often stirring or beautiful. The "Kay Nicte" in Maya, which means "Flower Song," is a poem about love and nature. When read aloud, it sets young Maya women to blushing. The "Story of the Tohueyno" is a bawdy, funny poem, with a grand melodramatic ending. The outlines of the story could have come from Chaucer or Boccaccio. Or it could have been an R-rated movie in our time, as the naked Tohuenyo conquers the heart of the king's daughter by dangling his "thing." The king, anxious to be rid of this lowlife and his "thing," sends the Tohueyno off to battle at the head of an army of hunchbacks, dwarfs, and other deformed people. The Tohueyno and his army of miscreants win the war, and the man with the "dangling thing" marries the king's daughter.

Other work by the Mesoamericans is not so sweet or funny. There is a great deal of speculation on questions of duration, both of the world and of the individual. The strain of millenarianism in the work may well be the best clue to the sudden disappearance of the entire populations of city-states. There is in it an almost overwhelming sense of despair about the fate of man. There is no heaven, no hell. There is an underworld, but it has no relation to the place imagined by Virgil or Dante. Nor is there ever a Beatrice or any other guide to the afterlife. The hero twins of the Popol Vuh travel together; Quetzalcoatl and most other heroes undertake their quests alone. The idea of twinning is everywhere in pre-Hispanic literature: the hero twins of the Maya, the Sun and the Morning Star of the Aztecs. The supreme god himself is named Two-God (Ometeotl) or god of duality.

The pre-Hispanic literature is often mournful, in the sense of mourning man's fate, but it is rich with heroes. Although there were no kings among the Aztecs, in the sense of an inherited throne, as there were among the Maya, entire city-states were given into the hands of one man. The mitigating forces were art and religion, the architect and the scribe for earthly posterity and the priests for the propitiation of the gods.

The gods had no human personalities like those of the Greeks, with the exception of Queztalcoatl. And while he saved man—that is, sacrificed his blood to resurrect the bones of man—there is no sense in which he saved man from sin, for there was no concept of sin in Mesoamerica. The Huehuehtlahtolli (Wisdom of the Elders) tells of a formalized system of behavior, as do the Bancroft Dialogues, but these works prescribe manners, largely by example; they do not offer divine punishment for offenses to custom.

All this makes for a literature of explanation, which is the function of premodern ("Neolithic" is not the proper term here) stories. The history of man explains his earthly situation, and the stories of the gods explain all phenomena that are outside the knowledge of humans and beyond their control. Among the Aztecs the literature took on definite forms. What we would call poems were divided into various categories, according to their content. And it is quite likely that they were spoken or performed with musical accompaniment. Among the Quiche (K'iche' is the modern spelling) Maya there were dance pageants, and fortunately one of them, Man of Rabinal (*Rabinal Achí*), has endured.[1] It is the story of a man who preferred a sacrificial death to betraying his city-state by joining the enemy. There is a similar story told by the Aztecs, indicating that the form may have been common across Mesoamerica, while the content distinguished each version.

The literature of Mesoamerica certainly goes far beyond what is generally termed folk literature. It includes, in separate categories, history, prayer, ontology, moral philosophy, etiquette, pageant, comedy, origin tales, and some hortatory works aimed at warriors. It is a significant world literature, and while it may not be "the foundations of heaven," it is surely the foundation of Mexico.

With the invasion, indigenous culture became a cut flower, pressed in the pages of the Florentine Codex of Sahagún, the undecipherable (at the time)

---

[1] The poet-translator Dennis Tedlock uses Quiché; the Guatemalan Maya poet Humberto Ak'bal prefers K'iche'.

Maya codices, incomprehensible (to the Spaniards) Raramurí rituals in the north, and the then lost Popol Vuh. But it was not to end. A second growth came up from the ashes, still in indigenous languages: the books of Chilam Balam, telling the history and culture of the Yucatán Peninsula; the first Christianized dramas, in which Jesus and the huey tlahtoani and Cortés all might participate; retellings of the life of Jesus in Nahua terms; the *Nican Mopohua*,[2] which tells the story of Juan Diego and the Virgin of Guadalupe. In the Christianized plays, poems, and histories, the task of the syncretizers bore fruit. For the Franciscans, it was the beginning of the end of native culture; later, for the Jesuits, it was the beginning of a new kind of Christianity. In both cases, the second growth was not so rich or beautiful as the first flowering.

A third growth began as early as the eighteenth century with the poems of Dzitbalche, a town in the state of Yucatán. These were tragic and beautiful works about subjects as varied as love and orphanhood. There is in them the sense of destruction and regeneration. But it was not only the Maya who began to write again. Work also came from the Mazatecs and Zapotecs and Nahuas. Poetry surfaced in dozens of indigenous languages. Some of it was romantic; other work was political or historical or biographical. Surprisingly little of it is angry; much more is concerned with love and nature. The writers are interested in sound, like Poe or Valéry or the serenaders and balladeers of oral literature. A Tzotzil novel has been written, and others in indigenous languages are in one state of completion or another at this writing. Writers like Natalio Hernández Xocoyotzin and Miguel Ángel May May have been appointed to federal or state government positions to nourish the languages and literatures of indigenous people. Miguel León-Portilla, historian and translator of indigenous literature, was president of the Colegio Nacional at the millennium.[3] Literature in indigenous languages in Mexico is thriving, but like small language groups everywhere, the native speakers and writers of Mexico live in an increasingly globalized and homogenized world; they will have to protect their treasure from the violence of necessity.

---

[2]The words of the title are Nahuatl and mean "Here is told," a common opening line for tales in Nahuatl.

[3]The National College is Mexico's version of the French Academy. Nothing like it exists in the United States. The position is not merely honorary in Mexico. Membership in the Colegio Nacional is limited to forty and includes a generous stipend.

ALTAMIRANO'S UTOPIA

Spanish language literature grew more slowly in New Spain. The seventeenth century belonged to Sigüenza y Góngora and Sor Juana and the struggle between science and religion. The eighteenth century saw the grand history of ancient Mexico by Clavijero, the Jesuit in exile. In the nineteenth century the literature of the struggle for autonomy and the War of Independence flourished alongside the romanticism of Guillermo Prieto and his Academia de Letrán. The academia gave powerful impetus to the writing of nationalistic literature. A government official, Ignacio M. Altamirano, born to indigenous parents in the state of Guerrero, led the movement, writing in virtually every form: journalism, poetry, criticism, stories, and novels.

Altamirano celebrated the jungles and beaches of his beloved Guerrero. He wrote of sun and shade and waves upon the beaches, of cane, cotton, alligators, jungle birds, mango trees with their gold and carmine apples, papayas, flowers that hang from the roofs in thousands of garlands. Then the slightly overheated lover of nature also wrote the most serious social novels, in which he attempted to find some meeting ground between the radical anticlericals of the Independence movement and the Church. His best-known work, "Christmas in the Mountains," as befits a true nationalist, is utopian.

Perhaps the most interesting aspect of Altamirano's work was his style. Along with Alfonso Reyes, he is considered one of Mexico's grand masters of style, or rather, he was until very recently, when a group of young writers in Mexico turned against nationalism, choosing Altamirano to represent what they thought should be avoided at all costs. Another of the nineteenth-century writers, Justo Sierra O'Reilly, produced the first Mexican historical novel, *La Hija del Judio* (The Jew's Daughter), describing the adventures of a former Spanish governor of Yucatán. He also fathered the historian and apologist for the cientificos, Justo Sierra Méndez.

WAR STORIES

Realism came to the Mexican novel at the end of the nineteenth and beginning of the twentieth century, more or less coinciding with the Porfiriato. Heriberto Frías, who was more a war correspondent than a novelist, has some historical importance because of his description of the Battle of

Tomochic. One of the interesting works of the school, *Los Parientes Ricos* (The Rich Parents), by Rafael Delgado, chronicles two families, one urban, the other rural, laying out the differences between classes and the cruelty of the middle class. The urban family invites the rural family to come live with them in the city and then proceeds to make life miserable for them.

The growing national dissatisfaction near the end of the Porfiriato drove many writers away from art and toward action; politics set the course for their work. Novels and poems continued to be written, but the period created a sense of urgency in the writers that the slower-moving influence of art could not accommodate. Mariano Azuela, a physician, had written a novel based on his experiences in a hospital, working mainly among the poor. When war broke out, he joined the Villistas as a physician and later wrote about what he saw in *Los de Abajo* (The Underdogs), one of the best novels of the period. Azuela was a writer of the kind of solid prose for which Alfonso Reyes is venerated in Mexico. He set down what he saw, no less and no more.

The civil wars did not leave much time for writing or reading, but the years following the end of large-scale hostilities produced a huge body of work—fiction, poetry, philosophy, criticism, journalism, some theater—and all in service of "the Revolution." Curiously, the one area that did not continue to hold the interest of the writers or their audiences was the philosophical revolution that had taken place, the turn away from positivism to a more spiritual, artistic view of human beings. It was overwhelmed by nationalism. Not only Vasconcelos but virtually all influential Mexicans agreed with Manuel Gamio's idea of nation building.

The civil wars were concluded. Everyone knew the country would survive the Cristeros and the occasional pronouncement of some self-proclaimed savior of Mexico. Invasion from the United States was no longer likely. The Monroe Doctrine, for all its imperialistic character, protected Mexico from another European invasion. At the same time, armed political revolution by the left or right would not be permitted by the United States. And democracy, with all its unwieldiness, did not affect the Mexican government, which enjoyed all the advantages and suffered all the flaws of a one-party system.

Literature, like the rest of the arts in Mexico during that long postwar period, depended on nationalist dreams and the Revolution for subject and soul. The Revolution was the true church, and art worshiped there. Works critical of the revolution may have been written, Orozco may have had his counterpart among the writers of the period, but the main theme was the Revolution of 1910, which became more and more glorious and less and less revolutionary with the passing years. Of the major novelists and biographers of the period, more than a few moved from "revolutionary" thinking to the hard political right, among them Vasconcelos and Martín Luis Guzmán, inventor of one of the versions of Pancho Villa. Guzmán, a member of the Ateneo de la Juventud in his youth, claimed to have known Villa well.

His *Memorias de Pancho Villa* was the best defense of the actions of General Villa and an interesting speculation on Villa's early life. Since then there have been many other books about Villa. Friedrich Katz wrote the now-standard biography. Luis and Adrián Aguirre Benavides, members of the family of generals who went from Villismo to fighting against Villa, wrote a memoir of the war. General Álvaro Obregón wrote another. Bitter works about Zapata came from the Carrancistas, including Gerardo Murillo (Dr. Atl).

Neither Zapata nor Villa had many supporters in the first years after the end of the civil wars.[4] As is the case in all wars, the winners were the heroes. Only very slowly and after Guzmán's *Memorias* did Villa become a hero. Diego Rivera's portrait of Zapata contributed to the change in his status, but Zapata still needed help from abroad, a fine biography by the American John Womack and a not so fine movie, *Viva Zapata!*, with a script by John Steinbeck. Womack took away Zapata's ability to speak Nahuatl, and then Steinbeck made him into a complete illiterate, the former a small and not indisputable oversight by a first-rate historian, the latter a cruel insult by a man whose novels were never kind or fair to Mexicans or Mexican-Americans.[5]

CONTEMPORARY POETS

The overwhelming nationalism of Mexican literature affected the poets as well as the novelists. Carlos Pellicer belonged to a group named and defined by a magazine, *The Contemporaries*, published in the late twenties and early thirties. Jaime Torres Bodet belonged to the same group. The Contemporáneos were purely Mexican, nationalists, Indianists, and talented. None of them had much luck with prose, but they could sing, and in

[4]Guzmán's *Memorias de Pancho Villa* (Austin: University of Texas Press, 1965) was not published until 1938, ten years after his *Águila y la Serpiente* (*Eagle and Serpent*, translated by Harriet de Onis [New York: Doubleday, 1965]) had established the author as a major figure in Mexican letters. The *Memorias* were a partial reconstruction by Guzmán, but generally accurate history.

[5]Movies about Villa abound; he has been portrayed by a series of unlikely castings, ranging from Wallace Beery to Yul Brynner, an ignominy that may atone for most of his sins.

the case of Pellicer, they could also laugh and speak of love. Pellicer had a grand design: He was deeply devoted to Mexico's indigenous past, which figured in his attempt to integrate all aspects of the world. In an interview with Mexican journalist Elena Poniatowska given late in his life, he spoke reverently of the meaning for him of the work of Father Ángel María Garibay K. and Miguel León-Portilla, citing the latter's *Aztec Thought and Culture* and his brief biographies accompanying translations of the works of *Thirteen Aztec Poets*.[6]

Among Pellicer's books were *Piedra de Sacrificios* (Sacrifical Stone) and other poems and *Hora de Junio* (June Hour), both of which are often quoted, anthologized, remembered. In "Horas de Junio," he gave each hour a different character, as in these stanzas. (It is useful to remember when reading Pellicer that he was born in Tabasco, where June can be stifling, hot and humid in the magnificent jungle, and a bit of shade or shadow is always welcome.)

> June gave me voice, the silent music
> of quieting a concern.
> June now brings, like the wind,
> hope most sweet and deliberate.
> Through my voice I produced the clean rose,
> the unique, eternal rose of the moment.
> Love did not capture her, the wind brought her,
> and the idle soul was merry.
>
> The fruits of my voice said in this way,
> and very privately, that in the year of
> the death of days, some days
> lived in the shade of this song.
> (Here, the voice breaks and the dread
> of loneliness fills the days.)[7]

In "Piedra de Sacrificios," he spoke of "an insolent noise that/ chills the sweet Mexican song," and of his dreams of eagle and jaguar princes on the hunt. Yet he worked within the Vasconcelos plan to educate Mexico through the arts as well as rural schools, and at the time he too wanted a single, Spanish-speaking nation.

---

[6]The attribution of poems to various poets is not quite certain, although the question does not detract from either the biographies or the poems themselves.

[7]These stanzas are from "Horas de Junio," one of the poems in the collection *Hora de Junio*.

HIGH STYLE

Alfonso Reyes, who was not a member of the same group as Pellicer, spent his childhood and early youth in the labyrinth of bargains and betrayals of Mexican politics. His father, General Bernardo Reyes, was close to Porfirio Díaz and a likely choice to succeed him, had the dictator resigned earlier or died. After Madero was elected, Reyes turned against the government and prepared to take charge himself. For his ambitions he was arrested and imprisoned. At the start of civil war in the streets, the Ten Tragic Days, the general was released from prison by forces hostile to Madero and given troops to command. On the first day of his last battle General Reyes was killed while trying to storm the gates of the National Palace.

The death of the general or an intimation of it appears in the most inventive story written by his son, Alfonso, who lived in Mexico City as a student and was a member of the Ateneo de la Juventud. Like the other members of the Ateneo, he opposed the cientificos who had surrounded Díaz and stayed on in the Madero administration. But Reyes must have been torn between opposition to the cientificos and love for his father. In an essay, "Thoughts on the Ninth of February" (the day on which his father was killed), written long after the death of the general, he spoke of "the greatest romantic" and ended with a brief description of the machine guns cutting him down. It is a touching piece, written in the lucid style for which Reyes was already quite famous. And it is not political, for that was not of interest to the writer then or ever during his long career.

By 1912 the young man, who eventually grew into baronial physical proportions, had written a story, "La Cena" (The Dinner), that may have been the beginning of modern literature in Mexico.[8] Another aspect of the story, and equally important, comes in its understanding of time. Although Reyes was a norteño, born in Monterrey, the story has a Mesoamerican sense of time, its directions, and its relation to space.[9]

---

[8]The story was not published until 1920. The scene about the portrait of the father of the writer may have been added after the death of the general in 1913.

[9]In Mesoamerican thinking, the gods escape time or live outside the ordinary movement of time. León-Portilla devoted a play, *The Flight of Quetzalcoatl*, to this theory.

The Mesoamerican view of time is similar to Newton's idea of past and future as two sides of an equation. Since an equation moves in both directions, time may also go backward or forward. Both concepts are relatively difficult to grasp, but give a good idea of the quality and complexity of Mesoamerican thinking.

The Reyes story begins: "I had to hasten across unknown streets. The end of my journey seemed to run ahead of my steps, and the appointed hour was beating in the public clocks. The streets were lonely. . . . I ran, provoked by a superstitious feeling about the hour. . . ."

He becomes frantic, hoping that by running through the streets, he will arrive on time. Soon he hears the sound of nine bells and a "a metallic chill came upon my epidermis."

The narrator, who we soon find out is a writer, one Alfonso, thinks of the reason for his appointment. He has been invited to dinner by two sisters whom he has never met. When he finally arrives, they invite him into their plain house, where he sees three Japanese masks on the wall and notes the sparse furnishings, which have the "cold luxury of things from New York."

The women are anguished, their mouths tremble, but they manage smiles, yet look beyond him, over his head. He describes the conversation as "a colloquy of sighs." They go out into the garden. A sister describes the plants; he thinks he hears her speak of flowers that bite and flowers that kiss. Alfonso, overcome by weariness and "the Chablis," dozes off. He awakens again to hear them speak of an artillery officer, a captain.

Somewhere in the house a window is opened, and a breeze blows out the candles. In the darkness the faces of the sisters are illuminated. Then he is taken from the garden, upside down, carried like an invalid. He finds leaves in his hair. He comes upon a picture of a soldier, not of Alfonso, but like him, almost a mirroring of his own face. "I was like a caricature of this painting." The painting falls from his hands, "And the two women [looked] at me with mock pity."

He hears a sound, "like a crystal spider dashed against the floor," and runs out into unknown streets, finally arriving at the door of his own house, where he hears the sounds of nine bells. "There were leaves upon my head, and in my buttonhole a little flower that I did not cut." And that is the end of the story.

Does the captain represent his dead father, General Reyes? Probably. The style, even in these brief bits, and translated, has the feeling of Poe or someone later. There is none of the tone of the works of earlier times in Mexico. If there is a timeline in literature that must be minded, Reyes appears after Poe and before Borges, at about the time of Valéry. In Spanish the prose has a distant sound, like a very slight echo, related to Poe by sound and to Borges by content. A similar sound appears eighty-five years later in *Diorama*, a novel by the Mexican postmodern writer Vicente Herrasti.

Yet neither of these connections reaches the deepest aspect of the story. It is Mexican. Reyes has bid good-bye to New Spain, to Cervantes and even to Sor Juana; he is Mexican. Only four or five years later he completed his major work about the indigenous world, *Visión de Anáhuac*. But "La Cena" was already a work rooted in Mesoamerica, all about time and space and the possibility of escaping from time into Time. It is difficult to imagine anyone, in 1912, who could have written such a story without strong Mesoamerican influence. "La Cena" is not science fiction, but fiction, so particular to place and culture that it is in itself outside time.

Reyes did not stop with the story or his book about Anáhuac. He wrote in every form on virtually every subject. He knew classical European literature and Daniel G. Brinton's early translations of Mesoamerican works, as well as the Molina dictionary of the Nahuatl language. He served in the diplomatic corps, like many Mexican literary men before and after him, but it appears that he mostly wrote and wrote and wrote. His collected works, published by Fondo de Cultura Económica, fill twenty-five volumes. Very little of this great output has been translated into English, and it is probably too late for that. His story "La Cena" was out of its time, but that of course would have suited the Alfonso of the dinner and his author. It was not realism, but it was not magical either; the issues were Mesoamerican, time and space; no one had green hair as in the potboilers of Isabel Allende, although the faces of the women did glow in the dark. The genius of the next Mexican reality would not appear until 1955.

Between the style of Reyes and the magic of Rulfo came the powerful realism of José Revueltas. The novelist was part of a trio of brothers who were all among the most accomplished Mexicans of their time, each in his own field: Fermín was a muralist, and Silvestre was a composer. José, who apportioned his life equally between politics and literature, suffered the repressions of the post-Cárdenas era in Mexico. Carlos Monsiváis lists his characters as "political prisoners, campesinos, repentant or obedient militant communists, street people, prostitutes, teachers persecuted by a fanatical mob." It is a good list, and Monsiváis is clearly admiring of Revueltas, in whose work he finds echoes of Dostoyevsky, Malraux, and Faulkner.

As a novelist and as a political man Revueltas lived on the edge, always critical in his politics, always seeking something new, some new form, some new kind of character, anything to express his distaste for the class structure that had grown up in Mexico. His life was difficult; he poured out novels and tracts with equal enthusiasm; he suffered physical illness as well as persecution by a government that took its economics from the soft left and its politics from the hard right. He saw a dark life in Mexico, not merely a dark side of life. As it made him the enemy of the government, it also made him the darling of the young leftists. The subject matter of his work during the twenty-five years of his greatest productivity, 1939 to 1964 was not new; it had been covered more than twenty years earlier, in the almost documentary descriptions of class differences, but José Revueltas was the first Mexican to bring modern stylistic techniques to the problems of a slightly postcolonial society.

HOME IN COMALA

Alfonso Reyes had made a great start on the incorporation of Mexican thinking into a modern story, but the story did not have any successors among his works, which were examples of brilliant style in the service of relatively unimportant thoughts. *Pedro Páramo* was the next step in Mexican literature. With that novel Rulfo freed Latin American literature from the bonds of conventional reality. He wrote about indigenous people, thought about them, photographed them, worked with them, mainly in his native Jalisco, but he was not himself indigenous; he was a fair-skinned man, balding as he aged, quiet, not public, never public, although not a recluse. In the last years of his life (he died in 1986) he became the center of speculation in the Mexican literary world. Why had he not written more? Why had he been silent since publishing his one and only novel? The speculation took many forms: cruel, sweet, or simply ignorant. There were complaints about his work from people who wanted something lighter, nicer. One Mexican critic, Felipe Garrido, was so concerned by such attacks he wrote an essay about Rulfo's smile, pointing out amusing scenes in *Pedro Páramo* and several stories. Others were not so kind. After Rulfo had entered into his thirty years of silence as a writer, there were rumors that he was a drunk or that he had nothing left to say or that he really did not know anything about indigenous people in Jalisco.

Some said he mumbled when he spoke; others carried on about his timidity. Critics, especially young ones, do not generally have much interest in lifting up the careers of older writers; "The king must die" is the battle cry of infants. So it was with Rulfo. Some said, "He writes too little," while others said, "He writes too simply, with no passion; it's boring." Rulfo's son said that writing, even a letter, was very difficult for him.[10] One critic, Héctor Manjarrez, who had talked with Rulfo, collected all the accusations and ended up saying that when he left Rulfo for the last time, he felt like crying. Perhaps he did not realize what he was saying, for pity is surely the harshest criticism of all.

The homages to Rulfo after his death were eloquent and generous: Fuentes, Paz, Poniatowska, García Márquez, Monsiváis, and Benítez, who wrote about his conversations with Rulfo. If there was ever any doubt about the origin of magical realism or the cyclical character of Mexico, including its literature, Rulfo put it to rest in the interview with Benítez. He said, "I like the ancient chronicles [of Mexico] because of what they taught me and because they are written in a very clear, very fresh, very spontaneous style." And after some conversation about another writer, he went on, "I have read almost all the chronicles by the friars and other travelers, the letter writers, the tales of the New Spain. What we call magical realism today originated there."[11]

In *Pedro Páramo*[12] the dead speak. There are noises, voices, murmurs. One of the characters, Dorotea, is addressed as Doroteo, which was the baptismal name of the man who later called himself Pancho Villa. Villistas appear in the novel. Those who die fall to pieces, like a pile of stones. Melquiades is the name of one of the characters, and curiously there is a Melquiades who appears in a García Márquez novel, an homage to Rulfo, as the Colombian Nobelist's colonel is an homage to Fuentes, and his rain of butterflies to the Cuban Alejo Carpentier. The return, the very concept of nostalgia belongs to Homer, but it is also the journey of the Morning Star, the hero twins, the Chichimecas who find the promised land where the nopal plant stands. In Rulfo's novel, the narrator returns to the place called Comala[13] to seek the past or the present, to find Pedro Páramo, who may be everyone's father. Rulfo works a basic myth, Telemachus in America, magical realism, universal magic; the novel becomes a Mexican monument quickly built by a pale young man who knows his native Jalisco down to the stone.

---

[10]On the other hand, Rulfo told Fernando Benítez that he wrote his novel in four weeks and each of his stories in a day.

[11]The Spanish words he used for "magical realism" were *real maravilloso*.

[12]A *páramo* is a high, parched plain.

[13]Tortillas, the Mexican staff of life, are cooked on a *comal*.

The climate of Comala is so dry and so hot during the summer that a man tells the narrator a joke: When people from Comala die and go to hell, they ask to be allowed to go back to earth for a few moments to fetch a blanket. It was the Jalisco Rulfo knew. He claimed to know everything about Jalisco, and it may be that he did. Surely, he knew everything about Mexico, from the first planting of corn to the grim aftermath of a decade of civil war to the corruption of the postwar government. No Mexican novel before *Pedro Páramo* had investigated the dreams that rose from the countryside; nothing had been so thoroughly imagined in Mexico since the fall of Tenochtitlán in 1521. The news of the novel was the novel itself, the genius of the form.

KILLING THE NEWS

After Rulfo, there were many writers in Mexico. The sensual Chiapanecan poet Jaime Sabines found a huge and adoring audience. Translations of writing or works of the oral tradition from the pre-Hispanic period improved. Paco Taibo II wrote detective novels and worked as a publicist for Cuauhtémoc Cárdenas during the election of 2000. Homero Aridjis wrote poetry and fiction, represented Mexico in international writers' groups, and tried desperately to preserve the environment of his beloved land. These were all talented writers and worth reading, but in the last half of the twentieth century in Mexico several overshadowing figures emerged: in history, León-Portilla and Cosío Villegas; in journalism, the publisher and editors and writers of Alejandro Junco's newspapers in Monterrey, Mexico City, and Guadalajara. Junco first got into trouble by criticizing the Echeverría government in 1974 in *El Norte*, his Monterrey flagship newspaper. More trouble came in 1985, when he published articles about voting fraud in the northern city. He took his newspaper business to Mexico City under the name *Reforma*, and met a new kind of resistance from the party-government. The PRI, which he opposed, convinced the newsstand vendors in the city not to sell the paper. Junco had a newspaper, no official censorship, but no way to get the paper to readers. He responded by starting his own distribution system.

Junco's newspapers have a distinctively North American look. He was educated at the University of Texas, and when he became serious about changing the nature of journalism in Mexico, he hired his former journalism professor, Mary Gardner, to train his staff. Junco supported Vicente Fox in the 2000 election and keeps close to the PAN view of the country and the world. In no small part because of his daring, the popular Mexican press was liberated from PRI domination and the Mexican presidency ceased to deal with the press only through speeches, carefully scripted interviews, and press releases and began to hold press conferences at which the president had to answer difficult questions. It may also be true that Ernesto Zedillo gave way rather easily to the idea of a free press.

The northern border with California has produced a group of journalists, almost all of them working for local weekly newspapers, who write about illegal drugs. Of these, at least twenty-five and perhaps twice that number have been kidnapped, beaten, and in several instances murdered. Benjamín Flores González, who ran a little newspaper he called *La Prensa* (The Press), was murdered. The most celebrated case did not result in the death of the journalist, but Jesús Blancornelas was wounded, and his bodyguard and one of the assassins were killed, in a gun battle on the street in Tijuana. Blancornelas survived and continues to publish his newspaper.

For years Blancornelas published a page in every issue of the newspaper accusing Jorge Hank Rhon, the son of one of Mexico's richest and most powerful members of the PRI, of complicity in the killing of Blancornelas's partner and cofounder of the paper. According to Blancornelas, Hank's bodyguard did the killing. The war between the drug dealers, their pals, and the newspaperman went on for years. Blancornelas's lawyer and accountant were murdered. But the Arellano Félix family drug cartel, one of Blancornelas's targets, has not fared so well either. The body of one brother, reputed to be the enforcer, was found dead and moldering in 2002. Another, probably the boss of the cartel, was arrested in the same year. Expectations on the part of the press and the government were that the deaths and arrests of the Arellano Félix brothers would lead to a gang war for control of the drug cartel. Blancornelas was sure to report on the war for as long as his bodyguards could protect him.

In nonfiction beyond daily or weekly journalism, Elena Poniatowska took the role occupied by Studs Terkel in the United States, publishing book after book of interviews. She preferred famous people of all sorts, from the actress María Rojo to the composer and conductor Carlos Chávez, who referred to her during the interviews as *criatura* [child]. The most extraordinary work of her career was her carefully done set of interviews about the 1968 Tlatelolco Massacre. By the beginning of the new century, as more information came out of government files and the memories of the dying participants, it appeared that if anything, Poniatowska's interviews understated the extent of the massacre, the mistreatment of the jailed student leaders, and the complicity of the government at the highest levels. Almost thirty-five years after the massacre, it is still not clear who gave the orders for the slaughter: President Díaz Ordaz or his secretary of the interior, Luis Echeverría.

The other writer of nonfiction whose work has emerged as both popular and influential is the conservative Enrique Krauze. He came to prominence as the student of two of Mexico's most famous writers, Cosío Villegas and Octavio Paz. In the later years of Paz's life, Krauze attended to him as an acolyte, and he could hardly have done better in choosing a mentor, although Paz had by then become an all but fanatical cold warrior and the enemy of anyone who could tolerate ambiguity on the subject of communism.[14] Krauze described his own politics as classically liberal, following Cosío Villegas, although his work takes a conservative stance on all issues, including the war in Iraq. Krauze wanted Mexico's United Nations delegate in the Security Council to vote with the United States. Although he is not yet old, Krauze's views moderated slightly with the years, and he became Mexico's most respected conservative writer.

In general cultural criticism, Carlos Monsiváis simply owns the field. The misfortune of a writer of his extraordinary talent is that his topicality and brilliant Mexicanidad limit his audience almost entirely to Mexico. His essays on virtually every aspect of Mexican culture are usually charming, always original, to the left of the Mexican center, astonishingly well informed, and stylistically unique, if sometimes difficult. No writer in American newspapers has the literary wit of this columnist in *La Jornada*, the slightly left-of-center daily often said to be the UNAM's newspaper.

Monsiváis employs a huge vocabulary, and he sometimes indulges a taste for arcane language and neologisms, which keeps his readers alert. The problem of one voice dominating the field is that it leaves the rest of the cultural critics in relative silence, in much the same way that the *New York*

---

[14]Krauze, who had spent more than two decades in daily communication with Octavio Paz, wrote a loving obituary of him, which appeared in English in the *New York Review of Books*, May 28, 1998. He said of his mentor, "Paz converted Mexico into a sacred text that cried out to be deciphered, to be revealed. He was a miner and an alchemist of Mexican identity."

Times shouts down other voices in the culture by the dominance of its voice. The good fortune, in the case of Monsiváis, is that he can be careful, choosing to write about what interests him and what he knows; he does not have to fill hundreds of columns every day or satisfy his stockholders. But over the years it is character that has won out as his most beloved offering to his readers. Monsiváis is not doctrinaire; he writes what he sees and says what he thinks based on what he has seen.

Alongside the looming figure of Monsiváis, Mexico has produced hundreds of essayists. A collection of literary essays by writers born after 1920 includes fifty different writers, not one of them without talent and many, including Enrique Serna, Silvia Molina, Alberto Ruy Sánchez, Sergio Pitol, and Juan Villoro, to mention but a few, whose work is extraordinary.

THE LABYRINTHINE

Two men, however, have dominated Mexican letters for the last half century, Octavio Paz (1914–1998) and Carlos Fuentes (1928–). One received the Nobel Prize for Literature, and the other is an annual candidate for the prize. Given the literate population of Mexico at the time of their birth (less than ten million), the production of two writers of their caliber, while not quite a repetition of the golden age of Athens, is extraordinary. Paz was born in Mixcoac (now part of Mexico City south of Tacubaya), educated at the UNAM, and took up writing early in life. Although he was not so prolific as Reyes, his body of work is as wide-ranging; his poetry is more affecting, his philosophy at a far more sophisticated level, and his politics at a different, much higher level of complexity. Like Reyes, Paz served in the Mexican diplomatic corps. His stay in India deeply affected his art and philosophy, and he wrote about it in both prose and poetry, but his major work is about Mexico and Mexicans.

Unlike most North American poets and novelists of the last part of the twentieth century, men and women who lived in and around the academy, Paz belonged to an earlier generation of writers who were engaged, willing to act in the world, like the British novelists and poets of World War I, even more like Camus, who edited *Combat*, the French underground newspaper during the German occupation of France. Along with engaged writers from around the world, Paz went to Spain to oppose Franco and the Fascists. And when he returned, he was among many Mexicans who had survived the

Spanish Civil War and took their battered idealism home with them after the defeat of the Republic.

In combination with an influx of Europeans, mainly Spanish leftists and Jews fleeing the Nazis, these veterans of the opposition to fascism infused Mexican cultural life with a new energy. Unlike Diego Rivera, who stayed out of Mexico during the turbulence of 1910–1920, Octavio Paz had put himself in the middle of the civil war of his time. Even after that, instead of retiring to the academic life, he started magazines, mentored young writers, criticized liberal capitalism, and ended up a cold warrior. No writer protested the Tlatelolco Massacre of 1968 more openly and firmly than Octavio Paz. He called the aggression of the government a form of regression, separating it from the response of other governments to the student unrest of 1968. Then, in a turn he might later have regretted, he compared their savagery with the behavior of the Aztecs.

He was an exceedingly complex man who treasured eros, art, thought, and democracy, perhaps in that order. Toward the end of his life he turned cranky, whining, writing *Itinerary*[15] about his critics on the left. He sent the young Enrique Krauze out to conduct his war on Carlos Fuentes, who had remained on the left, although not a Communist. The attack was not pretty or even reasonable: Paz/Krauze claimed Fuentes was not a true Mexican, because his father had been a diplomat in Washington, D.C., where Fuentes spent much of his early life and adolescence. Krauze said very clearly that Fuentes lacked Mexicanidad, which is a profound insult and, in the case of Fuentes, contrary to much of what he has said and done during a long life. Bitterness ensued, as could be expected. Paz had engineered a rift in Mexican letters that did not heal while he lived and will not heal now, because so much of it remains in print.

Every person of course has a natural right to play the fool, and Paz abused that right far less than most. His early work was spectacular. Having spent some time teaching in Los Angeles, he observed the *pachucos* (zoot suiters) and *pochos* (Mexicans in the United States; the word is now obsolete) and thought about Mexico. In 1950 the young professor published a collection of essays, *The Labyrinth of Solitude*. It was a brilliant and stylish display of mind. The book included the often quoted essay that delved into the connections among the story of La Malinche, the verb *chingar* (to rape, etc.), machismo, and the Mexican character. It was a ballet rarely equaled in the

---

[15]A brief collection of essays, translated by Jason Wilson (Orlando, Fla.: Harcourt, 1999).

musicality of the language and the choreography of the thinking, his first of many dances with words.

In 1970 he published *Posdata*, wisely updating his views of Mexico, which had undergone remarkable changes in twenty years, as had Paz himself, who resigned his post as Mexican ambassador to India to protest the killings in Tlatelolco. In 1979 he agreed to a conversation with Claude Fell, which was published as a *Return to the Labyrinth of Solitude*. He was sixty-five years old, erudite, accomplished, and famous. He spoke with Fell of the concept of myth, reminding him of the French structuralist anthropologist Claude Lévi-Strauss's idea that the decipherment of one myth is the creation of another. He applied the notion to *The Labyrinth of Solitude*, which he said attempted to "describe and comprehend certain myths" but created another, because it was a work of literature.

His poetry was widely read and always admired, but there is no one poem that every student at the UNAM seems to know, and it is Jaime Sabines rather than Paz whose poetry touched the hearts of Mexicans. Paz lived and wrote in a less accessible, less lyrical world. Of all his many poems, *Piedra del Sol* (*Sunstone*) is perhaps the best known. It is a long poem, and there is an unfortunate English translation by Muriel Rukeyser that is so "free" and far from the original it appears, in places, to have been written by a different person.

In photographs, the dour face with which he must have greeted such license is as often reproduced as a smiling Paz. The smile appears less comfortable for him; it weakens his chin and makes him seem supercilious. The other face is more memorable, more fitting. The great head, with its thick pile of hair and jowls of discontent, the eyes that contain black electricity, made him into a Roman or Mexica sage, a Caesar or *tlahtoani* of the mind, intimidating, even in old age, after a fire took his papers, when he was dying. When Octavio Paz spoke, people listened, but it was not responsive reading, there was no chorus singing, never that. He spoke; they listened.

One does not argue with Paz. It is better to hum an agreeable accompaniment to his poems while reading them. The same can be done with his prose, which is often as moving and richly written as his poetry. A pilgrim of the mind, mercurial, skeptical, a cool man who said he loved eros above all, Paz ventured into many fields. He saw nihilism where there was only pain, masks when there was only the hope of salvation from an impossible life. He pleased foreigners with such views of Mexicans; some Mexicans were not so sure he was correct. Although he loved eros most, he lived the critical life. He hated Stalinism, Maoism, and the market economy. He was not a salesman.

His grandfather had written the first Mexican novel with an indigenous theme; the family had been Zapatista when Zapata still lived, and they had fled to Los Angeles until it was safe to return. Ironically, Paz, like Fuentes, was accused of being a gringo by other Mexicans, for he came home to Mexico knowing English. Like Vasconcelos and Reyes, he was a universalist. He defended the Contemporáneos, who were accused of caring more for foreigners than for Mexico and Mexicans. India fascinated him, as did structuralism, existentialism, nihilism, and virtually every other idea of his time. In the end it is the Mexican work that will last. In 1990 he was awarded the Nobel Prize for Literature; in that moment he became officially a Mexican for the world. His acceptance speech ended with speculations on time, as befit a universal literary man or a priest of the classic period Maya.

A MODEL NOVELIST

During the long career of Paz, there were of course other Mexican writers. Rosario Castellanos wrote about indigenous people in Chiapas. José Emilio Pacheco wove fragments together in dark, bitterly ironic fictions. Juan García Ponce, who was often praised by Octavio Paz, produced a flood of novels, usually erotic, always protesting existing social mores, which he understood as the role of the artist. He effected no great change in form or style. His work was often compared with that of Robert Musil, but it was not overwhelming in a time dominated largely by Paz, Rulfo, and Fuentes. Rulfo, despite his small output, may have been the most important Mexican writer, but the best known is the still-dashing (in his mid-seventies) and multifaceted Carlos Fuentes. There has never been a Latin American writer who caught the fancy of the world so much as Fuentes. Neruda is beloved, as is García Márquez; Cortázar is studied, Gabriela Mistral is not, Asturias is still read with pleasure, Borges lives on, Rulfo is venerated, and Paz is admired, but Carlos Fuentes occupies a unique place: He is the novelist as the world would have the novelist be.

Fuentes entered the literary world with a story about a Chac Mool, a rain god, always seen reclining, his face turned toward the viewer, on his belly a little place for offerings, perhaps of hearts, perhaps of frogs. In the Fuentes story, the Chac Mool comes to life, a golem in Mexico, an old story and a new kind of telling, Mexican and universal, but not either so Mexican or so universal as the maturing novelist would become. A few years after the story,

Fuentes published *La Región Más Transparente*, known in English as *Where the Air Is Clear*. The irony of the title grew with the years, as the air over Mexico City turned yellow-brown, more foul than the air over Los Angeles and almost as murderous as the sulfurous air of Chinese industrial cities. The novel sprang into the world, an instant success. At the age of thirty, Fuentes had produced the first modern Mexican novel. Readers worldwide could at last find their way into the mystery of Mexico. Fuentes gave them the moment, the history, the middle class, questions of economics, and love, and he did it all in prose that could not catch its breath. Sentences went on for pages, often made up of lists of people, places, ideas intermingled to converge in the mind of the reader as one image, fractionated, held together only by the page itself. The novel, like Mexico, was light broken into parts by the prisms of three competing cultures: Spanish, indigenous, and universalist.[16]

Although *Where the Air Is Clear* presented itself as a modern novel, it also belonged to the Mexican penchant for nationalism, seeking to do what Vasconcelos and Gamio had advised, but not in quite the same way. There was, in Fuentes, even then a sense—although still vague and only underlying—of a pluralistic Mexico, which may have been the most modern of all the aspects of the novel. The literary modernism had roots in both the United States and Europe. He had read widely, and his fluency in English must have exposed him more successfully to the moderns. His nationalism probably grew out of several sources: his father's position in the diplomatic service and the nationalistic view it required, his family in Mexico, and his upbringing largely outside Mexico, which, he said many times, gave him a strong sense of otherness and a desire for the comforting bosom of language and home. Like Paz, the experience of growing up outside Mexico made of him both a universal man and a nationalist.

Like Paz, he loved his country with an open-eyed embrace, his critical sense sharpened by the constant battle between the polarities inside every Mexican. For Paz, who spoke the philosophical language of the Europe of his time, there were always "negations" to be considered. In the Hegelian ideas that drove much Mexican thinking of the time, the indigenous and invading people were the thesis and antithesis. The question before every artist

---

[16]Later, in *Terra Nostra*, Fuentes broke the Spanish culture down further, including Jews and Moors, as well as Christians. He also included African culture and its effect on the mestizaje.

was to decide which was the thesis, to locate his or her birth mother. Paz wrote *Sunstone* and *Eagle or Sun?*; Fuentes began with *Chac Mool*, wrote *Burnt Water, Terra Nostra,* and *Aura.* In both writers conflict between the cultures rages, and in Paz another, India, appears.

Born fourteen years after Paz, Fuentes had no experience of expulsion because of the civil wars. He was a child of the most politically and economically revolutionary period in Mexican history, the sexenio of Tata Lázaro. Fuentes often spoke of his awareness of the feelings of Americans after the oil expropriation. He said it made him feel his Mexicanidad more powerfully than ever. He was fourteen years younger, but an entire generation separate from Paz; Fuentes was eight years old at the height of the Spanish Civil War, when Paz went to Spain. He came to his maturity during the beginning of the Mexican Miracle and enjoyed his rise to prominence during that period. Paz saw the death of the republic in Spain; Fuentes saw the most hopeful period in Mexican history, a moment when cynicism had become a form of charm, a golden age of *cumbias* and boleros, when the *danzón* was outlawed in parts of Latin America because of the erotic character of the dance. The characters in *Where the Air Is Clear* argue economic policy, love, and history. Scenes from the Battle of Celaya, where Obregón's Yaquis with fixed bayonets stood in their places in the trenches of the muddied field and destroyed Villa's cavalry, set something like a time of birth for the novel, and a list of over 120 names in Mexican history begins on the first page of the last chapter of the book. Words poured out of Fuentes at a rate equaled only by Cantinflas, but the method of the comic's criticism was incomprehensibility, and the method of the novelist was clarification.

With the success of that novel, followed only four years later by *The Death of Artemio Cruz,* Fuentes had excited readers around the world. In the new novel an old warrior lay dying, rehearsing the days of his life. It had not been a good life. Once a revolutionary, with ideals, he has grown corrupt and lazy, and moreover, he had corrupted others. The form of a fiction related by a dead or dying person had given great latitude to other novelists—Broch and, closer to home in Mexico, Rulfo—and Fuentes used the structure in unsentimental, almost brutal fashion to assail the flaws in the spoils system that had beset Mexico after the fall of the Porfiriato. It was unforgettable storytelling, nationalism through criticism, a patriotic declaration of war on the history of his own country via the novel. For Mexican literature it was also an event in form, the first novel to employ stream of consciousness to tell a story. Fuentes had now broken through the old styles in both form and content. He was not yet forty years old, and his place in Mexican literary history was assured.

It was precisely the time for the critics to investigate the career of the still-young man who had become Mexico's breakthrough novelist. To make matters worse in the world of literary jealousies, Fuentes looked like a matinee idol and married a movie actress. The rich period of Latin America letters, the "BOOM," sprang from him, more than Paz, more than Rulfo, more than anyone but Cortázar and García Márquez. No Mexican writer, not even the Nobelist Paz, had such influence or reputation. Like the muralists, Tamayo, and Toledo, who had brought Mexico into prominence in the plastic arts, Fuentes brought Mexico into the literary world. He was prolific and popular; he could be as difficult as his modernist antecedents, as businesslike as Balzac, and more adventurous than any Mexican writer before him as he dared the world to read his literary history of everything connected to Mexico, his compendious and poetic *Terra Nostra*.

To some readers *Terra Nostra* was a monumental failure; to others his greatest success. It made little difference to the critics. They bit him, drawing a little blood here, a little there. Mexican literary criticism has a vicious streak. Academics in Mexico must produce vast amounts of work to maintain their bonus status in the university system. Publish or perish is about careers in the U.S. academic world; in Mexico the government keeps score, noting the number of published articles and books, the number of conferences attended. Those at the level of *investigador* (researcher 1, 2, or 3), who meet the minimum requirements receive bonuses of close to 100 percent of their salaries. Few people eligible for the bonus do not give their all to earn it, meaning the amount of inconsequential work published by academics in Mexico is as great per person as anywhere in the world, perhaps greater. On rare occasions a tenured professor in the United States has been known either to devote full time and effort to teaching or to vegetate. Both are considered crimes, but neither is punishable by starvation. In Mexico, publications have the flavor of food and drink. The idiom for producing a large volume of inconsequential work in Spanish is "making sausages."[17]

As his prominence increased, the criticism of Fuentes increased: He was not really a Mexican. He wrote for tourists. He wrote like a tourist. *A Change of Skin* was an international failure, thus a Mexican failure. He was universal. He spent too much time with celebrities. He was a celebrity. He wrote in

[17] *Hacer salchichas.*

too many different styles. Finally, as he grew older, one young critic said, as young critics in their foolishness must, he was repeating himself. Much of the criticism was senseless, sausages. He was too far left for some, too conservative for others. When he resigned his ambassadorial post to protest the appointment of Díaz Ordaz as Mexico's ambassador to Spain, some said his resignation came too late; after what Díaz Ordaz did in 1968 no Mexican should have served in a government post. Meanwhile, the United States refused to give Fuentes a visa. It was an archetypal literary life of the time, but not unusual in its complications; the best of his contemporaries, García Márquez to Arthur Miller, had endured similar problems.

And yes, of course, some of his novels were better than others, and he did enjoy celebrity. No Mexican writer, with the possible exception of José Revueltas, who was attacked during the last decades of his life by both the Mexican government and the Communist Party, had so interesting a life as Fuentes. Revueltas lived in a kind of public tragedy, while Fuentes lived a private one: His only son suffered from hemophilia. The writer with the charming wife, the journalist Sylvia Lemus, always the great conversationalist, daring to attack the Reagan administration for its Central American policy in a speech to the graduating students at Harvard, knew the promise of darkness.

He can also laugh. In 2001, Carlos Abascal, the ultraconservative secretary of labor in the Fox cabinet, attacked Fuentes's short novel *Aura* as pornographic, an affront to all good Catholics, especially the young. The Mexican newspapers put the story on the front page. Abascal had found out that a teacher in a convent school attended by the secretary's daughter had assigned the book. The secretary demanded the teacher's dismissal. The teacher was fired. The story played on. The book became a great best seller, and Fuentes, rather than complain, told the press he was so grateful to Abascal for the sales promotion he thought he should give the secretary at least 10 percent of his royalties.

Fuentes was not laughing when he supported the Zapatistas in their demands before the Mexican Congress. Nor did it take long before the novelist who had greeted the election of Vicente Fox as "a breath of fresh air" began to question the actions of the government. The détente between writers and the government after the defeat of the PRI did not last long. In a democratic society, writers had a role to play. Fuentes and Miguel León-Portilla, who engaged in public argument with President Fox over his treatment of indigenous people, were Mexico's *grandes,* and both men took the role seriously. Fox, unlike many past Mexican presidents, did not retaliate against his critics; rather, he appeared to be interested in what they said, although not convinced by them. Mexico had changed. The role of the writer had changed.

As one looks back at the long and far from completed career of Carlos Fuentes, the question that has dogged him for most of his writing life begins to be answerable. Is Carlos Fuentes Mexican, or is he a kind of tourist, peeking into Mexico to find material? The answer comes from the work. He began with a story that might have had antecedents in Alfonso Reyes and the rain god Chac and then published the first modernist Mexican novel. Next, he introduced stream of consciousness writing to the Mexican novel. *Terra Nostra* was a third form, *A Change of Skin* another; *The Hydra Head* came in the form of a mystery; *Aura* was gothic in tone and Mesoamerican in form; *The Old Gringo* spoke through the minds of two cultures and characters of two generations. And within all the books, on or under the surface, has been the writer's radical revision of the world, the dreamed revolution against the status quo. But the politics of literature alone does not answer the question.

The key to the work of Carlos Fuentes is always in the form. The content is Mexican, but anyone, even D. H. Lawrence and Malcolm Lowry, can write about Mexico. The Mexicanidad of Fuentes is the concern with form; the aesthetic experience of reading his work is in apprehending the "significant form." As in the first Mexican novel, the set of Olmec figures, all but one carved from the same material and all facing the different one, the form is the story; all the rest is hard work and stone.

CRACKERS

Keeping to the form of Mexican history, which is Mesoamerican in its cyclical nature, or a series of negations in the existential view of Paz, or Hegelian, as some on the left would have it, the (perhaps) successors to Rulfo and Fuentes announced their arrival in 1996 with nothing less than a manifesto, written by Jorge Volpi (born in 1968) and agreed to by four other young writers: Ignacio Padilla (also born 1968), Vicente Herrasti (b. 1967), Eloy Urroz (b. 1966), and the old man of the group, Ricardo Chávez Castañeda (b. 1961). Of the group, Volpi has made the most money, he and Padilla have won the most prizes, and Herrasti is the most intensely clear stylist.

They call themselves the Crack Generation, which is something of a pun, since it refers not to "crack" as rock cocaine, but to "crack" as in la Ruptura, which refers to painters of an earlier generation. It all calls for an elbow to the ribs and a *ja ja ja*, as one writes "ha, ha, ha" in Spanish. The Crack Generation (one is tempted to call them crackers) often define themselves by quoting a retired professor and translator from Kansas, John S. Brushwood. Why choose Brushwood over a Mexican or Spanish critic? one might ask. No doubt the primary reason is that Brushwood is not a Mexican; the crack writers are willing to be anything but Mexican. Another is that they agree with him about his notion of the "profound" novel, and finally, and perhaps most important, he said their work is "profound."

The Crack Generation has been compared with Generation X.[18] It has also been called the Aztec Invasion and the postmagical BOOM. The crack writers see themselves as a break away from the "BOOM" mentality of magical realism and nationalism. The charming, witty, and very magical novels of David Toscana, a contemporary writer from Monterrey, are to them old-fashioned, while Toscana sees the crack writers as part of a Mexico City Mafia. Toscana's novels are published in the United States, while the crack writers have taken longer to reach the English-speaking world. Volpi was the first; Herrasti and Padilla will not be far behind.

Volpi's prizewinning novel *En Busca de Klingsor* (In Search of Klingsor) takes place in Europe at the close of the Second World War. It is about mathematics, physics, and evil. Volpi and the other crack writers claim various antecedents, from Calvino to Broch to Poe to Thomas Bernhard, but to write a novel about Nazis and quantum mechanics and the evil of the twentieth century is to be a descendant of Thomas Pynchon and a relative of Don DeLillo, whether or not one mentions their names or knows their work. Unlike the magical realists, who sprang from the very soul of Mexico, the crack writers are alienated from their own ancestors, with the possible exception of Fuentes, who brought modernism to Mexico as they are attempting to bring postmodernism home. But where is home?

For the crack writers it is Central Europe more than anywhere else, but it is also Scotland, where Herrasti and Volpi studied and worked, and Germany. Anywhere but Mexico. Herrasti's *Diorama* is a descendant of Poe.

---

[18]A name that first appeared in a magazine, the *Baffler*, edited by a group of people under the age of thirty at or around the University of Chicago.

Roderick Usher lurks in the background; the descriptions, the unnamed menace, could have no other antecedents. Herrasti has published a novel about Gorgias, who was a Greek philosopher (483–378 B.C.) and the subject of one of Plato's dialogues. The novel, *Acarnia en Lontananza* (Acarnia in the Distance), is the first of a projected series of four historical-philosophical works. In it, Herrasti succeeds in turning the philosopher's last days into a series of intrigues, including murder, wild nightmare scenes, gravedigging, almost everything one would not expect in a novel about a perishing philosopher.

Herrasti's novel is about ideas. Volpi claims that his novel is about love rather than mathematics, physics, and evil. What is certain about this new generation of Mexican writers is that they are disgusted not only by the failings of their own government, their own society, as older generations of writers were, but by the failings of the world. They have a deeply Catholic sense of the existence of evil and a powerful sense of themselves. The painters of the Ruptura who produced the most brilliant work were those who said they never made a break with anything. Will the same be said of Mexican writers who are more concerned with their own work than making a public break with the past? Or will the universalist crack writers turn out to be the new postmagical boom? We shall know soon enough whether they are the inheritors of glory in their own time or merely alienated, ambitious, and well-spoken young men.

27.

The Reinforcement of the Worst

There is something like a national community . . .
—CARLOS MONSIVÁIS, *La Jornada,* September 9, 2001

The popular culture of Mexico, like the popular culture of any country in an increasingly globalized world, presents a problem of categories. In this book, Mexico is divided into its constituent parts, according to the way the Aztecs defined the centers of a person: the head, the heart, and the liver, home of the winds of life. Purely market-driven culture belongs in the last category, in the folder next to the one marked "economics." Art belongs here, in this category contained in the heart, as the Mexica knew. But which category should hold popular art, and how should popular art be distinguished from folk art in Mexico now? Liberal capitalism has invaded the handiwork of dreams, but unless or until the conquest is complete, popular art will have two homes. The Huicholes of Nayarit have put the yarn paintings and beadwork versions of their mushroom-inspired visions up for sale, but the visions are still theirs alone. The women of the indigenous villages of Chiapas still embroider their blouses in designs unique to each village. Don José, of the village of San Jacinto high on the side of a volcano, is ninety-five years old, and he still sings and plays the guitar and instructs younger men, some only in their sixties, in the performance of corridos (story songs).

To consign Don José to the world of the market would be to bury him while he still has many years to live.[1] And not only him. The work of the

---

[1] I mention his longevity only partly to convey the charm of him. At a fiesta in the village I was seated next to Don José at dinner. Earlier in the day I had tried and failed to keep pace with him as we climbed a steep path up to the community building. We had laughed and chatted during the morning meal and ceremonies. While we drank pulque before dinner, he told me he had been married at the age of forty-one to a sixteen-year-old girl. "You are a devil," I said. And he laughed.

428

Huicholes, more vivid and exciting than ever, now occupies entire walls in the Museum of Anthropology and History in Mexico City. While the work was being installed, I stood with one of the museum's art historians in the unfinished room, with ladders and carpenters' tools for a still life before the walls and no light but the sun reflected through the windows from the gray stone of the central patio, and the energy that came from the Huichol wall painting took my breath away.

The question then for Mexico, as for much of the world, is of intent. What impels the maker of a work of popular art to make the object, sing the song, produce the drama, or perform the dance? In the beginning, before Europe invaded what is now Mexico, popular art may have been the only form of art. What was plain was public, and what was arcane was public. The stelae incised with names and dates and the mnemonics of myths and history were on public view. Spectators attended the games in the Mesoamerican ball courts. The codices (folded books of deerskin or fig tree paper) were apprehensible to many, if not most, people. The Maya documents, which puzzle us today, were as easily read then as a rebus on the comics page of a daily newspaper. Dance pageants in pre-Hispanic Mexico were highly formalized representations of the history known to all who attended. Pre-Columbian societies had a class structure, with the upper classes exposed to more complex art and history, but most of the culture was observable by the public; a pyramid is hard to miss.

Not long after the invasion, culture divided into three categories: indigenous, European, and more and more a mixed culture, a mestizaje of culture to match the mestizaje of genes. In the mixed culture there were also African influences. The *sones*, dances of Oaxaca, adapted African rhythms to the performance of dances born of indigenous ideas. What impelled the dancers to invent the dance? Pleasure or religion, life or death? If it was religion, it functioned like the market before the market was invented. Religion examines the fears and desires of the people and then invents itself to cater to them.

When I asked why he had not brought his sweetheart to the fiesta, he said, "Because I could meet someone here."

"Yes?" I asked, putting the question as politely as possible.

And he nodded and smiled with mock shyness. Then he put a piece of pit-barbecued lamb in his mouth and ground it up with gusto on his sturdy brown teeth. *Ars longa, vita brevis?*

Or is religion at a different level, divinely inspired? The ethnocentric rule has long been: If it is our religion, it is divine; if it is their religion, it belongs to the market. But this is hardly the place to examine the nature of divinity.

Much of the popular art of Mexico was concerned with practical things; the rest was for God or the gods.[2] Among the practical things, most had to do with daily life—cooking or clothing—or identification. The separation of villages required a variety of designs. And then boys were unlike girls, men were unlike women. Classes were defined by dress, the popular art of couture. Anthropologists have done countless studies of the use of art to define aspects of society; there is no need to repeat them here, except to say that the very widely known and appreciated art of the time was what we would now describe either as art or folk art; popular art in contemporary terms is very different.

There was no popular art in the contemporary sense in pre-Columbian or colonial Mexico. Popular art as it is practiced now requires mass production and the concept of a market beyond the intimate circle of the producer; the consumer of popular art is objectified—studied and abstracted—and art is then made in a repetitive fashion to satisfy the desires of the objectified consumer. Marketing is perhaps the defining phenomenon of the modern age, and the production of art to satisfy market-driven tastes has had more influence on the culture than most of the great advances in technique, perhaps even more than the printing press.

The preceding is a simplified definition; distinctions between popular art and folk art in Mexico are much more difficult to determine. When an object, something as simple as the common Eye of God, a series of windings of colored yarn in the shape of a rectangle on crossed sticks, is repeated over and over, a hundred times, then a thousand, then tens of thousands of times, it passes from folk art to popular art. The 246,000th iteration may appear to be exactly identical to the first object, but it is not. Jorge Luis Borges, who compared repetition to death, told in "Pierre Menard, the Author of the Quixote" of a man who rewrote the Cervantes novel word for word, letter for letter, yet produced something entirely different. The first Eye of God made by the Huicholes of the state of Nayarit originated from a different

---

[2] It is perhaps unfair to suggest that religion comes in response to fear of death and punishment in the next life; the market for religion may also be seeking an ethical formula for living.

motive (to protect children) and to serve a different end from the hundred thousandth. Only the means is the same, winding for winding, on the crossed sticks.

In the realm of art in Mexico, there are many levels of production, all driven by economics, and by that measure the worst is best. That is not to single out Mexico among the countries of the world in this respect. All modern societies mass-produce popular art. The difference between Mexico and the United States in this area is that there is very little folk art and vast amounts of popular art in the United States, while Mexico is still in the process of commercializing its folk art.

HATS

There were no public toilets in Mexico City in the sixteenth century, when the elegant residents of the capital first became disgusted by the penniless, itinerant leperos who fouled the streets. Spanish cities of the time were much filthier, but between the horses and the poor immigrants, the streets of the capital were worse than the stables of Augeus. The pre-Hispanic occupants of the gleaming white, pristine city in the sun, who found the Spaniards foul-smelling and filthy at the time of the invasion, must have been appalled by the condition of the streets of the capital of New Spain. Today the problem for most people is in the air rather than the streets, but there are still no public toilets, and for Fernando, a boy of four years, and his grandmother María, who spend the day on the sidewalks of the city, the lack of public toilets is a tragedy. From the time the bus arrives in the center of the city to the time they return to the distant suburb where they live, they wish for toilets.

María Martínez González, the hatmaker of Santa María Ustlahuaca, estado de Oaxaca, thinks about toilets. All day, even on Sundays and holidays, her mind is filled with thoughts of toilets. This question of toilets would seem to belong to the distant past, to the infancy of persons and cities, but it is not so, not for her. She lives outside time, an anachronism in the realms of artisanship and plumbing. She lives in a one-room house with her daughter and Fernando. The house does not have a toilet either, but there is a private place with a door just outside the house, and they can use it as they will. To have access to a toilet is a kind of freedom. Of all the things the hatmaker has learned since she and her daughter and Fernando came to the capital, she counts the value of toilets and the frailty of her hands the most important.

Once, and not long ago, she said, her hands, which appear to be crumpled now and blackened, not with earth, like campesino's hands, but with some dark and viscous waste, were the quickest hands in Ustlahuaca. Adroitly, a sculptor with straw, fingers as agile as those of a violinist in full flight, she wove straw into crowns and brims that outlasted the men who wore them. A hat for a hen, she said. But that was long ago, when she also wove dolls and animals of straw. She could weave a straw family and its house too; she could weave an entire town, a marching band, a nativity scene or the crucifixion. Whatever she could dream, she said she could weave.

Abuela (Grandmother) María does not recall when the price of woven hats began to decline. It fell slowly at first, and then suddenly her weaving was hardly worth anything at all. There were stores in a nearby village where a hat could be purchased for less than a fourth of what she asked. The hats did not last so long as hers, nor were they beautiful or in any way connected to the village or the *municipio* (larger political and economical community, including the village). It made no difference; hats were purchased according to the price. She could not sell her hats, nor could she barter for them. Then a drought came and all but destroyed the village. Her family lost the tiny ranch where they had lived.

To survive, she hired herself out to make hats. The contractor paid eighty centavos (less than a dime) for a hat. The straw was not good, and she worked so fast she could make three hats in a day, but eighty centavos a hat was not enough, not even in Ustlahuaca. The family ate nothing but corn and chillis, and they had to walk up and back to another village to buy that food, because there was no store in Ustlahuaca, and without rain nothing grew. She and her daughter and Fernando left their village for the capital.

It surprised them to find so many indigenous people in the capital: Masawas, Zapotecos, Mixtecos, Otomis, Nahuas, Mazatecos, and speakers of many Mayan languages. So many languages. María knew only a few words of Spanish then, and she was already fifty-four years old and not five feet tall. When she smiled, she showed all her teeth; it made her somber face into an icon's visage, a form instead of a face. No one wanted her; no one wanted her hats. They looked like country hats, unfit for life in the capital. She found work as a laundress. Her hands were put to scrubbing, her back to lifting heavy loads of clothes. First, something broke in one hand, and then the other, and then she could not use one shoulder.

A neighbor instructed her in a new art, one that required only sadness.

She took to begging. Instead of eighty centavos a day, she said she earned thirty pesos almost every day, sometimes more. The work was easy. She did not mind the heat and she did not fear the cold. If it had not been for the problem of the toilet . . .

The boy, Fernando, stood beside her, slight and dark, underdressed for the cooling afternoon. He did not smile, having learned sadness from his grandmother. He danced a little, moving from one foot to the other, as children in need of a toilet do; that is how his grandmother and I came to speak of toilets and freedom and the effect of the modern world on the craft of hatmaking in Ustlahuaca. I offered to walk a few blocks with them to a hotel where I was known and where the boy could use the toilet near the hotel bar.

He went into the little room by himself, and when he came out after a while, I asked if he had washed his hands. He did not answer, but I saw that his face had changed; he appeared to have lost his sadness. His grandmother's face had also changed, although not so much as his; the iconic smile had been replaced by something softer. She said they were going home; their day was done. Only much later did I understand the damage freedom had done to the mood of the artist.

FISH

The village of Hunucmá, Yucatán, is not so far from the sea that no one there had ever seen a fish, but no one in Hunucmá would have considered making fish if Julio Maccosay, the lawyer, and his wife, Isela, had not come to the village with a proposition about economics and a cooperative to produce *artesanías* (handicrafts). With a little start-up money, they could invent fish. And then they could buy a lathe and a jigsaw and chisels and sandpapers and paints and brushes to make fish. A few men could work in the *taller* (workshop), and many women could be employed as sanders and painters and dryers and packers.

It would be art and craft, a place to earn a living for those who had been left out when the henequén market failed and then left out again when the Salinas administration suddenly cut off their welfare pensions. They located an unused house with some space out behind it for ovens and saws and big pieces of hardwood, and then they designed a fish. The first fish was as fat as a grouper and colored in stripes, an artist's version of the tasty fish that lives in the warm waters of the Caribbean.

Making the design into a fish was not so easy, but the fish became more beautiful with each iteration. Soon there were two kinds of fish and then four and then fish in big sizes and small and fish divided in the middle so that they could hold napkins or letters between their multicolored sides. The variety of fish increased until they had what is known as a full line of crafts, which the Maccosays helped them to sell to tourists in Cancún and Isla de Mujeres and Mérida.

The fish were pretty, and they fetched good prices from the shopowners, so the fishmakers of Hunucmá expanded. They took more orders and made more fish. Maccosay and his wife were pleased; the United Nations Development Program, which had put in some seed money, was pleased. In the workroom the women sang while they sanded and painted the fish. In the room behind them, the order books filled up. Artesanía, although it had to be taught to the Maya in the workshop, had returned to Hunucmá; the disasters of the henequén and Salinas had been overcome.

Soon, however, fish that looked very much like the Hunucmá fish began to appear in some stores. The lines were not quite so delicate, the surface not quite so smooth. The fish with imperfections were not set aside, as in Hunucmá. The competition paid lower wages than the cooperative of Hunucmá; the fish they made were repetitions of the repetitions of Hunucmá. Soon there were more fish than the stores could sell, and the price went down.

It was the same with the huipiles (long overblouses worn by Maya women) that had been embroidered in the villages. First, they were embroidered by hand, and then by one woman running one machine, and then in factories far from the villages where the designs had been invented. Tzotzil designs from Chiapas were copied in factories in Guatemala, as were the Yucatecan designs. The anthropologist Silvia Terán invented a new way to embroider the huipiles with much less labor, but the artisans still could not compete with the factories. The customers did not distinguish between the well-made fish and machine-made fish, nor did they find the quality of the embroidery on the huipiles of great importance. The artisans of the cooperatives are left to make new designs and to seek new ways to sell them. The profits belong to the sellers in the modern world, and if the makers are not the sellers, they cannot earn enough to survive. Folk art is succeeded by popular art in the age of repetitions; the hands of artisans are anachronisms. The dexterity of their fingers is more profitably used in the arrangement of silicon chips in patterns that will not suffer the variations of the artisan's touch.

CORRIDOS

The origin of the corrido, the Mexican version of the story song, is not entirely clear. Some historians say that it came to Mexico with the Spanish invasion, a New World form of the old Spanish *romance*. Others ascribe it to the ancient Nahuas, who had a glorious oral tradition, which was, like all orality, filled with rhythms, rhymes, and song. Nahua works range from stories of journeys, gods, and battles to comic tales to meditations on art and the brevity of life. The corrido probably has a bicultural provenance. Mesoamerican civilization was one of the few truly original civilizations on earth, but the similarities among humans are greater than the differences: Every written tradition is preceded by an oral tradition; every custom of writing down stories follows the custom of telling stories. So it would seem to go without saying that the Mexican corrido began with the Nahuas and the various Maya-language groups and the Purépechas, Mixtecos, Yaquis, Totonacos, Zapotecos, Raramurí, etc., and also with the Spaniards who sang ballads for love and history in the Middle Ages. The importance of the corrido in popular culture in Mexico would seem then to be carried in the genes of all who live in Mexico: Mesoamerican, Northern Indian, Asian, African, or European.

By the nineteenth century the form of the Spanish *romance* was used in a corrido to stir the rebels to take up arms against Spain in the War of Independence:

> *The gachupines* [Spaniards] *want blood,*
> *to kill our nation,*
> *but the truth is that if they get involved,*
> *we will make cracklings* [chicharrones] *of them.*

The corrido told of how the Spaniards had arms and munitions, but the rebels had stones and a lot in their underwear, meaning manliness.

Half a century later there were story songs about the "jail at Cananea," the town where the mineworkers' strike took place, and songs about the textile workers and the campesinos who suffered at the hands of the hacendados. The corrido was usually a song of the underdog, and when it told a story, it always had a resolution, although not always a happy one. There were romantic corridos, tragic corridos, outraged corridos. All of the secular world found its way into the corridos. Taken as a whole, the corridos were a history and a literature of Mexico. For centuries, there have been men sitting in the plazas, cantinas, and all the parlors and one-room houses of Mexico, holding guitars and singing. The style was nasal and high-pitched; the guitars twanged; even the gut strings had a metallic sound.[3]

The corrido served for storytelling and for news. A corrido could be written about something as eternal as love, as historical as Independence or Reform, or as topical as yesterday's railroad strike. The music of the corrido always sounded less consequential than the lyrics, at least to my ear, although there have been changes in the tunes and orchestrations over the last sixty years. The truest corrido or perhaps the original corrido is sung to the accompaniment of one guitar, and the singer is best when he is an old man with a wide repertoire. To be a grand singer of stories, he should be a story himself, venerable, but never sanctimonious, always willing to have a chat with the devil. All of this history and sly laughter must be sounded in the overtones of his thin, high-string voice.

During the first decades of the twentieth century the corrido had what are still its most cherished years. Corridos written about battles and heroes are still heard on records and now and then on a street corner. One can hear of the taking of Zacatecas or a dozen songs of the railroad, virtually every detail of the career of General Francisco (Pancho) Villa, and a few songs about his rival, First Chief Venustiano Carranza. There are corridos about guns ("Carabina .30-30") and horses ("Siete Leguas" [Seven Leagues]). Death in battle of one kind or another is a common subject, with the brave winning every encounter, even if they die in the process. The corrido is the people's novel, a story for those who cannot read, a history for those who have never held a book.

The corrido, with its mestizo ancestry, is a flexible form, capable of adapting to new content and new technologies: It was born of internal conflict in both its composers and the country in which they lived; it survived, but not in the solid state of national music. Unlike the Spanish *romance*, the corrido

---

[3]The corrido was originally in waltz time, although now it is usually a polka, especially in the north. There are four lines to a stanza, eight syllables to a line. The melodies are no more complex than the sentiments.

belonged to nations. It was quantum music, evolving in leaps. The form of the corrido changed radically, became all but unrecognizable, yet remained the same. Since it had been planted on the mercurial ground of the mestizaje, it could lose its music or its words, exchange rhythms, or take up new subjects and still remain the corrido, a Darwinian song, Heisenberg music; the modernity of mestizaje.

At the same time that the literate population of Mexico grew, the paper supply increased and the cost of printing declined, and the corrido was adapted to the comic book. With the civil wars largely in the past, the stories of battles became historical tales, and personal stories of the trials of life became the subject matter of the corrido. Instead of the stories being sung, they were drawn for *novelas*, cheaply printed comic books, smaller than the magazine-sized U.S. version. In the early novelas, contemporary life was portrayed as a soap opera: Family problems were always solved in the end; the god from the machine kept at it, story after story. During the beginnings of the corrido on paper in the 1930s and even today the dialogue is so sparse in these comic books, and the pictures so obvious, they seem to owe more to silent films than to the often witty corridos of the past. As the corrido turned into popular art, produced in vast quantities, the wit and charm faded. Rhyme and meter had no place in a comic book, and the pun, the staple of Mexican humor, could not be proffered to the semiliterate millions who read the novelas. Of the motives of the authors there can be no doubt: The market had been found, and the producers were not about to lose it. Like the denizens of Darwin's island laboratory, the producers of comic books evolved. The latest versions appear in full color, the more expensive ones with slick paper covers, and often as close to erotic as a comic book can be.

In northwest Mexico German immigrants brought a new sound and rhythm to the corrido. They added the accordion and moved the rhythm from a quick waltz to an even quicker polka. *Conjunto* (a small band) music started in Monterrey and moved across northern Mexico and into Texas. The political character of the music faded, and the melodramatic *romance* took its place. By the early 1990s the conjunto sound filled dance halls from Texas to Tamaulipas to Sinaloa.

Reversions to the old form of the corrido appeared a few years later to celebrate the birth of the Zapatista movement in Chiapas. They were written in Spanish, making them unavailable to the monolingual indigenous people of the state, the poorest of the poor and those meant to be aided and inspired by the movement and its songs. Like the amusing Internet messages of Subcomandante Marcos, the corridos looked to the world beyond the mountain and jungle villages of Mexico's poorest (in per capita income) state. And the corrido had a certain retro charm: The revolution called for in the corridos from Chiapas had as a subtext the Zapatista revolution in Morelos almost a century earlier.

It was not long afterward that the corrido began telling stories again, broadcasting the news. This time the stories were about Carlos Salinas de Gotari and his family. And the singer said his farewell "until another circus arrives and the same thing happens again." The news, as in most corridos, was surprisingly accurate and captured in amusing rhymes. In the case of songs of Salinas, it was a matter of giving the public exactly what it wanted. And it did not stop with Salinas. Vicente Fox had spent only two years in office when a group known as Los Tigres del Norte (Northern Tigers) took up what was becoming a national complaint about his failure to carry out his promises. They laughed at his campaign slogans, called him Zorro ("Fox" in Spanish), and leaned heavily on his Coca-Cola connection. Whether a song grew out of the singer's anger over the vast amounts Salinas stole or his unhappiness with the Fox administration or the appeal to the market is difficult to say, since almost everyone enjoyed the shame cast on Salinas and his party, the PRI, and the unhappiness with Fox was just beginning to gain a foothold.

Another version of the corrido appeared in northwestern Mexico in the 1990s. The first popular song in the new corrido was "Contraband and Betrayal." It told the sad story of a couple, Emilio Varela and Carmela the Texan, who crossed the border in a car that rode on tires filled with illegal drugs. The song follows the smugglers through the southwestern United States until it ends with a shooting and the usual farewell at the end of a corrido, in this case, ". . . that's all I know." The *narcocorrido* became immensely popular. The heroes were not addicts but smugglers. Pancho Villa had been replaced by the head of a drug cartel. Like the corridos about Villa, the narcocorridos represented the anger of people for whom there was no alternative but to flout the laws of an oppressive government. The narcocorrido celebrated the daring and the tragedy of anarchy: Flores Magón in postmodern lyrics.

One song lamented the arrests in Culiacán (in the western state of

Sinaloa) of the leaders of a drug cartel because the standard of living in the town would fall. The narcocorrido even has a patron martyr, Chalino Sánchez. His voice was ragged, and there was a brutal clarity in his lyrics. In "The Crime of Culiacán" Chalino told of two men who were killed and whose guts were eaten by dogs. It was not a pretty story, and neither was the life of Chalino. He was shot and wounded while onstage performing one of his songs in California. True to his music, Chalino drew a gun and shot four men, killing one of them. Not long afterward, back home in Culiacán, Chalino was arrested by several men who said they were police. They put two bullets in his head and threw his body into a ditch. If the story were made into a narcocorrido, it would conclude with the farewell line ". . . and that was the end of Chalino." But it was not the end. He endures as the revered founder of the narcocorrido, the bandit who extolled banditry, an antihero, the carrier of the quantum of the mestizo in his time; if not quite so talented as the fifteenth-century French criminal-poet of the streets François Villon, then surely just as tough.

MARIACHIS

The most familiar typical Mexican music, songs played by mariachi bands, came from the state of Jalisco, where it was played on stringed instruments at celebrations and weddings. The musicians wore charro costumes, waist-length jackets and tight-fitting trousers, embroidered and often spangled, and very large, heavy, highly decorated sombreros. The music they sang commonly dealt with betrayal, lost love, and vengeance. Every song was a cowboy movie or at least the plot and characterization for one.

While mariachi music can be lilting, very moving, even inspiring, the music and the movies that sprang from it are rooted in nostalgia, partly for the rural life, but more for the Porfiriato, making it one of the most curious aspects of Mexican popular culture. The country that suffered under Díaz could not let go of its nostalgia for that time. The very people who lived in peonage during the Porfiriato celebrated the costumes and the rural life of the time. Was it like Americans watching Fred Astaire and Ginger Rogers in formal clothes dancing through the Great Depression? A palliative in the form of a sweet dream on the big screen?

Mexico is different. Fred and Ginger said that money existed, was still possible in a time of poverty, in a country that was about money. Films and songs of the time of the Porfiriato were not about the present, but the past. The Porfiriato was, in memory, a time of honor, tradition, modernization, and peace. The period that appears as an ugly dictatorship to historians now did not seem so unappealing after the ten years of bloody civil war and the bossism of Calles and then the Cristero Rebellion against anticlericalism coming in the middle of a worldwide depression. The Mexicans were left hoping for the chance to rest for a moment and draw a deep breath of what was still fresh air. Just then the Depression ended, in a world war.

In the 1940s and 1950s ranchero movies and songs reached the height of their popularity. Jorge Negrete was Mexico's favorite singing cowboy. He defeated rustlers and crooks and went home with the girl. Honor, manliness, and a good Catholic heart won the matinee and the evening. But it was not all machismo; women could sing and ride too. No one had a more powerful voice or sturdy stance than Lola Beltrán. In the roseate moment of nostalgia, life appeared good again, moral. The mariachis and all the ranchero singers were proud, full of love and anger, and always swift to take revenge. The music was loud, louder still when trumpets were added to the guitars, and the voices of the singers, men and women alike, boomed out the lyrics. No man bent his knee, except before God or his own father. Everything was in order, good triumphed over evil; there were rules. A good man saved God the trouble of taking vengeance later: Vengeance is mine, sang the charro, and no decent man or woman had to whisper. It did not matter that ownership of a large ranch was a requisite of good character; the Mexican who saw himself in his nightmares not as the cosmic race but the muddied heritage preferred the triumph of clarity over justice.

DANZONES

In Mexico there have been two actresses named María who have affected the course of the country. The first, María Félix, was at the peak of her influence during the 1940s and 1950s. She was beautiful and wild, and because of the parts she chose, the life she led, and the way she spoke about other women, she insinuated egalitarianism in a country of economic extremes. La Félix or María Bonita or La Doña was, in her own way, perhaps inadvertently, a defender of the indigenous people of Mexico. She came out of the Cárdenas era, born of his revolution, as a goddess might be engendered by some divine plumage or the miracle of the sea. Beauty was her claim to goodness, but the two attributes could not be equated in Mexico as in ancient Greece; La Félix, the scandalous goddess, could not convince anyone about her goodness, at least not the traditional Mexican goodness of a woman. Nor did she want to; she made a different arrangement. She was the mestizaje in the movies, the child of a Yaqui father and a Spanish mother. One side was equal to the other in La Doña; she was the most beautiful, alluring, stylish mestiza anyone had ever seen, and she was the product of the antithesis of the wedding of Cortés and Malinalli, her mother had been the Spaniard in the pairing.

The mestiza, perhaps because she had a message about indigenous Mexico and about women, behaved like a movie star. If ever she stepped out of the role, no one knew. She was the woman who resisted, dangerous, beautiful, and never subservient. Even in the pictures of La Doña Félix with her son, she was the star as mother, never simply mother. She married Agustín Lara, who wrote love songs to her, and she married movie stars. La Malinche did the bidding of Cortés; there was nothing men would not do for María Bonita. She reigned, beyond law or logic, the star from the town of Alamos in the north, the one who was raised in Guadalajara and spoke the elegantly accented Spanish of that city. Lázaro Cárdenas had delivered a speech in an indigenous language and returned vast amounts of land to the descendants of the original owners, but María Félix rewrote the rules of the parlor and the bedroom. She was a woman as a woman could be. After her, after the eyes and the fire of María Bonita, anything would be possible for a woman in Mexico. From the tear-filled sea of more than forty films, most of which did not even aspire to mediocrity, a bronze goddess arose; the worst had somehow produced the best.

When María Félix died on her birthday, April 8, 2002, she was (at the very least) eighty-eight years old. She had been the subject of paintings and books and the most inventive gossip about her and her secretary. She had worked with Jean Renoir in French films, and Jean Cocteau had said she was the most beautiful thing that lived. Diego Rivera, Carlos Fuentes, Octavio Paz, Elena Poniatowska, Luis Spota, José Clemente Orozco all had found her fascinating. Most fell at her feet. Only Carlos Fuentes, who said after her death that he had always desired her, took another view in his short novel *Zona Sagrada* (*Holy Place*), in which Claudia, the vulgar, overbearing mother of an emotionally wounded son, is closely related to the life of La Doña María Félix.

In the mid-1990s Gloria Trevi, a buxom woman from Monterrey, sought the kind of fame and influence that had come so naturally to La Doña Félix. And found it. Even Elena Poniatowska could not resist writing about her and publishing a portfolio of pinup pictures to accompany an essay. Trevi was available, wild, beautiful, and vulgar. She was a thumb in the eye of respectability: big breasts and a round ass (to say "buttocks" in relation to Trevi would be to miss the point of her entirely) to oppose the chicken-breasted rich women who imitated French and American models. Trevi represented a revolt against the bourgeois hypocrisy forced upon Mexico by a government that went to mass on Sunday morning, had dinner with the family at three in the afternoon, and returned to the bed of its whore after dark.

Trevi wrote and recorded her own songs. She herded an army of little nymphs around the stage while she danced, and she posed for photographs half naked, partly naked, naked, in every erotic pose she or the photographers could imagine short of overt sexual acts. And then it all fell apart. The government accused her of abusing the little girls in her entourage. They charged her with holding orgies with minors. María Félix had left the country to make movies in Europe after a similar scandal, but La Doña had been the mistress of President Alemán. She simply left, even though the scandal involved a death. Trevi had no connections at that level of government. Félix knew the limits of the new; Trevi made a career of opposing limits. To avoid prosecution for sex acts with minors, Gloria Trevi fled to Brazil, where she was imprisoned while fighting extradition. After several years in a Brazilian prison, she delivered a child. She fought extradition, fearing for her life, she said. But at the end of 2002 it appeared that the Mexican government would have its way, bringing Trevi back for prosecution. She looked defiant and gorgeous. The *Washington Post* called her the Queen of Garbage, an insult that made headlines in the Mexican newspapers.

The other María of Mexican films appears at first to be a kind of Newtonian reaction to the first: equal and opposite. María Rojo starred in a movie that long held the box-office record in Mexico for Mexican films. *Rojo Amanecer* (Red Dawn), like the persona of La Félix, affected the culture and eventually the history of Mexico. No film made in the United States ever had such influence on the political life of the society. How much of the formation of the PRD, the candidacy of Cuauhtémoc Cárdenas, and the eventual defeat of the PRI is due to the film is impossible to estimate, but that it did affect the course of the nation is undeniable.

When *Rojo Amanecer* was completed and ready to be shown in movie houses, the Mexican government refused to allow it to be distributed. That was not the least bit difficult in Mexico, for the government, in addition to financing many movies, licensed them. For several years the government managed to suppress the film by using its licensing and police powers. The subject of it was perhaps the worst embarrassment Mexico had brought upon itself in decades, the 1968 Massacre at Tlatelolco. There had been books about the massacre, most notably the Poniatowska oral history, but the newspapers had not kept the story alive with investigative or retrospective stories. Tlatelolco '68 had begun to fade in the mind of the Mexican public when *Rojo Amanecer* was finally released twenty years after the massacre.

Its importance was greater in Mexico than it might have been in the United States or Europe. Mexico is not a country of readers, except for daily newspapers, and newspaper readership has fallen off since the advent of television. *La Jornada*, the center-left newspaper connected in the minds of its readers with the UNAM, sells about fifty thousand copies. Books are overpriced and often cannot be published without a subsidy by a university, the government, or a private source.[4] Movies offered the best means to reach very large numbers of people before television arrived in most of the country, and even afterward, because Televisa, the largest and most influential network, was, although privately owned, little more than a government voice. The situation has changed since the fall of the PRI in 2000, but the business plan at Televisa continues to call for it to be careful.

Rojo Amanecer was not careful in that way. It takes place in an apartment overlooking the Plaza de las Tres Culturas (Tlatelolco) on the late afternoon and early evening of October 2, 1968. The action never leaves the apartment, the camera never looks out the window, but the wounded and the dying who walk or are carried into the apartment tell the story. Such movies are generally made by unknown people, more often dedicated to politics than film, but the star of this movie was María Rojo, who was by then far enough along in her career for *Rojo Amanecer* to have been a risk.

[4]To avoid casting aspersions on the work of other writers, I will use one of my own books to make the case. A short novel, *En Yucatán,* in its Spanish version, published in the usual form, trade paperback with flaps, cost 179 pesos in 2001. In U.S. dollars, the cost at the 2001 exchange rate was a little less than $20, but per capita income in Mexico is about one-eighth that in the United States.

More than ten years later, in an interview with Poniatowska, she revealed what may have been her motivation, in both the political and theatrical sense. Rojo had been there in the plaza, in the third row of students, with her husband, Juan Allende.[5] When the shooting started, her friends hid her in a space filled with electrical equipment. She told Poniatowski she heard a wounded man singing a line from an old song, "*La vida no vale nada . . .* [Life is worth nothing . . .]," and the shooting and screaming. Afterward she and her mother, a schoolteacher, searched for days among the dead, asking everywhere for María's husband, who had been mistaken for one of the strike's leaders, taken to prison, and subjected to vicious interrogations by the military and the police.

Rojo Amanecer made Rojo the most famous actress in Mexico, a woman idolized, but not a star. A star was something else entirely. María Rojo was then, and has always been, a woman who did not understand her celebrity. She and her husband, Esteban, live in a comfortable but unpretentious house in a quiet part of Coyoacán. They sometimes invite relative strangers to visit. One evening the three of us had a light supper there and talked about politics and the movies. It had been raining heavily all evening, and the house and even the tiny street were difficult to find. I arrived late, carrying a damp copy of a book and flowers. Had I known that Rojo was dyslexic, I would have brought a shorter book.

The house was sparely furnished in the Mexican style but warmed by the vibrant colors of the paintings on the walls: reds, of course, bright yellows, and hot greens. We sat in the living room, around a very large, square coffee table, and drank red wine and ate cheeses and sausages and crackers. I said that my wife had been in the film business in Mexico and was very interested in the way the role of women had changed. We gossiped about the business for a while; then we talked about *Danzón*. The story of a telephone operator and the man with whom she danced, it is gentle, touching, accurate in its portrayal of the Mexican lower middle class but is mainly a film about a woman and her loves and longings. Rojo's performance and the serious and erotic grace of the dancers in the danzón halls of Mexico made the film an international success. As Rojo is quick to say, she is too short to be a star, too dark, but she was a new kind of idol for Mexican movie fans: She was real.

---

[5] Allende died of cancer in 1985. Rojo later remarried, to Esteban Schmelz, who had come to Mexico from his native Austria when he was a child.

The character in *Danzón* is passionate, but not vulgar; poor, but not cheap. A woman could be a woman, real, yet good, even virtuous. Movies could end in the tragedy of a routine existence. They could be like life, but not naturalistic, not documentary. Unlike *Los Olvidados* (The Forgotten), Luis Buñuel's brutally realistic story of Mexican children living in poverty, the new character was more to be loved than pitied. Rojo had become the woman next door, but heightened and liberated, feminist, leftist, symbolic and real. The sixties, which Mexicans call *la Onda* (the Wave), had produced one emblematic figure that transcended the changes of the decades. She sat curled on the black couch, toying with the zipper of the red sweater she wore over her dress, tugging now and then at the hem of her short skirt as she changed positions. Esteban and I sat opposite her. Schmelz is a handsome man, bearded, charming, fluent in several languages. He is outgoing, the owner of a large and successful travel business, offering tour packages, mainly to Europeans. She is shy. Her voice is strong; his is soft. Later, when I said to him that María looked very young for her years, he did not simply nod to the compliment, but explained, "She is a *traga-años*; you know, one who swallows the years and does not age."

During part of the conversation I thought she was speaking through me to my wife, who had been in the same world. Esteban said that was correct; she liked talking with women, part of the shyness and the feminism. Speaking of women in film, she said she did not like actresses who were simply beautiful, like models. She preferred Bette Davis to Grace Kelly, the latter hardly being an actress at all, in her view. Of her own career, she said that the director Arturo Ripstein had taught her a great deal about acting and film.[6] But making movies in Mexico was a difficult business proposition for actors as well as producers. When she worked in *Danzón*, which was one of very few Mexican films (*Like Water for Chocolate* was the other) that found an international audience during the last decades of the twentieth century, she was paid the equivalent of ten thousand U.S. dollars for her work. When the movie became a hit, there was more money, but she used the fee for

---

[6]Son of a Mexican film producer, Ripstein worked with Buñuel as a very young man and later directed many of Mexico's more interesting and innovative films. He is one of very few Mexican directors (Buñuel is a Spaniard) to establish an international reputation, although several young directors, Alejandro González Iñárritu and Alfonso Cuarón chief among them, have now moved to what can be called international status.

Danzón to make a point about economics and the Mexican film industry. Rojo earns her living from television, appearing in *telenovelas* to be able to afford to work in serious films. The money is in television, and television is still Televisa, and the network is still the word of the government. When Jacobo Zabludovsky, Televisa's star newsman, was asked why he didn't speak more openly about what happened at Tlatelolco in 1968, he answered the same way to every questioner: The government watches very closely. Popular culture in Mexico was caught between the government and the United States, all but helpless.

"Look in the newspapers," Rojo said. She and her husband then spread the entertainment section from that day's paper on the coffee table. They pointed to the number of U.S.-made films, talking about the vast distribution of them compared with the one Mexican film showing that day. "Mexican films cost under a million dollars," she said. "And we make only ten or twelve films a year now. The Mexican interest in American films has destroyed our industry." She blamed it on the open trade agreements between the two countries, which she thinks are unfair to Mexico. "Very few theaters in the United States show Mexican films, but U.S. films dominate the Mexican market. This is both economic and cultural imperialism."

Issues of culture and economics were already on her mind by the mid-1990s. She was an active member of the PRD and was chosen a delegate at large to deal with cultural affairs, including films, but not limited to films. She was interested in writers and painters as well as filmmakers. She quoted Octavio Paz in casual conversation, numbered Gabriel García Márquez among her friends, believes like most Mexicans that Juan Rulfo is one of Mexico's great writers, and draws the Paz/Krauze distinction when she speaks of Carlos Fuentes, whom she calls "a very important writer from Washington, D.C.," and then separates him from the true Mexican world of which she is such a vital part.

Nationalism and racism are difficult questions for Rojo, the emblematic Mexican woman, the real one who came after Félix the dream. She said, "Mexico is not a racist country, but in films, and even more so on television, there is a standard of beauty. . . ." She looks over at Esteban. The house in which they live is both Mexican and Viennese; the dog that lies half awake on the floor beside her is a German shepherd. The Mexican film industry seeks something less parochial now, less Mexican, but yet as international in its appeal as *Danzón*. The irony is that *Danzón* was the most Mexican of films starring one of the most Mexican of actresses.

María Rojo later appeared in a comedy based on a story by her friend Elena Poniatowska. It was supposed to be satire, a work about feminism, another critique of the middle class. With a lesser actress and a lesser writer, it might have been a better film. The two serious women were not destined to be slapstick satirists. After that, Rojo turned more closely to politics, dividing her time between her work in the national legislature and movies and television. She fought for the Mexican film industry as if she were fighting for her life. What emerged was not all art, not all appealing to the entire world, but the industry has been revitalized.

Although it did not find an international audience, *La Ley de Herodes* (The Law of Herodes) upset Mexican government censors in 1999. The story takes place during the Alemán administration (1946–1952), when corruption in Mexico achieved a new level of sophistication as the country was exploited by Mexican and U.S. interests. In a small village an indigenous family exemplifies that pattern, mercilessly abused by government and gringos. The gringo, a character who has no other name, mistreats the family and rapes the woman of the house. The villagers, who have meekly endured their suffering for years, even generations, will suffer it no longer. Enraged by a series of ugly incidents, the people of the village, with no one to turn to but a party hack in the mayor's office, an ugly, utterly corrupt man, attack the mayor and decapitate him. The governor of the state, wishing to avoid problems, covers up the scandal and appoints another mayor, loyal to the party, but not yet as corrupt as his beheaded predecessor. The success of the indigenous uprising even in a comedy at a time when the government was negotiating with the Zapatistas in Chiapas was more than the censors would permit. Party hacks themselves, they suppressed the movie. Only after protests and a long legal battle was the film released.

Amores Perros (an all but untranslatable title sold in the United States as *Love's a Bitch*) was released in 2001. It was a brutal attack on Mexican society at every level, from the economic bottom of the working class to the wealthiest celebrities, filmmaking as the art of social criticism, ugly, relentless, with only a crazy old intellectual, a dog-loving seer, to partially redeem humanity. The scenes included bloody dogfights and a model going mad as she lay helpless in her apartment, looking out the window at a giant photograph of herself on a billboard. The whole film revolved around a horrendous automobile accident that served to link the characters and the stories.

Amores Perros met no problems with censors because there were no rebels praised and all criticism of the government and Mexican society was implicit. The thirty-seven-year-old director, Alejandro González Iñárritu, who had learned his trade at Televisa, had not yet learned what had to be left out of a film. Some of the plot owed its origins to the telenovela and the corrido, and the style had been pioneered by Quentin Tarentino, but *Amores Perros* showed that the Mexican film industry had risen from the ashes. After *Amores Perros*, financing and distribution for Mexican films would be easier. An industry was developing again. Whether the industry would overcome the influence of American styles and American cash was still in doubt. González Iñárritu's career had progressed from rock and roll disc jockey to telenovelas to *Amores Perros*; the direction could not be more promising.

A different future for the Mexican film industry was suggested in 2002 by *Y Tu Mamá Tambien* (*And Your Mother, Too*), which was even more successful than *Amores Perros* in Mexico and around the world. The producers had to get over a censorship problem in Mexico, but not for political reasons. The scenes of sexual intercourse, cunnilingus, and fellatio were vulgar, although not erotic. When the government refused to allow adolescents into the theaters, there were protests across the country by the very adolescents who were banned from seeing the movie. The government relented. But not for long.

The defeat of the PRI had changed the interests of the censors from political to moral issues. There was soon a new official rating system for admission to films. The left, including María Rojo, who was then the PRD delegate from Coyoacán, opposed all six categories in the new system, calling it a return to paternalism, a way to inhibit Mexican filmmaking while permitting U.S. films to show to much wider audiences, a sop to George Bush and the "gringos."

Mexican filmmaking had undergone an even bigger change. The writer-director, Alfonso Cuarón lived mainly in New York City. He had learned about the commercial side of filmmaking from American movies, and not from the best of them. *And Your Mother, Too* was a version of American films about adolescent sex fantasies aimed at adolescent audiences; Cuaron had learned the formula of vulgarity without sensuality, a form of anti-eros. His film could have been called *Porky's Mexican Movie*. There was some social criticism in the film to redeem the vulgarity, but the heart of the movie was in its title. "And your mother too" is the rejoinder, as every Mexican knows, to an insult.

"*Chinga tu madre!* [Fuck your mother!]."

"Y tu mamá tambien!"

The film showed some class differences, a bit of heavy-handed sarcasm about wealth and skin color, but it never transcended the vulgarity of the title. Nonetheless, Cuarón had made a name for himself directing adolescents for adolescents, and he had broken through into big-budget films. His next job was directing a Hollywood production, the third Harry Potter movie.

In the same year that Cuarón made his successful film, which he told the *New York Times Magazine* was about "coming,"[7] the Mexican actress Selma Hayek was finally able to complete *Frida*, the film she had been trying to produce for many years. Hayek as Frida Kahlo was a far more beautiful creature than Frida could have dreamed herself, there were too few Mexicans in the film, Frida's physical suffering was largely kept in the background, but none of the flaws mattered very much, for the film was as lovely to behold as Hayek herself, a woman of Lebanese and Mexican ancestry who does not walk, but glides, her bearing regal and her smile as sweet as the mangos that ripen in Mexico in May. If it was not exactly the pain-filled life of Frida Kahlo, it was the stuff of life for Mexican films. Cuarón's film was a Mexican version of Monica Lewinsky's blue dress; Hayek's was a celebration of the Mexican heart and mind.

RACE

In the movie made of Carlos Fuentes's novel *The Old Gringo*, a young Mexican actor in the role of a Villista officer appeared in several scenes with Gregory Peck. The Mexican actor was tall, slim, handsome, and if he was nervous about being in the company of the American star, it was not evident on the screen. Peck had been advising the actor throughout the filming, calming him, leading him into Peck's comfortable acting style. In previous films the young actor had worked as a Plains Indian, dressed in a breechcloth, riding bareback on a pinto horse. He had changed his name to Pedro Damián to help his acting career along, and he continued to use the name when he returned to Mexico City to take up a career as a director-producer at Televisa, the Mexican network that for many years had all but a monopoly in Mexican commercial broadcasting. Then, as now, Televisa owned the

[7]March 23, 2003.

most popular telenovelas. The telenovela, the mestiza offspring of the Mexican corrido and the American soap opera, is still the leading form of popular art in Mexico. It began as a melodramatic version of the Mexican heart laid bare, but it is no longer the heart where authenticity lives; the telenovela has become a segmented study of the culture, the market version of the heart. It was this inauthentic heart that Pedro chose.

In Mexico, actors and directors can survive only by working in telenovelas. Damián had aspirations in the theater, he was attracted to all things avant-garde, but he saw himself bound to the inauthentic heart, and before long he was among the most successful producer-directors in the field.

Televisa is a corporate entity not unlike the now-defunct Hollywood studio system. It has its own schools for actors, directors, and technicians, and it is enormously profitable. Televisa has several studios in Mexico City, many of them located in a large complex in the south. From its Mexico City headquarters Televisa studies the audience, which it understands in precise segments by time of day and by age, gender, income, and preferences in every imaginable category. And then it produces programs to measure.

The audience for television is no less examined at TV Azteca, the upstart network, where the pay is less and the facilities are not quite so good, but where greater risks have been taken, although always with the market in mind. Prior to the national elections of 2000, TV Azteca scored great successes with programming critical of the government and Mexican society in general. There was no better predictor of the outcome of the elections. TV Azteca had studied the audience and delivered to the inauthentic heart exactly what it wanted. Research showed that Mexico had not chosen the PAN; it had suffered all of the PRI that it could bear. Zedillo was a weak and (for Mexico) permissive president, perhaps because of his weakness. The Salinas scandals and the assassination of the PRI presidential candidate, Colosio, had readied the market for satire. TV Azteca produced a bitterly satirical telenovela and succeeded with it, but Televisa was still the master of meeting the market for popular culture and Pedro Damián was as good as anyone in Televisa at dealing with the time slot the corporation had slated for young teenagers.

Televisa's offices in the main production center wind around an enclosed court, floor after floor of producers, marketers, accountants, executives, directors. Pedro Damián's personal office, on one of the upper floors, holds a desk and a small rectangular conference table. The interior wall is glass. A corkboard covers the space between the windows on the outside wall. Pedro dresses in soft shirts and blue jeans; he is still a young man, but hurrying, feeling time, counting. He paces, smokes, speaks quickly; there is a schedule. Popular culture exists in time; it has an ancient Aztec duration. "Only a little while here on earth," the poet said.

After the telenovela about to go into production, *Mi Pequeña Traviesa* (The Little Scamp), there must be another one, and Pedro is already working on it. There will be a circus. He has read a story about a circus, a very touching story, and he likes the characters. How he casts the actors in the circus story will involve an examination of the heart. Meanwhile, in his office he met with his staff to work on *Traviesa*. The casting had been done, the main location chosen. Photographs of the characters were pinned to the wall. There were two families, not exactly Romeo and Juliet in modern dress, but two families in conflict and a heroine whose name was Julia. Pedro talked, paced, took telephone calls, smoked one cigarette after another.[8]

After the meeting, which lasted only a little while, Pedro broke from his schedule to talk about *Traviesa*. He spoke of teenage gangs in Mexico City, how they wanted to emulate the gangs of Los Angeles in everything from hairstyles to music to automobiles. He wanted to know about the Chicano gangs of Los Angeles, *los vatos* (the guys,) and their girls. There was one difference in Mexico: Indians. The gang in *Traviesa* would have at least one Indian member. Ehecatl was his name. I told Pedro that it meant "wind" and was associated with Quetzalcoatl. He smiled. It was new information, useful. Everything was useful. In conversation, he showed gratitude for anything said. And the more it seemed impolitic, honest, the more it seemed to please him, no matter who was speaking.

As we looked up at the pictures of the two families neatly laid out on the board in an anthropologist's hierarchy, there was something that demanded to be addressed. "Pedro," I said, "forgive me, but as I look up at the wall, it appears that you are a racist. The good family is fair-skinned, and the bad family is dark."

He answered immediately. "They are archetypes."

"Stereotypes."

He did not respond. Instead, he invited me to watch the first day of filming.

---

[8] Before Televisa agreed to schedule the program, Damián filmed four episodes, cut them into one show, and gave it to Televisa's researchers to test.

Pedro Damián likes to work on location. For *Traviesa* he had selected an *unidad*, a lower-middle-class housing project on the wrong side of the freeway in Tlalpan, which is in the southern part of the Federal District, at rush hour up to two hours by car from the Central Historic District. Every problem that befell Mexicans after the financial crisis in the early 1980s and the even more devastating one in 1994 fell harder on the people who live in the unidad in Tlalpan, for they had no economic cushion; they were the lower middle class, and many of them lost their hold on that class. Their savings evaporated, the value of anything they owned fell by half or more, and the interest rates on any money they owed were suddenly raised so high that borrowers had to sell or forfeit their goods or property. At the end of the century they had still not recovered.

The unidad, built in 1957, during the last years of the Mexican Miracle, had become a dangerous and dilapidated place. The iron gate to Building C3, where the telenovela was to be filmed, could be opened only with a key. Across the street from the gate, in a row of small shops, two meat markets, a furniture store, a general store, and a candy store were armored with steel plates or a heavy steel mesh curtain. The sidewalks had cracked, the stucco walls of Building C3 had not held. The trees of the unidad, planted when the buildings were new, were tall and unhealthy, with empty spaces between the branches, like a series of spindle-shanked old men looking down on the street and the people. It all seemed to be collapsing and unremarkable, as if it were not meant for history's recollection. The terrible weight of it was on the people. They groaned. Even the children. This was the place chosen for the home of the heroine, who was to serve as an example to a generation.

Pedro had chosen a seventeen-year-old girl, born in Marshalltown, Iowa, to play the lead. She had been "discovered" on a beach in Acapulco, where her parents had bought a small hotel in 1985, using her mother's Mexican citizenship to get around the law prohibiting foreigners from owning property near the seashore. The hotel had gone into bankruptcy during the crisis. Perhaps it had never done well. The young actress, Michelle Vieth, said the only words her father knew in Spanish were *un vaso de cerveza* (a glass of beer). The thought made her laugh. She had perfectly regular features, fair skin, a pert nose, full cheeks, white teeth, and dark, slightly secretive eyes. There was nothing remarkable about her, except when she laughed, and then the mischievous cast of her features turned satanic.

Awaiting the first morning of filming, Vieth wandered the street in front of the unidad, nervous, but more bored. She had not finished two years of high school. No one knew her. Some of the other actors barely acknowledged her as she passed. The crew took no notice. There were no autograph seekers, no photographers. Makeup had been brief. She was a small, slim girl with pale brown hair cut straight, parted down the center, not quite touching her shoulders. Her T-shirt and low-slung blue jeans revealed her navel. By midmorning, as Pedro passed by her on the way to the video truck, he chanced to comment that she was starting to get a little belly. She looked down at her navel: "It's because I haven't been to the toilet. I've been looking for a toilet for two hours."

At midday the cameras finally moved through the iron gate into the center of the unidad. The housing project rose for eight stories around a naked courtyard, broken stucco, iron railings. Everything had been painted turquoise. The paint had rolled down the walls of the unidad and dried into turquoise berms at the bottom. In some apartments the residents fought the routine decay of the unidad. On the second floor someone had affixed shiny gold stripes to a supporting pillar. On the first floor the resident of one apartment had covered the window with a piece of plastic made to look like stained glass. Every apartment had another face for its window. The effect was of a struggle against the slow descent of death by routine. Pedro had made the right choice: In all the months of *Traviesa*, the unidad was the one consistent character, the one authentic heart.

When all the actors and the cameras were finally ready and the filming began, a group of perhaps a dozen onlookers collected at the entrance to the unidad and mingled with the crew members there. Among the onlookers were an indigenous woman and a child. The girl, who was in the fifth grade, had only recently come to Mexico City. All afternoon she asked questions about the cameras and the long wires and why the actors had to say their lines over and over. Near the end of the day, when the company raced against the dying sun, the director called for La Traviesa's doll. A prop man hurried up to the gate with the doll in his hand and stood there waiting for the assistant director to take it from him. The newly arrived girl edged up close to him and looked carefully at the doll. It had long blond hair, blue eyes, and very fair skin. The girl, whose skin was very dark, said, "Oh, a North American doll!"

The filming moved from place to place. Months passed. Infatuation entered the story: Traviesa had a boyfriend, an actor considerably older and more fair-skinned than the half-American heroine. The on-screen love affair continued after the filming was over. In the entertainment press, the man in his early thirties and the girl still in her teens proclaimed themselves lovers. The Televisa publicists put the story on the covers of magazines devoted to telenovelas. Michelle Vieth was famous. *Traviesa*, which had been aimed at a young audience, mainly girls, an after-school drama, grew into a national favorite. Televisa had defined Mexico's economic categories into four viewing segments, A–D, in descending order. Telenovelas appealed to the C and D categories. TV Azteca, with its satirical telenovelas, looked for the B and C categories, but the Mexican economy put the bulk of the audience in the lower categories. The very poor, perhaps a third of the Mexican population, including vast numbers of children, did not count at all. The D category included many people who were lower middle class or poor, but not extremely poor. The unidad was the reality of D.

Halfway through the months of filming Vieth developed an ovarian cyst. She became difficult, a sickly star. The cyst burst, Traviesa went to the hospital, and the entertainment press went with her. She had been a small, dim star, but the illness turned the teenager into a supernova. Her picture decorated newsstands across Mexico. Thousands of letters arrived at the hospital. Many candles burned on behalf of the impish heroine. Traviesa, Traviesa, what would happen next to Vieth, or was it Traviesa? Vieth's life had begun to shape itself into the form of a telenovela. She had but one obvious move to make after she left the hospital: She married her fair-skinned costar.

Traviesa returned to work; her husband fawned over her on the set. She claimed weariness. On location on a soccer field where the good gang and the bad gang, the whites and the darks, played feverishly, Traviesa reclined in her special chair, a nurse at her side. When they brought her out to do a scene, she fumbled the lines again and again, asking for water, medicine, shade. Between takes she screwed up her face to show her pain, to prove what a show business trouper she was when the camera was running. Finally she said could not go on any longer. With the nurse and her husband at her side, a car took her to a nearby Red Cross station.

"Talk to her," Pedro said to me. "She likes you. Tell her she must come back to work."

A member of the crew drove me to the Red Cross station, where Michelle lay on a padded examining table partially covered by a white sheet. We spoke in English. She reminded me that she was expecting her American birth certificate any day now. The satanic smile crossed her face; her eyes turned to pleading, and she made herself suddenly pale. She tried to speak, failed to produce any words, lay back, and closed her eyes, then made another effort at words. In the wavering voice of the desperately ill, she asked, "Do you know a good Hollywood agent?"

Pedro and Traviesa fought until the end of the series, which lasted through most of a year. By the time the telenovela reached the halfway point, he had turned most of the work over to the assistant director and moved on to a new telenovela. It was the circus story, the one he had been contemplating when *La Pequeña Traviesa* was still in its earliest stages. This time, however, there was no market testing. "I feel this story," he said. "I am doing it because I have an instinct." He said there were two families in the circus story too. "But you will like this: The good family is the dark one."

Book Three

THE LIVER

(Ihiyotl)

28.

Indio, Lepero, Pelado, Naco:
Four Stages of Race and Class

. . . racism is not a feature of the Mexican consciousness. . . .
—ENRIQUE KRAUZE[1]

Miguel Ángel May May, a writer and educator, born and raised in the state of Yucatán, explains the relation between the Maya and the *dzules* (non-Indians) this way: A Maya friend went to an automobile dealer in Mérida to buy a new pickup truck. The man, middle-class, dressed in clean informal clothes, entered the Ford showroom and began looking over a pickup truck on display there. A salesman approached him, and said, "I'll give you ten pesos to wash the truck."

In Mexico City, taxi drivers do not pick up dark-skinned people on the streets and fair-skinned people do not get into taxis driven by dark-skinned men.

Until quite recently Chamulas and other indigenous people had to step off the sidewalks of San Cristóbal de las Casas to permit whites or mestizos to pass. Such racist rules could not be written into law in Mexico, but custom had the effect of law in Chiapas.

A student at the UNAM, a young man, tall and slim and very fair, said, "When we get on the bus, the dark ones [*prietos*] are very aggressive toward people with fair skin [*blancos*]. They push us and sometimes insult us, but if you fight back, you find that the dark ones are afraid of us. They don't really want to fight."

One of Mexico's leading intellectuals spoke of racism in the media. "If you look at the television news," he said, "you would think you were in Switzerland."

The young daughter of a well-known leftist said in response to a question

---

[1] *Mexico: Biography of Power*, p. 787.

about how her father would react if she brought home a dark-skinned suitor, "He would say, 'Who is this *pelado* [low-class guy]?' " Ifigenia Martínez, a former federal deputy and one of the founders of the PRD, as well as the former dean of the School of Economics at the UNAM, referred to the election of President José López Portillo, a criollo, as the takeover by the whites.

In a restaurant in Monterrey, having lunch with a friend who was born there to a successful family, I noted that there was a hierarchy of color in the restaurant: The customers were white, the headwaiter was a very fair mestizo, the waiters were more bronze mestizos, and the busboys either indigenous or very dark mestizos. My luncheon companion, who is very fair, and I guessed from their size and accents that the busboys were mainly from the south.

Monterrey is the whitest and most productive big city in Mexico. Many of Mexico's largest and most successful businesses grew up there. José Maiz Mier, the patriarch of one of the largest family-owned businesses, described one aspect of the success of Monterrey in terms of its whiteness: "Here we killed all the Indians." Maiz holds his views in a community that does not admit Jews to its best clubs, offers little or no opportunity to people who are not Roman Catholic, and has a system of blackballing leftists, dark-skinned people, and those it considers troublemakers. Maiz Mier is no more prejudiced than many Mexicans; he is just more open about his views.

Mexican racism has a long and complex history. It differs from racism in the United States in that there is no clear one drop rule—that is, one drop of indigenous blood does not make a person indigenous. The vast majority of Mexicans are mestizos, with indigenous, European, less often African, and even less often Asian, ancestors. When Mexicans come to the United States, they encounter U.S.-style racism, which has regional variations and is somewhat modified by class. The size of the Mexican population in the United States affects the degree of racism: The more people of a different (non-European) group, the greater the racist feeling. There is no need here to rediscover the causes of racism, but it is worth keeping in mind the connection of racism to fear. The newest fear of the racist in both the United States and Mexico comes with democracy. When nonwhites make up a large percentage of the population in a democratic society, they may choose to take political power, determining within constitutional limitations the lives of whites.

This statue of Coatlicue, Serpent Skirt, mother of the gods, stands in the Museum of Anthropology and History in Mexico City. She symbolizes the dualism of the Mesoamerican world, the symmetry of nature, the awesome progress from life to the place where her clawed feet grasp the earth. She is the virgin mother of Huitzilopochtli, the tutelary god of the Aztecs, and of Coyolxauhqui, the moon, and all of her allies. Coatlicue was impregnated by a feather that fell between her bosoms.

Death mask of Hanab Pacal, Lord Shield Pacal (615–683), Maya lord of Palenque, conqueror of the region, builder of pyramids, entombed in the Temple of the Inscriptions. Ruled from 627 (when he was twelve years old) until his death.

Olmec statues arranged exactly as they were buried. Note that one statue is made of different material and faces the others. The Olmecs were masters of form in art. It is probable that the Olmecs (a Nahuatl word meaning "rubber people"; no one knows what language the Olmecs spoke) were the mother culture of Mesoamerica.

The Maya wrote on codices (folded books), most of which were destroyed by Diego de Landa in a great auto-da-fé in the sixteenth century. The remaining codices (this is named the Madrid because it is kept there) have been carefully examined, and their religious, historical, agricultural, and philosophical content is slowly being deciphered.

Anachronistic drawings of Nahua rulers were common. This drawing of Nezahualcoyotl (1402–1472), huey tlahtoani of Texcoco, is from the Aubin Codex. Nezahualcoyotl was a poet, lawgiver, and philosopher.

Motecuhzoma II (Xocoyotzin or Younger) reigned from 1502 until he was killed during the Spanish siege of Tenochtitlán. The postconquest drawing shows him looking at a shooting star, one of the omens he saw prior to the Spanish invasion of Mexico.

Cuauhtémoc (1502–1525), the heroic last ruler and defender of Tenochtitlán. The throne indicates his place; the bird at the upper left is his name sign, Descending Eagle, ironically a metaphor for the setting sun. The Spaniards captured him, took him south in search of gold, and finally nailed him to a ceiba tree in the jungle.

Pedro Alvarado, known to the Mexica as Tonatiuh, the sun, for his red hair. He was the cruelest of the Spanish invaders, a killer and torturer. He was killed in 1541 while trying to put down an Aztec uprising led by Tenamaztle (one of the informants of Fray Bartolomé de las Casas, the Defender of the Indians).

Hernán (Fernando) Cortés (1485–1547), who led the Spanish invasion of Mexico, conversed with Nahuas through his concubine and translator known as La Malinche. Cortés, trained as a lawyer, had never before led men in battle when he and his small force invaded Mexico. He used troops from Tlaxcala and other vassal states to conquer the Mexica. (See the map on p. 34.)

Carlos de Sigüenza y Góngora was one of the most important colonial authors, an Indianist until the riots of 1692 turned him against native peoples. He was a close friend of Sor Juana, whom he influenced as a writer and thinker.

Juan Ruiz de Alarcón, a playwright and poet, skewered the Spanish court in the early seventeenth century, laying bare its morals and mores.

Sor Juana Inés de la Cruz (Juana Asbaje) was perhaps the greatest Mexican poet. She was a feminist, who dressed as a boy to attend the university in the seventeenth century, and an Enlightenment scholar. Early in her life she lived at the viceroy's court, which she left to join the Convent of San José and later San Jerónimo. Near the end of her life she recanted her modern beliefs and attitudes in a document she signed with her own blood.

Quetzalcoatl (Codex Borbonicus), who is also known as Ce Acatl Topiltzin, One Reed, Our Revered Prince, Feathered Serpent, was a monk at Tula in the historical version and also the god who brought humans back to life before this last and final sun. He was born in the year One Reed, died in the year One Reed, and was expected to return in the year One Reed (1519). He was sometimes shown with a beard, like Cortés.

The Virgin of Guadalupe appeared to Juan Diego at Tepeyac in 1531. She is the patron saint of Mexico and the most powerful Catholic religious figure in the Americas. In Mexico the brown-skinned Virgin is the symbol of the nation and its most unifying force. The Mexicans carried images of her into the wars for Independence in the early nineteenth century. She represents Mexico after the invasion as Quetzalcoatl represents pre-Hispanic Mexico.

The *Nican Mopohua* (Here It Is Told) is the story of the Apparition of La Santísima Virgen de Guadalupe at Tepeyac.

Miguel Hidalgo y Costillo, a criollo priest, gave the famous grito of Independence in the town of Dolores in 1810. He organized a great, ragtag army under the banner of the Virgin of Guadalupe, but was ultimately defeated by the Spanish Army, captured, and executed. His head was displayed on the walls of the granary of Guanajuato.

José María Morelos y Pavón, of African and Spanish descent, was Hidalgo's student. He led the second War for Independence. Hidalgo had said he was a leader of the people; Morelos said he was the people's servant. He was defeated by Agustín de Iturbide in 1813 and executed. Under Morelos, rebels proclaimed an end to slavery, the caste system, and the unfair taxation of Indians.

Agustín de Iturbide, a conservative, shown here about to embrace Vicente Guerrero rather than go to war with him, finally led Mexico to Independence. Soon thereafter he proclaimed himself emperor but was driven into exile by Santa Anna. He returned to Mexico and was executed.

Miguel Lerdo de Tejada, one of the leading liberals along with Melchor Ocampo, helped write the Constitution of 1857; authored the Ley Lerdo, confiscating property of the Catholic Church; and provided much of the legal structure behind the reforms instituted by Benito Juárez.

Benito Juárez, president of Mexico, Liberal leader of the Reform, pictured with his wife, Margarita Maza. Juárez, a Zapoteco, learned Spanish, studied law, rose to chief justice of the Mexican Supreme Court, became president in 1858, fought the Conservatives, defeated them, then fought the French under Maximilian, and defeated them. Juárez held on to the presidency year after year until he died in office in 1872.

Matías Romero served Juárez as ambassador to the United States, confidant, and financial adviser. He later served in the administration of Porfirio Díaz. Romero was probably responsible for convincing the United States that its interests lay in the defeat of Maximilian and the return to power of the Juaristas.

Porfirio Díaz, dictator who ruled Mexico for thirty-five years until his ouster by Francisco I. Madero and the antireelectionists and liberals in 1910. Díaz modernized Mexico, bringing railroads, electricity, communications, and vast amounts of foreign investment. He was advised in this by the científicos, followers of Auguste Comte.

Justo Sierra Méndez, Mexican historian, supported the Porfiriato (Díaz government) and the ideas of the científicos. He wrote poetry, reorganized the university, and served as secretary of education. Born in 1848, the son of the novelist Justo Sierra O'Reilly, he died only two years after the ouster of Díaz.

Victoriano Huerta, who ordered the murder of President Francisco I. Madero, signed this photograph to Nelson O'Shaughnessy, who replaced U.S. Ambassador Henry Lane Wilson in 1913. Wilson was complicit in the overthrow of Madero. Huerta was defeated during the civil wars of 1910–1920 and exiled to the United States, where he plotted with the Germans, was arrested, and died of alcoholism in a military prison.

General Francisco Villa, who never aspired to the presidency, sits in the president's Eagle Chair after his triumphant entrance into Mexico City along with Emiliano Zapata (seated on his right). Tomás Urbina sits on the other side of Villa. Rodolfo Fierro (in the cowboy hat) stands on the right. It was the high point of the Zapata/Villa forces of the Convention.

Francisco I. Madero (bearded) and Felipe Ángeles. Madero led the antireelectionist movement, believed in democracy and spiritualism, thought of himself as Bhima, the hero of the Bhagavad Gita, governed naively, and died tragically, duped by the American ambassador and General Huerta. Ángeles, an intellectual and an artillery officer, remained loyal to Madero to the end, then joined Villa against Huerta and Carranza. One of the few unalloyed heroes of the civil wars, he was executed by order of Carranza.

José Vasconcelos, here shown in his youth, became secretary of education shortly after the end of major hostilities in 1920. He is known for having developed the idea of the raza cósmica, a single race comprising all the others. Vasconcelos gave grants to the great muralists of the postwar era: Orozco, Rivera, and Siqueiros.

Diego Rivera, self-portrait, is the best known of the Mexican muralists, both for his work, character, love affairs, and marriage to Frida Kahlo and for his famous contretemps with Rockefeller in New York, who commissioned him to do a mural, then looked at the Communist figures, and ordered it to be destroyed. Rivera's work appears in many American as well as Mexican cities, including his famed depictions of the Ford Motor Company plant in Detroit.

José Clemente Orozco, who lost a hand as a child, painted ferocious murals in which he depicted scenes of civil war, religion, Aztec gods, and Mexican historical figures. His great murals were done in Guadalajara, in the Orphanage and the Governor's Palace. His work was enigmatic, powerful, content submitted to the discipline of form.

First Chief Venustiano Carranza (bearded) and beside him General Álvaro Obregón. They led the northern Constitutionalists during the civil wars. Obregón defeated Villa at Celaya; Carranza approved of the betrayal of Zapata. Carranza governed Mexico until Obregón had him killed. His daughters borrowed the money to pay for his funeral.

Alfonso Reyes (1889–1959) was one of the founders of the Ateneo de la Juvented, a group of young Mexican intellectuals who opposed the Porfiriato and the cientificos. Alfonso Reyes is known for his literary style and prodigous output. He wrote in every form: stories, poems, essays, criticism. Although he spent much of his life in diplomatic posts abroad, he founded what is now the Colegio de Mexico.

General Bernardo Reyes, father of the writer, was a powerful conservative governor and army general. He plotted to unseat Madero, was sent to the Santiago Tlalteloco military prison, escaped, and led an attack on the presidential palace at the beginning of the Ten Tragic Days of civil war in the capital. He was killed on the first day, February 9, 1913.

Daniel Cosío Villegas (1898–1976), author of a multivolume history of the civil wars of 1910–1920, liberal professor, who taught in the United States for many years. He exchanged insults with Mexican presidents, retained his independence and the clarity of his ideas.

Manuel Gómez Morín, former rector of the UNAM, founded the Partido Acción Nacional (PAN) in 1939. The party grew very slowly at first, mainly in the northernmost states, where its members were persecuted by the PRI. Vicente Fox Quesada, a member of the PAN, became president of Mexico in 2000, but on an Alliance for Change ticket.

Plutarco Elías Calles, Mexican president 1924–1928, began his career as a leftist, with firm anti–Catholic Church views. He is credited with helping bring Mexico out of the turmoil of its civil wars. He ruled from behind the scenes until Lázaro Cárdenas forced him into exile. Calles ended his life a Nazi.

Francisco Toledo, photographed during an early gallery show. Toledo, now Mexico's leading painter, spent several years in Paris, where he was befriended by Mexico's other great Oaxacan painter, Rufino Tamayo. Toledo returned to his native Oaxaca, where he works and operates a workshop for young artists and artisans.

Rufino Tamayo (1899–1991) broke with the muralists to follow his own path in painting. Members of la Ruptura (the Rupture) claimed him as their own, but Tamayo, a Zapotecan from Oaxaca, who expressed his admiration for both the muralists and la Ruptura, said he did not belong to either. He was a brilliant colorist with a genius for what the critic Clive Bell called "significant form."

Juan Rulfo (1918–1986), shown here as a young man at the peak of his career, is one of the great Mexican writers of fiction. His novel *Pedro Páramo* (1955) was the forerunner of what became known as magical realism. Besides that novel and a book of spare, beautiful stories, *The Burning Plain* (1953), Rulfo did not publish any other work. In *Pedro Páramo* history and dreams meld, names change, time is cyclical, and everything is perfectly Tapatío, as a work by a writer so deeply rooted in his native Jalisco should be.

Actress María Félix (1914–2002) was described in Europe as well as Mexico as "the most beautiful woman in the world." Her beauty gave rise to popular songs and a long string of successful films in Mexico until a scandal drove her out of the country. La Doña, María Bonita, La Félix changed the way Mexico understood the role of women.

Mario Moreno, or Cantinflas (1911–1993), was Mexico's great comic actor, in his familiar costume of tiny hat, kerchief and undershirt, and trousers at half-mast. He was Mexico's Chaplin, but a Chaplin who spoke, satirizing the double-talk of bureaucrats. He portrayed the pelado, the poor soul from the countryside trying desperately to make his way in the city.

Jorge Negrete (1911–1953), one of Mexico's first great movie stars, established the role of the singing cowboy in a series of hit movies, usually in costume, always representing goodness, justice, religion. His films were nostalgic, portraying the order and high moral character of the hacendado during the Porfiriato. He married actress María Félix. Negrete died of liver disease, a result of hepatitis contracted in New York City.

A scene from *Los Olvidados* (1950), directed by Luis Buñuel and starring Roberto Cobo, which was an international success, establishing Mexico as a place capable of making quality films. It tells the story of a group of street urchins in Mexico City and includes a controversial scene in which a legless man is sent careering down a steep hill by the street toughs.

María Rojo, shown here at home with her husband, Esteban Schmelz, and granddaughter Fabiana, is Mexico's most important living actress, known not only for her brilliant portrayals in such films as *Danzón* but for her role in left-of-center politics, having been elected a federal deputy on the PRD ticket. She starred in *Rojo Amanecer* (Red Dawn), a film about the 1968 Tlatelolco Massacre. The government refused to allow the film to be shown in theaters, but public opinion forced it to change its position. It became one of the most watched Mexican movies of all time, alerting the country to its deepest problems. Sr. Schmelz, also in the film world, located an old copy of the poster for *Rojo Amanecer* shown here.

Octavio Paz (1904–1998) won a Nobel Prize in 1995 for his work as a poet and essayist. He was for many years the leading intellectual in Mexico, founder and editor of magazines, ambassador to India, a man of conscience, who resigned his post immediately after the 1968 Tlatelolco Massacre. Among his many works no poem was better known than *Piedra del Sol* (Sun Stone), and no prose works more than *The Labyrinth of Solitude*, which launched his career, and his biography of Sor Juana.

Carlos Fuentes, born in 1928, has been Mexico's most widely read novelist since he published *Where the Air Is Clear* in 1958, establishing himself as a Mexican modernist and one of the most important writers of the Latin American "BOOM." Since then he has published a steady stream of successful novels, always deftly written and always exploring the form of the novel as well as the content. In recent years he has been one of the leading voices of the left.

The only known photograph of all six writers who signed the Crack Generation Manifesto in 1996, breaking from traditional Mexican fiction and its nationalistic limitations: (left to right) Ricardo Chávez, Ignacio Padilla, Eloy Urroz, Pedro Ángel Palou, Vicente Herrasti, and Jorge Volpi.

Carlos Monsiváis was born in 1938 in Mexico City and still lives there, chronicling the politics, art, and culture of the country and particularly the city. He has written for most quality publications in Mexico over his career, and his work has been gathered into several books. His style is complex and inventive, and his thoughts are original. He is generally considered the best living essayist in Mexico.

Elena Poniatowska is Mexico's most prominent journalist, widely known for her brilliant oral history of the 1968 massacre at Tlatelolco. Poniatowska is also the author of a multivolume series of interviews (*Todo México*) of political and artistic figures.

Luis Echeverría (shown passing power to José López Portillo on the left) became president of Mexico after Díaz Ordaz. It is not clear whether he or his predecessor initiated the massacre. Echeverría governed from the left, admired intellectuals, and established Mexico's dirty war, in which anyone suspected of Communist sympathies was imprisoned or disappeared. He made a genuine effort to bring indigenous people into the general society.

The Carrillo Family—Seventy Years of Government Service

Photograph of Mexican President General Álvaro Obregón signed in 1923 to Alejandro P. Carrillo, then Mexican consul in Japan.

Alejandro P. Carrillo (right), Mexican consul in San Antonio with his son Alejandro Carrillo Marcor in 1927.

Former Mexican President General Lázaro Cárdenas with leaders of the Young PRIistas, Alejandro Carrillo Castro (far left) and Miguel Osorio Marban (left).

General Lázaro Cárdenas witnesses the wedding of Alejandro Carrillo Marcor's daughter in 1958. Carrillo Marcor was governor of the state of Sonora from 1975 to 1979. Earlier in his career he was a member of the left wing of the circle close to the former president.

José López Portillo, who became president of Mexico in 1976, congratulates Alejandro Carrillo Castro upon passing his law examination in 1965. Carrillo worked very closely with López Portillo during the early years of his administration and was rumored to be a candidate to succeed him.

Carrillo Castro and President Miguel de la Madrid. Carrillo headed the Mexican Government Employees' Social Service and Pension System (ISSSTE) from 1982 to 1988. He became part of the reform wing of the party as the PRI turned toward neoliberalism.

In 1986 (left to right) Carlos Salinas de Gotari, secretary of budget and planning; Carrillo Castro, head of ISSSTE; and Alfredo del Mazo, secretary of energy, mines, and state industries. Salinas and del Mazo were vying at the time to become President de la Madrid's choice to succeed him.

Carrillo Castro as Mexican ambassador to the Organization of American States, 1991–1994. When Zedillo was elected in 1994, he moved Carrillo to director of immigration, where he would suffer criticism from all sides. Prior to that he had been director of the Commission to Aid Refugees. In violation of existing rules he signed an order making thousands of undocumented Guatemalan refugees legal residents, and then resigned his post.

Carrillo Castro, currently president of the National Institute of Public Administration, which no longer receives federal funding and is finally free of party control, with his wife, one of Mexico's most popular radio and television talk show hosts, Talina Fernández.

Arturo "Blackie" Durazo (in uniform), President José López Portillo (1976–1982), Carlos Hank González (left). Durazo was a small-time tough whom López Portillo promoted to chief of police; in the job Durazo created the most corrupt police department in Mexican history. Durazo reported to Carlos Hank, who ran the Federal District under López Portillo.

Luis Donaldo Colosio, seen here with his wife, Diana Laura, and his father, Luis Colosio Fernández, was assassinated on March 23, 1994, in Tijuana while campaigning for president of Mexico on the PRI ticket. Colosio, who had been president of the PRI before being tapped by Salinas de Gotari to succeed him, was a reformer within a party in which reformers have consistently been pushed aside. Before his assassination he had openly attacked the government, the party, and Salinas.

Ernesto Zedillo Ponce, president from 1994 to 2000, was Colosio's campaign manager and took his place after the assassination. Zedillo was a fiscal conservative, in favor of globalization and austerity, but he opened the PRI to primary elections and strengthened the Institute of Federal Elections, leading to the most honest election in Mexican history at the end of his term.

This photograph of Rafael Sebastián Guillén Vicente appeared in the magazine *Proceso*. Sebastián Guillén is more generally seen wearing a balaclava and smoking a pipe in his revolutionary persona as Subcomandante Marcos. From the jungle of the Chiapas lowlands the former UNAM student became a world figure through his writings on the Internet. He is witty, well-read, intelligent, and his comments on everything from globalization to Mexican politics and indigenous rights have made him a hero to people throughout the world.

A fiesta in Chamula, photographed by Genaro Sántiz Gómez and published in *Camaristas, Fotografos Mayas de Chiapas*. Sántiz is a member of the Chiapas Photography Project founded by Carlota Duarte in 1992. Over two hundred men and women from ten different Maya ethic groups participate in the project. Its archive (AFI) is located near the Tzotzil village where the picture was made.

The Indigenous Photography Archive staff: Genaro Sántiz Gómez, Juana López López, Petul Hernández Guzmán, Maruch Sántiz Gómez, Xunka' López Díaz, Carlota Duarte, Emiliano Guzmán Meza. Their work has been exhibited in Mexico, Europe, and the United States. They have published two books and gathered an archive of more than seventy-five thousand images.

Jorge Castañeda as a young man, when his politics were on the left. The son of a Mexican secretary of state, he became secretary of state himself, as well as the author of many books and a professor at New York University and other institutions.

In 2003 Jorge Castañeda announced an exploratory campaign for president of Mexico, probably on a fourth party ticket. He had resigned as secretary of state in the Fox cabinet, saying that the United States had turned its attention away from Mexico after the 9/11 attack on the World Trade Center. Elba Esther Gordillo, shown with Castañeda, is a bridge between him and Carlos Salinas. Andrés Manuel López Obrador, mayor of Mexico City, is the likely PRD candidate. Roberto Madrazo Pintado is a likely PRI candidate. The PAN has little hope after the Fox sexenio.

Immigrants to Mexican border cities often settle on unimproved land, building three-sided shelters like the one shown, hoping to find employment in a maquiladora (assembly plant), move up to a rudimentary house, and improve their standard of living. Many of them are among the 30 percent of Mexicans suffering from malnutrition.

A couple from the state of Veracruz in their shelter in the colony named for Porfirio Muñoz Ledo near Matamoros. They have no running water, electricity, or sewerage. All their earthly goods are shown in the photograph. They are squatters but confident that the government will not move them off the land.

A view of the abandoned railroad tracks in Cuernavaca, where houses have been built up on both sides. A preschool and a university level course for their parents has been established there by a Baptist group from the United States and the Community Foundation of Morelos. Elena Cepeda, daughter of the former governor of Coahuila; Herlinda Suárez, daughter of the former governor of Chiapas; and Martha Galas, of a prominent Spanish family, three of Mexico's social doctors, support the work there.

The cover of a brochure distributed by the Streetwalkers' Brigade, "Elisa Martínez," in the Plaza Loreto section of Mexico City. The streetwalkers, in their sixties and seventies, serve the young internal migrants who are too poor to have girlfriends or to pay younger, more expensive prostitutes.

Raúl Murguía Rosete, the tall man in the white shirt in the first row center, manages and funds more than fifty projects for the United Nations Development Program on the Yucatán Peninsula. He is pictured here with students from Sihó, where UN-sponsored projects are helping grow medicinal herbs and educate students like those in the group pictured here.

Andy May Citúk (left) and José Chim Ku of Sihó work on reading ancient Maya writing. Chim is the young leader of the village. An oral history of his life as a young man, a student, and then the leader of his people appears in the Appendix. Both May and Chim have achieved national recognition as young leaders.

A group of students from Colegio Williams, a private school in Cuernavaca that sends almost all its graduates on to colleges in the United States and Mexico. Compare the size and robustness of these students with those of the older Maya. The Maya have diminished in size after nearly five hundred years of poor nutrition following the invasion.

Historian Alejandra García Quintanilla of the University of Yucatán was president of the faculty of the Escuela de Alta Cultura Maya—Hunab Ku, in which Maya language and culture were taught at a sophisticated level to young adults. García Quintanilla, a Fulbright scholar, holds a doctorate from the University of North Carolina.

Herlinda Suárez Zozaya de Valencia is one of the leading scholars in the field of education in Mexico. She is the author of numerous books and articles and is an investigador II, the second-highest rank in the Mexican university system. She has founded Clemente Courses in the Humanities to teach young adults in Mexico and Chicago, working with the UNAM, the University of Chicago, and ITESM (Monterrey Tec).

Gustavo Valencia is director of development at the Morelos campus of ITESM in Morelos. He holds a doctorate in mathematics. Valencia is also an important civic figure in Morelos, where he heads civic commissions, serves on the board of elections, and continues building the Morelos campus into one of the major sites of the largest private university in Mexico.

Javier Valencia, who worked as a research assistant on this book, is a student at ITESM. He and his sister Fernánda, a graduate student, are pictured here with the author. Both young people have studied in Europe as well as Mexico. Fernánda is multilingual and interested in foreign affairs. Javier is a philosophy major.

José Romero Keith, with his wife, Marcella Gavaldon, and his mother, Del Romero, continues the family tradition of service begun by Matías Romero during the Juárez administration. After graduating from Harvard, Romero helped bring modernizing technology to indigenous villages. He has been an executive in the Pan-American Health Organization and the Capacity 2015 project of the UN Development Program. He and his wife are among Mexico's "social doctors."

Porfirio Muñoz Ledo has held almost every major political office in Mexico: ambassador to the United Nations, secretary of education, speaker of the Federal Cámara de Diputados, president of the PRI, cofounder of the PRD, presidential candidate of a minor party, and ambassador to the European Union.

Sergio Aguayo Quezada has long been one of the leading human rights activists in Mexico. He received his doctorate from Johns Hopkins University. He taught there, at the Colegio de México, and the University of California at Berkeley. His wife, Eugenia, represents journalists in Mexico.

Rodrigo Rojes, shown here at age five, youngest grandchild of Ifigenia Martínez. Only three years later he and his grandmother were watching videotapes about the external debt in Latin America.

Carlos Salinas de Gotari, as a college student with some hair and no mustache, stands to the left of Ifigenia Martínez, La Maestra, then head of the economics department at the UNAM. Salinas, who was not a member of the class of '69 gathered for the photograph, ran to join the group and of course to stand next to the head of the department.

Cuauhtémoc Cárdenas, son of the former president, has been the moral leader of the PRD since it was formed, although Cárdenas, former governor of Michoacán, lost three presidential elections.

La Maestra in the Green Salon of the Cámara de Diputados in 2002. She was a strong supporter of indigenous rights and the Accords of San Andrés, which granted such rights but was never implemented.

Miguel Angel May May, the author, taught Maya language in the Sihó project of the UNDP. He is now the head of Maya language education for the state of Yucatán. He and Alejandra García Quintanilla and Raúl Murguía Rosete frequently work together with other NGOs.

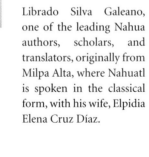

Cover of *Jump'eel Tzikbaal Yo'olal U Kaajil Kimbilá* by Miguel Angel May May, who is becoming one of the better known of many writers now working in the Maya language. May writes in Yucatecan Maya; a novel has now been published in Tzotzil Maya, and other works are being written in a new florescence of indigenous writing.

Librado Silva Galeano, one of the leading Nahua authors, scholars, and translators, originally from Milpa Alta, where Nahuatl is spoken in the classical form, with his wife, Elpidia Elena Cruz Díaz.

Cover of *New Songs of Anáhuac* by Natalio Hernández Xocoyotzin, who writes poetry and essays in Nahuatl and Spanish. Hernández Xocoyotzin has also been executive director of Writers in Indigenous Languages and works with the National Institute of Indigenous Languages. He has lectured and read his work in many countries.

The novelist and the historian when they were young: Juan Rulfo (left) and Miguel León-Portilla. Rulfo had by then written *Pedro Páramo*, and León-Portilla had written *Aztec Thought and Culture*, which changed the way the world thought of indigenous people. Rulfo was director of the editorial department of the National Institute of Indigenous Studies in the 1960s.

Miguel León-Portilla, Ascensión Hernández de León-Portilla, author of the major bibliographical work of Nahuatl literature and university professor, and their grandson Miguelito. León-Portilla is president of the Colegio Nacional (the Mexican Academy), professor emeritus at the UNAM, holder of eighteen honorary degrees from universities around the world, former Mexican ambassador to UNESCO, author of more than forty books, recipient of numerous prizes, and a defender of indigenous rights who has argued their case in his published work and in public and private with successive presidents of Mexico.

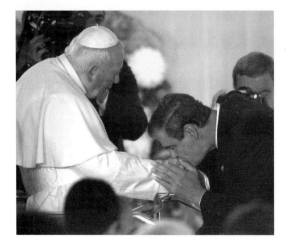

President Vicente Fox Quesada, who once hoped to study for the priesthood, kisses the ring of John Paul II on the Pope's visit to Mexico to celebrate the canonization of Juan Diego.

Don José plays the guitar and sings corridos. In 2002 he was ninety-four years old. He did not bring his wife to fiestas with him, he said, "Because I might meet someone." He has lived his entire life within sight of the great volcano known as Don Goyo (Popocatepetl). He was eleven years old when Emiliano Zapata was betrayed and murdered at Chinameca.

These children also live within sight of Don Goyo. During fiestas they sing in Nahuatl and dance to the sound of Don José's guitar. They dress for the occasion in the white cottons and red sashes that were worn by campesinos who fought under the command of Zapata.

In the Americas, racism also has colonial origins. Small numbers of invaders had to find ways to control large indigenous populations. The sooner the invader could use racist tactics to make the native population internalize feelings of inferiority, the sooner conquest could be completed.

The most curious thing about racism, in its Mexican form, is the ability of racial conflicts, like bacteria, to mutate to meet new conditions. A priori one would think the mestizaje would solve the problem of racism in Mexico or any other country in which two disparate sets of physical characteristics produced a third. A tidy progression seems only reasonable: Thesis, antithesis, synthesis, and that's the end of history for racism. History has a different lesson, however. Sweet logic comes to grief in Mexico; the metaphor of the bacteria prevails. It has so far gone through four stages.

Before the four stages are examined, a fifth—denial—has to be considered. All Mexicans will agree that the country suffers from racist attitudes toward indigenous people. The leaders of government, much of the press, and many intellectuals will argue that the racism has only to do with indigenous people. President Vicente Fox gave this quote to the newspapers during his campaign:[2]

> *Yes, we have three different Mexicos. The north is the vanguard both economically and educationally; it is the part that leads in development and has the best levels of education and economic development in the country.*
>
> *In the center we have a deep-rooted historical phenomenon. It is where the grand social movements required by the country have emerged. And day in and day out this area formed of Guanajuato, Jalisco, Querétaro, and Aguascalientes [with PANista governments] is going to provide much of what we speak of as the transformation of the country. I would say that the impetus for politics, democratization, federalization, and good government comes from the center.*
>
> *The south, unfortunately, is full of political bosses, scorpions, vermin, poverty, and ignorance, and not in vain do the PRI and PRD campaign where this situation exists, so they can sustain their successes because of ignorance, lack of education, poverty, and misery.*

The old man Maiz Mier, who was not campaigning for the presidency, put his racist views more openly and succinctly, but there was no doubt after Fox's quote that he held a certain view of Mexico's indigenous population.

[2] *La Jornada*, August 6, 1998.

He sold them Coca-Cola, his family owned huge ranches, where, according to *Reforma* and other Mexican newspapers, they employed children in violation of the child labor laws. Fox was not attacked on the question of race by either his PRI, PRD, or minor-party adversaries. He did, however, refer to his PRI rival as a *maricón* (queer) during the campaign, as if to clarify his cultural politics. In Mexico one does not raise the question of racism; race hatred is always described as the ugly situation Mexicans encounter when they cross the border to the United States.

Racism does exist in Mexico, but in a form unique to the mixing of races, the unresolved mestizaje. For example, Benito Juárez, whose ancestry was indigenous, is often spoken of as Mexico's "whitest" president. And the characterization has validity. Juárez was largely spared from the abuse suffered by indigenous people. He lived a hard life as a young man, losing his parents early, and his grandparents soon after. He went to live with an uncle, who gave him fieldwork to do and taught him to read. In his autobiographical *Notes for My Children* he spoke of poverty, of working as a household servant and in the fields, and of the great effort it took to become an educated man, but he did not speak of suffering abuse because he was indigenous either as a young man, a seminary student, a lawyer, and then as the leader and savior of a nation. Skin color, height, etc., all the physical characteristics that generally describe racial differences, both do and do not apply in Mexico. The irrational conflict between vaguely defined groups of people that would merit the name racism elsewhere requires a new name in Mexico. It is often connected to class, but not always.

Jaime and Elvira Montejo, two social workers who work with day laborers, pimps, thieves, and prostitutes in one of the poor areas near the center of Mexico City, see the issue of race in raw form, lacking entirely the niceties as well as the cruelties of the middle-class world. According to the Montejos, many of the people they work with come from mountain communities, where the culture is indigenous and the people are very proud of their culture. When they come to the city, however, they find a different situation. Elvira Montejo said, "If a woman is seen eating nopales [cactus] and other indigenous food, dressing her children in the style of her village, she will suffer discrimination. They learn quickly when they come to Mexico [City]. Even if people are Indian by blood, they don't show it." The racism she describes has more to do with culture than with physical characteristics. It involves class, even more than color, and the way a person behaves in the world. In Mexico no one of the three criteria for discrimination is sufficient in itself. Each has influence by itself, but not such great influence on employment, social life, politics, or academic life as to merit the word "racism." Yet racism has a defining effect on much of life in Mexico. A more inclusive name would be a more accurate denotation; perhaps *culturalismo* could serve, although it does not, at first glance, give proper weight to physical characteristics. It bears some relation to the problem for Mexicans living or visiting in the United States.

They encounter two kinds of racism. One kind will come from outside the extended group of people from Spanish-speaking countries known as Latinos or Hispanics. The other, which I have said elsewhere should be called *racismo*, will come from within the larger category of Latinos and be directed at people of Mexican descent by those whose ancestors (or who themselves) lived in Cuba, Puerto Rico, Argentina, Spain, and so on. Similarly, the Mexicans and Mexican-Americans will say the Cuban exiles are arrogant or Fascists, the Puerto Ricans can't speak Spanish, the Argentines are arrogant (buy them for what they're worth, sell them for what they think they're worth), and they will all accuse one another of ethnic disparagement, if not hatred.

Mexicans-Americans and Mexicans have very different views of each other. On the night of the boxing match between the great Mexican fighter Julio César Chávez and the Golden Boy from East Los Angeles Oscar de la Hoya, the director and professor of drama at UCLA José Luis Valenzuela and his wife, the writer and actress Evelina Fernández, had an argument. José Luis was born in Mexico and Evelina in California.[3] The argument was very funny and very theatrical, an amusement for their children and guests, but the same argument was not amusing in many parts of the United States and Mexico. There was no question of race in the boxing match, but the distinction between those who stayed in Mexico and those who went to the United States is a complication in the question of race.

The conflation of class and race began almost immediately after the arrival of the Spaniards. The invaders held all those who were not Spanish in low esteem but then distinguished between those who were pipiltin (nobles) and those who were macehuales (common people). As the generations mixed and mixed again and people of African descent came into the gene pool, the Spaniards developed systems for categorizing various com-

---

[3]Valenzuela of course favored the Mexican, and Fernández rooted for the Chicano.

binations. Two are shown in Santamaría's *Diccionario de Mejicanismos,* one from the National Museum and another from a series of numbered paintings in Michoacán.

Español con India—Mestizo
Mestizo con Española—Castizo
Castizo con Española—Español
Español con Negra—Mulato
Mulato con Española—Chino (curly hair)
Chino con India—Salta atrás (step backwards)
Salta atrás con Mulata—Lobo (wolf)
Lobo con China—Gibaro (peasant)
Gibaro con Mulata—Albarazado
Albarazado con Negra—Cambujo
Cambujo con India—Zambaigo
Zambaigo con Loba—Calpamulato
Calpamulato con Cambuza—Tente en el aire (hummingbird?)
Tente en el aire con Mulata—No te entiendo (I don't understand)
No te entiendo con India—Torna atrás (throwback)

The systems are similar, and there are many paintings, about half of them unsigned, depicting the various combinations of origins. It is clear from the paintings that the color of one's skin (on a scale of light to dark) determined the quality of life and labor. The peninsulares lived best, then the criollos, and then all the rest of the people on the color scale.

The paintings give a great deal more information than the names but still do not draw the class distinctions that existed among the shadings of white through brown to black. Fray Servando, who had his troubles, but ultimately had great influence on the Mexican drive toward Independence, was quite willing to say that he had indigenous ancestors, but the ancestor he chose to mention was not merely a noble: He claimed descent from Motecuhzoma himself!

At almost the same time that the experts in racial categories were at work painting the various destinies of nonwhites, another class had been defined in Mexico City. These were the leperos (lepers), largely homeless, poor Spaniards who had come to New Spain hoping to find wealth or simply relief from a difficult life on the Iberian Peninsula only to encounter class prejudice and what was perhaps worse, a lack of any means to earn an honest living, because the lowest forms of labor, those which the leperos could have done, went to indigenous people. The leperos gained a reputation as thieves and lowlifes, very much like the people later defined by merciless Americans as the underclass, a class of dangerous and dirty people who have never been dear to anyone. Neither Crown nor Church cared for the leperos; they were the untouchables of New Spain.

Indigenous people found no defenders through the end of the nine-teenth century, although there was always someone ready to praise their pre-Hispanic ancestors. Those who began to care about them in the early years of the twentieth century thought the only way to save them was to strip them of their culture. Meanwhile, the number of mestizos in Mexico continued to grow. The cosmic race envisioned by Vasconcelos was in the process of being born, but the world still belonged to the criollos. Power belonged to the northern generals, and they were fair-skinned when not white. Madero and the men who supported him in the north were all fair-skinned or white. The men of Morelos were dark, indigenous.

Lázaro Cárdenas was the first person with real power in the history of Mexico to support the humanity of indigenous people. His politics had lost much of its impetus during the last years of his term, but his effect was immeasurable. Open prejudice against the indios abated, if only a little, and the mestizos rose inside the Mexican political system. The PRI, which included farmers, workers, and intellectuals in the Cárdenas formulation, added the business community under Alemán. All of Mexico, including the mestizos with somewhat darker skin, had a voice in the party.

It was not until the election of López Portillo that the mestizos, especially those with dark skin and Indian features, began to fade in the power struc-ture of the party. Meanwhile, another phenomenon, most likely a result of the look of men who were pressed into service in the federal army during the civil wars, came into being, the pelado (baldy.) The federal conscripts had short haircuts. They were poor men who would rather have been doing something else, not career soldiers. The pelados had little money, lived badly, were docile, usually illiterate, and rarely, if ever, criollos.

Samuel Ramos, professor at the UNAM and author of *Profile of Man and Culture in Mexico*,[4] who had nothing good to say about indigenous people, describing them as uncivilized, "a race of minors who must be treated as

[4] *El Perfil del Hombre y la Cultura en Mexico*. English translation, *Profile of Man and Cul-ture in Mexico* (Austin: University of Texas Press, 1962).

children," also defined the pelado. Ramos said, ". . . the Mexican pelado . . . constitutes the most elemental and clearly defined expression of national character." When we keep in mind that Ramos said Mexicans suffer from an inferiority complex, the pelado becomes more important. "The pelado belongs to a most vile category of social fauna; he is a form of human rubbish from the great city. He is less than a proletarian in the economic hierarchy, and a primitive man in the intellectual one."

Ramos goes on: "[H]e is an explosive being with whom relationship is dangerous, for the slightest friction causes him to blow up." Here his pelado sounds a lot like Octavio Paz's view of Mexicans, although the pelado is not so dissembling as to wear a mask. "He is like a shipwreck victim who, after flailing abut in a sea of nothingness, suddenly discovers his driftwood of salvation: virility. The pelado's terminology abounds in sexual allusions which reveal his phallic obsession.

"He lives in distrust of himself and in continuous fear of being discovered." The poor pelado: Ramos will not even afford him the truth of his dreams of sexual prowess. So it is possible, then, that the Paz notion of the mask has an antecedent in Ramos. He finishes the case of this distrusting, masked person with "The Mexican does not distrust any man or woman in particular; he distrusts all men and all women." And to be certain nothing has been left out: "He is the least 'idealistic' person imaginable."

Not long after Ramos, head of the humanities department at the UNAM, published his book, a pelado, a fellow who played a drunk in the tent shows that were set up in poor neighborhoods in Mexico City and tried to make people laugh, made a movie. When he worked the tents, he made people laugh at his stumbling, double-talking act. "*En la cantina tú te inflas* [You fill yourself up in a tavern!]," they shouted in appreciation. The entertainer, who had tried his hand at boxing and dancing and fighting bulls, had a wry sense of humor, so he used two of the words to give himself a stage name: Cantinflas.

He not only saw through the double-talk of the official party and the pretense of revolutionary ideals but provided a perfect riposte to Ramos's racist, classist views. Ramos, like many Mexican intellectuals of his time, was educated at the Sorbonne, while Mario Moreno Reyes, the exemplary pelado, learned his trade in tent shows and in the streets. They were Mexico's polar opposites. Ramos saw the pelado as the worst aspect of Mexico and the Mexican character, and Cantinflas, who never finished high school, loved the people, as they soon came to love him.

Cantinflas, who played the same irreverent, insouciant role in almost all of his movies, presented a face of Mexico available to interpretation by any group, according to what its members wanted of the world. To those who ruled during the movie career of Cantinflas, laughter was an escape valve; it calmed the people while successive administrations, beginning with the Alemán regime, abused power in pursuit of money and pleasure.

To those of all classes who were abused, Cantinflas unmasked the deceptions of language and policy used by government to control and deceive the masses. He skewered the left as well as the right, the president as well as the local cacique. Cantinflas was George Orwell speaking to a vast Mexican public.

To those who opposed the government and its abuses of power, Cantinflas was both confirmation of their views and hope for the future. He was neither a leftist nor a rightist, he liked elegant parties and beautiful women, he adored being adored, but he opened the door just enough to let in a thin shaft of the light of possibility.

To the pelado, the man[5] despised by Ramos and the rest of the middle class and the intellectuals, Cantinflas played the part of redeemer. Like the Virgin of Guadalupe, he represented the dark-skinned people; he loved them; he was their hope, not for heaven, but for some small victory on earth. Cantinflas proved again and again that any poor pelado, with his trousers falling down and his mustache too wispy to appear truly manly, could win life's lottery. Every Cantinflas movie was a melodrama; he always defeated the pompous, and if he didn't get the girl, he made sure the girl ended up with the good young man instead of the wicked businessman.

The logic of Cantinflas was inescapable in the eyes of the poor of Mexico. If a pelado, one of them, born in a poor neighborhood to a family supported by a man who had a low-level job in the post office, could become Mexico's biggest movie star, how bad could pelados be? He was Charlie Chaplin talking two miles a minute, and he was a survivor. Cantinflas could literally beat the devil, as he showed in one of his most famous films. Lucifer himself, complete with tail and pitchfork, could not endure the antics of the pelado and sent him back up because it was the only way to be rid of him.

Yes, Cantinflas and his scriptwriters said, life was hell, but the pelado

[5]Women were not considered of importance in Mexico then, even during the bravura years of La Félix.

could escape the worst of it simply by being himself. The very characteristics Ramos found irritating and debasing were the pelado's salvation. Perhaps God did not appear to love the pelado, but He had not consigned him to the eternal fires. Those were for the criollo in the dinner jacket. The years of the pelado were a mix of racism, classism, and ethnocentrism—in short, culturalismo. The pelado was dark, docile, and often drunk. If he lost his temper, he showed his anger to another pelado. Pelados did not attend nightclubs, they did not attempt to look like their "betters," and they did not upset anyone. Like the black bit part players in U.S. films of the thirties and forties, pelados provided comic relief in Mexican life. Everyone in the comfortable classes had a funny story to tell about a pelado. Rich people wandered through Mexico's Thieves' Market to amuse themselves.

For half a century and more, the pelado, the bumpkin from the country who never really comprehended the ways of the city, no matter how many generations he spent in urban squalor, played the butt of the joke to Mexico's urban elites, and he had no defenders but Mario Moreno Reyes and the Virgin of Guadalupe. With a school system that weeded out the poor and little money available to the poor and lower middle class to buy a house or start a business beyond the informal economy, the pelado had little chance to rise into the middle class until the Mexican Miracle began after World War II, with immigrant energy and education bolstering government-funded internal growth.

The race and class problem of the "miracle" came in the making of it. As Mexico transformed itself from a rural to an urban economy, the government made the mistake of centralizing industry in a few large cities, mainly the capital. Mexicans who had not been able to make a living on the farm or ranch brought no marketable skills to the factories and offices of the city. They could not survive in the city, so they moved to suburbs, vast areas of shacks and unbearable squalor, where they were prey to local bosses, landlords, and other kinds of thieves.

In only a few years the pelado, who lived his hapless existence serving the rich with his labor, beating his wife, and now and then shooting or knifing one of his drinking companions, turned into a new, utterly despised character, the naco. And no one loved the naco, not even the naco himself. He had no Cantinflas to sweeten his self-image. He had lost the world of the countryside and gained nothing from the city. His name probably came from Totonaco, a group of indigenous people who had once lived in the present-day state of Puebla but had been driven out by the Toltecs or

Chichimecas. Most of the Totonacos settled on Mexico's east coast in the current state of Veracruz. They mixed with the local people there but lived under the rule of the Aztecs at the time of the invasion.

The Totonacos are the eighth-largest indigenous linguistic group in Mexico, with about 450,000 speakers of all ages. How their name came to be associated with the naco is not clear.[6] Nor is the definition of "naco" clear, although as many as 6 or 8 million people in the capital alone could be identified as nacos under the broadest definition. The word has no pleasant connotations. The pelado may be considered charming as well as mercurial, a sweet or wily innocent in the city, but the naco has no saving grace. For those who despise and fear him, the naco is a mistake of man and nature, the result of technology, globalism, and overpopulation in a country without the natural or human resources to resolve its problems.

Both Enrique Serna and Carlos Monsiváis, Mexican essayists, have written about the naco. According to Javier Valencia, a philosophy student and researcher, the definition depends on who is speaking: "Among my friends everyone has a different definition. For some it is a person whom they see as ugly or simply someone different. For me, a naco is a person who has a great lack of culture. And to be a naco it is not necessary to be poor, because there are also rich nacos." When one puts his definition together with theirs and with observation and experience in the capital, an idea of the naco emerges.

The naco is a unique mixture of class, race, dislocation, overpopulation, and cultural distortion; he is deracinated and without hope, despised because his very presence has disturbed the structure of Mexican urban life. Attempts by some on the left to embrace the naco and his world are self-serving at best and patronizing at worst. The naco responds to both his attackers and defenders with disdain. Serna explains why: "Treated sympathetically in telenovelas, government campaigns, and art films, the naco has been the victim of doubletalk: his patrons claim they really care about him, but every time he tries to lift his head, they sock him so hard that he bows it again."[7] There are few criollos who would be termed nacos, but it is possible. A vulgar word or gesture at an inappropriate time, an error in compre-

[6] At one point "naco" meant "someone who wore white cotton trousers, a peasant," according to Santamaría's *Diccionario de Mejicanismos*. In Central America the word means "coward." The Larousse dictionaries do not deal with it, either in the standard dictionary or the dictionary of neologisms.

[7] *Las Caricaturas Me Hacen Llorar* (Mexico: Joaquín Mortiz, 1997).

hending the dress code proper for his generation, the wrong address, a lack of money—any of these could drag even a criollo into the world of the naco.

Money alone is rarely the way to climb up out of the social pit where the naco lives. At one time, "naco" referred mainly to the new rich—that is, newly arrived in the middle class. Indigenous people were still indios, and some people still used the term "pelado" for the lower classes. A naco may have money enough to copy French or American styles, but he never gets it quite right. The color of his shirt is too loud or he wears his trousers too low or she has too large a jewel buttoned into her navel or too large a tattoo on her ankle. The naco is an arriviste; in New York City, a naco might be called a member of the bridge and tunnel crowd.

If that were the limit of the definition, it would be clear and useful, the detritus of an expanding economy. It began that way, during the last years of rapid economic growth in the sixties and seventies. The naco was the last person to join the rock and roll generation. As the economy sank in the eighties, the definition of the word "naco" expanded to include practically everyone who was not well enough connected to have gotten his or her money out of the country before the peso collapsed and the government prohibited trading in "hard currency."

The declining economy turned the naco bitter. Those who had jumped up fell back. It was the classic anomic situation described by Émile Durkheim: the sudden fall, the loss of confidence in the rules, lawless behavior. Jorge Pinto, former Mexican consul in New York, expressed the idea in the clearest terms. "What else is a poor person in Mexico to do? Crime is the only opportunity."

By then the naco's victims had expanded the definition to include criminals. All dark-skinned people became nacos, unless they lived outside the capital, in which case they were still indios. As the population of the city in its golden years (the 1950s) doubled and doubled again and again and again and the peso collapsed and it became impossible to survive on the minimum wage, the advent of that confluence of racism, classism, and cultural snobbery resulting in the naco was inevitable.[8] It was a combination of social and economic errors that went back for a least a century.

---

[8] Here I think it is fair to say that the idea of the naco is a good example of culturalismo, but the behavior is not necessarily indigenous. The naco's style ranges from *cursi* (cheap, tasteless) to *rascuache* (poor, miserable), the latter being a word rescued from its past and changed to mean "genuine" or "the people's work."

The history of the naco begins with the decision by the cientificos at the end of the nineteenth century to invite investment and management from abroad, turning the country into a labor market, a role from which it has never recovered.

The centralization that began in the 1950s utilized the labor market but did not create the critical mass of capital investment and education required to build the manufacturing and technological base of a first world economy.

U.S. economic and cultural hegemony inhibited the growth of a uniquely Mexican culture, one that might have resolved the issues of the struggle out of colonialism. Instead Mexico entered into a second stage of colonialism, one in which the country remained legally independent but economically and culturally dependent on the United States.

The spread of the media, which quickly displaced much of what remained of indigenous and European culture with manufactured and marketed culture, created its own kind of envious and aggressive person.

And then there was the metro. As long as the poor Mexican stayed in his suburb or wandered around the Zócalo or went on a pilgrimage to La Villa de Guadalupe, he was a pelado, and if he spoke no Spanish, he was an indio. In either case, the poor Mexican was his own (or his neighbor's) worst enemy. And then came the Metro, depositing poor and lower-middle-class Mexicans in every part of the city. The Zona Rosa, across the Paseo de la Reforma from the U.S. Embassy, was the liveliest area of Mexico City before the advent of the Metro. Art dealers, restaurants, nightclubs, shops, and hotels made it a desirable area day or night. It was a highlight of Mexico City for both residents and tourists. After the Metro, it slowly fell to the nacos. At the end of the twentieth century the Zona Rosa had become so dangerous that armed guards holding attack dogs on short leashes stood outside many of the cafés at night to protect the customers from thieves, robbers, and beggars, all of whom now fall into the category known as nacos.[9]

The income gap in Mexico may eventually become the best definition of the naco. Although Mexico, according to the World Bank in 2002, had the ninth-largest economy, it ranked sixty-ninth in per capita income. The World Bank said income distribution in Mexico was among the least equitable in Latin America. The top 10 percent of Mexicans had 42 percent of national income, while the bottom 10 percent had only 1.3 percent. Accord-

[9] Among the successes that endear Mayor Andrés Manuel López Obrador to *capitalinos* has been the rejuvenation of the Zona Rosa.

ing to the World Bank, which defines poverty at a very low income level, 46 percent of Mexicans are poor and 16 percent live on a dollar a day or less. Other estimates show more than 70 percent of the population of Mexico City living below the poverty line. If those figures are correct[10] or even close to correct, the number of nacos in Mexico City and its environs exceeds 12 million, using a definition based on class alone. Many of these, however, at least one-third, are small children or old people.

Nationally, the income gap on a per capita basis is astonishing. It ranges, according to the National Population Council's 2003 data, from $40,000 a year in the richest ward (Delegación) of Mexico City to $149 a year in Santos Reyes Yucuná, Oaxaca.[11] Illiteracy ranged from 1 percent in the Federal District to 70 percent and more in parts of Oaxaca and Guerrero, and the lack of literacy in indigenous areas should not be attributed to resistance to learning the Latin alphabet, for many indigenous languages are now successfully transliterated. Overall, the quality of life in the Federal District, measured in dollars per capita, is six times better than in Oaxaca or Chiapas.

In comparison to other parts of the country, life in Mexico City looks adequate, if not prosperous, but averages are skewed by the layer of the very rich across the top of the society, and the very poor at the bottom are mobile, timid about answering questions, difficult to locate. Poverty rates in the Federal District depend upon who is counting. The number of nacos also depends upon who is counting and according to which definition. When race, style, and addiction to U.S. culture, including imitation of teenage Mexican-American gangsters (*cholos*), are added to the definition, the number of nacos increases. The great megalopolis breaks into two ill-defined groups, a pitiless tension between the envied and the despised, anomie. Society breaks down. No one is safe on the street; no one is safe at home. No one dares leave a house empty even for a weekend, a night. There is always a naco watching, waiting for the opportunity. Armed guards with automatic weapons stand in front of the banks. Stores operate from behind bulletproof shields. Anyone who can afford it hires a bodyguard.

Criminals are nacos; beggars are nacos; taxi drivers are nacos unless they are architects or university professors who can't find other work. The police are nacos; the military is made up of nacos; the whole informal economy is made up of nacos. And the old rich call the new rich nacos. Ask anyone in

[10]More information about Mexican income appears in Chapter 33.
[11]*La Jornada*, February 17, 2003.

Mexico who is behind the loss of public civility in the city, and the answer will be "the nacos."

Yet the naco holds a few surprises in the class war in Mexico. He has not lost the Mexican sense of generosity, and the closer he is to his indigenous roots, the more likely he is to be generous, which is not to say that in his next encounter with a stranger he may not be picking the stranger's pocket or pointing a gun at him. Anomie has a fractured character; it obeys no laws, it lacks a structure, even an internal structure.

In a book of transgressive art published by the Universidad Iberoamericana, the artists and writers, all of them tattooed and imprisoned, nacos by any definition, show no conception of social structure. "I saw it, I wanted it, I did it" is a kind of refrain that runs through the conversations with the artists. The work is not interesting; it lacks the sense of outrage common among men and women in U.S. prisons. The word "transgression" seems inappropriate; one must be aware of the rules to break them, and the salient of the naco is the void where the social structure once existed. He has left the traditions of the village and come to an incomprehensible city.

If the naco has any political loyalty, it is to Tata Lázaro, and even that dims with each succeeding generation. The young naco with the purloined gold chain wandering the Zona Rosa may never have heard of Lázaro Cárdenas. He would probably not know the names of such people as Nezahualcoyotl or Madero or Juárez or Cuauhtémoc were they not names of streets and wards in Mexico City. In the democratization of Mexico, however, the naco has proved useful. He votes against. He has no heroes outside the gang or the soccer club; he has only antagonists. It makes sense to him to vote against. If the naco has his way, the PAN will lose the next presidential election in 2006, for nothing is more offensive to the disaffected than the continuity of power. Unless power is his.[12]

GORDO

In the northern tip of the state of Oaxaca, where it meets with the states of Puebla and Veracruz, there is a river of butterflies, the Río Papaloapan. Flowers, fruit, tobacco, rice, coconuts, and sugarcane grow in the valley.

---

[12]See Book Four for a discussion of the question of alternation vs. democracy by Alejandro Carrillo Castro, president of the National Institute of Political Administration (INAP).

Great fields, cultivated for more than a thousand years, lie between the tributaries of the river. Porifirio Díaz declared his Plan of Tuxtepec in the town beside the river. Until 1955, when the Miguel Alemán Dam was completed, the Papaloapan had drained the mountains, the flatlands, and the marshes; it lay languorous in dry seasons, turned torrential in the hurricane years. The Aztec traders had come south through the valley, and before that it had belonged to the El Tajin culture on the east. Something about the river made the people docile: perhaps the ease it provided, perhaps the flowers it nourished. Like butterflies, they circled the flowers and drank and let themselves be carried on the wind. The Aztecs named the land and the rivers and the towns. "Tuxtepec" comes from the Nahuatl *toci* and tells with the suffix that it was a hill where rabbits lived. It was perched high above the Papaloapan, "the place of butterflies."

The Aztecs exploited the river plain, taking tribute, the traders stopping on their way north and south to pick up what they could, whatever would survive the trip back to the Valley of Mexico. After the Aztecs the tobacco planters came to the plains along the tributary of the Papaloapan, the Río Valle Nacional, and they took the people in peonage and worked them until they died.

For as long as anyone could remember, there were fish in the Papaloapan, and the original people who lived along the river, the Mazatecs, cast their nets into the water and took fish for food and barter. It was a rich life. The men were strong, and the young women were famed for their beauty. When the dam was completed in 1955, the fishing was even better in the huge lake it created. The floods that had made the plains a gamble for farmers came to an end, more and different crops were planted, and the fishermen lived well.

The family of Agustín López Placido had fished in the river and then in the lake for as long as anyone could remember. They had taken big robalo, the firm-fleshed favorite of Mexico, and the little mojarra that cut through the water like a knife, and crayfish and freshwater shrimp too. They had lived well, and Agustín, who was young and strong, married a woman from just across the state border in Veracruz, and she was as beautiful as the women are said to be from that side of the lake. There was a great wedding, and her father, who played the guitar and composed and recorded songs, mainly cumbias, wrote a song and he and his friends played music and everyone ate and danced, and it was all quite wonderful.

Agustín had done well as a fisherman. He had a boat that was big enough to hold him and two boys who worked the nets with him and a great haul of fish. Every day but Sunday they fished. For a man who owned his own small house and had a beautiful wife and two children, it was enough. They were not rich, but they had enough, and to have enough in the eyes of the López Plácido family was to be rich.

After the crisis in 1994, the price that Agustín was able to get for his fish fell precipitously. At three pesos for a kilo (about fifteen cents a pound), he found that after he paid the boys who helped him, there was very little left. He did not have to pay rent, and he had plenty of fish to eat, but there was nothing left for shoes or clothing or even a bottle of beer. He was an experienced man in negotiations, because he had to hire boys to help him and bargain for the price of fish. It gave him the idea that he could do better in the capital than in the tiny towns of the river basin. He packed up his wife and their children, sold whatever he did not think they would need, and bought second-class bus tickets for the City of Mexico.

The trip takes twenty-two hours, and the bus is always on time. Children who ride the second-class bus do not often cry, and there is no television set blaring from the top of the barrier behind the driver's seat as in deluxe buses, but there is no bathroom either. They had been to the capital before, but only for a few days. This time they came to stay, for there was nothing to go home to. And they had an idea about surviving in the city, in the very heart of it. Agustín had been a fisherman; logic told him that people had to eat. The price of fish had fallen, but in the city there were no fish and no fishermen; in the city people bought food on the street; he had seen it, people had to eat. The only questions were how much to pay for the ingredients and how much to charge for the food they sold on the street. Agustín knew about such things. He could negotiate.

And he had another idea. He was a Mazateco, strong and sturdy, but not much to look at; his wife, however, was one of the beautiful butterflies that lived in the river basin. She would be the street vendor. In a marketplace filled with fat men and pockmarked men and stringy women with no buttocks and fat women with babies on their apron strings and old women with widow's frowns, la señora López Plácido would be an attraction, no matter what she sold. Her very presence would improve the flavor of the food.

Every woman in the town where they lived had a wide repertoire in the kitchen. They made tamales of every kind of fish and fruit and meat in the river basin, and they made tamales filled with such sweet rice no one could resist them. They made the dough, filled it with any of the variety of available foods, then wrapped the tamales in banana leaves and boiled them. Yes, tamales, they agreed, but there was a problem. To buy banana leaves in Mexico City was difficult and expensive, and the Mexicans there had no taste for the styles of tamales made in the Papaloapan river basin. La señora López had to learn to cook all over again.

Agustín found work here and there, in a shop in the market, sweeping out a tavern at the end of the night, picking up trash after the wrestling matches, good jobs, but jobs he could have for only an afternoon or a night or two at most until the regular employee returned from a sick day or some other emergency. Meanwhile, they had found a two-room apartment in a vecindad in the center of the city. It was expensive, but they had a dream: to have a place in the Zócalo, a spot of their own right there in the city's main plaza, where Juana, the beautiful butterfly of the river, could stand and sell tamales.

They made an arrangement with the "leader" of the vendors in the Zócalo, who sold them a place on a nearby side street and protection from thieves for twenty-five pesos a week; a place in the Zócalo itself was still beyond reach. They worked together in the morning. Agustín mixed the cornmeal and lard in the center courtyard of the two-story complex of tiny apartments. They cooked the first lot early in the morning. He helped her carry out the pots of hot tamales before the lunch hour. And while she sold them, he boiled more. He did not like standing in the Zócalo. His skin was dark and he wore workman's shoes and there was about him the look of the country. He was a fisherman. The Zócalo was not his place. People there insulted him. The merchants tried to cheat him. A boy picked his pocket and danced away, holding out Agustín's billfold, extracting the money, and then throwing the billfold as far as he could, into the middle of a crowd. Agustín did not know whether to retrieve the billfold or chase the boy. In the end he chose the billfold, which had his voter identification card and his many licenses and receipts.

A few weeks into the grueling schedule, he began drinking while he kneaded the dough and formed it with his hands. By early evening he was drunk. Every day was the same: He prepared the tamales, drank beer, and when the last batch was done, he went to a tavern down the street from his house or bought huge bottles of pale yellow beer, the cheapest he could find, and sat on the floor in the tiny apartment and watched television and got drunk. The strong young fisherman from the Presa Miguel Alemán grew fat. By the time I met him, no one spoke of him as Agustín. He was Gordo. And to be certain everyone knew which of the Fatsos they referred to, his name was accompanied by the sign for a drunkard, a fist with the thumb and little finger extended and a movement toward the mouth.

In June he cut his thumb with a knife while chopping pieces of pork for the tamales. He put the wounded thumb in the *masa* which stopped the flow of blood, kept it there for several minutes, and went on with the work, drinking and kneading and forming the masa to be filled, wrapped in corn husks, and boiled. His thumb did not heal properly. When he lived as a fisherman, he had cut himself a hundred times; his fingers and hands were marked with tiny scars and more than a few that were not so small. But this time his cut did not heal. His thumb hurt, but as long as he drank enough beer, he could work and sleep. The thumb swelled to three times its normal size. Pus oozed from the cut. He kneaded the dough and made the tamales, and his wife sold them on the side street near the Zócalo.

One day, in the middle of July, in the early afternoon, it rained so hard that all the vendors abandoned their posts in and around the Zócalo. His wife came home early, and his cousin, Marcelino, who lived with them and the four children and two teenage nieces in the two-room apartment, went to the tavern with Gordo. The rain fell all afternoon and into the evening; it flowed in rivulets down the gutters, carrying papers, plastic bottles, lottery tickets, corn husks. It had such force that bottle caps and even a small rubber shoe were borne along on the water. Gordo spent the day in the tavern alongside Marcelino, who greeted every man who walked in with a rubbery smile, a handshake, and "Marcelino am I, *Marcelino pan y vino.*"

Business had not been good of late. There had been rumors in the street about the quality of their tamales. Someone who had seen Gordo's thumb had told someone who had told someone else who had passed the word on to a competitive tamale vendor. Even the "leader" had asked questions. The merchants of the Zócalo had a certain reputation, he said. But a beautiful butterfly provides absolution from all sins. The leader did nothing.

Gordo and Marcelino walked home through the rain, watching the gutters, hoping to see something of value floating by. They were, after all, fishermen. If something of value passed . . . But there were no fish in the gutter. When they arrived at the vecindad, Marcelino pounded on the door until an old woman who lived on the first floor came out of her apartment to see what all the noise was about. She opened the door for them and turned around to show the other neighbors with her fist and extended thumb and little finger that Gordo was in the usual condition.

In the center courtyard, where Gordo drank Sol Azteca (an inexpensive beer) and made tamales, a flood had begun. A neighbor woman shouted blame at Gordo, saying he had plugged the drain with corn husks. "*Tapado, tapado, tapado* [stopped up]," she shouted, standing in her bare feet in the water. Gordo shrugged. He staggered on the way up the stone steps to the second floor. There was no handrail. He put out his hand with the swollen thumb to balance himself against the wet stone wall. At the top of the steps his niece huddled in the arms of a man. She turned to look at Gordo as he and Marcelino passed. Lipstick had smeared across her face. She had a big red clown's mouth and viperous eyes. The man smiled. In the rain, his hair hung over his face in black ringlets. "Good evening," he said, bowing his head diplomatically.

"*Pinche lluvia* [fucking rain]," Gordo said.

"*Pinche lluvia*," Marcelino said.

The man agreed. After Gordo and Marcelino had passed by, he and Gordo's niece resumed their embrace.

The front room of the apartment was no more than ten feet by twelve. The back room, which was piled high with beds, layered one atop the other, was not so large. Plastic grocery bags, pink and white and green, hung from nails around the upper perimeter of the room. There were two chairs and a small, narrow bed in the front room. A girl lay on the bed, a blanket pulled up over her head. Juana, the beautiful butterfly of the river basin, sat in one of the chairs, with her feet in a bucket of water. All day, every day, she stood on the cobblestone street near the Zócalo, and at night she sat and nursed her aching feet and doled out pesos to the children to buy ice cream at the store on the next block. All the children had grown fat, like their father, in a matter of months. The oldest girl sat next to her mother on the only other chair. She was not pretty, not like her mother, who was still a butterfly, orange and black curves, a spot of yellow, a slash of white, and eyes like black diamonds.

In a corner above the two chairs, the television set, mounted on a piece of wood just below the confluence of the walls and the ceiling, showed a wrestling match, followed by a ranchero movie. Gordo and Marcelino removed their shirts, spread blankets on the floor, and sat with their backs against the wall. The oldest girl went inside and brought out two large bottles of Sol Azteca.

Gordo and Marcelino drank the beer. They talked about going home for the annual fiesta. "We'll dance," Gordo said. He instructed his daughter to bring the tape player and the tape her grandfather had made. She climbed up on the chair and reached into one of the plastic bags that hung on the wall. Gordo sat for a long time contemplating the machine and the tape. His body was brown and smooth, and his belly bloomed over his trousers. He told his daughter to whistle "La Cucaracha" while he made the muscles in his arm jump in time with the song. She whistled and he flexed his muscles and everyone laughed, except for the girl who lay on the bed. She pulled the blanket up further over her head, as if it could block out the sound of laughter.

Gordo and Marcelino finished off one of the bottles of beer. Gordo put the tape in the machine and turned it on as loud as it would go. He and Marcelino rolled sideways onto their hands and knees, and then they struggled to their feet. The music was loud, and the singing had a bit of the whine of Veracruz in it, but the rhythm was quick, and Gordo and Marcelino began to dance. They laughed and tapped out the rhythm with their heels, and Gordo's fat shook like happiness itself. And the butterfly laughed and even the girl under the blanket raised her head and looked at the two drunken men dancing and she laughed too.

After three songs, Marcelino staggered backward and leaned against the door. Gordo fell back to his place on the floor and drank off more of the beer while the tape recorder continued playing. When the tape was finished, Marcelino asked Gordo to play another song.

Gordo looked up at him and smiled. He raised his eyebrows and tilted his head down and slightly to one side, like a dog. In English, he said, "Watt do dchu want, meestair?"

"*Gringo!*" Marcelino shouted.

"*No, Amerinaco!*" Gordo said, and laughed. His belly shook and his arms flapped and his swollen thumb banged against the floor and he kept on laughing.

Everyone laughed at his self-deprecating joke, his marriage of the word "naco" with "American," a creature twice despised—that is, everyone laughed except the beautiful butterfly, who sat quietly, looking at her husband, who had been a strong and slender young fisherman, and it was impossible to tell whether the look in her eyes was love or pity.

29.

A Savage Bite

A revolution is shaped on battlefields, but once it is corrupted, though battles are still won, the revolution is lost.
—CARLOS FUENTES, *The Death of Artemio Cruz*

Mexicans say there are two basic kinds of corruption. The first, which has been practiced for five hundred years but did not achieve its full sophistication until 1914, during the civil wars, is known simply as corruption, and it does not disturb people very much, although it has, at times, been accompanied by disappearances and torture. The theory of this kind of "endemic" corruption in Mexico is that it was, in its least injurious form, a sort of tax without legal or ethical basis, a means of gathering capital, which was then used to build resorts, factories, housing, and infrastructure, to advance the country. President Miguel Alemán epitomized the mixed character of this kind of corruption.

Another kind, which by comparison has only a brief history, has earned the name *corrupción salvaje* (savage corruption) and enriches only ten, twenty, perhaps thirty people, who gather up the money and send it out of the country to banks in Switzerland or the Caribbean or the United States. The seeds of the new corruption were planted by President López Portillo, who raised the amount of wealth amassed by a Mexican president into the stratosphere while sending the political character of the presidency to the depths. Miguel Alemán was also corrupt, but he was a builder of cities, bridges, resorts, dams; Alemán's corruption was massive, but still of the old style. There may have been an assassination or two in his background, but Alemán was the son of a general. He stole to put money in his own pocket, but in his curious way he also amassed capital for the development of Mexico.

Savage corruption did not begin to sprout until after the Mexican Miracle of 1950–1975. Mexico's "dirty war" began in 1968, but corruption remained largely in the old form. The head of Gobernación (the Department of the Interior, but with far more power than the department of the same name in the United States; as its name says, governance of the nation) in 1968 was Luis Echeverría, whom Díaz Ordaz chose to follow him as president in 1970. It was apparently Echeverría's special brigade, not the army, that had done the work at Tlatelolco and again when they dressed like students to foment the trouble that led to the Corpus Christi killings of young leftists in 1971. But Echeverría had another side. He proposed to bring Mexico's indigenous population into the burgeoning economy. His economics were almost as far left as those of the people he was killing and imprisoning, and he had a plan for intellectuals, which was to bring them into his government, to "co-opt" them, in the common term of the day.

An intellectual who worked with Echeverría might become an ambassador, like Carlos Fuentes, or hold a cabinet post, like many members of the UNAM faculty. He was generous to them and respectful; he liked being in their company. On his frequent trips abroad, Echeverría took an entourage of intellectuals with him. On the other hand, whoever frightened him—Communists, suspected Communists, guerrillas, suspected guerrillas—was killed or taken to the nightmare of tortures in White Camp One.[1] In the twenty-first century, under the freedom of information laws promulgated during the early years of the Fox presidency, the extent of Echeverría's human rights abuses finally began to surface.

Long before that, however, people knew. The reality of Mexico under Echeverría was being told as early as 1989, although few people listened. There were witnesses, timid people, afraid to give their names, but witnesses nonetheless. In a conference of human rights workers in Tijuana, a woman told of her sister, a schoolteacher in Ciudad Juárez. "She was a leftist, but not a Communist," the woman said, and then, while she wept, she told of the torture of her sister. She said they, meaning the army, burned her sister's genitals. She used the word *chicharronear*, which means "to make cracklings." "Then they took her to White Camp Number One, and my mother and I have been searching for her, for any information about her, ever since."

---

[1] While it is hardly a defense of Echeverría, the United States engaged in the Iran-contra affair and supplied military equipment and training to extreme right-wing governments in Central America during the Reagan administration. Revolutionary success by the Sandinistas had panicked the United States as well as Mexico, and Mexico had the added concern of proximity.

She said all this outdoors, in a noisy café, where no one else could hear, not even the other members of the human rights group having lunch together there. The conversation, two of us leaning forward at the side of the table, heads close together, speaking in something close to whispers, was like a bad movie, too obviously surreptitious, clumsy. She described her sister standing in the classroom, a good teacher, one who cared about the children. Then taken, gone. A few words leaked from the prison where she was tortured. Then she was moved to the White Camp and never heard from again. Her mother and sister wrote letters to the government, asking the whereabouts of the schoolteacher. Her mother went to the offices of the police and the army. She insisted. The officials responded with threats. The woman who sat beside me said she was not afraid, yet she had been frightened since the day her sister was taken.

The actions of the Echeverría administration were not then known as the dirty war. People knew something about the massacre at Tlatelolco and about the Corpus Christi killings and the provocateurs known as the Falcons, but the extent of the dirty war was then unknown, incredible. No one knew then how the government feared armed revolution spreading into Mexico from Central America, Echeverría's nightmare of disorder. Echeverría patterned himself after Lázaro Cárdenas, but misunderstood Cárdenas, thinking that to be like him was to be a demagogue. He was a nationalist to such extent that he refused investment from the United States. He suffered from logorrhea. As an economist he was a disaster. During his sexenio the value of the peso fell by almost half, and the foreign debt got completely out of hand, rising by 600 percent. Echeverría could not find an honorable place for himself in history, although it became the aim of the last years of his sexenio. He gave a medal to Cosío Villegas, and Cosío said that Echeverría was *nuts*. In return, the government published a paper deriding Cosío as a dupe of "Uncle Sam."

Echeverría's administration was open, at first, and his politics were clearly with the left. But then he turned on Julio Scherer, who ran *Excelsior*, Mexico's best newspaper at the time. Echeverría managed to force Scherer out of the paper, but the scheme backfired. The end result of his manipulations was the emergence of the newspapers *Unomásuno*, then *La Jornada*, and several magazines, among them *Nexos* on the center left and *Vuelta*, Octavio Paz's magazine on the anti-Communist center right. For *Excelsior*, the result was not so good. The group Echeverría put in power at the paper supported the government, but lost credibility, and when *Excelsior* tried to come back in 2000, it fell into bickering and protests, the end-stage chaos that comes to newspapers that have outlived their usefulness. Echeverría supported Fidel Castro and Salvador Allende, although he did little to help either of them. He made no secret of his dreams of glory—he lobbied for a Nobel Prize, a major international post—but no one loved him for what he had done, as if the whole country, the whole world, knew that underneath all his wishes to embrace the left, to talk his way into history, to limit financial corruption with a barrage of words, he was the man who invented the dirty war. Even the vast army of bureaucrats he had hired despised him. They called the bureaucracy "the system," and while they enjoyed it, they hoped to escape it. When Echeverría went to the UNAM to speak, the students attacked him, throwing stones, forcing his bodyguards to put him into a car and speed away to save the president from further embarrassment and perhaps danger.[2]

In 1976, Echeverría passed on the presidency to his finance minister, José López Portillo, a man who held himself in high, if slightly loony, regard. He read Hegel and thought of himself as the reincarnation of Quetzalcoatl. The country Echeverría passed to his "fingered"[3] successor suffered from crushing external debt, inflation, devalued currency, a gigantic bureaucracy, and a full-blown dirty war. The army, which had not fought a foreign enemy since Maximilian was executed in 1867, had become the arm of government responsible for internal security but not responsible to anyone, including the president. It had been almost fifty years since an army officer had attempted a coup, but the officer cadre was paranoid, corrupt, independent, and wildly anti-Communist.[4] Echeverría had left Mexico with two, possibly three threats of instability: the economy, the army, and, the unlikely third, the radical left. A fourth, savage corruption, was brewing in Colombia, in the dark alleys of U.S. cities, and in the relationship between the incoming president and Blackie Durazo, the *cuate* (pal, literally twin) of his childhood, who worked as his bodyguard.

[2]Enrique Krauze wrote in his unflattering portrait of Echeverría that his bodyguards tossed him into the trunk of the car.

[3]The *dedazo* (fingering) was the common expression for the naming of the next PRI candidate and until 2000 the next president.

[4]By the end of the century the number of men on active duty in the army, navy, and air force had exceeded 150,000. Complicity in drug trafficking and human rights abuses by the Mexican military was common knowledge.

THAT OLD-TIME CORRUPTION

Everything, including corruption, must have a beginning. Even when there is a dispute about the cause, the beginning of the effect can often be located. In Mexico, however, it is in dispute. The best-known theory of the origins of corruption in Mexico was adopted by Carlos Fuentes in his novel *The Death of Artemio Cruz.* A dying old revolutionary general tells of his life, from war to wealth. Indeed, there were many such generals, men who took vast tracts of land in return for their service to one of the sides in the civil wars of 1910–1920. This spoils of war theory is a good one, and it was true in Mexico, as it has been throughout human history, but it does not account for the other four centuries of Mexican history, nor does it explain why corruption spread through the society and lodged so deeply that it became one of the foundations of Mexican business and government.

Corruption in Mexico at its ordinary day-in and day-out level is known as la mordida (the bite): a bribe, a tip, the grease of the machine of civil— or not so civil—society. Mexico is not alone in this; most of the world practices one form or another of la mordida. The Scandinavian countries are not very good at it, the United States is best at hiding it, the Middle East has made an art of it, and Mexico is famous for it.

Corruption in pre-Hispanic Mexico took the form of political, economic, and military hegemony. The most widely studied system belonged to the Aztecs, who exacted tribute from much of their known world. In their own city, particularly the great marketplace at Tlatelolco, petty corruption was kept to a minimum. The social structure itself, however, comprised various classes, and there was little upward or downward social mobility. Poverty existed among the Aztecs, as did prostitution and some forms of exploitation, especially for labor. Less is known about the classic Maya, but at the time of the invasion, a similar system of classes existed within the postclassic Maya world. The system of exploitation through inherited social and economic positions may indicate a form of moral corruption, but it is not in itself what we think of today when speaking of corruption.

Systematic corruption in Mexico did not occur until after the conquest, when it affected not only the conquered but the conquerors as well. Nuño de Guzmán was no saint when he fought alongside Cortés, but his actions after the conquest, when he became one of the practitioners of corruption, may have so rotted what some might call his soul that when he embarked on his journey north and west to conquer territory and take slaves, he behaved like a beast, with no sense of limits.

The Spanish system for managing its conquered territory divided the land into districts, adding new districts as it brought more and more land under its control. As the Spanish hegemony spread outward from the center, the number of settlers and managers grew thinner. To accomplish the administration of the land without making large grants, the crown developed a system of *corregimientos*, each one overseen by a corregidor, which translates into English as "magistrate" but comes of the word *corregir*, which also means "to correct" or "to punish." Corregidores received no salary, in some cases having to buy their positions, and their initial appointments were for four years, with a possible extension. To put food on his table and clothing on his back, the corregidor had to levy taxes in his district. These were "special taxes," separate and above those collected for the crown.

The natives governed by the corregidor lived according to his rules, without the right of appeal. And they had little hope of help from the churchmen who were stationed in the same areas, for the priests were often as corrupt as the corregidores. By the middle of the sixteenth century the Nahuas had learned to put their cases in writing, albeit in their own language: In 1560 the community of Huexotzinco wrote to Philip II of its problems, and in 1595, a man in the Nahuatl-speaking village of Olinalá wrote a letter to the ecclesiastical inspector[5] complaining that his wife had been seduced by the local priest.

Since the corregidor had the role of administrator and judge, he could charge whatever special taxes he liked, and since he was also the mercantile connection between the natives and the rest of the world, he could buy their produce at whatever price he chose and sell manufactured goods to them, also at whatever price he chose. If he made an error and bought too many pairs of shoes to sell to people who did not wear shoes or too many bolts of fine cloth to peddle to people who were used to white cotton, he had only to insist that the natives purchase his goods at the price he designated. It was a system of protected marketing, beyond mere monopoly, the unmitigated corruption of colonialism.

There were, no doubt, some honest corregidores, but the system invited

[5]See "Olinalá, the Seduction in the Confessional," in León-Portilla and Shorris, *In the Language of Kings*, p. 360.

corruption. Corregidores appropriated the entire crop produced by native people in a district, then sold some of it back to them to use for seed. As the sixteenth century wore on, the corregimiento system developed into a bureaucracy. By the end of the century almost every district had its *ayuntamiento* (city hall) and increasingly long lines of people—natives and the first mestizos—applying for licenses, complaining, paying taxes. The corregidor became mayor of the village or town as well as judge and mercantile conduit.

The system ended with Independence, but the hierarchical rules of corruption it installed remain in practice today. They are the universal practices Voltaire described in *Candide.* Someone steals and must pay someone more powerful for the privilege. Corruption begins at the bottom, but it is made possible by the top. Conversely, it can be said to begin at the top and be made possible by the bottom. In either direction, the system produces profits all through the chain of corruption, with the most accruing to those at the top.

The corregidores began the system in the form of a tax, then added other transactions (or thefts) to the tax to further enrich themselves. Since the Spanish crown first designed the system, public servants in Mexico have been underpaid, with the mordida serving as a tax on the public, providing income to public servants, from the cop on the beat and the clerk in the office of the Department of the Interior to the president of the Republic. At the lowest level, the mordida generated a small amount of money, and the tax collector, immigration officer, customs inspector, policeman on his motorcycle, or any other bureaucrat was expected to pass a considerable bite out of his take to the person at the next level up in the chain of corruption. A police sergeant might have twenty men reporting to him, perhaps more. Each of the twenty had to deliver 10, 20, or 30 percent of his take to the sergeant, giving the sergeant an income two to six times that of the motorcycle cop shaking down drivers on a favorite street corner.

At each succeeding step in the chain of corruption, the multiple of the original corrupt payment increased. At the highest levels the take was enormous. And at the top was the king of Spain or the president of Mexico! The pyramidal pay scale could have been devised by the "human resources" department and board of directors of a late-twentieth-century U.S. corporation. To grasp the enormity of such a scheme, imagine as little as 1 percent of the earnings of half a million corrupt public officials! If each person in the chain stole an average of ten thousand pesos a year, the person at the top of the chain would receive fifty million pesos. If 10 percent passed through to the top, it would amount to half a billion pesos. And if the person at the bottom stole a hundred thousand pesos a year, which is currently a little less than ten thousand dollars, it would amount to five billion pesos every year. And even in pesos five billion is a lot.

Logically, one would think the best way to end the system of corruption would be to interrupt it at either the top or the bottom. One cure would be to bring honest people into government at the top. A test of that theory has not yet been completed in Mexico.[6] It almost happened when Ernesto Zedillo, a man with more academic than political credentials, took office. He brought some either naive or honest academics with him. Unlike previous Mexican presidents who had filled their governments with law school cronies and foreign-educated economists, Zedillo allowed a few genuine scholars to slip into his administration.

One of these, an undersecretary, told his academic colleagues of his introduction to the system, and the story leaked. The undersecretary's friends were careful to protect their source but glad to tell the tale. As time went on, the story was edited and perhaps embellished.

On his first day in office the new undersecretary sat in his fine leather chair behind a very large desk. He opened one of the desk drawers. It was filled with money. He opened another drawer: More money! And another. All the drawers of the desk were filled with pesos. Thinking there must have been some terrible mistake, he telephoned his superior, described the situation, and asked what he should do.

The response came back accompanied by laughter: "Clean out your desk!"

Perhaps the answer lies at the other end of the chain. Writers who deal with corruption in Mexico always point out that the police are poorly paid. In *La Capital*, a history of Mexico City, Jonathan Kandell wrote that policemen had to buy their revolvers and even their badges from their superiors. It is the same all over Mexico. The pay scale for the Mexican police rivals that of the corregidores. It is low at the beginning, not much above the minimum wage, and it does not rise very much in the highest ranks. It would seem only logical that raising the salaries of policemen would release them from the temptations of corruption.

---

[6]Accusations of corruption in the Fox administration have not been serious, so far, but it may be due to the lack of accusations rather than the lack of corruption.

I suggested this to Ramón Sampayo at the end of his term as mayor of Matamoros, when he was weary of politics and anxious to return to his business. Instead of offering generalizations about corruption, he gave details. The logical answer to the problem of police corruption, he explained, did not take the system into account. Young policemen, according to Sampayo, did not become corrupt because they were underpaid. He said they came on the force ready to be honest, and in the beginning they were. But then they encountered the system. He gave the example of a tavern that kept its doors open after the legal closing time. The policeman wrote a citation and gave it to the prosecutor, who refused to prosecute. The prosecutor had begun honestly, but when he brought a case before the judge, the judge refused to convict. Everyone up the line had been bribed.

Soon, according to Sampayo, the policeman understood the system. He accepted a small bribe from the tavern owner. The tavern owner did not mind paying the bribe because it allowed him to keep his establishment open as long as he had customers. Moreover, it was less expensive to bribe the policeman than to buy a license that permitted a later closing time. The city received less money in license fees, which it made up by paying less to its police force.

Paying more to the police would not, according to the description given by Sampayo, solve the problem. The police became corrupt because the system was corrupt. A mayor might control part of the system, but not all of it, certainly not the courts. Without the ability to remove all the corruption from the system, it was impossible to remove any of it. Then, one might ask, why were there so many people in prison in Mexico? And the answer of course is that almost all of those who are convicted and sentenced to prison are guilty of having no money. In that respect, the Mexican criminal justice system is just like the American system: The poor go to prison, and the rich, except in rare instances of gruesome murder or sudden spurts of morality by the government, enjoy the spoils.

There are serious differences, however, in the way the systems operate. In the United States, only some of the rich and many corporations avoid paying taxes. In Mexico, tax collection is impeded by a form of the mordida. The word for this business is *transar*, which means "to settle" or "compromise." One can almost always make a deal with the tax collector or customs agent. As the journalist Rosaura Barahona noted, the practice resulted in a popular saying, *Si no transa no avanza* (if one doesn't compromise, one doesn't get ahead). The joke is that *avanzar* may also mean "to loot." In the United

States, tax avoidance depends upon using loopholes in the tax laws. The Mexican system is, in certain respects, more efficient in that costs for accounting and legal fees do not siphon off so much of the money.

Corruption so thoroughly institutionalized leaves a Mexican reformer in a difficult position because it may not be possible to rid the country of corruption without vast changes in both government and culture. Nonetheless, reformers constantly test piecemeal solutions. The problem in Mexico City had become so bad in 1998 that Alejandro Gertz Manero, a newly appointed chief of police under a new PRD administration, decided to hire women as traffic cops, thinking for some reason buried in the depths of machismo that women are less corrupt than men. They are not.

The flaw in the system designed by Gertz, who had been the rector of a university before taking on corruption in Mexico City, was that it made driving more expensive. Instead of giving a traffic cop twenty or fifty or as much as one hundred pesos for a serious offense, citizens had to pay fines of five hundred pesos or more. Some people either had no money for bribes or preferred the ticket to the bribe. And with good reason. Those drivers who did get tickets refused to pay them. The chief of police told a press conference that 90 percent of traffic tickets went unpaid. The choice then for the chief was between dishonest traffic cops and scofflaws. Tinkering with one part of the system produced no good effect.

In 2002, Andrés Manuel López Obrador, the populist mayor of Mexico City and the leader of the ambitious centrist faction of the PRD,[7] had another plan to tinker with the system. He hired former New York City Mayor Rudolph Giuliani to advise him on lowering the crime rate in the capital. López Obrador agreed to a fee of more than four million dollars, which was to be paid by a consortium of businessmen, led by Carlos Slim Helú. López Obrador praised Giuliani's zero-tolerance policy, which meant arresting and incarcerating people for petty crimes. It was what he and Slim

[7]Party President Rosario Robles, who had earned a reputation as a troublemaker and a Maoist while a student at the UNAM, had moderated her views and now led the center left. One-time mayor of the Federal District and three-time PRD presidential candidate Cuauhtémoc Cárdenas led another faction of the party, which opposed López Obrador, whom it considered a man determined to be an old-fashioned caudillo. Early in 2004, both Robles and López Obrador were involved in scandals, Robles directly and López Obrador as the mayor whose appointees were caught on videotape accepting bribes. It was not certain whether López Obrador was involved in the scandals himself or was simply a poor manager. In either case, his political career was damaged.

wanted for Mexico. Giuliani, whose draconian policies led to accusations of greatly increased police brutality in New York, was also to change police procedures. Whether Giuliani's methods would work in Mexico was immediately brought into question, but there may have been more behind the move than an attempt to reduce the crime rate in the capital.

The tie between López Obrador and Slim was curious. The two had fastened on several ideas for improving life in Mexico City. They wanted to clean up the area around the Zócalo by moving the street vendors out to a distant area. Slim, head of Mexico's telephone monopoly and a director of the state-owned oil industry, had offered a huge sum to set up the new market and to move the vendors.[8] Friends of the mayor and Slim revealed that there was a plan to gentrify the area around the Zócalo after the peddlers were moved out and the area was cleaned up (Giuliani and zero tolerance were announced later). Slim Helú, who had previously shown no interest in public administration, pushed the new initiative hard. And a man with at least ten billion dollars in his pockets can generate considerable momentum. The influence of Slim Helú showed up in many places as he mounted a campaign to get rid of the peddlers: The Mexican Chamber of Commerce joined the campaign (October 27, 2002) at its annual meeting when its president, Juan Manuel Arriaga, announced the dire effect of street vendors on legitimate business. Because of street vendors, thousands of legitimate businesses had been forced to close, the chamber claimed.

Before the campaign began and the projects to move the peddlers out were announced, there were stories about new hotels in the historic district near the Zócalo and fine new apartment buildings and shops. And a small notice here and there about Slim Helú, who had been buying up property in, of all places, the run-down streets around the Zócalo. There was nothing illegal in the transactions, although they had no regard for tradition or for the people who lived or worked in the area. Peddlers had been selling every-

[8]Telephone rates in Mexico, particularly for long-distance and international calls, rank among the highest in the world. Slim Helú owns many other businesses. He is ranked by *Forbes* as one of the richest men in the world. He owns one of the largest collections of Rodin sculptures. His business interests extend to computer stores and ownership of a large stake in the holding company that owns Televisa, the dominant Mexican television network. Slim is the most prominent member of the thriving Lebanese-Mexican community, descendants of people who emigrated to Mexico during the chaotic nineteenth and early twentieth centuries in the Middle East.

thing from foodstuffs to arts and crafts from their blankets and portable stands (*tianguis*) there since long before the Spanish invaders marveled at the cleanliness and order of the market in the early sixteenth century. Perhaps it was time for the tianguis to move on.

Cuauhtémoc Cárdenas had thought so. He tried to move the peddlers out when he was mayor of the city. Perhaps there was an authoritarian streak in the Mexican left that could not bear the disorder of the ambulantes (peddlers). The PRD is so splintered it is always difficult to understand its thinking. The case of the chamber and Sr. Slim required less cogitation. Nothing as elegant as the Platonic sense of how to order a Republic played any role. It was money. Gentrification in Mexico City would follow the pattern of cities in the United States. The vast profits that would come out of the process harked back to the fortune made by President Miguel Alémán through his premonitory investments in property about to change from worthless to astonishingly valuable. And always because of government policy. At least since the Alémán sexenio, corruption had been blamed on the PRI, although its roots had been established four hundred years before the party was born and they were nourished by the spoils system that began during the last years of the civil wars that finally ended in 1920. The PRI was no doubt guilty of corruption, but it was the old-fashioned kind: Alémán reinvested his gains in building Mexico. Salinas de Gotari was a destroyer. He wounded his country and brought down the PRI. But changes of political parties have so far had no great effect. The PRI in Mexico City simply exchanged roles with the PRD. Where once there were protesters from the PRD carrying signs and claiming the PRI officials in their neighborhood were corrupt, there are now people from the PRI standing in front of office buildings, shouting and carrying signs saying, as one group did, that PRD officials unfairly distributed housing in publicly funded projects, giving all the apartments to members of their own party. And complaints against the PAN began the moment it came to power in northern cities and states.

Few countries other than those in Scandinavia can claim to be free (or close to it) of corruption. Certainly not the United States. The chief difference between the countries is that in Mexico the infection too often takes over a person's character, growing insidiously from a bribe here and a threat there to rape and murder. Like Nuño de Guzmán, the corrupt lose all sense of limits. But Mexicans are not unique in this. How can anyone be a little bit corrupt? No moral code allows it. The Aztecs had draconian punishments for people who broke their moral code; after the invasion, there was no enforceable code, except as it applied to the most outrageous cases. There was an effort by Charles III, who sent José de Gálvez to Mexico to reform its corrupt practices but Gálvez did not succeed. Arriving in 1761, he stayed long enough to clean up some corrupt practices but is better remembered for participating in the expulsion of the Jesuits and for ordering many, many executions throughout New Spain. Gálvez provided no model on which to build a code.

Americans exploited Mexico; Spaniards exploited Mexico; the French exploited Mexico. Spain took all of it; the Americans took half of it and kept what they took; France took all of what was left, but only for a little while. The behavior of the conquerors was rarely benign and never incorruptible. Spanish Catholicism could not control the culture as the indigenous religions had, in part because it was focused on the next world but mainly because the Church itself was an instrument of colonialism: It blessed those who murdered and stole in the name of God. In New Spain the possibility of absolution and eternal life in paradise made corruption far less risky than an Aztec stoning or the removal of a hand. The Church did not condone corruption, but the Church forgave it. And as Octavio Paz pointed out again and again, a critical counterforce to the Church never developed in Mexico, as it did in the United States, where Protestantism had brought its critical sense to the country with the English landings on the East Coast. During the most anticlerical periods in the history of Independent Mexico, heaven, as defined by the Church at the Council of Trent, which concluded in 1563, still held sway. With a priest at his bedside, a corrupt man could die in peace.

QUETZALCOATL'S BODYGUARD

José López Portillo had the face of a Spanish Fascist, balding, with heavy eyebrows, an arrogant glance, and a stepmother's mouth. And it was all a mask. Like the Spanish rebels who had been propped up by the Germans, López had long been an ambitious man, but not one who could begin anything. He did what he was told. When Echeverría anointed him as his successor, López Portillo ran a campaign against corruption and for maintaining the strength of the Mexican peso. He entered office with a plan for the peso and put his personal safety and that of the public under the care of his old chum Blackie Durazo, a *pistolero* (thug) whose luck had gone sour when the gangster he worked for was sent to prison. Echeverría's administration had been corrupt, but in no more than the usual way. Echeverría said he loved the poor, and perhaps he did, but he bought huge tracts of land in Morelos and built resorts in Cancún, enjoying the fruits of those and other prescient choices and civic projects in the manner first used by Miguel Alemán.

López Portillo, his secretary of the treasury, promised to put an end to all that. He was the first criollo president in many years, and he thought of himself as the reincarnation of that other criollo of Tula, Quetzalcoatl/St.Thomas. But a criollo in a land of mestizos had to prove himself a man as well. López Portillo devoted a good part of his presidency to machismo, riding horses, flaunting his sexual affairs, and building mansions and complexes of mansions. He saw to it that some of the most corrupt men in Echeverría's government went to jail. At the same time López Portillo was pushing corruption beyond the limits the Mexican people would tolerate. His party became known as the "institutional corruption party" instead of the Institutional Revolutionary Party.

The most astounding case of corruption in his administration was aired in a book by José González, who worked as a bodyguard for Police Chief Blackie Durazo and then told all his secrets after Durazo lost his job at the end of the López Portillo sexenio and fled the country to avoid prosecution. In the annals of police corruption Durazo may hold the record. He had been indicted on a felony drug charge before López Portillo appointed him to the post, and he went on from there. His police force stole, murdered, tortured, extorted, raped; they were a band of felons, and they all knew enough to send the money up the chain of command, with everyone taking a share of the loot and passing it on until it reached Durazo (and perhaps López Portillo). Durazo built a mansion for himself, often traveled to work by helicopter, took what he wanted from whomever he wanted. He was a bandit with limitless power until the end of his term.

Shortly after he was replaced, he fled to the United States, but even after being extradited to Mexico, he almost got off without being indicted. No one wanted to testify against Blackie Durazo. In the end, the prosecutors, who may also have been bribed or afraid of Blackie, charged him with illegal weapons possession.

López Portillo, whose administration brought Mexico to the edge of bankruptcy, did not limit corruption to stealing a few million for himself while keeping Blackie in office. At one point he wanted to appoint his mistress secretary of education, but was convinced by sounder minds that Rosa Luz Alegría was not quite the contemporary version of Vasconcelos, although she had an advanced degree from the UNAM. He made her secretary of tourism instead. And to be sure the downgrade in cabinet posts did not leave her feeling unhappy or perhaps unloving, he bought her a large house.

He put Carlos Hank González[9] in charge of Mexico City. Among other things, a long stretch of the Metro was built during Hank's tenure. It was one of many huge construction projects during López Portillo's sexenio, all of which appear to have enriched everyone in the government. The extent of the thieving led Mexicans, who had been tolerant of corruption under many presidents, to say there was simply too much corruption; it was harming the country. Corruption of such magnitude, they realized, was different in kind.

It is impossible to say when the new kind of corruption came into being in Mexico. It may have been at the end of the López Portillo term in office, when people were shipping their money out of Mexico as fast as they could. López Portillo tried to stop it, but it was too late. There was an international financial attack on the currency. Everyone in the world sold pesos, and no one wanted to buy them. López Portillo had claimed he would defend the peso, "like a dog," but no currency can endure such an attack. The bill for all the economic errors López Portillo and Echeverría before him had made— mistakes in pricing oil reserves, a bizarre run-up in the foreign debt, vast corruption, unimaginable ostentation by government officials—came due. People who had dollars sent them out of the country. López Portillo made it unlawful to take money out of the country. He nationalized the banks. But nothing could hold off the disaster. In 1982 the peso collapsed.

---

[9]Hank died in 2001, still claiming that he was not a member of the Atlacomulco Group and that the group never existed. Hank, who was nicknamed Genghis, was known as one of the most powerful of the "dinosaurs" who were and still are the old guard of the PRI. The Atlacomulco Group was said to have controlled presidential and other nominations within the PRI. The former governor of Tabasco Roberto Madrazo Pintado, speaking to a reporter, Fernando Benítez, at Hank's funeral, confirmed the existence of the group but said it was merely a group of friends who wanted to do their best for Mexico. Madrazo became the president of the PRI after the party lost the presidency in 2000. He is a likely PRI candidate for president of Mexico in 2006. Men like Carlos Slim Helú, although fabulously wealthy, were not part of the Atlacomulco Group. Slim was an outsider, only second generation in Mexico.

The near bankruptcy of the government, the flight of capital, the sudden loss of income were catastrophic. According to Ricardo García Sainz, who managed Mexico's social security system under López Portillo, real salaries in 2002 were still only 75 percent of what they had been twenty years earlier. The fall changed the sense Mexicans had about both public and private institutions. Except for the very rich, life was not the same in Mexico after 1982. The sudden descent changed the character of the country: Crime and corruption took over more and more of life, resulting in anomie. Durkheim's idea of the breakdown of norms took hold then and grew more pronounced with each new economic catastrophe.[10]

Something else happened during the López Portillo sexenio that may have helped set the stage for the new kind of corruption. Blackie Durazo did not get out of the drug business when López Portillo named him chief of police; instead, he used the police force to market illegal drugs in Mexico City and to protect drug traffickers in the city. It was common knowledge at the time, but most people discounted it as among the least of Durazo's crimes.

Durazo had two supervisors: the president, because Mexico City was part of the Federal District, and the man in charge of the district, Carlos Hank. López Portillo had put together a government of many cronies and one mistress, but that was not unusual in Mexico, nor would it be unusual in the United States, although neither John F. Kennedy nor William J. Clinton, nor Eisenhower, Johnson, or Roosevelt offered cabinet posts to the women they used. Hank was a standard presidential crony, a rich businessman with an interest in politics, "public service," and corruption. While Durazo was making a fortune out of drugs and shakedowns, Hank and López Portillo were also getting rich, taking kickbacks for the vast government contracts let largely during the later years of the 1976–1982 sexenio.

Hank may have had other business with Durazo, and it may have involved Hank's son, Jorge, and Carlos Salinas de Gotari. How the Colombian drug cartel established itself in Mexico may never be known, but Durazo surely knew his suppliers and the people at the highest echelons of government. In 1988, Hank held a dinner at his house in Lomas de Chapultepec to which he invited the richest men in Mexico. The result of the dinner was estimated at hundreds of millions of pesos for the election

[10]Described in his 1897 book *Suicide.*

campaign of Carlos Salinas, under whose administration the drug cartels reached into every part of Mexican government.

On May 24, 1995, Jorge Hank was arrested at the Mexico City Airport with $46,500 and "jewel-encrusted" items valued at much more in his possession. The next day the *Los Angeles Times* reported that U.S. and Mexican investigators had told them the Hank family was involved with the PRI and the Colombian drug cartel. Hank denied it in an interview broadcast on National Public Radio. Jesús Blancornelas, the courageous newspaper editor who exposed the drug cartels in Baja California, claimed in a raft of articles that Hank was involved in the killing of the coeditor of the paper.

Given Carlos Hank's position as kingmaker in the PRI, it is unlikely that the cartel could have penetrated so deeply into the Mexican government without his help or at least his tacit approval. Hank must have thought he was in some danger in Mexico during the López Portillo administration because he bought a house in Connecticut; a purchase that did not endear him to other Mexicans, who had begun to hate the *sacadolares* (people who sent dollars out of the country). It has since become common practice for wealthy Mexicans to keep their money in U.S. banks or securities and to own property on or near the border, especially in an elegant section of Tijuana or an expensive high-rise apartment building in San Diego, which they laughingly refer to as Taco Towers. Hank, however, set the pattern. To be able to get out of Mexico to a safe place without enduring the tribulations of the refugee's life was vital, almost as important as keeping money in an American bank.

By the end of the century the tentacles of savage corruption had not only reached into government but become public, material for newspaper headlines and movies (*Traffic*) in the United States, Mexico's largest trading partner. A PAN official in a border town lamented the publicity as much as the crime. "We'll never get rid of it. Our only hope is to turn it into something like the Mafia in the United States. It exists. It corrupts, but it doesn't control the government." The fear then was the "Colombianization" of Mexico, meaning a fall into something near anarchy in which the federal army, various paramilitary groups of the left and right, and criminal organizations in the drug business battle for power.

The results of corruption and economic mismanagement struck at the heart of Mexico. The middle classes fell, the poor fell even more, and the numbers of the extreme poor, those who lived on a dollar a day or less, grew.

With the near bankruptcy of the country, life outside the cities became more difficult. The poor sold off their little pieces of land and moved to the hope of the impoverished farmer, Mexico City. The great urban slums expanded, encircling cities all across Mexico. Squatters' colonies began, won the right to the land under Mexican law, turned the colonies into urban slums, and the inhabitants worked at anything they could, including crime.

If López Portillo left behind a single idea that would affect Mexico for centuries to come, it was his acceptance of an idea given him by Jesús Reyes Heroles, one of Mexico's leading liberal intellectuals. Reyes Heroles gave his president a way to legitimize a government that had lost almost all credibility. Nothing would save the peso or raise the price of oil—López Portillo had bet the national economy and lost—but Reyes Heroles suggested that López Portillo revise the way the Congress functioned, changing the number of federal deputies, adding a hundred more, with the proviso that at least one-fourth (one hundred) of all the deputies would belong to opposition parties, guaranteeing debate, new ideas, opening up a Congress that had simply been a rubber stamp for the president since the 1917 Constitution was adopted. With the president's blessing, the idea became part of the Mexican Constitution. A decade later, according to a column in *Reforma*,[11] Manuel Bartlett, secretary of the interior under Salinas, sought a way to subvert the idea, proposing a new organization of the lower house that would guarantee 51 percent of the votes to the majority party, thus keeping the PRI in control for the foreseeable future.

Although López Portillo's step toward more equitable representation in Mexican government could not withstand the assault from the masters of darkness, it loosened the stranglehold of the PRI on the country, if only for a moment, and gave hope to the opposition. The man who thought he was Quetzalcoatl was not entirely machismo and mistakes.

WITH ALL DUE RESPECT, MR. PRESIDENT

During the 1970s the Mexican family, which until that time could not be broken except by death, began to come apart. President Echeverría's son divorced a woman who then became the mistress of López Portillo. It was

[11]December 7, 2002, in a column by Graco Ramírez, who is also president of the PRD in the state of Morelos.

not a model for social change, but evidence of it. Education had made women free. They went to school, then they went to work, and they went their own way when their husbands irritated them; the Church could not hold the line against the newfound freedom of Mexican women. By the year 2000 divorce was common enough in Mexico that Vicente Fox, a divorced man, won the presidential election and then married Martha Sahagún, a divorced woman. But the change did not take place only among the Americanized and the rich; it spread through the society.

Among the poor and the newly poor the change was driven by economics as well as by the new sense of liberation. Families from rural areas came to the cities, could not survive as family units, and broke apart. The children were often left to fend for themselves. A great population of street urchins grew up in the city, coupled with each other, and produced children who also lived in the streets. On July 23, 2002, an article in *La Jornada* declared them the "black numbers," saying there were now street urchins who were the grandchildren of street urchins. Without those "black numbers," Mexico had thirty-three thousand children between the ages of twelve and fourteen who were either married, living together, separated, divorced, or widowed. Of thirty-two million children below the age of fourteen, more than twenty million were not eligible for any of the benefits of the social security system, according to INEGI (National Institute of Statistics, Geography, and Information). They had, in the popular phrase, fallen through the safety net.

By the end of López Portillo's term the collapse of the Mexican Miracle and the Mexican family could no longer escape notice; a great, slow-moving revision of the politics, economy, and social structure of Mexico was under way. Mexicans within the PRI as well as those openly in opposition—the PAN, the Communists, the guerrillas in the mountains, the last remnant of the Sinarquistas, the disaffected intellectuals—saw what was coming. It angered them, but not so deeply that they united to do something about the system. For many of them, their first act of participation in the inexorable remaking of Mexican society was to shed their mates. While they attended the divorce courts, the economic decline continued. By the end of his sexenio López Portillo had sent the country to the edge of bankruptcy, and to make matters worse, he had let the dope dealers in at the top and created the circumstances for a wave of crime at the bottom.

The Colombian cartel, protected by the army and the federal, state, and local police, moved in. They had developed an almost foolproof system for winning people over to their side. According to Dr. Broglio,[12] many of whose patients had joined the Colombians in Michoacán, representatives of the cartel appeared at a farmhouse one day and made an interesting offer to the farmer: If he joined them, doing whatever they asked, he would be paid ten thousand U.S. dollars and provided with an automatic weapon and ammunition. If he chose not to join them, they would kill his wife and children and leave him to mourn his mistake.

A farmer had nowhere to turn for help. Since the beginning of the Echeverría sexenio, the government had been systematically and purposively corrupting the army, slowly ridding it of the elite officer corps that might have executed a coup, rotting the army's morale by permitting drug dealing and extortion and using soldiers to capture, torture, and execute dissidents. Federal, state, and local police, many of whom had done obligatory military service, knew how the army worked and hoped for equal or greater profits through corrupt practices.

The new, savage form of corruption was destroying the sense of limits at the core of civil society when Miguel de la Madrid, elected in 1982, brought with him yet another blow to the struggling country. He was Harvard-educated, an aristocratic banker with little experience outside banking. When foreign bankers demanded austerity to fight inflation, reinvigorate the peso, and pay off or at the least stop increasing foreign indebtedness, de la Madrid, a neoliberal, accepted the prescription. Instead of demanding a lower interest rate or some other diminution of the debt, he followed the International Monetary Fund's stern conditions for survival of his government: He let the Mexican people pay.

Inflation stayed up over 100 percent a year, but salaries did not rise to meet it. No matter how hard he (and now she, as more and more women came into the labor force) worked, the average Mexican got poorer. At the bottom, crime was a better and better alternative to misery. Social scientists learned to divide poverty in Mexico into two groups: the poor and the extremely poor. Yet Mexico did not become Colombia. What may well have saved the country from descending into chaos was the tradition of providing help through government programs. At the beginning of the neoliberal years Ricardo García Sainz, managing the social security system during

[12]See Book One, Chapter 11 for more about him.

much of this difficult period, not only continued but was able to increase his programs to build and maintain medical centers and supply full pensions to workers who had completed twenty-eight years of employment. The problem was that García Sainz began from a low base in medical care and the employment situation enabled only a relatively small number of workers to participate in the social security system. Nonetheless, the social programs begun before the neoliberal conversion steadied the country as the quality of life deteriorated.

De la Madrid could do little else to solve the country's problems. He did not have the stomach to prosecute López Portillo, who had fingered him for the presidency, nor did he dare to take on Carlos Hank, whose Atlacomulco Group held sway over the PRI and thus the government. Before the sexenio was over, de la Madrid, the criollo aristocrat, was also widely accused of corruption, but not on a scale comparable to that of López Portillo. De la Madrid was a caretaker of sorts, a man who tried to squeeze Mexico and Mexicans back to health, and all the while the drug cartels grew more powerful and the great corruption under Carlos Salinas de Gotari was yet to come.

At the very end of his term a curious thing happened to President de la Madrid. During his final informe (State of the Nation speech) on September 1, 1988, a dissident, the former president of the PRI itself and a former secretary of labor and education and Mexican ambassador to the United Nations, stood up to challenge the ideas and the magisterial authority of the president of the republic of Mexico. Porfirio Muñoz Ledo was already known for his impulsiveness, but the challenge was not made casually. Muñoz Ledo had surely consulted with his friend and former deputy U.N. ambassador Ifigenia Martínez and perhaps with Cuauhtémoc Cárdenas and others who considered themselves part of the Democratic Current that had been organized in 1986 by reform-minded members of the PRI. De la Madrid, who had negated a PAN electoral victory in Chihuahua, had shown nothing but disdain for Cárdenas, Martínez, Muñoz Ledo, and the other new upstarts on the left; in fact, he welcomed their decision to leave the PRI and start a new party.[13] And now Muñoz Ledo showed disdain for de la Madrid, the PRI, and the office itself. He leapt from his chair and shouted, "With all due respect, Mr. President . . ."

---

[13]The Democratic Current formed in the fall of 1986. The political party, comprising many parties in opposition to the PRI, then known as the Democratic Front, was formed later.

He was shouted down. "Son of a whore! Traitor!" Governors and congressmen swung their fists at him. Fidel Velázquez, head of the vast Mexican Workers' Union (CTM), threw a punch at Muñoz Ledo, missed, and hit a reporter instead.[14]

Nothing like it had been seen in the world of Mexican politics for decades. No member of an opposition party had ever dared respond to the president during the ritual of the informe. In less than one complete sentence, all that he was permitted to utter, Muñoz Ledo's brash move dispelled the aura of invulnerability that had surrounded the party and the presidency. The great public moment of opposition is known today as a key element in the fall of the system, but it was only a beginning. Neither Muñoz Ledo nor García Sainz nor the courageous members of the Democratic Front nor the unstoppable reformers in the PAN and the less daring reformers who had remained in the PRI, nor a majority of Mexican voters could stave off the election of Carlos Salinas de Gotari and the ethical nadir of Mexican politics. The fall of the system took another twelve years to complete.

[14]By 2002 response to the State of the Nation address had changed into a meeting of catcalls, whistles, competing applause, and a grand gesture by Rosario Robles prior to the moment when the PRD turned its back on the president and walked out. She laid a funeral wreath at the foot of the podium. It was a sign that the style of the sixties had ended; a funeral wreath was considerably more dignified than the pig's head mask worn by Marcos Rascón, a PRD federal deputy of an earlier period.

30.

A Dearth of Beginners

*W*hen *I was a young man, living and working in Ciudad Juárez, my next-door neighbor was a prostitute. We rarely spoke. She was all business, and business took place in a house across town. Since she worked the swing shift, on very hot summer afternoons she left the door of her room open to catch the breeze while she slept stark naked on her bed.*

On one such afternoon my mother telephoned to say that she and an aunt who was visiting from Chicago were coming to the hotel where I lived. "No. Please don't," I said, thinking of my neighbor's idea of dishabille.

She insisted.

What could I do? I went to my neighbor's room, knocked on the screen door, told her of my mother's impending visit, and asked if she would mind closing her door for a while.

"It's too hot," she said.

"In that case, would you mind covering yourself with a sheet?"

"It's too hot."

"Could you get dressed?"

"It's too hot."

It was then that my neighbor and I made history: A young man in a Mexican border town paid a prostitute to put her clothes on.

By the crudest measure of gross national product Mexico has one of the ten largest economies in the world, but in terms of per capita income it ranks among third world countries (sixty-ninth), making it a country of the poor but not the idle. President Vicente Fox proudly points to the Mexican unemployment rate,[1] which was under 3 percent during his first years in office but

---

[1] A person who has worked as little as one hour in a given year is not counted as unemployed by the definition used to gather statistics in Mexico.

rose to 3.96 percent in 2003. At the same time, 45.73 percent of the population lived in poverty, according to the very conservative estimate by the World Bank (July 2002). Extreme poverty had grown much worse in rural areas, comprising 25 percent of the population, said the World Bank, but had fallen in urban areas. Sociologist Julio Boltvinik writing in *La Jornada* in March 2002, estimated poverty in the Mexico City metropolitan area at 70 percent. Boltvinik is a brilliant maverick, often disputing "official" figures, but he did not announce the worst of the poverty figures. That was official: Over eighteen million people lived in extreme poverty, which means they survived on less than two dollars a day. In some rural areas, mainly in the south, many people had no monetary income at all, managing to survive by hunting birds and small animals and foraging for edible vegetables. President Fox announced in June 2003, as a sign of the success of his administration, that the number of households living on less than one dollar a day had fallen from 9.7 percent of households in 2000 to 7.4 percent. Inflation over that period was more than 10 percent.[2]

Boltvinik, who has doggedly pursued the question of poverty in Mexico, attacked government figures and World Bank numbers, describing the issue of poverty statistics in Mexico as a "hot potato," saying that there were two sets of figures. He described the two as the "technical figures" and the "official figures."[3] Following Boltvinik, the technical committee appointed by the secretary of social development (SEDESO) determined that poverty in 2000 in Mexico had reached 65 percent. The government had revised the definitions, eliminating one category at the top of the group formerly considered in poverty, so that the number fell to 54 percent in the official figure. To put the figures in some perspective, the levels of poverty in Mexico range from "extreme" (about one-sixth of the U.S. poverty level) to "poor" (less than one-third of the U.S. poverty level). Since families in the United States have nowhere near a decent standard of living at or near the official poverty level, the Mexican numbers are bleak.

Maldistribution of income in Mexico, among the worst in Latin America, accounts for some of the problem, but something else must be going on if the ninth-largest economy in the world cannot provide a decent living for nearly two-thirds of its citizens. With so much money around and so few

[2]Quoted in *La Jornada*, June 22, 2003.
[3]*La Jornada*, August 16, 2002.

people officially out of work, anyone looking at the numbers would have to conclude that a few Mexicans are very shrewd and the rest, the great mass of people living in poverty, have no head for either labor organizing or business. The reality is very far from both hypotheses. Mexican labor unions played a role in overthrowing the Porfiriato. The leaders of large unions, who have ranged from leftist intellectuals to thugs and thieves, much like their counterparts north of the border, made labor one of the pillars of the PRI during its seven decades of dominance; labor was never without a voice at the highest levels of government, but in a corporate state all the officers of the corporation follow the leader.

The Mexican Constitution of 1917 afforded many guarantees to labor, but only enough to give it equality with capital. Venustiano Carranza had been no friend to labor; he gave the unions only as much as he had to, and then he schemed to take control of all that he had given them. As Ramón Eduardo Ruiz wrote, "Article 123 [of the Constitution] did not do away with classes, or the poor, but simply made the state the protector of the worker. . . ."[4]

Before and after 1917 Mexicans have been very good at labor organizing, although they were not strong enough to have a voice in the writing of Article 123. Carranza's scheme worked. The government, their protector, soon took control of unions and their leaders. After the corporatist state became institutionalized under Lázaro Cárdenas, the power of the president of the country over the unions increased. Cárdenas supported the Communist intellectual Vicente Lombardo Toledano, who founded and led the huge CTM (Mexican Workers' Confederation), but after Cárdenas was succeeded by Ávila Camacho, the labor situation changed. When labor leaders became bothersome, as did Lombardo Toledano in 1942, the government simply pushed them out.

A century after the unions helped bring down the Porfiriato, Mexicans are still organizing, hoping independent unions can break the stranglehold of the CTM, the amalgam of unions that controls the lives of workers in Mexico, holding wages down and keeping workers docile. The rebels have had little luck, however. An attempt to organize an independent union in Mexico can result in beatings, jail, and sometimes death.[5] A widely

---

[4] *Triumphs and Tragedy* (New York: W. W. Norton, 1992).

[5] I have described the problems of union organizing in Mexico in the novel *In the Yucatán.*

John R. MacArthur describes problems in labor organizing in maquiladoras in *The Selling of Free Trade* (New York: Hill and Wang, 2000).

reported (*New York Times,* etc.) union election at a plant in Mexico City affiliated with the Dana Corporation, a U.S. manufacturer of auto parts, offers a good example. The vote was held inside the plant, where workers had to make public declarations of their choices while CTM goons stood by, noting every vote.

At maquiladoras (assembly plants) in the state of Tamaulipas, workers who are dismissed for infractions of the rules or for annoying the foremen or attempting to start a non-CTM union cannot return to a maquiladora for six months. All assembly plants there are part of the NAFTA agreement, and all are organized by the CTM. Employment takes place through the union, which administers the punishment. One aspect of NAFTA was to be the protection of workers on both sides of the border. The agreement allows the United States, Canada, and Mexico to monitor each other's labor practices and particularly to review complaints.

Since wages are held down by collaboration among the government, employers, and the unions, all of which respond to the pressure of world markets in a very open economy, the opportunities for Mexicans must come in something other than wage labor, which means the professions, government, and corporations. The rest of the population belongs to the informal economy. In the July 2, 2002, issue of *El Universal,* Raúl J. Lescas of the University of Mexico estimated the number of people employed in the informal economy at 25.5 million. It is probably as good an estimate as any, since the informal economy is not easy to catch in the demographer's net and Mexico maintains its claim of a low rate of unemployment by putting the vast number of people without work into the informal economy.[6] With the percentage of people suffering from extreme poverty at 18 percent and the number of unemployed at less than 3 percent, it is clear that a lot of what the government calls employment is not well paid. The Mexicans have no choice but to be good at business, albeit mainly on a small scale. The competition is fierce, and resources in the informal economy are limited to a person's wits and prayers. The stakes are high, malnutrition and survival are on the table, but the amounts of money involved are minuscule.

[6]The government concedes, however, that employment in the informal sector is growing more rapidly than job creation in the formal sector. Those numbers were compiled before the loss of five hundred maquiladoras in the first half of 2002.

Mexico must create more than a million jobs a year to keep up with the number of young people entering the job market.

There are of course many large Mexican-owned corporations and tens of thousands of other businesses of varying sizes. Many of these are successful, but they do not feed the majority of workers (only fifteen million were eligible for social security medical or pension benefits in 2002, according to the government statistics institute, INEGI). It is the genius of the microentrepreneurs of the informal sector that saves Mexico from economic and social catastrophe. In 2002 these energetic wheeler-dealers of the street corners and puestos (market stalls) were the fastest-growing segment of the economy. With the maquiladora industry in retreat, losing hundreds of thousands of jobs to Asia and Central America, and employment in Mexican-owned industry stagnant, a simple rule for survival prevailed in Mexico: If you want a job, you must create one.

FOR THE LOVE OF JUAN

On some days in Mexico City I am the secretary to Josefina Nuñez Morales, who lives in a vecindad across from El Jardín del Carmen in Tepito.[7] She is a careful woman, the owner of many locks and many tragedies. On the days when I am her secretary life is carefree for Josefina as she goes from place to place in the great open market of Tepito asking her customers what ails them, where they ache, and what they dream. When I am with her, she can work for many hours, because I write down the names of her customers and a word about their sufferings in my notebook and later tear out the page and leave it with her. If I were not there with my notebook, she would be able to serve only as many customers as her memory would

---

[7]Not her real name.

A vecindad can be as large as the one where *Mi Pequeño Traviesa* was filmed or as small as twenty apartments or even fewer.

Oscar Lewis recorded interviews with individual members of a family in Tepito, then a neighborhood of poor and working-class Mexicans. *The Children of Sánchez*, an oral history of a family, their domineering father, and the illegal and sexual activities in the vecindad, became a popular success in the United States. The Mexican government was outraged by the book and banned it. The government's position was overturned in the courts, and the book was published in Mexico. The interviews took place half a century ago.

Since then Tepito has become a center of narcotics trafficking and crime in Mexico City.

permit, for Josefina can make out the names of her customers and the simple words I print beside them, but she never learned to write, and she says she is too old and too busy now to study.

So there is, at the end of the day, a list. Because some of her customers have the same first names and she can make out only first names and a few simple words, which she recognizes as if they were pictures, my list includes María *joya* (jewel) and María *blusa* (blouse) and María *dulce* (candy), and for the other María who also sells candy but is not such a longtime customer, María 2. Their ailments are a litany of the human suffering of the world of the puestos, the little stands or stalls that line the marketplace: knee, foot, feet, liver, headache, swellings, tears, stinging, diarrhea, stiffness, toothache, bellyache, and one man who said he suffered from a bad taste in his mouth that would not go away.

In the category of dreams, for which Josefina offers potions made of herbs, she heard only the worst of the inventions of the night: *muertos* (the dead), *llorando* (weeping), *temblor* (earthquake), and tales of endless falling through a darkness filled with devils and snarling beasts, this last so common that beside the name she said merely to note *s* for *sueño* (dream).

Josefina's garden was a supply of tiny tins and bags and boxes all filled with grasses, leaves, roots, and flowers. The receptacles of hopes occupied a nest of shallow drawers and shelves along the north wall of her personal room. She kept neither songs nor incantations in her garden of cures, although she hummed along with the radio and joined softly in songs heard in the street. She was a woman from the mountains, a widow with a gold tooth and hennaed hair, brown-skinned, in the beginning of her wizening. She was expert in tragedy, in barrenness and loneliness. The neighbors gossiped about her. The women hanging their wash across the courtyard of the vecindad stared up at her apartment on the second floor. A plant had died in the stone urn beside the door at the top of the concrete steps. It stood stern and stiff in the bright sun, the sign of her house, the sign of her. She did not laugh; she scurried, although she was too big, too thickly built to scurry.

"My mother died when I was very young," she said. "We lived on a farm in the state of Mexico. I had to work, so I could not go to school."

We went often to restaurants to talk. It was a long walk from her place to the Plaza Garibaldi, where the mariachis gathered in the evening, but she liked to be away from Tepito. We lunched there, in the middle of the afternoon, Mexican style. In an outdoor restaurant, a place neither clean nor

amiable, we ordered *carne asada*. The waiter, who studied her face as we
ordered, brought us each a large spoon along with a bowl of beans, rice, and
a thin piece of grilled steak. He brought no utensils but the spoons, as if to
say he knew something about her origins. She did not complain. She held
the meat with the edge of the spoon and tore off pieces of it with a folded
tortilla. Before she ate, she touched each item on the plate with her forefin-
ger, putting a taste of it on the palm of her hand. Then she touched her
tongue to her hand to examine the food. "Don't eat the beans," she said. "The
pork in the beans is not good. It will make us sick."

She did not complain to the waiter, but she did not eat the beans. It did
not occur to her to think about the meaning of the spoon. In her house she
ate no large pieces of meat; she ate only with tortillas. The knife lay on the
counter beside the sink; I never saw a fork. A big spoon hung on the wall.
She lived in a place of few things and many treasures: herbs and photographs; a radio as old and fat and out of date as Mexico's época de oro
(golden age) that gave out the tin sound of contemporary newscasters'
voices; a television set on which real ghosts appeared in the unreal scale of
grays. She lived in three rooms: a kitchen, her own room, and the room she
rented to an old man. The old man's face and weary limbs had fallen into
trustworthiness; he shuffled across the floor to his room, intent upon a nap,
wishing her good afternoon in courtly tones. Yet she had asked her suitor, a
man who knew something about carpentry, to construct an impenetrable
door to her private room and to secure it with not one lock but two.

Josefina did business. All was business, carefulness. She did not laugh, nor
did she show any emotion in her daily life. But when she spoke of the man
she had married, she could not hold back the tears. He was a good man, she
said, and he had taken her from the laborious life of the country into the
City of Mexico, where he had worked hard and treated her well. But first she
became ill and endured an operation that left her barren; then he became ill,
and he died slowly, in pain. She did not know what had killed him, perhaps
a demon, some creature that had entered his blood and eaten the life out of
him. She was alone then in the city. He had left behind a small amount of
money in an insurance policy paid for by the factory where he worked. Josefina, bereft and weary, had not been foolish about the legacy; she used the
money to buy the apartment.

She did not want to be a fool; she went about life as if it were a game of
chess, anticipating dangers two or three steps ahead of the moment. Every-

where we went in Tepito, she introduced me as her cousin from Chicago: "You see what an accent he has!" It was to prevent gossip, she said. Not about lovers, although she had a lover who visited often in her apartment; no one cared about lovers, it was strangers they feared.

In the middle of the morning she began her tour of the labyrinthine open market in Tepito. She tucked her house keys and the few pesos she might need into her brassiere. No woman who lived in Tepito carried a purse, she said; it would be stolen in ten minutes. She carried herbs in a plastic grocery bag and the goods of her other business, one by one, never more than she could afford to lose. She stored these other goods in a box on a shelf in the room she kept for herself. They came from an American company, and they were very valuable, she said: lipsticks, perfumes, everything a woman needs to be beautiful, to attract men, to feel better. She held up a bottle of cologne. "Imported from the United States," she said. "Ah-bone." She was the Avon Lady as well as the physician of aches and dreams. What she could not cure, she made beautiful.

Every day, in the middle of the morning, she goes to the open market to make her rounds. On the way she stops at the indoor market to bring food to Juan. He is her man, her lover but not yet her protector. She feeds him, but he does not live with her. They are together, but she remains alone. Juan too is in business. In the middle of the first floor of the market, between the counters filled with shoes, among mounds and bins of rubber and leather, counterfeits and counterfeits of counterfeits, amid the odors of feet and foot coverings, not far from the stockings of all shades and a rainbow of socks, like a tree in the river of shoppers, amid the din of acquisition, stands Juan and his cart of ices. He cries out to the children, and the children cry out for him, his ices and sweet syrups. He has ices, he has flavors; he says the flavors in his flat, gruff voice; he names the fruits, long lists of fruits; he makes an arboretum among the shoes.

Juan does not like children very much. They pester him; they spill their cones of ice and ask for more. He glowers, he shows the darkness of his brow; he is the father not the friend, a humbled brute who serves the babes who pester him. He shows no more gentleness to Josefina than to his customers. He takes the food without a word; immediately there is a child calling for a cone, a mother with pesos in her extended hand. There is no kiss for Josefina, no embrace; the children take his glance from her. The crowd pushes in two directions through the narrow aisle, catching Josefina in the flow. She has left him his lunch. He will not come for dinner until evening when the market has closed and he has returned the cart to its place. There is no leisure, often not even a place to sit for Juan. He eats.

One day of Josefina's rounds is much like another. The market runs in long aisles divided into blocks. Although a great deal of money passes through the market every day, and there are pickpockets and robbers and drug dealers, and every imaginable kind of confidence man, counterfeiter, mugger, and fiend wanders the aisles, the people who stand or sit in the puestos have no fear of them. "The leader takes care of them," according to Josefina. "There is a leader for each part of the market and a leader for the whole market. To have a puesto, you pay the leader, and the leader takes care of the authorities and the criminals. No one is afraid in the market; it is very safe."

The market, however, is not as it appears. The tiny stalls are four feet deep, six feet wide and ten feet high. At first glance the stalls appear to be places of struggle, women and a few men hoping to make a sale here and there, individual entrepreneurs. In the stalls that sell clothing, they reach up with long sticks to bring down a wedding dress or a blouse from the highest part of the puesto so a customer may inspect it. Josefina's friend and customer, who has a tiny dress shop in her puesto in the northwest part of the market, looks more prosperous than Josefina. She and her husband sit on comfortable padded chairs inside the space and eat and laugh. Josefina treats the woman's pain in the shoulder, but on the day we spoke she felt no discomfort, and Josefina did not attempt to sell her a preventive remedy.

"We have six puestos," the woman said to me. "They are in all the parts of the market. My husband goes around all day to collect the money." Like Josefina, the woman who owned the dress shop was a Nahua who had come to Mexico from a small town. She spoke Nahuatl as well as Spanish, and she said it was sometimes a help in doing business. Although she and Josefina were friends, the owner of the puestos and her husband had a different life. They had children who attended college and preparatory school, they were part of a buying cooperative that used the leverage of its size to get better prices from wholesalers, and they had long ago moved out of Tepito to a small house in the north of the city. It was not a good place, the woman said, and she and her husband hoped to move soon, but they were glad to have been out of the center of the city when the 1985 earthquake killed so many people and brought down the factories where some of the clothing had been made for her business. "It was God's vengeance on the Jews who owned the factories," she said, the common refrain in Tepito. Around the corner, surrounded by the most garish blouses and decorations—flowers painted on black velvet, dragons printed on rayon, the face of Sting, and something that might have been the Yellow Submarine—sat the oldest woman in the market, according to Josefina. She was María blusa. She beckoned to Josefina to come near and to bend her head down close to the old woman's lips. Professional ethics kept Josefina from repeating what the old woman said, although she hinted that it might have to do with dreaming. The old woman said in a loud voice that she was ninety-four years old and she did not like the heat. It was not clear why she wore a woolen sweater and kept a blanket over her knees.

All morning and into the afternoon, through the heat and the yellow haze that saddened the sun, Josefina walked the aisles of the market, collecting nightmares and woes. It was a day of many notations. The gigantic woman in front of the bakery bartered two sweet rolls for a headache powder. The vendor of clay jars complained of his fingers. At the wedding dress puesto Josefina promised to bring a sample of the newest lipstick from Avon the next morning. In the late afternoon we ate and then brought food home to Juan, who was due to arrive just before sundown.

He entered with a key, went immediately to the sink to wash, and sat at the narrow end of the small rectangular table covered with green and white plaid oilcloth that served for everything from meals to food preparation to a workplace in the kitchen. The dishes were in one small open cupboard; a few pots and pans hung on the wall. Josefina lit the two-burner stove and warmed his food in one pan and tortillas in the other. He ate like an animal, grunting, tearing the food with his tortillas and his hands. His conversation was monosyllabic, words spoken with the food momentarily tucked into a huge lump in his cheek. At the end of the meal he drank a cup of Sanka, picked his teeth, and delivered his opinion of Mexico's three main political parties.

Josefina said but little, serving him, bustling between the stove and Juan's place at the table, filling his plate with rice, replacing every tortilla he ate with the next fresh one off the griddle. "Business is poor," he said. "The PRD is more corrupt than the PRI, and the PAN are all sons of whores from Monterrey." He tapped his elbow on the table to indicate the stinginess and greed of people from Monterrey.

Josefina turned on the radio; Juan chose the station. She trembled before him; all the wisdom and wiles had fled. He ordered her about; he did not touch her. When she asked if he had enjoyed the food, he merely grunted. He too had a gold tooth and another inlaid with gold. He wore long sideburns and a Zapata mustache. His eyes were dark, and where they should have been white and clear, they had become yellowed. Everything about him promised violence.

They had been together for a long time, but Josefina did not speak of marrying Juan. He worked only a few days a week. The rest of the time he devoted to his mother. He wanted Josefina to sell her apartment and give him the money to buy a pickup truck so he could go more often to visit his mother, who lived in a small town in the state of Mexico. She refused. "The apartment is all I have in the world," she said. "And Juan."

DEAD CAPITAL

Mexico, like many countries still outside the modern legal and economic system, follows Roman law in its view of property.[8] The law leans very heavily toward the protection of the owner and makes the transfer of property or any other transaction involving construction or the start-up of a business extremely slow, difficult, and costly. On January 22, 2002, the Mexican newspaper *El Economista*, perhaps in an effort to spur changes in Mexican law

---

[8]Given Mexico's adherence to Roman law, which is very different in execution from Anglo-American case law, property rights are often in doubt. Roman law, brought from Spain to Latin America, is a highly formalized system, a written code allowing for little interpretation by the courts. In a system of Roman law, a property owner may have the right to recover his property under certain circumstances, even after a legal sale has been made, if it can be proved that there was the smallest error in the sales contract or that it was not properly notarized. Banks have become increasingly unwilling to make loans for housing or business development. Should the mortgagee default, it could take a bank five or seven years to take over the property or business under Mexican law. As a result, down payments are high (25 to 40 percent) and the banking system prefers credit cards, which are a form of personal loan at what would be considered usurious interest rates for anything else.

In Mexico's system based on Roman law, the notary becomes a very important figure because any contract not properly notarized is open to dispute. It is the unfortunate buyer who neglects a comma in a Mexican contract, for the buyer may wind up without the property or price he or she paid for it.

and to prod the government to lessen corruption, published a long article on this flaw in the Mexican economic system, the cost of doing business according to the law.

The paper made its point with a list of transactions, the time needed to accomplish them, and the cost expressed in U.S. dollars[9] and months of work at an average wage job. A real estate transaction took twenty-four months, and cost $2,500 (six months' salary). To get a mortgage also took twenty-four months, but cost $7,100 (twenty months' salary). A mortgage guarantee took forty-three months and cost $11,920 (thirty-three months' salary). In sum, it could take forty-three months and cost almost six years' pay at an average salary to buy a house legally with all the protections of a legal mortgage in the United States, and that is in addition to the cost of the property. Instead of paying the monetary costs and enduring the years of legal complications, the transfer was as often as not done illegally.

Once a property was obtained illegally, the capital invested in it had no value. It was, in the language of economics, dead. It could not be used as collateral in seeking to raise working capital, and it was anything but liquid. The money was taken out of the economic system. In Mexico, a country that has been thirsting for capital since the day it became independent, the loss of working capital in its own economy means the money has to come from foreign sources. Because the informal economy is so large in Mexico and loses so much capital through illegal or (to avoid the stigma of criminality) "extralegal" transactions, Mexico has had difficulty becoming a modern economy, dependent upon its own extractive, agricultural, and manufacturing sectors to produce goods from start to finish. In other words, Mexico does not have enough money to get rich. Not in the modern industrial world. The painful truth is that much of the capital used to improve the standard of living in the country during the quarter century of the Mexican Miracle was amassed through corrupt practices or international debt taken on at high rates of interest: Mexico became richer, although not rich, by stealing from itself for itself. After the "miracle" was over, in the savage form of corruption, only the thieves got rich.

The ongoing problems, at least in terms of lost capital, may be ameliorated by streamlining Mexico's legal system to make extralegal transactions

[9]A quick way to compute the value of the peso in 2002 was to multiply the number of dollars by ten.

less appealing, but in an economy that produces more jobs through the informal than the formal economy, capital will continue to disappear, lost forever in the netherworld of informality. Unless the situation changes, and the government returns to managing the economy more adroitly, Mexico will continue to sell itself off to accumulate capital or fish for investment (with many strings attached) from external sources, and the labor of its citizens will continue to be the product in an ongoing sale of distressed merchandise.

In 2003 the Fox administration tried to attack the problem of what he saw as useless regulation, cutting taxes on rents of all kinds and investments, also making it easier to open businesses, transfer properties, import all sorts of goods, including animals, and so on. He proposed changing the rules for twenty kinds of dealings, reducing or removing red tape and fees. His purpose was to bestir a lagging economy and produce jobs. His ideas were in many instances conservative solutions, involving the Mexican Institute of Social Security, further weakening the arm of the government that made life better for the working class.[10] At the same time, he announced a program to help the poor by providing them with twenty-seven cents a day per household. But expenditures on social services in Mexico continued to decline overall, becoming among the lowest of any country belonging to the Organization for Economic Cooperation and Development (OECD).

TAKE ME OUT TO THE BALL GAME

José Maiz Mier, the octogenarian founder of Constructora, one of the largest and most successful construction companies in Mexico, had a theory about running a construction business. He said that when he went out to a job site, he never dressed in fine clothes, had a chauffeur, or drove an expensive car. There was no sense, according to Maiz Mier, in making the people who were working on the sites feel bad. There is some irony in that, because the Maiz family owns, among many other things, the Mercedes-Benz dealership in Monterrey. Constructora itself has two thousand employees and does more than a hundred million dollars a year in business. The company slogan is "There is no project so big we cannot build it and no project so small we would not do it."

Constructora has built highways, international bridges, shopping centers,

[10]*Reforma,* June 17, 2003.

skyscrapers, factories for General Motors, General Electric, John Deere, and Seagate, as well as many of Mexico's largest businesses. Its offices, true to form for the patriarch who still oversees the character, if not the dealings, of the firm, are in a building owned by the family, but the entrance to its offices is not at the impressive front of the building. Constructora's customers and employees enter through a modestly marked door on a side street and climb a flight of narrow stairs to a small landing where a woman answers the bell by opening a small frosted sliding glass window and asking if the visitor has an appointment. It is Dickensian Mexico, and it epitomizes the abstemiousness for which Monterrey is famous.

The founder of Constructora, José Maiz Mier, descendant of the family of Fray Servando Mier on one side and Basques who arrived at the end of the nineteenth century on the other, is a tall, slim, very upright man, of Spanish elegance and Basque toughness, a modest grandee, with white hair and a neatly trimmed white mustache in the style of Spain before the Civil War. He chooses to accept visitors in the company conference room, a cramped place of dark wood under a low ceiling. It looks small-time, old-time, downtime. A black dial telephone sits on the table near the head. It rings with the now-startling bell of mid-century. For a man whose personal wealth was estimated at a quarter of a billion dollars or more, Maiz Mier told a modest tale. He has had one passion outside family and business, and in the end it led him to great pleasure and a terrible mistake.

He told his family history from long before the time of Francisco Madero, whom he referred to as Pancho, offering a bit of gossip about the reason for Madero's interest in overthrowing the Porfiriato. He qualified it with "There are various reasons for Madero's participation in the Revolution. One is that they [the Maderos] had business problems. They went broke.

"My great-grandfather was the governor who had Madero a prisoner here when he was campaigning for the presidency before Porfirio renounced. They asked my great-grandfather why he did not put Madero in front of a firing squad, and my great-grandfather said he did not execute political prisoners."

He spoke of Bernardo Reyes, who would have succeeded Madero, in his opinion, had Reyes in rebellion not been shot at the gates of the National Palace. But curiously, Maiz's grandfather sided with Huerta, who made him governor of Jalisco. "He remained loyal to the institutions of government. Then Obregón attacked Guadalajara. While my grandfather led the battles, my mother fled for her safety to Ciudad Alemán. My grandfather would not surrender, and he was assassinated. They sold the family properties, and my mother and father left on a freight train and went to live in New York."

Maiz Mier said, "I have always been in the opposition. Lázaro Cárdenas was a socialist, very radical; he wanted to institute a socialist education here in '34, and we students went on strike in protest and stayed out until he sent the army after us, and we were obliged to leave. We went to Mexico City, where we rested for a few months. The rector of the university had been the founder of the PAN [Manuel Gómez Morín] , so we were welcome."

With a degree in civil engineering, he started his business at home in Monterrey, working, he said, "on public-sector properties: water, sewerage systems, and so on. We worked from eight in the morning until four in the afternoon. At four in the afternoon, I started work with another group, and we worked until eight. We did that every day." He and his brothers started Maiz Mier, Civil Engineers. "Then we separated, and I went on alone. When we changed from professional engineers to builders, I founded a corporation in 1961. Then there was an opportunity for my sons."

The Maiz family worked on bigger and bigger projects, many of them for American companies. Maiz Mier described Monterrey as halfway between a Mexican and an American city. His advertising and much of the information his company put out on the Internet were in English. And Maiz Mier had a passion for something else American, baseball. He founded the Monterrey Sultans baseball team and then built the largest baseball stadium in Mexico, seating twenty-five thousand, as a home for them. The greatest moment in baseball for Maiz Mier came when the Los Angeles Dodgers catcher Roy Campanella visited Monterrey, and the greatest moment for Monterrey came when its team played in the Little League World Series in 1957.

Maiz was Monterrey's ultimate baseball fan. He was the president of the team and the builder of the stadium, but he was also a figure in civic organizations, and with his oldest son, José Maiz García, and others of his twelve children, he moved beyond baseball. His love of sports connected him to Jorge Lankenau, the owner of a soccer team. Lankenau persuaded Maiz Mier to join him in a venture bigger than anything the Maiz family had attempted before: "Banca Confia—Have confidence in Mexico!" It had eight hundred retail branches and was among the largest banks in Mexico. The system had been privatized again after López Portillo's nationalization, and banks were seen as highly profitable investments. Maiz Mier had confidence in Lankenau and Banca Confia. He bought in deeply. Then the peso crisis of 1994 crushed the banks. Banca Confia was eventually bought out by Citicorp, which wanted its retail outlets.

Lankenau turned out to be a less than perfect partner. His shady dealings, which Maiz Mier had not followed, led to federal prosecution. The Maiz family suffered enormous losses. For a family considered among the most astute of the famously shrewd businessmen of Monterrey, it was an embarrassment as well as a financial loss. Of the great error of his long business career, Maiz Mier had but three brief sentences to offer: "We were in Banca Confia. The head of the bank is in jail this evening. We lost a lot."

Then he put aside the mistake, and his toughness took over. "There is a reason why we are successful here in Monterrey," he said. "This is a semiarid zone, where it is difficult to survive, so the people always had to work. In the southwest they have many blessings; you can just put out your hand and cut off a stalk of bananas or a coconut from a tree, and you can survive. Here we don't have that. You have to work."

NIPPLES OF THE NORTH

Prisciliano Siller said, "I have only two planes now, but in my life I have owned thirty-seven." It is his way of introducing himself and his success in business. Once it was Niples del Norte and a hardware store, but that was all in Mexico. Siller is a special kind of Mexican, one of those known as a sacadólares (takes out dollars). He began in Mexico, where he considered going to law school, then changed his mind and started working in a hardware store. He was fourteen years old. Soon he and a partner had a store together. Siller said, "I liked doing business. To do business, you have to have two things: First, the vision; then you have to be strong, work." Although he never gave up the hardware store, he earned a law degree, then built a company called Niples del Norte, a plant that made the small metal nipples through which lubricants are inserted into machines. "We had three hundred employees," he said. "Sixty percent of my production was exported to the U.S. and Latin America. In 1994 we had sales of forty-eight million dollars."

Siller had no competition. Then, in 1994, the peso fell, and NAFTA rules allowed a U.S. firm to open a factory in Tijuana. Niples del Norte was finished. "I sold the factory to Jews," he said. "They took advantage of me. I had to sell at a low price. I had my way of doing business. Consultants came in and offered to improve my productivity after the plant opened in Tijuana, but I had always done business my own way. I didn't need their advice.

"I like the big, not the small. I don't like to rest. I develop big things. Small things don't please me. I invest too. Javier Pérez in Merrill Lynch is my broker." He smiled; he grimaced. He looked like the former Mexican president Díaz Ordaz, the same skeletal mouth and teeth, the same calculated smile. He had tight eyes, measuring. Siller liked airplanes and country clubs. He counted his life by his properties. The hardware business was still his, still in Mexico, although he lived in the United States. "I have one hundred employees in one large store. We do thirty to thirty-six million dollars in annual sales of tools, business and industrial tools. I buy precision tools from the United States and sell them in Mexico."

Siller is Mexican, but his investments, except for the hardware store, are in the United States. He owns property in Laredo, San Antonio, and McAllen, Texas: shopping centers and office towers. He bought and sold Mockingbird Plaza in San Antonio. Siller is aging now, bringing his burly red-haired son into the business, spending time at country clubs, eating carefully, caring for himself. "I remain restless," he said. "If an idea presents itself, I do it."

He continues to operate a business in Mexico, but the capital flows out to the more stable country. The cycle followed by Siller and thousands of other Mexicans strips the capital value of Mexican labor and ships it north or to Europe or to investment in other Latin American countries. His hardware business pays wholesale prices to U.S. manufacturers, sells the goods in Mexico, and recycles the profits to investments in the United States. He puts money back into Mexico through Ciudad de las Niñas (City of Little Girls), a charity, but not through business. The policies of the Mexican government and the economic and political power of the United States have created Siller's business practices. Like any good capitalist, he pursues his own self-interest and leaves the rest to the "invisible hand."

NO SUBSTITUTE FOR LOSING

Mexican economists ranging from Ricardo Pascoe to Ifigenia Martínez to Monterrey business consultant Manuel Sama all see the major current problem for Mexican business beginning with the sudden lifting of tariffs on manufactured goods by the Salinas government and the end of import substitution.[11] Carlos Slim broke his usual public silence to tell a Chilean news-paper that the problem in Mexico was "neoliberalism gone wild," com-plaining that "the Washington mandates" do not allow Mexico the chance for internal growth.[12] That they share the view gives it credence, for they are not cut from the same cloth. Slim is, according to *Forbes*, the richest man in Latin America. Pascoe, who studied economics at New York University and worked with the Allende government in Chile, became Mexican ambassador to Cuba in the Fox administration. Martínez was head of the economics department at the UNAM and a figure in the PRI and then the PRD. Sama, a partner in the consulting firm of Sama, Cueva y Valencia, is also a profes-sor at ITESM, where he runs the strategic planning seminar in the M.B.A. program.

Slim owns the Mexican telephone company, Telmex, Sanborn's restau-rant chain, real estate, broadcasting, and so on; his interests are national and international. Pascoe and Martínez are oriented toward Mexico City. Sama has clients in several Mexican cities, but the bulk of his work is in Monter-rey. There are more than a dozen fairly large corporations there, several of which would be considered very large by U.S. standards. Sama has served as a consultant at one time or another to many of them. The first three listed below have sales of more than three billion dollars annually, all the rest have sales of one billion dollars or more. The business of the three banks at the end of the list, of course, is not measured in the same way. Cemex is the third-largest cement company in the world. Pulsar produces one-fourth of the entire world supply of seeds. Maseca produces corn flour (masa), the basic food of the Mexican diet and the flour used in almost every tortilla sold in the United States as well. Almost all the companies are conglomerates. Junco is a newspaper publishing empire. All the companies are Mexican-owned.

---

[11]A policy common in less developed countries. Using tariffs and other means, it encour-ages domestic production in the place of imports, raising domestic income and indus-trial growth and supporting internal markets through greater labor utilization. The policy is debated among economists, with those who favor free trade, like the Interna-tional Monetary Fund, the United States, etc., claiming greater benefits through foreign investment and export, utilizing low labor costs as the major economic engine. Many developing nations would like to be able to use all the policies at the same time—that is, import substitution, export growth, foreign investment, all with relatively low wage rates. China appears to be doing this to good economic effect.

[12]*El Mercurio*, November 24, 2002.

As a city Monterrey abounds in anomalies, nowhere more obviously than in the business community. Every businessman in Monterrey points to the city's cultural connection to the United States, but Monterrey is the most nationalistic business community in Mexico. Monterrey is one of the most conservative Roman Catholic cities in Mexico, but it is the only city where the Protestant Ethic dominates. Everyone in Monterrey's business community talks about politics, but the key difference between Monterrey and Mexico City is that business in Monterrey does not survive on political connections (until the 2000 election the business community was, like Maiz Mier, in the opposition) while Mexico City business lives by government outlays and favors. A glance at the names of the owners of Monterrey's largest enterprises points to a different set of connections. Many of the names are the same, most are of Sephardic Jewish origin (although all are practicing Catholics); the list defines an extremely tight community, usually allied by marriage, like the royal families of Europe.

Cemex—Zambrano family

Alfa—Garza Sada family

Femsa—Garza Laguera family

Vitro—Sada González

Pulsar—Alfonso Romo and Alejandro Garza Laguera

Axa—Jorge Garza

Maseca—Roberto González Barrera

Imsa—Clariond and Canales families

Soriana Organization—Martín family

Cydsa—González Sada family

Copamex—Maldonado family

Editora el Sol—Junco family

Bancomer—Garza Laguera family

Serfin—Sada González family

Banorte—Roberto González Barrera

During the years of the Mexican Miracle, when the country used tariffs of up to 100 percent in an effort to allow Mexican enterprises to grow, with their markets protected from foreign competition, the major businesses in Monterrey used the breathing space to grow strong. Their behavior was not common in Mexico. As the government centralized the country, Monterrey went its own way, grumpy, industrious, religious, conservative, American-ized, and tough. Pascoe on the left and Sama in conservative Monterrey have the same fear for the future of Mexico: It could become one huge maquiladora.

The two from the capital are political, economists, with grand designs; Mexico City, despite its size, at heart is a government town. Manuel Sama, in Monterrey, makes plans for businesses. He works behind a planner's clean desk, in the studied modernism of the firm's offices. Sama speaks quickly, then stops, asking for time to organize his thoughts. He wears gray suits, has graying hair; the colors in his office are muted, as if to allow his ideas to be the one salient. Although his voice is high, almost shrill, he has a charming way of saying quite suddenly, "Yes, that should be done, but I don't know how to do it." All three are multilingual, highly educated, well traveled, nationalistic, and worried. Only Sama was educated entirely in Mexico.

All three have a pugnacious view of the place of Mexico in a global econ-omy: Mexico must engage in global markets. Sama argued that when the peso fell in 1994, it was not because of the maquiladoras. He added that Mex-ico's trade with the United States and Canada was more or less balanced. "Asia," he said. Then he explained what he viewed as the great Salinas eco-nomic error. "Mexico was a closed economy for forty years, but it did not produce enough jobs. Employed people were happy, but unfortunately we needed a million jobs a year, and we were producing five hundred thousand. So that's why we had to open the economy. But maybe we opened the borders too soon. We had forty years to prepare, but then we opened the borders too fast, forced the international situation. Maybe we should have taken twenty years. But that's history.

"Some businesses became competitive, and many others went broke before they discovered they had to change. I think the government made some very serious mistakes. For example, before NAFTA we used to have import duties going up to fifty, seventy-five, one hundred percent. Suddenly they decided no import duties higher than twenty percent.

"Only with Canada and the U.S.? No, no, no! With everybody. That was crazy, stupid. That's one of the causes of the '94 crisis. The crisis was not cre-ated by NAFTA. The huge deficit was with Asia, because they don't import anything from Mexico and we lowered the tariffs to twenty percent for them. Then we started to negotiate with the Americans from twenty down. They should have lowered from a hundred to forty and then started negotiating. We should have had a slower transition. And now, from twenty, we lower the tariffs to ten."[13]

He took a moment to recover from his upset at the error, which he believed hurt Mexico where it was most vulnerable, in the area of mid-size business, which he defined as companies with sales of a hundred million dollars or less."

"We have three Mexicos: the Indian Mexico in the south, the mestizo Mexico in the center, and the northern Mexico, which is very influenced by the gringos. The difference is becoming greater and greater between the north and the others. Northern corporations are oriented to exporting—thirty, sixty, seventy percent in exports. Our major conglomerates are becoming international, learning to manufacture outside Mexico. For example, Cemex has more than fifty-five percent of its production outside Mexico. They have plants in Spain, Venezuela, Colombia, Panama, and Malaysia. This example has been followed by other corporations. Bimbo, for example, the producer of bread, has plants throughout South America and now in the U.S.[14]

"Femsa is in Buenos Aires, with a large bottling plant. Imsa, which makes batteries for cars, has plants throughout South America. First, they became competitive, then international. There has also been a switch in education. Monterrey has been influenced by Monterrey Tec [ITESM], which was founded by MIT graduates, trying to copy MIT. The Tec now has thirty campuses, exchange agreements with universities in the U.S. and Europe, distance learning in South America. It's a dramatic switch from local to international."

And then he came to the problem and his charming moment. "The big challenge is to develop mid-size industries, and I don't know how. If you go to Europe, you find hundreds, thousands of mid-size companies that are internationally competitive. In the U.S. there are tens of thousands of com-

---

[13] And on agricultural products from the United States to zero in 2008.

[14] At the end of 2003 Jorge Castañeda, who was trying to find backing to run for president of Mexico in 2006, said that this multinational trend in Mexican business was wounding the national economy. He described it as a new method for sending capital out of the country (personal interview).

panies in a special niche with a special product. If only the huge conglomerates grow, the concentration of wealth and power is too great. It's not good for a country. We have to develop mid-size industries, not microindustries."

He groaned at the thought of most business in Mexico. "It's very parochial, serving only a small market, not competitive, always managed by the owners. There's no sense of competition in the universities here. Outside Monterrey, the juniors, the sons and daughters of the owners, don't feel the need to compete. In Mexico City of course you can find anything, but in the rest of the country there is this complacency. They don't realize you can buy anything from anywhere in the world."

There is no computer in Sama's office. He works on paper. The computer is outside, in another room. It leads to the most basic question about Mexican business. There is virtually no research and development. Mexicans have become efficient managers of what others invent, build, and sell to them. "Generally speaking," he said, "our corporations are not leaders. We are a satellite of the U.S., and that's not good. We should invest not ten times, but a hundred times more in research and development. But we don't. That's why we are becoming a maquiladora country. The reality is that if we don't invest in R and D, we will become only subsidiaries of U.S. corporations. As I tell my classes, the first step is to open borders, the second is to become competitive, and the third is to plan for twenty years from now. The difference between the first world and the third world is the planning horizon. In the third world it is no more than one or two years."

Then he paused to think about the future of a maquiladora country. He shook his head when he thought of the wage rates, the ultimate danger. "If the maquiladora workers put too much pressure on for higher wages, they will lose their jobs. The plants will move to lower-wage countries."

The closing of the maquiladoras began in 2001; in 2002 the number of plants in operation had fallen from the peak of thirty-five hundred to below three thousand. The jobs followed the path Sama knew was inevitable: Asia was taking another slice out of Mexico, and the move toward democracy had not brought prosperity with it. By midsummer 2002, Mexican industrial production had fallen for seventeen months in a row.[15] The U.S. economy was shaky, and the major export markets of the Monterrey conglomerates, Brazil, Argentina, and Colombia, were on the edge of chaos.

[15]INEGI, reported in *La Jornada*, August 13, 2002.

EFFICIENT ESCAPES

Raúl Cárdenas Cavazos (no relation to the late President) operates an efficiency and management consulting firm, Productivity de Mexico, out of offices in Monterrey. Cárdenas teaches industrial operations how to motivate and train employees to use modern equipment and methods, mainly Japanese methods, Kan Ban, or just-in-time, various quality-control procedures, etc. The firm has won major contracts in competition against Stanford Research Institute and other U.S. competitors. Its clients include major U.S. operations, like a Ford assembly plant in Mexico.

Cárdenas Cavazos was an academic at Monterrey Tec when he was lured into the business world by Metalsa, part of the Zambrano family empire devoted to making metal frames for light trucks and now owner of a heavy truck operation in Roanoke, Virginia. Cárdenas quickly moved into management at Metalsa. In 1991 he left Metalsa to start his own consulting firm. Cárdenas is a brusque man, with a deep voice, who speaks English without accent. He wastes no time, as one would expect from an efficiency expert. His views of his country come in succinct portions. "We are a very corrupt country, have no doubt about it. We depend on the U.S., but no cure for Mexico's ills can come from outside. When you believe the solution for Mexico's problem is outside of us, a solution is out of our reach. We, the Mexicans, have to do it for ourselves."

Democracy is the start of the cure for Mexico, in his view, but politics alone cannot change the economics of a country. Democracy is not in itself a producer of wealth; there will also have to be research and development, new Mexican industries. The NAFTA agreement merely exacerbated the problem because it prohibited technology transfers from the United States to Mexico, leaving Mexico in the same difficult and expensive position. "We are very rich in natural resources, but we buy technology. It will take at least fifteen years for us to begin to take leadership positions."

Educated, efficient, visionary about the need for Mexico to begin to behave like a first world country in its business sector, Cárdenas Cavazos, like Manuel Sama, works at the heights of the manufacturing world. His son, who calls himself Raúl Jr. in the American style, belongs to the next generation. Known to his friends as Dos Metros because he is six feet two inches tall, he holds a degree in computer engineering. His heroes are Steve Jobs and the geniuses of the cybernetic world. In his late twenties, he worked as the salesman for his father's company (he is as smart as Raúl Sr. and very,

very charming) and dreamed of starting ancillary businesses, perhaps something that would challenge AOL (America On Line) in the Internet access business. His idea is to sell Internet access on a small scale, offering superior service.

His father worries about Dos Metros's leaving the company to work more in his own world. Another son, also a computer engineer, has already done so. Work in Mexico at his level of engineering skill was not available. He moved to Germany to work for Siemens, then to the United States, seeking both opportunity and intellectual stimulation. Dos Metros has already been to school in the United States; it will not be long until he follows his brother.

As Mexico enters the age of efficient industrial work, the rest of the world is moving beyond it into a new age, driven more by information than industry. As with all new ages, the preceding one will not disappear. Agriculture faded with the industrial age; it did not disappear, but agriculture was changed by the new age. Not in Mexico, however, where agriculture has not become highly sophisticated even as tens of thousands of small farms have been abandoned. Mexico imports corn and corn products from the United States. Corn syrup exported from the United States closed down the sugarcane industry in the state of Morelos, leading to strikes and protests by cane workers in the fields and mills. Mexico uses corn from the United States to feed vast numbers of hogs, whose excrement poisons the water and fouls the air for tens, eventually hundreds of miles around the pens.

The old world based on the "three saints"—corn, squash, and beans—did not survive intact and healthy as the new age produced crops at much lower cost. A similar future awaits Mexico in the industrial world. It provides cheap labor, made cheaper by technology and efficiency, but it does not have the information age skills to initiate new businesses, and it does not yet understand the need to develop them if it is to survive.

Mexico, which once imported 100 percent of its manufacturing and engineering talent, is now a net exporter of engineers. It does almost no basic research, although agricultural experts, like Luis O. Tejada Molina, are looking into imaginative ways to cultivate, can, and export new products from the south of Mexico. Tejada has an idea about canning guanabana and exporting to the United States.[16] Monterrey Tec, headquartered in a city so

---

[16]Guanabana (also known as soursop) is grown in many parts of Latin America. It is most common in the Caribbean, where fruit with a gentler flavor is produced. The fruit, sometimes a foot in length, can be cut open and eaten with a spoon, or it can be made

different from the rest of Mexico that the senior Cárdenas says some people think of it as a separate country, is modeled on MIT but does not do the same kind of scientific research and does not teach science at the highest level. It is an institute of technology, as its name promises. Monterrey Tec has not produced a great deal of originality, nor has either Mexican business or its educational establishment nurtured new ideas. Of all the patents granted in Mexico, 96 percent are held by foreigners. In Mexico, genius has few sponsors. In February 2003 the World Economic Forum released its technology rankings for the preceding year: Mexico had slipped from forty-fourth to forty-seventh place in the world, behind Botswana.

The hope of Mexico in the information age may lie in its connection to the intellectual accomplishments of pre-Hispanic Mesoamerica. The genius may still exist in the genes. There are signs, promises. The poet Natalio Hernández Xocoyotzin was born in the mountains of Veracruz. His parents were Nahuatl speakers, but country people, not citizens of a great urban center like Tenochtitlán or Chichén Itzá. One of the sons of Hernández Xocoyotzin holds an advanced degree from the UNAM in computer science, with a special interest in graphics. The trip from a mountain village to computer science in only two generations is remarkable, but it was nothing compared with the intellectual journey of the Maya, who went from mere counting to the discovery of the concept of zero and the beginning of mathematics six hundred years before the idea was known in Europe. Mexico has only to take advantage of its birthright in the mathematical foundation of the age of information to come to prominence, but that will take interest and investment on the part of government, which does not appear to be forthcoming.

---

into a rich-tasting drink when sweetened or mixed with milk. There is, at present, a very small market for guanabana in the United States, but it could be sold in many forms, including a carbonated soft drink.

31.

Maquiladora Nation

TIME IS MONEY

—THREE ENGLISH WORDS ON THE COVER OF
Inversionista, SEPTEMBER 2002[1]

In 1994 the North American Free Trade Agreement, known everywhere by its acronym, NAFTA, went into effect. In the United States the battle over the agreement had been fierce. In a famed television debate between Vice President Albert Gore, Jr., and H. Ross Perot, a Texas billionaire and self-propelled presidential candidate, Perot uttered the often quoted phrase about the "sucking sound" that would be heard as American jobs went south. Gore and the president, William J. Clinton, representing the interests of the conservative wing of the Democratic Party, put aside their connections to the labor unions that opposed the agreement and, with the help of business lobbyists and public relations firms, pushed the bill through Congress.

On the Mexican side, the agreement had been invented by President Carlos Salinas de Gotari, whom many people, including most of the media, then saw as a visionary Harvard-educated economist intent upon privatizing and modernizing Mexico to further stabilize one of the longer-lasting governments in the hemisphere.[2] U.S.-Mexico trade was already enormous, and the only real problem between the two countries was the ever-increasing number of immigrants from Mexico, and even that was not a real problem.[3] The

---

[1] "A Magazine of Personal Finance." The cover illustration was a drawing of a pig with a coin slot in place of its navel.

[2] He earned a degree in political economy, not in economics.

[3] Water, which has become a critical issue between Mexico and the United States, was not a widely recognized problem in 1994. Rainfall had been fairly plentiful, and farmers on both sides of the border had benefited from water-sharing agreements. It was not until 2000 that the two countries came to open and unpleasant confrontation over Mexico's water debt. U.S. farmers in Texas, suffering from drought, claimed the Mexicans had stolen their water. In actuality, the Mexicans owed the United States billions of gallons.

immigrants were mostly young, providing energy to an aging America, and willing to work for miserable wages, which kept the price of everything from produce to chickens to construction low enough to raise the standard of living for Americans. On the Mexican side, immigration was a safety valve for an economy that could not provide jobs or hope for millions of its citizens. The immigration problem was an American chimera; if the United States could not count on immigrants from Mexico, it would have to find them elsewhere or suffer sudden price increases in food, housing, and services. Farmers, businessmen, retailers, food service industries all wanted Mexican immigration to continue. As did the Mexicans. Jorge Castañeda, Fox's former secretary of state, estimated the Mexican need for emigration to the United States at 300,000 a year through 2012–2015, after which the decline in Mexican population growth (to only 1.47 percent in 2002 and perhaps even lower in the future) would solve the problem. He and I did not argue the question, but given the fact that Mexico now has 33 million people fourteen years old or younger, his prediction sounds very optimistic.

NAFTA was a different question. Workers coming north could be dealt with by the usual repressive measures: racial, cultural, and linguistic discrimination; unions closed to immigrants; poor schools; limits on all forms of redress. Factories going south to take advantage of wage rates one-tenth (or less) of those paid for the same work in the United States posed a different kind of problem: Where would it end? Why would anyone engage in manufacturing in the United States? What would happen to wage rates in the United States? And to the already moribund union movement? Hence Perot the populist and the sucking sound.

On the Mexican side, NAFTA looked good, at least in the short run. U.S. companies, which had already been building factories in a narrow strip along the border to take advantage of special tariff rules agreed to by both sides, would build more plants, pay more wages to Mexican workers, and vastly increase the size of Mexico's international business. Some side agreements, including those involving the U.S. ability to monitor and act on labor practices and air and water pollution took a long time to negotiate. UNAM

An interim settlement was reached in 2002, when the United States agreed to help Mexico upgrade its irrigation system and the Mexicans agreed to repay at least some of the water debt.

economist Teresina Gutiérrez Haces, one of the Mexican negotiators, thought the United States wanted to be able to use the pollution agreement to put Mexican plants out of business if their success endangered a U.S. competitor.[4] Other side agreements covered the export of corn and other agricultural products to Mexico, technology transfer, trucking in the United States, and so on. It was a complex document, and the Mexican negotiating position was not good.

The actual problems caused by NAFTA did not emerge immediately on either side of the border. In the United States, as predicted by unions, factories did close.[5] On the other side of the border no one had imagined the social and infrastructure problems, the stagnation of Mexican national industry, the ruin of farms, or the other consequences of a basic rule of capitalism, which is to increase profit through reducing the cost of producing goods by any means possible. NAFTA should have been seen by the Mexicans as a long-term trap rather than a short-term blessing, but Salinas and the neoliberal Mexicans apparently did not understand capitalism. Salinas adored free markets; he knew that the era of import substitution (protected markets) had to come to an end in Mexico one day, but he did not know how or when. Meanwhile, his "Solidarity" plan called for job creation.

NAFTA was the brilliant stroke that would provide a strong spine for the new Mexico. But Salinas does not appear to have understood that businesses in the United States (and the world) must continually increase profits to meet the demands of an insatiable stock market. They can do it through innovation, greater productivity, increased market share, tax avoidance, or lower labor costs. The first three require some imagination, the next is a question of ethics, and the last is the bludgeon of globalization.

NAFTA is about tariffs and the bludgeon. Suddenly reducing tariffs left Mexican business vulnerable, as Manuel Sama and many others have said, but the maquiladoras were expected to provide more jobs than those lost to lowered tariffs. What the Salinas government hoped was that NAFTA would replace import substitution. It was a bad equation. Gutiérrez Haces said the

---

[4]Pollution along the Rio Grande has caused high rates of cancer and other diseases on the border, because plants on both sides of the border dump toxic chemicals into the river. Efforts by conservation groups on both sides of the border have had little effect on the problem. I have seen children who became ill by playing near the river. It is not necessary to drink the water to be poisoned by it.

[5]See MacArthur's *The Selling of Free Trade* for an accurate and readable account.

increase in manufacturing jobs in Mexico brought by NAFTA (at its peak) was the same as the total increase in manufacturing employment during that period. In other words, NAFTA brought no more in than the lowered tariffs sent out. Mexico had gained little other than a new form of economic vulnerability and a new social problem. The charming little Harvard man with the shiny pate had left his country's businessmen and workers to deal with sudden competition from abroad and a labor scheme that turned much of Mexico into a human cog in a foreign-owned machine.

The social problems manifested themselves quickly; the economic costs took more than six years to come clear. The profound change wrought by the assembly line itself would not be noticed for nearly a decade. In Ciudad Juárez, which boasted of 180,000 young women working in maquiladoras at the end of the twentieth century, the newspapers were filled with stories of the murders of 200 of those women. On the eastern end of the city, away from the hills where colonies of squatters lived, new hotels and restaurants in what was known as the Golden Zone sprang up to serve the prosperous Mexicans who sold the land on which the maquiladoras were built and provided some of the services they used. Not all service providers were happy, however. A Mexican citizen who ran a security service for maquiladoras came home to his house in the elegant east side neighborhood of Cuidad Juárez one night to find his home burglarized; the thieves had even taken his treasure of treasures, a pair of beautiful hand-tooled cowboy boots. He moved across the border to El Paso but continued to run his security business in Mexico.[6]

Maquiladoras bought paper, printing, fuel, electricity, building supplies, and so on for the plants. They did not buy the parts they assembled and sent back to the United States. The parts came in free of tariffs and went out with no tax on the value added by the labor in the maquiladoras. The managers pressed for ever-increasing productivity. Turnover in maquiladora employment reached 30 percent a month in some plants. And still the managers pressed for more output.

The men who manage the maquiladoras speak "off the record" of the docility of women, particularly those who come up from the south to work in the plants. These are the employees they want. And in a poor country the

---

[6]The operator of the security service, a friend of my sister and brother-in-law, asked for obvious reasons that his name not be used.

rich can always get what they want. They recruited young women from southern Mexico and the mountains of Veracruz, uprooting whole families with offers of free transportation to a better life. Originally, maquiladora workers along the border put in forty hours a week and were paid for forty-eight hours, but as competition for low-wage work increased from Asia and Central America, the assembly plants shifted to a forty-eight-hour schedule, meaning a cut of 20 percent in hourly wages. The government reported increases in maquiladora wages that year of 5 percent, which left the real cut in hourly wages along the border at 15 percent.

As maquiladora wages in various plants rose, pushed upward by the threat of independent unions operating outside the corporatist state, and the U.S. economy slipped into recession, the reality began to dawn on Mexico. If workers in another country could do the same work for less, the work would go to that country. And it did. From the beginning of 1995 to September 2000 the maquiladora industry grew at the rate of one new plant a day; exports of assembled goods tripled. And then the growth stopped. After that employment fell. In 2001 and 2002, according to federal sources, 529 maquiladoras closed their doors and went to China, Taiwan, the Philippines, or Central America.[7] The state of Chihuahua lost 115,000 jobs, 80,000 in Cuidad Juárez alone. The total loss of jobs because of closings in Mexico in 2001 alone was 228,500, according to Bancomer.[8] Between 1994 and 2000 the number of jobs in maquiladoras had increased by an average of 109,000 a year. More than 3,450 plants remained, but the losses had just begun. Investment in assembly plants was down 8.2 percent in 2002. Mexico had higher taxes than China. Mexican wages averaged over a thousand dollars a year more per maquiladora worker. Proximity had some value, but not enough for the added 15 percent or more to assemble goods in Mexico. A change in the international economic situation, the globalization of low-wage work, had now pitted people at the bottom of the wage scale against each other. It was a question of working for less than the other poor of the world or not working.

Some of the newly unemployed went home to the cities and towns they had left for opportunities in the maquiladoras. Others went north to the

[7]Bancomer put the number at 462 and counting through the first nine months of 2002.
[8]INEGI reported 243,716 jobs lost in maquiladoras from the time Fox took office in December 2000 to June 2003. *La Jornada*, June 4, 2003.

United States. For many, the experience had been tragic. It was physically difficult for the women and emotionally corrosive for the men. Drug dealers, thieves, and serial murderers (the plural is not a typographical error) plagued the *colonias,* where the workers, many of them squatters, lived. A measure of the destructive effect on the Mexican family is the number of children born out of wedlock in Ciudad Juárez, 55 percent.[9]

Despite its overall negative effect, the maquiladora industry led to some basic technical training for many Mexicans, sent tens of thousands to technical schools to get the minimum preparation necessary to work in a modern factory, and gave more than a few Mexicans the opportunity to move into management positions. Unfortunately, NAFTA reduced the possibility of industries invented, engineered, owned and managed by Mexicans. It was a dream killer. In part because of NAFTA there would be no Mexican computers, no Mexican cars, no Mexican washing machines, no Mexican television sets, no Mexican stoves or hair dryers or razor blades or subway cars. Salinas had given away the Mexican possibility, and for nothing. He had, in effect, sold the country into servitude. The Spaniards had begun the process, the Porfiriato had internationalized the process of selling off the country, there had been a nationalist pause with Cardenismo, a period of Mexico as a closed market, and then came globalization. The richest of the rich countries prospered, and the poor of the world, including Mexico, sold their renewable resource, labor.

The rule of the maquiladora industry was simple: Get high-quality production at low cost. The Mexican Constitution of 1917 stated very clearly that Mexicans and foreigners doing the same work would receive the same pay. The maquiladora industry preferred Mexican managers, especially at the level of foreman. The Mexicans were said to understand the culture, to be able to get more production out of the workers. It was an ancient colonialist rule put to use in a very sophisticated kind of colonialism. And the foremen and managers, like the overseers of another time in Mexico, were paid for what they delivered. Some earned as much as fifteen thousand pesos a week and managed a decent standard of living. For the middle-class, educated Mexican, the maquiladora was a good job, but for the great majority of the people in the plants, those who worked on the assembly lines for between five hundred and one thousand pesos a week, life in the maquiladora world was always grim and sometimes worse.

[9]Reported in *La Jornada,* October 27, 2003.

THE REFUGE

At the bottom of a hill, in an old neighborhood of the City of Juárez, set in a garden among aged cottonwood trees, there is a house where people come to die. If the neighbors knew, they would drive out the occupants and punish the men and women of Los Compañeros who conduct the traffic in the dying and the dead. For fear of the neighbors, few visitors are permitted to come to the house, and the dead and their belongings and the mattresses on which they slept are removed in the dark of night and taken away to be burned. Perhaps none of these precautions is necessary, perhaps the dying would have no visitors and no one would be frightened by the removal of the dead, but the managers of this refuge for the dying must be careful; they know that Mexico has not learned tolerance for the disease, and death is not a joke celebrated with sugar candy skulls when it comes slowly, accompanied by great suffering.

One evening at the end of autumn when the nights grow cold in the high desert, only two residents remained in the house. All the others had been carried out during the last few nights. There were several small rooms, already cleaned and disinfected, each one with a new mattress lying on the floor, awaiting the next to arrive at the refuge. The two residents, a young man not yet twenty years old and a woman, very worn, and not quite so young, sat in the common kitchen. She had cooked dinner for them, but they ate different dishes: He ate to stoke whatever fire remained in his body, and she sought to save her feet and the last light in her eyes.

They were grateful for the refuge; they did not complain about dying. They had many diseases now; they were opportunities for microbes and viruses. The nurse who came now and then to see them offered comforting words and no predictions. She did not stay long.

The house was very clean. It was part of the duty of the dying to keep the house, an agreement made in exchange for refuge. All the surfaces of the house were of linoleum or tile or porcelain or glass or shiny enameled wood, surfaces that did not require burning. The residents did not offer food or drink to their guests, and they were surprised by a hand extended in greeting; they did not expect anyone to touch them.

AIDS devoured the boy. He was as thin as the edge of the night wind, and when he smiled, he looked like death. On the days when he felt well enough to work, he rose at four in the morning and ate some tortillas and an egg and went out into the end of the night and climbed the hill to the road to wait for

the bus that took him to his job in a maquiladora, where he assembled moth-
erboards for computers. He was a delicate man, both spidery and sweet, with
the gestures and dexterous hands of a young woman. His workday began at
six, and he did not come back to the refuge until late afternoon. He slept for
a while until the woman awakened him to the dinner she had cooked. They
watched television together for an hour, and then he went to his room to lie
down on his mattress and sleep until four the next morning.

His family lived in a small Nahua village in the mountains of the state of
Veracruz. His parents had entertained great hopes for their firstborn son and
had sent him to the public school in the village and then to the secondary
school in the county seat. He returned their love by going northwest to Ciudad Juárez to make his fortune in a maquiladora. The poster in the county
seat had promised work at good wages, but not ordinary work: computers!

Once every week he telephoned his parents, always on a day when he felt
well and his voice was strong, and he still sent money home. He said he
would send money to them for as long as he could work, until his production declined and the foreman or the union representative at the
maquiladora told him not to come back.

He and the woman who lived in the house with him contributed what
they could to their upkeep; it was a rule of the refuge. But she could no longer
go out to work, for she had been diabetic since childhood, and when she
became a prostitute, she had no resistance to the microbes and viruses
inserted into her body, and she soon became a swarm of diseases. To make
her contribution to the refuge, she spent her days forming scented candles
and chocolate candies. He coughed and wheezed when he fought to breathe;
she sat very close to the small television set to discern the movement of the
figures. She was still fat-faced and full-bosomed and scheming. On the days
when she was well enough to make candies and he was well enough to work,
he took the candies she made to the factory and sold them in the lunchroom.

The product of her recent days of work lay spread upon the linoleum-
covered table, tiny chocolate hearts wrapped in pink cellophane. "They are
for him to sell to the Americans," she said, "to celebrate their day of
Thanksgiving."

FAMILY VALUES

*In August 2001 Mexican human rights groups and the National Program
against Family Violence reported a sudden increase in violence in Mexican*

*households. The surveys compared violence over an eight-year period that
included six years since the implementation of the NAFTA agreement. The rise
may simply be coincidental, or it may have been caused more by the crisis of the
devaluation of the peso at the beginning of 1994 than the destruction of the
Mexican family brought about by the maquiladoras. The newspapers headlined
the key finding: One of every three Mexican households suffered some form of
family violence. Two years later the Office of the High Commissioner for
Human Rights of the United Nations reported that there were ten million incidents of family violence every day in Mexico. The cost to Mexico, according to
the high commissioner's office is 1.5 percent of the gross national product.*

In Mexico those who move to the city are immigrants, radicals, true revolutionaries, willing to be converted to a new ways of living and thinking.
They want to throw off the culture of centuries of farming or husbandry,
although not their desperate attachment to the land. In much of Mexico
they are the new politics; in Ciudad Juárez they are briefly politicized, critical, the new electorate, the new workers, but when they come to the border
and stand on the western hills of the City of Juárez and look to the north,
they see the buildings and the electric lights of El Paso, Texas, in the country where the owners and the managers live, and they think about what they
have done, where they have come, and are suddenly bereft of the political
life, victims of their own critique of the life they left behind. They understand that once they leave the rhythms of rural life, they are no longer free
within the limits imposed by nature. In the city there is no freedom for the
poor, no matter where they are or what they do. The ancient Greeks were
right about necessity; it is a form of violence, like the gaze of the foreman
and the insistence of the line.

But the disappointment of the maquiladora is more than intellectual.
There is also the life. The maquiladora system violated one of the cardinal
rules of the traditional Mexican family. Women are more desirable than
men in the assembly plants. They find work, but their men do not. There is
the question of docility, but also of wages. The average income for a male
head of household in Mexico, according to Laura Frade Rubio of the World
Bank, is 2,234 pesos a month compared with 735 pesos for a household
headed by a female.[10] Women's wages fell during the Salinas and Zedillo
presidencies. Maquiladora wages for women were close to the national average for female heads of household and not far from the average minimum

---

[10] *La Jornada*, January 9, 2000.

wage.[11] But along the border, where prices are high compared with other parts of Mexico, the maquiladora worker never gets out of poverty, no matter how hard she works.

Some women, especially the unmarried women, change jobs regularly, but the factory managers have learned to take advantage of marianism, the notion of the woman as the divine sufferer, the perfect complement to machismo, to keep the maquiladora worker in her place. Marianism more than anything makes the women who work on the line docile. The idea of holiness in work and suffering sends the women to the assembly line and to tend to the house, care for the children, and serve the men. Marianism makes a woman go on with an unbearable life.

Marianism, machismo, and the maquiladora tear the family apart. Machismo—the means by which the man who has no place in the world, no reputation, no power gathers respect through violence—runs wild when the woman of the family becomes the breadwinner. What can the man do but make the household a world in which he dominates? Whom can he beat but his wife? Whom can he threaten but his children? He cannot even get a job; the assembly plant that recruited his wife has no use for him. The fall of a poor man whose wife brings him to the border provokes the kind of pain no man can bear. He becomes a brute at home, or he leaves home to behave as a brute in the street. He must do that or disappear.

Following the marianist tradition, the woman he has beaten and betrayed takes misery as her due; she suffers. Whatever her husband has not taken, she gives to her children. Like Sor Juana Inés de la Cruz, she says, "I am the worst of all," and devotes herself to the needs of others until she is worn out and, if not dead physically, dead to all forms of life but labor and suffering. Unlike Sor Juana, she never knew comfort. Youth, her only glory, had no duration.

TWO DIMES A DANCE

The mission founded in the pass between the two great mountain ranges along the river known to the tribes that wandered in the area as Tibuix had a curious beginning. It was named La Misión de Nuestra Señora de Guadalupe de los Mansos del Río Bravo. *Manso*, which means "tame" or

---

[11]On a maquiladora worker's forty-eight-hour contract, the wages had risen almost 90 percent in five years to $1.50 an hour ($73) a week.

"gentle" or "cowardly" (in the case of bulls), was something of a misnomer since the natives turned out to be "hostile and unsociable."[12] After the first effort failed, the mission to the peaceful ones was finally established a quarter of a century later, and a place of worship was built. The original mission, which still stands beside the newly renovated nineteenth-century cathedral, boasts one extraordinary feature: It does not contain a single nail. The local people, apparently having been socialized by God's will and the sword, musket, and sacramental wine, used wooden pegs to hold together the beautifully hewn beams that have withstood time and civil war and the withering desert heat.

Now, more a tourist attraction than a church, dwarfed by the cathedral next door, the mission marks the northern edge of the Cuauhtémoc Market. During the day the market is filled with tourists who mingle with the local shoppers picking among fruits and vegetables, curios and clothing, and herbs for cooking and curing from every part of Mexico. The market has the usual atmosphere of haggling and acquisitiveness. Clay pots, woolen shawls, and baskets of flowers give it a crowded, haphazard beauty, and although the food does not taste quite so good as it smells, it can be pleasing enough.

As evening comes, the Cuauhtémoc Market, like the Mexican sun, enters the underworld. The vendors close their puestos and leave them in the center of the street, shrouded or shuttered, like heavy beasts, barring the walkway in the night. Music emerges from the dance halls that open after dark; the sound rushes out of open doors, subsiding as they close. Glass breaks; whistles and atavistic howlings mix with the music. There are no shadows on the main street of the market, Calle La Paz, only shapes in the faint yellow light. A crude sense of menace hovers in the street. It feels cinematic, intended, not night but *noir*, a made-to-order ambiance, like a sign, an advertisement for despair.

Transgression never wants for meeting places; it is a public business, like machismo, the opposite of prayer; the location of the Calle La Paz, the market of the night, at the side of the ancient mission describes a certain symmetry, the dualism of the Mexican world. The dance halls and whorehouses and crowded bars of Calle La Paz describe another dualism, this one with the day: Timeless and disorderly, they are the opposite of the regimentation

[12]According to Ignacio Esparza, the official historian of the City of Juárez (personal conversation).

of the maquiladoras. The dance halls and the assembly plants are not separate from each other, distinct; they are the components of one, as light and dark produce a day.

Inside the halls, in the warmth and smoke and the yeasty smell of beer, the men stand at the bar or sit at tiny tables. There is a heaviness of middle age about them, in the curled toes and sweat stains of their cowboy hats, the careworn collars of their woolen jackets, the amplitude of their mustaches. They have thick hands, stone fists, scars, and they do not look at the world, they squint, as if in search of someone, something to serve their craving for vengeance. There is no laughter in the dance halls; machismo requires recognition, it has a face, it is a sign, a threat. When the sign fails, the macho must act.

"Get up. I was sitting at this table. I went to dance." Or "This was my table; I went to piss."

Arturo Herrera of Los Compañeros and I abandoned one table and then another and finally stood at the bar. Herrera knows La Paz; he works the streets there. Herrera comes out of the Mexican radical left tradition. His uncle, the family hero, was one of the men who attacked the military barracks in Ciudad Madera on September 23, 1965. Herrera calls his uncle's work a "social movement," drawing no distinction between armed rebellion and his work in the streets. He is interested in the tenor of the room, the transfer of money. Herrera is an enemy of machismo, a saddened observer of marianism. He watches.

Across the room, sitting on tiny chairs arranged in two long rows, arrayed in organdy or denim, spangles or spandex, facing the dance floor, the women talk to each other or smile at the men who may ask them to dance. Two pesos a dance, and the men want to dance close, close enough to feel breasts through the wool of a winter jacket or let the woman have a poke of manliness between her legs, as if she wanted it, as if she were dying for it.

When the music changes, the dancers do not change their steps. The dance is not about the music or the bodies of the dancers, although they press together as if in love; it centers on the faces. The maquiladoras fill the dance halls with desperate men and dour women acting out a ritual of courtship and remembrance. The effort in the room is in the unmaking of reality. Everything happens as if the bus will not pass through the colonias in a few hours and the assembly line will not be waiting on that February morning.

The women had painted their faces, but they had not been able to paint over the signs of the long day that had passed in the maquiladora or the anticipation of the day that was to come. They shuffled slowly to the sprightly music, marathon dancers in need of two pesos, and two pesos more, and more and more to pay the rent, feed the children, send something home. There were no norteños among them, not the women or the men. There were no descendants of explorers, no cowboys, no tall men. They had come from the south or the mountains of Veracruz.

When they arrive in the maquiladora towns, the men find little work, because they are not docile and their hands are too thick. If they are not lucky enough to earn even the minimum wage, they grab the paychecks their wives bring home from the maquiladoras, cash them, and take the money for their own. The glowering men pay for their beer and desperate shuffling with the labor of their own women, who also rise before dawn to work in the maquiladoras. Weariness is the lot of the women who have work; tragedy is the fate of the men who have none.

WITNESSES

An assembly line, the principle of production designed by Henry Ford, immortalized in the murals of Diego Rivera, made more efficient by the Japanese invention of the just-in-time parts system, requires people and machines to observe the rigorous discipline of the line. The slightest deviation from this discipline produces errors in the product, which means the manager of an assembly line must pursue two goals: to reduce the number of exceptions and to speed up the assembly process. The tension in the assembly process comes of the antagonism between time and accuracy. The latter is the craftsman's desire; time belongs to the world after the Protestant Reformation. There is no more eloquent expression of the Protestant notion of time as money than the assembly line. And there is no more Catholic country than Mexico. An assembly plant in Mexico denies the decisions of the Council of Trent and the Counter-Reformation. It requires of its workers a modern view of time and money and a willingness to accede to the views of the owners.

For the first six years after NAFTA went into effect there was a labor shortage on the border. Plant managers were desperate for bodies to fill the places on the line. New plants opened almost every day in one border town or another, and the turnover rate on the assembly lines hovered around 30 percent a month as people grew tired of the work or the life and quit.

Culture caused the problem. There is a powerful work ethic in Mexico, but it is not modern, not industrial. One plants corn or beans and prays for rain. The work is hard and must be done, but it is understood by task, not by time. The goal of the maquiladora manager is to introduce the worker to a different view of God and man, to cause her to put aside everything sacred and profane that was believed by tens of generations, to abandon the old sense of time, to internalize the idea of a God who hoards His moments. It is the new Reformation, and it is taking place not only in the maquiladoras but all over Mexico. It is tied to emigration and to the Protestant evangelicals who have moved into every corner of the country.

Emigrants are the true revolutionaries of our time, because they are willing to throw over many past beliefs. They make a profound political decision by emigrating, which opens them to a new sense of time and money; emigration is an act of criticism, an expectation of the new. For that reason, Mexican immigrants in the United States, like all American immigrants before them, are desirable citizens and workers.

Whoever comes to the United States comes willing, if not wishing, to adopt the Protestant Ethic. There are only economic Protestants in the United States, although people pray in many languages and many houses. No more Protestant country has ever existed, and no country has benefited more than the United States from the idea that time is money, a concept now expressed euphemistically in the word "productivity." For example: the company headed by Raúl Cárdenas Cavazos, Productivity de Mexico, has as its basic function the implementation of the Protestant Ethic, the imitation of the United States. His work is to continue the transformation of Mexico begun by President Miguel de la Madrid and the International Monetary Fund in 1982.

Since then neoliberal policies in Mexico—austerity, productivity, and the shame of indebtedness—have sought to turn the country into a Protestant nation, based on the belief imposed by the rich nations of the world that no other kind of nation can fully adopt the capitalist spirit. The crime laid at the feet of McDonald's and rock and roll, the destruction of Mexican culture, is at its deepest level the work of the assembly line and the worship of austerity. Monterrey is the model for Mexico. While it is the most Catholic city, with the possible exception of Guadalajara, it is the most Protestant city in terms of its life-style and thinking. Monterrey is garbed in darkly puritanical colors, prim and diligent in the management of the Lord's time.

The other model for Mexico is the assembly plant, whether it is in Puebla or Nogales, making automobiles or assembling computers. The managers of the plants must be evangelists, teaching Calvinism, proving by the paycheck that those who are the richest are the elect of God. Every day at the dinner table or the supermarket or the shopping mall, the lesson of God's chosen is brought home.

There was a time when Mexico had other notions of chosenness: The Spaniards thought they were chosen to evangelize the Indians, and those who loved the Indians thought the original peoples were chosen because they had journeyed like the Israelites, and the criollos thought they were chosen because God had granted them a country of great wealth. Now it seems to be coming clear to every Mexican that the rich are the elect, and in a country where so many are so poor, one who has come from near starvation on a tiny farm to a debilitating job on an assembly line must try to understand how God chooses. From there it is an easy step to accepting a new ethic under the cloak of the old religion or to accept a new religion entirely, to become a Protestant in name as well as belief.

If one were to construct a laboratory for this theory of the conversion of the Mexicans, the creation of a Protestant body within a Roman Catholic skin, it would be among internal "immigrants," all of them connected in one way or another to an assembly line. The reality of modern Mexico necessitates choosing internal immigrants because the country has only recently been transformed from rural to urban. People are still connected to some piece of land, but it has diminished over the generations from hectares (2.5 acres) to *metros cuadrados* (square meters). The internal immigrants represent the next generations in Mexico. The assembly line, setting aside economic considerations, represents the modern world (exploitative as it may be) in Mexico.

There is such a laboratory, and I came upon it by accident. I had gone up into the hills west of Ciudad Juárez to visit the colonies where the squatters had made their homes. There was no real purpose to the visit other than nostalgia, for I had spent quite a lot of time among the first squatters there in the 1950s, and I was curious to see how the colonias had changed. With Arturo Herrera and María Elena Ramos of Los Compañeros, I went to the Colonia Felipe Ángeles. There are about thirty-five thousand families in the colony, and almost all of them include a woman who makes the two-part journey, climbing the hills to the bus stop, then taking the bus every workday morning down the hills to one assembly plant or another.

If the colony has a core around which it turns, it is the store owned and operated by María de Jesús Hernández, a middle-aged woman whose most prominent feature is the frilly apron she wears over her dress. Sra. Hernández quickly makes it clear that she lives according to a hierarchy of values: business, gossip, and flirting. If a customer enters her store while she is in the midst of a coquettish smile and a slight shivering of her shoulders, she gives one last blink of her dark and fetching eyes and becomes a nineteenth-century New England merchant. After the customer leaves, there is a little gossip about what this one owes and how she loaned money to another to pay her medical bills, but there is nothing malicious, nothing terribly revealing; it is a kind of happy gossip, chitchat.

"Yes," she said, "everyone works in the maquilas. They earn five hundred and twenty, maybe seven hundred pesos a week."[13]

She described the hours of the women who work. "They have a little soup to eat. Then the bus comes at four and brings them home at six." They work fourteen hours; she works fourteen hours. Her store is open from seven in the morning until nine at night, and she tends it alone. "On Sundays I rest," she said. "I close at seven."

Most of the people in the colony cannot get to a supermarket; they must pay the higher prices in a store like hers. Few of them can keep up with the cost of food. Almost everyone has a page in her book, where she writes down the cost of what they buy, adding it up. Some owe four hundred pesos. One woman's account went up to fifteen hundred. If someone is sick, she loans them money to buy medicine or pay a doctor. She is the center of the world around her.

At the end of a long conversation, interrupted by customers buying soft drinks or strips of pork or tortillas (because the price is fixed by the government, tortillas cost less than the flour used to make them) or an egg, I chanced to ask her there in her little cube of a building, which stood like a beacon in the dark, the only electric light on the hill, "Are the people good Catholics in the colony?"

[13]I have changed the numbers to bring them closer to current pay rates. When I spoke to her, she put the low figure at four hundred pesos. In actuality, pay then averaged a little less than two dollars an hour, but decreased, bringing Mexico into competition with China and Central American and Caribbean countries for low-wage work.

The decrease came as workers were asked to put in longer hours for the same wages. Figures here are for take-home pay. They do not include benefits or other costs that may be apportioned to hourly wages for accounting purposes.

"Very few. The majority are Jehovah's Witnesses. You know Jehovah's Witnesses: Protestants, evangelists. We have very few Catholics in this colony."

María de Jesús Hernández is not a trained census taker. Her information may be better or worse. The Protestant and anticlerical movements have a long history in northern Mexico, but she said there were very few norteños in the colony. Almost everyone had come there from deep inside Mexico. If the managers had recruited only Protestants, they knew something profound about the assembly line, but it seemed unlikely, as it seemed unlikely that only Jehovah's Witnesses had applied for work. One of every six maquiladora workers lived in the Colonia Felipe Ángeles. They were a test. The circumstance of their lives, the change in the perception of time, had broken out of the confines of tradition. What was happening on the inside of many Mexicans had come to the surface of the people in the Colonia Felipe Ángeles.

There is no way to know how many will remain Jehovah's Witnesses or for how long. Some will go back to the Catholic Church; others will move on to different evangelistic religions. None will ever be able to return to the stifled world of the Council of Trent and the Counter-Reformation. They have become critics, individuals, servants of time in its smallest increments.

If there is a certain loss of joy in Mexico because it is being harnessed to the tick of God's own time, there is also an end to obedience in the political world. The harness of modernity is also a criticism of the past. Mexicans, still mainly Catholic, still devoted to Nuestra Señora la Santíssima Virgen de Guadalupe, have internalized the idea of time as money, the most Protestant of notions, and at the same time abandoned their obedience to the hierarchies of Church and State. Democracy is about autonomy and criticism. In one of the anomalies of the modern world, the routine of the assembly line produces a taste for autonomy and the freedom from tutelage of democracy.

32.

Where the Future Falls

Mexico is the country of inequality.
—ALEXANDER VON HUMBOLDT

Driving south from the center of Mexico City, at the place called Santa Fe a metaphor arises to explain the future of Mexico. This metaphor straddles a very thin line between entering the first world and drowning in the colonial catastrophe of a few pockets of opulence amid poverty and economic servitude. On one side of the road the architecture leaps skyward, solid and shining, more interesting and contemporary than the New York City skyline or the low buildings of London or Paris or the gray of St. Petersburg. But the leap forward is no deeper than one building, or at most two. Behind the row of glass and steel buildings just across the freeway from the newly built campus of Universidad Iberoamericana, the question about the future of Mexico arises. The outstanding building belongs to IBM, and just behind it on a series of the steepest hills in Mexico City live the very poor. Not the poorest of Mexico anymore, not the starving, but the poor, internal migrants who spent the early years after their arrival picking through the garbage of the great dump of Santa Fe, an entire colony bent over, fishing in the trash of the city, unionized, terrorized, exploited, extorted, holding their ground, bent and befouled until they could find a way to stand.

On one side of the freeway, facing IBM, the students of the main campus of Universidad Iberoamericana, the daughter of Carlos Salinas de Gotari among them, learn philosophy, history, art, literature, and logic. It is a classic Jesuit university. Ibero, as it is known, is fraught with problems of management and a student body more conservative than much of its faculty. Vicente Fox received his degree from Ibero in 1999 after a hiatus of many years spent in the Coca-Cola Company. It is an illustrious degree in Mexico, like that of the Colegio de Mexico or some parts of the UNAM or ITESM (Monterrey Tec), but it is not Harvard or Princeton or the Sorbonne in the eyes of Mexicans, who have always looked to foreign universities for the best education.

The difference in the lives of people facing IBM and those behind the building defines contemporary Mexico as well as any metaphor can. The people of Santa Fe are largely literate, although at a very low level. Mexican law now requires that children complete secondary (junior high) school (*secundaria*), but few of the children in Santa Fe will go on to high school (*preparatoria*). Some will go to technical schools, the low-level training schools that seem to occupy the second floor of almost every building in every commercial street of Mexico; most will not go so far as that. Most of the young in Santa Fe, like their parents, will have only labor to trade for sustenance.

Those who face IBM are far fewer, of course. Ibero is a small university, a few thousand students, nothing like the UNAM or Monterrey Tec, with its campuses spreading across Mexico and through distance learning to most of Latin America. Nonetheless, Ibero produces students whose influence will be felt in Mexico, for they are the children of the rich. It is, however, a university that graduates students of curiously limited imagination. Like Monterrey Tec, although with emphasis on humanistic studies, it is severely limited. The Tec produces people who know how to use the technology invented in other countries, a cadre to carry out the imperatives of the Protestant Ethic, but not to invent either tools or methods. Ibero produces students with limited perspective on the humanities, comma counters and sales managers, but not dreamers.

Only in the highest aeries of the UNAM and UAM (Universidad Autónoma de Mexico) and the Colegio de Mexico do Mexican students think of science and dreaming, entering the world of the new. And even that is limited, for the quality of higher education in Mexico has fallen over the last decades. To teach in a university no longer requires a terminal degree or brilliant research. The government has created an unimaginably stultifying system, managed by bureaucrats rather than educators, in which professors are required to grind out useless and unimaginative books and articles and hold tedious conferences at a rate more like an assembly line than a university.[1] The reality of it comes through in the retirement system for university professors. A professor's base salary, according to Sergio Aguayo, a well-known Mexican author and human rights activist, is about twenty thousand dollars a year (2002), but the professor's real salary, if he or she meets all the requirements of publishing, giving conferences, etc., is two to four times that

[1] See Book Two, Chapter 26.

amount. Aguayo and other academics are pressing for a change in the law to have retirement income computed on the real salary rather than the base.

Given the system, the possibility of a professor in any field devoting his or her time to the kind of deep research needed to do major innovative work in the physical or social sciences is too often limited by the demands of the belly. Without the bonuses paid for grinding labor, a professor would hardly be able to earn a living. There are of course exceptions. Extremely successful professors, like Miguel León-Portilla or the political philosopher Enrique Leff or the political scientist and former rector of UNAM Pablo González Casanova or the philosophers Luis Villoro and Adolfo Sánchez Vázquez, and the UNAM's highly respected astronomers or mathematicians, or Aguayo himself, are exempted from some of these dreadful demands. Artists too, like Tamayo and Toledo and many lesser painters, have also found a comfortable life in Mexico. A burst of imagination in one's youth is repaid with the time to have a long and fruitful intellectual life, but that is the exception, not the rule. It is not quality so much as labor that is rewarded in higher education in Mexico.

Were the government to change its policy on labor in the universities, were Vicente Fox Quesada to rescind his opposition to spending money on research (he cut the budget for research to almost nothing in 2002), were more than 20 percent of Mexicans to expect any higher education at all, were the universities to raise their standards for professors and students, the system of higher education in Mexico could recover quickly enough. The UNAM was a glorious university, but it has been systematically wounded, in part perhaps because it produced the radicals of 1968 and 1971, and Subcomandante Marcos, and the strikers of 1999. Perhaps the Mexican educational system no longer holds the dreams of the young men of the Ateneo de la Juventud. It belongs more now to the dream of an industrial elite, which the cientificos understood as the leaders of Comte's third stage of development. Perhaps the Mexican business community follows the same rule as the university community (or is it the other way around?): Business rewards labor rather than genius; it has no interest in genius. And it apparently has precious little interest in college graduates. According to the National Higher Education Evaluation Center, 40 percent of the college graduates in Mexico in 2001 could not find employment. Of the 60 percent who did find employment, almost a third had to work outside their chosen career fields, and another third who did find work in their fields earned less than two thousand pesos a month.[2] For more

[2] *El Universal,* July 3, 2003.

and more graduates, the choice was between emigration and an economic life bordering on poverty.

If this weakness were a passing phenomenon, it would have but a small effect on the future of Mexico; the promise of the country would be based on overcoming the lull in education, but the country belongs to the ideas of a businessman at least until 2006, and the businessman belongs to the religious conservatives. The decline has become a fall. Mexico has 1,333 institutions that call themselves universities, according to the National Association of Universities. Of these, 803 are private institutions of "dubious quality." In 2000 only 27 were true universities, and of those, only 18 were research universities.[3]

On August 27, 2001, Pablo González Casanova described government attacks on education as "a new cold war against culture and knowledge." Among the leaders in the "cold war" none stood out more than the Neanderthal secretary of labor Carlos Abascal, who first embarked upon a campaign to censor reading lists and, having done that, set out on another campaign to purge the books that offended him from school libraries. Authors and educators howled, but there was no public reprimand from the president. Abascal had religious motives, or so he said, and Fox was the most openly religious (and most deeply loyal to the Protestant Ethic) Mexican president since the liberals of the mid-nineteenth century had released Mexico from the political and economical grip of the Church.

The failure of education extended from the universities down through the kindergartens. Mexico suffered from both an unimaginative and antiquated educational philosophy and a desperate lack of money. In the United States, life bifurcates at the college level, with college graduates earning almost twice as much over a lifetime as those with only high school diplomas.[4] In Mexico, education determines a permanent separation between those who have any hope for a decent life and those who will live in or near poverty, and the separation takes place earlier than in the United States. Among indigenous children in Mexico, only 24 percent complete grade school, according to a study done by the Center for Research and Graduate Studies in Social Anthropology (CIESAS). The sorting in the rest of Mexico is done in junior high school, the last mandatory step. Whoever can manage to go on to high school is entitled to hope. All the rest will become commodified, labor.

[3] *La Jornada,* July 7, 2003. Other studies say Mexico has only nineteen universities altogether.
[4] U.S. census figures reported in the *Christian Science Monitor,* July 18, 2002.

In Mexico the distribution of expenditures on education is more elitist than in other OECD countries, about thirteen times as much for a postsecondary student as for a student in primary school. The system all but guarantees that the upper economic classes will be protected for yet another generation. President Fox has promised more funds for education, but not in amounts or with innovations that will make a great difference. With two million children between the ages of five and fourteen not attending school at all, some two hundred thousand of them for the lack of a birth certificate, progress toward a functional democratic society will continue to be slow.

ANNUAL REPORT
THE PANORAMA OF EDUCATION 2002
ORGANIZATION FOR ECONOMIC COOPERATION AND DEVELOPMENT

The report was presented by the chief OECD statistician, Andreas Schleicher, in a videoconference on October 29, 2002, and reported in *La Jornada* and other publications of the following day.

Annual Expenditure per Student

(It is important to note that the buying power of a teacher's pay in the Federal District fell 79.5 percent between 1982 and 2003. Among primary school teachers 52 percent worked at a second job.)[5]

Primary School: Mexico—$1,096 Average of Member Countries—$4,789[6]
Secondary School: Mexico—$2,226 Average—$5,919
High School: Mexico—$4,789 Average—$9,210

Classroom Hours per Teacher

Primary School: Mexico—800 Average—792
Secondary School: Mexico—1,482 Average—720

Class Size

Secondary School: Mexico—34.8 Average—15

Children Fifteen to Nineteen Years Attending School

Mexico—50 percent Average—80 percent

---

[5]Center for Multidisciplinary Analysis, UNAM, reported in *La Jornada,* May 15, 2003. The teachers' union during much of that period was headed by Elba Esther Gordillo, now one of the leaders of the PRI and at one time the darling of its "dinosaurs."
[6]When compared to the average of expenditures at every level in OECD countries, the U.S. expenditure is about double. Thus the United States spends eight times as much per primary school student, and so on.

Mexican students have less access to computers than the average student in the OECD member countries. Of fifteen-year-old students, 44 percent read below grade level. Among persons between fifty-five and sixty-four years old only 11 percent have completed high school. The number climbs only to 25 percent in the twenty-five to thirty-four age-group.

THE DEFEAT OF THE WALLS

Six hundred years ago, in Texcoco, there was a huey tlahtoani who was not merely a ruler but the author of some of the greatest pre-Columbian poetry. This poet-ruler, Nezahualcoyotl, was a strange man. He sent his best friend off to die in war so that he might take the man's wife for his own. He was also one of the first of the Aztecs to consider the idea of a nonanthropomorphic god. His poetry, which accepts the apocalyptic notions of Mesoamerica, asks many of the questions that have interested philosophers from the pre-Socratics to the existentialists. In the early 1960s people from many parts of Mexico were attracted to the place where the covetous moralist Nezahualcoyotl had lived and loved and posed the philosopher's questions. They did not hesitate to name the place where they settled after the poet-ruler of Texcoco, and in a very short time the place where Nezahualcoyotl had reigned became the largest slum in the history of Mexico.

On the six hundredth anniversary of Nezahualcoyotl's birth, the suburb of Mexico City named for him was Mexico's fifth-largest municipality, home to over 1.5 million people. Since its founding, Neza has lost some of its reputation as the unthinkable slum. Valle de Chalco, south of the city, has taken on that role because the migrants came later and still live largely in houses without sanitation. Moreover, Chalco floods regularly and in 1999 was inundated with tens of thousands of gallons of sewage when a huge pipe that carried waste out of Mexico City burst and the government had to choose between flooding Mexico City or Chalco with the filth and excreta of millions. It chose Chalco. In the 1960s it had chosen Neza to accept its overflow, leaving the people to live with sewage and garbage and drugs and crime.

By the end of the century most of Neza had electricity, sewerage, telephone service, and running water. It was not a pleasant place to live, but most of it was habitable, and many of its residents had found their way up from extreme poverty into a more bearable level of poverty and even the lower middle class. In a hotel along the Paseo de la Reforma half the staff, including most of the dishwashers and maids and waiters and bellmen and perhaps a few clerks, made the one- to two-hour journey from Neza. No one was ashamed any longer to admit to living in Neza. It had survived, and it had not forgotten its namesake.

One of the first secondary schools built in Neza paid homage to ancient culture with its name, Calmecac, the name the Aztecs gave to their school for nobles. Nezahualcoyotl had studied in the calmecac, but it had been different then; it had not been a shattered metaphor. In its thirty-fifth year, Calmecac Technical Secondary School, in the First Section of the Colonia Metropolitana of Neza, had begun its surrender to gravity, weather, poor construction, the fragility of glass, and the careless vitality of thousands of students. Windows had been broken; walls had started to crumble; a leak in the roof of the library had caused the ruin of most of the books and left the building shuttered. The decay of the physical plant hung over the students like an ancient prophecy, punishment for the hubris of naming such a place Calmecac.

Students attend the Calmecac School in two shifts, beginning at seven in the morning. In autumn, when school starts, it is still light at that hour. The mothers of the children stand in the street outside the iron gate and gossip into the morning air, birds of early middle age, dressed in the drab plumage of breakfast clothes, housecoats and sweaters, and puffy jackets, and all of them pleased to have arrived with their offspring safe. "This is our morning dress," the mothers say. "You should see us later in the day." And laugh.

Until seven they arrive, the last ones hurrying, urging the children along, the first-year students in their dark red uniforms, the others in green. The purpose of the uniforms was to avoid distinctions between children of different economic classes, but the students had learned to tell whether a classmate was richer or poorer by looking at his or her shoes. "The rich ones are the leaders," the teachers said.[7]

Rich and poor alike waited outside the gate. It had rained the night before, as it always rains in the afternoons and often into the night in Sep-

---

[7]The small middle class in Nezahualcoyotl generally comprises owners of small stores and taxis, anyone who can contract for labor performed by others, and a few technicians. The lower-middle-class workers are those who earn more than the minimum wage: taxi drivers, service workers, and clerks. The poor are generally the newcomers, some of them still living in one-room shacks made of laminated cardboard. Illegal activities are often profitable, and crooks, like intellectuals, are classless.

tember around Texcoco, which once held a lake where islands floated and foodstuffs and flowers grew. Now at the place where the state of Mexico meets the Federal District there are no flowers, and the huge fenced-in yard in front of the school has but a little grass and almost no trees. It is simply ground, *terreno baldio*, uncultivated land, useless. The children do not walk there but follow a narrow path to the front of the school and enter the central patio, then disperse into their separate classrooms.

The morning begins in order, and the day will continue that way. In *official* (public) schools, deportment is a key issue. In the Calmecac School, it will not always be possible to maintain order everywhere. Each student must spend eight hours a week in a technical class, and with the exception of mechanical drawing and secretarial work, the technical classes—construction, soldering and plumbing, woodworking, electrical work—are noisy. Most of the technical courses take place in a series of open rooms, like giant cubicles, under a high ceiling, with large areas of glass poorly painted to keep out the heat of the sun. The woodworking noise carries over onto the banging of the carpentry class, while the students of electricity sit at long benches attempting to draw diagrams of imagined circuits. The tools belong to an earlier time when the school was first opened, and some of them were ancient even then. The government provides no money for tools or maintenance. Parents must pay 250 pesos a year toward the upkeep of the physical plant. Students must buy their own uniforms and most of their books. The lunchroom is a series of open-air stands in the central courtyard, where students may purchase rice or tacos. Nothing is free; there are no gifts, not even for the poor. The public school, like many in the United States, cannot cover all the costs of education.

Textbooks have been printed by the federal government for the last forty years, but there were no textbooks at the Calmecac School. There had been a scandal about printing costs; everything was delayed. Without books, one history teacher simply stood at the front of the class and dictated the outline of the textbook in a harsh, wounded voice: "With black pen, in capital letters, write . . ." And then: "Now, under that heading, in red pen, write Two A: The difference between animals and humans. And under that, in black ink, write the number one. . . ."

The civics teacher had found another way out. She prepared her students for a debate on the subject of abortion, dividing them into two groups, each one to choose debaters and researchers to prepare for the debate. "They do not read," she said of her students. "They do not know basic grammar. But we are teaching them; they must now read Kafka and Gárcia Márquez."

In the biology class the teacher spoke in metaphors about cell physiology. DNA was king, ruler of the cell. The art history teacher sat at her desk while her students attempted their own version of a still life. She explained how the still life developed in France because of food shortages. Fruits, cheeses, bread, and wine became very precious, she said, subjects worthy of the artist.

A tiny woman, properly bespectacled and serious for one so engaged in the study of the French still life, she was quick to place herself outside Neza, in the world of art. "My husband works in the Bellas Artes [concert hall]; one of my sons dances in the Mexican Folkloric Ballet; the other has his doctorate in philosophy. Yes, I love French art, but I prefer the art of Mexico. Mexican art!" She lifted her eyes to the muse.

The low point of the school came in another history class, where the professor, the tidiest of the men, the only one wearing a jacket and tie, did not appear to understand the role of the opposable thumb or the importance of language in distinguishing humans from their animal predecessors. At the end of his class, he asked for an opinion of his work. And then, before I could answer, without preface, he said, "I have been here thirteen years, except for one year when I was in jail. They accused me of molesting a student, but I was found not guilty." The assistant principal and the chief social worker, who stood beside me, looked away from him. He smiled and hurried to prepare for his next class.

He could not teach, he did not know his material, but for some of his students it made no difference. When he asked questions of the students, a chubby, pale boy, who had chosen to sit at a desk along the wall rather than in the center of the room with the rest of the class, gave long encyclopedic answers. There was no question he could not answer, no information he did not have. "I want to be a medical doctor," he told me later, speaking precisely in the poignant soprano of the last days of childhood, "a surgeon. From here I will go to the prepa [high school] at the UNAM and then on to medical school."

There are no special classes for gifted children at the Calmecac School, but there are many gifted children. In the course of sitting through a dozen classes, one sees the gifted ones, the extraordinary students, bobbing up like corks in a rain barrel. It is the same with the teachers. There are half a dozen besides the fin de siècle art teacher whose talents or whose will to teach make them extraordinary. But it was not until I was about to end my time at the school after many hours in the classrooms that the common quality among the best teachers came clear. We had just finished going over the curriculum. Besides the eight periods a week spent in workshops, the students studied Spanish, science, mathematics, civics, geography, history, English, and art.

No class seemed more attentive to their work than the students of mechanical drawing, who used their compasses and rulers and triangles to precisely reproduce the dimensions of complex forms. They stood at their drawing tables or sat on high stools with their surgically sharp pencils and drawing instruments, silent, absorbed, more girls than boys in the room, dreaming even as they worked, they told me later, of the life and work of architects and engineers. In the hushed room, the teacher, Sergio Márquez Ángeles, took a series of spiral-bound books from a cabinet and opened them one by one, thumbing through the pages. The drawings, pale in pencil, robust in ink, were excellent. I thought they were his, the models for his students, but they were the work of students.

Márquez is a young man, with very regular, slightly squared features, more like a jai alai player than a secondary school teacher, and he preened the work of his students as if it were himself. While he opened binder after binder of the work, two of the school administrators, Natalia Castillo and Elizabeth Sánchez, pointed out that the mechanical drawing teacher with the open collar and the athletic stance, had graduated from Calmecac School. When I asked if there were other teachers who had come back to the school to teach, the administrators listed five, and all were among the best teachers. Sergio said, "We all live here in Neza too. Every teacher has an obligation to his students. We have dual obligations, because we come from the community."

Of the students who emerge from their years in the broken building, having survived the noise and the leaks and life in Nezahualcoyotl, 80 percent go on to high school, half of these to a technical school and the other half to one of the high schools in the UNAM system of higher education. Few public secondary schools in Mexico can claim a better record.

LAS ISLAS BRITÁNICAS

Nothing distinguishes students in private secondary schools in Mexico so much as their size. Private school students are taller, wider, with bigger bones and more solid musculature, as if they belonged to a separate species, one related to public school students, but not identical. It is both a metaphor and a physical reality. At some point, hundreds of years ago, there appears to have been a bifurcation in the species *Homo sapiens* in Mexico: The poor were diminished and the rich enlarged. The brain took what it needed, all that was available to nourish it, and the body made do with what was left.

Public and private school students may have the same innate capacity for thinking and dreaming, or so one hopes, but the public school students must dream inside narrower confines. They will never achieve the size of their private school counterparts. If they have good luck and get beyond junior high school, they may improve their English, learn French, discover how to manipulate a computer, but they will never make the same kind of physical impression in the world.

The difference in size betokens a barrier to dialogue between the two groups, the impossibility of communication that the contemporary German political philosopher Jürgen Habermas says is symptomatic of colonialism. It is another surface of the complex metaphor of rich and poor in Mexico:

> great and small :: conqueror and conquered

During secondary school the rich evolve into the role of giants, and what hope have the others among giants? Here and there an Odysseus emerges to defeat a one-eyed giant or a Napoleon Bonaparte comes on the scene and commands armies, but there cannot be a nation of Napoleons, eighty or ninety million diminutive conquerors surrounding a field of giants. A public school girl or boy may grow up to succeed; it is not impossible, but in most cases the Mexican educational system prevents the necessary dialogue that would rid the country of Habermas's conversational colonialism. The private schools educate giants to their proper place, and the public schools teach the poor that only a few of them will not live in unspeakable poverty. It is the rule in Mexico, and it has been so for generations.

As the Calmecac School represents the better public secondary schools attended largely by children whose families have escaped the extreme poverty of internal migrants, so the four Colegio Williams schools, in Mexico City and Cuernavaca, represent the better schools for children of the upper middle class and the rich, almost all of whom attend private schools.

A shift toward religious school might have been expected during the Salinas sexenio, when the Catholic Church became emboldened in Mexico, taking a larger and stronger role in education, but almost a decade later less than 4 percent of all Mexican secondary school students attend religious schools.[8] Instead, Opus Dei and other ultraconservative movements within the Church exert a growing influence on secular education in Mexico through their connection to conservative elements in the government.

The problem for Mexico in the growth of ultraconservative influence in secular and religious (Catholic, Protestant, Jewish, and Muslim) schools has to do with the limitations it places on thinking. The system teaches obedience rather than daring. The dreams of Vasconcelos for a brilliant intellectual Mexico, rising from the raza cósmica, degenerated after his period in office, then rose again during the great splurge of public works spurred by the discovery of vast reserves of oil. Illiteracy fell dramatically; schools spread from the cities to the countryside. López Mateos fostered the idea of free textbooks for every student. And then with the decline in the price of Mexican oil, the fall in the standard of living, the high birthrate, and the terrible austerity forced on the country by international bankers in 1982, the system fell into a swoon.

Mexico had never resolved its most basic educational problems: inequality; a teachers' union that managed to be both weak and corrupt; a sense of technical versus intellectual achievement that dated back to the influence of Moisés Sáenz in the 1920s, when he served as director of the National Preparatory School and then as a major figure in the office of the secretary of education, an idea that went back to nineteenth-century notions of training; a lack of funds to maintain schools and provide free food to the poorest students; and a cynical, although unspoken, view of the educational system as a means to maintaining social stability.

With a young population and the tension of the mestizaje that might produce genius as well as paralyzing internal conflict, Mexico has nowhere to turn but to its people. Most of the land is not arable, estimates of oil reserves fell sharply at the beginning of the new century, and the United States is forcing Mexico more and more into subservience. The only alternative to a maquiladora nation is in nurturing the minds of its people, and Mexico may not have the will or the money or the capacity for dreaming required to save

[8]According to the Catholic Missionary Union, 293,000 of 7.5 million in 2002.

itself. Schools do not choose thinking or dreaming as their primary goal; discipline is the first order of Mexican public education. I have visited classrooms in public secondary schools where the entire blackboard was taken up with rules of deportment, except for one small space in the corner for the day and date.

Then there is the question of the giants. Sylvia Schmelkes, a sociologist in charge of bilingual education for indigenous students, has long argued that the basic problem in Mexican education is inequity, pointing out that the government spends four times as much per student in urban areas as it spends for rural (mainly indigenous) students. UNAM Professor Herlinda Suárez Zozaya has written books and articles on the question of *rezago* (falling behind) in the Mexican educational system. Suárez agrees that Mexico treats its public school students unequally but also points to higher education in Mexico, where the system has built a wall between the humanities and the vast majority of college and university students. Her views do not vary greatly from those of the students who participated in the recent strike at the UNAM. Carlos Fuentes, in his essay *Por un Progreso Incluyente* (For an Inclusive Progress),[9] argued for a balance between history and modernity in Mexican education, but his key point in the entire essay was that without a greater emphasis on education Mexico could not progress. Something terrible had happened to Mexican public education since the ideas of young Vasconcelos and the glory days of the UNAM; it was no longer likely that future presidents would come out of the public school system and the national university. The aspirations of the lower economic classes, never widespread in Mexico, not even during 1910–1920, when civil war and radical dreams raged side by side, had suffered a great fall as the turn of the century neared.

Private schools, like the Colegio Williams, had become the training ground. The giants prepared, and preparation was expensive. At Williams in Cuernavaca the cost of a year of study in secondary school was 33,550 pesos;[10] high school cost 40,744. And it is not the most expensive of the secular private schools in Mexico. Williams has a British provenance, as does the London School; other private schools stress their French heritage, and

---

[9] Mexico: Instituto de Estudios Educativos y Sindicales de America, 1997.
[10]Divide by ten (in 2001–2003) for a rough estimate of the dollar equivalent. The figure is for eleven monthly installments.

there is of course an expensive and desirable American School. Until World War II the German School was considered one of the best in Mexico, but it declined along with the Fascist and Communist parties. Education at a private school like Williams follows the pattern of private schools throughout the Western world. Its student–faculty ratio is nine to one, and 95 percent of its graduates go on immediately to college. By the time they graduate, the students are highly proficient in English, less so in French, but still able to deal with the language. The most appealing thing about the school is the restlessness of its leadership. Led by Alfonso García Williams, its director general, it has recognized the problem of rote learning in Mexican schools and it is determined to change Williams into a place where García Williams said, "We educate to think and create, to teach the new values of this [twenty-first] century: ecology, involvement in service, citizenship. We want to develop critical thinkers. As part of that change in our educational pattern, we have begun to hold discussions with major figures in the humanities here in Mexico. Our students read philosophy, from Plato to Habermas. They read pre-Columbian philosophy, Vasconcelos.

"We are working now with the International Baccalaureate Organization in Switzerland, which is helping us to stay aware of the new trends in education and to implement them here. We also have an exchange program with the Friends School in Philadelphia." And then, as if to emphasize how far Mexico had fallen behind in its methods, he referred to an idea that dates back to John Dewey: "It is a great change in Mexican education to put the student in the center."

The faculty at Williams, where the buildings are white and the grounds are immaculate, all have college degrees. Twenty hold graduate degrees, and two have earned doctorates. The three-story building complex contains a swimming pool, gymnasium, and soccer field, as well as classrooms and an auditorium. An Englishman named Williams founded the school at the end of the nineteenth century, and it has been a family business ever since. The Cuernavaca campus was founded by a descendant of the original Williams, in 1976, and García Williams carries the family name. The founding dates correspond, respectively, to the period when the Porfiriato sought outside investment in everything and to the last years of the Mexican Miracle, which was fueled by what was imagined to be an endlessly profitable supply of petroleum.

But it has been a long time since Mexico had a robust economy. The senior faculty at Colegio Williams worries about the future of its students. Employment for educated people in Mexico has become more difficult to find since the devaluation at the beginning of the Zedillo sexenio, and nothing during the first years of the Fox administration has helped. Students will have to look beyond Mexican business and industry for jobs. Going to an English school may help. English is now the international language of technology. But a school that concentrates on English offers more than the rudimentary knowledge required to operate Microsoft's clumsy programs. It increases the possibility of work with a U.S. company inside Mexico or legal emigration to the United States and a successful career. Mexican emigrants are no longer solely campesinos; engineers and architects and scholars are leaving too, mostly for the United States.

Curiously, in a school where the administration points to graduates who have attended Notre Dame, Stanford, and various U.S. state universities, the teacher in an eighth-grade civics class has no internationalist leanings. He teaches pure nationalism. Not history, not government, not concepts of democracy, but nationalism. He asked the students to stand, one by one, and read the essays they had written on the subject "My civic attitude toward the national symbols."

Under that heading he began a list, taking his cues from the essays written by the students. There were two categories, but he did not define them. He put some virtues in one category and some in another.

no cynicism	love
pride	honesty
respect	
fortitude	

After the virtues were listed on the blackboard, he turned to the glory of those Mexicans who died fighting for their country, the story of the Niños Héroes, the young cadets who chose to wrap themselves in the Mexican flag and leap from the walls of Chapultepec Castle rather than surrender to the Americans. The anniversary of their deed would be celebrated soon, and according to legend or history, there was a connection to the students in the classroom: The heroic young men had not been much older than the students who were asked to venerate them that September morning. "Studying is also your duty to your country," the teacher said, and went on to compare it with the loyalty of a soldier or sailor.

From the cadets wrapped in the flag as they leapt from the walls, he turned to the flag itself, the eagle standing on a cactus devouring a serpent. "Tenochtitlán," he said, "where the people called the Tenochas lived. Tenochtitlan means 'place of the cactus.' " But he did not ask why a cactus, nor did the students raise questions about the choice of a cactus. Why not a rose? I asked the students if they knew where the cactus came from. Was it always there? Did they know the story of the wizard Copil?[11] They did not. The history they learned had no depth; they had no urge to probe the story of the founding of Tenochtitlán. They listened; they repeated what they heard. This was a class in nationalism; the critical thinking so treasured by the school administrators did not make an appearance. The administrators would not have been surprised if they had been in the room that afternoon; they had said they were concerned, as they should have been, not merely for the Colegio Williams but for the Mexican system of education. The plea of Octavio Paz for a critical tradition that would permit the modernization of Mexico had not yet arrived in the civics class.

Nor had it arrived in the history class, where Victor Hugo Chávez, a slim, bespectacled young man, dressed in the style of the radicals of 1968 and 1999, author of a soon-to-be-published book about Emiliano Zapata, spoke to his students on a more contemporary subject, a film they had seen showing the September 11 attacks on the United States. Chávez talked on and on, giving his own views of the context of the attacks. The students slumped in their chairs, and when at last Chávez gave them a chance to speak, they followed what appeared to be the routine of the class: They offered no ideas of their own but asked questions of him, as if he were the oracle of Delphi seated at the small desk in the front of the room.

Mexican educators, even in this very successful school, have not abandoned the methods of Descartes; they simplify, as he would have them do, and instill the simplified ideas in their students; they do not develop knowledge in the student, they pass it down. The system works; the method is efficient up to the moment when repetition fails, dying at the entrance to the new.

---

[11] According to legend, the heart was torn out of the body of the evil wizard Copil and buried in the ground. A prickly pear cactus (tenochtli) sprang up from the burial place. The legend of Copil is key to understanding the "founding of Tenochtitlán." See León-Portilla and Shorris, *In the Language of Kings*.

THE GIANT OF TEMIXCO

After the unpaved streets and routine houses in the dry, stony, sun-scorched town of Temixco, Morelos, the entrance to the *telesecundaria* comes up suddenly around a corner, as if from another world, a place where shade trees grow and dark green vines line the walkways and there are sweet and promising scents of flowers. The introduction lasts but a few paces, past the gate and up an unpaved road that opens onto a large square surrounded by white stucco buildings and watched over by plump, leafy trees. Compared with the secundaria of Nezahualcoyotl, the school in Temixco looks rich or, if not rich, solid, like old Mexico, the Mexico of the imagination, of the neat austerity of rural life, not fully escaped from the clutches of the seasons, beholden to the rain god Tlaloc, but dignified, like white cotton and straw.

Luz María Uribe Quintanilla, the principal of the school, has the auto-matic response of the best administrators to a scrap of paper fallen on the school grounds. She will not wait for the wind to take it but reaches for the scrap herself. It is after all her school, her place, her duty. She organizes; she manages; she is devoted. In such a principal, one expects a bit of exaggera-tion, a softening of the edges of life, a slightly poetic presentation of the world as she would like it to be. But she is like the director of the Colegio Williams in that she knows what is and what must be done. The difference between them is money.

There are no giants in the school at Temixco. The school hero walks on crutches and bears the hesitance of palsy in his speech. He is perhaps the world's best swimmer among children his age, with physical disabilities sim-ilar to his. He took first place in swimming among his peers in Paris the pre-ceding year, and he will probably win again, unless the school cannot raise the money to enter him in the competition. The principal will try very hard to find the money. Carlos represents possibility, and in the old town of Temixco there are very few possibilities.

Among the other problems of Temixco, nothing looms so large as this absence of prospects, which begins for most students with breakfast, for there is no breakfast. The Mexican government provides a free breakfast only for six- and seven-year-old children. The rest must make do with what-ever their parents (or parent) provide. The problem of breakfast has also affected Uribe Quintanilla, the director, for when she speaks of breakfast, a darkness of old tears comes into her eyes and the pitch of her voice takes on a ragged and cutting edge. "The children don't have to say they are hungry; you can see the signs of malnutrition: thin, yellow, with blotches on their faces. They sleep. If they spend time in the sun, they faint. In class they sleep. They are children who have been hungry for a long time. They grow because it is natural, not because of nutrition. It makes them different, those who have had breakfast and those who have not, and the one who ate yesterday and the one who did not.

"It is very difficult to learn when you are thinking about hunger. We hope that through the foundation [Fundación Comunitaria Morelense] we can get food for the most humble, because they sleep."

She never uses the word "poor," only "humble"; only "virtue," never "failure."

"We want them to have something before school starts, a glass of milk, a little sandwich, a piece of fruit. It would be good if they had to pay only a peso. Or nothing. Colegio Williams is helping. We are going to make a kitchen here in the school." She bustles, she tries; her weapon is honesty, but of a distinct kind, said in Spanish as *coraje*, which means "righteous anger." "The children are beset by problems," she said. "There is little work, many single mothers, many women who work. The economic situation here is a bit difficult, so the children are often alone, and we have no resources, no facilities to continue activities after school. These children have no one to look after them. They are at the age when they like to form groups [gangs], and we don't want them to do that. There is no park, no place for healthy distraction. We have only a tiny library.

"On most streets in town they have water, electricity, and about sixty percent have sewerage. But they are short of food. Either they don't work or they are ill paid. Many earn less than the minimum wage. Unemployment is very high here; about half are unemployed."

"But the president claims unemployment in Mexico is only two-point-nine percent," I said. (Since then the number has increased to 4 percent.)

She understood the comment as a cue for laughter. "That's what he says, but the truth is different. There's some hourly work, perhaps on the weekends in the stores, but they don't pay minimum wage [about four dollars a day in Temixco]. People earn twenty, thirty pesos. This is not employment; it's not secure. These are not jobs that one can live with. And others have no work at all. They just don't have it."

Uribe Quintanilla tries to counter the problems of behavior and nascent juvenile delinquency through a parents' organization. Four women, all of whom have children in the last year of the secundaria, sit on the executive committee. Three are mothers, portly and proud, or so they present themselves until they begin to unravel the woven cozy of euphemism and pride that hides their lives in Temixco. The fourth, a thin woman with white hair and long, bony arms draped with the crepe of age, wearing the short-sleeved housedress of the grandmothers of the humble, her face narrow and angular, as if she were facing into a powerful wind, had a grandson in the school. Her daughter long ago ran off to the United States, leaving the child with no father, no siblings, no one but his grandmother. Now and then the woman sends money home to care for her mother and son, but she has not seen the boy for more than five years.

The mother has married in the United States. The grandmother does not know whether she has other children, nor does she know where the mother lives. Somewhere in the United States, in the north, in a city, some city. If the mother sends money back for him, the boy can go on to high school; if not, he will have to go to work. But there is no work. The grandmother raises her head, looking again as if she were facing into a storm, not beseeching, holding her ground.

Aurelia Carbajal, the president of the parents' organization, did not lose her husband to despair or a lack of interest, like many of the other women of Temixco; her husband died. She cannot work now because of a back injury, but she gets along better than most. Carbajal serves as the psychologist of the school, not educated as such, but able. She deals with children who misbehave, who do not come to school. When parents mistreat their children, when the children form gangs, the problem always goes to Aurelia Carbajal, who comes full-faced, still young, and aching always, unable to alleviate the pain in her back, and speaks to the problem. Violence is the problem, according to Carbajal and the members of her committee, violence at home, where the wives and children are beaten, and violence in the streets, and even in the school. One can feel the violence everywhere, force waiting to explode into action. It manifests itself in both crude and subtle ways, in the children posing for a photograph, making gestures that require retaliation, wanting to imprint them forever on another student.

A surround of force, which is as common among the poor in the United States as in Mexico, makes violence the only answer in the hurried world, where reflection takes too much time.[12] The poor in Mexico have nowhere to turn; almost everything in their lives functions as a force turned against them: violence, hunger, filth, racism, knives, the absence of hope, class distinctions, ugliness, roofs that leak, toilets that overflow, the angry sun, disease, and on and on until the only haven—and only briefly at that—is the school or the arms of the one parent who may not at the moment hold a stick or a strap in his or her heavy hand.

Violence occupies so much of the lives of the students in Temixco that the women of the parents' association have developed a school for the prevention of it. They bring together as many parents as will come, especially those whose children show marks of violence or who report violence at home. And then Carbajal and her committee try to teach restraint. A war against machismo while living within a surround of force would seem a fool's errand, but the women persevere. They talk about the task, their work, not the results. They use everything at hand, and they have nothing at hand but themselves. They write and perform plays to teach the parents and students about violence and sex. With no worldly objects, no money, no education, no expectation, they carry on their battle of mind against fate. And they are everywhere in the throes of television.

The committee cannot say for certain what television means. It surrounds their children, first in school, and again after school, when the children watch television, unless they can afford to play video games. Sra. Carbajal says the children like cartoons; another member of the committee says they prefer comedies. In the afternoons and evenings the students gather in the houses of those who have television, as Americans did half a century ago. And during the day, for the first seventeen minutes of every class in the telesecundaria the students watch a television presentation. In the afternoons and evenings they also watch television. The video does not pacify them but makes them passive—observers, battered versions of Eliot's Prufrock, but lacking the time and temperament to reflect on their passivity.

Not all, of course, have been caught in the net of violence. Sra. Carbajal's son has no time for it. When he leaves secondary school at the end of his day,

---

[12]See *New American Blues: A Journey through Poverty to Democracy* (New York: W. W. Norton, 1997) and *Riches for the Poor: The Clemente Course in the Humanities* (New York: W. W. Norton, 1999) for a full discussion of the surround of force and its effect upon the poor.

he goes on to a technical school in Cuernavaca, where he is learning to repair computers. He comes home late, with homework to do, and watches television until it is time for bed. He does not expect to go on to high school. Computer repair interests him, and if he learns his trade well, his only problem will be finding work in a country where the number of home computers is still extremely low and very few businesses will want to put their complex electronic machines in the hands of a fourteen- or fifteen-year-old boy from Temixco.

The study of computers would seem a logical outgrowth of a system based on imparting information via television. Everything in the system has been programmed: The television lectures, which are crudely produced, like World War II army training films, lead into workbooks containing questions about the material in the films. The students repeat what they have just heard in response to the questions in the workbook. Geography, for example, consists of imprinting a map on the minds of the students.

"Where is Mexico?" the film narrator asks. And answers, "Between the United States and Central America. That is why the Aztecs said Mexico was the navel of the universe." It does not occur to the students to ask what the Aztecs knew about the United States or Central America in the fifteenth century. They do not raise the issue, nor does the teacher raise the issue with them. The film announces, and the workbook insists upon the veracity of the film. It is not a roomful of questions, but a new form of Cartesian instruction.

Estela Múgica Calderón, the teacher, claims not to approve of such rote learning. She says she is afraid the children will be turned into robots, yet she follows the rules of the system. She must. Tomorrow there will be another seventeen minutes and another page to cover in the workbook, and on and on, and it will not change, unless somewhere a teacher or a student rebels by raising a question.

It will not happen soon. The school of the old town of Temixco lacks options. To produce giants requires breakfast. And lunch. To produce genius requires a combination of elements so complex and so perfectly balanced that like some unimaginably tiny component of a neutron, it can be changed forever simply by trying to see clearly what it is. It is not farfetched to say that geniuses, like atoms, are better tended than examined. I do not know how to recognize genius in a child, but anyone can catch a glimpse of possibility. Forecasts can be made, although revisions must also be made. Of the children who attend the secondary school at Colegio Williams, all go on to high school, and most to universities. Of those who attend the Calmecac School, about a third go on to the UNAM's preparatory school system, and it is not known how many of those go on to the university itself; there are no formal studies, but the number is presumed to be small.

At the end of the last required year of public education at the secondary school in Temixco, almost no one goes on to high school, and the number of those who complete high school and go on to college must be left to dreaming. The problem of Temixco does not grow out of the failure of teachers, and it cannot be solved by the scent of flowers or the drone of television. Breakfast would help. Nothing would help so much as breakfast. But there will be no breakfast in Temixco, certainly not soon. "We do not bother to ask the government for it," the principal said, "for we know there is none." And for this, because of this, there is that darkness of old tears about her.

Yet she had one thing more to say. In the large square between the buildings, under leafy trees, in the shade, there are several picnic benches. Sra. Uribe sat at one of the benches and waved to a young man to join her there. He sat down with some formality and examined the other faces around the table. He did this with an air of curiosity, sitting straight, watching hard. Although he was no taller than the rest of his class, and not wide, except for the fullness of his cheeks, he did not look like the other students. He claimed the stature of giants. In the deep shade he appeared luminous. His eyes shone; the reflected light seemed to come from within him.

He observed, but not passively. He saw and he wished to be seen. He did not look away when speaking to older people, as many Mexican children are taught to do. The principal introduced him and offered him a glass of cold water from a clear plastic pitcher. The boy brushed back a lock of hair that had fallen over one eye. He had the sausage fingers of well-fed children, but he was not clumsy. He took the glass the principal served, without shyness, as if he expected it, yet he showed no arrogance but was instead polite, as giants are taught to be. "I am going to preparatory school next year," he announced. "And then on to university to study law, although I have also considered becoming a doctor. But right now I think I prefer law."

He considered his career, looking over at the principal for confirmation. He was the dream student of Temixco, the brightest, the most ambitious; he would not suffer hunger, nor would violence come into his life. He had decided; he would not permit himself to fail. "Oh, I do not think I will be the president of Mexico," he said, feigning a sigh. Then he smiled as if to wink, "But it's possible."

33.

The Science of Dismal Prospects

Mexican Population
1859 — 8,000,000
1895 — 12,632,427
1900 — 13,607,272
1910 — 15,160,369
1921 — 14,334,780
1930 — 16,552,722
1940 — 19,653,552
1950 — 25,791,017
1960 — 34,923,129
1970 — 48,313,438
1980 — 66,846,833
1990 — 81,249,645
present — 106,000,000+ (est.) [1]

THE RESPECTFUL DIVAS OF PLAZA LORETO

In the center of the City of Mexico, not far from the Church of Loneliness, respectful women stroll, and when luck is with them, they make assignations. The women work there every day and into the night in the old section of the city, where age is sometimes mistaken for history. In this thoroughly policed part of the capital, where extortion is the rule, the day begins slowly. By afternoon Plaza Loreto resembles the colonial heart of a provincial town, a mournful common where storekeepers treasure shade and the few shoppers and sellers hurry along, huddled close to the façades of buildings, as if to escape the slant light of the sun.

In the dark the air appears to be clear. A frenzy has begun, like the open-

---

[1] The 1859 figure is a combination of estimates by Miguel Lerdo de Tejada and Antonio García Cubas. It is perhaps the best estimate of Mexican residents after the Treaty of Guadalupe Hidalgo at the end of the Mexican-American War. The other numbers, except the final estimate, appear in the Porrúa encyclopedia (*Diccionario Porrúa de Historia, Biografía y Geografía de México*, 6th ed. [Mexico: 1995]).

ing of a long-anticipated sale. No one wants to pay the asking price in the plaza, for nothing in the plaza or the surrounding streets quite fits his expectations. The night turns gaudy with sex shows and rock bands and mariachis and the growling laughter of machismo at play. Along the perimeter of Plaza Loreto, the respectful women stroll and hope. A few sit on benches facing the street. Night lasts a long time, and already their feet hurt.

The boys have arrived, an army of provincial invaders transported by third-class buses and the battered Volkswagen buses they call *combis*, and not a few of them have walked great distances over weeks or longer, from Estado de Mexico, or Morelos, or even farther. And here is one from Guerrero still speaking Nahuatl in a version no Aztec of pre-Hispanic times would have understood, still dressed in country clothes, lacking city shoes, a villager in a New Orleans Saints T-shirt and worn blue jeans. He could be twenty years old, perhaps younger. He is very short, and although he does not seem malnourished, he has a weary look, an older man's step, and his eyes do not accurately reflect the light.

Two Chilangos, city men, natives of the capital, one in a black leather jacket with a torn zipper, inspect the strolling women. The women are respectful, but the city men have come to jeer, perhaps to mourn the scant contents of their wallets, which have sent them here to Plaza Loreto and not to the streets off the Reforma, where beautiful women pace on spike heels. The Chilangos are prepared to participate in the bargaining that accompanies the sale; the smirk is the naco's chip. The country boys are uncertain; they have what they have, no more, and if they buy a beer or two, not enough will be left.

The women who stroll or rise to meet the men are old. They have swollen ankles and wide waists; their breasts have descended to meet their bellies. One has the bowed legs of rickets, another shows a scar, but they are shod tall, pulled up, pushed in, dyed, creamed, and painted. They are not painted for the street but for the stage—opera or ballet. In the semidarkness, if they had but been women of age and not warriors against history, they might have been beautiful as history is beautiful, but their eyebrows are blacked as thick as thumbs, and they have painted marks to extend the perimeter of their eyes. They plump their lips red and incompletely round, like ripe, wet strawberries. And on every woman's cheeks two red circles: one for Petrouchka and the other for Pagliacci. They carry their chins like Mussolini to hide the folds of their necks. Some waddle, some mince; the bowlegged woman merely advances. After the men have passed by and the street has gone empty for the moment, the women continue walking, but the strawberry mouths pinch and the eyes narrow a little more, for there is no one to see them but each other, and their feet hurt.

On a good night a woman can earn two hundred pesos. So many lonely boys. One who shoveled, the palms of his hands as hard as toenails. Another who hammered his thumb flat. Before the social workers formed the Brigada Callejera (Streetwalkers' Brigade), the police took thirty pesos from each woman in the morning and thirty pesos in the evening, and if a woman had no money, they beat her for a lesson in marketing. Then the social workers came and formed the Brigada Callejera. What the Sisters of Holy Obligation could not do, what Carmen Río, the Spanish nun, could not do with her lovely Italian face and madrileña accent, what her gray-touched, softly curled hair and the light in the lightness of her eyes could not do, what no one else had been able to do for decades, if not for centuries, the social workers accomplished. They saved the women from the police.

No one was more grateful than Yolanda, the widow of the composer and singer from the Yucatán, for she was a thinker and a saver and a listener, and of all the women of Plaza Loreto there was no one more respectful than Yolanda. Nor was there another woman strolling along the plaza more worn, more used up than Yolanda. Not Cela, the bandy-legged woman from Veracruz, who had adopted a baby girl twelve years ago and lived with her in a house in the place called Ecatepec, where José María Morelos was executed in 1815. Cela stayed in a hotel near Plaza Loreto in the good times, and when times were bad, she slept in a dormitory in the care of the Spanish nun, and in the worst of times Cela slept in the street. Some men preferred her African features. There were also some who preferred tall women, and Cela would have been very tall if her legs had grown straight and lifted her up to her genetic height.

Cela didn't speak much to her clients. Only the social workers and Yolanda really knew who chose the women of Plaza Loreto. "I don't like just to do it," Yolanda said. "I like to talk to them first. They are mostly bachelors, sometimes men who have problems in love. The young ones choose me because I show them respect. And I teach them."

In the afternoon old men visited her: old customers who did not mind that her ankles had swollen or that she picked constantly at her upper teeth with her fingernail. When the social workers introduced condoms to Plaza

Loreto, Yolanda used them regularly, but she said there was something wrong with them, they were defective. Every time she used a condom with a customer, it broke. And she liked the condoms, she said. They were very good for the skin. She opened the little packages and rubbed the lubricant on her face before she put the condoms on her customers.

When the young men visited Yolanda, she never failed to ask where they were from, what work they did, what they wanted of her, and she never showed anger when they said they could not afford the beautiful young prostitutes who strolled along the Reforma, nor would any young woman want a beau who was so poor. She commiserated, she comforted, she was Nuestra Señora de Papachos,[2] and she told stories; she won over her customers, she made them friends as well as lovers. She spoke to them as equals, no longer boys; that was how she respected them.

One Friday afternoon Yolanda ate in the restaurant in the corner of the church building, where the comida corrida[3] was filling and economical, and they offered seconds of vegetables and rice. The customers were mainly prostitutes and thieves, but of the kind who prayed. Even so, the food was served on disposable plates and eaten with plastic utensils. The nuns who ran the restaurant were not fools. They knew their customers loved Jesus but stole the crockery.

Yolanda sat there, picking and pushing her upper teeth. Her teeth hurt more than her feet. She could not chew at all with them. The moment her food was served, she removed her upper false teeth and put them in her purse. Instead of the expected line of dark pink flesh, she showed a row of small, white triangular stubs, as sharp as shark's teeth. It was no wonder she wore the painful denture! Without it, she would have had no customers at all.

Every evening when dusk descended over Plaza Loreto, she completed the application of her greasepaint mask, and put in her teeth, and did her best with elastic and plastic and ruffles and wood to disguise her belly, enhance her backside, and corral her lolling bosom. Trompe l'oeil, and if not, at least to distract the eye from her swollen ankles and the folds of flesh the lubricant had failed to erase. The boy who chose her one evening had journeyed

[2]Our Lady of Caresses (of the kind usually given to children). "Papacho," from the Nahuatl for "flutter."
[3]Daily lunch, like a blue plate special. A hearty four-course meal for eight people cost less than twenty-five dollars.

from the heights of Popocatepetl, the great volcano that he called Don Goyo, for that is the name country people use. He spoke to her of fruit trees and cool water originating in snow. And then of loneliness. What woman would have a boy who had no money, who slept in dormitories, on church pews, and now and then lay all night in the courtyard of a vecindad molested by dogs and moonlight and the sound of a cousin's sick child?

She was all he could have. They sat side by side on the neatly made narrow bed, in the tiny room for which he had paid, and she told him her story, as she told everyone, as if she were a novela illustrated by her own paints and lumps and swellings. "My mother was a pocha [Mexican-American] from Troy, Michigan, and she married my father and went to Acapulco, but he died of cirrhosis of the liver and left her there alone with her children. She could not work; she knew very little Spanish. When I was old enough, I went north, *mojada* [wet], to pick strawberries and harvest apples. Then I met my husband. He was a Yucateco, a singer and composer and a member of a trio. We had eight children. He had money; he owned two pieces of land by the beach south of Tijuana.

"And one day he was going with his trio to play, driving by the water on a curve along a great cliff, when a horse trailer turned out in front of them, and they crashed. My husband went through the windshield from the crash. '*Salgo* [I am leaving],' he said. '*Salgo.*' And he became a *volante* [flier], flying, flying over the cliff.

"He was a composer. He wrote many songs and made recordings. He wrote songs to me." She sang, "When you kill me, it is a rose that kisses me ..." And another: "Yolanda, lovely Yolanda, countenance of the rose, I will make a gift to you ..."

She had a soft voice, very gentle, an incongruity, and when she sang the second song, her voice started to tremble, and during the third song she wept. The boy applauded. People always applauded when Yolanda sang. "He died twenty-two years ago. We lived in Acapulco. It was very beautiful then."

Before she had finished talking and the business of the night had begun, she sang once more, and said, "*Ai, óotsil,*" which is Yucatecan and means "Oh, woe is me."

At the end of the night the boy, who had spent more than two days' wages, seventy-five pesos, on four bottles of beer, a room, and Yolanda, went back to the vecindad to sleep with the dogs and the moon, and Yolanda washed and changed into soft shoes and put her teeth in a glass and finished packing both her suitcases, for she had a ticket to Baja California, where she had built a tiny house on one of the pieces of land her long-lamented Yucateco had left to her so that she might have a place near the beach, like the place where they had lived in Acapulco when Acapulco was still beautiful.[4]

MANY MEXICANS

During the 1950s, when Mexico enjoyed its Golden Age, a popular "witticism" claimed that "the trouble with Mexico is that there are too many Mexicans." Two million people lived in Mexico City then, and successful Mexicans were comfortable enough to make such self-deprecating remarks. A few years later Ifigenia Martínez raised the issue of the population problem in Mexico. She looked at the high birthrate, the falling infant mortality rate, increasing longevity, the paucity of arable land, and predicted trouble unless population growth in Mexico slowed. Neither the government nor the public paid much notice to the prediction. These were the best of times in Mexico; no one wanted to think about long-term problems. Besides, Lord Keynes had said that in the long run we are all dead. And even if Mexico had paid attention to the problem, what could have been done? Neither machismo nor history nor the rules of the Roman Catholic Church were likely to be changed by a university professor's work. Mexicans were still largely rural people who thought of children as a twofold blessing: familial love and farm labor. The economics of the large family were undeniable: more children, more work; more work, more corn.

Those who thought the birthrate should be blamed entirely on Mexico's Roman Catholicism have since been proved wrong by Italy, which possesses both the Vatican and the lowest birthrate in the world. Martínez had

[4]For help with interviews and information I am grateful to José Romero Keith, Ph.D., then of the Pan-American Health Organization; to La Brigada Callejera and social workers Elvira and Jaime Montejo, who helped organize the Streetwalkers' Brigade; to Carmen Río of Hermanas Oblatas del Santísimo Redentor; and to Cela, Alicia, and Julia of La Brigada Callejera, who gave interviews and permitted tape recordings but asked that I not use their family names. None of the men I spoke to was willing to give his name, allow tape recordings or note taking. Most of all, I am grateful to Yolanda, who spoke to me at great length, told me her story as she said she told it to her clients, and allowed me to use a tape recorder.

it right long before the problem became apparent to the rest of the world: Mexico's population explosion was not caused by religion alone. It came out of the culture, including religion, and it would affect every aspect of Mexican economic (as well as social and political) life. When Martínez published her warning, the 1950 census had reported 25 million inhabitants in Mexico. The current annual growth rate of the population is the lowest in many decades, under 1.5 percent. If it remains at that level, the Mexican population will increase to 130 million by 2020. The old joke has come true: The trouble with Mexico is that there are too many Mexicans. How the country will accommodate yet another 25 million people by 2020 is the Mexican problem.

Although the issue is seldom discussed and the birthrate has been falling, many of Mexico's economic problems and its hopes for the future can be traced to the population explosion. If the preceding statement appears to be a conundrum, it is. Both the problem and the hope are realistic. Hope comes from the possibilities inherent in a young, educated population, while the problem comes from the sheer magnitude of the population and its requirements. In 2003, Foreign Secretary Luis Derbez made the argument for hope in curious fashion. He said that Mexico and the United States had "complementary" populations. In the United States, he said, forty-three percent of the population was over forty years old, but in Mexico only 23 percent was over forty. "We offer the kind of population they want," he said.[5] The offer of people in exchange for better relations with a neighbor commodified the people. In the view expressed by Derbez, who had been the cabinet officer in charge of economics before moving to foreign secretary, Mexico was raising people, like hogs or beef cattle, and using them for export.

It sounds a bit Malthusian to base so much of a country's predicament on population growth, and the number of people who must divide up the pie is certainly not the only Mexican economic problem. But all the problems not caused directly by the burgeoning population are exacerbated by it. For the last quarter of a century it has been common in Mexico among the left opposition parties to say that economic democracy must be preceded by political democracy. Exactly what they mean by economic democracy is not the same in every case, but it always includes the reduc-

[5] *La Jornada,* July 17, 2003.

tion of all kinds of poverty and the elimination (so far as possible) of extreme poverty.

Political democracy seems now to be possible in Mexico, although the country has yet to create fully functional democratic institutions. Meanwhile, here gathered in a single list are some of the issues related directly or indirectly to accommodating rapid population growth. Taken individually, they seem manageable; viewed in the aggregate, the effect is quite different.

Mexico can no longer feed itself. It imports many foodstuffs, including over seven hundred million dollars' worth of corn a year from the United States. It also imports beef and pork. Food and other imports have increased steadily and will take another leap upward because a provision in NAFTA removes more tariffs from U.S. agricultural imports beginning in 2003 and all tariffs by 2008.

About eighteen million people live on little more than a dollar a day in Mexico, according to the World Bank.

Estimates of the number of people living in poverty vary from 48 percent[6] nationally (or 57 percent or 64 percent, depending on who is counting) to as high as 70 percent[7] in the southern and southwestern states and in the Federal District, this last according only to Julio Boltvinik in *La Jornada*. In the spring of 2004 Raquel Sosa, secretary of social development in the capital, said 62 percent of the people in her jurisdiction lived in poverty, and announced efforts to eliminate poverty in the city. She said that the winter campaign of 2003–2004 had provided 642,440 dinners and 4,275 blankets to the indigent.

Mexico's product per capita fell from $5,070 in 2000 to $4,940 in 2002, according to the Bank of Mexico, and the decline in world markets that continued into 2003 promised yet another fall. In Mexico, 42 percent of the wealth is held by the top tenth of the population, but the bottom tenth has only 1.3 percent. Mexican officials like to compare their country with Spain, but in 2002 the split in Spain was 25.2 percent and 2.8 percent.[8]

The distribution of wealth in Mexico is far worse than that in the United States. In both countries the decile figures no longer reflect the true con-

[6]World Bank, 2002.
[7]Organization for Economic Cooperation and Development, *Reforma*, September 27, 2002.
[8]World Bank, 2002. Mexico has the third-greatest concentration of wealth of any country in the world. The wealth of the ten richest people is equal to 5.8 percent of Mexican GDP.

centration of wealth and power. The top 1 percent or less has enough money
and power to exercise control over many aspects of the society, including
government. The wealth of the top 1 percent dwarfs that of the bottom 40
percent in the United States. In Mexico, the bottom 50, perhaps 60 percent
has no economic power. Poverty in the United States is figured at twelve dollars a day per household of four persons; in Mexico, extreme poverty is
defined as two dollars a day.[9] In both countries, the economic pattern affects
the political pattern.

The U.S. middle class declined during the 1990s; the Mexican middle
class fell after austerity was imposed by the International Monetary Fund in
1982 and again in 1995 after the peso devaluation. Of course, the patterns
function at much different economic levels. Mexico has a greater extreme at
the low end. And the loss of the middle class in the United States and Mexico came about for opposite reasons: Mexico had too little money, and the
United States had too much. The U.S. middle class became relatively poorer
while the Mexican middle class became absolutely poorer.

Another major difference lay in the kinds of economic activity in the two
countries. In Mexico the informal economy was growing at twice the rate of
the formal (salaried) economy and being encouraged by the Fox administration's concentration on funding microindustry. Of more than 40 million
economically active people in Mexico, about half had no health, welfare,
medical, or pension benefits. Although Mexico claims a little under 4 percent unemployment, there were 3.5 million people counted as workers who
were not paid anything at all. Among female workers 13.2 percent were not
paid at all.[10]

In demography, as in all work related to statistics, it is not the counting
but the definitions that matter. In Mexico, definitions have been manipulated to show it as one of the world's leading industrial nations, with one of
the world's lowest levels of unemployment. But there are very few people

[9] The president also speaks of those living on one dollar or less a day.

There are many definitions of extreme poverty, one of the most common is income
less than the cost of the basic food basket. But the basic food basket is defined by the government, which may choose to manipulate the items or quantities to raise or lower the
number of people in extreme poverty.

[10] INEGI (National Institute of Statistics, Geography, and Information) and International Labor Organization figures, July 2003. When there are differing results for studies
of the same group, the INEGI figures are generally more conservative.

who believe the government's assertions. In September 2002, for example, the government noted, with astonishment, that unemployment in Mexico had risen to more than 3 percent. In bustling Monterrey, it had gone up to 4.6 percent. In Monclova, Coahuila, to 7.3 percent. Total unemployed in that month came to 1,659,250, a relatively small part of those who were considered economically active. A year later, when the number rose to 4 percent, there was less astonishment and more consternation. The value of being economically active in Mexico, however, may not be very great.

MINIMUM WAGES 2003

Zone C (Federal District, Acapulco, Baja California, Ciudad Juárez) 43.65[11] pesos a day
Zone B (Monterrey, Guadalajara, Tampico) 41.85 pesos a day
Zone A (southern and rural states) 40.30 pesos a day

Figured against the basket of goods in the areas where the minimum wage applied, each day's wages was worth 4.4 pounds of beans and 4.4 pounds of tortillas or about 2.6 pounds of chicken. Daily wages for "professions" were higher:

Truck driver	65.10 pesos
Gas station attendant	56.35 pesos
Cashier	56.45 pesos
Construction supervisor	63.60 pesos
Reporter on metro daily	130.75 pesos

There are several other numbers to be taken into account: critical conditions, defined in Mexico (INEGI) to mean the situation of a person who works less than thirty-five hours a week or who works more than forty-eight hours for less than double the minimum wage. That group accounts for another 7.48 percent of the economically active population, adding 3 million people to those who are not really employed. Add those to the 2.4 million officially unemployed, and the total goes over 5 million. Add that to the 25

---

[11]To convert figures to dollars, divide by ten as a general rule. The exchange rate floats, however. When the new wage rates were promulgated, the salary in the Federal District, including Mexico City, was worth only $4.24 a day.

million (62.7 percent of economically active persons) Mexicans who live in the informal economy, which could also be called the hand-to-mouth economy, and there are about 30 million economically active Mexicans who do not earn enough to enjoy a decent, by which I mean secure, standard of living. In other words, the worst of the numbers is correct: Seventy percent of the people in Mexico are either living in poverty, spending some time each year in poverty, or living at the edge of poverty. Since the population grows faster than the economy can produce jobs, even the government admits that the informal economy will grow faster than the economy of secure enterprise and employment.[12] And Mexico, like other countries still in development, has sought new ways to move people from extreme poverty to the informal economy.

President Fox proudly announced Mexico's participation in the worldwide program of microloans, giving people just enough money to buy a pushcart or a taco stand or an ax and a burro to enter the firewood-collecting business. He told an audience in New York City on November 11, 2002, that these microloans had reduced the number of people in poverty in Mexico from 18 to 15 percent.[13] But microfinancing contributes more to the moral than the economic health of a country, and the loans, like the informal economy itself, are concentrated in three areas: the states of Mexico and Jalisco and the Federal District (Mexico City and environs). The numbers can be deceptive, however, because they do not include people in the agricultural sector.

Furthermore, the informal economy and the unemployed produce nothing for export. Members of the hand-to-mouth economy often trade in very cheap imported goods, mainly from Asia. Street vendors sell flimsy T-shirts, tape recorders, toys, cameras, blue jeans, film, crockery, tapes, CDs, even copies of pre-Columbian artifacts imported from Asia. Mexico cannot manage its trade deficit with Asia, which has set out to capture part of the market at every economic level.

[12]Some economists have labeled these toilers in the hand-to-mouth economy "capitalists" or "microcapitalists." It would be difficult to imagine a more foolish designation. INEGI, the Mexican statistical institute, claimed that 28 percent of the economically active population was employed in the informal economy in 2002. Two years earlier the OECD put the percentage at 57. Banamex, a Citigroup company, put the percentage at 62.7 at mid-year 2003.

[13]The president apparently meant the percentage of the population living in extreme poverty.

To accommodate its growing population as much as anything else, Mexico devised the North American Free Trade Agreement (NAFTA). President Salinas saw it as an alternative to the informal economy and underemployment. By 2001 the maquiladora sector accounted for half of all trade between the United States and Mexico. And 85 percent of Mexican exports went to the United States. Nonetheless, *Excelsior*, a Mexican daily, wrote on March 20, 2001, that this meant declines in maquiladora exports would have little effect in Mexico. A huge loss of jobs in the industry—190,000 in the first months after the article was published—gave the lie to the *Excelsior* argument.

Mexican debt in autumn of 2002, both internal and external, was equal to 56 percent of its gross domestic product, most of it in current account expenses, meaning that very little had gone for development, argued Federal Deputy José Antonio Magallanes Rodríguez.[14] The Fox administration had, except for a brief time, been able to keep inflation below 5 percent and reduce the debt despite the recession in the United States, worldwide losses in stock markets, and the concomitant slowing of growth in Mexican GDP, but the performance had slowed in 2001 and 2002, and 2003 looked worse. By 2004 it was clear that the Fox administration had produced the worst three-year period of economic growth in the last fifty years. The performance looked good at first glance, but a more careful examination showed the Fox administration playing the money markets; as interest rates fell, Mexico took on new debt at lower interest rates to pay off the old debt. The net amount came down, but the IMF projected an end to the game. Its economists projected interest on the debt at ten billion dollars, still roughly equivalent to two-thirds of the revenue Mexico earned from its oil exports.[15] The foreign debt was over $140 billion in 2003, which came to 23 percent of gross domestic product.[16]

The danger for Mexico in all of this, as it must be for any country still in the process of development, is an attack on its currency. The country runs

---

[14]*La Jornada,* October 10, 2002. External debt alone in September 2002 was $152 billion, which amounted to 26.3 percent of GDP. By July 2003 the Bank of Mexico said that $71.36 of every $100 Mexico received in foreign investment went to pay interest on the foreign debt.

[15]The U.S. Department of Energy estimated Mexican oil revenues for 2003 at $16 billion, up 21 percent from the preceding year. Mexico estimates $50 billion in 2004.

[16]Secretaría de Hacienda estimate for March 2003.

short on dollars, begins seeking dollars by offering higher interest on them, and the devastating spiral begins. Mexico has been running a current account deficit for the last seven years, meanwhile paying a staggering amount of interest on the external debt.[17] In the midst of an economic downtown, the governors of the Mexican states have been pressing Fox to give them more money out of the federal budget, which would increase the current account debt.

In financial terms, it looks very complicated, but the economy is still "the public household." Spend more than you make and run up debts larger than your savings, and very soon people think you don't know how to manage your house. Instead of being part of it, they want to get away from it. You beg them to stay with you by giving them a little more of your house until there is no more house to give. And they take control of your house. The problem comes in the inability of anyone to predict accurately when the international bankers will decide to sell the currency. At this moment the Mexican economy appears to be stable. Bankers are generally conservative and the president is a conservative; the chance of continued trust in his ability to manage the Mexican public household is good. Compared with his counterpart in the United States, he appears to be both wise and prudent about debt. But the chance that someone will decide tomorrow to sell ten or twenty billion pesos and trigger a run on the currency is not out of the question.

Meanwhile, outflows of money to banks and investments in the United States and other countries continued to have a negative effect on the availability of capital. And the reforms promised by Fox, some of which would have enraged his critics on the left, had not come about. He had not dealt with the poverty problem; education policy and expenditures had slid backward; corruption had suffered a dent, as had the illegal drug business, but Mexico was hardly incorruptible, and Fox had been accused of violating Mexican election laws by accepting contributions from foreign sources. He had promised his country and the world the rule of law in Mexico, and he had not delivered.

In 2002, Mexico was still unable to connect with overseas markets (other than the United States) on either the supply or demand side. The largest

---

[17]In the second quarter of 2003 the current account deficit was $11.5 billion, according to Hacienda.

companies seemed to prefer investing in foreign factories to exporting from Mexico. It still sent less than 10 percent of its production to countries other than the United States. At the annual Pacific Rim trade conference (held in Cabo San Lucas), Mexico was trying to finalize negotiations for a free trade agreement with Japan. Mexican officials told the press they had learned from experience with NAFTA how to negotiate such an agreement so that it was more beneficial to Mexico. At the same meeting President Fox tried to buttonhole his American counterpart on such issues as agricultural subsidies and legalization of the status of undocumented Mexican immigrants in the United States. He had no luck. He had no choice but to keep at it. If the United States shut down the border or, even worse, began deporting large numbers of undocumented workers, his government would collapse, and his country would be thrown into chaos.

Oil prices rose with the tensions in the Middle East, but Pemex, the Mexican national petroleum company, was a mess. Both the union and management were involved in corruption scandals. The union was judged guilty by the Federal Election Institute (IFE) of putting vast amounts of money into the PRI presidential campaign in 2000, resulting in what came to be known in press jargon as Pemexgate, a case that became a disaster for the PRI, resulting in the largest fine ever levied against a Mexican political party, one hundred million dollars.

Management fared no better than the union or the PRI. Fox had caused a stir when he took office by appointing wealthy and powerful businessmen—Carlos Slim Helú of Telmex, Lorenzo Zambrano of Cemex, and Rogelio Rebolledo Rojas of Pepsi-Cola, among them—to the board of Pemex. The left feared it as a step toward privatization; the business community cheered it as a step toward efficiency. After two years it had proved to be neither. Oil sales continued to pay for a third of the entire federal budget, but Mexican refineries still could not produce enough gasoline to supply Mexican demand: Mexico still exported petroleum to the United States and imported the refined product (gasoline), leading to consistently higher prices for gasoline in Mexico compared with the United States. The relation of Pemex to the population is not merely incidental on either the supply or demand side. Petroleum revenues had paid for much of the Mexican Miracle. Oil prices may go up or down, but as the population increases, the share per person of national resources (both renewable and nonrenewable) decreases, and the demand for gasoline (imported) increases.

Pemex has had problems increasing oil production and has made very lit-tle progress in enlarging its refining capacity. One group of Mexicans wants Pemex to contract with U.S. oil companies to drill, pump, and refine Mexi-can petroleum. The argument in favor of this notion holds that it is better to pay part of the increased revenues to the Americans than to have only the current revenue. The idea is to let the burden of the capital investment fall on the Americans.

The other theory, held by nationalists who claim to have a long-term view, is that Pemex and the other state-owned industry, electric power gen-eration and distribution, should be forced to use Mexican technology. It is a good argument but naive: The technology does not exist in Mex-ico, NAFTA does not permit technology transfer, and the investment in devel-oping the technology might not pay off for years, if ever. Research and development are expensive, often taking many years; Mexico's oil reserves are running out, and the cost of extraction rises as reserves decline. There is no good answer to the problem in either industry. Foreign ownership of power plants has already begun.

Since 1521, when Tenochtitlán fell to the Spaniards, the outside world has been interested in the extractive industries in Mexico: a little gold; a lot of silver; a vast amount of copper; enough oil to have fueled a boom when prices were high and a bust when prices fell in the early 1980s. The problem for any country that bases its economy to a large extent on extracting commodities for sale overseas is that it has no control over fluctuations in com-modity prices, as the Mexicans learned when they tried to set the price for oil. For five hundred years Mexico has been dividing the mined and pumped portion of its nonrenewable resources by an ever-increasing num-ber of people.

To alleviate the population pressure Mexico has nowhere to turn but the United States. But who is looking after the millions of Mexican citizens in the United States? What is the Mexican government's responsibility to its cit-izens abroad? To answer the question, the Fox administration appointed Candido Morales of Northern California to head a new department serving Mexicans abroad (*en el extranjero*, but really meaning the United States). Morales, a small, soft-spoken man who had worked successfully for many years on behalf of Mexican migrants and immigrants in Northern Califor-nia, was introduced on October 1, 2002, to the press and various community organizations by Georgina Lagos Dondé, the Mexican consul-general in San

Francisco. Sra. Lagos, a former journalist and a political conservative, who has taken the consulate from a bleak and weary office in a run-down building to new headquarters and active participation in the life of the Bay Area, towered over Mr. Morales, who has the face of an Olmec statue (although he is from Oaxaca). Both the elegant consul and the down-to-earth Mr. Morales spoke of the suffering, lack of health care, poor schooling, inadequate housing, and so on of Mexicans in the United States. The new department may be no more than a ploy to win votes, but neither the eyes of Sra. Lagos nor the history of Mr. Morales are cynical.

The department will be staffed by a hundred people in the United States and about twenty in Mexico. The economics of the operation are clear. Mexicans in the United States send vast amounts of money home (estimates for 2003 range from fifteen billion dollars up), and the amount that actually arrives in Mexico has increased since the cost of sending money there has gone down, although Wells Fargo Bank in California was still charging 12.5 percent (the U.S. Postal Service charged less than one-fourth of the Wells Fargo fee), and banks, led by Wells Fargo, were developing lower-cost methods for electronic transfers. Competition for the service, which had once been provided mainly by Western Union, was fierce. Mexico has only three major money-making sectors: oil, tourism, and money sent home from the United States. So Mexicans in the United States are an investment worth protecting, both economically and politically. The economic return on investment is clear; the political return, should Mexicans abroad be allowed to vote, may be more interesting.[18]

The number of eligible Mexican voters in the United States (under most of the proposed plans) is equal to 16 percent of the electorate, exactly the percentage of the vote that went to Cuauhtémoc Cárdenas in the 2000 presidential election. Should the great majority of Mexicans in the United States vote for one party, they could determine the outcome of any Mexican election, including the presidency.

As long as the Mexican population increases and the United States maintains its appetite for low-wage workers, the exchange of people for

---

[18]The social cost of breaking up families by sending the young fathers and mothers to the United States for long periods (often years) is difficult to estimate. Some children survive, prospering by the ability of their parents (usually fathers) to feed and clothe them and even to send them to private preparatory (high) schools. Others despair.

cash will continue. But sooner or later there will be serious opposition. Unemployment in the United States could cause problems, as it did in the 1930s, when thousands of people of Mexican descent, including many U.S. citizens, were deported. Or the issue may be founded on cultural discontent. Many Americans, including Americans of Mexican descent, want to restrict immigration. Whether the trigger is cultural or economic, the dispute is unavoidable. The outcome will likely be to limit immigration, but not for long and not to zero or anything close to zero; neither country could endure that.[19]

A possible solution to the population problem and its economic results shows up now and then in the conversation of Mexican economists, social scientists, journalists, and even government officials. They envision a North and Central (and eventually South) American version of the European Common Market. Such a common market in the Americas would allow the free flow of labor as well as capital, technology, raw materials, and manufactured goods. The stumbling blocks are the inequalities. One country dominates the hemisphere. Under what circumstances would it consider commonality? To arrive at an agreement would require something close to a miracle, but in the dreams of Mexicans who think about the economic future and political stability of the country, the difference between a good

---

[19]Mexico faces an immigration problem on its own southern border. It does not want immigrants from Guatemala, and it makes a great effort to stop them from entering the country. It is not a gentle effort. Human rights activists complain of the mistreatment of immigrants by government troops and bandits, particularly in the jungle near the Usumacinta River, which defines part of the border.

There are checkpoints all along the highways in southern Mexico, both in Chiapas and the Yucatán Peninsula. Cars are stopped; buses are boarded. The Mexican Army apparently does little or nothing to stop bandits from preying on the immigrants. And there are rumors of bandits' sharing their loot with the army. The practice has gone on for at least fifteen years. Guatemalans who were robbed and beaten after they crossed the border into Mexico are willing to describe their experiences once they reach the United States. As the bandits and their accomplices know, immigrants do not report these incidents to the Mexican authorities for fear of being robbed of whatever the bandits missed, beaten, threatened, and deported.

Mercedes Olivera, formerly of the office of the UN High Commissioner for Refugees, has written extensively on the subject of mistreatment of Guatemalans in southern Mexico, including the use of young Guatemalan (as well as indigenous Mexican) women in brothels serving Mexican Army troops in Chiapas.

night's sleep and the sweat of anxiety depends upon the possible opening of hemispheric borders.[20]

Meanwhile, Mexico suffers the loss of its human potential. In many small towns in the state of Puebla, which has lost a huge part of its most promising population to the United States, there are no young men. Every evening, starting at dusk, boys nearing the age of emigration stand listlessly on street corners in the center of the town in which they live, waiting for their time to come. Those who go and later come home leave their youth across the border. Those who go and never come back are a loss for Mexico. They send money home, but that is all. Wanderers intrigue us; they are all members of Odysseus's crew, adventurers, no matter what comes of their journeys. But emigrants are the true heroes, whether walking across an icebound strait ten thousand years ago or lying seasick and hopeful in the stinking hold of a weary ship on its way west from Europe or east from Asia or running north through the night into the desert. All through history emigrants have been the best of suffering nations: the boldest, bravest, and brightest. That is the cohort Mexico gives up in order to relieve the pressure of population.

AHUITZOTL'S WATER

For more than five hundred years, water has posed a problem for Mexico, in the capital, in the breadbasket of the bajío, and in the semiarid and desert areas of the north. At the end of the fifteenth century the bellicose and impetuous Aztec emperor Ahuitzotl (reigned 1480–1502) realized, according to Fray Diego Durán, "that the beauty and fertility of Mexico depended upon great quantities of water entering the city. The Aztecs had built floating gardens and orchards where they had sown maize, sage, squash, chilli, amaranth, tomatoes and flowers. With all these plants the city was greatly

---

[20]In 2003, with terrorism feared at home and Iraq at the top of the agenda, the Bush administration paid scant attention to Mexico and questions of immigration except to tighten control of the southern border. Fox and Castañeda had proposed giving legal status to undocumented Mexicans in the United States, and Bush had expressed interest in the idea, but that was before September 11, 2001. Interest in Mexico remained high for people involved in business, labor, the environment, human rights, agriculture, petroleum, tourism, and so on, but Washington had turned its attention to the Middle East: American soldiers were dying almost every day, and the people in the Department of Defense who had promoted the war had no idea of what to do after the war was "over."

beautified, but their freshness would be lost if they should lack water. . . . So it was that the king sent two messengers to ask the ruler of Coyoacán to allow water to be brought in [from the great spring there]."

The ruler of Coyoacán refused, and Ahuitzotl had him killed. Then the Aztec emperor called upon his allies to help construct a dam and a huge water pipe. When it was completed and water flowed into the city, "Ahuitzotl welcomed the water with florid words. . . . A few days later the water began to increase in such quantities that it flooded some of the floating gardens. So it was that the nearby cities and towns were asked to come help build [a] dike. . . .

"However, all of their efforts were useless; the more they tried to stop the water the more damage it caused. It began to enter the homes of many inhabitants who abandoned their houses and their city. . . . The cornfields with their tender cornstalks were lost, and so were the chilli, tomato, amaranth, and flower plantations."[21] To save Mexico City, Ahuitzotl ordered the destruction of the pipes and the dam.

During Ahuitzotl's reign the population of Tenochtitlán and Tlatelolco probably reached 250,000. By current estimates the population of Mexico City is over 8 million, the metropolitan area more than 13 million, and the market area somewhere between 20 and 29 million. The great lakes (north to south) of Zumpango, San Cristóbal, Texcoco, and Chalco have been filled in, dried up, disappeared. Only a part of the lake that supported the floating gardens of Xochimilco remains. The water supply of pre-Hispanic Mexico (from the current U.S. border south to Guatemala, but not including the territory ceded to the United States in 1848), which played a vital role in the ability of a civilization to develop and prosper, cannot meet the needs of 100 million Mexicans. And as the population increases, the water problem will only grow worse. Everything depends on water: agriculture, sanitation, health, the very ground the capital stands on, life itself.

Water and the rain that brings it remain so important in Mexico that virtually every citizen knows the name of Tlaloc, the Aztec god of rain, and more than a few can talk about Chalchiuhtlicue (Lady of the Jade Skirt), the goddess of water. Tlaloc means most in the countryside, although people in the capital take note of him when the city floods after a rainstorm. Chalchi-

[21]From *The History of the Indies of New Spain*, translation by Doris Heyden and Fernando Horcasitas (New York: Orion Press, 1964).

uhtlicue controls the great aquifer under Mexico City. No one quite knows the size of the aquifer, how much water it contains, how long it will last, how much untreated sewage is working its way down through the soil to contaminate it.[22] Only the sinking of the city can be accurately measured. Downtown Mexico City has sunk twenty-five feet during the last hundred years, but since the wells around the center of the city were capped, the rate of fall has diminished to a few centimeters a year. The great cathedral, the Bellas Artes concert hall, and other grand buildings have survived.

The problem of subsidence (the technical term for the sinking caused by drainage of the water table) is more serious now in areas outside the center of the city; in Chalco, the dry lake bed, well below the level of the ground around it, floods every year, and the waste from outhouses floats free in the street. Mexico City too suffers from leaking sewer pipes and raw sewage that leaches into the ground in various parts of the city and the surrounding area. As the bacteria find their way into the aquifer, the water supply, although disinfected by the city, becomes unhealthy. According to INEGI, 585 of every 100,000 people in Mexico died of infectious intestinal disease in 1995. Dr. Andrea Navarrete, who practices in one of the hospitals in the Federal District run by Mexico's social security system, said that while illness caused by parasites is now rare in the capital, bacterial infections remain all too common.

Sewer pipes and water pipes run side by side in Mexico City, and both systems leak. The city loses more than a third of its water through leakage, water meters have still not been installed in many areas, some parts of the city have an irregular water supply, while others have no water at all except what they can get from public taps, and the cost of electricity used to pump water keeps the entire system deep in the red. Fixing the water system in an ancient city is a Herculean task, yet successive city governments have each made a little progress. If population growth and water use stabilize, the government should be able to stabilize the system, with end users paying more and more of the cost. A considerable amount of used water is being recycled for industrial use, the water department continues to install meters, and repairs to the ancient pipes go on apace. But the system remains fragile, and there is no shortage of ecologists, hydrologists, geolo-

---

[22]Estimates have a fairly wide range, perhaps 1,150 billion cubic feet, which would last two hundred years at the current rate of use, although contamination is a serious problem.

gists, and journalists predicting doom. Another earthquake, like the one in 1985, or a sudden release of great amounts of contaminants into the aquifer could be catastrophic.

The water problem in northern Mexico raises a different issue. There will never be enough water in northern Mexico to supply the farms and orchards that have sprung up in the border states from Chihuahua to the Gulf. In 1944 the United States and Mexico made an agreement about water for farms in south Texas and northern Mexico. Mexico would supply 350,000 acre feet[23] a year from the Río Conchos basin to southeast Texas farmers, and the United States would supply a little more than four times that amount from the Colorado River to Mexican farmers. Over the years Mexico has consistently provided less than the amount it owes the United States under the agreement. In 2002 the Mexican water debt was 1.5 million acre feet (502 billion gallons), and it had turned into a serious issue between the two countries. At one time Presidents Bush and Fox were to meet to discuss the water debt, among other issues, but the United States executed a Mexican citizen, and Fox canceled his trip to Texas because of Mexico's opposition to capital punishment.

Texas farmers, suffering from drought, claimed the Mexicans were wasting water, taking more than their allotments. The United States agreed to loan money to Mexico to repair its agricultural infrastructure to reduce the waste of millions of gallons of water in return for a Mexican down payment on the water debt. Texas farmers and legislators contended that Mexico had been rewarded for failing to comply with the agreement. "Why did the money go to Mexico instead of U.S. farmers?" they asked.

Perhaps the United States had good reason for making the gift of a loan to Mexican farmers. Texas farmers needed the water, the Mexicans were claiming they could not pay the debt, and the United States was about to deliver another blow to Mexican agriculture. On January 1, 2003, the North American Free Trade Agreement (NAFTA) ended duties on pork, poultry, beef, dairy products, wheat, rice, barley, and potatoes, all of which receive heavy U.S. government subsidy either directly or indirectly. The United States was already undercutting the prices Mexican farmers needed to make a profit on corn. The flight from the farms to the cities and across the border would be redoubled. The number of emigrants as well as the population of Mexico City would grow a little faster, there would be more need for

[23]An acre foot is the amount it takes to cover one acre with one foot of water, 325,851 gallons.

water, and the government would have to patch the pipes and pay for the electricity to pump the water. Water could not be separated from Mexico's other problems: population, food supply, and, increasingly, relations with the United States.

The Fox administration, driven by necessity, had spent its first year and a half buttering up the Bush administration, especially the president, who spoke a few words of Spanish and had what his father called "little brown ones" in the family.[24] Fox expected Bush to help get legal status for millions of Mexicans in the United States who had no documents. But after the attack on the World Trade Center, Bush lost interest in Mexican problems. He wanted the water debt paid so his fellow Texans could irrigate their crops, and every time he went to an international meeting where Fox was present, Bush seemed to have no interest but Iraq.

Fox had been severely criticized in Mexico for being too close to the Americans, but when Mexico became a member of the UN Security Council, Fox opposed the U.S. resolution on Iraq, and no matter how Bush pressured him, Fox held his ground. Even after the United States invaded Iraq, Vicente Fox refused to join what Bush called the coalition of the willing. Mexico was unwilling, even though it was certain that Bush would punish it for its pacifism. And he did; he even canceled the Cinco de Mayo celebration he had instituted in the White House, an act some people found petty.

On his own side of the border Fox had massive political problems, among them legislative stalemate and open rebellion against his budget and policies by the governors of the thirty-two Mexican states.[25] And underlying all the problems, the unrelenting pressure to find a million new jobs a year in an economy that had not shown really healthy growth for most of the last twenty years.

AMERICA FIRST

For the last 250 years Mexico has been economically, and some would say politically, in the hands of the United States, except for Maximilian's brief tenure. The only aggressive Mexican response to American hegemony came

[24]The first President Bush was referring to the children of his son Jeb and his Mexican wife.
[25]Mexicans commonly speak of 32 states, including the Federal District in the number, although it is not technically a state.

during the brief social revolution led by Lázaro Cárdenas, starting in 1934, when he took back Mexico's petroleum reserves from Standard Oil. Recent Mexican governments—and "government" meant "the presidency" until 2000, when the PAN won the presidency but not the Congress—have been utterly dominated by the United States. Mexican nationalists from all the major political parties speak of the situation in dire terms. They use the phrase "maquiladora nation" to describe the economy, but in their anger they see something worse: Mexico used, a form of servitude. Shoes are shipped from New York City to the Yucatán to be resoled. False teeth go by air to poorly paid craftsmen in Mexican plants and then back to the United States and into American mouths. Some Mexicans think the maquiladora is a more dignified business than catering to the American foot and mouth.

On the day Salinas de Gotari signed NAFTA, Mexico officially relinquished control of its own destiny. Following the signing of NAFTA, Salinas saw his troubles mount. Mexico, like many developing countries since then, found its currency under attack. At three pesos to the dollar, Mexico had to spend its dollar reserves to protect its currency. To increase the reserves, Mexico had to pay higher interest rates. It offered *tesobonos* (dollar-denominated bonds, known as Brady Bonds) to attract foreign capital, and the Wall Street banks took all they could get. After all, in the 1980s, Walter Wriston, head of what was then known as Citicorp, in his role as the genius of global capitalism, had said, "No country ever went bankrupt."

As the bankers attacked the peso, demanding higher and higher interest rates to hold peso-denominated money, Mexico teetered on the edge of what Wriston said could never happen. Robert Rubin, U.S. secretary of the treasury, President Clinton, and Alan Greenspan, chairman of the Federal Reserve, determined to protect the U.S. banks. Over the objections of Americans and Mexicans, they arranged a bailout of the Mexican system, heading a consortium of banks that guaranteed Mexico almost fifty billion dollars. It could not have been a more profitable arrangement for the banks and a worse arrangement for Mexico. To negotiate NAFTA, which Salinas claimed was his idea—dreamed up one night during a conference of international financiers and government leaders in Davos, Switzerland—he had had to give up some of Mexico's sovereign right to manage its own economy. To negotiate the fifty-billion-dollar loan, he had to give up much more.[26]

---

[26] Jorge Padilla Olvera went to Washington to lobby against the bailout (see Book One, Chapter 9).

Washington took over management of the Mexican economy and insisted that Salinas privatize the banks, lower taxes on corporations, hold down wages, use every weapon the PRI had at its disposal to impose austerity on Mexico. Since it was a corporatist party, made up of sectors, including unions, rather than individuals, Salinas was able to do as Washington demanded.

Ernesto Zedillo took office in 1994, in a time of terrible doubt in Mexico. He devalued the peso and then bore the burden of the results of the U.S. loan of fifty billion dollars to Mexico. The terms of the loan were so strict and forced Mexico into such deep austerity to meet the payments (it was actually repaid ahead of schedule) that the economy cracked. Mexico had to allow foreign institutions to buy into its banks. The external debt, the bête noire of developing countries, continued to eat into the wealth generated by the Mexican economy. Leftist economists, often joined by their competitors on the center and the right, did not propose to default on the external debt, but they asked forgiveness of some of the interest, at least. The interest on the external debt had grown to the point of devouring Mexico's oil revenue.

And Zedillo held on more tightly to the United States than ever before. Mexico belonged to Wall Street. U.S. banks, in part through the International Monetary Fund, were able to dictate interest rates in Mexico, which could not afford another devaluation. The standard of living rose slightly after Washington took over management of the Mexican economy, but the privatizations had skewed the Mexico distribution of wealth just as the Clinton presidency had done in the United States (the United States had the largest income gap of the industrialized nations). The rich became wealthy beyond their most avaricious dreams, the middle class never got back to the standard of living it enjoyed in 1980, and the poor suffered. The problem of income distribution in Mexico had first been raised in 1960 but had been shrugged off as something that would be solved by development. In fact, the income gap exceeded the worst predictions; in 1960 no one could imagine the ravages of privatization.

As Mexicans went to the polls in 2000 and 2003, a country still lost in the traps of history could continue looking backward and still not see what had gone wrong. The new conquistadores had come from Wall Street and Washington; the new culture was mass culture; the new religion was consumerism; the viceroys were the heads of the drug cartels; foreign investors were as voracious as France had been when it sent Maximilian to rule; and the United States was as deep into Mexican politics and economics as it had been when U.S. Ambassador Henry Lane Wilson participated in the over-throw of President Francisco Madero's government, which began the murderous civil wars of 1910–1920. Spain had taken control of Mexico's economy in 1521, and in the twenty-first century Mexico had still not regained its economic sovereignty.

34.

Alternations

Sophrosyne [temperance] was not a quality peculiar to any one party within the state, but the harmony of the whole, which made the city [Athens] a cosmos and gave it self-mastery. . . .
—JEAN-PIERRE VERNANT, *The Origins of Greek Thought*

. . . in our state, if anywhere, the governors and the governed will share the same conviction on the question who ought to rule.
—PLATO, *The Republic*, IV, 431

Sovereignty has no heritage in Mexico. The Aztecs conquered the Valley of Mexico and much of the surrounding world. Then came the Spaniards. Mexican Independence, achieved in 1821, lasted only a few years. In 1848 half the new Republic of Mexico was lost, and not long afterward Napoleon installed Maximilian as emperor of what was left. Mexico regained its sovereignty with the defeat of the French, but soon afterward Porfirio Díaz began selling off the restored Republic to foreign investors. After the United States allowed the Mexicans to finally get rid of Díaz, it played a prominent role in the overthrow of Madero and the outcome of the civil wars that followed. Tata Lázaro brought Mexico close to sovereignty in the 1930s, but the United States was too close and too powerful, and Mexico was soon willing to settle for the illusion of Independence. Mexico supplied materials for the U.S. war effort, settling into an economic relationship in which the United States was so dominant it could dictate the terms of sale of both imports and exports. Within a few years after the end of World War II, Mexican nationalists clamored for independence from the United States.

It was unlikely. Mexico had no important markets to the south, and it was separated from Europe and Asia by vast oceans. The gringos could do what they would with Mexico, and they did. When Samuel Ramos wrote of the Mexican "inferiority complex," his idea was driven in no small part by U.S.-Mexican relations. Mexican slang referred to the dollar as *oro* (gold) and the peso as *plata* (silver). In 1982, through the IMF, the United States

591

took control of the Mexican economy, extending its control through NAFTA and the terms of the fifty-billion-dollar bailout.

Once the Colombian drug cartels began using Mexico to run cocaine and heroin into their major market, Mexico submitted openly to the United States stationing agents of the FBI and the Drug Enforcement Agency (DEA) in various parts of the country. The CIA and the military Counter Intelligence Corps (CIC) had been operating in Mexico for many years. When the left became interested in the Zapatistas, U.S. supporters flooded into Mexico, expecting to be able to operate with impunity. They treated Mexico as if it were a colony and they were the colonists.

At the beginning of the new millennium hardly anyone in the United States, right or left, considered Mexico other than a corrupt, poor, and poorly managed U.S. possession with magnificent beaches, a few billionaires, and dangerous lettuce. The theory behind the United States' assuming management of Mexico's economy and politics was that open markets and fiscal austerity would assure the establishment of democratic institutions. Wall Street, the IMF, the World Bank, and the Mexican neoliberals made one serious error, however. They forgot the origins of democracy. It has always been the case that to be a democracy, a state must first be sovereign.

Democracy in Mexico faces two basic problems: sovereignty and education. Like most postcolonial societies, Mexico has not only a huge income gap but an education gap as well. There is a blossom of well-educated people at the top, a situation that Mexico fosters by spending sixteen times as much per student in college or graduate school as in primary school. The weakness at the beginning, the number of dropouts, and the rate of failure to learn to read and think in an ordered way mean a majority of the people do not have the ability to become fully functional citizens in the original sense of a democracy. Vicente Fox claims education is the backbone of development and promises that 8 percent of Mexico's GDP will go toward education, but other than building a small number of new libraries and classrooms, he announced no plan. Moreover, he expected a significant part of the expenditure to come from private sources, assuring the continuance of a two-tier (public/private) educational system.[1]

---

[1] On November 23, 2002, Fox told the graduating class at Mexico's Naval Academy that he would raise expenditures to 8 percent of GDP, with 1.4 percent to come from other than federal sources.

To judge by Mexico's history of underinvestment in education, those who control the country are apparently pleased to have it so. In other words, Mexican systems are geared toward maintaining a political and economic ruling class of a million, perhaps two million people. This class is defined by its ability to deal easily with the colonizers and in many cases to represent colonial interests.[2] Mexico's foreign secretary at the beginning of the Fox sexenio, Castañeda, said so when he divided Mexico into those who were connected to the United States and those who were not.[3]

The question then arises: How can a colony have an open market? The answer, which Mexico found out during the Salinas sexenio, is that its markets can be open, even though they are open almost exclusively to the colonizer. In Mexico the open market did not produce independence, democracy, or democratic institutions. Like any colony, Mexico cannot engage in full self-rule, and its people cannot be citizens in the fullest sense.

The corporatist state that developed in Mexico further limited the development of democratic institutions. A corporatist state, uniquely suited to dealing with a colonizing power, has a curiously representative form of government, with only three well-defined representatives: union, army, and business. A fourth group has recently become important again in Mexico: the Catholic Church. Like the party during the seven decades of PRI rule, the Church spans the other three groups, but unlike the PRI, it can influence the others but cannot manage them.

In such a state, the second level of the leadership, the heads of the army, unions, and business, negotiate with the leader. No one, other than the representatives of these parts of the corporate state, has the power to negotiate. The rest of the society is, for all practical purposes, mute. If Salinas de Gotari

---

[2] As in the United States, an unreflective class can be easily manipulated into voting against its own interests. In Mexico, it leads the populace, which votes in much greater numbers than in the United States, to vote for the interests of the colonizers and their beneficiaries in the plutocracy.

[3] *Mexican Shock.* Castañeda had a successful career as an author, a columnist for *Newsweek,* and a professor at New York University before accepting the post of secretary of state. Since then he has been pelted with eggs by students and attacked by *La Voz de Aztlán* as a Zionist in a stream of anti-Semitic rants on the Internet. Castañeda is the son of a Jewish woman of Russian descent. The anti-Semitic propaganda began after Castañeda, who had written a book about Cuban revolutionary hero Che Guevara, chilled relations with Cuba while he was secretary of state.

wanted to negotiate a trade agreement, he had only to discuss it with the army, the heads of two unions, and the representatives of the business community. His government, unlike that of Lázaro Cárdenas, was not obstreperous in the eyes of the colonizer. Salinas was an American darling, a heroic figure in the press, the cover face on newsmagazines; his government provided what the United States wanted when the United States wanted it, and at a price that pleased the U.S. economy.

The two countries have lived in this uncomfortable symbiosis for over 125 years, the United States often as a safety valve for the Mexican population problem, and Mexico as a relief for U.S. economic problems, from raw materials to the labor supply. Were Mexico to become a truly independent country, able to develop democratic institutions and to protect them from foreign interference, it might well choose not to serve U.S. economic or political interests. Unlikely as it seems, the colonial relationship could be terminated.

If the word "colonial" seems too harsh, what word could be substituted for a country that does almost 90 percent of its trade with one other country?[4] Perhaps it would be more accurate to describe U.S. relations with Mexico as something closer to that of the Aztecs (Mexica) and the Tlaxcalans, who provided labor, foodstuffs, and sacrificial victims to the Aztecs, yet maintained some control over their internal situation. Tlaxcala fit the definition of a vassal state, and "vassalage" might serve better to name the relation of Mexico to the United States. The *Wall Street Journal* gave its view of the vassal state of Mexico on October 30, 2002, when it shook its finger at President Fox's refusal to support the U.S. position on a war with Iraq; the *Journal* warned that Mexico would pay for its actions. A *New York Times* editorial spoke of the poisoning of the friendship of Fox and Bush. A week later, after Mexico had joined in a unanimous vote on a U.S. resolution offering the Iraqis disarmament or war, the *New York Times* (November 9, 2002) headlined the story MEXICO'S INFLUENCE IN SECURITY COUNCIL DECISION MAY HELP ITS TIES WITH U.S. Fox had shown his people that he was not merely a pawn of the United States, but then he acceded to American wishes. A few days later, in London, he told the press that Mexico did not have to fol-

---

[4]An argument has been made in some academic circles that Mexico was never a colony because of the intermarriage (mestizaje) of invaders and natives. The absurdity of the argument has not deterred its proponents.

low the advice of the IMF or of U.S. Federal Reserve Chairman Alan Greenspan, who had praised Mexico for behaving in ways that Adam Smith, the eighteenth-century British economist, would have deemed wise. Fox said he would take no advice on having to lower Mexico's external debt but soon began a serious effort to do exactly as he was told.

Then Fox changed his mind about supporting the U.S. position on Iraq, condemning the idea of a rush to war, insisting on continued inspections by the UN to determine whether or not Iraq had weapons of mass destruction. For his future relations with George W. Bush the Mexican position would most likely prove catatastrophic. Bush, who is a born again Christian, is not noted for turning the other cheek.

Despite Fox's defense of Mexican ideals, Independence was not secure for Mexico; it was at best a dance, a waltz of a giant and its geographical mate. Vassalage, concubinage, colonialism—by whatever name, a country that cannot determine its own destiny does not inspire its people to think they can share with those who govern them "the same conviction on the question who ought to rule." The question of democracy in Mexico had to be put off for generations because the country could not achieve real independence. Since the 1980s, however, with the coming of age of the post-Tlatelolco '68 generation, a quest for democracy has been brewing in Mexico. Believing that no other situation can be stable over a long period, the U.S. government attempted through various forms of economic coercion (IMF), public influence, and funding to move Mexico in that direction, beginning with open markets and an end to the party-state system. What U.S. policy makers have not been able to understand is that sovereignty is the necessary precursor of democracy and that by definition, democracy cannot be imposed.

From the U.S. point of view, stability in Mexico occupies a key place in foreign relations. Mexico had a serious flirtation with communism in the 1930s, and it rubbed shoulders with fascism during the same period. Since the early 1950s radical revolutionary groups have been operating in Mexico, although their numbers have never been large and they cannot seem to coordinate their activities beyond importing a few weapons (the Zapatistas, like Fidel Castro's band of Cuban exiles in Mexico in the mid-1950s, train with wooden guns). But when the Zapatistas took San Cristóbal de las Casas briefly in 1994, they alerted the CIA and other U.S. agencies to the danger of a rebellion like the Sandinista movement in Nicaragua.

Since U.S. foreign policy holds that the preventive medicines to stop the spread of radical left politics in any country are market capitalism and a democratic movement led by people sympathetic to U.S. interests, the Mexican democracy movement could find no more willing advocate. U.S. foreign policy turned toward this new road to stability. The PRI had maintained the desired stability for seven decades, and the United States made no effort to change the situation. Recent PRI leaders had been educated in the United States (Harvard, Northwestern, Yale, and so on), and they had accepted the idea of economic management by U.S. banks. They had even permitted a U.S. bank (Citigroup) to buy into what had been the most powerful bank in Mexico. The trouble with the PRI (viewed from Washington) lay in its connection to the drug cartels, the blame it had accrued through the disgrace of the Salinas presidency, and the failure of the Zedillo administration to resolve any of the country's major problems. And then there were the Zapatistas. With stability on its southern flank no longer a given, the United States had to move: Mexico had to become a democratic society.

WASHINGTON'S DARLING

But the problem of the precursor remained. U.S. foreign policy had to figure out a way to have the stability of democracy without the potential problems of Independence. When Carlos Salinas de Gotari was chosen by outgoing President Miguel de la Madrid to be the PRI candidate in 1987, Washington and Wall Street believed they had found the answer in one young man. He held a degree in economics from the left-leaning department headed by Ifigenia Martínez at the UNAM, but he had gone on to earn an M.A. in public administration and a Ph.D. in political economy and government at Harvard. From Washington the situation looked good. De la Madrid, who had pointed the finger (dedazo) at Salinas, had conceded to IMF policies on open markets, and Salinas was sure to continue to accept the demands of the IMF, perhaps to go beyond them in pursuit of free trade. He had been in finance for most of his career, and he was well versed in PRI thinking, having been part of the party's leadership training institute. When elected (the PRI nomination depended on the dedazo, and the nomination assured election), he would be the youngest president since Tata Lázaro took office in 1934 and the most thoroughly versed in free market economics.

Salinas the candidate was not a powerful, prepossessing figure. He had a fringe of black hair around a shiny pate and a slightly Chaplinesque mustache. With a towel over his arm, he could have passed for a waiter in a second-rate restaurant in Madrid. But not in Mexico; he was too fair, a criollo. There was also something a bit haughty about him, in the way he carried his small frame, in the ease of his laughter. His father, a man known more for rectitude than brilliance, had been a member of the López Portillo cabinet, a member of Congress, and ambassador to the Soviet Union. As many people who knew the family now suggest, the father might have done better to have paid less attention to his career and devoted a little more time to instilling that sense of rectitude in his children, for something went awry between the generations. The amateur psychologists say Carlos Salinas's behavior was a reaction to his strict socialist father. It is certainly possible, but amateur psychologists have a spotty record.

The election did not go easily or well for Salinas. During the de la Madrid sexenio a split had occurred in the PRI. On one side, most of the inner circle of the PRI was criollo, for free markets, and corrupt. On the other side were the reformers: mostly mestizo, in favor of a strong state, and under the moral leadership of Tata Lázaro's son, Cuauhtémoc, a decent man who had been an undistinguished governor of the state of Michoacán. At a dinner in the home of Ifigenia Martínez, the leaders of the dissident movement within the PRI decided reform of the PRI was impossible, they could no longer stay in the party. That evening, sitting around the long black Scandinavian-style table in Martínez's house of high ceilings and colonial timbers, with its paintings and art objects collected from around the world and its huge two-story library in a separate building at the back of the garden, the left made its decision: It formed the Democratic Front, precursor to the PRD. It was agreed that no one who attended the dinner, neither Muñoz Ledo nor Cárdenas nor any of the others, would accept the new party's nomination for president.[5]

Nonetheless, Cárdenas accepted the nomination, apparently without a qualm. It was perhaps a harbinger of the factionalism that would weaken the center-left party. Yet there was more than nascent factionalism or personal ambition involved. The group had a practical side. If anyone in Mexico could defeat the PRI, it was the son of Tata Lázaro. In the rural areas of Mexico, where Tata Lázaro had achieved mythical status, the PRI was strongest. Tata

---

[5]See the brief oral history of Ifigenia Martínez in the Appendix for more details on the split and the reasons behind it.

had made it that way. He had defined the modern PRI and made it invincible. Mexico was about to witness a remarkable contest between myth and power, memory and money. Salinas and Cárdenas campaigned hard. Salinas had all the machinery of a party that had been in power for generations.

Who is Salinas? the voters asked.

The PRI.

No, not the PRI. Cárdenas is the PRI. Tata Lázaro founded the PRI.[6]

Then who is Salinas if not the candidate of the PRI?

Who knows?

And for whom will you vote?

For the PRI.

The election could not have been more confusing. Cárdenas won, but how many of the people who voted for him thought they had voted for the PRI is impossible to determine. Surely, there were enough such votes to have given the election to the PRI. But people, not parties, run for office. Salinas and the PRI apparatus resolved the problem of intent. They stole the election.

Afterward many people urged Cárdenas to contest the vote, to call for the people to take over the government. Had the fraud taken place in an earlier time, he would surely have "declared," but the time for such uprisings seemed to Cárdenas to be over. A decade later he told interviewer James R. Fortson, "In 1988—in my personal view—the conditions did not exist that would have enabled us to reverse the election."[7] He accepted the results and vowed to run again. And he ran and lost in 1994. He won the contest for mayor of Mexico City in 1997, but in the 2000 presidential election, he got only 16 percent of the vote. His career was over. The moral leadership of the PRD went into retirement; the center was gone: Cárdenas, Muñoz Ledo, Ifigenia Martínez. It became a collection of factions, with the new mayor of Mexico City, Andrés Manuel López Obrador, and the head of the party, the former Maoist, Rosario Robles, contending for power. And in the middle of the fray, Cárdenas again, apparently unable to accept a series of defeats, to remain in retirement, to write the book or books of rationalized history expected of old politicians. In Michoacán, however, another Cárdenas, the son of Cuauhtémoc, campaigned for governor, and won.

---

[6]The party was then called the PRN, the National Revolutionary Party, but it was the PRI by an earlier name.

[7]*Cuauhtémoc Cárdenas: Un Perfil Humano* (Mexico D.F.: Grijalbo, 1997).

Salinas did not leave such a legacy. He came into office with a plan to open the economy, and he did. At the same time, he made some small but important moves toward establishing a more democratic government. He claimed he was trying to break up what he called the political-economic mafias, while he sold off Mexico's lifeblood to them at bargain prices in return for a nice cut. He did get rid of the head of the corrupt oil workers' union, although he was replaced with another corrupt PRIista. There was one curious step forward, however: The Federal Election Institute (IFE) was a Salinas creation.

The PRI lost a gubernatorial election in 1989, when the PAN took Baja California Norte, but in 1991 the PRI came back to its former prominence, winning more than 61 percent of the vote in the midterm elections. The PAN had a little less than 18 percent, and the PRD only a little over 8 percent. Moreover, the election was probably the freest in Mexican history.

All the while that he was weakening the traditional PRI stranglehold on the legislature, without diminishing in any way the enormous power of the executive, Salinas ran a vast public relations campaign under the slogan "Solidarity." He was giving the country away to the very rich, partly by destroying the last vestiges of the ejido system of communal farms, and at the same time promoting the solidarity of the great majority under the PRI/Salinas banner, selling his politics to the very people he wounded. His presidency could have been invented by Cantinflas or Chaplin: double-talk out of the mouth of the Great Dictator. And it seemed not to matter to Salinas, because the Mexican Constitution prohibited reelection. Unless the solidarity campaign was a Salinas move toward something more ominous. As the end of his sexenio came near and he refused to devalue the peso even though Mexico dollar reserves had disappeared, there were rumors that Salinas planned to put off the election, that he had made certain deals with his *socios* (pals, partners) in the business world, the men with the real money and power in Mexico. The Mexicans who knew him well, those on the inside of government, from the Perredistas (PRD) to Alejandro Carrillo Castro of the PRI, wondered aloud if Salinas intended to be reelected. Juárez had done it. Porfirio Díaz had held the office for more than three decades. Salinas was younger than either Juárez or Díaz. He did not have to succeed himself immediately; he could hand the term over to an underling, lie in wait for one, perhaps two terms, then come back. He had time and billions of dollars. Solidarity! The presidency again. Why not?

What went through the mind of the young president is impossible to know. Did he care about either economic or political democracy? From the vantage of a decade the question remains moot. What really interested him (*and still interests him*) was power and the money that went with it. In retrospect, his actions were those of a man confused and maddened by the power of the presidency. Under his administration Mexico moved farther from Independence, away from self-rule, yet he wanted the world to see him as a president who believed he could lead the country to democracy. His plan was simple. He had only to pretend to follow orders from the north, hoodwink the gringos, and everything would fall into place: money, power, and a curious kind of democracy, one that operated under the tutelage of the leader.

People in Mexico made jokes, comparing his policies to perestroika, the Soviet economic policy.[8] *Salinastroika* they called it. And Mexico's dollar reserves sank. Salinas, in his frenzy to accumulate money and affect posterity, perhaps to become the first Mexican president since Porfirio Díaz to serve more than one term, had attempted to reverse the stages of democracy so that economic democracy preceded political democracy, which in turn came before Independence. He had misread the order of history, but knowing history would not have helped with his next problem. His brother's arrest, conviction, and imprisonment for his involvement in the murder of José Francisco Ruiz Massieu cast a shadow over Salinas.

The Raúl Salinas story in detail would require another book. The key in terms of his brother, Carlos, is that Raúl was convicted of the murder of his former brother-in-law, José Francisco Ruiz Massieu, and on January 1, 1999, was sentenced to fifty years in prison for the murder and various other crimes.

On September 28, 1994, Ruiz Massieu, then the secretary-general of the PRI, left a meeting, walked to his car, and was shot to death with a machine gun. Ruiz Massieu had been married to Adriana Salinas, the sister of Raúl and Carlos. They were divorced in 1979. Raúl Salinas de Gotari then, or perhaps before then, became Mexico's most outrageous playboy. There is a famous photograph of him sitting on a sailboat with his partly clothed, inelegant, but nonetheless gorgeous girlfriend astride him.

[8]In 1985 Mikhail Gorbachev inaugurated policies to revamp the Soviet Union: "Perestroika" meant economic liberalization (literally restructuring), an alternative to socialist policies, and "glasnost" meant political liberalization, an end to censorship, more democratic institutions.

As the court cases made public over the years between his arrest for murder in 1995 and the sentencing in 1999, Raúl Salinas was involved in everything from money laundering to the drug business. He did not kill Ruiz Massieu himself, but was convicted of ordering the killing. Why he did it, how his brother, the president, was involved, if the president was involved lead only to speculation. The court and the world did not speculate, however. The disgrace of the president was quick and thorough. But Carlos Salinas, who fled the country, was not convicted of a crime. Within a few years he began making brief visits, then longer visits. Jorge Castañeda, former secretary of state, had met Salinas in Brussels. Rumor had it that they engaged in secret negotiations. Castañeda assured me that the rumors were not true. He said that he knew Salinas from having interviewed all five living former presidents for his book *Perpetuating Power*[9] and that President Fox had instructed him to consult with the former presidents on matters of foreign policy. When I asked if he agreed that Salinas was again the manipulator of political power in Mexico, he said Salinas wanted "to give that appearance, but it was all smoke and mirrors." It looked different immediately after the 2003 elections, when photographs of Carlos Salinas casting his vote appeared in the newspapers and on television.

The attention paid to him in the press, and the rumors he was able to generate made it clear to everyone in Mexican politics that Salinas was back. Of that there could be no doubt. Had Castañeda engineered a deal with the PAN? Was Salinas about to become the gray eminence of the PRI? Mexican government, which is presidentialist, with the president holding enormous constitutional power during his term in office, had come to a complete standstill. Congress and President Fox had been at loggerheads since the day he took office at the end of 2000. Would Salinas become the catalyst of a working relationship between the PAN, the PRI, and the president? López Obrador, the mayor of Mexico City, spoke for the PRD and perhaps much of Mexico. In López Obrador's view, the news could not have been worse.

TROTSKY'S INTERNET

On January 1, 1994, just as NAFTA took effect, the Zapatistas took San Cristóbal, and initiated the first postmodern Revolution. For a moment it

[9]New York: New Press, 2000.

looked as if the Mexican government might fall. And if not the government, the way it governed. There had never been anything quite like Subcomandante Marcos in Mexico or anywhere else. Marcos planned a world revolution from his place in the jungle: Trotsky on the Internet. Not long after Marcos began distributing his writings on the Internet, Carlos Fuentes described him as the (literary and political) son of Carlos Monsiváis, which was high praise for the wit, style, intellect, and politics of the masked man from the jungle. That was in the beginning, before Monsiváis took his first critical look at Marcos seven years later.

Marcos, whose real name is apparently Rafael Sebastián Guillén Vicente, adopted tactics and ideas from whatever appealed to him: Faulkner, Marx, Sendero Luminoso (Shining Path guerrilla movement), García Márquez. His immediate constituency was indigenous, but his goals from the outset were secular. His references were exclusively Western. In 1984 he wrote to his parents, telling them he had gone to live with the Tzeltales and Tzotziles (Maya) in the jungle. Until then he had been a student at the UNAM and a professor at the Autonomous Metropolitan University (UAM). His scholarship had earned him a medal given by President López Portillo. He studied philosophy, sociology, and aesthetics, and his heroes, strangely enough, included Mario Vargas Llosa, the novelist and center-right candidate for president in Peru. If he had any interest then or now in indigenous language, art, or literature, it does not appear in any of his many biographies, nor are there important references to indigenous ideas in his writings.

An important distinction must be drawn between the Zapatista uprising in Chiapas and the earlier rebellions, among them, the Tzeltales (1712), the Chamula War of St. Rose of 1868, and Pajarito's War of 1910. Indigenous people led these rebellions, which most often intended to expel the *ladinos* (whites) from their world.[10] The Zapatista rebellion had the son of a furniture store owner from Tampico at its heart. It demanded a better material life for the indigenous people of Chiapas and the rest of Mexico, but it did not have an indigenous worldview.

Without Marcos, who immediately captured the attention of the outside world with his mask, his pipe, his wit, erudition, and interest in connecting the Chiapas uprising to other political questions in Mexico and the world, things would have taken a different turn in Chiapas. There is no reason to

---

[10]Gary Gossen has recorded and translated much of the oral history of these movements.

think the Mexican government would not have handled the Zapatistas the way it did other armed indigenous insurrections. The indios would have been killed, and that would have been the end of it. Killing Marcos was another matter.

Indeed, Salinas sent the army into Chiapas. For two weeks they fought. Hundreds, including civilians, were killed. At least sixty thousand people, perhaps more, were displaced. Then Salinas changed his mind. He realized that this rebellion was different. Marcos was not isolated, unknown, another *guerrillero* whose death would go unnoticed by the world. Marcos had drawn a shield of publicity around himself and the Zapatistas. To strengthen the shield, he looked to Bishop Samuel Ruiz, who participated in the first negotiations between the Zapatistas and the government. For all the carping about him by people in the government, the church, and even some on the left, Ruiz was the closest thing to Fray Bartolomé de las Casas since the "defender of the Indians" had been bishop of Chiapas in the sixteenth century. With worldwide attention and Bishop Ruiz to protect him, Marcos was bulletproof. So were the Zapatistas.

The army moved into Chiapas in strength, but the Zapatistas had held San Cristóbal only long enough to make a point, then disappeared. The EZLN had not intended to confront the army. Nor did the Zapatistas commence a series of guerrilla attacks. This was a new kind of war, a different revolution. The words came out of the ether and appeared on computer screens around the world. What could an army do? Who could shoot the Internet? The Zapatista National Liberation Army had a few guns, many masks, and an endless supply of words. Marcos had occupied San Cristóbal only briefly, but the office of moral authority was his for the duration.

While Marcos remained in contact with Mexico and the world, Salinas, who still had almost a year left in his presidency, could do no more than shake his fist. Mexican military planes flew over the jungle, a military operation was mounted against Marcos and his Zapatistas, but Salinas quickly abandoned the idea of one devastating large-scale attack. Instead, paramilitary groups were formed and apparently instructed by . . . the government? The PRI? . . . to attack and kill Zapatista sympathizers. The worst of the paramilitary killings happened later, under Zedillo, and the killings continue, but sporadically now, in small numbers so that no one notices. A man is killed in the mountains; a husband and wife are murdered in the jungle; someone disappears, and the body is found weeks or months later. The paramilitary group called Paz y Justicia (Peace and Justice) usually gets blamed for the killings, but no believes the work begins with them.

As his sexenio neared the end, Salinas had trouble from every side, economics, politics, and family, all this while completing the theft of hundreds of millions, perhaps billions of dollars from Mexico. And then he chose Colosio, pointed the finger at him, the far left of the PRI, the true reformer, only to have Colosio turn on him and declare Mexico a country living in third world conditions. Then Colosio was dead, assassinated. And Salinas pointed again, this time to Colosio's campaign manager, Ernesto Zedillo.

THE MASKED MAN AND THE CARETAKER

Unlike Salinas, the son of a Mexican diplomat and legislator, Ernesto Zedillo Ponce de León came from the poor end of the middle class. His parents were internal migrants, people who had moved north to Mexicali, Baja California, in search of a better living. Zedillo went through the Mexican public university system and on to Yale and then to the great Mexican bureaucracy. Like Salinas, he had found a home in the system, but unlike Salinas, he did not think economic democracy could precede political democracy, or so he implied. And he lacked Salinas de Gotari's rapacious sense of governance.

It is still too soon for historians to have fully investigated Zedillo's presidential career. There are rumors about Zedillo using the powers of his office to get rich, but so far the only evidence is his membership on the board of directors of Procter & Gamble, ALCOA, and other corporations and his arrangements with Coca-Cola (Fox had severed his relations long before) and Daimler Chrysler. If his economic views were ever in doubt, becoming a columnist for *Forbes* makes them clear. He shares the space with Caspar W. Weinberger, who was a member of the Reagan cabinet, rightist historian Paul Johnson, and Lee Kwan Yew, a Singapore government minister. Zedillo may not be quite so reactionary as the man from Singapore, but he promotes similar views of the benefits of globalization and free trade for developing nations in his writings and at Yale, where he is director of the Center for the Study of Globalization. When the PRI candidate, Francisco Labastida, lost to Vicente Fox in 2000, Zedillo did not seem at all unhappy. Zedillo was quick to announce the results and very pleased by Jimmy Carter's observation that the election was "almost perfect." He did not say a great deal about economic policies, but his involvement with U.S. corporations and his writings since then suggest that a conservative government led by Vicente Fox did not displease him.

Zedillo's presidency could not have had a worse beginning. Salinas had left him a rebellion in Chiapas, a national economy with its monetary reserves used up, low growth, inflation, and the need to devalue the peso. Zedillo began with the devaluation, setting the Mexican standard of living back by at least twenty years. The great economic bubble of the last half of the 1990s helped resuscitate the Mexican economy, but Zedillo could not solve the problem of Chiapas. The bureaucrat from Yale was no match for the postmodern genius from the jungle.

A six-year struggle began on the day Zedillo took office, and when Zedillo handed the presidency over to Fox, he had made no progress in meeting the demands of the Zapatistas or quelling the effect of Marcos on the outside world. Zedillo made a try at defeating him militarily, and by February 1995 the president gave up. He accused Marcos of being manipulated by outside forces, when the opposite was true: Young liberals and leftists around the world were reading the words of Subcomandante Marcos and rethinking their views about peace, justice, human rights, globalization, and indigenous people in Chiapas.[11] A year later, in San Andrés Larrainzar, an accord was reached between a congressional Commission on Concord and Pacification (COCOPA) and the Zapatistas guaranteeing the ten million or more indigenous people in Mexico the rights to pursue their own traditions, a decent standard of living, and management of their own affairs—autonomy.

This last was the sticking point for Zedillo. Mexico's intellectuals tried to draw the distinction between autonomy and sovereignty. Miguel León-Portilla published his explanation to Zedillo in *La Jornada*, but Zedillo either could not or would not understand the distinction. Negotiations between the government and the Zapatistas collapsed. The negotiators left San Andrés Larrainzar, now partly in the hands of the Zapatistas, and nothing more happened except for the killing of Zapatista supporters by the paramilitary groups. From the outside the Zapatistas appeared to be as strong as ever, stronger, but the pressures of guerrilla life in the jungle began to have

---

[11] During the same period the Pine Ridge Reservation in South Dakota had the highest unemployment rate in the United States and often the lowest per capita income. American leftists and human rights activists went to Chiapas instead of Pine Ridge.

some effect. The Zapatistas took up the ancient Greek practice of ostracizing people as a way of maintaining control. It was certainly preferable to killing them, but as the Greeks knew, to be banished from the state was tantamount to death.

Anthropologist Mercedes Olivera reported tensions between women's rights groups, one of which she founded, and the Zapatistas. The Zapatista organization became more hierarchical while at the same time following the old rules of consensus on questions of lesser importance. Meanwhile, the presence of the Mexican Army in and around San Cristóbal brought taverns and whorehouses to serve the soldiers. Some of the people displaced by the uprising and its aftermath came to the city, like the Protestants who had been expelled from San Juan Chamula by the traditionalists; others started little villages of their own in the mountains. The Lacandones, some of them still with long, unkempt hair and knee-length white cotton tunics, fought to save the lowland jungle, where they lived in a mix of intellectual sophistication and Neolithic disregard for material progress. But in the postmodern world of Internet warfare, the cutting of hardwoods in the Lacandón jungle could not be stopped. Displaced people cleared the forest for the sake of cash and corn. They sold the lumber and planted corn in the ashes of the sticks and leaves they could not sell.

On December 22, 1997, in the tiny community of Acteal, the government lost a battle in the war against the Zapatistas. The defeat did not come in postmodern fashion, words in the ether, but with guns and machetes. It was bloody and unfair, as war has always been, and among the dead there were many women and children. Much of the killing took place in a chapel, but that was not all of it. The killers hunted down the few who got out of the tiny Tzotzil village. The victims left evidence of their terror in the mud as they fled. They ran out of their shoes. One here, the other there, left in the mud as they ran. And at the ends of the trails of shoes and pieces of clothing caught in the forest, the searchers who arrived on the next day after the massacre found the last of the forty-five bodies—twenty-one women, fifteen children, nine men.

The dead, all of whom had been displaced from their homes by the war in the jungle, belonged to a Roman Catholic group known as Las Abejas (the Bees). They spoke Tzotzil and perhaps some Spanish, and it is possible that they were Zapatistas, but it is unlikely. Their connection to the struggle in Chiapas was Bishop Samuel Ruiz. They had put their faith in his faith. They were farmers, Catholic, but also Tzotzil. They dreamed of returning to their land, of being farmers again. Perhaps they dreamed they were farming again, preparing the land. According to the Tzotzil photographer and collector of sayings of the elders Maruch Sántiz Gómez, *Mi chijchabaj ta javaechtike, yu'un oy buch'u chcham*: If one dreams of working in the fields, someone is going to die.[12]

The Bees were buried on Christmas Day, and on the ninth day after the massacre a novena that was said for them was widely attended by the journalists and human rights activists, who filled the hotels and motels and hired all the rental cars of nearby San Cristóbal de las Casas. No one who came to the novena was arrested, and no foreigners were expelled for violating Mexican sovereignty by participating in the mass.

If the novena had been the end of the Bees, the government might not have lost the battle, but the dead of Acteal (municipality of Chenalhó) were to engage in a perpetual war on behalf of indigenous rights. On March 22, 1998, four months after the massacre, the anniversary occasioned a gathering of members of the Zapatista Front, the civilian wing of the movement, at the monument to Mexican Independence on the Paseo de la Reforma in Mexico City. The gathering was originally scheduled for noon, but changed to three o'clock to accommodate the schedule of José Saramago, the Portuguese leftist writer who was to deliver an address.

Those who arrived at noon were told to come back at three. No one grumbled. After all, Saramago was coming to speak to them, and he had a schedule. He was not García Márquez, but there were rumors about a Nobel for Saramago. So they went across the paseo to the Zona Rosa to have a beer or to browse in the shops, and those who had brought their families looked for a place out of the sun while their children played on the steps of the monument, hiding around corners, pretending to shoot at each other.

A small crowd assembled. Not so many as had been expected. No reporters, no television cameras came. At three the flower bearers appeared and one by one they laid their sad bouquets on the steps of the monument: forty-five bouquets, one for each of the dead.

There were not so many speakers as had been expected, and none spoke for more than a few minutes. In the beginning, the speeches had to do with the aims of the EZLN, the military wing of the Zapatistas, and the much-

---

[12]*Creencias*, published by CIESAS et al., 1998.

broader Zapatista Front, which had members—that is, supporters—throughout the country. There was some talk of Indian rights, the preservation of Indian culture. No Tzotziles, no Tzeltales, no Tojolobales, no Choles appeared. The grand boulevard had been designed with defensible traffic circles in imitation of the boulevards of Paris. The monument was built for the 1910 celebration of the hundredth anniversary of Hidalgo's grito of Independence. Since then Mexico had become a vast urban center. Two million Indians were said to live in and around the city, an army of the displaced and indigent, but none came to the monument that afternoon. This was an urban memorial.

A woman speaker mourned the Tzotziles with references to their god Quetzalcoatl, as if the Tzotziles would have known his Nahuatl name. Another spoke of the forty-five dead having gone to the *inframundo* (underworld), the Xibalba of the Popol Vuh, but the murdered Tzotziles were all Catholics, who feared the fires of hell. At the close of the speech about the inframundo a car pulled up to the edge of the monument grounds. A man in his mid-seventies stepped out, gray and thin, wearing pale eyeglasses, on the edge of old age. It was Saramago. The crowd applauded. He mounted the steps, walking carefully, as if uncertain about the abilities of his knees. He spoke for several minutes and was gone.

The man who had spoken first took the microphone again. He said, "We make this prayer for our indigenous brothers, that they may hear our words and know our love for them." And then he led the tiny gathering in a prayer, spoken in Spanish for the ears of the dead, who knew only Tzotzil.

From there Saramago went on to Chiapas. He spoke often about the massacre, and what he said was in the press, along with the words of Monsiváis and León-Portilla and Cárdenas and Bellinghausen and García Márquez. Later that year Saramago received the expected Nobel Prize, and afterward he continued to travel to Mexico to speak in defense of the Zapatistas and the Tzotziles. His voice was louder then, but not so loud that Zedillo heard him. The accords reached after the long negotiation at San Andrés Larrainzar were not implemented during the Zedillo presidency, and even though seventy-seven people had been arrested and sentenced for taking part in the massacre, no one among them had possessed the power to order the killings.

Ernesto Zedillo became a pariah in the PRI after the party lost its grip on the presidency in 2000. The loyal PRIistas say now that he gave the presidency away, that he made some sort of deal with Fox or Coca-Cola or the PAN. Those who do not reproach him for the election remember the conditions he accepted for the fifty-billion-dollar U.S. bailout. He stays out of the country most of the time now, teaching in London or at Yale or attending board meetings of U.S. corporations. Zedillo remains a trim, vigorous man, with a bureaucratic face, slightly longer than symmetry would dictate and always marked by the reflected light from his rimless eyeglasses. The eyeglasses hold the key: octagons of impeccably clean, geometrically perfect glass, utterly transparent, yet distorting.

Early in his presidential career he spoke of democracy in Mexico, but no one paid much attention to his promise. It seemed that Mexican presidents had always given their words to democracy, their attention to economics, and their hearts to corruption. Zedillo had gone a step further by giving real power to the Federal Election Institute (IFE), and then he did something undreamed of in the PRI. He instituted primary elections. When asked whom he would point his finger at to indicate his choice for president, Zedillo looked into a mass of television cameras and reporters and held up his thumb. Everyone watching understood the gesture. A Mexican voter's thumb is marked with indelible ink after casting a ballot, making it virtually impossible to vote more than once. The famous dedazo (finger pointing) had now become the *dedo gordo* (thumb) of free elections.

Then Zedillo saw to it that José Woldenberg headed the IFE, and Woldenberg took the job seriously. He invited foreign observers into Mexico for the election, but foreign observers are few, many do not speak Spanish, and the thefts of elections do not take place in the open. Woldenberg knew the history of Mexican elections. He had foreign observers for public relations purposes and young professors and scholars from the universities as the real watchdogs of democracy.

Woldenberg had been given enough money to set up elaborate communications systems in the IFE organization. On election day 2000, the representatives of the IFE were everywhere. In San Antón, a village within a city, a place of steep hills, where the name does not refer to St. Anthony, but to Analco, the ancient Nahua name of the place, the polling places opened late. At 10:00 A.M. the first people in the long line at the side of the federal election table cast their ballots and gave their thumbs to be marked. From there they had to go to the state table, wait in line again, vote, and give the other thumb to be marked with ink of a different color.

As the morning wore on, a sense of carnival came into San Antón: long lines of chattering people; crowds in the street; vendors selling ices and souvenirs. Then a bus pulled up past the polling places and parked twenty feet down the road, its back decorated with a huge PRI sign. The complaints began. The anti-PRIistas went in search of the IFE representative. "It's too close," they said, speaking all at once, a knot of democrats, men and women. One man so old he appeared mummified croaked his complaint about the placard attached to the back of the bus.

The mummified man went to the window of the bus to interrogate the driver, who answered with shrugs and a smile. He offered his excuse to the mummified man, "I'm not a PRIista. I'm a humble person who is being paid to sit in this bus here with my wife." The mummified man was not satisfied. He went to look for the IFE representative, someone who was in charge.

When the IFE representative arrived, a crowd gathered around him. They shouted for his attention but not with anger. He represented fairness, and it was fairness they sought. Luz María Alanis Beltrán was the first to present her case: "Señor, I was in the PRI for many years; then we left the PRI. Now, because I am no longer in the PRI, I lost my vote. Look on the lists! You'll see that my name is not on the lists. Here, here is my voting registration card, but my name is not on the list."

Sebastián López, the official from the IFE, was half the woman's age, tall and slim, and he wore his hair in a crew cut. López was a candidate for an advanced degree at the UNAM, a patient man, young, but imposing by his height and his easy demeanor; he had a psychotherapist's calm. Perhaps it was natural with him or else the IFE had trained him into such calm. It worked to disarm the crowd. They spoke harsh words about the PRI: "kill, cunt hair, bastard, asshole, thief, crook." They complained to the young man from the IFE, but they did not blame him. And when he answered them, it was with the reading of the election laws. For every question, every complaint, he had a reference in the law. He gave the same answers again and again, patiently, without variation, in his quotations from the book of election laws.

Again and again he heard the same complaint: "When I was a member of the PRI, I was on the voting list, but not now. Yes, of course I am a registered voter. My child goes to school. Don't you know the rules? If you don't have a voting card, you can't register your child in school. Why is my name not on the list?"

But the registration had been years ago. Her child was already out of school, married, and with children of her own.

The other complaints, the most serious complaints, were all directed at the poll watcher from the PRI. He stood near the federal polling place and scowled. To teach the voters the lesson of the PRI, he knit his brow, distorting his heavy eyebrows, thick as black caterpillars, and under them, half hidden, his dark brown, almost black, eyes registered the faces in the voting queue. He did not speak, he did not gesture; he gave not a nod, a smile, a wink, nothing; he could have been made of stone, he was as heavy as stone, granite in a gray, zippered jacket and brown trousers, heavy, like the great Aztec monolith Coatlicue, an entire life cycle and the next life too; and the people hated him.

With the IFE standing there on the street, the people could speak, but the PRI could not. The tall, slim student with the crew cut from the UNAM trumped the PRI, and its own president, Ernesto Zedillo, had allowed it to happen. How the PRI would come to hate him!

The people gathered around the young man from the IFE. They wanted him to move the bus with the PRI placard on the back; they demanded the removal of the PRI poll watcher. Christina Sotelo, a woman in blue denim pants and jacket, an accountant dressed like a ranch hand, a handsome woman who lived down the steep hill off the main street, as tall as the man from the PRI and with the same granite weight in the world, watched the election for a while, then walked down the steep street to her house. She was the *topil*, the elected traditional leader of San Antón, a woman not of stone, like the PRIista, but of gravitas. At the end of the steep street of stones and ruts, the door to her house opened on to another world, of leather couches, stereo equipment, finely made modern furnishings, the ambiance of a Mexico City high-rise apartment building, but with windows that looked out on adobe houses and sun-baked streets so steep that everything looked ready to fall into the river somewhere below. *Antón*—in English the town would have been called Riverside. After a thousand years or more, it had chosen a woman to lead it.

She lounged on one of the leather couches, drank a glass of water, and went back up to the street. Then there were two knots of people on the street: those who complained to the young man from IFE and those who complained to the topil of San Antón. She stepped out of the center of the crowd for a moment to say of the PRIista poll watcher: "He menaces us more with his looks than any words. There are people here who are weak, who can be induced to vote for the PRI. To me, the hell with it, they couldn't change my vote with a pistol."

The PRI lost everything that day. It was over, or so it seemed on that July evening in 2000. Labastida, the PRI candidate, chosen through the first open primary, had been defeated by a coalition of parties opposed not merely to the PRI but to the system. It had called itself an Alliance for Change, and it had gathered people into the effort from other parties, other times: Muñoz Ledo, the man who had hoped to be the first president from the PRD, had joined them; so had Jorge Castañeda, a leftist professor. How Vicente Fox would govern would depend on the nature of the alliance he had crafted. Had the PAN won or had it been a different kind of victory, the triumph of anyone but the PRI? Anger or democracy?

ALLÁ EN EL RANCHO GRANDE [13]

In July 2000 the film changed at the Mexican movie palace. For half a century Mexico had been watching a tearjerker in the movies and on television. The screen had been dark, shadowy, populated by men with thin mustaches who wore pinstripe suits and snap-brim fedoras. The exact source of their power was seldom known, but every viewer, from early adolescence on, knew that the men in the dark suits were connected to power. Had they been insiders, they would have called it the system, the interlocking party-state. That these men in dark suits had some relation to the PRI was no secret, but just how, just where, with whom, remained a secret. The stories in these dark melodramas seldom varied much: desperate women misused by powerful men, sometimes saved, often left with an illegitimate child.

In the films and telenovelas the women often came from the countryside to the city, innocents caught in the great Mexican centralization scheme begun by Miguel Alemán. They never understood the origins of power, nor did they question its legitimacy. Men who questioned power ended up badly. And underneath this acquiescence to mysterious power, there was a growing reaction; first from María Félix and then even more brazenly from María Rojo. The undercurrent represented egalitarian notions left over from

[13] "Over There on the Big Ranch," the title of the first popular ranchero or cowboy movie, made in Mexico in 1936.

the civil wars and the Cárdenas revolution, and women carried the burden of it.

The other film, the one that replaced the tearjerker in 2000, was a ranchero movie. The first ranchero movie was made in 1936 and starred the singing cowboy Tito Guízar. *Allá en el Rancho Grande* was a hit movie, the birthplace of a song so widely known in the world that Elvis Presley sang it. After that, ranchero films were ground out at the studios in Churubusco like the long strips of fried and sugar-coated doughnut dough known as *churros*. Ranchero films were as rural as the tearjerkers were urban. The hero was almost always a cowboy with a big sombrero, big mustaches, a *pistola*, a fine horse, and a strong but sweet voice. As the tearjerker belonged to the present, so the ranchero belonged to the past. The power of the ranchero was always clear; he or his father owned the rancho. The *peones* served him gladly, and the women servants had no fear of him. He was just but firm. A thief might be whipped, or a bandit could be shot. There were no courts to worry about. Justice belonged to the Porfiriato's "shot in heat."

Everything in the ranchero referred back to the Porfiriato, the simple clarity of it. There were no crowded cities, no dark corners, no mysterious system. Men were men, all good people were good Catholics, women were virgins on their wedding day, and there was no social mobility. In ranchero films, everything always turned out well. The noble rich and obedient poor remained as they were, in happy symbiosis. Guitar strings never broke; no hero ever died. One film, *The Cemetery of Eagles*, was produced in 1938 to honor the Niños Héroes who had thrown themselves from the walls of Chapultepec Castle in 1847 rather than surrender to the gringos. But the movie was a ranchero: All the cadets could not die. One, the cadet played by the immortal cowboy Jorge Negrete, survived.

Ernesto Zedillo had cast some light into the darkness of the system when he opened the PRI to primary elections, but the appearance of Fox offered a new show altogether. Zedillo did not have the dark side of Salinas or Echeverría or Díaz Ordaz, and he was not egocentric like López Portillo; nonetheless, he had come up in the system. He permitted the alternation that many thought would lead to a democratic society, an act for which he will be well remembered by historians, but he could go no farther. Whether Zedillo acted out of principle or naiveté or on orders from the United States may never be known. Of the three possibilities, none is certain. Mexican presidents do not write tell-all books about their careers, and when power is tightly held by the president of a country, he has no need to share his views during his term in office or afterward, and no matter what he says, most Mexicans will not believe him.

Years earlier Cantinflas had exposed the language of the bureaucracy, the fake intellectuals who did the daily work of Mexico, many of them educated at the UNAM, in France, or in the United States. No one could understand what they really meant or how their statements affected life in Mexico. It was the Mexico of lawyers and economists, the language of educated incomprehensibility. The ranchero offered an antidote to the double-talk of the darkness. He was plain-talking, blunt except when speaking of love, when he resorted to music and rhyme to overcome his inarticulate style. The ranchero was as clear as the Indispensable Leader had been. There was something else about him, something unknown to the children and their mothers: When the ranchero was in his element, among men, he talked like a man, one could be certain of that. He was a real *chingón*, a man with *un par de oro* (golden balls), macho.

Mexico needed a hero, an end to the language of lawyers and leftist intellectuals; it needed Jorge Negrete, and Vicente Fox Quesada appeared to have been born for the part. Until 1993 it had been closed to men like him, for he was not the child of Mexican parents. His mother, Mercedes Quesada, was an immigrant, a Basque. His father, José Luis Fox Pont, was Irish and Mexican. But the Constitutional Amendment of 1993 gave every Mexican-born citizen the chance to become president. Any one of the nine children born to Mercedes Quesada de Fox on the Rancho San Cristóbal in the state of Guanajuato could have been president. As the children grew up, Vicente was probably the most unlikely choice for the office; he wanted to study for the priesthood.

Vicente's parents had other ideas for his career. They sent him to Mexico City to study business administration, but they did not send him so far from the Church that he would feel isolated from his religion. He enrolled at the Jesuit Universidad Iberoamericana, but did not complete his studies there. The rigorous curriculum at the university did not engage young Vicente, or perhaps it was his country ways in the urban atmosphere that made him uncomfortable. He left the university to enter the business world rather than study it. The Coca-Cola Company offered him a job as a route supervisor in its Mexico–Central America operation in 1964. The boy who wanted to be a priest remained Catholic, but Coca-Cola was a transnational corporation, where American attitudes and business practices prevailed; to get ahead, one had to adopt the Protestant Ethic.

He gained a reputation for hard work and honest business practices. Before long he was given responsibility for distribution, and then, in 1975, Coca-Cola put him in charge of the entire region. He took a business management course at Harvard and set out on his own in 1979, building his own Grupo Fox, expanding the business into agriculture, food packing, feed, and ranchero-style leather goods.

Nine years later he joined the PAN, which quickly put him in charge of state party finance, and chose him to run for federal deputy. It was his first election, and he won it. Fox ran for governor of Guanajuato in 1991 at the end of his term in Congress and lost. He ran in the next gubernatorial election and won, with 58 percent of the vote. By 1997 he thought he could be president of Mexico, and he began courting political leaders around the country, listening a little, talking a lot. He held social weekends in Guanajuato, in the city of León, not far from San Francisco del Rincón and the ranch along the Río Turbio where he had grown up in a world not unlike that of Jorge Negrete and the ranchero movies. He was a big man, a genuine ranchero in his cowboy boots, a man with a booming voice and big mustaches. He seemed to belong to that older time, that older Mexico of the ranchero movies. Fox supported an orphanage, adopted four children, and went to church. He did only one thing that would never have happened in a ranchero movie: He divorced his wife.

Other than the divorce, Fox was the man of light in the dark world of Mexican politics; he had not grown up in the system. It interested him only as something to be avoided, to be broken down, and he believed he was the one who could do it. He would come riding in on his horse and conquer the sinister forces of the city. After all, he was from Guanajuato; history was on his side. Fox was from the western part of the state, and he was not a priest, although it had been his ambition, but the revolt against Spain had started in Guanajuato in 1810, why not the revolt against the PRI?

At first, he campaigned in the language of the ranchero, but not the idealized ranchero of the movies. There was something almost thuglike about Fox the candidate. In debate he insulted his major competitors, and compared with the high moral tone and soulful countenance of Cárdenas, he seemed almost brutal. He represented the PAN, but he could not have won were it not for several factors beyond Fox's control. The PRI had shot itself in the foot with the choice of Labastida, a colorless, weary product of the system. Cárdenas was turning into the Mexican Harold Stassen of Minnesota, a man who ran for president every four years for decades. And there was of course the legacy of Salinas. Furthermore, the PRI could no longer steal elections because of the IFE and the foreign observers. It was a contest. Whether by accident or design, Zedillo had seen to that.

Among his accomplishments, Fox listed his experience in business and his success as governor of Guanajuato. He had improved the economic situation there, but he had not left Guanajuato a Mexican paradise. The literacy rate in 2001, according to the federal secretary of education (SEP), was the fifth-lowest of the thirty-one states and the Federal District: Of the adults in Guanajuato, 15.3 percent could not read. In the northern states, along the U.S. border, the literacy rate was 95 percent, and it was even higher in Mexico City. Fox had said that early in his life he had lived among the farmworkers along the Río Turbio and that he knew poverty and wanted to eliminate it. He had been a probusiness governor.

To win the election, he needed something beyond the PAN, which had been contesting the PRI in elections in Mexico for more than half a century and had enjoyed very little success at the federal level, although it grew consistently stronger in the northern states. Fox needed something akin to a trick, a different kind of party. The Alliance for Change became the Fox party. He took in people from the left as well as the right, made them his advisers, all but promised them major cabinet and ambassadorial posts. As Mexican presidents had once co-opted intellectuals by bringing them inside the house, Fox planned to co-opt his opposition. He went so far as to ask Cárdenas to join him, promising an important role for him and the PRD and the defeat of the PRI. Cárdenas declined.

Zedillo did nothing to stop the Fox campaign. He left the grass roots machine of the PRI exactly as it had been, a carrot and stick system, with no politics. The PRI had systematically hampered the Mexican entrance into a truly political system since the last years of Tata Lázaro's sexenio. The party had opposed the notion of self-government by the people; it had been the opposite kind of system, secretive and dictatorial, the darkness of the Mexican melodrama. An Alliance for Change was the sunny world of the rancho. If it was politically conservative, so had the ranchero film been politically conservative, and Catholic, and open, with a hierarchy as clear as the sky over preindustrial Mexico.

Fox was also a salesman, had been a salesman, and would continue to be a salesman. He made promises: 7 percent growth in GDP; a solution to the question of the Zapatistas "in fifteen minutes"; a solution to Mexico's poverty problem, a great improvement in the national infrastructure; an economic and social renaissance in the southern states; the beginning of the end of human rights violations. Mexico had not had such a "promising" candidate in many years. He had campaign advisers and media consultants from the United States, and he had money. The PRI, as usual, was getting money from unions, bank deposits it controlled, and businesses it had favored. Fox was accused during and long after the election of accepting funds from foreign (meaning the U.S.) sources, which is illegal under Mexican law.

The contest was brilliantly engineered: change vs. status quo. Change won. On his fifty-eighth birthday Vicente Fox became president-elect of Mexico. He took office with a month left in the year and showed Mexico and the world that he did intend a change not only in political parties but in the way Mexico was governed. He did not fill the cabinet and the government with PANistas, but with members of various parties, people who held differing views. The secretive corporate state that had existed for almost seventy-one years could not survive a mixed government. He had brought his cowboy openness and businessman's practicality to the presidential residence at Los Pinos. What he could not bring was any experience in government at the federal level. From his first days in office, the mixture of openness and lack of comprehension of how a mixed government could be managed was to cripple his administration.

He could not hold his own party in line. The president of the PAN, Luis Felipe Bravo Mena, joked that after Fox there would be a president from the PAN. The lower house of the Congress split, with no one party clearly in control. The PRI still controlled the upper house, and it could join with the PRD to stop Fox wherever he turned. The government was largely paralyzed. Fox had promised supporters on the right that he would begin the process of privatizing Mexico's electrical system and parts of Pemex, the state oil monopoly, but the Congress blocked every move in that direction. On the left he had promised a solution to the Zapatista question and a great effort to resolve problems of poverty. Two years into office he claimed to have reduced poverty by 3 percent, using microloans to the poor. But the figure he gave for poverty in Mexico, according to the newspapers, was ludicrous: 15 percent.

The September 11, 2001, attack on the World Trade Center ended any chance of meeting his other promises. Economic growth slowed, then stopped. Unemployment increased. Inflation was higher than promised. Maquiladora plants left Mexico to find cheaper labor markets. And at the beginning of 2003 the NAFTA plan to eliminate tariffs on imported farm products from the United States and Canada was about to destroy Mexican agriculture. Salinas had left a time bomb in the agreement. Late in 2002 Fox began demanding that the United States stop subsidizing farmers. With little hope for such action, Fox looked to his own treasury to help Mexican farmers. But there was no money in the budget to handle the problem. He told the farmers he would increase the budget for agriculture by 3.9 percent. The farmers paraded their anger in the streets on the same day that Fox announced his satisfaction with NAFTA on its tenth anniversary.[14]

He encountered another problem he had not expected, the revolt of the governors. Mexico, unlike most other OECD countries, collected less than half of 1 percent of its local budgets from property taxes. Municipalities and states depended upon the federal government to provide for their needs. As Fox prepared his third budget, the governors revolted: not just PRIistas and Perredistas, all the governors. The method the PRI had used to keep the states under control, centralizing government through the purse strings while giving it the appearance of a federalized operation did not work for a mixed government. Everyone wanted to be a ranchero in post-PRI Mexico.

The greatest embarrassment to the Fox administration came after one of his most brilliant political moves. On March 11, 2001, at the end of a long trip through many states, Subcomandante Marcos, many masked members of the EZLN, and thousands of sympathizers arrived at the Zócalo in Mexico City. When they had first announced the caravan, it seemed a dangerous idea: armed rebels traveling through Mexico. It was only a question of who would kill or imprison them: federal police, state police, the Mexican Army. Once more Marcos had made a breathtaking move. But this time Fox was quick, and far wiser than his predecessors had been.

The president invited Marcos to his house for a chat. He suggested they

---

[14]The agreement was signed in 1992, although it did not become effective until 1994. Carlos Salinas de Gotari, George Bush, and Brian Mulroney met in Washington on the anniversary to celebrate their work. Of the three, only Bush had not been officially disgraced. Bush praised Willam J. Clinton for completing work on the agreement, Salinas blamed Zedillo for the farm problem, saying he had not properly supported the farmers, and Mulroney smiled.

have a face-to-face meeting in the residence at Los Pinos. He went beyond that. As long as the march was peaceful, the Zapatistas would not be harmed. The governors growled in several of the dozen states through which the caravan of thousands had passed, but Fox prevailed. The buses and trucks and cars filled with unarmed Zapatistas passed through Mexico unharmed.

Under the tutelage of Marcos, the visit in 2001 was peaceful and orderly. The caravan traveled north, entered the Federal District, went first to the campus of the UNAM to a great rally, and then into the center of the city. There were more rallies, more speeches. The government at every level accommodated the caravan. The Zapatistas were invited to speak to the Mexican Congress. For the first time in the history of the country a masked person addressed the Congress. The scene angered the PANistas and some other members of the Congress, but there was no violence.

Marcos declined the invitation to take off his mask and have a chat with Fox, the Zapatistas gathered themselves up, and the "Zapatour" went home. Marcos left feeling triumphant. The left-of-center Commission on Concord and Pacification (COCOPA) had promised new laws to guarantee the autonomy and civil and economic rights of indigenous people. Fox was satisfied. His own party, if it really was his party, the PAN, had behaved badly during the Zapatista stay in Mexico City, but the president had behaved admirably. It looked to all the world as if Marcos had accomplished his goals. As promised, he had brought the Zapatistas to the capital, and he had won a better life for them then and in the future. Only one outcome could possibly have been better: martyrdom. And Fox had not allowed it to happen.

Then the Congress began amending the COCOPA version of the legislation. When it passed and went into law, the indigenous people of Mexico had fewer rights, less autonomy, no more economic assistance, and less claim to their own dignity than they had before the Zapatour. Worse, the Fox administration toyed with funding for indigenous projects. It cut off the money for one of the main Indian cultural efforts, the Organization of Indigenous Writers, whose magazine offered the only national and international publication for the writers. Everything for indigenous people got worse rather than better. The Zapatour had been a catastrophe. Marcos called the behavior of the Fox administration a *burla* (mockery, a cruel joke). Then he was quiet. There were rumors that he was sick, suffering from malaria or worse. Another rumor held that he was contemplating a new role for his Revolution, a more common political role, as a legitimate party. The civilians of the Zapatista Front remained loyal, but Marcos and

Fox had a problem in common, publicity. Castañeda complained privately about the mistreatment of his boss by the press in Mexico and the lack of interest in Mexico in the United States, while Marcos, in his self-imposed silence, had faded from the headlines.

When Castañeda, who had been Mexico's most arrogant and unsuccessful foreign secretary in many decades, resigned after two years in office, he made a public display of his petulance. In response to a question about his reputation for arrogance, Castañeda told me, "There is no question. I am self-assured, and on occasion I speak too bluntly. There are opinions people have about public persons." In a conversation that went on for more than an hour, he gave no sign of his reputed arrogance. On the contrary, he was charming even when the questions were not entirely flattering, such as the question about arrogance. Then again, a man who is considering a run for presidency of his country is not likely to be unpleasant to a writer. As secretary, however, he had made enemies everywhere he turned, in the Mexican government, in the Bush administration, and with the Mexican press. Among Mexicans, it is considered a cultural flaw bordering on treason to be *agringado*—that is, to have adopted American habits, politics, and a gringo view of Mexico as a backward, corrupt country. As a schoolboy in Mexico Castañeda was known as George because of his gringo ways. Castañeda pressed the United States aggressively on the one hand, and on the other he told the members of the Mexican press their problem was that they could not speak English, preventing them from reading the *New York Times*.

Although Castañeda had romanced the U.S. press for years while teaching at New York University and assiduously courted *New York Times* correspondents during his two years in office, the *Times* gave his resignation a few hundred words in the January 9 editions, with the headline FOREIGN MINISTER IN MEXICO WILL QUIT, FRUSTRATED BY THE U.S. Castañeda blamed his frustrations on the new priorities of the U.S. government after the attack on the World Trade Center. The Bush administration, with unusual sarcasm, said it would miss the "pleasure" of working with him. Given the importance of U.S.-Mexico relations, Jorge Castañeda had turned a public relations problem during a tense time in the world into a diplomatic problem for Mexico. His boss had not chided him for his petulance; instead, Fox told the press he did not know if he was going to accept Castañeda's resignation. But he did, and quickly. Luis Ernesto Derbez, cabinet secretary in charge of economics, with whom Castañeda fought over many issues, was named foreign secretary. The pity of it all was that what Fox had wanted from the United States—residency for undocumented workers, some way to spare Mexico from subsidized U.S. farm products undercutting their own farm prices and destroying Mexican agricultural businesses—was fair and decent from almost any viewpoint. And Fox and Castañeda had botched the job. As Derbez, the new foreign secretary, pointed out, Castañeda had asked for the "whole enchilada" instead of taking a bite at a time, and he had failed to take into account extreme poverty in Mexico as the root cause of the migration issue. Clearly, two amateurs at the helm of a government had been at least one, if not two, too many.

It was not yet the end of Castañeda's political career, although Derbez lambasted him mercilessly in the press. He was very close to a leading member of the PRI, Elba Esther Gordillo, the former president of the Education Workers' Union (SNTE) and still said to be the power behind the throne. Gordillo, national secretary of the PRI, had been considered for secretary of education by the Fox government. Castañeda's connection to Gordillo made it possible that he would have the support of one faction of the PRI if he ran for president on a fourth-party ticket.

No one knew what to think about El Sub. In Chiapas, Sister Carlota Duarte, who knows the Tzotziles and their needs very well, said, "I admire his silence. Everyone seems to have his or her interpretation, which adds to the myth-making." To questions about his leadership style and the Eurocentric nature of his ideas, including those first raised by Andrés Oppenheimer,[15] she said, "I think there may be an element of envy in the commentary. For me, the alleviation of oppression and suffering, on all levels, of people here is what matters most."

At the end of 2002 Marcos surfaced with a tantalizing announcement that left open the possibility of a new political party. Or something. As everyone knows, guerrillas survive by not giving away their plans, surprise being their most effective weapon. Marcos broke his silence to laugh at the thought of his illness, sending a letter of support to a new magazine, *Rebeldia,* dedicated to Zapatismo.[16]

Marcos once again demonstrated the literate, witty, slightly arrogant

[15]*Bordering on Chaos: Mexico's Roller-Coaster Journey to Prosperity* (Boston: Little, Brown, 1996).

[16]With no explanation or comment, *La Jornada* (November 18, 2002) published the letter, dated September 2002, from Marcos to the magazine.

voice that had endeared him to the educated left around the world. The work was incomprehensible to the people with whom he lived because many of them could not read, and in the eight pages there were no references to Maya culture that would have made his indigenous audience comfortable. He did, however, take a paragraph to tip his hat to feminism, perhaps in response to his feminist critics.

Marcos had five main points and a trail of postscripts. In the first point, he spoke of the role of criticism and self-criticism of the left in Mexico. But it was the second point of the letter that charmed: "In Mexico at present, political and cultural practices are filled with myths." And then he mentioned a few of these, beginning with:

"There is, for example, the cultural myth that reads: 'Enrique Krauze is an intellectual,' when everyone knows that he does not go beyond being a mediocre businessman."

He complained about María Félix, who he said was not a diva at all, and then went on to politics:

> "The Partido Acción Nacional is a party of the right." Well, it is neither a party of the center nor the left. In reality, the PAN is nothing more than an employment agency for management posts.
>
> There is also the myth of the Democratic Revolutionary Party, "The PRD is an alternative on the left." And it will not be an alternative on the center or the right; the PRD simply is not an alternative to anything.
>
> Or you have the myth: "The Institutional Revolutionary Party is a political party." In reality, the PRI is a cave with 40 thieves uselessly waiting for their Ali Baba.
>
> Or there is another myth beloved by the rusty left that reads, "To go against globalization is like going against the law of gravity." On the other side, the marginalized of all colors everywhere in the world challenge the one and the other; and neither the laws of physics nor the International Monetary Fund can avoid it.

Finally, of the myth "The Zapatistas are finished," he wrote. "The only thing that is finished is their patience."

He had nothing good to say about the ultras, the most militant group in the last strike at the UNAM. For him, they were just new members of the PRD. It was history that concerned him, "The role of the rebel is to smash the labyrinth of history," and he did not care if the rebel used his head as a hammer, not that rebels had hard heads, but because "to break the traps of history, with its myths, is work that one does with the head, that is to say, intellectual work."

And then came a bizarre letter about a Spanish judge and the president of Spain and the Basque separatists. It is difficult to understand why he wrote a letter larded with crude references to flatulence and clowns and praise for terrorism. Monsiváis and the left attacked him for the politics, the style, and the timing of the letter.

It was very different from the early days of the Zapatistas. When Marcos first began his Internet revolution, Fuentes and Monsiváis, the grand novelist and the best Mexican essayist, welcomed him as a writer as well as a political figure. And Marcos has remained a writer in the ether. Like every writer, he is only demeaned by his personal appearances. And every interviewer, no matter what her or his personal politics, seeks now to unmask the myth, to be the Joseph Campbell of reporters. And Marcos knows. Perhaps he has come to the old age of gods and writers: A smile, a frown, a burst of intemperance, an ill-chosen epithet, no more than an instant in human form, and he is dead.

The Spanish judge challenged Marcos to a debate, and the masked man accepted, choosing the Canary Islands as the place. But a few days later, Luis H. Álvarez, who was responsible for seeking peace in Chiapas, told the newspapers that Marcos and those closest to him, perhaps Comandantes Tacho and David, had been forced aside and that the EZLN had broken up into tiny groups in the Lacandón forest.

Fox did not, of course, reply to the message from the ether, nor did any of the three political parties reply. The president had his own troubles. He had married his press secretary, Martha Sahagún, and the elegant ladies of the capital gossiped. They said she dressed "like an Avon lady." Fox himself put his foot into the intellectual world when he tried to levy a 15 percent use tax on food and books. Virtually all of Mexico attacked him. Intellectuals insulted him over the books, and the left and center complained of what the tax would do to the poor. The Congress did not pass the tax. And Fox and his wife were once again the bumpkins in the city, as he had been at the Universidad Iberoamericana in his student days.

At midnight, in Mexico City's finest restaurants, there were no cowboys. In the hotels of Polanco and Lomas, the older men in their midnight blue suits chose wines offered by comical sommeliers in anachronistic garb and toasted the "nieces," who sat as upright as mannikins and raised their softening chins to the light. The men in the midnight blue suits had been the men of the long darkness of the PRI, and they had no respect for the ranchero, no matter what property, what opportunity he wished to give them, for he had taken away Mexico, which had been their grandest possession. There was Manuel Bartlett in one restaurant, dressed in his black Italian suit, growing old, but still so sleek he shone with prosperity. And arrogant as only the men of the long darkness could be. He flattered the famous and ignored the rest, going from table to table, leaving behind him a trail of vicious whispers.

If any one person could be blamed for Fox's problems, it was Bartlett. He had been a senator, the governor of Puebla, the head of the Department of the Interior, and campaign manager for Carlos Salinas de Gotari in 1988, when "the computers voted for the PRI." He had presidential ambitions, and he obviously intended to preserve the power of the PRI for himself, but the open primary before the 2000 elections chose Labastida instead of him or Roberto Madrazo Pintado, who was to become president of the PRI. In his late sixties, with no place to go, the man from the darkness had once tried to set up the Congress to guarantee the continued influence of the single-party system and stymie the efforts of any president who was not a soldier in the PRI.

As Fox's popularity declined and his promises faded, he took up foreign affairs. He distanced himself from Fidel Castro—the first Mexican president to do so since 1959. And Fox traveled. In difficult times Mexican presidents had always traveled. All the promises had begun to melt away from the ranchero; even the promise to shine a light on the dirty war of the past. There were no revelations from deep inside the government. Past presidents chose not to testify, waiting patiently in their old age for death to deliver them from the bite of the ranchero's big horseflies. Had 46 been killed at Tlatelolco or 406? If there had been 406, where were the bodies? Who gave the orders?

Sergio Aguayo published *La Charola* (The Badge), his revelations of corruption, with pictures of CIA headquarters in Mexico City. He gave details, but the big revelation, the role of the presidents, did not come. The attorney general could not deliver what Fox had promised. With more than two years to work on the human rights problem, Fox had done little or nothing, according to José Luis Soberanes, chairman of the National Human Rights Commission (CNDH). He told EFE, the Spanish-language news service,[17] that there had been much talk and little action since Fox took office. According to Soberanes, who had the role of ombudsman, there had been no diminution in torture, abuse of rights, discrimination. He said that human rights violators "continue to enjoy complete immunity." To drive home his point, Soberanes said that Mexico ought to treat immigrants from Central America with the same dignity it demanded for Mexican immigrants in the United States.

There was no improvement in the standard of living, and the poverty problem had proved intractable. But no problem loomed larger for the rest of Fox's sexenio than the paralysis of government. A mayor, like López Obrador, could get things done in Mexico City, the impossible, unmanageable capital. He evicted—for whose benefit would not be known for some years—the ambulantes and their carts and serapes from the Historic District and reopened the streets, and he planned to build a second level on the Periferico, the clogged main freeway in Mexico City, widely known as "the world's largest parking garage."

López Obrador proved that some problems could be solved in Mexico, some progress could be made, but when Fox tried to build a new airport in Mexico City's San Salvador Atenco area to supplant most of the service at the overcrowded international airport, where the main runways flooded and airplane wheels sank into the mud after thunderstorms, he failed. The residents of the area protested, captured members of the government, and marched through the streets. Armed with machetes and a few rifles, they threatened to fight to the death. Fox could neither cajole them nor frighten them into permitting the construction of the airport. He abandoned the plan. After more than two years in office, Revolution Day, the celebration of Madero's pronouncement of 1910, went badly for the president. A newspaper columnist took up Subcomandante Marcos's idea about myths, accusing the president of making a myth of the Revolution by failing to solve problems of hunger and oppression in Mexico. In Morelos, hundreds of farmers blocked the toll road into Mexico City, demanding to see the secretary of agriculture, asking for help to survive the bad growing season.

The irony was not lost on the Mexican press or the public. Almost a century earlier the farmers of Morelos, led by Emiliano Zapata, had complained of their poverty and oppression to Francisco Madero, a democrat, but not a

---

[17]November 22, 2002.

social or political radical. And on Revolution Day 2002, Vicente Fox Quesada, also a democrat with no radical social or political ideas, had spoken of Madero as the true hero of the Revolution. He had not mentioned Zapata.

WHAT IS DEMOCRACY?

Plato, who was not a democrat, asked what he thought was the key political question, Who ought to rule? In the middle of the twentieth century, Karl Popper, an Austrian philosopher living in England, responded to Plato by restating the political question. He was not so interested in establishing governments as in removing them. How does one write a constitution that enables the bloodless removal of a government? When Popper raised that question, he was already well known for his work on the scientific method, which he saw as a system of trial and error, one in which there was no certainty. It should be applied as well, he thought, to governments.

With the first new government in seventy-one years in Mexico stuck in a mire of contentiousness, Popper's question carried as much importance as Plato's. Had the replacement of the party-state system been an error? If so, should the idea of democracy in Mexico be considered no more than a trial run, to be replaced by some other system? A return to the one-party state? The 1917 Constitution gave enormous power to the executive, but the Fox administration had seen the power of the president eroded, challenged everywhere, on the streets as well as in the governor's mansions and the halls of the Congress. Much of Mexico was no longer under Mexican control. As the various parts of the North American Free Trade Agreement went into effect, Mexico lost more and more of its economic sovereignty. The essayist Carlos Monsiváis called Mexico "a U.S. franchise," and demanded a more nationalistic policy.

Mexico had become a democracy, but the meaning of democracy for Mexico was not clear. The problem of definition was not an academic exercise. By the simplest definition—majority rule—Mexico had achieved democracy, but majority rule, as Popper had pointed out in *The Open Society*,[18] can be a dangerous business: Hitler had come came to power through majority rule. Popper was not the first to worry. Since Plato and Aristotle first raised questions about the path of majority rule, philosophers and political scientists had been seeking a better definition. A nation could sat-

[18]London: Routledge, 1945.

isfy Popper's theory by substituting one oppressive government for another; it had happened all over the world.

We often speak of democratic institutions, by which we mean a system of civil and criminal justice that is more often fair than not, an executive branch balanced and checked by both a legislature and a judiciary, a constitution that guarantees certain rights, and so on. Both Benito Juárez and Porfirio Díaz headed governments *for many years* that were by most measures democratic. Virtually all the commonly named democratic institutions were in effect under the PRI.

Participation adds another requirement to the definition of democracy, but the degree of participation in government by citizens of the United States is in serious question, and it is a democracy that has been stable and functional for more than two centuries. Mexicans still participate by taking to the streets, waving machetes at the government, or blocking roads. The Zapatista uprising, no matter how Marcos defines it, has so far been the participation of a coherent group, with a much larger amorphous group at the fringe. The vote has not yet been accepted as effective in much of Mexico. One registers to vote in order to be able to enroll children in school, but to stop the building of an airport or to demand help to survive a drought, one takes to the streets. Since no one trusts the newspapers and television has been an arm of the PRI for most of the history of the major network, Televisa, the demonstration and the corrido (in its many incarnations) continue to be the major forms of participatory democracy. *Manifestaciones* (demonstrations) take place almost daily in Mexican cities, especially the capital, blocking streets for hours on end. When Mexican farmers realized what would happen when tariffs were lifted on U.S. farm products under NAFTA, they took to the streets, threatening to block international bridges. Salinas had sold them out, Zedillo had paid no attention to their problem, and Fox was incapable of negotiating their survival.

If democracy can exist only when the vast majority of the population enjoys a healthy diet, decent housing, the opportunity to be educated at public expense, access to health care, and work that is not onerous, then it bears too great a resemblance to paradise to be likely to occur in a large country soon. A modern constitutional democracy requires a powerful element of justice, which the philosopher John Rawls described as fairness in his *A Theory of Justice*.[19] There is an economic component to democracy,

[19]Cambridge, Mass.: Harvard University Press, 1971.

fairness extended beyond politics to the private household, fairness at the dinner table and the kindergarten, quotidian fairness, unimpressive, uninteresting, except that without it, democracy is simply another way of dividing up the spoils. Perhaps all anyone can hope for is a society that is *for the most part* fair, as well as participatory, through democratic institutions. Popper's system of constitutional trial and error is not enough, but it is the sine qua non of a democratic society, a beginning. On July 2, 2000, Mexico embraced that idea.

DEMOCRACY TAKES A TAXI

At the end of the day, when the PRI had always been able to find a way to maintain control of the country, the counting of the *casillas* (boxes of votes) began. The state election commission of Morelos had been in session since morning, housed in a large empty house in an upper-middle-class section of the capital city. All day the precinct workers of the IFE, the federal commission, and the Morelos commission had been going from casilla to casilla, settling the inevitable disputes, writing down the claims of fraud. The serious complaints had been forwarded to the group in the empty house.

By nine o'clock in the evening the PANistas were already celebrating in the streets of the center of the city, singing, shouting, honking automobile horns as if they were the bells of another time. Around the state election headquarters the streets were silent, quieter than usual. State police had set up roadblocks in a huge circle around the headquarters. For half a dozen blocks in any direction cars were not permitted to enter the area unless the occupants had business at election headquarters or lived in the neighborhood. The police were polite but firm; they did not hide their automatic weapons.

There were no police inside the headquarters, although there was an elaborate identification system of printed nametags laminated in plastic. Only members of the commission and one observer from each party were allowed inside the room where the actual counting was to take place. The casillas themselves, small boxes containing the paper ballots, which had been counted at the polling places, had been coming into the headquarters slowly since a few hours after the polls closed.

The commission members sat behind a long table. At the far end, with his laptop computer open on the table in front of him, Gustavo Valencia, a mathematician, director of development for the growing Morelos campus of Monterrey Tec (ITESM), listened intently, entering every number in the grid on his machine. A tall, handsome man with a very carefully kept beard, Valencia was not voluble. He was a definite man, serious about his work and his career, stern, until he smiled, showing a sweet face of such optimism that he seemed an innocent. No one doubted either his ability to process the details of the situation or to represent fairness in a dispute.

Leonor Orduña, the president of the Municipal Election Council, sat at the center of the long table, an elegant woman, proprietor of a fashionable store, combed and made up as if she had just come to the meeting, although she had been there all day and would remain there long into the night. On the wall facing her, a gigantic chart showed every section of every election district. The other members of the council, seated to either side of her, represented various parts of the city: business; labor; the university community. To the left of the table, six folding chairs had been set up. An observer from each political party sat in one of the chairs. I had been given a council credential to sit in the remaining chair.

Behind the chairs a young man worked at a huge Compaq computer that projected the material on its monitor onto a white wall behind him. At the top the computer-generated chart said, "Microsoft Excel Cuernavaca 2000." As information arrived, it was recorded on his computer, on the wall chart facing the council members, and on Gustavo Valencia's laptop. The computer-generated wall chart showed running totals of the vote for every party and every candidate in every district, section by section. The tally for any box of votes could be located instantly.

Every two or three minutes a young man, a volunteer, carried in a box of ballots, passed a tally sheet to Srta. Orduña, and waited while she called out the totals for the candidates. When the council was satisfied, the volunteer carried the box to a large room. There was an instant of quiet, and the next volunteer carried in the next box. There was very little conversation; no one laughed, no one commented. The scene had the spare grace of a mathematical equation. But for one person, one voice.

In the second row a man in a black leather jacket, thickset, with a neat mustache and thinning black hair combed straight back, the observer from the PRI, sat with his cell phone close to his lips, whispering. He sweated profusely, holding the cell phone in one hand, using the other to draw a huge handkerchief from his pocket and wipe his face. Every number he saw, every word he spoke agitated him; he looked like a kettle about to boil over. Finally he was unable to bear it any longer: the room, the heat of the moment, the unhappy glances from the council members whenever his whisper rose into interference. He bolted from his seat and out through the French doors into the garden. On the other side of the doors, like a character in a silent film, he gestured wildly as he spoke. He had passed beyond unhappiness, beyond agitation; he had the eyes of a man attending his own execution. Seen through the French doors, he was all teeth and eyes, glistening with fear. The news could not have been worse for him: The PAN was not only carrying the presidency but sweeping the state and the city.

After a long time the man from the PRI came back into the room and sat quietly, without his cell phone. He had not complained about the counting; his party had been defeated by the voters and again by the orderly electoral process. After this election, no one would be able to joke that the computers voted for the PRI.

Later that night, standing on the crest of the hill above the house where the votes were being counted, Professor Herlinda Suárez de (Gustavo) Valencia and two members of the state election institute, watched the ballot boxes being delivered from all the parts of the city of more than a million people and the surrounding area. The boxes were brought in white, four-door taxicabs. As each taxi pulled up under the portico at the entrance to election headquarters, the young volunteers who worked in the headquarters opened the trunk and took out the boxes of ballots. The young men tossed the boxes from one to the other in a line leading into the house. The boxes moved quickly down the line of the brigade of volunteers.

When the boxes had been removed from one taxi, it pulled away, and another taxi came to take its place. The driver popped the trunk, and the volunteers reached for the ballot boxes. All the taxis were white, and every one had a banner on the hood proclaiming its duty. The line of taxis wound up the hill that led to the headquarters and down the other side and up the next hill and down. There were more than three hundred taxis, every one with its yellow parking lights shining in the darkness of the July night. The line moved slowly, the stopping and starting of the engines carried on the light wind of the night. The young men had tied kerchiefs around their heads. They looked like dockworkers. They slammed down the trunk lids and gave them a slap to send the taxis on. As each taxi was relieved of its cargo, the line came to life, and another yellow light came over the top of the near hill and the far. There was no end to the row of yellow lights.

At the top of the hill one of the members of the election commission looked out at the long, undulating line of taxis, rising and falling with the geography of the hills, yellow lights visible to the horizon in the clear night air, and said, "I see democracy."

35.

Doctors

Worse than sadness is filth. Poverty fouls the house, the bed, the body and the soul. It chokes on its vomit. Come to life to agonize.

—JAIME SABINES

The conversation took place some years ago when José Romero was an executive at the Pan American Health Organization (PAHO). We were on our way to dinner in an old restaurant in Mexico City's Historic Center, talking in a mixture of Spanish and English, alternating the languages by paragraph or subject, when he said, "You know, Earl, there is an epidemic in Mexico, but inside the epidemic there are many doctors. They cannot stop the epidemic, but they can save many of the afflicted."

For a man who was managing PAHO's project on AIDS prevention to speak of sickness in Mexico was no surprise. AIDS had already traveled south from the United States. The first victims were homosexual men, but the disease had also reached women whose husbands had crossed the border without papers to do farmwork or construction or to pull the guts from chickens.[1] Lonely, without much money, the men engaged in opportunistic sex with other men or visited prostitutes, and when they came home, AIDS came with them. But Romero was not speaking about AIDS. The epidemic he spoke of was a metaphor; it represented all the ills—medical, social, and economic—suffered by Mexico. The doctors were of many kinds, again a metaphor; they were the goodness that exists in Mexico, and like the problems, the goodness is not inconsiderable.

The troubles affecting the country, the effects of what Mexico's richest

---

[1]According to the National Center for the Prevention and Control of AIDS, the ratio went from twenty male patients for every female when accurate statistics were first gathered to five to one at the beginning of the new century. *Reforma* of December 1, 2002, reported the story under a headline telling of the cases doubling. There were 50,000 cases of AIDS and 177,000 cases of HIV infection in Mexico.

man, Carlos Slim Helú, in his newfound nationalism calls a neocolonial society, manifest themselves in many kinds of suffering, but for a time, before neoliberalism and AIDS, physical health was not chief among them. During his long tenure as a director of programs in the Mexican Institute of Social Security and then as a cabinet officer, Ricardo García Sainz had made a good start on a national health program, with many first-rate clinics and hospitals serving workers and the poor. During the Salinas sexenio the system had begun to weaken, suffering from lack of funds, and García Sainz had resigned from the Salinas administration for that and many other reasons. No one with either his managerial talent or his drive to bring health care to the poor had taken his place. In the Zedillo and Fox administrations, the problem was no longer how best to expand pensions and medical care, both of which came under social security, but how to manage the system down as the austerity imposed by the United States and the IMF and the World Bank bit deeper into the lives of Mexicans. Where to find the money was the problem: Mexico still had not been able to modify its laws to collect taxes from the rich. On the other hand, for those within the shrinking social security system, care in some hospitals was still good. As in the rest of the world, it was best in metropolitan areas.

In the finest hospitals, including some in the social security system, the quality of medicine rivaled that in the United States or Europe. Dr. Andrea Navarrete and I toured the social security hospital where she is on staff in pediatrics.[2] It was newer, cleaner, and more orderly than most large U.S. general hospitals, and as well equipped. Her major concern was that she did not have a portable MRI machine she could bring to the incubators where at-risk newborns were kept. There are of course no such machines, at least not yet, but Dr. Navarrete and her colleagues were anxious to have new medical technology as soon as it was available, always trying to anticipate the possibilities.

On the other hand, many people in Mexico, especially in rural areas, still

[2]Hospital #1 serves almost a quarter of a million people, members of the social security system and their families in the Gabriel Mancera area. The hospital has 212 beds and 1,753 people on staff. It was opened in 1996, replacing an old hospital destroyed in the 1985 earthquake. It offers a full range of services, from surgery to psychology, and has modern equipment for dialysis, utrasound, tomography, and so on.

Social security dues in Mexico are very low and shared by employee and employer, as in the United States. Retirement payments, however, are also very low.

rely on traditional indigenous medicine, a skill that has declined in many places, sinking into something very close to fraud. In a tiny village on the slopes of a volcano, I watched a woman healer treat a client by passing an egg over her body. I expected her to follow the ancient rules, giving the egg to her client, with instructions for the proper burial of the egg, which had become the vessel containing all the spirits that caused the sickness. But the curandera merely set the egg to the side to use for the next patient or to cook for dinner.

IBERO

The declines concerned Romero, of course, but he was not speaking about problems of physical health; it was a metaphor. His thought, said with a sigh, took a broader view of Mexican society and character. The doctors he spoke about were social physicians, many of whom are nuns or priests. Cross the freeway from the Universidad Iberoamericana, walk between the gleaming office buildings into the slum behind them, and there are church-funded social service centers, grade schools, and a home for troubled young women.

In the primary school on the steepest street in Santa Fe, far too steep for cars to pass, as steep as the steps up the side of a pyramid, the children have the interest and the aid of the university across the freeway. The classrooms have been put in order, and the children have been supplied with much of what they need. The teachers are well trained, and the methods are modern. It is a public school, but a public school supported by social physicians from across the the freeway. Outside the school, on the street that falls for a thousand yards, women carry their children in rebozos and their groceries in baskets balanced on their heads, as if they belonged to another time and place.

The home for troubled women in Santa Fe gleams with order; surfaces shine as if they had been lacquered. Outside the building, in the garden seen through glass, the plants have been labored to perfection. It is a ferociously loving place in which the women follow a daily routine detailed to the moment. "Strait is the gate and narrow be the way unto life"—Matthew 7:14—might well be the motto of the treatment. Yet the director claims a record of success, few women falling back into drugs or crime.

But the social doctors of the church cannot bring their clients across the freeway to the place that could transform their lives. Iberoamericana is an elite and expensive university. The system does not belong to the doctors; they work with one child, a tiny school, fifteen troubled girls. Romero's metaphor holds here, as well. It is not for a lack of doctors that Mexico suffers but for the size of what he calls the epidemic.

PERIPATETICS

Other doctors come to Mexico from other churches, other places, from the governments of Italy and Sweden: Mennonites from Philadelphia, Baptists from all over the United States, and, from the rest of the world, the social doctors of the United Nations Development Program. Among the doctors one finds the peripatetics, those who go from country to country, epidemic to epidemic. In the low jungle, Lucidi Sigismondi, an Italian agronomist, rides his bicycle, raises his children, is generous to his scholarly wife, and tries to re-create an industry that disappeared when the valuable hardwood trees were cut down by the thousand and the forests died. "What is wood worth?" Sigismondi asks. He knows wells, water tables, the need for fertilizer, but he cannot make the topsoil deeper, and he does not control the rain; for rain the people look to saints or Chac, the god of rain. Sigismondi greets the world with shrugs, shouts, broad gestures, limitless enthusiasm. He would like to teach the descendants of the ancient occupiers of the jungle what their ancestors knew. Behind his great blond beard, he lives in irony, in his native Italian and pragmatic Maya.

A hundred miles southeast of Sigismondi, in Dzulna, Quintana Roo, there is a Spaniard who was in Africa until he came to Mexico. The jungle around him is high, putting his house in constant shade. It would be a refuge for mosquitoes were it not for the surrounding screens. On the porch of his house, behind the metal screens, tethered by a thick chain, a huge dog, a beast the size of the animals that came with Hernán Cortés, growls. A Maya cook provides food both Spanish and Mayan; the favorite beverage of the household is made of purified water and exotic fruit that has no English name.

The question of exotic fruit interests the social and economical doctors all over Mexico. To strangers in the jungle it seems that anything could grow there. They read history. There was a time when the land was fertile. The peripatetics think it could happen again. A few miles outside Dzulna, on a UNDP-financed experimental farm, the Spaniard taught the local people how to make compost and mix it with the red clay of the area to produce rich soil. In that part of the jungle he was the doctor of the earth.

SUPERBARRIO

An epidemic requires many kinds of doctors. Some are comedic, but doctors nevertheless, and of the Mexicans, many have spent time in prison, for there was a time in their lives when they thought drastic measures had to be taken to halt the epidemic. The government, which they blamed for the spread of the troubles, feared them. In the time of the dirty war the Mexican government imprisoned, exiled, tortured, and killed many of the country's best and did the work in a totalitarian way, secretly, with no rules but the rule of power. It has not changed over the decades. When a human rights activist is murdered in Mexico, even now, during the Fox administration, the killer will rarely be found, making the practice of that kind of medicine a dangerous business.

The comedic physicians do not expect to be assassinated, but they find it helpful to drive fast, maneuverable cars. Marcos Rascón, the amusing and slightly mad federal deputy who wore a pig's head to a joint session of the two houses of the Mexican Congress, drove such a car and tended to look over his shoulder now and then. "I am only worried about a parking ticket," he said, with a smile that did not match the quickness of his glance. Although he denies it, with the same smile, Rascón was the inventor of Superbarrio, the masked character dressed in a wrestler's costume, including a cape, who stepped into the public spotlight in the 1990s to defend Mexico's poor. The barrio is the neighborhood, a place where poor people live. And wrestling in Mexico is, well, an art form.

Wrestlers always appear masked, whether representing good or evil, in the tradition of Mexican art depicting the gods, who were mainly anthropomorphic[3] but, unlike Greek gods, did not reveal their human faces. And wrestlers are serious fellows. I recall entering the stage door of a television studio in Mexico City behind five stocky men, including a dwarf, all dressed

---

[3]Coatlicue, the greatest artistic rendition of a Mexican god(dess), has no human form. Two serpents form the head of the statue, and its feet are clawed. Neither does Ometeotl, the god of duality, have human form. Similarly, the Maya god Hunab Ku, the Unified God, has no human form.

in matching pale blue suits and vests, all carrying small black bags. When the star of the television show announced that they were her next guests, the five dour men took five dour masks from the small black bags, put on the masks, and marched out onto the stage. They spoke with the dignity befitting divinities.

Superbarrio, masked defender of the poor, in his tight, revealing body suit did not have quite the physique of the men in the light blue suits. He looked a lot more like a certain federal deputy. Soon after his early, unsolicited appearances, Superbarrio was in great demand, so he cloned himself. There were Superbarrios everywhere, at every protest. Whether it was a gathering in front of the Peruvian Embassy or a Mexican government office, Superbarrio was there.

His inventor, Rascón, began his career as a reporter for *El Fronterizo* in Cuidad Juárez. Then, Rascón said, "I spent three years in jail in Chihuahua [the state] after I and other young radicals held up a bank to get money for the revolution." Rascón is a chubby, funny, very open man, a fixture in the Mexico City café society world through his wife, the well-known singer Eugenia León. When we met, Rascón appeared in his SUV, which he said, delightedly, he bought with the ten thousand dollars, expense money every federal deputy gets upon entering the chamber.

Had Superbarrio raised the country's interest in the problems of poverty? I asked. He did not answer. His term in office was coming to an end, and the Superbarrio joke was growing tired. He had been a comic god of resistance, a physician of fearlessness and hope. And fat. A hero to people who lived on one or two dollars a day could not be otherwise; there were no thin wrestlers behind the masks, no emaciated doctors.

CATARACTS

Romero himself is a social doctor. A big man, with a great head of curly hair and a Mexican mustache, the son of a charming Australian woman and a Mexican newspaper columnist, Romero had been a sixties youth, a sociology major at Harvard, a graduate student at the UNAM, and an assistant professor, before he went out into the world,[4] first, into the rural areas of

[4]Our families have known each other for more than half a century. His father, Pepe Romero, wrote in English for the now-defunct *Mexico City News*, exhibited his paintings

Mexico as national coordinator of bilingual/bicultural education, then into rural areas again to bring technology to the countryside. Before joining PAHO, he worked on nutritional problems for the rural poor. After the AIDS project came to an end, Romero joined the United Nations Capacity 21 project to create and support sustainable development programs in Latin America.

It was all government and NGO (nongovernmental organization) work, in large bureaucracies. Then one afternoon I overheard him talking about his need for an airplane; I could not imagine why. Beyond his work at PAHO and the UN, he and his wife, Marcella Gavaldon, had put together a project to bring eye surgeons to rural villages where the bright sun at high altitude frequently caused cataracts. As is common with cataracts, over time blindness occurred in one eye and was followed by the clouding of the lens of the other. The villagers, who had no access to ophthalmological surgeons, saw a haze and then an impenetrable cloud came over the world.

The cataract project trucked in the equipment for portable operating rooms and brought the surgeons in by air. The surgeons, who donated their time, could do thirty operations in a day. It was the only time I heard José or his wife, Marcella, a beautiful and very stylish woman, with long dark red hair, speak of the work. It is his life, and she is in agreement with it. If you ask him about the work, he will change the subject. Or tell you there are many doctors in Mexico.

THE SWIMMING POOL OF LAS VIAS[5]

The address of the small rectangular building known as La Buena Tierra (the Good Earth) is Calle San Juan, *sobre la via del tren* (over the train track). And it is true that only a few feet from the school, in the narrow, unpaved

---

in galleries in Mexico City and New York, and published two books written in English. José's great-granduncle Matías Romero was the Mexican ambassador to the United States during the first Benito Juárez administration, which began in 1858, and later served in the Díaz administration as secretary of finance from 1877 to 1879 and again in 1892 and 1893. Like Juárez, Matías Romero was from Oaxaca. Pepe Romero's widow, Del, retains her Australian accent undiluted even after many years of living in Mexico City, making her Spanish unusual. Her combination of Australian openness and Mexican generosity results in *abrazos* and laughter.

5Las Vias (the Tracks) is a section of houses built along an abandoned railroad spur.

alleyway where the garbage blows in the wind or mixes with the summer mud and the dogs snarl and scavenge, two narrow ribbons of steel lie half buried, wasted, not even saved for scrap. In the Mexican style, in which the burden of history can never be set aside, people call the alleyway Las Vias. All along the track, people constructed domiciles. Not all houses, as houses are known. Although some have grown sturdy over the years—one is brick, one is stone—most are made of lamina, the reinforced, waterproofed card-board that is the chief building material of the urban poor in Mexico. The flaw in lamina is that it cannot bear much load beyond its own weight; a window made of glass would cause it to crumple, like paper in a fist. Behind the fences made of wire and wood, which are in reality no more than flimsy prayers to fend off thieves and dogs, many doors and few windows face the alleyway.

In the first years of the population of Las Vias life went along calmly. The difficulty of mere survival apparently occupied the residents. Then, over time, the single rutted space that provides entry to Las Vias from the major parallel street became a dividing line. Neighbors allied with each other on each side of the tracks. The alliances turned into factions. Open hostilities broke out. The parents and children fought over slights or rights to the necessities of life: water; electricity; the disposal of human waste. Then a Baptist church in Mexico City and the Fundación Comunitaria Morelense, IAP (the initials indicating that it is a private rather than public assistance institution) started a kindergarten and a prekindergarten in the rectangular building divided into small rooms and outfitted with tiny tables and chairs.

La Buena Tierra served families from both sides of Las Vias, and after a time, because their children went to school together, the intensity of the feud diminished, if not everywhere, at least in things pertaining to the school. The women cooked together in the kitchen of the school, and they formed a society of mothers to serve the children. They read the Bible and spoke of the gentle ways of Jesus, but the feud simmered on, the dogs snarled every-where along the tracks, and no house lacked a fence.

One afternoon three of Mexico's social doctors and I visited the school along with Elizabeth Marroquín, the director of La Buena Tierra. The chil-dren in the classrooms, only three and four years old, were unafraid when we talked, but careful only to glance at us as we entered. In one room they cut pictures from magazines to match a word the teacher had told them. They were too polite and perhaps too thin, but they had already begun to consider their way in the world. If a survey of dreams had been taken, most of the boys hoped to drive taxis, while the girls wished to be nurses. But they were all open to encouragement. After one boy said he wanted to be a doctor, the other boys changed their dreams and took up medicine too. Save one, who pulled himself up very straight in his tiny wooden chair and said in the loudest voice, as ominous as the flute sound of a child's voice could be, "I will be the police."

The doctors had been born to lives as far from Las Vias as one might imagine. All were elegant and attractive, each in her own way. Elena Cepeda, who headed the private foundation in Morelos, was the daughter of the former governor of the state of Coahuila and the wife of the president of the PRD in the state of Morelos. Her skin was as fine as parchment blushing, and she was very brave, having defeated a deadly disease. Martha Galas, who worked with her at the foundation, was the second generation of two families of Spaniards in Mexico. Although she did not whistle her sibilants, she had the quick, forceful accent of the Spanish north and the confidence that is the special quality of attractive Spanish women. Herlinda Suárez, through whom I met the others, is the daughter of the former governor of Chiapas. She is not part of the foundation, but there are few social doctors like Suárez, who still dresses in blue jeans and looks more like a student than an *investigador 2* (the second-highest rank in the Mexican university system) as she goes striding through slums and isolated villages, protected only by the confection of a knowing smile and her presumption of the goodness of the people she meets.

When they walk the alleyway of Las Vias, disdaining the menace of the dogs, chatting with the women who come out to greet them, the three doctors—sweet, formal, and quick—could not be more out of place or more at home. They have connected La Buena Tierra to the Colegio London, one of the best private schools in the city. They and the director of La Buena Tierra would like the children of Las Vias to have all the advantages of the children who attend the private school. All of them wished for a swimming pool so that the children might have healthy exercise, but there was no space and no money for such a grand project. The director said, "So we found a space and we painted the ground blue like a swimming pool. We told the children to step into the blue area and move their arms as if they were swimming. All of them went into the blue, but one. 'Why don't you go in, like the other children?' I asked.

" 'I can't,' he said. 'I'm afraid of the water.' "

THE CLANDESTINE DOCTOR

On the wall in the room where I work there is a photograph of Raúl Murguía Rosete and twenty young Maya men and women in a village not far from the ruins of Kalkini. They are lined up in front of a low building with a space for a door and two windows. It is clear from the hard lines of light and shade in the photograph that the sun is ferocious. People in the photograph squint rather than smile. Murguía towers over the Maya students, none of whom rises to his shoulder. He has a black-and-white beard, full but neatly trimmed. His hair is black and gray. He wears thick eyeglasses, although the lenses do not distort the shape of his eyes as seen by the camera. Because of Murguía, who represents the United Nations Development Program on the peninsula, the young people have built the structure, which they are making into a cultural center and a classroom and a place to learn about computers, if ever the amperage of the electricity in the village becomes stable enough to power a computer.

They named the course of study, which Murguía made possible, Escuela de Alta Cultura Maya—Hunab Ku (School of High Maya Culture—the Unified God). At the first meeting of the course, the students brought the few small tables and chairs they could carry from their houses to form a semblance of a conference table. The course had become a problem for the students. When the tables and chairs were in the schoolroom, no one could sit at a table in their houses. A few days later Murguía loaded tables and chairs and a blackboard and other materials into the back of his van and delivered it all to the village.[6]

The young people of the village trusted him, as do the Maya all over the Yucatán Peninsula. Murguía administers fifty-five programs (at last count) for the United Nations Development Program. He does it with a staff of one, a van, and very little money. There are two distinct sides of Murguía. One is a man of Mexicanidad, an intellectual with a deep voice, a commanding laugh, and a nose for the ironies of life; that side drinks tequila or scotch whiskey (if he must), enjoys good food and interesting women. The other is a tough-minded administrator who watches every program, wasting noth-

---

[6]Murguía also assembled the faculty, including Dr. Alejandra García Quintanilla as *presidenta*, Miguel Ángel May May to teach the Yucatecan Maya language (the students all knew Maya, but not at the level they would achieve after a year with May May), and Silvia Terán, the agronomist and anthropologist.

ing, checking, checking, always traveling, always looking, counting, evaluating. It is not an entirely pleasant side; waste money, botch a program, and Murguía will terminate it, even if the program belongs to a close friend.

I will not tell you the details of his life, how he came to his work, what incident or incidents formed him, although it is a long time since we met and we have spent many, many hours together drinking tequila or traveling in his van from place to place on the peninsula. Once, on a long road trip, I asked if he would agree to a formal interview. "No," he said. "I am a *clandestino*." It was a curious adjective to convert into a noun, for he did nothing clandestine. He was a social physician, not a secret physician. We rode in the silence of disagreement for a long time, more than an hour. Perhaps his answer was motivated by modesty, in which case I have betrayed him.

Perhaps the best way to explain Raúl Murguía is to tell about one day. It was quite a long time ago, and I suppose much has changed since we went to Carolina and Xtobil. We picked up Sigismondi, the Italian agronomist, on the way, and stopped in a grocery store to buy bottled water, which came icy cold and appetizing. When I took a handful of pesos from my pocket to pay for the water, Murguía pushed my hand aside and told the grocer, "His money is counterfeit." And we all laughed. It is Murguía's style: expansive, laughing, and tough, nothing like the dour face of a "do-gooder." There was a time when the Mexican government feared him. He is the UN's man now.

Murguía promised lunch in the "best restaurant in Xtobil" that afternoon. It was served in a hut made of sticks and thatch about fifty yards off the highway. We dipped water from a barrel into a bucket to wash our hands before eating. The woman who ran the restaurant, which had one table and four chairs, took the bottled water we had brought and mixed it with powder to make *horchata* (a sweetened mixture of grain and water). There were no decorations inside the hut except for an old deer rifle hung on the wall. Shooting deer was illegal in the state of Yucatán, but shooting one's neighbors was not so frowned upon. There were feuds, shootings; villages split apart, and new villages were started. It was like the beginning or the end of human society.

Lunch was spit-roasted chicken, cooked again in a pot filled with vegetables and a few noodles and filled out with stacks of tortillas made by a woman who sat just outside the hut cooking them on a long piece of iron, part of which extended over an open wood fire. When the tortillas were cooked on the hot part of the griddle, she picked them up, one by one, and moved them to the part of the griddle farthest from the fire, where they stayed warm, but did not burn. There were no utensils. We ate the chicken with our fingers and used the tortillas to scoop up the thick stew, and we also salted the tortillas and ate them just for the flavor of the local corn. At the end of the meal each of us picked up his bowl and drank the remaining soup. The chillis, which were served in a separate dish, were as hot as any I have ever tasted; only the salt could take away the sting. And while we ate, a turkey, which was all legs and neck, like a scrawny old man, paced the dirt floor of the hut and a tiny enclosed yard next to the woman who cooked tortillas on her metal comal.

After lunch, we washed again, and paid for our meal, and drove down a rutted road into Xtobil. The meeting Murguía and Sigismondi had come to attend was to be held at the pump house, four kilometers into the dense, dry forest. For many years the village had lived mainly from crops planted in its milpas (small farms) cut into the low jungle or forest. The beans, squash, and corn, along with a few chickens and a rabbit or an agouti here and there and a pig for the Day of the Dead had kept them alive. Then two bad things happened. The PRI gave the village several foot-powered sewing machines in exchange for their votes, and the women decided they would rather embroider than work in the milpa. Then the pump broke down, and there was no more well water for irrigation. Until the pump broke down, the villagers had been able to grow pineapple and a few bananas, as well as the three saints of survival, and it had been enough to sell to earn money to buy cloth and thread and cooking pots, a bicycle to share.

We trudged through the forest, pushing aside low branches, following the villagers until we came to a sudden hill, with a cement-block pump house at the side. Perhaps it had been the site of an ancient temple, long overgrown, covered over with windblown earth and grass until it became a hill. The men and women of the village had gathered there, waiting for Murguía and Sigismondi, who would help with speaking in Maya. The village had been damaged by a hurricane and was just recovering. It was not prosperous, but with the new pump it might become prosperous again, if there was also rain, and the women came back to the milpas, and no hurricane came again soon.

The villagers were scattered around the hill. Murguía and Sigismondi sat at the top with the leaders of the village. It was very hot, and there was not much shade except in the narrow early-afternoon shadow cast by the pump house. I stood at the bottom of the hill among several women and a few old men. One woman nursed her child. An old man whispered to me that he spoke Spanish and would interpret for me what the village leaders said in Maya. They spoke of the hurricane and the rain and the pump, which would enable them to plant and harvest crops beside the three saints again. Before the hurricane they had been beekeepers, but when the hurricane passed through the village, the wind blew the bees away, and they lost an important part of their livelihood. They thanked Murguía and asked for his continued help. Then it was his turn to speak.

His voice was strong, and they could hear him well even at the bottom of the hill. He was much taller than the Maya, but he chose to stand just below the top of the hill so that he did not dwarf the village leaders. He said he wanted to help them, but he imposed certain conditions. He explained that he did not represent either the Catholic Church or the government; in their work with him they would be free of both influences, able to make decisions for themselves. He did not speak of democracy, but he described the beginning of the process, and he said, "I am interested in helping you only if there is no discrimination on the basis of gender or color or politics or religion. I am interested in working with you only as long as you live together this way, as comrades."

While his words were translated into Maya, he stood very still, with his arms folded over his chest, a tall man of sixty years, dressed in a short-sleeved polo shirt. All around him, on all the levels of the steep hill, in the sun and in the shade of the shadow of the pump house, the people of the village listened. Afterward they would talk about what he said and make decisions together. But it was already clear how they would decide about these aspects of democracy, for it was the first time in more than 2000 years that a meeting to decide the future of the village had included women.

36.

The Ninth Mexican

A definition: Mexican-Americans are not Mexicans,
just as German-Americans are not Germans.

One Saturday afternoon, long ago, on the way to Agua Prieta to buy gasoline, I asked my father if we could invite the old man to our house. He said the old man could come back to the house with us in the car, but he would have to get home by himself. While my father and the mechanic at the gas station tinkered with the recalcitrant motor of the old Packard, I made the invitation. The old man shook his head. "I am a red bone Mexican. From here, from this side."

He said no more to me that afternoon, although I recall standing there in the dust of his front yard for a very long time. Our acquaintance was not the same after that. He said very little. Or perhaps I had run out of questions. The Saturday trips came around relentlessly, like the news about the war, but the distance to Agua Prieta seemed to have increased since the afternoon of his declaration. The old man and I had become strangers, our friendship sundered by an imaginary line. It had been his advice to begin with history, to examine the provenance of the dust, and then he showed me the line as if it were the end.

Had he lived for a hundred years, he would never have crossed the line. He had other dreams, other expectations; he was Mexican. The land, whatever the wind left, belonged to him. He built his house and put his chair on his land and waited for rain. He would have owned a cow if grass had grown on the sand. In March, in the high desert, the wind came and rearranged the surface of the land. Then in the hottest part of summer, the tiny tornadoes we called dust devils came and lifted the dry, dusty land into the air and carried it for miles and miles across borders and fences, up and back, this way and that, and although the dust devils did no harm, they were unstoppable.

LUPITA AND ST. PAT

At nine o'clock on the morning of December 12, 2002, a man dressed in
the attire of an Aztec prince climbed ceremoniously to the top step leading
to St. Patrick's Cathedral on Fifth Avenue in New York City. His arms and
legs were bare; his breastplate, breechcloth, gauntlets, greaves shone red and
gold. On his feet he wore only leather sandals. As he reached the top step, he
removed his crown of towering peacock feathers, knelt on the icy stone, and
bowed his head in prayer. The temperature was close to freezing, but there
was no wind. He knelt for a long time, more than five minutes, perhaps ten,
and he did not shiver. He crossed himself, and he arose and backed down the
steps as ceremoniously as he had mounted them.

The torch was coming, carried by relays of runners from the Basilica of
Guadalupe in Mexico City across the states of Hidalgo, Puebla, into Veracruz, and up the coast through Tamaulipas, crossing north from Mexico
at Matamoros, and then through Texas, Louisiana, Mississippi, Alabama,
Georgia, the Carolinas, Virginia, and into Washington, D.C., where members of the U.S. Congress turned out to march beside the torch in a
parade, and then the runners headed north again, through Maryland,
Delaware, Pennsylvania, New Jersey, and on the morning of the birthday
of the La Virgen de Guadalupe, the young men completed their 3,133-mile
journey. On the forty-fifth day a young Mexican, in the company of great
portraits of the Virgin, carried the torch into St. Patrick's Cathedral. The
organizers of the journey of the torch said she had come across the border
"wet," meaning the Virgin of Guadalupe was undocumented, illegal. In
this, she was like the crowd that gathered in the cathedral to sing "Las
Mañanitas" (the birthday song) to the Virgin, while a mariachi band
played and the sound of the trumpet came through the great doors of the
cathedral out onto the street, where yet more of the faithful awaited the
arrival of the torch.

They came from parishes and parish schools, dressed in white sweatsuits
with the words (in Spanish) "Messengers for the dignity of a people divided
by a border" printed in bold letters across the front. As the hour of the
arrival of the runners neared, the crowds grew, the organized school groups
on the steps, facing the avenue, and another crowd on the street facing them.
The students on the steps cheered the Virgin, and their chants and shouts
were reminiscent of high school football cheers, but for one:

Aquí estamos,	(We are here,
y si echamos,	and if you throw us out,
nos regresamos!	we are coming back!)

And then the football-style cheers again:

I see it,
I feel it,
The Virgin is here!

As the hour of arrival approached, they took up yet another shout, more like a demand:

Amnesty!
Amnesty!
Amnesty!
Now!

They were undocumented, and there on the street, setting up sawhorse barricades, were the police, yet the undocumented were not afraid. Like La Virgen, they said, they were "wet." They had made her into the patron saint of the "wets."

When the torch came down Fifty-first Street, held high in the runner's hand, moving slowly, in keeping now with the huge portraits of the Virgin, the crowd on the steps, the Aztec dancers in their suits of pre-Columbian markings and the folk dancers in their white costumes and tall straw hats, the press, and all the people who had brought videocameras to record the moment—as if memory, which had been the library of their ancestors, would no longer suffice—parted graciously in honor of the Blessed Virgin who had come without papers across the Rio Grande.

Amnesty now!
Viva Mexico!
Amnesty now!
We are Mexicans!
Viva Mexico!

This was one of the oppositions of the morning. One was caused by the Aztec prince, the symbol of Ce Acatl Topiltzin Quetzalcoatl (Our Revered Prince One Reed Quetzalcoatl) who was Indian Mexico. It was the celebration of the arrival of Guadalupe, yet a man in breechcloth and breastplate

of red and golden yellow had knelt on the steps of the cathedral, his crown
of peacock plumes tucked in his left arm so that he might make the sign of
the cross with his right. Had he come to surrender to the Church in a symbolic reenactment of the Colloquy of 1524? Or did he insist that there were
still two routes to syncretism? He spoke to no one. He endured the cold on
his naked skin. He knelt before the Church.

A boy, not yet twenty, as undocumented as the Virgin and as slim as a stick,
said, "I cannot go back; I am Mexican, yes, but I am accustomed to New York."

> Viva Mexico!
> Amnesty now!
> We are Mexicans!
> Viva Mexico!

The cry was for amnesty for 3 million Mexicans (or 6 million or 10 million or 13 million, no one knows how many) who lived and labored in the
United States. It is probable that one of every nine Mexicans lives north of
the border. In 2000, the IFE estimated that 8.83 percent of all Mexicans of
voting age (6.2 million people), not including the 1 million Mexicans who
had become naturalized U.S. citizens, lived in the United States.[1]

The young people on the steps of the cathedral, led by the strong voices
and cadence-counting arms of their teachers, chanted and cheered and said
they were Mexicans who wanted to become Americans, but they did not say,
"Viva los Estados Unidos." It was another opposition, and it would not be
easily resolved now as it had been once before when there was an amnesty
for undocumented workers. Amnesty meant residence papers, the treasured
green card, the ability to come and go between the two countries, stability,
higher wages, and most treasured of all, amnesty opened the way to citizenship. But nothing had come of the negotiations between Bush and Fox.
Instead of making the border more open, the Americans had narrowed the
passage after the attack on the World Trade Center. Vicente Fox could not
accomplish an amnesty, but there was still the Virgin of Guadalupe; perhaps
she would perform one more miracle.

[1]For more details on Mexican voting in the United States, see Raúl Ross Pineda, *Derechos Políticos de los Mexicanos en el Extranjero,* copyright by the author. Ross is a columnist for *Exito!,* the Spanish-language weekly publication of the *Chicago Tribune.*

In 2003 Latinos were declared the largest minority group in the United States according to the Census Bureau.

Inside the cathedral they prayed, and because it was the year of the beatification of Juan Diego, they brought their small sons in the costume of the new saint so that they might approach the altar and be blessed. All through the mass the little boys in white sat or stood, and knelt when required, and in the back of the cathedral, which was filled from the altar to the doors, in the flat space where hundreds stood, unable to see the distant altar, watching the mass on television screens attached to the pillars, the boys in the guise of Juan Diego sat on the floor and waited to become the particularly blessed of the morning.

When it came time for the homily, Bishop Josu Iriondo said, "We ask you, Father, for the intercession of our Queen and Mother, the Virgin of Guadalupe, that we may, with the force of being a united people, organized in struggle, move the hearts and minds of those who govern this country that they give Permanent Residence to the nine million undocumented immigrants,[2] that we may enrich this country with our labor, our talent, and our culture." After the homily the mariachi band played and everyone sang "Mi Virgencita Ranchera," the song in which Mexicans say that the Virgin gave them this beautiful land (Mexico) for their country and blessed it, for it was her desire to have a sanctuary close to heaven.

The morning belonged to the Pope, for it was he who had chosen to make a saint of Juan Diego, to take the converted of Mexico to the bosom of the Church as never before, to raise the banner of the Virgin of Guadalupe forever above those of Quetzalcoatl and Martin Luther, and to solidify the claim of the origin of Mexico in a Catholic miracle. For those who lived anxiously the limited life of the undocumented the Pope had that morning succeeded as rarely before.

"Aquí estamos, y si echamos, nos regresamos!"

And who would stand beside them, who other than the Virgin? Joel

---

[2]James B. Wilkie, of the University of California at Los Angeles, sets the number of undocumented workers at four to five million, which, on the basis of my anecdotal experience, seems low. No one knows how many undocumented Mexicans, including women and children, live in the United States. A good number may be ten million, but it could be as high as twelve or fifteen million, given that there are more than five people in the average Mexican household, according to the 2000 U.S. Census. The number of persons per household times the number of workers does not produce an accurate figure. Many, many households include four or five unaccompanied workingmen, who have wives and children in Mexico.

Magallan, the Jesuit priest who heads the Asociación Tepeyac,[3] the one who hovered over the entire day, the inventor of the idea of carrying the torch, the originator of the Asociación Tepeyac, a busy, burly man from Zacatecas, born to breathe deeply in the high altitude of the ancient mining town and home of the great civil war battle—what Mexican marching band could not play "La Toma de Zacatecas"—said there would be no help from other Latinos, not from Puerto Ricans or Dominicans, the two largest groups of Latinos in New York. Help, when it came, he said, always came from the Anglos. But that may not always be the case, for Silvana Bonil, an Argentine psychologist, and Juana Ponce de León, a Colombian editor, agree that other Latinos do not help the Mexicans, yet both donate their days to Asociación Tepeyac.

Joel, as everyone calls him, not Padre Joel, is like Gregory Boyle, also a Jesuit priest, who heads the Guadalupe Mission in the most dangerous and difficult neighborhood of Los Angeles. Boyle is known as G-Dog which is what the gang members he works with in the neighborhood call him, but like Joel, he devotes much of his work to the newly arrived. They come to the mission carrying a small piece of paper with the address written on it. At night, in the mission church, the men who cannot be housed elsewhere sleep in the pews. They are clean and weary, and they will work as day laborers or dishwashers until they have enough money to move on.

They are a stream of labor and dreaming, the three million or five million or nine or thirteen million, and they follow many routes once they enter the country. The limitations on their rise to citizenship and the comforts of the working class are enormous: language, prejudice, lack of skills, and always, like a persistent nightmare, the terrible failure of the Mexican system of public education. Those who came from the cities fare better than those who came from the rural areas. It has always been that way in the United States: The Poles who came from the farms took longer to rise than the urban Germans; the Italians from the poverty-stricken south were at least a generation behind those from Rome. Nonetheless, the emigrants who crossed oceans were adventurers, the brightest and most enterprising, and although the journey from Mexico is not so final as the crossing of an ocean, emigration, especially from the farm to the city, is still a trip to another world. Every immigrant arrives dreaming, and when the dreams do not

[3]The Virgin is said to have appeared to Juan Diego at Tepeyac.

work out, as is too often the case for Mexicans, the first generation turns sour on dreaming and life, and succeeding generations must lift themselves by a heroic act of will from disappointment to success, if not happiness.

In an attempt to gauge the politicizing effect of emigration on Mexicans, I walked down long lines of immigrants waiting to get Mexican identity cards (*matriculas*), asking them two or three simple questions. Are you a Mexican citizen? Are you a registered voter in Mexico? If you were able to vote in the Mexican elections while remaining here in the United States, would you vote and which party would you choose? The people were of various ages, both men and women, and all but one of perhaps sixty people said he or she would vote. Most chose the PAN, a few the PRD, but not one said the PRI. When I asked if they wanted to explain their choice, almost everyone who answered the question said the same thing: because of what the PRI did to Mexico.

To use this tiny survey to define the character of Mexican emigration invites skepticism; nonetheless, the consistency of the answers shows that coming to a new country engages a person in what Pericles defined as the political life. What it does not show is when the political life came into being. Is a sense of politics what drives migration? Or does arrival in a new country lead to the political life? In the past the economic and political ideas of Mexicans who came to the United States and secured citizenship papers often moved from political liberal and social conservative to political and social conservative. They were political liberals at first, because it was in their interest; liberals have traditionally been more willing to accept and protect immigrants and those least able to protect themselves. And immigrants saw themselves in the role of underdogs, people in need of liberal policies. Conservatism is bound more closely to the protection of property and the tenets of religions. The distinctions between the two kinds of politics are not entirely about the haves and have-nots, but the categories generally hold.[4]

---

[4]On social issues many Mexicans and Mexican-Americans often side with conservatives, mainly for reasons of religion, as in right to life vs. choice questions.

Mexican culture is divided on gender issues along economic and geographic lines: Urban, educated, middle-class women in Mexico have progressed at least as quickly as those in the United States, but women from rural and disadvantaged backgrounds tend to want to stay at home until they are married and then to have children and live as *amas de casa*—literally, "homelovers."

Young Mexican and many Mexican-American women either are kept at home by

As those who were once Mexicans shed memories of the past, some chose to protect their newly won property.

It would be a mistake to think of Mexicans as a monolithic political body, but there are patterns, and there have been changes over the last few years. The newest arrivals now come with a different politics. They have lost faith in the center-left policies that grew out of the 1917 Constitution; the new arrivals have no quarrel with conservative policies; their interest was in democracy as it was represented by the fall of the party-state system; they accepted agreement with the conservative ideas of the PAN as a means and put themselves in the hands of hope. But to be a political person does not automatically permit political life at any level beyond the family and the immediate community.

In 2006, Mexicans abroad may be able to vote in Mexican elections. Several proposals have been put before the Congress. During his sexenio Ernesto Zedillo favored voting by Mexicans abroad, and José Woldenberg, head of the IFE, said he thought the conditions were right for voting abroad for the presidency in 2006. The battle for voting rights for Mexicans abroad has been going on since 1929, when the Los Angeles Spanish-language daily *La Opinión* raised the question. It is almost as easy for Spanish speakers in the United States as in Mexico to keep current with Mexican issues. They can follow the news on two television networks, many radio stations, and a great many newspapers. The *Dallas Morning News* provides excellent coverage out of Mexico for those who read English. *La Opinión*, owned by the *Los Angeles Times*, provides good coverage in Spanish. In Chicago, it's the *Tribune's Exito*. The *Miami Herald* has the best coverage of Latin America overall.

When permission for Mexicans abroad to vote will finally be granted is difficult to know, given the current stalemate in the Mexican legislature. The PRI, which still controls the legislature, is not the likely favorite for Mexicans abroad. The PAN sees these voters as theirs and courts them

---

their parents or feel uneasy when leaving home to attend college or find work. Sex education is an issue for the parents of young children. They may also favor complete bans on using fetal tissue for research.

It is not at all uncommon for those who have arrived in the United States from Mexico to want "to shut the door behind them," opposing amnesty for undocumented people and other policies liberalizing immigration.

assiduously in preparation for the day when they are able to vote. But there are many issues to be resolved: Who is a Mexican citizen? (U.S. citizens are able to hold dual citizenship status. Mexican citizens cannot hold dual citizenship.) Should people who vote in U.S. elections be allowed to vote in Mexican elections? What are the laws regarding dual citizenship and voting in the United States and Mexico? How would those Mexicans without voting credentials secure them? Finally, how would Mexicans vote? By absentee ballot? Or would there be polling places for Mexican voters throughout the United States?

There is also a U.S. side to the issue. To hold a foreign election on such a vast scale in the United States will surely not sit well with a large part of the populace. In 2000 there were "symbolic" elections in the United States. Some fifteen thousand Mexicans cast their votes in eighty places in six states. The results put the PAN far ahead, the PRD in second place, and the PRI, with its weak candidate, Labastida, last. There were no serious questions of sovereignty raised about a "symbolic" election. When Mexican citizens, many of them undocumented, go to Mexican polling places in the United States, they are certain to face protests from nationalistic Americans. The nationalists did not complain about thousands of Brazilians voting at their consulates in 2002, but Lenin was correct when he said that quantity equals quality: Thousands and millions are different in kind.

The voting question affects millions of Mexicans in the United States, including virtually all undocumented people and many who have residence papers. They are disenfranchised on both sides. They have no legitimate power outside home and family; their situation borders on statelessness. José Martín is one such person. He arrived in the United States when he was twenty-two years old and had been working in a garage in Guanajuato for eleven years. He crossed the border at Tijuana and went on to Sacramento, where he washed dishes all afternoon and into the night and slept in a rented space in the back seat of a car. It took two paychecks for him to get enough money together to move into a tiny apartment with five other men. At thirty-two he is a slim, handsome man, tall, with regular features; like many Mexicans, Martín has a strong sense of his own presence as a man. "I'm a writer," I said by way of introduction, and before I could go on, he said, "I'm a mechanic." He held out his hands, palms down, to show the blackness that would perhaps never come out from under his fingernails. He smiled, both to show his sense of irony and to inaugurate a tale of bitterness and warmth.

Martín married a few years after he arrived. His wife had come to California from Jalisco when she was two years old, and she had never looked back. She is a citizen, a child psychologist working for both state and private institutions; he has a residence permit good until 2006, and they have three children. The main problem in their lives is that Martín does not belong anywhere. He has mixed feelings about U.S. citizenship, although he does not want to go back to Mexico, where he says he and his family would starve: "Yes, I want to be a citizen because I want the benefits. And no, because I am Mexican *de hueso colorado* [to the depth of my bones; literaly, red bone]."

He speaks only a little English, and he is not interested in learning. "If I knew English, if I went to high school, I could take the test to get my certification as a mechanic," he said. "But they give the test in English, and I can't pass a test in English."

At home he is the cook as well as the father, and he tries to make light of it, but it is difficult for a man with blackened fingernails to be the cook in his own house. "I don't cook Tex-Mex food," he said. "I cook real Mexican food, food that stings [*pica*]." We made jokes about chillis, habaneros compared to jalapeños, but there was something else on his mind. There is a problem arising now in the Martín house. Eventually he decided to talk about it: "My son is eight years old, and he speaks English. In my house we speak Spanish, but he speaks English to me. He doesn't understand many Spanish words."

It hurt him to say this, to admit that he, the ironist, had lost control of the irony. When a man in Mexico cannot any longer be a man, he may be forced to turn to machismo to defend his honor. It is the last gasp of irony, the person who has been made into nobody insisting upon existence with his fists or his willingness to die or even by reaching for the bill when his pocket is almost empty.

For a moment Martín appeared to be relieved by revealing the problem, abandoning irony for a few sentences. But he soon changed his mind and tried perhaps to heal, more likely to hide his troubles in irony again. He showed the unhappy smile; it thinned his lips and narrowed his eyes as if he had just discovered a joke had been played on him. He said, "Every day I give my son green chile and a prickly pear smoothie [*licuado de nopales*] so he'll know he's a Mexican." And laughed, but such laughter does not relieve the anxiety of an ironic existence. He is a lost man; he has no voter registration card for Mexico, and he is not a citizen of the United States. He has no home. He belongs only to language, family, and the inner workings of machines.

WHY THERE IS NO GOOD MEXICAN FOOD IN NEW YORK

As José Martín knows, the palate is as important to a culture as to a body; when the cuisine is lost, the culture cannot be far behind. The process for Mexicans in the United States is not quick, and the path does not go straight from one culture to the other. Tex-Mex food and Spanglish (the mixture of English and Spanish) do not belong to the culture of any country; they are the world of the between. Tex-Mex food has very little resemblance to Mexican food other than the use of corn tortillas, which are more and more replaced by big, tasteless tortillas made of wheat flour. A burrito in a Mexican village in Puebla is a freshly made corn tortilla flavored with a pinch of salt and rolled up into a warm and pungent cylinder; it is not a big flour tortilla filled with the ingredients of the classic "Mexican plate": Spanish rice, refried pinto beans, a glob of puréed avocado and cream, shreds of meat or chicken, and a tomato and onion sauce that may or may not ever have met a chilli.

Spanglish is a complex, variable, and limited code. It is not a matter of enhancing the flavor of English with a few Spanish words that have the savor of home and the intimacy of shared secrets. Nor is it a matter of code switching between English and Spanish. Spanglish is less the introduction of new words into either language than the distortion of the sound and meaning of Spanish or English words. The difference between English, which is the most inclusive of all languages on earth, and Spanglish is that Spanglish has no core. It does not adopt words into a grammatical and syntactical structure, and it has no standard vocabulary; it is not the language of Antonio de Nebrija, the grammarian, or the historical principles of the *Oxford English Dictionary*. East Coast Spanglish and West Coast Spanglish are different, and neither is like Texas Spanglish. There are as many versions of Spanglish as there are national origins of Latinos and geographical variations in English vocabulary and diction.

The tragedy of Spanglish is more social than linguistic, for it does not signal the death of either English or Spanish. People who use Spanglish exclusively, many of whom are young and living in ghetto circumstances, are excluded from full participation in the general society. Spanglish-only speakers have trouble completing high school. The national dropout rate for Latinos is 35 percent (for students of Mexican descent in California it reaches 40 percent), and those who complete high school have the lowest college completion rate, far lower than either blacks or whites. Some of the social content of Spanglish appears in the way a fair-skinned Spanglish speaker may refer to educated dark-skinned people as whites. It follows the pattern in African-American ghetto schools, where good students are called whites and frequently ostracized.

In 2003, more than 50 percent of all children born in California were Latinos, most of them Mexican-American. These children will follow one of two paths: poverty, misery, a lack of formal education, an inability to speak either Spanish or English well, and very little hope for themselves or their children. Or they will be proficient in one language, often in two, and find a comfortable life in a society increasingly influenced by Mexican culture.[5] Much will depend upon beginnings. The life of the immigrant generation often determines the generations that follow. Children of people who immigrated successfully were long known among demographers as the skyrocket generation. The pattern can be seen among public persons.

Henry Cisneros held a cabinet post in the Clinton administration until a relatively inconsequential error cost him his political career: On his financial disclosure forms he had failed to report payments to a woman with whom he had an affair. Undaunted, he went on to become a success in media management, then in real estate. Cisneros grew up in a middle-class section of San Antonio knowing that he was descended on his father's side from a man to whom Spain had given a land grant in what is now New Mexico.

Cisneros was not the only Mexican-American member of the Clinton cabinet. Federico Peña, the former mayor of Denver, served as one of the leaders of the Clinton transition team, secretary of transportation, and later energy secretary. He is a quiet, polite, efficient man, who devoted most of his life to public service. Peña's father had been a cotton broker in Laredo, Texas.

---

[5]People from many Spanish-speaking countries now influence life in the United States, and dominance changes by area, with Mexican culture dominant from Chicago west to the Pacific Coast and south to the Mexican border. Caribbean culture was dominant in the eastern United States for many years, first Puerto Rican, then Dominican and Colombian as well, but now Mexican culture has become very influential in the East as well as in the rest of the country, because of both the number of Mexicans and the proximity of Mexico.

Henry B. Gonzalez was the first Mexican-American in the U.S. Congress. He served for thirty-eight years, headed the House Banking Committee, and seldom swerved from his Democratic populist positions. When he retired in 1998, the congressional seat stayed in the family. His son, Charlie, took his place. The Gonzalez family immigrated in 1911, during the Mexican civil wars. Like many of the Mexicans who came to the United States during that period, they were well prepared for life in a new country. Henry B. Gonzalez's father had been the mayor of the town of Mapimi, Durango.

Early on, Mexican-Americans were almost all Democrats, but that has begun to change. Ronald Reagan appointed a Mexican-American to his cabinet. George W. Bush speaks a few words of Spanish, producing no more solecisms in that language than in English. Bush's official lawyer, the solicitor general, is Mexican-American. Jeb Bush, the governor of Florida, is married to a Mexican woman. San Antonio and Southern California, especially Orange County and the suburbs, are producing large numbers of Mexican-American Republicans. Some pundits have argued that the long history of left-of-center politics in Mexico will make California an even more liberal Democratic state. It may be so, but there are many other factors to consider: the results of the 2000 elections in Mexico, the influence of neoliberalism, and the changes wrought by life in the American middle class. Mexican-Americans are not Mexicans, even when they speak fluent Spanish and have relatives in Mexico, and although many are poor, to think of Mexican-Americans remaining in poverty is to discount the effects of all the civil rights work of the last seventy-five years, from LULAC (League of United Latin American Citizens) to Chicanismo and to discount completely both the effects of immigration and the continued existence of the extraordinary willingness of Mexicans to work long and hard in service of their families.

The history of their rise to economic and political equality began at Pearl Harbor, when Mexican-Americans responded as well as, or better than, those whose ancestors had fought in the American Revolution. After World War II, when Mexican-Americans had demonstrated great courage under fire, winning many decorations, including Congressional Medals of Honor, their lives began to change. Many of them had the experience of serving as officers or noncommissioned officers who gave orders to Anglo troops. These veterans came home with a different understanding of themselves and their possibilities in business, education, health, housing, and civil rights. The GI Bill gave them the opportunity to go to college, and they took it. Until then relatively few people of Mexican descent had attended college in the United States, with the exception of some Catholic colleges. St. Mary's in San Antonio, for example, produced a stream of successful men through its college and law school, including Henry B. Gonzalez and civil rights leader Willie Velásquez.

In the 1960s politically active Mexican-Americans began to call themselves chicanos. Willie Velásquez of Southwest Voter Registration and Education and Joaquín Ávila, Jr.,[6] of the Mexican American Legal Defense and Education Fund led the fight for voting rights and more equitable distribution of funds for education in Texas. Rubén Salazar moved from the *El Paso Herald-Post* to writing a column in the *Los Angeles Times*. In the summer of 1970 Rubén, my friend since childhood, told me the Los Angeles county sheriff had threatened him, saying he had "to stop stirring up the Mexicans." Days later, during an antiwar march, a sheriff's deputy shot Rubén in the head with a tear gas projectile, killing him. It looked for all the world like murder, but a coroner's inquest ruled the killing accidental.

As the Latino—mainly Mexican and Mexican-American—population of California, Texas, New York, Illinois, Colorado, Georgia, and other states grows, more and more Latinos are elected and appointed to public office, but they are not a homogeneous political group, and they do not make up the majority in any state legislatures, so that their political power, like that of blacks, is still limited to choosing which side to agree with on any issue. Within the next decade, two at most, the role of Latinos, most of whom are of Mexican descent, will change, especially in California, where Latino population growth will no longer be driven by Mexican immigration. Demographic power is political power; their votes could determine most elections if they voted as a bloc. However, there is no reason to think that will happen, except on single issues. As Mexican-Americans move into the middle class in great numbers, people who now expect them to vote like recent immigrants and poor people will have to revise their views entirely.

California politics and policies will change. Racist tactics for maintaining people of Mexican descent at lower social and economic levels will not be acceptable to a controlling bloc of voters. However, California will not

---

[6]Ávila was one of the first Mexican-Americans to attend Yale College. He grew up in Compton, California, in what was then a working-class neighborhood, but he lived in a cultured home; Ávila's mother had served briefly as a secretary to Lázaro Cárdenas.

become a "Mexican state," tied body and soul to Mexico. People of Mexican descent will continue to identify with Mexico, but over time in a more distant, nostalgic way; the idea of Mexico as home will largely have disappeared. Even now they identify more with each other than with Mexicans. Their attitude toward new immigrants, like that of their countrymen, will depend largely on economic factors—theirs, that of the United States and of Mexico. Liberals may be no more welcoming to immigrants than conservatives. Whoever thinks otherwise has only to look back at the history of amnesty for Mexican farmworkers. Cesar Chavez, organizer of the farm workers' union and in most matters a champion of the downtrodden, opposed amnesty on the grounds that it would endanger the jobs of members of his union.

The Chavez argument against amnesty was defeated by the farm lobby. The farmers wanted more low-paid labor. The Mexican workers seeking amnesty were just what the farmers ordered: good workers at low wages. The farmers won the amnesty; the Mexican migrants could not have done it. Mexicans have no political power in the United States. The U.S. Constitution grants many protections to them under the Bill of Rights, which applies to persons, not merely citizens, but they are foreigners, strangers. Having residence papers makes little difference in their political value; they make appeals to justice and morality, but they can never rise above the unenviable role of supplicants. If they want to return to Mexico, they must show either a Mexican passport or a matricula, an identification card proving they have registered with the Mexican government at a consulate. People with U.S. residence cards as well as undocumented people must have the card to return legally to their own country. The Mexican government hoped the matricula would serve as proper identification for undocumented people in the United States, enabling them to secure drivers' licenses, open bank accounts, and so on. Several states agreed to accept the matricula, but New York, where there are now a million undocumented Mexicans, and California, where millions of undocumented Mexicans live and work, had both refused to accept the card as legal identification until California Governor Gray Davis, in a cynical attempt to win Mexican-American voters during a recall election in 2003, suddenly reversed his position and agreed to accept the matricula. Mexican-American voters weren't fooled. Davis was recalled.

A carpenter without a driver's license may have trouble getting to a job, a gardener may not be able to bring his tools, a cleaning woman may not be able to work so many jobs, a plumber may not be able to get to a leak quite so quickly. A person without a bank account has no safe place to keep savings, must pay high fees to cash checks, and so on. Refusing to recognize the matricula had no other function than to make life miserable for undocumented persons in the United States, keeping most of them below or near the poverty level.

The excuse was the September 11 attack on the United States. After that, Bush backed away from the idea of amnesty for undocumented Mexicans, and New York refused to recognize the matricula. The Pataki administration in New York gave its reason as "homeland security," but there was no mention by either Bush or Pataki of the undocumented people who had been killed in the attack, as if they had not ever existed. Mexican Foreign Secretary Jorge Castañeda continued to demand amnesty, which only irritated Bush and the U.S. Congress. Castañeda held the moral high ground on the issue of amnesty: It was surely merited, earned with hard work, tax contributions, and so on, but moral arguments, especially when presented aggressively by foreigners, have not often been successful with Washington; they are more likely to produce the opposite of what they intended. By 2003 U.S.-Mexican relations had deteriorated, pushing an amnesty farther into the future.

At the start of the 2004 election campaign President Bush announced a plan to give undocumented Mexican workers a three-year amnesty during which time they could work legally in the United States and travel up and back to Mexico. In his proposal, the period could be extended for another three years, but no more. After that, the Mexican workers would no longer be allowed to stay in the United States. There were varied responses to his proposal. President Fox, who wanted to please both Mexican workers and his counterpart in the north, immediately agreed to the idea. Political pundits in the United States said the proposal was simply a ploy to win Mexican-American votes in the November election; it would never be passed by a Congress dominated by conservative Republicans. There is yet another way to consider the proposal. It has many of the aspects of indenture, but indentured servitude in the early years of the English colonies and later the United States led to the opportunity to become a citizen at the end of the period of indenture. (U.S. President Andrew Johnson began his career as an indentured apprentice.) The Mexicans who work in this new form of indenture will have nothing at the end but voluntary or forced deportation.

The lives of the undocumented extend from comfortable, if a bit difficult, to nightmarish and are always subject to caprice. Rosa María Tellez Ortíz has seen and lived almost the full range of undocumented life, and she is only thirty years old. She comes from Chila de la Sal, Puebla, a mountainous area where, she said, salt is mined, washed, and dried in the sun. Her father left the town when he was a young man and spent a decade in Mexico City, working on the bottling line in a dairy. In 1982 he left Mexico to make his fortune in New York City. His wife, who was from Xixingo de los Reyes, Guerrero, and their daughters returned to Chila de la Sal. Seven years later Rosa María's mother sent her daughters north to find their father and bring him home. Rosa María took her younger sister by the hand, and she and the weeping fifteen-year-old set out for Manhattan. Rosa planned a career, she had studied to be a hairdresser; her sister had no expectations but to find their father and bring him back to the dry mountains of Chila de la Sal.

The smugglers, known as *coyotes* or *polleros* (chicken herders), charged nine hundred dollars each—money the girls would have to pay back later— to bring them across the border. Their route was Tijuana, Los Angeles, Sacramento. In Sacramento, the coyote gave each of them fifty-five dollars to take a bus to New York City. They had crossed the border through a sewer pipe, crawling for ten hours along a ledge above the sewage; then they had traveled with two other people in the trunk of a car from the border to Los Angeles, and north on Interstate 5, through the great farmlands of the valley, to Sacramento. When they finally arrived in Manhattan, Rosa had only a telephone number for her father. She dialed, the number answered, her father said he would see them, and the girls set out to meet him on West Ninety-fourth Street in Manhattan. Although their father spent much of his time with his girlfriend, he lived in a studio apartment with seven other men. Three slept in the full bed, Rosa's father and uncle slept in the twin bed, and the other three men slept on the floor. Rosa was seventeen years old; her weeping sister was two years younger. Their father negotiated a space for them on the floor.

Looking back on her introduction to New York, Rosa María, at thirty, speaks of it with a mix of sadness and nostalgia. She presents herself carefully. Her hair is smooth; her face is soft; she dresses as young matrons do in the borough of Queens, where she lives. She is a folk dance teacher and a folk art teacher and a writer and editor and human rights activist and wife and mother and hairdresser, and everything she knows and does is self-taught, except for hairdressing. A woman of composed surface, she excels at makeup and the coif of her thick black hair. And then at a word, a thought, some glimpse into the past, the composure comes under attack from the remembered moment: The dancer stumbles, the hairdresser's hand turns unsteady, a gray cast suffuses the smooth brown skin, and she must stop to defeat the gray, to push it back down inside her rather than to allow it to drain off in tears. "On one side," she said, "I laugh. On the other side, I cry."

She speaks easily and well, in proper Spanish not yet wounded by life in the city. "My father was very tough with us, hard. When we arrived, he stopped living with his girlfriend and went back to the studio. It made him angry, and he often came back to the room drunk. He wouldn't help us. He wouldn't give us money for clothing or food. He told us to go out and look for work.

"I looked and looked. I walked from Forty-second to Twenty-sixth, asking for work. Finally, I had an aunt who worked in a factory who taught us to cut and sew fabric. I found work in a place owned by Koreans. They paid two fifty an hour, ten hours a day; they took out no Social Security, nothing. One day I caught my finger in the sewing machine. I was bleeding. The Korean woman put some oil on it and told me to get back to work.

"My sister didn't work then. She stayed in the studio, but it was not a good place. The men came home drunk, and they made a lot of noise. We had to leave because a man tried to attack us. We moved to the Bronx, then to Queens. In Queens, everyone speaks Spanish. I don't speak English, because I don't use it.

"My sister got work in a Korean deli, but the owner of the deli tried to abuse her, so she ran away. The saddest is when Mexicans do this to Mexicans. Mexican restaurants are the worst. The pay from six at night to eight-thirty in the morning is ten dollars, and they don't even let you eat there. You have to bring your own food and eat it in secret, because they don't want the customers to see you. You can't sit down, and if you give no sexual favors, you're gone. If you don't do what they want, they fire you and they don't give you your money and they say they are going to call Immigration. And when you have no papers, who are you going to complain to?"

She expanded the categories: any undocumented person, any employer. Perhaps she meant to imply a political component to the exploitation: "They do it to men too. I know men who worked for homosexuals, all kinds, Greeks, Jews, Italians, Mexicans too.

"I want to be an insurance broker, but you have to pay forty dollars for two months of classes."

When she returns to speaking of her father, her eyes grow distant; there is a faint glitter of tears; they could be tears of sadness or anger; then the gray, like a dusting of ashes, comes into her skin, and the direction of her story is set: "After I got pregnant, my father changed his attitude toward me. He became very helpful. He worked as a deliveryman for a grocery store near St. Luke's Hospital. Every Sunday he rode his bicycle to Queens to visit us, to see his granddaughter. He bought her clothes; he was very good to her.

"My father was forty-nine years old when he died. He was thin, he didn't smoke, he rode his bicycle to Queens, and he believed in the Virgin of Guadalupe. They said he went to work, got a fever, went to St. Luke's, and died. The doctor said he was vomiting, and he died. I saw him on a cot in the hall, blood was running out of his nose, and he died. He had no papers, so they didn't pay attention to him.

"When my father died, the world fell. I took him home to be buried. He didn't want to live there; he liked the city, Manhattan. Friends and family helped me. The owners of the store where he worked helped me; they gave me two thousand dollars. When I came back, I had to pay two thousand dollars to a coyote.

"I live sometimes with my husband. I am living with him now. He hit me once, only once when he was drunk. My father used to beat my mother. I saw it a lot.

"My husband doesn't want to support us. Our apartment costs sixteen hundred seventy-five dollars a month. My sister, two other women, and a baby live with us. Besides the rent, there is the gas and electricity. It's very expensive.

"My husband is a cook in a Mexican restaurant. He didn't know how to cook Mexican food when he came here. He was from Toltecamilla, a mining town. When he came here, he worked for a Greek who owned a taco cart in Far Rockaway [Queens, New York]. There was a Pakistani who worked for him too. Then the Greek died, and they lost the cart. So the Pakistani borrowed money to open a restaurant. The Pakistani learned to cook Tex-Mex from the Greek, and then he showed my husband how to do it, and now my husband is the cook in the Mexican restaurant owned by the Pakistani, who learned from the Greek, who died."

She thought about food for a moment, careful not to smile at the ironies of her husband's culinary career or the Mexican restaurants where she had waited on tables and mopped floors. "When I go home to see my mother in Chila de la Sal, the real Mexican food makes me sick; I'm not used to Mexican food. I try to go to the next town, where they have a pizzeria."

After a long time, after talking about the little magazine she edits for Asociación Tepeyac and how life has improved since she learned her rights, she came up against the wall that bars people like her from well-being. She said of her daughter, "She is very quiet, very reserved. She speaks English well, and she has a U.S. passport. She asked me, 'What is undocumented?'

"And I told her, 'It means that you can go by plane, and I have to go on land.'

"But she doesn't understand. She was born here. She is eleven years old and she has a passport and I am her mother and I am undocumented."

DRYS

Ten years ago, thousands of people crossed the border at Cuidad Juárez, Tijuana, Tecate, and Matamoros. The danger was almost entirely from bandits who waited along both sides of the border. Near Matamoros (Brownsville) on the Mexican side at dusk bandits stepped out from the cover of the heavy brush that grew along the river and fired at the passing Border Patrol vans because they interfered with the business of banditry. At Cuidad Juárez people without documents cut through the wire fence on the U.S. side of the Rio Grande and ran and ran until they could take cover in the stream of shoppers browsing the stores of the South El Paso streets. On the Texas border the bandits worked the Mexican side. At Tijuana people ran across through an open sewer to get to the American side of the border. If they did not wear plastic bags on their feet when they crossed, the stench identified them to the cholos, the toughs who waited on the other side, tracking them like dogs, waiting to sniff them out in the darkness and strip them of anything they owned, even the unsavory shoes and clothes that had soaked and splashed in the thickened water of the sewer.

It is a different crossing now. The Border Patrol has built more fences, added more sophisticated equipment, forcing undocumented people to move away from the cities and towns to remote areas or to allow themselves to be packed like animals in the airless, killing heat of tractor trailers. The danger in crossing the border in the open now comes from the desert itself and from a pack of thugs who ride or walk along the border, brandishing weapons, claiming to protect the United States from "criminal elements." They are of course the truly dangerous element, vigilantes and racists who are more likely to shoot unarmed women and children than to interdict terrorists or drug dealers. But even the vigilantes are not so dangerous as the desert.

In early 2003 a Mexican newspaper ran a supplement advising people on how to cross the desert to enter the United States. The supplement was more warning than advice. Despite the efforts of the Border Patrol to rescue lost immigrants and the placing of water tanks by people concerned with the danger of the Arizona crossing, it is easy to become lost in the strangeness of the desert. Most of the Mexicans who come across now are from the south or the center of the country. For example, most of the young men and many of the young women of the town of Hueyapan, on the border of Morelos and Puebla, which is known for its fresh mountain water and fruit trees, have come north. These migrants understand hunger and poverty, but they have no concept of desert life. The land in Hueyapan is steep, and the bones of the earth have been reorganized into forbidding houses and streets in the high reaches of the town, but there is fresh, cold, clean water from the melting of snow above the town on the slope of the volcano. There is no water in the desert.

In summer, in the high desert of New Mexico, Arizona, and the westernmost counties of Texas, after the trickle of runoff from melted snow or December rain has dried in the gullies and rivulets, and the March winds have fanned the heat, there is no water. The sun and the distance between places that offer fresh water leave many people dead. The high desert, which does not look like the Sahara or the Gobi or the Mojave, can be deceptively rich in vegetation, but it offers no shelter, no shade, no food, nothing but myths about the wealth of water in the center of fat cactus. It takes ten acres of forage to support one steer in the desert along the border with New Mexico. To eat the core of a nopal (prickly pear), which grows along the New Mexico border in particular, it is best to boil off the thorns and strip away the outside. But there is no water to boil, and a machete is heavy. No one comes carrying a machete to split cactus. When the prickly pear flower turns to seed, the fruit is covered with thorns as thin as hair, so many that no tweezers, nothing but time, can rid the grasping hand of their itching sting. And the temperature in summer rises to 115 degrees in the shade, but there is no shade, nothing but sun. Thirst is not the only killer in the high desert; there is also heat, the want of salt, and then despair, for the mountains are always very far away, and if a walker reaches the mountains, it is only to find that the stones are sharp and the slopes are dry.

Migrants come to the high desert because they are strangers and because the desert hides behind myths. Vultures do not wait for the end of things. I saw one attack my dog when I was a boy, and we lived in the next to last house before the desert. The bird screamed, the dog screamed; I threw stones at the bird until it rose slowly into the air. It could have been a dreamed bird had it not been for the stench and the whimpering dog it left behind.

Only those who know the desert know the aggression of it, the way cactus thorns jump and snakes do not warn in the shedding season and vinegaroons stink and sting and the sun penetrates hats and shirts and sears flesh from the ground up, using every stone, every shiny slice of mica for a weapon. The Mexicans come to the desert: city people and all those who dwelt along rivers and streams and within walking distance of wells and oceans of water. They bring one plastic bag filled with clothing and only a little water, because the load grows heavier with every mile, and they must walk for many miles. They die. And although the desert has the silence of emptiness, many things come to eat the fallen. I do not know at what stage of dying they begin their attack. Ants eat carcasses from the inside out; I have watched them at their work.

As fences are extended east and west from the busiest crossing points and the ground is dotted with sensors that announce every footstep, the migrants are forced out farther from populated areas, deeper and deeper into the desert. Now, the remains of hundreds of Mexicans are found in the desert every year. And more are not found. These are the cruelest deaths. People look for the lost for decades. Luis Pérez, now a U.S. citizen working in the vineyards of California, where he has become an expert in grafting the vines, is fifty-six years old. In 1969 he heard from his brother who had reached the border and was planning to come across. Pérez was in Chicago then, sending money back to his brother, who was in Tijuana.

Pérez waited, but his brother did not arrive. He began a search for him. He went to Tijuana to ask for his brother, combing the streets, the cheap hotels in town, and the houses above the canyon west of the city where the migrants waited for a cloud to bring the moonless moment when the coyotes would lead them across, running down through the steep-sided canyon into the night, racing against the revealing wind, with their hands clutching wives, children, a grocery bag filled with all the possessions of their lives.

In all his searches Pérez found nothing. He does not know what happened. There was no news, no sign. Coyotes keep no records and entertain no questions. They are the villains and the heroes of the crossing points. Pérez could not find out where his brother had gone, whether he had entered the United States or he had gone east, beyond Tecate, beyond California, then north into the desert, and disappeared.

GEORGE W. BUSH'S UNDOCUMENTED MAN IN CALIFORNIA

In 2003, President Vicente Fox, who could not reach an agreement with the Bush administration on amnesty for undocumented workers, took another tack. The Mexican government began seeking social security payments for people who had worked and paid into social security in both countries, arriving at a total of the required quarters (ten in the United States) needed to be eligible for retirement benefits. The United States has an agreement with many countries to make such payments. Estimates of the cost came from various sources, but they agree on something near a billion dollars a year, if money was paid to all 162,000 Mexican nationals brought into the system under the rules sought by the Mexican government.[7]

The more interesting question was Social Security payments to people who had worked in the United States using nonexistent Social Security numbers. In American cities and towns, all day, every day, people walk up and down the streets of neighborhoods that cater to recent immigrants offering Social Security cards of the dead, and now with the help of computers, any number not yet registered. Undocumented people buy the Social Security numbers because an employer must pay federal and state (when applicable) withholding taxes and Social Security even though he may say he assumed the person had legal status and did not ask to see a residence (green) card. Gabriela Lemus of the League of United Latin American Citizens (LULAC) told the *Washington Post* twenty-one billion dollars paid into Social Security may have come from undocumented Mexicans.

But there is no clear definition of what is meant by a Mexican in the United States. Do only noncitizens count? Is a person of Mexican descent a Mexican, unlike a person whose ancestors came from Germany six generations

---

[7] *Washington Post*, December 19, 2002.

ago? Should residents be counted differently from undocumented people and people with visitor or student visas? Is the definition genetic—i.e., based on indigenous ancestry? If genetic, what about criollos? What about the children of Europeans who emigrated to Mexico during World War II? Former Foreign Secretary Jorge Castañeda, in an argument with Carlos Monsiváis,[8] claimed that one-fourth of Mexico's economically active population worked in the United States. Converted to numbers of people, Castañeda said that of the 38.7 million whom statisticians at INEGI reported as economically active, 9.68 million worked in the United States. Castañeda's statement appears at first glance to be absurd, too high by at least a third, but his point has merit; if his figures were even close to correct, Mexico has lost sovereignty over its own labor market. Unemployment in Mexico has risen to 4 percent, but the loss of the safety valve in the United States would increase Mexican unemployment to 28 percent, a full-blown economic depression.[9]

The United States could absorb the loss of the workers, but without them the cost of the labor component of many foodstuffs and services would double, triple, quadruple; prices would skyrocket while profits disappeared in the middle of a severe economic downtown. The point is that the two economies are inextricably linked. The United States cannot get along without a source of low-wage labor, and Mexico would have great difficulty absorbing the flood of workers and the loss of the thirteen billion dollars they send home every year. For a long time, people on the left in Mexico have

[8] *La Jornada*, November 21, 2002.

[9] The economic forces that drive Mexicans to cross the border make much more sense in light of the full tally of Mexican labor problems released by the government institute INEGI. In June 2003 it published data showing *urban* Mexico suffering employment problems very close to depression levels. The number used by Fox had then risen to 3.17 percent, but there were also 3.74 percent not seeking work for one reason or another, 4.69 percent in the process of changing jobs, 4.4 percent who worked less than thirty-five hours a week, and 8.9 percent who worked more than thirty-five hours but earned less than the minimum wage. The percentages do not include those people, mostly rural, who live on about one dollar a day, another 1 or 2 percent of the work force. For the same month Banamex reported more people in the informal sector. And the United Nations had just formed a commission on economic problems led by former Mexican President Ernesto Zedillo and including former Mexican Foreign Secretary Carlos Castañeda. The UN Commission favored free trade, which meant globalization. Given the INEGI statistics, one could only hope that the ideas of Zedillo and Castañeda would not prove to be contagious.

demanded that labor flow up and back across the border as easily as capital. In fact, it does. The Immigration and Naturalization Service, which operates the Border Patrol, is at times brutal, but never efficient or effective.[10] It is hopelessly understaffed and underfunded, unable to slow the flow of labor across a border that runs for two thousand miles along rivers, across deserts and mountains, and through cities and towns.

The INS has a less than sterling record in the treatment of undocumented people whom it refers to as "illegals" or "wets" or "tonks." This last refers to the sound of a flashlight banging on a person's skull. Beatings, violations of rights under the U.S. Constitution, racial profiling, and other crimes have been shown in testimony in U.S. district court to be common behavior by the INS.

Silvestre Reyes, who spent many years heading the Border Patrol along the Texas-Mexico border, has since been elected to the U.S. Congress as a Democrat from the Sixteenth District, centered in El Paso. His record on immigration both before and after his election was scrutinized by Americans for Better Immigration, a xenophobic organization, and published in the form of a report card. Over the course of his career Reyes has consistently earned grades of F and F– from the anti-immigration zealots. The Border Patrol was far from perfect under Reyes, but apparently living intimately with the issues of immigration for many years leads a person away from xenophobia and toward recognition of the gift immigrants bring to the country.

Not all undocumented immigrants make the best citizens, but many do. At Cristo Rey High School, a new, still small school in a businesslike brick building in the heart of the Mexican and Mexican-American section of Chicago's Pilsen and Little Village neighborhoods, all the children are of Mexican descent, and presumably some are not citizens or legal residents. The school, like the New York City Department of Education, does not distinguish between documented and undocumented students. Cristo Rey has a dropout rate of 1 percent. Every member of the graduating class of 2002

---

[10]The Immigration and Naturalization Service (INS) has changed its official name since becoming a part of the Department of Homeland Security, formed after the September 11, 2001, attack on the World Trade Center. It is now the Bureau of Citizenship and Immigration Services, but bureaucracies, like brides who marry late in life, continue to be known by their maiden names.

was accepted by a college. Of all its graduates at the time, 87 percent have gone on to college.

The school has a work-study program that places its students in law firms, brokerage houses, advertising agencies, and so on, where they enjoy a kind of apprenticeship and earn money while attending school. Many of the students are from the state of Michoacán, but a show of hands in a group of sixty or seventy students produced none who knew they were of Purépecha descent or that *michi* means "fish," as in the name of the place where they or their parents had come from. They were interested in law and banking; Mexico was another time, another place for these scrubbed children. What they had brought with them was the Virgin of Guadalupe and a taste for the future. Some had crossed a river or crawled through a drainpipe to get to Chicago, and they were not interested in going backwards. The undocumented studied and worked and prayed to the Virgin of Guadalupe for amnesty.

Not far away, in an alternative high school, there were also undocumented students. They talked tough, looked tough, mixed easily with the black students in the same "last chance" setting. Their language was a mix of black English, Spanish, Mexican slang, and standard English. In a small group that came with no notice to talk about Mesoamerican literature, there was a young woman who carried her poems in her backpack and another who wanted to write a novel. But they could not say what they felt or thought in sensible sentences. The gangs had touched them: They showed tattoos, the girls wore purple or dark red fingernails as long as tiger claws, and one of the boys had a gang insignia on his cheek.

They represented the two paths for Mexicans in the United States, the two faces, the two sides, the economic duality carried across the border. That the undocumented could survive, perhaps succeed, was clear enough in Pilsen. That the newcomers and the children of newcomers were at risk was also clear. More than 150,000 people live in the Pilsen–Little Village area of Chicago. In 2002 the public high school dropout rate for the area was 65 percent.

The question raised by the undocumented students at Cristo Rey High School is one of great importance. These undocumented students, who are among thousands graduating from U.S. high schools every year, are prohibited from receiving financial aid and made to pay high "out-of-state" tuition at public colleges and universities in many states. They are not eligible for federal aid, and worse, if they receive scholarships, even from private sources, they may find when later applying for residence papers that they are denied on the grounds of having been "wards of the state."

In New York and other states, these rules against the hopes of children have been dropped, and undocumented high school graduates may attend institutions of higher learning like any other students. Senator Orrin Hatch of Utah has tried to make the New York attitude toward undocumented students a national policy. The alternative is to turn excellent students by the thousands into people with little hope of success, to waste them. That can hardly be seen as in the interest of the United States or Mexico. Whose interest is served by ruining the prospects of students who have already proved their seriousness about education and demonstrated their quality of mind is not clear.

Most of the people who emigrate are adults for whom school is no longer a question. They have completed primary or more often now secondary school. Interestingly, a political transformation takes place in these people even if they cannot get residence papers, becoming immigrants in the legal sense. It is the case with Carlos Lara, who crossed into the United States when he was twenty-six years old, divorced, and the father of a child. Immediately after arriving, he went to school to learn English. He came for the better life, which for him means economics, but he did not come from poverty. His family lived in Durango, where his father was the foreman on a cotton farm. The Lara family lived in a two-bedroom house in Durango. There was always food on the table, but never enough money to go to a restaurant. Lara's brother emigrated first, found work in Vacaville in Northern California, then brought Carlos along, writing to him about the good life in California.

When he arrived, Carlos worked in restaurants at miserable wages, then moved into construction work as soon as he learned enough English to be able to communicate on the job. Now he belongs to the carpenters' union, has health insurance through the union, and prefers to speak English. He sends seven hundred dollars a month to his ex-wife in Durango, who spends a good part of it to pay their son's tuition at a Catholic school. Lara opposes the idea of parochial school for his son, but there is nothing he can do about it. His son is now eleven years old, and Lara has not seen him for ten years.

Lara had a California driver's license for a while, but when he applied to have it renewed, the state checked his Social Security number, found out it was false, and took his license. Lara shakes his head about the driver's license. "California is the worst state as far as concessions to immigrants." It is the driver's license that bothers him more than anything. "Where I live," he said, "the bus comes by once an hour. It comes by on time, but I have to go when the bus goes."

Lara is a burly man, smooth, tall, made entirely of round surfaces, heavy shoulders, full cheeks, not fat, but fatted, smug in the full-bellied way of a man leaning back in his chair after a good meal. He has theories. He does not fear the *migra* (INS), but he finds his situation irksome: "The state takes and takes and gives nothing back. We don't ask for much. Amnesty would make things easier; it would mean I could work anywhere. We're not supposed to work, and sometimes it's hard for undocumented people to find jobs. As you get better jobs, they check your ID more carefully. You can only go so far. But it's still better here. In Mexico I had to work twice as hard, and I didn't have the things I have here, food, clothes. You have to work a whole week in Mexico to buy a pair of Levi's."

It was February 2003 when we talked. The United States was on the brink of war with Iraq; there were peace demonstrations around the world, many in California, but not for Lara. He admired George W. Bush and thought Bush was not making a mistake about Iraq. He said he would vote for the PAN if he could vote in Mexican elections. Lara had become politically conservative; his life had pushed him that way; he wanted to be just like every other middle-class person, that was what he admired. He came back again and again to the role of the undocumented: "We don't hurt anyone, we're working. I work construction; eighty percent of the construction workers are illegal. In plumbing it's fifty percent, and landscaping, a hundred percent."

He had a view of life in the United States. "We work," he said. "We don't take anything for granted." And then mechanically, as if the thought were always appended to the idea of work: "Welfare is an abuse to working people; I think the system has been abused."

He stood in silence for a moment, touching his mustache, the wisps of hair few enough to count, and summed up what he thought about the country he said he would never leave. He did not say he felt welcome, but he wanted it understood that immigrants were not parasites, not supplicants. He said that people like him were permitted to live in the United States, "as long as you pay your taxes."

BEST LOVE

To celebrate the success of another immigrant group in a nation of immigrants is to celebrate the ordinary, for there is nothing unusual about a defined group of people from another part of the world entering the United States, enduring more or fewer generations of struggle depending upon whether they were urban or rural people, and then following the existing social and economic patterns. A Mexican engineer in Atlanta moves quickly into the society, living well, finding himself a charming guest, a welcome professional, a desirable neighbor; a psychologist in Texas and a professor in California have the same lives. A Mexican student may choose to attend the University of Chicago's Mexican studies department, which is headed by Friedrich Katz, one of the best living historians of Mexico. A Mexican-born scholar may try to reorganize the University of California. A Mexican-American businessman in Texas spent tens of millions of dollars of his own money in the 2002 governor's race only to lose to George W. Bush's Republican choice.

Had San Antonio Mayor Henry Cisneros not suffered the results of a much publicized extramarital affair, he might very well have been the candidate for vice president of the United States on the Clinton ticket. Cisneros was highly educated, articulate, a successful mayor, a man of both great charm and effectiveness, and he had Clinton's not quite liberal political views. To be a Mexican in the United States is a matter of class rather than race. To be a Mexican-American is an entirely different question with an entirely different set of problems and possibilities.

Most Mexicans in the United States work hard, collect very little in return for the taxes they pay, and are, in short, a huge net profit. Other people pay less for food and services because of the low wages Mexicans earn and enjoy more for their tax dollars (including Social Security) because Mexicans get less in the way of services for their contribution. Keeping undocumented Mexicans in that situation serves the interests of U.S. citizens. However, all Mexicans in the United States are not perfect. Some are like Roger Gutiérrez, a man of twenty, as aggressive as a bullet.

He says he murdered a man, shot and killed him. He was still a juvenile then, a "gang-banger,"[11] part of the 18th Street Gang, a Southern California gang connected to the Mexican Mafia, one of the two big prison gangs, the

[11]Slang for a person who participates in gang wars.

other being the Northern California gang La Familia. For his crime, he was sent to juvenile facilities, where the guards had trouble controlling him, so they moved him to boot camp, which is usually a six-month stay. They kept Roger in the rigid discipline of the camp for two years.

Roger rages against the world; he is a collection of slights, insults, racism, sexual aggression, wounds, hatreds, a twenty-year-old loaded with the explosives planted by poverty and prison. When he was being transferred from one prison to another, carrying his papers, he was "beaten by the police. A black dude in the prison beat me down, hit me so hard I woke up in the hospital." Roger is short, round, muscular, with a shaved head and the wispy mustache and beard of an old Asian man. He can speak only a few sentences before his words turn into pure aggression; his stance changes, he begins moving forward, crowding the other person, pushing the space between them, devouring it; he cannot keep his hands down, he runs on reflexes; at the age of twenty he boils up out of his own past, ready to turn the fire on whoever is near.

He knows everything that has gone wrong for him. He blurts out his wounds and responses: "Why do people make it so hard for us? You got to look white, I guess."

The conversation is disjointed; he speaks in bursts of lightly accented English. He moves forward a step, closing the distance, a man who likes to fight inside: "White girls are easier than Mexican girls. I got kicked out of my house. I had a truck, and I moved to Virginia, where I met a lot of people who went to school. I don't gang-bang anymore. If I keep gang banging, these white girls wouldn't look at me. White girls. White girls are easier. I like white girls." He moves his face up close, fabricating a hint of drool as he talks about white girls, anything to create discomfort, to challenge, to gain some advantage. He probes, jabbing and jabbing, the rest of him cocked like a heavy left fist.

"They brought me across the line at Tecate. I'm from Oaxaca, Tehuantepec. I want to go back at Christmas. They don't do nothing here at Christmas. It's real active back there. I have a residence card; all I need is the matricula.

"You know, my mother works so hard. When I killed somebody, it made her very sad. My father, he left us. I don't talk to my dad. He did nothing for us. He's married again now; fifty-two years old, and he has to change diapers. That's a punishment for what he done to us."

And then, for a moment, he presents another face; "I have a GED, but I want a high school diploma. Right now I go to Contra Costa College. I get As and Bs in school; the white teachers like me. I work construction, welding, driving a forklift. I work 'til four P.M., go to school at six-fifteen, get home at nine-thirty; then I'm at work at seven. I'm the first one in my family to go to college. But my cousins, they had the family together; they weren't hungry like us. Their parents helped them; they even paid for them to go to college."

He raised his fists and turned them over to show the tattoos on his knuckles: "BEST LOVE." "The police don't know what this means," he said. "It's a secret." He went on to tell the secret of the Spanglish code on his fingers: "*B* is for Barrio, *E* is for Eighteenth, *ST* for Street. *LO* is for 'los,' *V* is for 'vatos' [pals], *E* is for Eighteenth. BEST LOVE."

He turned to probing again, using women, economics, exploitation, jabbing and jabbing, like a heavyweight boxer, like a big man looking for the killing blow. He had no sadness, no sweetness, he suffered no slights; at the age of twenty he had not yet learned the difference between the bullfighter and the bull.

AN EXIGENT KIND OF LOVE

A long time ago, when Mexico obeyed the marriage rules of the Church of Rome, there were many sinners and few divorces. Hollywood stars and dissatisfied women from Park Avenue and Glencoe, Illinois, and Ladue Road in St. Louis fled just barely south of the border to Cuidad Juárez, where they were pronounced no longer wives. Divorce was then common only among the relatively well off in the United States. In Mexico it was rare, for women had no money of their own and no prospects. To be a widow in Mexico was a tragic but respectable life; to be divorced was a moral and economic catastrophe, except in the world of movie stars. With greater opportunities for higher education and more careers outside the home open to them, Mexican women learned to object to a husband's having a *casa chica* (a trysting place) or delivering a beating at home when other things went wrong in his life. Women went to work and to the divorce courts. Vicente Fox Quesada, the first divorced man elected president of Mexico, was not the first husband of his first lady. To make matters more complex, he was also the first Mexican president to kiss the Pope's ring. Divorce was not sanctioned by the Pope, but it had become as routine in Mexico as in Rome.

The rich were the first to divorce in Mexico, as elsewhere in the world, but it soon enough came time for the middle class and the poor. Educated women worked at good jobs, the poor and uneducated worked at maintaining the households of the educated women, and the breaking of the bonds of family trickled down. At the income level where two people cannot maintain two separate households on Mexican wages, the choice often comes down to emigration or malnutrition. The weak or weary or frightened do not attempt to emigrate. A sorting process takes place; the daring come north. The character of immigrants, if there are enough of them, defines to a large extent the country that accepts them. It happened in the United States, meaning that by defintion every immigrant is already an American.

It is so even with the divorced and those who lived at a level and in a place where there was no hope for their children. They did not submit; they emigrated, embracing responsibility for those they left behind as well as for themselves. So Silvia Salas, who married at seventeen in Cuidad del Valle, in the state of San Luis Potosí, to a man who worked in the fields and in auto repair shops, came to be an American without documents in California. She is a tiny woman. She could be made of filigree, an ornament of sorrow; her face turns old when she smiles. In San Luis Potosí, Silvia's family lived in closeness without limit. When an aunt died in childbirth, the infant she left behind came to live with Silvia and her mother. Silvia speaks of her as "my sister." They live together now in a studio apartment: Silvia, her sister, her brother-in-law, and their three children. Silvia's brother-in-law has residence papers, her sister has applied, but Silvia has yet to find a sponsor, although she has several employers.

From eight in the evening until seven in the morning she works as a custodian in a public school. When she leaves the school, she tends to private houses. To care for a four-bedroom house, she earns another $150 a month. In the end, after state and federal income tax and Social Security and worker's compensation, there is not much, and she must pay her share of the rent, utilities, and food. Whatever is left, after her own expenses for transportation and shoes and such, she sends home: never less than $400 a month to care for her mother and three children. She also sends money for schoolbooks and the 250 pesos she must pay toward the public schooling of each child. She understands the world as a place of work without end, dilemmas without solutions. "I have no time to enjoy life," she said. "I came here to labor, not to rest."

Silvia left Mexico when she was twenty-nine years old, divorced, and the mother of three children. There was no money for food or clothing. She could not bear to see her children suffer; to save them, she had to leave them. It has been seven years since she last saw the children. Once a month she speaks to them by telephone, and that is all.

The unwillingness of the United States to allow passage home and back to Silvia Salas has produced the moral equivalent of Sophie's Choice.[12] The pain of the dilemma appears on her face. Over time Silvia Salas has developed the demeanor of saints. She is Sor Juana's woman; her eyes do not entirely focus, as if somewhere in the distance she sees a moral death. Although she shows no sign of ill health, she appears to have been diminished in size, not wizened, not sickly, but dwindling, like a wooden pencil often used.

She said, "My children asked if I would come home for Christmas, but I said that if I went, I could not send them the money to live. If I brought them here, I would have no one to look after them. If I go home, I would not have the money to pay a coyote to return. If I stayed home, I would see my children suffer."

[12]This was the Nazi question to the woman in a concentration camp asking which of her two children she wished to save, as portrayed in the novel by William Styron and the film based on it.

Book Four

TONALAMATL

37.

The Book of Predictions

Some thirty years after saying good-bye to the old man of Agua Prieta, I went back to look for him. In the waning of the afternoon the wind had risen, and the dust was as it had always been, the enemy on both sides, like the ancient warrior god Yaotl. The wind had sculpted stone, eaten away at paint, etched glass, and did not permit trees or corn or anything but mesquite and the invincible barbed and poisonous things of the high desert to survive. The gas station was gone: the measuring globes, the hoses, the ramp that raised the cars, the shallow pit below, no wider than the mechanic who lay with his tools on his chest and looked up into the greasy darkness of the transforming age of the machine.

The house still stood. I ran toward it, calling, "*Viejo, maestro, anciano.*" I did not know his name. I never knew his name; he was only "old man, teacher, ancient one."

No chair stood in the dusty patch that had been his front yard. What the wind does not disperse, I thought, what the wind does not disperse.

Chickens remained.

A child pulled aside a piece of gray cloth that hung in the doorway. And smiled. And disappeared.

"*Viejo-o-o-o!*" I made my own echo.

Sixteen years later the house was gone. The field where the last remnants of the last brigade of General Francisco Villa's Northern Division lay dying, begging for water, crying out to God to permit them one last time to lay their heads on the bosoms of their mothers and be introduced to death as they had been born to life, the unrelenting expanse where the machine-gun bullets had danced in the electric light of Woodrow Wilson's wish, that bloodied dust had been buried in expanses of concrete. The old man's gift had been history; he had left me that glance into the future.

THE LIFE AND TIMES OF MEXICO

The *Tonalamatl*, the book of naming and auguries, is an old book, and only those who know the past may read it. When I retraced my steps to the house where the pomegranate tree grew in the garden and the stunted palms flourished in fat-bellied dignity on the front lawn and my sister laughed until her long curls frolicked and her eyes closed in innocent delight, the house and all that went with it were gone.

RED BONES

In the last months before completing this book, I visited with two intellectuals in the world of Mexican politics.[1] We talked about the country, their parties, and the implications for the future of Mexico. They represent two paths for Mexican politics: reform of the old and the birth of the new, a two-party system modeled on the United States and a volatile multiparty system, more like that of Italy. Neither one is satisfied with the status quo. Although they are both professors, well versed in U.S. as well as Mexican history, politics, and culture, their styles and origins are very different, almost as opposite as their politics. One, a well-known human rights activist, Sergio Aguayo, had been instrumental in creating a new political party, Mexico Posible. The other, Alejandro Carrillo Castro, often described as a red bone PRIista[2] because of his loyalty to the party, had just been named to head the National Institute of Political Administration (INAP), a private institution that functions as a combination of the Kennedy School of Government at Harvard and the Woodrow Wilson School of Public and International Affairs at Princeton, although not yet the equal of either one. Every year six thousand scholars, government officials, and political aspirants spend all or part of the year at INAP. The Mexican institute is connected to the International Institute of Administrative Sciences in Brussels, where Carrillo is a member of the academic committee. For many years INAP was considered the training ground for the PRI (Salinas once headed it), but it now appears

---

[1] There was a third conversation, with Jorge Castañeda, but we could not get beyond a series of "canned" answers, although I think we both tried. He is a wary man, as a man of great ambition must be. With the other two, there was true dialogue; the calculations were relegated to the background. Perhaps Castañeda thought his conservative, proglobalization politics would not sit well with me. Or that I would frown on his connection to Salinas and Gordillo.

[2] The red bones are the vertebrae just below the skull of a cow that hold its head up.

to be less partisan as Carrillo attempts to connect INAP more closely to a university. The Fox administration helped clarify the future of the institute when Ramón Muñoz, the head of Fox's Presidential Office of Innovation in Government, put an end to government funding of INAP. Carrillo described it as a healthy setback, for now INAP was free to be much more like graduate schools of public administration in democratic countries.

It should be noted that both Aguayo and Carrillo have been subjected to ferocious criticism at one time or another, Carrillo the more so because he has held high government office, including the unenviable position of commissioner of immigration, which earned him a reputation for suppression of journalists and human rights activists in Chiapas: Those without proper visas were told to leave the country. Carrillo, fiercely nationalistic, has long argued that the difference between U.S. and Mexican rules for visas was unfair.[3] Aguayo has not escaped criticism based on U.S.-Mexican relations either, especially in *La Jornada*, the newspaper he helped start.

By most accounts, Carrillo represents the "new PRI," while the national president of the party, Roberto Madrazo Pintado, represents the "dinosaurs," the old, moneyed power brokers who reaped fortunes out of the corporatist organization of the party and the country. Rumor has it that the "dinosaurs" belonged to a secret society, the Atlacomulco Group, fourteen men, including Madrazo's father, centered on the late Carlos Hank González. Hank insisted the group never existed except as a gathering place for old (and very wealthy) pals, but no one accepts his denial. Aguayo represents an academic approach to politics; his Mexico Posible Party is studious, naive, quixotic, middle-class, and unfamiliar with power outside the groves of academe.

Before taking the position of director of INAP, Carrillo was a professor

---

[3] U.S. citizens automatically receive visas at no charge upon entering Mexico via airports and seaports or may ask for them at international crossing points. Mexicans, including Carrillo Castro, when he was appointed consul general in Chicago, must pay a fee of one hundred dollars and wait up to six months or more for clearance. He had, he said, discussed the question with the U.S. ambassador, asking why there was no reciprocity. When he raised the issue with Mexican officials, the response was clear enough: If U.S. citizens had to wait six months and pay a hundred dollars to get a Mexican visa, they would vacation in other places and Mexico would lose billions in tourism revenue every year. The Yanqui dollar was invincible.

When American citizens descended on Chiapas, ostensibly as journalists or self-appointed human rights workers, Carrillo apparently understood it as an affront to Mexican sovereignty.

of law, former Mexican consul in Chicago, head of immigration,[4] and deeply involved in the presidency of López Portillo. He is the son of a man who was a friend to Lázaro Cárdenas and the grandson of a man who worked closely with Álvaro Obregón. Carrillo is the author, most notably, of *El Dragón y el Unicornio,* "The Dragon and the Unicorn" (Aguilar, 1999), an investigation into the social, psychological, philosophical, and mythical history of world culture. The body of the book curiously excludes Mesoamerican culture, but Carlos Fuentes repaired the omission in a long introduction devoted to Coatlicue, the mother goddess of the omitted culture.

Aguayo is not only a professor of international relations at Colegio de Mexico, he has taught at Johns Hopkins, from which he holds a doctorate in international relations, and the University of California at Berkeley. He is the author of several books and has a long history as an advocate for human rights and democracy. He has received the democracy medal from the U.S. government—an award sponsored by the National Endowment for Democracy (NED). Aguayo said he grew up in a poor neighborhood in Guadalajara, escaping to the academic life through a scholarship to the Colegio de Mexico, while many of his friends from the barrio chose radical left politics, joining guerrilla movements.

The men come to their intellectual status from opposite backgrounds, but they are both gracious. Carrillo Castro is more nationalistic, more wary of the United States than Aguayo, who professes not to be cowed by the power of the United States. Both have grown children and are married to extraordinary women. Aguayo's wife, Eugenia, a Spaniard from Catalonia, is an agent for newspaper columnists. Carrillo is married to Talina, a star of Mexican radio and television. Eugenia Aguayo complains of prejudice against her because her hair is blond and she has a slight Catalonian accent. Talina is famous enough to be recognized on the street, another kind of problem. Carrillo is more literary, Aguayo more academic. Carrillo has held positions of power, helping him avoid flights of political fancy; Aguayo is prone to making the grandiose pronouncements of amateurs. Carrillo is

---

[4]As head of immigration Carrillo "regularized" the status of eighteen thousand Guatemalan refugees who had fled to Mexico to avoid being slaughtered by the Guatemalan government. He did so for humanitarian reasons, knowing that his actions violated Mexican law. He submitted his resignation as director of refugee aid immediately afterward. He later became immigration commissioner.

very comfortable, perhaps "wealthy" would be the correct word; Aguayo lives on a professor's pay. Carrillo and I spoke Spanish, although his English is impeccable; Aguayo spoke in heavily accented but correct English.

Before our conversation, Sergio Aguayo was kind enough to offer a glass of white wine in a delicate long-stemmed glass appropriate to the wine. Eugenia Aguayo prepared a light supper. She teased her husband a bit, as if she wanted to calm him. I wondered if he knew I had read that a replacement for the CIA had been the source of the funds for some of his prodemocracy work?[5] Asking a man if funds for his work came from such a source is like asking if he beats his wife. Either he says he beats her or the story is "X denies beating wife." Whether it was true or not mattered but little. Was there anything in Mexico—from the ownership of its major banks to the election of its most important government officials to the price of corn—in which the United States did not have a hand? General Motors was still one of the largest private employers that paid a living wage, U.S.-owned maquiladoras had accounted for almost all of the growth in jobs in manufacturing during the last decade, U.S. money and power had determined the history of Mexico since it took half the country in 1848; it would be a great surprise if the United States had not invested in Aguayo's work, probably not for moral reasons but in the interest of stability on its southern flank.

Carrillo asked if I would join him in a glass of tequila. I accepted, and his wife, Talina, set two glasses and a fresh bottle of Herradura (*reposado*) tequila, on the table. It is an old business in Mexico, a test of manliness and intentions, and I have had the good luck to have enjoyed the test many times, although not always with such fine tequila. Carrilo and I had a drink,

---

[5] Aguayo headed the Alianza Cívica, which was partly funded by an arm of the U.S. government, the National Endowment for Democracy. Aguayo served on a steering committee of a branch of the NED.

In the *Washington Post* of September 22, 1991, Allen Weinstein, founder and first president of the NED, said that the organization was formed (in 1984) to do overtly what the CIA had done covertly. The NED most recently had a $150 million annual appropriation from the U.S. Congress. The connection does not implicate Aguayo in CIA activities, but it is proof of the involvement of the U.S. government in internal Mexican politics.

Aguayo describes himself as a "leftist," but the NED has historically been connected to the political right. Sergio Aguayo and my old friend Primitivo Rodríguez, a columnist for *La Jornada*, have had a falling-out. I do not know the cause, but their disagreement is public, played out in the newspapers.

the first of more than a few, and began our conversation. It was eleven o'clock in the morning.

Later, at a Sunday afternoon lunch in Polanco, I asked Carrillo's sister-in-law, Marcella Gavaldon, if he always started drinking before noon. She laughed. "He doesn't drink."[6]

AGUAYO

Sergio Aguayo lives in a comfortable condominium apartment in a small building in San Jerónimo in the southern part of the city. He laughs easily but abruptly turns serious. Then he leans forward and his rimless eyeglasses dominate his face. His field is the study of U.S. attitudes toward Mexico. It is, however, the future of Mexico that we have in mind and the political party he helped found. The party, of itself, is not to be taken seriously, but it is a party whose principals have had some influence in Mexico, both in the academic world and in various civic and human rights organizations. Why they started a political party is not clear, but there is precedent for academics having success in politics in Mexico. After all, the PAN was founded in 1939 by Manuel Gómez Morín, the former rector of the UNAM, who was its president for ten years while the party struggled to survive.

Just as the PAN was tarred with its connections to the radical rightist Sinarquistas all through its early years, Mexico Posible and its cofounder Aguayo have been tarred in the left newspaper *La Jornada* with being an instrument of a political wing of the U.S. government, the National Endowment for Democracy. For the NED it was a wise use of influence. Mexico Posible was unlikely to win any elections, at least not anytime soon, but for the U.S. government it was a chance to court college professors and professionals in Mexico. And perhaps to reach into government in Mexico. Aguayo himself said he had been offered two positions in the Fox government, one in foreign relations and the other a domestic post. He turned down both offers, he said, because he did not agree with the conservative ideas of the Fox government.

Aguayo recalled the beginnings of the party: "Patricia Mercado, president

---

[6]Carrillo said later that he is not a teetotaler. He enjoys food and wine and even an occasional glass of tequila. But to say of someone in Mexico that "he drinks" means he is "a drunkard."

of Mexico Posible, and a group of friends and I had breakfast together in a cafeteria a few days after President Fox was elected. As we started to talk about the election, we realized that we represented several sectors of society, although not every sector. We were the orphans of Mexican political parties, because they did not deliver what they promised, like the PRD, which is full of decent people, who have been incapable of organizing themselves. We had some credibility, but no political party represented our interests. Therefore, why not start a party? The idea of creating a party of civil society had been around for many years.

"That was the beginning. We began talking with other people, the responses were good, and we spent a year organizing. The party was originally called Equidad y Ecologia [Equity and Ecology], but we soon realized that the name was not very good. So we looked at three thousand names of political parties, came up with five, and organized focus groups to evaluate them. As [members of] nongovernmental organizations we have learned to combine specialized knowledge with our activities, which is characteristic of NGOs. We chose the name the right way, and the vote was unanimous. Peru Posible was the model.

"We succeeded in getting enough names on a petition to be recognized as a legitimate political party by the Federal Election Institute and funded by it. In 2003 I think we will get to Congress. And we are evolving. Today we are urban, middle-class, above average in education, with experience in social organizations—intellectuals. I think ninety percent of us have a university education."

He described Mexico Posible as a party that used psychoanalysis, among other techniques, to train its people to resist frustration. "What distinguishes us from the rest is that we are not afraid to experiment. We have a seminar for leaders on how to create self-esteem, how to handle criticism."

Like almost everyone in politics in Mexico, he defined his party by characterizing the others: "The PRI is an old political machine, very professional, the party of organized groups—corporate.

"PAN is the best-organized citizen party, made up of individuals, citizens involved in a party. It has the best by-laws, a very solid party.

"PRD is the most important party of the left in Mexican history, but look at the by-laws: It incorporated the seeds of its own disunity. Also, they cannot resolve the cultural differences among the groups because the left is made of diverse political cultures." He said that the PRD did not know what to do with the idea of moral leadership, that it might not work in the world of practical politics. It was a touching admission, for moral leadership was clearly his goal.

And Mexico Posible's offer: "We can promise that we are different. And we know where to concentrate our resources. An NGO [most of Mexico Posible's members were either professors or employees of nongovernmental organizations or both] is like a guerrilla, here and there, and when you are a guerrilla, you choose where to hit."

Sergio Aguayo quickly put his finger on what he saw as Mexico's major problems: "There are three contradictions in Mexico: (one) free elections without functional democratic institutions, (two) poverty, and (three) the fact that we are a neighbor of the U.S., which is not usually incorporated in planning for the future. Castañeda has written that those involved with the U.S. will be the leaders in Mexico." Castañeda, who is one of Aguayo's friends, speaks of the sweet, quixotic character of the party, wishing, like most other sophisticated Mexicans, that there was a place for such a party in Mexico. Would Castañeda have been the Mexico Posible presidential candidate? The question is academic; the party did not get enough votes to retain its registration.

But then it became very difficult to find out just what the party proposed to do about the "three contradictions." The platform is vague, based on civil society, an idea that originated with the German philosopher Hegel.[7] Aguayo would not discuss the economic platform of Mexico Posible, even when pressed. It is a curious position for a man who claims to be on the left. He answered the question the same way each time it was posed: "We are developing programs aimed at specific groups because that's the size of our party. If we prosper, we will have to develop an economic program for the whole country."

What seemed to interest him most about Mexico Posible centered on local government, on developing a process in which the entire community got involved in such things as deciding the budget, which would be an interesting process in a centralist country like Mexico, where most of the money

[7]In the most basic terms, a civil society is one in which people depend on each other while maintaining their individual personal and property rights. The state would be composed of a series of corporations of people, and these corporations would assure that the needs of the people were met.

for state and local expenses comes from the federal government. How Mexico Posible would accomplish its idea of direct government was not clear: "I don't mean a government in which everyone decides about everything; that's utopia. It does not work; that's not efficient." But then he went on to say that they would "incorporate the people in deciding with us, making the economic choices at the local level."[8]

The Mexico Posible platform includes almost every buzzword in modern politics: environmentalism, choice for women, sustainable development, social justice (meaning an end to poverty), education, gender equality, homosexual rights, human rights, participation, less crime, and so on. It contains a curious section that reads, "We want to leave behind those programs that only perpetuate the dependence of the poor on their political 'benefactors.'" And then it says Mexico Posible doesn't want to divide up the pie differently; rather, it wants to create a larger pie. The two planks in the platform could have been written for the old Rockefeller Republicans in the United States. It is difficult to know just what Aguayo and Mexico Posible intend. The party attempts to appeal to everyone but homophobes, torturers, and antiabortionists. It is progressive on social issues, but not on the fundamental political question of redistribution of income. There is in fact no major political party in Mexico willing to consider the redistribution of wealth; that idea went out with Tata Lázaro, and it is unlikely to return soon.

Regarding international relations, Aguayo followed his friend Castañeda's concept of a more assertive attitude toward the United States, although he admitted this would be difficult because of the question of the disequilibrium between the one remaining world superpower and a developing nation. At the same time, like everyone else, he favored a more global context for Mexico.

Then he resorted to informed dreaming. "In this world you are tied to an economic order that is imposed on you. You can campaign on one platform, but when you take office you realize that seventy to eighty percent of your economy is in the hands of the World Bank, so I think that eventually, when we [Mexico Posible] become large enough to compete for the presidency, we will have to propose a plan that includes the world pattern. Any political program that does not include external factors is just fooling itself.

[8] In 1989 the city of Pôrto Alegre, Brazil, adopted a system of participatory budgeting that Aguayo said was the model for his idea.

"Mexico is in a peculiar situation because we are in NAFTA and that ties our economy to the U.S. and Canada. Recognizing this fundamental reality, we'll start this new policy. We'll have an internationalist policy."

Then he thought back on what he had said and chuckled at his own hubris. "I understand that this may sound a bit too strong. One has to experiment. Unless you experiment, it's going to be difficult to attack Mexican problems. We will incorporate ideas that have been blossoming all over the world. We are part of the new reality of the postmodern world."

Mexico Posible is a dreamy party, a crusade of naifs, but it has a voice in the national debate. Aguayo writes a column that runs in sixteen newspapers in Mexico, including the leading conservative daily *Reforma*. Mexico Posible passed its first test when it was recognized by the IFE; it faced another in the 2003 elections when it had to get 2 percent of the total number of votes cast to continue to be funded by the IFE. Newspaper columnist Graco Ramírez, president of the PRD in Morelos, where Mexico Posible hoped to win a seat in the lower house of the national congress, with Aguayo as its candidate, said before the election that Mexico Posible could not win enough votes to continue to get federal funding. Ramírez, who tends to put things bluntly, is loyal to his party, which carried less than 20 percent of the vote in Morelos in 2000 and stood to lose some of its adherents to Mexico Posible. But not many.

At the moment there are many political parties in Mexico, but only three of any consequence: PRD, PAN, and PRI. The choices for the near term are to become a multiparty country, with a chaotic legislature and a series of presidents who represent fewer and fewer voters, or a two-party system, like the United States and Britain. Sergio Aguayo prefers the former, at least for now. If Mexico Posible fails? "Well"—he shrugged, knowing that it was inevitable, at least for 2003—"I am an academic; I will return to teaching." Meanwhile, there was one thing he said without qualification: "Mexico Posible is not a stalking horse for a Jorge Castañeda presidential bid in 2006." That had been the rumor early on, when the party was formed, but as it moved closer to the election, the rumor faded. People had learned that the members of Mexico Posible were like the Laputans of Swift's *Gulliver's Travels* who were so often lost in speculation they required their servants to bop them in the mouth or on the ear with an inflated pig bladder to bring them back to reality.

For Mexico Posible the analogue of Swift's pig bladders was the 2003 election. Graco Ramírez had been correct in his assessment of the party of professors and dreamers. In the end it turned out to have almost as many candidates as voters. Mexico Possible managed only nine-tenths of 1 percent of the vote nationally, less than half of what it needed to continue as a registered party receiving funds from the Federal Election Institute. Patricia Mercado, the president of the party, said after the election that Mexico Possible would continue, that it was not a mass party, but one of ideas. Sergio Aguayo, writing in the newspaper *Reforma,* on July 9, 2003, only three days after the election, did not mention his own party. He criticized the PAN for being timid, for trying to reach some accommodation with the PRI, for being the party of big business. And he said the *mapaches* (literally raccoons, but meaning party hacks and fixers) of the PRI were back at work.

Aguayo got a little more than two thousand votes in his race in Cuernavaca, which put him near the bottom in a long list of candidates for federal deputy. The professor's investment had been small, the risk negligible. Shortly after the election the United Nations high commissioner for human rights invited him and several others to write a report on Mexico. He was back to doing the work he cared about most. And once again in a maelstrom of criticism.

CARRILLO

The other point of view about the future of Mexican politics came from the PRI's intellectual. Alejandro Carrillo Castro began his case with the origins of democracy in ancient Greece and came forward through Mexican history to the moment and beyond. His conversation was an astonishing performance; it could not have been more Mexican: History explains everything. The PAN is the party of the man who brought Mexico its Independence, the conservative, self-proclaimed emperor Iturbide. Reform of the PRI will be like the reforms of ancient Athens; the corporatism of the PRI (its version of clans) will be replaced by a true federalism. Instead of business, unions, and the army, the three pillars of the Mexican corporatist state, it will be the districts, the cities and towns and states, each one with elected officials representing the interests of his or her constituents; it will, in brief, be a constitutional democracy. He spoke openly of the need for change, of the triumphs and errors of Mexico. There was but one subject he did not discuss, corruption in the PRI. But leaving aside that taboo territory, he acknowledged the social failures of the party-government and allowed himself the luxury of saying that Salinas de Gotari had probably been preparing to have more than one term in office when the scandal over his brother's involvement in the killing of Ruiz Massieu ruined his hopes.[9] After that, Salinas simply had taken the money and run, leaving behind a huge "system" of men and women who had spent their lives in government, among them Alejandro Carrillo Castro.

Some of the members of the system had hoped to reform the party from within; Carrillo resisted the temptation to join Cárdenas, Muñoz Ledo, Ifigenia Martínez, and others who said they had abandoned hope in the halls of the dinosaurs. He said the PRIistas who left the party to form the PRD had not abandoned hope for reform of the party; in his view, they had lost hope for higher office for themselves in the PRI. The careers of Muñoz Ledo and Cárdenas, each of whom wanted to be president of Mexico, had been stymied; they were getting older; they had to do something. In Mexican style they declared, but not for a bloody revolution, as in the past; they formed a new party.

Remaining in the PRI had apparently not been personally hurtful to Carrillo. When we talked, he apologized for the state of the household, saying that he and his wife had given up their big house now that their children were grown and were in the process of moving to a smaller, although commodious, house in Tecamachalco, the new "in" neighborhood in the most desirable section of the city. Some of the art the Carrillos had collected was just being unpacked, and it was brilliant, original, wildly colorful Mexican painting, in contrast with the more subdued sense of taste in the Aguayo house.

After we had chatted for a while and had the first glass of tequila, I asked if he thought there had been a revolution in 1910 or a civil war. He answered for almost an hour, pausing only to sip at his tequila and to take a bite of lime. "We were part of the great social revolution of the twentieth century," he began. "We had a civil war, lost a million people, and had a period of reconstruction under General Calles, a grand visionary. It was a civil war that changed into an uncontrollable movement. You can't offer a linear explanation. What we call the Mexican Revolution was a thing that came at the fin-

---

[9] His view is not unique. Many people who look back on the Salinas sexenio believe he wanted to change the Constitution or simply flout it in order to hold on to the office.

ish of thirty-three years of Porfirio Díaz. When Díaz decided to open the markets to Europe, the U.S. decided it was no longer worth maintaining the dictator. Madero received help from the U.S., as did Vasconcelos, and later Fox . . . not so much from the government as from interested groups in the U.S. This current generation went to public school under Alemán and learned the myth that the Mexican Revolution was socially progressive, concerned with the well-being of the majority. We have not been able to accomplish this in seventy years.

"Article Three of the Constitution said not only that the education we impart would be democratic but that by 'democracy' we mean not only a system of political justice but a system based on the constant improvement of the social and political lives of the people." Then Carrillo, who apologizes frequently for his legalistic terminology, reminding his listener that he was trained in the law, turned to Article 27 of the Constitution of 1917 and its three central ideas: Return the stolen lands (Zapata); break up the latifundias (Villa); preserve the small properties (Obregón). "It was like trying to keep three balls in the air. Cárdenas took the country to the left to carry out the promise of the 1917 Constitution to the campesinos. The U.S. helped create the PAN [in 1939], not for them to win the election but to maintain some balance in Mexican politics. Then Alemán from the right and the Partido Popular and Lombardo Toledano to balance him from the left."

Always, all through his conversation, it was history and the actions of the United States that explained Mexico. Carrillo had been secretary of international affairs for the PRI and Mexican consul general in Chicago, as well as commissioner of immigration, always in the part of the system that lived in the shadow of the United States. He argued Mexico in terms of its own history and the history of the United States. When members of the U.S. Congress came to Mexico, they told him it was not a democratic country because there was no alternation of political parties, and he replied, "With the Boss [Mayor Richard J. Daley], Chicago is not democratic, because the same party has been in power there for more than fifty years."

Then he turned back to the Mexican civil wars of 1910–1920, to explain the seventy years of the PRI: "When a group wins in a civil war, not a paper war, but one in which many people die and very powerful interests clash, as in the American Civil War, it is expected that one party may remain in power for some time, because they did not win with votes, they won with blood. In your case the Republicans held power for thirty-seven years.

Then the Democrats won some governors' offices and finally the presidency. But the Republican Party did not disappear after losing elections. Neither will the PRI disappear, although for a different reason: The PRI affords the country stability, because it unites the various interests.

"The federal system and the presidency tend toward bipartisanship because it's too expensive to have alternation between more than two parties. When there are two parties, every time one goes out of office, the party that comes in has people who have been in various posts before. When there are three or more parties, the costs and adjustments multiply exponentially.

"Mexico is passing through a phase. We shall come to alternation quietly. I don't know whether it will be called the PRI or the PRD, which is a splinter of the PRI, but I think the alternation will be with the PAN. One day we'll function much like the Democrats in the U.S. or the Social Democrats in Europe. Meanwhile, the PAN will become more like the Republican Party, conservative, but nationalistic, a defender of more orthodox Catholicism. One party (the PRI/PRD) will identify with Hidalgo, Morelos, and Juárez, and the other (the PAN) with Iturbide."[10]

He turned to the change in the interpretation of the three colors in the Mexican flag. "Today we say the green stands for hope, the white for the pure snows of the mountains, and the red for the blood of our soldiers. Originally (under Iturbide), the white stood for the same religion as Spain and the red the same blood as Spain."

The Catholic Church and PAN were on his mind. He recalled when Carranza said education should be the province of the cities and when Salinas wanted to move the responsibility to the states because the cities had no money. His view was clear: "If education is not in the hands of the government, the Church will return to the old model [after Independence, before the Reform]. This is a little bit of what is happening now with the PAN.

"My generation thought that after World War Two we were entering a joyous time in the world. We had twenty-three years of economic stability. The peso did not move. Inflation was one-point-two percent. GDP grew at an average six percent. Then came 1968. Not only in Chicago, but here too because the government did not fulfill its promises. The youth made demands. The old structures had to change. But a system becomes impacted

[10]Hidalgo and Morelos tried to bring about Independent Mexico from the left; Iturbide, the royalist conservative, succeeded from the right and then named himself emperor.

if it has no alternative. And the moment arrived when the leaders were of my father's generation, not mine; they were eighty years old, the same men who led the Revolution—in theory pluralistic, advancing, et cetera; in practice still centralist, outdated, authoritarian, and not very democratic.

"The PRI, with its right and left wings, might have defeated the PAN for another twenty years, but it broke apart because the formula it had no longer worked." And he pointed to Miguel de la Madrid and the neoliberals.

But always he returned to the idea of alternating power between the two major parties. It seemed not to matter to him that Fox had won so much as that Mexico had entered a system of alternation. He saw it as the means to progress, and he feared only that the most conservative elements of "the PRI and the PAN are not prepared to see the normality of alternation in governments, a democracy revitalized by change." To him, the puzzling failure of Mexican politics was that under Calles and Cárdenas, both interested in Marxist ideas, the government spoke against capitalism while it helped Mexican industry to grow. "Now the neoliberals espouse capitalism and give no help to Mexican industry."

In the elections of 2006, the PRI will once again face a PAN nominee and one from the PRD, as well as the smaller parties, although not Mexico Posible, not then, if ever. "The PRI is something that might unite again and win in three or six or ten years, because it is not like the Communist Party; it has no specific dogma. It was formed for Mexico. We are the party of the Maya, the Aztecs, the party of Hidalgo, against Iturbide, the party of Benito Juárez, who showed that an Indian could be president of Mexico; we are the party of Villa, Zapata, Obregón; the PRI was a sack in which to put all the Mexican heroes, so to be PRIista is to be Mexican, with all its problems, good people and bad. I believe that the other parties will decline; Fox deserves great merit for beginning the alternation. But the alternate is not forever: Alternation is alternation."

ALTERNATING CORPORATIONS

In both views of the political future, the two-party and the multiparty system, the corporate character of the parties, which has been the dominant form in Mexico since Lázaro Cárdenas completed the organization begun by Calles, will continue for some time. The PAN, although often described as a party of individuals, was elected by incorporating many groups. Whether the party holding the presidency in Mexico now is really the PAN or simply an anti-PRI party is a matter of conjecture. Fox has had and will continue to have problems with his own party. The PAN has its own corporate structure: the powerful orthodox sector of the Catholic Church; the Monterrey, Guadalajara, and parts of the Mexico City business communities. For a time Fox was so strongly supported by U.S. business and government they could have been considered one of the corporate sectors, but that support, especially from the U.S. government, has diminished.

How long these corporate bodies within the PAN will stand by it is the question. During the reign of the PRI, the corporate party-state left no other place for its component parts to go. The PAN and the PRD slowly picked apart the atherosclerotic body of the PRI until it finally collapsed. With a president who represents at least some of the PAN's views, the country suffers—falling GDP, rising unemployment, rising inflation, a peso losing its value against a weak dollar, maquiladoras shutting their doors and moving elsewhere, a costly cooling in U.S.-Mexico relations,[11] an agricultural sector in serious difficulty, and a Congress that refuses to allow Fox and the PAN to achieve their promises—and the corporate bodies making up the PAN may look elsewhere. If not in 2006, then in 2012. The PRI, the PRD, and even the tiny parties, like the deregistered Mexico Posible, now wait to pick the bones of the PAN as the other parties once waited for the weakening of the PRI.

In the 2003 elections for federal deputies (the lower house of Congress), the PAN lost 50 seats; the PRI, along with its allied parties, increased its total to 252 (an absolute majority); and the PRD increased its total to 95. Clearly, the PAN was bearing the burden of three years of stagnation during the Fox presidency, and with the PRI vote passing 250, the stagnation would almost certainly continue for the next three years.

A pattern has begun to emerge in Mexico, much like the pattern in the United States, in which the Republicans control the towns, the suburbs, and the South, and the Democrats control the cities, the North, and California. In Mexico the PRD controls the great capital city (about 30 percent of the

---

[11]At the end of 2003 Fox and Derbez were trying desperately to improve relations between the two countries. Fox had more than moral reasons for wanting to find a way to "regularize" the status of undocumented Mexicans in the United States: Remittances from the United States had become equal to one-third of oil revenues.

entire electorate), the PRI controls the countryside, and the PAN still controls much of the north and the great Mexican breadbasket, the bajío. Under these circumstances, it is not difficult to see how the future of Mexican politics depends almost entirely on the eventual defeat of the dinosaurs of the PRI. If the party can rid itself of them, it can unite with the PRD under one name or another or perhaps compromise on a third name. The result would be a two-party system: one center-left party and one center-right, very much as Carillo envisions it.

As long as the dinosaurs control the PRI, these aging autocrats will keep Mexico a multiparty system, a nation partially paralyzed, largely ungovernable except by the United States, which will manipulate the politics and economics of Mexico using all the tools of a colonial power: bilateral trade, investment, gifts, and, if need be, threats. Any serious instability in Mexico would bring U.S. military power to bear.

The PAN no longer seems likely to win the presidency in the next election. However, Mexican voters in 2003 did not punish only the PAN. The turnout, 45 percent of registered voters, was the lowest in many years. Mexicans appeared to be throwing up their hands, as if they had tried democracy and democracy had not improved matters at all. That was the story in the newspapers: Abstention had won the election with 55 percent of the votes. But a closer look reveals a victory for the PRI, and not for the Carrillo Castro wing of the PRI. It was the dinosaurs who won, Roberto Madrazo and Elba Esther Gordillo's wing of the party. One election went against the grain of Mexican politics: the loss of the governorship of Nuevo León, the cradle of the PAN. The winner there, Natividad González Parás, a member of the PRI, had been head of INAP before Carrillo. Professionalism in government service had a champion in office in the most Catholic yet most North American state; only Monterrey, Nuevo León, rivaled Mexico City in industrial and economic power. If there was to be a reorganization of Mexico into a two-party system, with the PAN on one side and a second party comprising liberal elements of the PRI and PRD on the other, González Parás was as likely a member as Carrillo.

There was one other very important person involved in the victory of the PRI. On election day the newspapers printed photographs of the former president of Mexico casting his ballot. Carlos Salinas de Gotari, the most corrupt president in a long line of corrupt leaders, had spent most of five years in exile in Ireland and Cuba and then quietly came to Mexico, where his daughter was finishing her undergraduate work at the Universidad Iberoamericana. While in Europe, Salinas had met with Jorge Castañeda. Both Salinas and Castañeda denied that some kind of political arrangement was negotiated during the meeting, but Salinas had met with other members of both parties, and two more ambitious men had not been born in Mexico.

As if to celebrate his return to public life in Mexico, Carlos Salinas de Gotari presided over a great party in celebration of his daughter's marriage. Azcárraga of Televisa was there, as were Elba Esther Gordillo and Jorge Castañeda Gutman and Roberto Madrazo Pintado, representing control of the largest union in the country, the factions of the PRI, connection to President Fox, and, in Castañeda, raw ambition. José Woldenberg, lately of the Federal Election Institute, former secretaries of energy and interior, the head of Banorte, journalist Raúl Velasco, and others came at the bidding of Salinas. The surprise was the failure to appear of Carlos Slim, the richest man in Latin America. But the man who put Salinas in office, former president Miguel de la Madrid, came to the festivities. Power had put shame to flight. Jorge Castañeda had consigned the influence of Salinas to the disgraced ex-president's dreams; he called it "smoke and mirrors," but he did not turn down the invitation.

Castañeda had told a close friend, Georgina Lagos, whom he had appointed to a choice overseas diplomatic post, Consul General in San Francisco, that he intended to make a run for the presidency in 2006 and that it was going to be as the candidate of one of the major parties. But which one? Or would it be a major party? He had also said he would be a candidate on a fourth-party ticket.

Castañeda had been a Communist, become a more or less liberal professor, moved to the United States, where he had opposed NAFTA from his perch at New York University. He told John R. MacArthur how thoroughly opposed he was to the very idea of NAFTA.[12] Then he became foreign secretary in a conservative administration and supported NAFTA. Castañeda, who had long favored the legalization of some drugs, was rumored to have become allied with billionaire currency speculator George Soros (an alliance Soros denies), who believed legalization could solve the world's drug problem. With the backing of Soros and Salinas, Castañeda's candidacy gained credibility. His dealings with Salinas pointed to the PRI. He would have

[12] *The Selling of Free Trade.*

some support in the party from Elba Esther Gordillo, who still controlled the votes of more than a million members of the national teachers' union. Their friendship was widely known; they were close enough that he lived in the apartment below Gordillo in a building she owned. And Gordillo was tied to Salinas and through Salinas to Fox.

The other possibility was that Castañeda would run on the same kind of alliance ticket that Fox had used, with support from Gordillo and Salinas and a base in the PAN. No matter which party, if any, put him on the ballot, the problem for Castañeda would be arrogance and perfidy; he had never been able to hide those aspects of his character. He was, in that, not very different from Porfirio Muñoz Ledo, a Mexican who had jumped from one political party to another, driven by irrepressible ambition, until finally he lost all credibility. But the war within Castañeda's soul was different: His father was Mexican, his mother a Russian Jew. Like Muñoz Ledo, he had become a political grasshopper, and like Muñoz Ledo, he was very bright, but not for the public taste. It would take a great deal of training by political consultants to make him into an acceptable candidate.

Salinas posed a more interesting question. If he supported Castañeda, Salinas would make Castañeda pay. The newspapers suggested that in return for his support Salinas might want the release from prison of his brother, Raúl, who had almost half a century left to serve on his sentence for murder. But Salinas would never agree to accept so little in return for the presidency; Raúl's release would be no more than a side agreement. Many people thought Carlos Salinas de Gotari wanted more than one term as president of Mexico. In 2006, Salinas would be only fifty-eight years old. His problem was how to circumvent the constitutional prohibition against reelection. But he had been out of office for two terms; in a sense, reelection was no longer an issue. Changing the Constitution to permit reelection after two terms out of office was not impossible. And he had hoarded the power he gathered during his years in the party and his term as president. On July 27, 2003, the head of the PAN told the press he was interested in negotiations with Carlos Salinas de Gotari. After that announcement, anything was possible.

Salinas had spectacular intelligence, he was ice-cold, a brilliant manipulator of power, but wisdom had always eluded him. He toadied to power (the United States) to gain power; he had always been a second-class man. And such a man is dangerous; if there was anyone in Mexico who did not harbor some fear of Carlos Salinas de Gotari, that person had misunderstood Carlos Salinas. He was the second son (Raúl was first) of a man who had himself dreamed of the presidency, and in Mexico primogeniture still means a great deal. Carlos was born in the schemer's position, and he had learned to excel in the art of scheming. Of all the schemers in Mexico, there was no one like Carlos Salinas de Gotari. And he had admirers everywhere.

Enrique Krauze, the influential conservative Mexican journalist, helped open the door to power for Salinas, expressing his admiration for the ex-president to the New York Times.[13] Krauze's mind ran in that direction. He subscribed to Carlyle's view of the hero as the force of history, and Salinas's ability to take and manipulate power appealed to him. He neglected to speak of Salinas's catastrophic economic failures, did not discuss the growth of the drug cartels in Mexico during the Salinas sexenio, but put his blessings on the leadership qualities of one of Mexico's worst political villains: "He has tremendous drive and a strong understanding of how to exercise power." And to be sure there was no doubt about his views, he added, "I have always thought he brought the most important modernizing reforms in recent history."

In his emotional capitulation to heroic figures, Krauze represented the strain in the Mexican character that has played a key role in the country's failure to achieve a real democracy. It grew out of the Spanish invasion and the defeat of the native peoples. The mixing of the races had exacerbated rather than relieved the tendency to capitulate to a powerful oligarchy, especially one with a series of whites (criollos) alternating as leaders, like de la Madrid, López Portillo, Salinas, Zedillo, and Fox; and of the likely candidates in 2006, all but López Obrador were criollos. The war-torn character of a people whose internal cultural and racial conflict had lasted almost five hundred years still sought peace in tutelage. The Fox presidency had not only failed politically and economically, it had been unable to replace the tutelage of the party-government system.

The movement toward a democratic society had provided no comfort, no single center of power that could subsume both the European and native parts of the Mexican soul and relieve its terrible inner tension. The vote in 2003 expressed the people's disappointment with the nascent democracy. Whether the abstentions were a vote for or against the risky business of freedom would not be known until the election of 2006 or 2012. If Salinas

[13]July 19, 2003.

could rig the contest as he had rigged the vote in 1988, Mexico would return to the state-party system it had endured for seventy years until the election of Vicente Fox. As in the past, when Plutarco Elías Calles had manipulated the presidency from behind the scenes during the late 1920s until the election of Lázaro Cárdenas in 1934, an ex-president had great, perhaps overwhelming influence in Mexico. Whether he sat in the presidential chair or merely stood behind it, as Tlacaelel did for the Aztec rulers, Carlos Salinas was, in all respects, the perfect leader for a nation under the tutelage of another. Enrique Krauze had been wrong to call the history of Mexico a history of caudillos; there had been no caudillos in Mexico since 1521. After the fall of Tenochtitlán there had been only caciques, except for Lázaro Cárdenas, and he had capitulated in less than his half dozen years in office. Until Mexico becomes a fully democratic society, it cannot produce leaders, only secondary men, presidents who live in response to the nation on the north.

AND THE PRD?

At the end of 2003 the Carrillo Castro prediction was beginning to take shape. The PRI was torn in half by a fight between Elba Esther Gordillo and Roberto Madrazo Pintado. Unions broke apart over the Gordillo-Madrazo battle. Small groups left the amalgam of government employees' unions. The governors of the states urged peace within the party but split their loyalty between the two factions. President Fox flouted the constitutional separation of powers by inviting members of the PRI to Los Pinos in an attempt to settle the dispute. The struggle within the party resulted in a drop in the value of the peso against a weakened dollar. In early December 2003 the peso fell to 11.55.

A crisis was brewing within the party and the government. No one in the Mexican political world could say whether it would pass easily or in some kind of earthshaking upheaval. In three years of democracy no democratic institutions had emerged. The courts remained corrupt; the army did police business; the murders in Ciudad Juárez remained unsolved; the president meddled in the affairs of the legislature; the stalemate in the Congress continued. The first signs of crisis had erupted in the lower house when a majority of the PRI members voted to remove Elba Esther Gordillo from her post as the leader of their delegation. She remained general secretary of the PRI, but her public connection to Fox and continuing allegiance to Salinas made her suspect. On another side, the Green Party sometimes voted with the PRI and at other times with the PAN. Meanwhile, urban Mexico, especially Mexico City, belonged to the PRD, and it was no more united than the PRI.

Andrés Manuel López Obrador, the mayor of Mexico City, is the most likely PRD presidential candidate in 2006. Should the reform wing of the PRI bolt the party and the left and reform-minded center left unite, he could win the presidency. He has been an activist mayor of Mexico City, far more effective than any other political figure in the country, and has shown himself open to ideas from the right as well as the left. Even so, López Obrador's chance to win the presidency depends on another split in the PRI, like the one that produced the PRD in 1988, and that is unlikely. How PRIistas like Carrillo Castro tolerate the return of Salinas de Gotari is the unanswered question. And whatever they think, neither Carrillo nor the other members of the tiny reform wing have made their opinion public.

Following the 2003 election, López Obrador said he would not campaign for the presidency. Although he was the most popular figure in the PRD and it had doubled the number of seats it held in the lower house of the Congress, the PRD was a collection of warring factions. López Obrador and Cuauhtémoc Cárdenas headed two of the wings. Rosario Robles, the head of the party, appeared to have her own ideas. The PRD had made great strides in the 2003 election, but having slightly less than 20 percent of the federal deputies gives it a voice in the lower house, no more than that. Cárdenas took 16 percent of the vote in 2000. The party seems to be stuck at that level, give or take a few percentage points.

The hopes of López Obrador took a terrible fall early in 2004 as scandals erupted in his administration. Had he benefited from illegal payments made to high-ranking members of his administration, or had he simply let the administration get out of control? Whichever it was, his reputation had been damaged. The corruption could not be denied. Federal prosecutors had videotapes of the bribe money being passed from one person to the next. But who had made the tapes? Some of those involved fled the country to avoid prosecution, including Gustavo Ponce, former secretary of finance, who was living the high life in the Hotel Bellagio in Las Vegas, according to Sanjuana Martínez of *Proceso*, who interviewed him there. A rally in support of López Obrador produced a huge crowd of supporters in Mexico City, but such rallies are party functions in Mexico and generally not meaningful. The problem was the party itself. Corruption had reached into it at the highest levels. Rosario Robles, who had preceded López Obrador as mayor of Mexico City, resigned from the party in the midst of a scandal. She had been president of the PRD. A businessman, Carlos Ahumada, was accused of being at the center of most of the scandals. And Ahumada was not partial to the PRD. He was also videotaped in a transaction involving a man from the party known for its rectitude: The attorney general of Mexico had charged the PANista president of the Federal Senate, Diego Fernández Cevallos, with drug trafficking.

Perhaps the fact that all three parties had been penetrated at very high levels would negate the effect of corruption on any of them in the 2006 elections. The greater problem lay with the disgust the electorate had shown for the midterm candidates. The Mexican public had learned that voting out one party did not produce paradise on earth. Nothing got better, only worse. The PAN could not govern; democracy appeared not to have progressed beyond the ballot box. In the coming election the public would have to make two decisions. First, they would have to decide whether the vote would produce democracy or merely worse conditions in their lives. If they decided for democracy and went to the polls, they would have to choose a candidate, but which one? Fox had seemed so sure of himself. He had said he could solve great problems in fifteen minutes. He had called his party an Alliance for Change, but there was no change. Was there anyone who could solve Mexico's problems? If stalemate in government was the problem, the choice was clear. And if it was help for the poor and the voter was poor, to whom could she turn?

In the three-way presidential election of 2006 the PAN will have no chance to win the presidency unless it runs against the Fox record, claiming he was an anti-PRI coalition president, not a real PANista. Or forms a new coalition around another candidate. On its own, the PAN would have to hope for a miracle. The PRI faces the problem of Salinas, who could insist upon a change in the constitution, point his finger at the PRI candidate he prefers, or join a coalition in return for what baseball fans know as "a player to be named later." And no matter what happens, Salinas faces the problem of a deceptively strong man becoming the next president. Everyone in Mexican politics knows that Cárdenas drove Calles out of Mexico after taking office in 1934. It could happen to Salinas. And while many politicians would mourn the departure of their mentor, the public might be pleased. Many

Mexicans are not so anxious as Krauze, Castañeda, and the dinosaurs to praise him, although it should be reiterated that for public consumption Castañeda says that the influence of Salinas is overestimated and that Zedillo is far more important.

The character of the dinosaurs, the kind of men Salinas de Gotari controlled, was revealed in the battle over a hundred-million-dollar fine levied against the PRI for accepting fifty million dollars in illegal campaign contributions through the petroleum workers' union. The party appealed the conviction before the board of the Federal Election Institute, but after a powerful attack from the PRD and a weak and disorganized defense by the PRI, the board ratified the fine. Responses from PRIista senators and party officials were bitter, promising revenge: "The measure you use against us today will be used to measure you tomorrow" and "Today's butcher is tomorrow's beef."

After the hearing, one issue still remained to be solved. The PRI and the press had raised it all through the process: Fox had also been accused of accepting illegal campaign contributions in the form of funds from foreign sources, money sent from the United States to his election committee, Amigos de Fox. The IFE had promised to investigate before the 2003 midterm elections.

Complaints of PRI corruption were old news. If Fox and the PAN had been found guilty of accepting illegal campaign contributions from the United States, it would have been a different question. The PAN had always run against corruption. The character of the old PRI had been a foregone conclusion; the judgment was a matter of wounding its finances. Fox and the PAN had more at stake. Not just the 2003 election but 2006 as well. On election day 2003 the IFE had convicted the PRI and done nothing public about the allegations of wrongdoing by the sitting president. According to IFE, the Alliance for Change, as the Fox campaign was called, had not broken the law. Only after the election did the IFE find reason to fine the PAN for its electoral practices. And then there was the indictment of its powerful senator on drug charges.

No matter who wins the election in 2006, the federalizing of Mexico cannot go forward until the states and localities control more of their own budgets. The battle between the federalists and centralists continues, with the governors on one side and people like Jorge Castañeda on the other. Oil supplies over one-third of Mexico's income at the federal level, money that is then distributed to the states and localities. Federal control of the budget remains so severe that should a town have financial problems, the federal government, not the state, is empowered to step in and take over the management of the locality. The state governors are balky, wanting greater autonomy, challenging the Federal government. Unable to work with the Congress, Fox faces something very close to revolt by the states. But the governors have their own management problems. Accomplishing effective taxation at the local and state levels is no more likely than it is at the federal level. Neither the rich nor the poor pay taxes in Mexico; the burden, as in the United States, falls disproportionately on the middle class.

The governors of Mexican states have demanded more money and more control of the money disbursed by the federal government, but their demands are so far still mainly in the form of pleas; it is a federalism of unhappy mendicants, and that is hardly federalism at all. The only weapon the state governments have is their prerogative in the distribution of federal funds, and that control is not unlimited. The Mexican budget is not effectively the province of the federal legislature, but of the secretary of planning and budget, who serves at the pleasure of the president.

Mexico remains a country with a strong president, but not nearly so strong as in the past. He cannot effect change without the Congress, even though the real power of the legislators is only to agree or disagree with the president. Since two decades after the adoption of the Constitution of 1917, Mexico has not had a Congress controlled by any party other than the PRI and its predecessors. Mexican tradition has been to govern by enforced consensus. Until it becomes comfortable with the democratic idea of the rule of slim majorities, it will continue to enjoy the stability of paralysis.

And there is always the question of bloody revolution in a country where the poor are in the majority. For a time it appeared that the EZLN, the military wing of the Zapatistas, might attempt some form of revolutionary action, but after the Zapatista march on Mexico City in 2001 resulted in the passing of a law that actually reduced the rights of indigenous people, the influence of Subcomandante Marcos declined. El Sub turned out to have had an agile tongue, but no teeth.

There are many other revolutionary groups in the country, a thousand members here, a few hundred there, each with its own agenda. Were they all to come together in a concerted action against the government, there would be bloody days or weeks, but corrupt as it may be, the Mexican Army is strong, well armed, well provisioned. And the United States has never hesitated to intervene militarily in Mexico when its interests appeared to be threatened.[14]

Although it may take either of two paths—alternating power or a stagnating multiparty system—depending upon the staying power of the dinosaurs of the PRI, Mexico is neither Cuba nor Colombia. Unless the United States mistakes the importance of Mexico and drives it into economic chaos through relentless pursuit of colonial policies, Mexico's promise includes both political stability and increasing comfort with democratic institutions and practices. But to realize its promise, Mexico must address the potentially destructive problems in the economy.

THE WEALTH OF NATIONS IN SUM

Oil is not forever. Of all the dangers looming in Mexico's economic future, none compares with the inevitable end of Mexican oil reserves. Long before the middle of the century, in as few as ten years, Mexico will become a net importer of oil. Instead of supporting a third of the cost of government with oil revenues, Mexico will have to look to taxes, tariffs, the export of labor (maquiladoras, etc.), and goods manufactured and sold abroad by integrated, Mexican-owned manufacturers. Little, if anything, is said publicly in Mexico about this aspect of its future. Discussions still center on how to pump more oil rather than extending the lifetime of the reserves.

There is, at the moment, no reasonable prospect for Mexico other than money sent home by Mexicans or Mexican-Americans that can produce revenues equal to oil. For the last century oil has played a decisive role in Mexico's economy. Fluctuations in oil prices have determined the careers of

[14]Although I have heard from several sources that the Zapatistas were allied with the other revolutionary groups until Marcos broke an agreement with them, I cannot confirm the story. It may be that a nationwide uprising was in the early planning stages when Marcos saw the public relations advantages of attacking San Cristóbal on the first day of the implementation of NAFTA. If the story is true, he may have saved many lives that might have been lost in the uprising or ruined the chance of a successful revolution. Whichever is the case, his effect on the medium of exchange for political commentary was profound. If as Marshall McLuhan said, "The medium is the message," Marcos was a true genius. On the other hand, readers of Marx or Jefferson might argue that the message transcends the medium.

presidents and affected the lives of the entire population. Mexico's foreign policy has been largely an oil policy; everything else has been ancillary: tourism, domestic manufacturing, mining, even the sale of labor to foreign manufacturers. Only the fourteen billion dollars in remittances from abroad have the potential to exceed oil revenues.[15] And barring an economic catastrophe in the United States, that will continue.

At the end of 2003 the Fox administration engaged in a gamble that had more than once proved disastrous for Mexico: It based its budget on a price for Mexican oil higher than the historic average. Twenty dollars a barrel for Mexican crude was $3.50 above the average. If oil prices declined to the average, Mexico would be unable to meet budgeted expenses without either cutting programs or borrowing heavily. Pressure from the states would make cutting programs very difficult. Borrowing would almost certainly lead to a fall in the value of the peso, perhaps another devaluation. On the other hand, if Fox guessed correctly, his administration would be seen as prescient, even wise. He could only take his idea to the Congress and pray that he was correct. But oil reserves and prices are only one of the problems looming in Mexico's future.

Mexico, at one time a rural nation, does not have enough water to become a major agricultural country. The end of tariffs on agricultural products under the provisions of NAFTA portends the further weakening of Mexico's agricultural industry as if by drought or plague. Unless the agricultural provisions of NAFTA are changed or the Mexican government pays much larger subsidies to farmers, more of the twenty-five million Mexicans who live in rural areas must migrate to the large cities or cross into the United States.

Industry in Mexico will not be able to accommodate the displaced farmers for many reasons, one of them being the lack of sufficient electric power, which Fox wants to solve by inviting more foreign-owned companies into the industry. As Mexico's oil reserves decline, selling off Pemex will become more and more attractive, although selling the company and holding on to the subsurface rights is an option.[16] And while Mexico is mired in a multi-

[15]Thirteen billion may be more accurate or fourteen billion may be far too low. Estimating the amount of the remittances is very difficult.
[16]There are some Mexicans, Castañeda among them, who see oil reserves as virtually limitless. But long-term planning based on hope is not a definition of prudence.

party standoff, getting rid of the gross inefficiencies in either industry is impossible. The PAN does not understand how to make government as efficient as business, the PRI cries nationalism and tries to protect what remains of its turf, and López Obrador alone in the PRD has a record of managerial accomplishment.

Alternatives exist for the short term, but the end of oil requires a new approach to economics in Mexico, one that has so far appeared not to interest the IMF, the World Bank, or the neoliberal Mexican government of the last quarter century. A weak and indebted state, a poorly educated people, and dwindling natural resources do not portend a good future absent a radically different approach to the problem.

The United States, as in the past, will play a key role. Economic exploitation, the conversion of the country into a giant maquiladora, control of government policy to the advantage of the United States, and the closing of the border (to the extent possible), could threaten the stability of Mexico. On the other hand, neither unlimited immigration nor enlightened altruism can be expected of any country. The Bush administration has thrown the United States back into gigantic deficits, selling the country off to the rich through tax law reductions in much the same way that Salinas sold off Mexico to the rich. In such circumstances the United States has few options for helping its neighbor. Alan Greenspan, chairman of the Federal Reserve, has repeatedly warned of the dangers of such enormous deficits. Failure to help its neighbor might be among the least of them.

An economic depression or even a prolonged recession in the United States would be the worst nightmare for Mexico, even worse than the end of its oil reserves. The peso would collapse, the closing of American-owned factories and assembly plants would put hundreds of thousands of Mexico's highest-paid workers on the street, subsidized U.S. exports would flood Mexican markets, and Mexicans living in the United States would return home by the hundreds of thousands or even millions.

During the Depression of the 1930s Mexico was more than 75 percent rural and had to feed, clothe, shelter, and employ fewer people than now live in the capital. Cárdenas nationalized the oil industry, import substitution was the rule, and the country survived, although the government toyed with the idea of an alliance with Nazi Germany to strengthen its economy. None of those safeguards and ameliorations exists now, and there is no country, friend, or foe that could rescue Mexico from a collapse in the economy to the north.

The development of export markets in countries other than the United States may be a hedge against such economic catastrophe in Mexico, but a deep recession in the world's largest economy would affect every other economy, wounding or eliminating Mexico's markets in those countries too. Greater self-sufficiency is a better long-term program and a better hedge against difficult times, but it requires the building of Mexican industry and enough backward integration to spread the benefits of industry through the economy.

Foreign investment can be helpful in the future, if it is financial investment in Mexican-owned industry, but foreign investors are not so much interested in developing Mexican national industries as in building and operating industries of their own in Mexico to take advantage of low labor costs. At the beginning of the twenty-first century, Mexico and China receive the greatest amount of foreign investment, and China has now passed Mexico to become the leading exporter of goods, in terms of dollars, to the United States. Labor is cheaper in China, but there is the question of distance and the cost in time to transport goods. China continues to improve its infrastructure, while Mexico's highways belong to private investors, its major international airport cannot handle any more traffic, its sewer systems pollute the underground water supply, and no workable solution to its electric power problem has been put forward.

Unless Mexico finds a way to improve its infrastructure, educate its people, and develop its own industries and products, China will wound it from one side, the Caribbean and Central American countries from another, Africa from another, and Indonesia from a fourth side. The economic future looks difficult for Mexico, but it is not for nothing that economics is known as the dismal science. Mexico has opportunities too. It has the world's richest market next door to the north and to the south a vast population that speaks the same language and could join with Mexico in a huge common market like that of Europe.

The North American Free Trade Agreement will have to be amended to remove the disadvantages to Mexico. For both moral and economic reasons U.S. immigration laws will have to give amnesty in the form of resident status (green cards) to Mexicans who come to this country without documents and live and work here, paying taxes and contributing to the national economy.

In the end, however, Mexico will prosper only as the United States comes to recognize that the two economies are mutually supportive; a healthy Mexico is a market more than a third the size of the United States in population and three times as large as Canada. As the Mexican economy grows and if the wealth is better distributed, Mexico will become a stabilizing force for the U.S. economy, distributing economic risks as well as rewards across a much larger and more diverse society. Much of this will depend upon the improvement of education in Mexico, which must first, require completion of K through 12 rather than end with junior high school; second, improve the quality of instruction by ridding the SNTE (teachers' union) of corrupt hiring practices; third, make certain that all children, not merely those in the first two years, have some breakfast and a decent lunch so they are not weary and distracted by hunger; fourth, vastly enlarge and at the same time develop standards of quality for the publicly supported system of higher education; and then make certain through a system of internships and apprentice programs, in Mexico and abroad, that those who complete four years or more of college are not relegated to becoming the world's best-informed taxicab drivers.

All thoughts of the future are built of smoke. Politics are married to economics, and the variables in any economy are so great that many people are willing to agree with Adam Smith about the unseen hand of some omniscient and omnipotent, if not apparently either just or merciful, God. Despite my disclaimer about the future, some unresolved issues are available to analysis, especially as they involve the past. The fundamental Mexican infirmity remains the debilitating conflict between the two sides of the Mexican soul: European and American origins. The infirmity is capricious, hidden, metastatic, usually left unspoken, yet curable. To prescribe for it, knowing the intractable nature of the future, is a vanity, which follows.

THE GOD OF DUALITY

Only the Indian can rescue the whites and mestizos of Mexico from the inner conflict that aches within every person, at every level of society. Unless indigenous people achieve full equality, both under the law and in the minds of the majority of the people, Mexico cannot give its full attention to the other problems that bedevil it. For almost five hundred years—since the bedding of La Malinche by Cortés—the battle has raged inside the soul of the Mexican, genetically and culturally, in the blood and behavior. Until it is finally resolved in the creation of a unified person, the war within will continue to drive the two faces of Mexico apart, the poor representing the indigenous side and the rich and middle class the European side. And as the rich side in the soul of every Mexican despises the darkness of the poor, so the poor side in return despises the whiteness of the rich.

To hide the inner conflict, the Mexican wears a mask—the wrestler, the revolutionary, the religious celebrant, Superbarrio the seriocomic hero, Tonantzin in the guise of La Virgen, the tears of the man who drags the cross and imitates the crucifixion in the Easter pageant—or a costume, which is but another kind of mask: the mariachi, Cantinflas, the mustache that regularizes the faces of rancheros, the cowboy president astride his horse. The mask presents a symbolic face: unified, clear, at peace with itself even when it is the mask of the guerrilla engaged in war. The effect of the conflict is a certain unease in the person and the country, a hesitance, as if awaiting the outcome of the war before choosing the right side, but the mask grants permission to act.[17] Everything is done "in the meanwhile"; there is no long-term planning; only the foreign companies look beyond the next few years, as if they would not accept the Maya date of 2012 for the end of the world.

Behind the mask the two Mexicans are safe; it is the veil of their corporation; their motives cannot be deciphered, their next move cannot be predicted. The PRI was a successful mask for the many parts within it, a symbolic unity of warring factions. A similar mask of clarity in the multifaceted opposition of 2000 was required to defeat the PRI, to hide the warring factions beneath.

Under the mask the Mexican is constantly choosing who will encounter the world, and why. Will it be the original part that identifies with its poor brothers and wishes to create a government that distributes great parts of the wealth and land among the campesinos or the invader's part that covets the land and labor of the natives? From time to time dominance shifts in the conflict of blood and conscience, but the rage is never-ending; there is no peace, no balance, no order in disequilibrium.

A country of such people is enfeebled in the world; it wears a mask of docility to hide its rage and wastes its will in an inner war. Cárdenas was too left, too Indian, the assertion of one aspect of the duality; the PAN came to life to represent the other side in the conflict; it could not have happened any

---

[17]Octavio Paz used the concept of the mask differently but to very good effect in *The Labyrinth of Solitude*. Mesoamerican gods were generally shown masked.

other way in Mexico. But as the two characters behind the mask face each other, the caprice within manifests itself. Mexico and Mexicans sway from pole to pole: Calles and Vasconcelos end as Fascists; Castañeda and Pascoe and Muñoz Ledo leap into bed with the PAN. And always Mexico worries about its image in the world, the appreciation of its mask, for if it allows the world to look behind the mask, the conflict will be noted, Mexico will appear to be forever unstable, dangerous, poor for a reason.

It is a country far stronger and more promising than most Mexicans imagine, not suffering an inferiority complex, as Samuel Ramos said, but possessed by a war within. Worn down, bewildered by the alternating rages and lethargies of constant war, they cannot picture their own happiness as they careen from surrender to rapacity. The clarity of resolution may yet be brought about by the rise to equality of the indigenous Mexican, but that will come only with difficulty and only through the will and the genius of the indigenous people themselves. No one can do it for them; not even a well-meaning revolutionary can break the endless deadlock of duality.

Had Subcomandante Marcos been indigenous instead of resolutely European in his culture, he might have made great progress toward the end of the internal strife. But it was not to be: He was the *white* man who spoke. And here it is worthwhile recalling that the word "Nahua" means "clear speaker." To the Nahuas all those who did not speak clearly were barbarians. The Nahuas made clowns of them, imitating their babbling languages. Nahuatl represented the great triumph of the human mind, language. Marcos was the "clear speaker" among the indigenous rebels of Chiapas; he may have claimed to be no more than the speaker, but the speaker is the tlahtoani, Motecuhzoma was the speaker, not a king, but the great speaker among "clear speakers." According to the Aztec definition, all the rest, all the silent ones in the jungle, were barbarians. And it was not as if the Zapatistas did not understand the meaning of language, the use of it in the world. The possession of the ability to read was a treasure among the people who constituted the Zapatistas; they knew the white man's secret, the mestizo's economic ladder. They distributed it as if it were gold or quetzal feathers; they valued it by the withholding of it, they doled it out: In the autonomous Zapatista villages there were many who were not considered worthy of learning to read.

The moment the whites and mestizos and Indians in Mexico examine the war beneath the mask and choose to end it by making the two sides of the duality equal, the possibility of peace exists. There will always be personal conflicts, no human being is without them, but the enfeebling conflict of two persons within one can be overcome. The redress owed by history and the state is a matter of self-interest, like the Socratic notion of virtue leading to happiness, for everything the country does to bring its indigenous citizens to equality moves the whites and mestizos and the society itself toward the end of the great civil war within. The wounds of a five-hundred-year-long civil war will not heal in one generation, but autonomy for indigenous people and the right to be the speaker who is heard, the rhetorician and the poet, the essayist and the statesman and the theologian, will start the process. Mexicans can heal themselves: Quetzalcoatl and Guadalupe can embrace like brother and sister, for they are of the same blood, and they are sick to death of the civil war of the soul. The work has begun; the hope for sweet surcease has many mentors.

IN THE HOUSE OF MEXICO

On the street in Coyoacán where the famed Mexicanist Miguel León-Portilla has lived for nearly forty years the house numbers have no apparent order; 33 may be followed by 15 or 85. To be at home on such a street requires the resident to live in history, for the houses are numbered according to their birth. On the street where the Mexicanist lives, time is a road.

In this way Mexico differs from its neighbor to the north and from much of the rest of the world. Time and space cannot be separated in the Mexican mind. Nothing can be considered in one dimension, nor can anything move in a single direction, for time in Mexico, said the Maya, is a road in five directions. As a result, Mexicans have a penchant for abstraction and complexity, a wish for analysis that extends from at least as far back as the classical period of Maya civilization to the conjunction of time and space in Coyoacán. The conjunction also gives root to the religiosity of the Mexicans, for the concern with time has universal implications; it involves men and gods, death and the millenarian expectation.

The scholar of Coyoacán is treasured by Mexicans now, much the way Octavio Paz was during his lifetime, and like Paz, who was almost a full generation older, León-Portilla looks down to find a younger crowd nibbling at his accomplishment. The pre-Columbian world is only a construction, the nibblers write, something the Spaniards dreamed. He smiles; there is a pre-

Columbian temple in the center of the largest city in the hemisphere; the evidence of his argument exists in stone. But the greater truth is in the effect of the indigenous world on the mind of Mexico, for nowhere in the European mind is time a road in five directions.

This thinking about time, the historicism of the Mexican, has expected origins. The great Mesoamerican civilization was obsessed with death and its corollary, time. It was so in the fifth century and the fifteenth century, and it is so in the new millennium. Death, as often has been said, gives meaning to time. No other force but death drives history, makes historical beings of us. For the Mesoamericans, as for us, the present serves but to divide "the not yet" from "the no longer." The Maya, like Sir Isaac Newton, thought of time past and future as the two sides of an equation. And since an equation functions in either direction, one may proceed from the present to the past or the future. The historicism of Mesoamerica differs from the irreversible timeline of Europe, and that is not only the source of many of Mexico's problems but the best hope for its future.

The manipulation of history began with the Maya, who said they could predict the past. It took a different turn when Tlacaelel, the gray eminence behind the throne of several Aztec rulers, burned the painted books containing pictographic records so revisionist historians might give his people a past more in keeping with their military and political power. In the seventeenth century the figure of the Virgin of Guadalupe came to symbolize Christian Mexico, replacing Tonantzin, who had been the beloved mother of Indian Mexico.

In 1794, Fray Servando Teresa de Mier, announced that Quetzalcoatl and St. Thomas of Mylapore were one and the same. He was a mestizo who used history to redefine the mestizaje as a wedding of equals; he dreamed of the resolution of inner conflict that has yet to be accomplished. In contemporary Mexico, history has a home in Coyoacán. The resolution in equality of the two sides of the great mestizaje has another champion. Here, behind the walls, beyond the garden, in the commodious house of scholars, history has been gathered and put in perfect order in the books that line the shelves of the library rooms. Here the ancient books, bound in leather, have their separate place, their honored cases, for they are the foundation and the proof, the analogues of incised stone, history, the hope for resolution in the soul of Mexico.

If there was once a single Mexico, if there is again to be a unified Mexico, it cannot be a found place. There cannot be a happenstance nation, a conquest simply because it was in the way, a culture merely to fill a void. Mexico, like any nation, must have both a historical foundation to stand on and an intellectual superstructure to give it order, longevity, and the inner peace to proceed. The foremost architect of that cause today, the one the Mexico City daily *Excelsior* describes as the nation's leading humanist, labors here. He sits at an antique desk, working in the intense light needed to look through a magnifying glass at manuscripts written in the sixteenth century. Today's newspapers are beside him; often they contain his thoughts on war and peace, disjunctions and embraces, in Mexico and the world. In the house of Mexico history is really an equation, Newtonian and Mayan; time flows in either direction.

Theory has been married to practice here in Coyoacán. The scholar's grandson, Miguelito, enters, and he and the septuagenarian scholar grin at each other. Then the scholar points a finger at himself, and says, "Nehuatl," which means "I." And points to Miguelito and says, "Tehuatzin [you]." The pronunciation is perfect, the second-person pronoun includes the honorific ending; it is classical Nahuatl, history alive in language. The grandson of the president of the National College hears the sounds of the "clear speaker," the symbol of equality within the Mexican, the hope for him and his generation.

It is a tense time in Mexico. The government suffers stalemate. Drug traffickers go about their business of corruption and killing. A part of the superstructure of a political party that was also the state has collapsed. The new party in power is failing. What institutions other than history and the Church are *de confianza* (trusted) in Mexico now? And if it is no other than the Church, is it the sweet, dark Virgin of Guadalupe's Church? What of history, the foundational being, Coatlicue? Is the mother of the gods not the mother of all the gods?

If in the house of the history of Mexico time is an equation, one must ask what the Mexica did, how the Maya retained control, whether the Spaniards used anything other than the sword and the plague. The history of Mexico is a history of God and gods. Answers will be found in religion for almost every question about the history of the land between the Usumacinta and the Bravo. That too is a room in the house of Mexico.

What of the future of the historian himself, his work, the work of artists and thinkers in Mexico? Surely, the house will stand. Like Paz, like Rulfo and Fuentes, Nezahualcoyotl and Sor Juana, Chimalpain and Cosío Villegas, the

Olmec sculptors and Rufino Tamayo, the house will remain. History will be contained in their work, and their work will influence the future. They are part of the equation.

Some people now say that the scholar who lives in this house on the street where time and space merge is a "nation builder," as if there had not yet been Mexico. The evaluation is simplistic; what interests the scholar is pluralism, a nation of many autonomous nations, a harmony of the unique, the calm of equity in the mirror of the mind.

In the house of Mexico, memory has many rooms, and hope also has its place. Many languages are spoken in the house of Mexico, English among them, although not foremost, not unaccented, but familiarly, for the house of Mexico, like the house of hegemony built by the Aztecs, has many outposts. The task of a nation builder is to establish equality between the center and the outposts, to cure the conflict. All this in the face of the greater danger to Mexico, which is that it could become nothing more than an outpost of the superpower to the north.

A different democracy, a realistic implementation of the ideals behind the Constitution of 1917, could become the rule in the house of Mexico, but on all the shelves in all the library rooms of the scholar's world on the street where time is a road, there is no precedent in more than two thousand years for the equalitarian democracy of the scholar's dreams.

If time does indeed return and history is not immutable, perhaps a nation can be built by inserting freedom and fairness into its past in order to change its future. Perhaps there will be other creations, a sixth sun, and in this next iteration the house of Mexico will be filled with flowers. Once, long ago, the Aztecs asked who could bring down the great city-state of Tenochtitlán, who could "shake the foundations of heaven." Tenochtitlán fell in a matter of days to an alliance of Spanish and indigenous armies. Who would have thought the PRI could fall so far in a single day in the year 2000? The present provides no comfort in Mexico, and history may point to hope or despair, equality or the stunning itch of the war within.

In the house of Mexico, in the rooms of history and ideas, the Mexicanist and a vast assembly of allies labor to complete the mestizaje, to build a nation of autonomous citizens, equal cultures, as timeless as death or the moment, unmasked and democratic. It is a good place to begin.

The Political Life of
Ifigenia Martínez, La Maestra

*I*figenia Martínez is known in Mexico by her nickname, La Maestra, which comes of her having been head of the Department of Economics at the UNAM. Although she serves now mainly as an adviser on economic issues to the PRD, she has had a long and influential career in Mexican politics and she may decide to run for office again. She was one of the first women to serve as an executive in the national government of Mexico and among the first to serve in the Congress.

Her descriptions of Mexican politics and economics over the past half century are informed by personal experience; she lived close to the center in finance, the national legislature, and the founding of the PRD. The most difficult choice in her political career came when her friend and colleague of many years Porfirio Muñoz Ledo left the PRD to campaign on his own for the Mexican presidency, ultimately to join the campaign of Vicente Fox Quesada. Long a friend of the Cárdenas family, La Maestra was forced to choose between her dear Cuauhtémoc and her dear Porfirio. She remained loyal to Porfirio until he abandoned his own campaign, but never lost her love for the Cárdenas family and the PRD.

Our conversations took place in Sra. Ifigenia Martínez's home in Coyoacán, Mexico City, at various times from 1999 to 2002. The living room of her home is filled with works of art and mementos collected over many years of travel, both personal and on behalf of the Mexican government. Here and there are photographs of her with presidents or prime ministers; she is always smiling confidently, for she was surely the most beautiful woman in Mexican politics.

She is now passing on her passion for politics to another generation. I recall one evening when her youngest grandchild, Rodrigo, then about ten years old, was visiting in her house. "Rodrigo," she said, "let's watch a videotape. Here is one you will like." She handed the tape to him, and Rodrigo put it in the *machine. A series of agonized faces from across Latin America appeared on the screen, martial music filled the room, and the title of the video appeared in huge block letters:* La Deuda Externa (The Foreign Debt).

My father, Jesús Martínez Elizalde, was born in the north of Mexico, in a tiny village called Jimulco, Coahuila, now a railroad stop. He was the youngest child, so the family saw that he had a good education. They sent him to Guadalajara, where he studied in the American Business College. He learned English and French. When he finished his studies, he went to work in the office of the Mexican National Railroads, and as far as I know, it was the only employment he had until he died. Eventually he rose to general superintendent of freight.

What impressed me most about my father were his library and his friends. He was a very cultured man who had a private tutor and read literature in French and English. He had friends who were bohemians, poets, writers, painters. His political inclinations were, at first, in Masonry. I don't know how, but he was deceived by the Masons and later became a Marxist and a Communist. He died still a member of the Mexican Communist Party. When I entered the university, my father told me that he did not want me to join the Communist Party, which had many student members. I didn't understand what he meant, because it had never appealed to me. (I was never convinced of their doctrine in economics; I supported a mixed economy.) I asked my father, "Why are you telling me this?" And he said, "Because there are lowlifes, thieves slipping in through the cracks." And now I understand, because in political parties, including the Communist Party, there is never a shortage of these rascals slipping in through the cracks.

My father died in 1955; it is a long time. My mother was ninety-seven when she died. She lived here with me after she was widowed. She was a very domineering woman, who spanked us—many times unjustly! Nonetheless, she took good care of her children. And when I married—the first time—she looked after my daughters and only son. I was never able to fit in with my mother. Nevertheless, the great part of my career has been because of the help she gave me. When my father died, I had three daughters, the youngest only a few months old, and my mother came to live with us. I left the administration of the house to her, because it made her happy.

My father was a feminist and had in his library a famous book by Frederick Engels about the family. I was the eldest, my father's favorite; he never allowed me to do any of the chores in the house. When I went to school, it was the choice my father made, the best school in Mexico, the Colegio Alemán [German School]. Even in grade school all the instruction was in German: history, mathematics, everything. When World War Two started, it was a terrible conflict for my father, because he was completely against Hitler and the Nazis. When Stalin signed the pact with Hitler, my father was not pleased. And when they broke apart, he was very happy. My father talked a lot with me; we talked a lot about politics. In the German School they had tried to indoctrinate us. Every day we had to sing three anthems: the German anthem; "Deutschland über Alles," the song of the Nazis; and the Mexican national anthem.

For secondary school, I went to an official [public] school. There were very few women, so the women were favored. After that I went on to Preparatoria Number One, the most famous school in the national university system. In preparatory school there was total freedom. You could go to the classes you wanted, go around with anyone you liked, total freedom. The professors were excellent. There were very few women in preparatory school, but more than in secondary school, perhaps twenty percent. There were some outstanding students, like Pablo González Casanova [sociologist], who had been my friends since secondary school . . . so many; Diego Rivera's daughter was my friend. So it was a lot of fun.

For me the great decision was law or economics, a new discipline in Mexico. I wanted to go on to study law. But my father said, "Not law, economics. Lawyers live off the disagreements of society, and economists study how to bring more goods for all; economics has a social function." I studied five years at the National School of Economics with but little enthusiasm for what I learned, old-fashioned economic doctrines. In that time, the forties, I don't recall any women as government executives. I knew many women, had a circle of women friends who were my constant companions, but none of us was interested in politics. The war years were not a time of abundance. The population was growing, and it was a time of limited supplies and high prices from 1940 to '46, so we had the problem we called *la carestía*, which means limited goods that become more expensive every day. Scarcity and inflation affected the popular classes, so we had to hope that the people's lives would improve at the end of the war.

The Sinarquistas were out in the countryside then, a rural movement, very close to the clergy. My father said he was a liberated person, one who had no religion, and we grew up that way. My mother was Catholic but not practicing. So we were not indoctrinated; not one of us was baptized, because my father thought baptism an injustice since the children had nothing to say about it.

At the end of the war Miguel Alemán [president, 1946–1952] opened an era of intense public expenditure that brought deficits. We had devaluations, which were not well accepted, especially by the leftist movements, including some famous economists who were in the government and had to resign their positions. They left because of the great devaluation of 1947, a postwar adjustment of the rate of exchange.

Mexico quickly lost the reserves accumulated during the war. Nonetheless, Alemán followed an expansionary policy, stimulating private companies and private investment. But the corruption of the Alemán regime brought about a great deal of justified criticism, so the next government took great care to straighten out public affairs.

During the Ruiz Cortines [president, 1952–1958] government, the administration began a program of fellowships to study economics at the best foreign universities.

It was a generation of outstanding Mexicans who contributed to the building of the country. Among them was the father of Salinas de Gotari. This select group was sent to work with the American and British governments. The American government provided grants to train them in the Bureau of the Budget and other offices so the Mexicans could learn how to manage public affairs.

Some Mexicans went to U.S. universities, others to the London School of Economics. My first husband, Alfredo Navarrete Romero, was one of this group. He had gone to the U.S. to work in the Bureau of the Budget in Washington and to study at the American University when we were married in 1946. My father was not in favor of the marriage. He said, "I educated you to have good judgment. I can only give you some hints, like what you should choose for a career, but not in more personal affairs." I was married here in Mexico City. And we went off to Harvard. I was not in the Mexican government fellowship program, so when I arrived, I had to struggle; interviews, applications, and finally, I was accepted in the Graduate School of Arts and Sciences, without a grant or government sponsorship. To get the money together for tuition, I worked at MIT, doing calculations for supersonic aircraft at the thermodynamics laboratory.

We had to return to Mexico in 1949, because Alfredo had an agreement with the government, but he didn't like the post they gave him, so he decided to complete his theoretical studies at the International Monetary Fund [IMF]. We spent three years in Washington [from 1950 to 1953], where we started a family. My two oldest daughters were born Americans, but they gave up their U.S. citizenship when they turned eighteen.

In 1953, Alfredo was hired by the secretary of finance, Antonio Carrillo Flores, who formed a group of young, well-trained Mexicans who had an idea of what the country needed. They created institutions, wrote laws, and sought the financial resources necessary for balanced economic development.

When I returned to Mexico City, married, with two daughters, Raúl Salinas Lozano [father of Carlos Salinas de Gotari] offered me the position of chief of the Fiscal Policy Office. I was able to grasp what the government needed, and we went ahead, but I had problems with the Bank of Mexico, because they had then, as now, a restrictive policy. At the Fiscal Policy Office we were in favor of an expansionary policy, using public funds.

I had very firm opinions, and I did not respect the hierarchy. I have never respected them when they interfere with well-founded reason. It's a matter of giving an honest opinion. Well, Carrillo Flores, the secretary of finance, said, "Let us avoid conflicts. It will be best if Alfredo continues his career in public financial policy and Ifigenia goes to the academic life." As always, I was very docile where my husband was concerned. I said, "Very well, I will go to the academy." So I went to the UNAM.

After I joined the economics faculty, I began doing research and writing books about economics. Later I became involved in the population problem and its effects on the development of Mexico.[1] We had a demographic explosion: 3.6 percent growth per year. I had a professor who said that we don't have to worry about population growth, because as Mexico had more people, it would have more demographic weight, more brains, more brilliant people to face the powerful United States. Others saw the population explosion as a burden that would not permit the country to improve its standard of living but would instead produce misery and poverty. It was going to be a problem. The answer was to have investment and education to

[1] She published her views in *Overpopulation and Economic Development* (Mexico City: Dirección General de Publicaciones, UNAM, 1967), p. 34.

support the growth in population. We know from history that the rate of population growth is inversely related to the rate of earnings and education, especially of women. With economic progress overpopulation diminishes. The rise in the status of women is related to the decrease in population growth.

The question of family planning interested me very much, but at the time it was sacrilegious. The Church had some influence on the population problem, but the real problem was that when a woman went to the social services clinic, the doctors were opposed to family planning. When I returned to the United States after the birth of my first daughter, the doctor asked if I wanted a system of birth control, ". . . and what method would you like?" Here in Mexico it was different. The problem of abortion was certainly a social problem, because there were no health services, nor did women have any information on how to prevent pregnancy.

Another subject that interested me was the financing of public education. I could not accept the official view that there were many children and no money, so I published three articles about the subject in the Sunday supplement of the journal *Novedades*. Dr. Jaime Torres Bodet, the new secretary of public education, read them and invited me to be his economic adviser for his eleven-year plan for the extension of primary education. That marked a turning point in the commitment of the government to provide for universal education.

Later I did the first estimate of the distribution of personal income in Mexico. The thesis was that in the process of rapid economic growth, everyone benefits, but those at the top of the scale of wealth move more than those at the bottom. The state had to moderate this tendency with social policies. This was in 1961, when López Mateos was president. The top public officials were political liberals, but in economics they were state interventionists, the position established in the 1917 Constitution.

And then the neoliberals, beginning with López Portillo [president, 1976–1982], based everything on the export of crude oil. They reduced and reduced and reduced the public economy and increased the number of poor people. The United States had great influence in reducing the public sector, because they do not understand anything, well, very little. And the Mexican officials at the Ministry of Finance and the Bank of Mexico, instead of defending the Mexican point of view, have been willing to give in.

In 1977 I was divorced, after thirty-one years of marriage, almost a full lifetime. Two months after we were divorced, he married again. A year later he suffered a severe depression from which he never recovered. He was ill from about 1979 to 1999, when he died. It was very sad, and so was the way he was treated. He was ultimately sent to a clinic for young drug addicts. What was he doing there? It had to do with the fact that he had money and a good pension.

My daughters were just starting out on their medical careers and had no influence in their father's care. Both daughters were at the UNAM. The older one prefers research to practice. My second daughter is very serious and committed. She always wanted to be like [Sor] Juana Inés, so when the time came to go to the university, she chose medicine and specialized in pediatrics. She works at a National Institute of Social Security hospital and has a private practice. She has three handsome young children [including young Rodrigo]. My next child went to the Liceo Franco Mexicano. She married a Frenchman and has two daughters and a completely French life. I've either lost her or gained a French family.

The idea of becoming a member of the Congress did not appeal to me. I rejected it three times. The fourth time I accepted because it was proposed by Porfirio [Muñoz Ledo]. At the time there was not a single woman in a position of power in Mexico. There was discrimination, but I never felt discriminated against because I am a woman. On the contrary.

I remarried in 1980, to a nuclear physicist, a wise man, charming and well educated. He always behaved properly during our life together, which lasted seven years. He knew everything that I didn't know: astronomy, mathematics, and physics. He's a quiet man who doesn't drink, smoke, or dance. He has no friends. He told me that he tried, but he couldn't live my life, he couldn't take it.

I told him I understood, because I couldn't change myself either. Then he said it would be best to separate. It was a very friendly divorce. We respect each other. It just wasn't possible for us to live together. I have to live my life around politics, but here in Mexico women live their lives through their husbands. And it's not possible the other way around. In our marriage everything revolved around me, my interests, my friends. I would come in late and find my husband sitting in a chair, waiting for me to come home. He said he couldn't sleep until I came back. He was very paternalistic. Mexican men think they have to pay for everything. We had to live modestly, but that didn't bother me. I never put what I earned into our joint bank accounts. I didn't do it with my first husband, and I didn't do it with the second, even though he was a full-time professor and had very little money.

Things have changed in Mexico. A woman who is well educated can get an interesting job and earn a lot of money, which enables her to have domestic help. That makes a big difference. In the old days women couldn't work, or they could if they had their husbands' permission. They had to agree on that. But now it's much easier. Two earners are needed to cover a family's day-to-day expenses. In my time that did not happen. Few women worked outside the house.

I myself am sympathetic to the men's cause. Some might say I am not a feminist but a masculinist. In my first marriage, Dr. Navarrete took care of our finances. I didn't even know how much we were spending, because his office took care of all that. All the bills were sent to his office and paid for. The money I earned was my money. Now both partners contribute. My daughters put their money into the pot. Their husbands need their contributions. Times are hard.

Today husbands are expected to share the work in the house. Some Mexican men are still very macho. They won't do anything around the house, but they don't fully support the family. If the men are macho, it's very difficult for the wives. Women work outside the house but have to do housework too. It's not fair. If they need their wives' earning power, husbands must help in the house, share duties and rights. Democracy starts at home. Otherwise, the wife and mother has a double burden. This is not good for the marriage. I was very lucky because I had my mother in the house.

My life in politics started when a group of women from the PRI wanted me to represent them in the presidential campaign [1964–1970]. They came to my house to invite me to speak at the opening of the campaign and to beg my husband to allow me to participate. He absolutely refused. But for one reason or another I soon was involved in political events. It made my husband very angry. Finally, he gave up and accepted my political career, but our marriage was already on the rocks.

Porfirio [Muñoz Ledo] and I met when he was the president of the PRI. He told me I should be a member of Congress. I said that I wasn't even a member of the PRI, because I didn't believe in the legislative work they did. In fact, I had no faith in the political system at all. But he told me that because I knew public finance, I could lead an important debate on the budget and taxes in Congress.

I spoke with the incoming president, López Portillo, who told me it would be wonderful if I went to the lower house. I said that I didn't like the work; I was accustomed to working at what I really enjoyed. He told me that it didn't matter, I should at least try a campaign to see if I liked it. I won in all the polling places but one—where the bankers lived.

In 1976 I took office as a deputy in the House of Representatives. It was a three-year term. I liked being a member of Congress, but it only lasted three years. After that, nobody could figure out where to put me because they didn't like my criticisms. I was mentioned for various posts, but somehow the influential people always objected. Porfirio, who was ambassador to the UN in New York, was the only one who accepted me. He said he needed an economist with the rank of an ambassador. He went to López Portillo with a list of three candidates. López Portillo said, "Doña Ifigenia is on your list. Aren't you afraid of her?"

Porfirio said, "No, I'm not afraid of her."

"Well, in that case, it's good that you want her. It's done."

Then I met the president here in Coyoacán, where he had come to attend an inauguration. He said, "Doña Ifigenia, I have found a place for you." The political class to which I already belonged was a kind of fraternity, so some job had to be given to me.

When Miguel de la Madrid, a man trained at the Bank of Mexico, took office [1982], the neoliberals came with him. That's why I came back from the UN in New York: I was very worried about the Mexican foreign debt. I told the secretary of foreign relations that the economy couldn't grow with that heavy burden in 1980 to 1981. The secretary said that [Carlos] Salinas [secretary of the budget under de la Madrid] was saying something different.

We talked for ten or fifteen minutes. Then he stood up and said, "I don't know why I am discussing all this with you."

So there it stood. We had to pay.

When Porfirio returned to Mexico in 1986, he said to me, "There is a lot to do. We have to criticize what is being done; it's not right.

"You don't believe me, do you?

"We have to have a meeting in your house. You have to realize that I'm serious. I will even send you the wine."

He was too hard on everyone. I asked a friend of his, "Do you think Porfirio is sincere? Do you think he really believes in his criticisms?"

At the time people on the left thought the economic model of import substitution was exhausted and a change in policy was necessary. They did not accept that what had worn out was the political system, presidentialist and authoritarian.

Before our first meeting we made a list of the better-known politicians. Porfirio wanted to know who would take part. I said to him, "Do you realize that Cuauhtémoc Cárdenas [who was then governor of Michoacán] just made a speech and he said exactly what we have been talking about [neoliberalism, presidentialism, the system, failed economic policy]. We have to invite him."

Porfirio said, "I'm having lunch with him tomorrow."

We made our list, sent out the invitations, and had about seventeen who attended. Cuauhtémoc accepted the invitation.

Porfirio was the first to speak. He said that the elections were coming up and that things weren't going well, that our economy wasn't being run correctly, nor were our international relations. Everybody present was a political heavyweight, people who were part of the system. Some of the participants were frightened and sat in the back. They thought they were in danger of losing their jobs, of losing their positions or reputations.

Cuauhtémoc was serious and stern-looking as always. From a look he gave us, I knew he was with us. He said that he couldn't fully support us until his term as governor ended, which was to be in a couple of weeks [September 15, 1986]. In the meantime, he asked us to produce a written manifesto.[2]

I was married then, and my husband agreed with all this. In fact, both my former and present husbands did. My former husband telephoned me during the meeting to say that he felt the same way I did. I had no fear myself, but many of the others were worried. If they couldn't earn their living because they were working outside the system, what would happen to them and their families?

Then President de la Madrid started to move his chess pieces, and we began to lose people. A few days later all the important people started to leave us; we were left on our own. But then Cuauhtémoc said, "They may be leaving, but more people will eventually join us." And many people—from all parts of the country—did join us. We continued our work the next year, 1987, but the government made a great effort to marginalize us in order to

[2] See Luis Javier Garrido, *La Ruptura: La Corriente Democrática del PRI* (Mexico: Grijalbo, 1993), which Sra. Martínez recommends.

make us fall in line. The president called Cuauhtémoc and Porfirio. He wanted to know what it was that we wanted, what our demands were.

The head of the party saw us twice, once in Cuauhtémoc's house, where he listened to all of us. We were about ten or twelve, the rebels. He promised, after listening to us, that he would do something. But he did nothing, and finally he was removed because he couldn't deal with us. They put someone else in his place as the president of the party, someone who was more experienced.

The first thing this man did was to have a huge party in his home, which is very close to my house. I can walk there from here. He invited every important politician in Mexico, together with those from the Corriente Democrática [Democratic Current]. Everybody was very cordial, and afterward the new president of the PRI called on each member, one by one, to offer whatever help he could and to say that they [the PRI] would gradually integrate [pay attention to] us. He said that the cabinet secretaries would meet with us to discuss our views.

Then came the Thirteenth PRI Party Congress. We were invited to present papers with our views. Cuauhtémoc Cardenas was there, and another friend, Oscar Pintado, a very young, very sharp, very intelligent young man. They both presented papers on the electoral system, seeking to change the method of picking candidates. Oscar suspected it was a trap. So he left.

But Cuauhtémoc didn't do that. He presented his paper asking to democratize the selection of the PRI's candidate. And it was a trap. His proposal was put up for a vote, a procedure that never had happened before, and it lost. So he left—very angry.

The next day was the inauguration of the Thirteenth Congress. Porfirio, who was a former president of the party, was there on the podium. The speech made by the new president of the party was full of criticisms and allusions to the Trojan Horse. I didn't even get the point at first. I thought they were against the PAN. When he finished, I applauded, but Cuauhtémoc continued to look very angry.

The next day a letter from Cuauhtémoc appeared in the papers, attacking the people in the party. And the fight began. Porfirio said, "I will send another letter to the papers," and he sent one that was even stronger. We were not out to defeat the system, but to change it. It was possible, because we were right. We're still right.

In 1988 Cuauhtémoc began to travel, because he wasn't governor anymore. He visited many parts of the country, where they were anxious to talk to him, because they agreed with what he believed in. It was what his father had done.

Finally, they sent someone to negotiate, here in my house, to say that the president wanted to see both of them [Cuauhtémoc and Porfirio] but under the proper conditions. Everything was becoming public, all of Mexico would know about it. I asked what these conditions would be. The representative answered, "Cuauhtémoc stops traveling, and Porfirio stops talking to the press."

I asked, "Are you saying that we should sacrifice our personal rights, our freedom of movement and free speech?"

Then the PRI published a long letter in the newspaper rejecting what Cuauhtémoc and Porfirio were doing. They said it was not authorized by the party, but there was no expulsion; it never happened. However, this was enough. We started to get letters of support from people all over the country who thought as we did. We said that we wanted a change in economic policy, a change in the electoral process, a change in the party itself. We finally put together a petition, a platform telling what we believed in. Cuauhtémoc was very involved in this; he wanted it all to be written down. So that's what we did. We put it on record.

Various political parties subscribed to it, and about twenty civil organizations. The signing of this pact took place in Jalapa, Veracruz. We all went there for the official ceremony. But before that, we wondered who would be our presidential candidate. We had to choose someone. Porfirio said our best option was Cuauhtémoc, "for many reasons. First of all, he has name recognition. His name promises a certain kind of government. He has a permanent staff, a group of forty or fifty supporters, because he was a governor, and he has experience in government, recent experience in state affairs. So for all these reasons, he should be our candidate."

Then I asked, "Have you told him about your plan?" Although there were some rumors that Porfirio himself wanted to run, he realized that Cuauhtémoc was the ideal candidate.

Again I asked, "Have you told Cuauhtémoc yet?"

"No."

"Then run and tell him." Which is what he did.

When Cuauhtémoc joined our group, he accepted under one condition, that he wouldn't be a presidential candidate. I was very surprised to hear this. But politicians always say no to something they really want. Cuauhté-moc finally accepted and asked for a platform. Porfirio worked hard on it. So did I and the rest of the group. We all contributed.

But we needed a recognized political party to register our candidate to compete for the presidency. A small party, representing people who dis-agreed with PRI methods, the Partido Auténtico de la Revolución Mexicana [Authentic Party of the Mexican Revolution—PARM], contacted us, saying they were willing to support Cuauhtémoc. We accepted.

The Frente Democrático Nacional [FDN], our group, ran a very success-ful campaign. Most political analysts agree that Cuauhtémoc won the pres-idency, but after several incidents of a very dubious nature, the government gave only 32 percent of the vote to the FDN. Adolfo Gilly, a political analyst, summarized the contest, saying the people voted for what they thought was the good PRI and the best candidate, a member of the historical political elite, and voted against the bad PRI. It was a heavy blow to the system. For the first time they lost the absolute majority in the lower house. From then on they lost ground until they lost the presidency.

Translated by Sylvia Sasson Shorris

The Education of
José Chim Kú

*T*he village of San Antonio Sihó, which lies in an area that was once low
jungle on the border of the states of Yucatán and Campeche, is a lesson in
globalization. Until the end of the eighteenth century, it was a farm community. People used mainly ancient, although efficient, methods to plant and harvest corn, beans, and squash. There was an abundance of wild animal life in el
monte (the forest) and a magnificent array of forage food. Medicinal plants and
herbs were also available in profusion in the forest. The need for twine to use
with mechanical harvesting equipment as well as to make mats and rugs and
so on gave birth to the henequén industry. The henequén was planted, harvested, and shredded in the Yucatán, then shipped out of the port of Sisal (from
which the product draws its common name) to be used around the world.

The people who worked on the henequén plantations suffered terrible abuse.
Yaqui Indians, defeated by the Mexican Army, were sent off to work in the
fields, where they suffered and died in the unfamiliar heat of the jungle. The
plantation owners became wealthy, while the laborers in the fields and processing plants lived and died of heat, overwork, beatings, hunger, and disease.
As the world market expanded, the owners demanded more production. Vast
tracts of land were cleared and planted with henequén. The ecology of the
peninsula was largely destroyed. In the forests themselves, the hardwoods were
clear-cut, with no thought of the future. Everything went to the world markets.

Since both indigenous culture and modern Spanish-language education
were considered impediments to productivity, the Maya culture was forced
underground, the language was prohibited, and the little schooling available
through the Catholic Church was insufficient to bring people out of their virtual slavery (some workers were actually locked into cells at night). The
henequén industry continued to thrive, serving a vast global market, until
someone discovered that baling wire was more efficient than twine for use in

binding machines. At almost the exact same time, competition in the sisal mar-
ket arose from Africa, the Philippines, and other places around the globe. Price
wars drove a sinking market toward oblivion. The vast henequén plantations
receded, like waters after a flood. What was left was the tragedy of globaliza-
tion: land destroyed by years of supporting a single crop, people deracinated and
sickly (the average height of the Maya declined during the period), a language
largely gone from the plantation areas, and a culture left in ruins after years of
prohibition.

By the end of the twentieth century the village of Sihó had 1,400 residents,
about 120 of whom worked in the henequén industry, where they were paid
eight pesos a day to work in the fields or in a small processing plant that had
lost one of its walls to time. The equipment in the plant was ancient, but func-
tional, powered by an engine imported from Germany. The global industry in
Sihó had been born as a result of a technological whim of the makers of
machines made to harvest wheat on farms a world away. And the industry had
died as the result of a different whim, a new way to use wire instead of twine.
All that was left was poverty and the ruined forest and the wreck of the land.
Labor was cheaper in Africa and Asia, although little labor was needed any-
more.

The carts that carried the leaves into the plant to be shredded were pulled by
burros in Mexico, by oxen in Asia. The same sun dried the shreds to be woven
into rope; similar species of flies gathered by the thousands to eat the juices the
shredding machine spilled. The United Nations Development Program sought
to fill the void left by the caprice of globalized business and culture. Develop-
ment in Sihó had not been sustainable.

José Chim Kú of Sihó is a stocky man with a sweet face who chain-smokes cig-
arettes that he buys two or three at a time from the only store in the village. He
has been a leader of political, social, and cultural efforts to improve the quality
of life in the village since he was a very young man. He is married, with chil-
dren, and he lives in a house made of stone. It has many rooms, but only dirt
floors. There is no potable water in the village, but Chim, his wife, and children
are all healthy, and the food they cook, which I have eaten often, is delicious. It
is very hot and humid in the interior of the Yucatán Peninsula during much of
the year, and like everyone in the village, the Chim family bathes frequently in
cooling water, often more than once a day. Chim works on community projects
with his friend Andy May Citúk. Although José Chim Kú is still a young man,

he is acknowledged as one of the leaders of the village. Chim, May, and several young women who have studied Maya culture in a UN-supported project[1] now teach Maya language and culture in the local primary and secondary (junior high) school. I asked him to talk about his life. He gave the following account without my asking a single question.

I want to speak a little bit about my family. I am going to begin with my grandparents. My paternal grandfather is like the strong part of me; he is the one who has impelled me toward the work I do now. My maternal grandfather is like the more sensitive part, the more reflective part. So this permits me to have some balance as a person. Fortunately, they are still alive. My grandfather, on my father's side, is eighty and still very strong, and it's from there that I get the vitality for my work. And my mother's father is also still alive. He is a very calm person, very noble. So at times I feel that I carry both parts inside me. Sometimes I am very enthusiastic, and at other times more reflective, more analytical. That's why I say the two personalities are in play inside me.

My father is a very calm person, in his life, his home, his daily life; nothing can be taken away from his virtues. He does not mix in problems, nor does he try to find solutions; he lives his own life.

I was born one sixteenth of February of 1964. I was born. I suffered a lot when I was a boy. My father drank. The little he earned, he spent on his drink, his liquor. So I lacked many things.

At age six, when I entered school, I had not had any preschool; I entered directly into grade school. Because of this beginning, I complained and quarreled a lot, because I had not been able to learn to read or write. My head was as hard as a nutshell.

I started to become more and more fond of reading. And the part that had the most influence, was this part of my grandfather. It allowed me many things, my love of books, which I did not share with my pals in the school, because they did not approve of me being full of books. And I did not like the games, I preferred to participate in the school activities, like the evening get-togethers.

The schools in Sihó at this time did not go beyond the fourth grade. Those who had some economic resources were able to send their children to the county seat [Halachó]. I repeated primary school twice, the fourth

[1] See Earl Shorris, *Riches for the Poor* (New York: W. W. Norton, 2000).

year, because there was nothing more, and there was no money, so I could not get what I needed to go to Halachó to attend secondary school.

I had to go into farmwork, which is henequén. I wanted then to learn everything about the work, the cutting, everything, and later I worked in the plant. But I still had the desire to continue studying. Later I knew a professor whom I told that I wanted to continue studying, and he helped me, and I was able to complete the sixth grade.

After I left there, I was able to enter a secondary school in Progreso, a boarding school for young men. And there you had to make your own decisions and be very independent. I had to take on the strong character of my other grandfather so that I could survive in this place where people came from different areas, even different states. In the first year I was the leader of the group, but [in order to do that] a lot of things had to happen. I had to get rid of one personality to put on another. One had to be strong, from your physical being to your character.

In this school, you had to get up at five in the morning so that everything was in order. Breakfast. Honor the flag. The classes lasted ten hours. There were four technical courses. One for fishing, where you had to learn all the arts of the fisherman. There was a workshop for motors. There was another that I liked very much, the seaman's workshop, where studies were in an integrated form: astronomy; physics; a lot of mathematics; cartography. I spent five hours a day in this workshop. Outside the normal ten hours a day of classes, I dedicated another two or three hours in the library.

In the second year I was able to continue in the workshop. It was a difficult course. I had to learn to steer a boat, learn the course of the winds, how to use the wind to sail the boat. I liked the work in this discipline.

I spent three years in this school, where I had to go without seeing my community. The third year I began to have a desire to get involved in politics. I was president of the student body. That's where I developed my career, because it depended on one's understanding politics. If one understands the politics, he can bring himself to a place where he can serve. So I took this road, a very wide road, perhaps a beautiful road, but one in which a person must follow his conscience. The black road won't let him sleep, because he is making use of his position for his own benefit. That is a bad road.

The political person, the honest person, the honorable person, gets the same from his close pals. He would never be part of the underhanded dealings of the director of the school.

The school had one bus, so the "gentlemen" used it for their own freight, and the money never got back to the cashbox of the school. The bus was not serving the students. We said that the school's vehicles had to be for the use of the school so that the money went for the benefit of the students and the school itself. It was there that I began to understand the reality of politics.

I lacked one semester for completing secondary school. We called a strike, and then my companions backslid; they accused me of being an agitator, of creating a sinister movement among the students. So I had to leave school. And because of this, I lost a very great opportunity. I had gotten a scholarship to study in Veracruz. And after that to go to a Japanese school to learn marine work, all of that. But the school said they should not give it to me, so I lost everything.

But it made me very happy, because I was able to be here with my people—this is my community—and it has enabled me to do many things that perhaps I could not have done if I had completed my studies. But before that time, before I returned to Sihó, I was in Cancún, around one year. I lived the whole story over there. I began to drink, I smoked, even marijuana, everything, because I was in a house with a lot of guys and gals. There was great promiscuity. But I had to think about it. This was a kind of cowardice, because I was losing something, I was losing something very important, which was the opportunity to serve, to feel useful.

When I returned, I got involved in the daily activities of the community. We formed a farmworkers' theater group, a youth group, in which we showed, in theatrical form, everything about social problems: alcoholism; drug addiction; prostitution; cultural underdevelopment; the disintegration of the family. We showed all this in an hour of theater, giving messages to the people. First, we went to the county seat, then to other municipalities. And then in many parts of the state, and then we got invitations from places outside the state, including Amecameca in the state of Mexico, Oaxaca, Veracruz, in various parts of the Republic.

Outside of this, two pals were working in Mexico with Professor María Alicia Medrano. This work was not for ourselves alone. It included other people, enabling them to develop themselves, not merely economically, not merely physically, but so that one could feel the satisfaction within himself. I think this is very important, because if a person pursues only riches, he will feel useless. Everything we did had a philosophical component that kept us alive.

We worked within the community, starting a preschool. We did this with a group of women from the community and a group of friends, on our own initiative, working with materials from the region, because the government did not give resources to do this, although we needed them. We started out one afternoon to build a little school of red earth and straw, and this gave the educational authorities the desire to authorize the school—once it was already there.

For economic reasons, we had to leave these activities to return to work. I worked in many things. I worked as a salesman in Mérida, going house to house, selling beauty products, selling electronic articles, to earn my living. Later I worked as a plumber's helper, as a construction worker. I worked for almost a year in the state of Tabasco in a laundry. But I always carried a book with me, some book. I always carried a pencil with a notebook or a piece of paper to write on.

It was about things, dreams, because if a person does not write it down when he imagines something, it will often disappear. But if you write, you can go back and read it. So I always went about that way, with something in my briefcase. These were my preferred weapons: a book, a notebook, and a pencil. So in this way I was able to get rid of the hopelessness in my life and work with the good things one lives with, because it is very, very, very bad not to have good things in life. When one comes to appreciate life, he appreciates himself as well. He finds good things; even a stone has something good.

I returned to this community, and we are again working with young people. People were saying at the time, "We suppose Mexico is a free and democratic regime. We criticize Cuba, but we are even worse," because it was considered a mortal sin to criticize the government, a very grave sin to complain about the party, which was then the PRI. I took on the responsibility of giving people the idea that as a social force we are very strong, because there are so many of us. I realized that there were two forces, management and the state. The politics of the state threatened to overwhelm the people, because they never succeeded in organizing themselves. They weren't able to unite.

So people began to say that as soon as they could unite, they would become very powerful, and then we could make decisions about our own development: what do we want; how do we want it to happen; how can we participate. But I also became aware of something else: For people to believe in what I was saying, I had to try to accomplish a unity of my own, the unity of only one person. At times your senses are separated from your body. Your body wants to prevail; your mind soars. Then you do nothing because you can't unite your own thoughts. The things you know go in one direction; your actions go in another direction. And your abilities go in yet a different direction.

Because of this awareness, I was able to take on a very responsible position. I didn't want it, but I had to accept. For three years I was a member of the [management] committee of the ejido. I had many problems during that time. It was a golden rule that whatever type of authority, communal or ejidal, had to yield and follow the hierarchies of the party [PRI].

I took a position on the side of the people who trusted me, which caused me many difficulties. It wasn't the usual position of those in authority. The authorities are supposed to serve their immediate superiors, not the people. I saw that such conduct leads to conformity. So I said, "What for? Whatever happens, we're screwed."

To be a leader, you must be a kind of conciliator, you must know how to be inclusive. You should take a firm stance, but do it in a subtle way. You must be able to turn your friends into brothers and your enemies into friends.

I have had a lot of experience since that time, which gave me the tools to know how to work with the community. Often I had to confront the power of the local politicians, but I was never afraid, because I sensed the power of the community, of my community, of my people.

In 1992 the government said no more subsidies, every group will have to fend for itself. Many people emigrated from the community. They went to live in Cancún, in Cozumel, the tourist places, taking their families. Others became bricklayers, house painters, to see if they could survive, if they could pay their bills. It was difficult for them. Our ancestors were decapitated. During the era of the hacendados, they cut off their thinking apparatus and left them with their bodies and the ability to work. That's what they did to our indigenous ancestors. Now we are learning how to think again.

When the Zapatistas had their conference in Yucatán, we took in some of them here, and it caused us a lot of trouble with the community. The head of the town council manipulated it. But we didn't weaken. We gathered about two hundred people from the community so that they could listen to their comrades the Zapatistas.

I spoke to them: "Look, friends, these people are not assassins, as you've been told. They are human beings, poor people, like us. They are peasants who are fighting for themselves. Our cause is different, because we don't use firearms. But ours is also a struggle, and one of the aims of our fight is to remove the veil from our eyes."

Many people asked me why the Zapatistas covered their faces. They thought it was because they were cowards. But I told them, "Look, my friends, they are not cowards. Under their hoods they have the same faces, faces of indigenous people, as we have. We are all connected."

I think we are on the verge of finding the energy that the old Maya had and the light that emanated from them. This light was what made them brilliant architects, brilliant astronomers, as well as great ecologists. This is why they were able to live in harmony with nature. I think it won't be long until this will be revived in all of us, the Maya who survive in this part of Mexico.

We won't start a movement to kill or to throw out people who are not of our race. Our cause will be one of inclusion, to take in everyone, so that we can all live in peace and harmony. We want to be respected for what we are, for how we think, for our origins. It's not a fight to the death; it's a fight for life.

Translated by Sylvia Sasson Shorris

In Place of a Bibliography

Any work about Mexico must be a conversation with many writers: Octavio Paz, Juan Rulfo, Alfonso Reyes, Miguel León-Portilla, Fray Bernardino de Sahagún, Jesús Silva Herzog, Nezahualcoyotl, Daniel Cosío Villegas, Sor Juana Inés de la Cruz, José Vasconcelos, Ricardo Flores Magón, Fray Bartolomé de las Casas, Munro Edmonson, Jaime Sabines, Gongora y Sigüenza, Alarcón, Clavijero, López Austin, Durán, Siméon, and Mexico's literary jaguar, Carlos Fuentes, these among the many grand voices; and also Ricardo Bonfil, Carlos Monsiváis, Luis Villoro, Elena Poniatowska, and, from the right, Enrique Krauze. And many others whose names appear in the body of the book, if only as footnotes. And for no other reason than my fascination with Pancho Villa, Federico Cervantes, Gildardo Magaña, Aguirre Benavides, and Obregón's endless memoir of the civil wars.

The Cassasola five-volume pictorial history of Mexico is a pleasure to look at, but dangerous for the working writer who does not want to lose an hour here and there just looking.

Of course I have already left out the Popol Vuh, Bernal Díaz del Castillo, poor little Motolinia, and Father Garibáy, as well as Alfonso Caso, Nezahualcoyotl's son Nezahualpilli, all the rest of the original Mesoamerican authors to whom specific works may or may not be attributable and their bibliographer, Ascensión Hernández de León-Portilla. And as I will not be the last, I am not the first of my countrymen to write about Mexico; John Reed, Anita Brenner, John Womack, Jr., Friedrich Katz (an Austrian who went to Mexico and then came to the Unite States), John Kenneth Turner, John R. MacArthur, Alan Riding, Dibble and Anderson, James Lockhart, and Thelma Sullivan are among those whose work is indispensable to the conversation. Also the writers about the 1910–1920 period: Roeder, Cockcroft, Cumberland, Ross, John Reed, Mariano Azuela, and now Alan Knight. There are also many histories to consult. The grand reference work is from *Porrua:*

Diccionario de Historia, Biografía, Geografía de México, and the other, the *Historia General de México* from the Colegio de México. In English, there are many histories, among them *The Cambridge History of Latin America* and Meyer and Sherman's *The Course of Mexican History.*

Then there are those writers who are both Mexican and American, among them Eduardo Ruiz, Ilan Stavans, and many others.

The extent of the conversation has grown over the fifty years and more since I first happened upon John Lloyd Stephens's book in the stacks of the old El Paso Public Library. At one time, during the writing of *Under the Fifth Sun,* I had lined the walls of my office with books about the Revolution of 1910. All those books and hundreds more have taken part in the conversation, and it goes on, with pleasure. And then more walls and more libraries were required for *In the Language of Kings.* And now even more. The writer of a book such as this lives not only in the real world but in the world of books written by others. I am indebted to all of them.

Here follows a list of some of those who have participated in this conversation. More than a few of them would disagree with what I have written here. All of them, I am certain, could add to what I have said. I have not footnoted the history to any great extent, since this is not an academic history of Mexico, but an essayistic version. Some of the history has been on an intimate level during my own lifetime, but I depended almost entirely on secondary sources for earlier periods. I will not try to list the writers, editors, and various texts from which I have gathered the material for the history of New Spain and Mexico. None of them can be held responsible for errors of fact or interpretation; those are my contributions. While I have rarely quoted directly from these works, unless noted, at times I may have listened too intently to one or the other. At other times, especially those when the material came in the form of whispered gossip about people ranging from María Félix to the wife of President Ruiz Cortines to the perverse sexual activities of the chairman of a huge corporation, I thought it best to leave the most damaging gossip in my notes.

Inevitably, there will be phrases or sentences in this book that I have read or heard or dreamed I read or heard over the more than sixty years of my acquaintance with Mexico. Again and again I have been pointed in the proper direction by the conversation of friends or the advice of other writers past and present. There have been moments when the work or the life of another writer brought tears to my eyes:

At the end of volume 15 in the complete works of José Revueltas, Andrea Revueltas and Philippe Cheron coolly list the incidents in the last years of his life, which were the years of repression following the Massacre of October 2, 1968, at Tlatelolco. Revueltas had spent years in prison. He had corresponded with Arthur Miller, then president of PEN International, and with intellectuals around the world, some of whom agreed with his leftist politics, many of whom did not. Pablo González Casanova, then rector of the UNAM, had asked for amnesty for political prisoners arrested in conjunction with the 1968 Massacre. And Revueltas had continued to write.

"Finally, Revueltas came out of jail on the 13th of May, 1971, free under protest. Days before his death, the judge announced that the process by which he had been free under protest had been revised. Revueltas, ill, was found in bed by his friends who came to give him the news. He asked his wife to help him dress. He did not want to go again to prison in his pajamas, as he believed was going to happen. He died, still under sentence, on April 14, 1976."

There was no literary tragedy, perhaps no tragedy of any kind, so great as the early death of the poet and essayist Sor Juana Inés de la Cruz, yet her work was uplifting, intellectually exciting, even the final work, the one she signed in her own blood. One of the writers was battered by the repression of the Church and the other by the repression of the government. Homologues.

The last part of the last chapter of this book is about my dear friend Miguel León-Portilla. We have talked a great deal about the book over the years. There would have been many more errors, omissions, and misinterpretations had it not been for his books and our conversations. If my characterization of him is that of a scholar buried in his books, it is not accurate. He is a witty, lively, now and then acerbic man, one who loves to laugh. We worked together for years on *In the Language of Kings: An Anthology of Mesoamerican Literature—Pre-Columbian to the Present*, which was the first book to consider contemporary work in indigenous languages as the continuation of the literature of the Maya and Nahua classics rather than something from a debased culture. It is, in itself, an argument for the equality of the two sides of the mestizaje, a step toward ending the inner conflict of centuries. And we made it clear in Spanish as well, with the publication of the Spanish-language edition.

Mexico has been generous enough to award me its Order of the Aguila

Azteca, and for that I am most grateful. As my wife is fond of saying, I must have been a Mexican in another life. I take her view as permission to see Mexico as if I were a native, with a loving, but critical eye.

The list above includes but a few of the many writers who together are the vast literary wealth of Mexico and its gift to the United States and the world. More appear in the text itself. I commend them (and all those I have overlooked) to you.

Acknowledgments

In 1956, Sylvia Sasson and I were married in Las Cruces, New Mexico, by a justice of the peace who could not pronounce my first or last name. We settled in a small apartment I had rented in a newly constructed building in Cuidad Juárez, Mexico, but the Rio Grande ran dry that very week, and we moved north across the border in search of fresh water and a shower. In the ensuing years I came to know Sylvia's Mexico, which was nothing like mine. Of late, I have taken to addressing her, with a wink, as La Estimada (*Estimada/o* is the polite salutation on a letter in Spanish), but in fact there is more than a little merit in the name.

There are hundreds of others to whom I am indebted, for sixty years is a long time, and many lessons are given. This book is owed to everyone who appears in it, especially these families: León-Portilla and Romero Keith (including Marcella Gabaldon and Florencio Martínez Martínez), also García Reyes, Suárez Valencia, Martínez Navarette, Carrillo Castro, Murguía Rosete, Hiernaux Gutiérrez, May May, Téran, Maccosay (Julio and Isela), Cárdenas (of Monterrey), Perez Bustillo (Camilo and María de la Luz and Centli and Xilo), Fernández-Valenzuela; in El Paso the families Salazar, Silva, Tellez, Para, Navarro; to my pal Primitivo Rodríguez, Alicia González, Javier Valencia, Margarita Roque, Estela Eguiarte, René Columb, Pepe Treviño, Antonio Mondragón, Susie and Victor Chellet, Victor Clark Alfaro, Rosaura Barahona, David Behar, Eleuterio Po'ot Yah, Mercedes Olivera, Horacio Gómez; to *los chavos* who were killed on September 23 and those who survived, to my schoolmates at the old Morehead School, to the first paracaidistas in the north, to Natalio Hernández Xocoyotzin and his family, José Ramón Tirado, Rubito Hernández, Alejandro del Hierro, Jesús Delgadillo El Estidiante, Rubén Hernández, many people in D.F., Cuernavaca, Mérida, Monterrey, Guadalajara, Chalco, Nezahualcoyotl, Matamoros, Ciudad Juárez, Oaxaca, Temixco, San Cristóbal, la selva Lacandón, the offices of

CIESAS, Tijuana, San Diego, Anenecuilco, Milpa Alta, Carolina, Delicias, Chihuahua, Los Charcos, Canatlán, Celaya, Torreón, Xtobil, Carrillo Puerto, and cities and towns and villages in virtually every other part of Mexico, north to south, east to west; to Consuls General Jorge Pinto and Georgina Lagos and her staff at the Mexican Consulate in San Francisco and especially my friend Bernardo Méndez (how Secretary Derbez could have fired her is one of the ugly matters of partisanship in the spoils system of politics). Few people taught me more than our students in San Antonio Sihó, and I am still learning from our students in Las Vias.

I am pleased to have been married to the town of Hueyapán, where the children learn to sing in Nahuatl, and to have eaten spaghetti made of long slices of nopales from Francisco Morales Baranda's farm after the presentation of my friends Elena and Librado Silva's book in Momozco Malacachtepec.

There would have been very few pictures in this book if not for Salvador Reyes Equiguas, who researched the photographs, digitized them, sent them north, and cleared the rights. He is a fine young scholar, and I am pleased to have worked with him.

Thanks to Harold Evans.

Pearl Hanig fact-checked as she copy-edited. She saved me from my memory, my penchant for misspellings, and my erroneous beliefs about such things as the ownership of gerund phrases. *Qué Dios la Bendiga!*

And to Don Rifkin, thanks for the kind words and great care.

At W. W. Norton: Debra Morton Hoyt and Eleen Cheung made it look good on the outside, and the talented people in the production department made it look good on the inside.

Streetcars race toward the desk of Morgen Van Vorst, and with good reason! While making her selection, she could not have been more patient and helpful. And smart! She and her mentor are more good luck than any writer can expect.

To Starling Lawrence, he of the graceful prose, *una vez, más gracias.*

Photo Credits

Coatlicue. Miguel León-Portilla. *Códices. Los antiguos libros del Nuevo Mundo*. México, Aguilar, 2002.

Jade mask of Pacal. *Arqueología Mexicana. Los tesoros de Palenque*. Special edition, No. 8.

Olmec figures of jade and sandstone. *Arqueología Mexicana*. Vol. V, No. 27.

Madrid Codex. *Historia de México*. Vol. 13. Edited by Miguel León-Portilla.

Nezahualcóyotl. *Códice Ixtlilxóchitl. Arqueología Mexicana*. Jan./Feb. 1995, Vol. II, No. 11.

Motecuhzoma Xocoyotzin. *Códice Durán*.

Cuauhtémoc. *Códice Cozcatzin*. Rafael Tena Studio. Mexico, INAH/Benemérita Universidad de Puebla, 1994.

Pedro Alvarado. *Arqueología Mexicana*. Aug./Sept. 1994, Vol. II, No. 9.

Hernán Cortés. Oil on silk, 17th century, anonymous, Museo Nacional del Virreinato. *Revista Arqueología Mexicana*. Vol. IX, No. 49.

Carlos de Sigüenza y Góngora. *Historia de México*. Vol. 13. Edited by Miguel León-Portilla. Salvat.

Juan Ruiz de Alarcón. *Historia de México*. Vol. 13. Edited by Miguel León-Portilla. Salvat.

Sor Juana Inés de la Cruz. *Historia de México*. Vol. 13. Edited by Miguel León-Portilla. Salvat.

Quetzalcoatl. *Codex Borbonicus*.

Virgin of Guadalupe. Horacio Senties. *La Villa de Guadalupe. Historia de estampas y leyenda*. Departamento del D.F., 1941.

Virgin of Guadalupe. Horacio Senties. *La Villa de Guadalupe. Historia de estampas y leyenda*. Departamento del D.F., 1941.

Miguel Hidalgo. *Historia de México*. Vol. 13. Edited by Miguel León-Portilla. Salvat.

Morelos. *Historia de México*. Vol. 13. Edited by Miguel León-Portilla. Salvat.

Guerrero and Iturbide. *Historia de México*. Vol. 13. Edited by Miguel León-Portilla. Salvat.

Lerdo de Tejada. *Historia de México*. Vol. 13. Edited by Miguel León-Portilla. Salvat.

Benito Juárez and Margarita Maza. *Historia de México*. Vol. 13. Edited by Miguel León-Portilla. Salvat.

Matías Romero. Courtesy of José Romero Keith.

Porfirio Díaz. Retrato. *Historia de México.* Vol. 13. Edited by Miguel Leon-Portilla. Salvat.

Justo Sierra. Complete works, México, UNAM, 1977.

Victoriano Huerta. *Historia de México.* Vol. 13. Edited by Miguel León-Portilla. Salvat.

Francisco Villa in the Presidential Chair. *Jefes, héroes y caudillos.* Fondo Casasola. México, 1986, CNCA/INAH/FCE.

Madero and Ángeles. *Jefes, héroes y caudillos.* Fondo Casasola. Mexico, 1986, CNCA/INAH/FCE.

Vasconcelos, ototeca FAPEC-FT. Reproduction authorized if source cited.

Rivera. *Self-Portrait. Salon de la plástica mexicana. México, Culural Program of the XIX Olimpiad,* 1968.

Orozco. *Autoretrato. 40 siglos de arte en México.* México Moderno.

Obregón. *Historia de México.* Vol. 13. Edited by Miguel León-Portilla. Salvat.

Alfonso Reyes. *Revista Universidad Nacional.* No. 477, Oct. 1990.

Bernardo Reyes. *Historia de México.* Vol. 13. Edited by Miguel León-Portilla. Salvat.

Daniel Cosío Villegas. *Seventy Years of the Faculty of Philosophy and Letters.* UNAM, 1994.

Gómez Morín. *Seventy Years of the Faculty of Philosophy and Letters.* UNAM, 1994. Fototeca, No. 18. "El banco de México hace setenta años." Reproduction authorized if source cited.

Calles. *Historia de México.* Vol. 13. Edited by Miguel León-Portilla. Salvat.

Toledo. "Juárez soñado por la muerte." Photograph by Caslos Alcazar, courtesy of Galerla Lopez Quiroga. From *Arqueología mexicana.* Jul./Aug. 1997, Vol. V, No. 26.

Tamayo. *Arqueología mexicana.* Aug./Sept. 1993, Vol. 1, No. 3.

Juan Rulfo. *Historia de México.* Vol. 13. Edited by Miguel León-Portilla. Salvat.

María Felix in *Rio Escondido. Historia del arte mexicano.* Filmoteca UNAM.

Cantinflas and Joaquín Pardabe in *Ahi está el detalle. Historia del arte mexicano.* Filmoteca UNAM.

Jorge Negrete in *Ay Jalisco no te rajes. Historia del arte mexicano.* Filmoteca UNAM.

Roberto Cobos in *Los Olvidados* of Luis Buñuel. *Historia del arte mexicano.* Filmoteca UNAM.

María Rojo. Photograph courtesy of Ms. Rojo.

Red Dawn poster. Courtesy of Ms. Rojo.

Octavio Paz. *Historia de México.* Vol. 13. Edited by Miguel León-Portilla. Salvat.

Carlos Fuentes. *Historia de México.* Vol. 13. Edited by Miguel León-Portilla. Salvat.

Crack Generation. Courtesy of Vicente Herrasti.

Carlos Monsivais. *Seventy Years of the Faculty of Philosophy and Letters.* UNAM, 1994.

Elena Poniatowska. *Seventy Years of the Faculty of Philosophy and Letters.* UNAM, 1994.

Luis Echeverría passing on the symbol of presidential power to López Portillo. *His-*

toria de México. Vol. 13. Edited by Miguel León-Portilla. Salvat.

President Obregón. Courtesy of Alejandro Carrillo Castro.

Alejandro P. Carrillo. Courtesy of Alejandro Carrillo Castro.

Young PRlistas. Courtesy of Alejandro Carrillo Castro.

Wedding witness. Courtesy of Alejandro Carrillo Castro.

López Portillo. Courtesy of Alejandro Carrillo Castro.

Miguel de la Madrid. Courtesy of Alejandro Carrillo Castro.

Salinas. Courtesy of Alejandro Carrillo Castro.

Ambassador to OAS. Courtesy of Alejandro Carrillo Castro.

Talina. Courtesy of Alejandro Carrillo Castro.

Arturo Durazo, José López Portillo, and Carlos Hank González. From Gonzalez, José. *Lo negro del negro Durazo.* México, Ed. Posada, 1983.

Luis Donaldo Colosio, Diana Laura, and Luis Colosio Fernández. *Revista Quién.* 19, June 2003, Vol. 4, No. 43. Arículo "Hijos de la política" by Benjamin Ortega Chávez, designed by Socorro Toxtli. (Photograph not credited.)

Zedillo. Cuartoscuro.

Sebastian Guillén. *Revista Proceso,* special edition, "Zapatistas." Jan. 1, 1999.

Fiesta. Indigenous Photography Archive.

Staff of Indigenous Photography Archive. Courtesy of Carlota Duarte.

Young Jorge Castañeda. Courtesy of Dr. Castañeda.

Gordillo. Courtesy of Dr. Castañeda.

Shelters. Courtesy of John R. MacArthur.

Couple. Courtesy of John R. MacArthur.

Cuernavaca, Courtesy of Herlinda Suárez Zozaya.

Brochure. Courtesy of Brigada Elisa Martínez.

Múrgia Rosete. Author's photograph.

Andy May. Author's photograph.

Colegio Williams. Courtesy of Colegio Williams.

Historian. Author's photograph.

Herlinda Suárez. Courtesy of Gustavo Valencia.

Gustavo Valencia. Self-photograph.

Javier and Fernánda Valencia. Courtesy of Gustavo Valencia.

José Romero and family. Courtesy of José Romero.

Porfirio Muñoz Ledo. *Proceso.*

Aguayo. Courtesy of Sergio Aguayo.

Rodrigo Rojes. Courtesy of Ifigenia Martínez.

UNAM class. Courtesy of Ifigenia Martínez.

Lazaro Cárdenas. Corbis.

La Maestra. Courtesy of Ifigenia Martínez.

May May. Author's photograph.

Book cover. Courtesy of Miguel Angel May May.

Librado Silva. Courtesy of Herlinda Suárez Zozaya.

Songs cover. Courtesy of Natalio Hernández Xocoyotzin.

Index